COMPLETE GUIDE TO

WALKS & TRAILS

IN SOUTHERN AFRICA

COMPLETE GUIDE TO
WALKS & TRAILS
IN SOUTHERN AFRICA

JAYNEE LEVY

STRUIK

Dedicated to Nicholas Penny,
who passionately loved the mountains
of the Cape.

Struik Publishers (Pty) Ltd
(a member of The Struik Publishing Group (Pty) Ltd)
Cornelis Struik House
80 McKenzie Street
Cape Town 8001

Reg. No.: 54/00965/07

First published as *Everyone's Guide to Trailing &*
Mountaineering in Southern Africa in 1982
First published as *The Complete Guide to Walks and*
Trails in Southern Africa in 1987
Second edition 1989
Second impression 1991
Third edition (revised and updated) 1993

Publishing Director: Marje Hemp
Managing Editor: Angela Sayer-Farley
Assistant Editors: Christine Didcott, Sandie Vahl
DTP design, typesetting and layout: Kevin Shenton
Cover design: Neville Poulter
Maps: Pam Eloff and Sally Adam of Technodraft
Editorial contributors and assistants: Belinda Bresler,
Brenda Brickman, Tracey Hawthorne, Brian Johnson-
Barker, Lindsay Norman, Janet Paterson, Marielle Rensen,
Christine Riley, Jan Schaafsma, Fatima Williams.
Proofreader: Tessa Kennedy
Indexer: Sandie Vahl
Photographic Researcher: Nicola Newman

Reproduction by Unifoto (Pty) Ltd, Cape Town
Printed and bound by Tien Wah Press (Pte) Ltd, Singapore

Poem on page 39 by Helen Frazee-Bower. It first
appeared in *Good Housekeeping*, a magazine published
by the Hearst Corporation, in March 1939.

ISBN 1 86825 448 8

HALF-TITLE PAGE: *Pinnacle Rock near Graskop in the*
eastern Transvaal, South Africa.

TITLE PAGE: *Klein Leeukoppie, overlooking Sandy Bay,*
mirrors Cape Town's Lion's Head in the distance.

THIS PAGE: *Natal Drakensberg hikers head up the*
Injasuti Valley.

PAGE 6: *Bathed in autumn sunshine, hikers take to South*
Africa's favourite Otter Trail.

PAGE 7: *Malawi's Mount Mulanje is a challenge to*
the fit hiker.

PAGE 9: *Inviting accommodation on the popular*
Swellendam Hiking Trail in the south-western Cape.

CONTENTS

PHOTOGRAPHIC CREDITS

Shaen Adey: pp. 14 (NPB); 168; 172, right; 191, top; 220, bottom (NPB).
Anthony Bannister: pp. 31; 150 (ABPL); 237, top left; 274; 312 (ABPL); 313 (ABPL); 315 (ABPL).
Richard Boycott: p. 229.
David Bristow: pp. 128; 252; 258, top.
Duncan Butchart: pp. 244 (AI); 304, right (AI).
Cape Nature Conservation: pp 16, top; 66, bottom; 68, bottom; 69; 134, bottom left.
Peter Comley: pp. 292, bottom; 293, bottom.
Mike Coppinger: p. 336 (ABPL).
Gerald Cubitt: pp. 28; 126; 159, top; 179; 194, top; 196; 224; 227; 278; 280; 296; 304, left; 309, top.
Ian Davidson: pp. 320; 322; 325; 326, bottom; 327; 328; 329, bottom.
Roger de la Harpe: pp. 10 (NPB); 12 (NPB); 16, bottom; 18 (NPB); 86 (ABPL); 170; 171; 172, left (NPB); 174; 176; 182, top and bottom; 183, top; 185 (NPB); 186, top (NPB) and bottom (NPB); 187; 188 (NPB); 192; 197, top and bottom; 204; 205; 215; 216; 217 (NPB); 221; 256, bottom; 337 (NPB).
Nigel Dennis: pp. 200 (ABPL); 207, bottom (ABPL).
Equus Trails: p. 340.
Neil Griffin: pp. 102; 104; 232; 234; 246; 254; 256, top; 261.
Lesley Hay: pp. 258, bottom (ABPL).
Lex Hes: pp. 27; 231, bottom.
Peter Hill: pp. 17, top; 74, top; 330; 332; 335, top.

Leonard Hoffman: pp. 61, bottom (SIL); 74, bottom (SIL); 137 (SIL).
Andrew Ingram: p. 17, bottom.
Carl Konrad: p. 237, top right.
Walter Knirr: pp. 1; 4/5; 32; 51, top; 122; 136; 142; 158, top; 160; 166 (PA); 202; 206; 210; 211; 212; 213; 234; 235 (PA); 259; 264; 265; 266.
Jaynee Levy: pp. 8; 43; 44, bottom; 48; 57, top; 61, top; 70; 73; 76, bottom; 78, bottom; 79; 108, right; 110; 115; 120; 124; 138; 144, bottom; 148, top; 151; 157; 159, bottom; 165, top; 180; 198; 201; 207, top; 226; 231, top; 237, bottom left; 243; 253; 262; 263; 273; 283, bottom; 290; 335, bottom.
J Matthews: pp. 106 (Landmarks); 108, left (Landmarks).
Rick Matthews: pp. 7; 35; 245, top and bottom; 310; 316.
John McKinnell: pp. 13; 117.
Salome Meyer: pp. 292, top; 293, top.
Natal Parks Board: pp. 47, bottom; 255.
Nicola Newman: pp. 53; 68, top; 341.
Robert C Nunnington: pp. 183, bottom (ABPL); 193, top (ABPL).

Derek Odendaal: pp. 144, top; 145; 146; 148, bottom; 154, top and bottom; 156, top; 161, top; 163, top; 164; 165, bottom.
Willie and Sandra Olivier: pp. 9; 64; 94; 134; 149; 134, top; 250; 269; 275; 281; 282, left and right; 283, top; 285, top and bottom; 286; 287; 288; 295.
Colin Paterson-Jones: pp. 6; 26; 40; 45; 47, top; 50; 54; 55; 56; 57, bottom; 58; 60; 66, top; 76, top; 84, left and right; 85, top and bottom; 87; 90; 91, top and bottom; 93; 95; 96; 97; 100, left; 101; 107; 132; 134, bottom right; 135.
Marek Patzer: pp. 314; 318; 319, bottom.
A Peter: pp. 105 (Landmarks); 109 (Landmarks).
Herman Potgieter: pp. 33 (ABPL); 161, bottom (ABPL); 194, bottom (ABPL).
Eric Reisinger: p. 82 (ABPL).
Peter Ribton: p. 2/3.
T Rooyen: p. 162.
Kevin Shenton: pp. 46; 305, bottom.
Michael Slater: p. 239.
Andrew Snaddon: pp. 78, top; 127.
Lorna Stanton: p. 241 (ABPL); 259 (ABPL).
David Steele: p. 248 (PA).
Peter Steyn: pp. 298; 299; 301, top and bottom; 303; 305, top; 307, top and bottom; 309, bottom; 323, top and bottom; 326, top; 329.
Dirk Swagger: p. 220, top; 222.
Mark Tennant: p. 195 (AI).
Mark van Aardt: pp. 29; 191, bottom; 308; 335.
Chris van der Merwe: pp. 208; 271, bottom; 289, top; 319, bottom.
Hein von Hörsten: pp. 24; 42; 44, top (ABPL); 63; 72; 98; 289, bottom.
Patrick Wagner: pp. 99 (PA); 100, right (PA); 158, bottom (PA).
Zelda Wahl: pp. 20; 51, bottom; 52; 59; 62; 65; 77; 80; 81; 88; 89; 92; 111; 112; 113; 117, top; 119 top and bottom; 121; 123; 131; 133; 138; 139, top and bottom; 141.
F. Weir: p. 125, top.
T Wooldridge: p. 163, bottom (Landmarks).

FRONT COVER: **Hein von Hörsten**. *Tsitsikamma Trail.*
INSET LEFT: **Peter Hill**. *Mountain biking near Graskop, eastern Transvaal.*
INSET CENTRE: **Charles Didcott (Felix Unite).** *Canoeing on the Orange River.*
INSET RIGHT: **Roger de la Harpe (NPB).** *Hillside Horse Trail, Champagne Castle, Natal.*
SPINE: **Neil Griffin.** *Sunset on the Bushman Trail, Kruger National Park.*
BACK COVER: **Walter Knirr.** *Injasuti Valley, Drakensberg.*

ACKNOWLEDGEMENTS

This book is a culmination of the work of many people – not only those experts who assisted in compiling the manuscript but also those hikers who are familiar with exciting and/or new walking and trailing terrain and who enthusiastically contributed their knowledge and experience. The publishers and the author wish to thank all of them, and to acknowledge the contributions of certain individuals and organizations in particular.

Cape Nature Conservation were extremely helpful; Lesley Richardson, of the Nuweberg office in the Hottentots Holland Nature Reserve, was always ready and patient with advice, and Mark Gentle helped to clarify the trails administration structure. Trevor Dearlove of the National Parks Board willingly shared his extensive knowledge of the wilderness walks in South Africa's national parks. Cathy Knox of the National Botanical Institute brought us up to date with walks in gardens administered by the Institute. George Gundry of the Hiking Federation of South Africa, and Anne Bush, who administers the walks and trails database set up by the Geography Department of the University of Pretoria, provided general information.

Mike Lundy, one of the western Cape's most prominent (and most genial) hiking personalities, offered many useful suggestions based on his considerable experience of walking in this area. Colin Paterson-Jones, with his penchant for accuracy and love for the fynbos environment, was a source of valuable research on the western and southern Cape regions, as well as on Namaqualand, the northern Cape and the Karoo.

Hugh Parry and Mary Yates kindly took time out from exploring the Eastern Cape to offer a wealth of relevant advice.

Derek Odendaal of the Department of Education and Culture in Bloemfontein contributed useful suggestions, based on his comprehensive knowledge of

hiking in the Orange Free State and QwaQwa. Sarie Mehl of Jacana Country Homes and Trails deserves thanks for her prompt responses to our many queries on trails run by her organization. The QwaQwa Tourism and Nature Conservation Corporation, especially Lewis Roberts, was always eager to supply any details that we required.

The Natal Parks Board updated much of the trailing information on the Drakensberg and the rest of Natal, while the KwaZulu Bureau of Natural Resources supplemented our information on this area. Geoff Nichols of the Durban City Council gave us permission to extract relevant information from his well-researched book *Day Walks in and around Durban and Pietermaritzburg*. David Bristow offered the benefit of his vast experience of hiking in many parts of the country, especially in the Drakensberg and the Eastern Transvaal. Bernard de Souza, well-known hiking figure in the Eastern Transvaal, also assisted by scrutinizing the text for this region.

Willie and Sandra Olivier, veteran explorers of Namibia, contributed many useful suggestions on hiking in that country, while Heinz Kramer of Namibia Tourism in Cape Town enthusiastically assisted in gathering information.

Edward Chindori-Chininga of the Zimbabwe Tourist Development Corporation was extremely accommodating of our many requests for information. The Department of National Parks and Wild Life Management in Harare provided the latest details of their wilderness trails.

Peter Comley and Salome Meyer verified and updated the data on the walking opportunities in Botswana.

The Department of National Parks and Wildlife in Malawi and the Malawi Department of Tourism gave comprehensive responses to our many queries on that country. Peter Steyn also added practical advice, gleaned from his many years of bird-watching in both Zimbabwe and Malawi.

From their considerable experience of travelling and hiking in southern Africa, Ian Davidson and Colin Bell of Wilderness Safaris and Chris Badger of Central African Wilderness Safaris offered many useful hints.

Marek Patzer, now living in Zambia, assisted with pertinent comments on wilderness walking opportunities and river rafting in Zambia.

Greg McCulloch, in association with ROMP, shared his expertise and enthusiasm for the blossoming sport of of mountain-biking. As a freelance river guide, Bill Mitchell provided up-to-date information and advice on white-water rafting and canoeing trips.

Finally, special thanks are due to Pam Eloff and her assistant, Sally Adam, for the many hours they put into perfecting the maps in time, and to Kevin Shenton, the book's designer, for whom nothing was ever too much trouble.

PUBLISHER'S NOTE

This book has been extensively revised and updated to reflect the substantial changes and expansion in the realm of hiking on the southern African sub-continent. While many of the entertaining anecdotes and personal observations are as relevant as they were when Jaynee Levy compiled the previous editions, and have been retained, most of the trail descriptions have been compiled and updated from new data supplied to the publishers by the various trail authorities, and vetted by experts in their respective areas, including Mike Lundy, Colin Paterson-Jones, Derek Odendaal, Bernard de Souza, David Bristow, Willie and Sandra Olivier and Peter Steyn.

Approximately 160 hiking trails and day walks have been added, along with a Special Interest section, containing a further 100 new trails, which includes mountain biking, horseback, pony-trekking and camel trails, as well as canoeing and river-rafting trips, an underwater trail and trails for the disabled. We hope to see this section further expanded in future editions. This edition also contains a chapter on Zambia, which now offers guided wilderness trails in big game country as well as river-rafting trips, and is becoming a popular destination for those wishing to experience untamed Africa.

The trails in this book are mostly more than 2 km long and situated on land that is over 50 ha in extent. Where kilometres and times are given, these figures should be used as guidelines only and are not absolute. We have tried to be comprehensive in the information and maps provided, but advise the

hiker before setting off to seek further details from the authority in charge.

During the compilation of this edition we noticed that some privately owned facilities insist on applying their own rights of admission based on race and colour. We dissociate ourselves entirely from any form of discrimination, and trails that to our knowledge are managed on such a basis have been omitted from this book.

Any guidebook grows out of date with time. New trails are constantly being opened (as the Stop Press section of this book attests), and established

trails rerouted or closed altogether. Whenever you encounter a change which may affect the information in this book, we would be grateful if you would advise the Editor, *Complete Guide to Walks and Trails in Southern Africa* in writing, who will ensure that such details are incorporated in a future edition.

While every effort has been made to ensure that the text and maps are accurate and the routes described are safe, neither the author nor the publisher nor the cartographer will accept responsibility for any damages resulting from the use of this book.

Trails: Living in a multilingual country such as South Africa, confusion often arises as to the correct form of proper names. Every attempt has been made to use the standard, accepted version of place, mountain and river names; where doubt existed, we used the English form.

In the trail descriptions, the available literature is obtainable from the authority which issues permits and/or takes bookings, unless otherwise stated.

Maps: It should be noted that the maps in this book have been designed as simple visual guides to the area concerned, and are not intended for use in the field. Every effort has been made to ensure the accuracy of the maps, which are based on the best available source material. However, this material varied considerably in quality from area to area, and this variation will inevitably be reflected in the maps presented in these pages.

We wish you safe and happy hiking!

ABOUT THE AUTHOR

Jaynee Levy has been intricately involved in outdoor recreation and environmental education development in southern Africa since 1975, when she joined the South African Forestry Branch of the Department of Environment Affairs. During the 12 years she spent in southern Africa, she assisted in the development of the National Hiking Way System, and has served as Environmental Education Officer for the Cape Province, Tourist Development Consultant for the Ciskei Tourist and Holiday Trust and Chief Recreational Development Officer for the Ciskei Tourist Board.

Born in America and educated at Cornell (B.Sc.) and Yale (M.F.S.) universities, Jaynee served both in the Environmental Conservation Department of her native New York State and in Israel, before arriving in Africa.

A highly experienced backpacker, having hiked in more than 36 countries in Africa, North and South America, Europe and Asia, Ms Levy finds this the ideal way of pursuing her other interests of nature photography and bird-watching. Jaynee is also a keen canoeist, mountain-biker, skin-diver and skier.

AUTHOR'S PREFACE

I came to South Africa in 1975 to assist in planning the National Hiking Way System – an exciting position within a burgeoning recreational activity. The potential for expansion and development in the field of outdoor recreational and environmental education was wide open. My work was multifaceted – I was either bushwhacking up a slope with a team of foresters, lecturing to 'Veld and Vlei' participants, constructing a trail through thick indigenous forest with a group of youngsters, being an interpretive naturalist on the Wild Coast, or selecting backpacking gear for the mountain catchment team. I developed a deep respect for the mountains and their animals and plants. Weekends and public holidays found me exploring new ranges, peaks or gorges and, during my annual leave, I flew to neighbouring countries to investigate their mountains and trails. My professional life and private hours fused – and I loved it.

My first book, *Everyone's Guide to Trailing and Mountaineering in Southern Africa*, was written out of sheer self-defence for, invariably, whenever I went hiking, one of the members of the party would trigger a barrage of questions. How long is the Outeniqua Trail? Is it more difficult than the Boland Hiking Trail? How many nights do you sleep out? Where can I make bookings? What about the Wild Coast? I heard you organized an expedition up Mulanje – how was it? Have you hiked the Fish River Canyon? Would my children be able to manage it? What footwear do you recommend? The questions were endless and I encountered them every time I hit the trail. Willingly providing advice and information to each hiker, it struck me as ironic that I, an American who had lived in southern Africa only a few years, was the target of all these queries. It also emphasized the very real need for a practical and comprehensive book which would answer this sort of question.

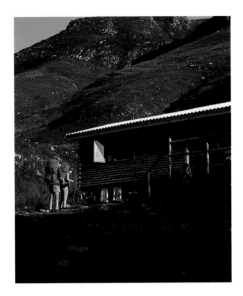

Although I knew that all the information existed somewhere, it became obvious that nowhere did it exist in a single reference work. So I reluctantly traded mountaineering time to combine the facts and experience that appear here. Compiling up-to-date information on trails in southern Africa is like trying to write the latest reference on world politics – both are constantly developing and changing. Although the directory of trails is as comprehensive and accurate as possible (as of July 1993), alterations to routes and other changes are inevitable, and it excludes the late-comers listed under Stop Press at the back of the book.

Some mountaineering and kloofing regions have been purposely excluded at the request of their landowners. Coverage of parks, nature reserves and

bird-watching spots which offer the opportunity to walk, but no set routes, has had to make way for descriptions of the many newly created walks and hiking trails. Likewise, it was decided to omit trails (historical or otherwise) that travel urban streets, as the publicity associations of the towns and cities concerned already do an excellent job of promoting these. The book nevertheless remains the most comprehensive of its kind and more than one hundred and sixty new trails are described, all of which have been developed or redesigned since the previous edition of this book. The trails concept has been broadened to include over one hundred mountain-biking, canoeing, white-water rafting and horseback, pony-trekking and camel trails, as well as trails for the disabled. All information on equipment, resources and references has also been brought up to date.

By popular demand, the basic structure of the book has remained the same as that of the previous edition: the trails are arranged geographically (by province – and, on occasion, neighbouring state/s – or country) to facilitate practical needs when planning a trailing holiday. The information on southern Africa's various ecological zones has been retained, however, in order to assist understanding of a trail's natural environment.

I hope that the third edition proves to be not only as popular as the first and second, but also a practical and inspirational guide for everyone's exploration of southern Africa's rich natural and historical heritage. Trailists and mountaineers should unite as an active voice, encouraging wise use and preservation of the land on which they tread.

This book is my tribute to the magnificent mountains and other natural areas I have been introduced to and the wonderful people I have met while in southern Africa.

INTRODUCTION

THE DEVELOPMENT OF TRAILS IN SOUTHERN AFRICA

Hiking as a widely accepted recreational activity is growing exceptionally fast in this sub-continent. The number of active hikers increases daily as more and more people seek to escape their stressful urban environment and explore new territory, becoming one with nature.

The myriad trails in southern Africa today, most of them established less than 18 years ago, are stirring up the question: 'Are trails a positive influence in the ecology, or are they merely another human means of manipulating nature for selfish goals?'

Some people are of the opinion that hiking trails should not be built because wild lands are shrinking, and that those remaining should be closed to the public and saved for future generations. Another argument is that by having your ability to explore and move where whim takes you limited, you develop 'tunnel vision' and your interest in the outdoors is destroyed. Others are concerned that trails create an artificial need and avenue for people to explore our natural areas, and by doing so, over-populate them. Arguments are heard that inexperienced people, unsupervised by clubs or guides, destroy the environment and so the experience for the 'real' hiker.

Some arguments point to the ills of hiking in the USA, where millions of hikers utilize hundreds of thousands of kilometres of hiking trails annually, and solitary experiences are shattered by the popularity of the pastime; *Giardia*, a water-borne disease, is spread by backpackers to remote high altitude streams; the 'carrying capacity' of a camp site is inversely proportional to the distance campers must walk to collect dead firewood; and prime camp sites and trails are littered and show other ugly scars of overuse.

Strangely, I, who have dedicated the past 16 years of my life to planning and constructing trails, and publicizing and using them for environmental education, sympathize with these arguments. I recall how excited I was when I arrived here in 1975: southern Africa seemed, in comparison to my American homeland, a big wilderness area, where I seldom met another hiking party on a peak or traverse, where I could drink from every mountain stream, and where the animals were not yet food-raiders and tent-invaders. So I am asked, 'Why do you do it? Why do you plan more trails and write trail guides? Why are you updating this book?'

The answer is simple. The world's population is increasing, and while people are acquiring more leisure time and dispensable income, development and technology are creating more stress and moving humans further from their natural roots. People are looking to our untouched areas for relaxation, education, exercise, spiritual, mental and physical refreshment, and as pleasant places to reunite with their families, friends and lovers. By creating a hierarchy of trail types – physically easy to strenuous, one hour to one week, on the beach to the high escarpment, self-guided to group involvement, walking to canoeing and mountain biking, primitive camping to luxurious overnight lodges – we cater for the diverse levels of interest, degrees of involvement and physical capabilities of the public. Hiking, mountain biking, horse-riding and canoeing trails are relatively low-impact developments with high-impact benefits. We compromise some natural regions for the purity of others: by creating financially viable recreational zones, we prevent these areas from meeting worse fates – industrial and agricultural developments, overgrazing or resettlement. By awakening and exposing more people to the beauties and challenges of their natural heritage, we develop a population of alert individuals, a pressure group who will join the others in influencing public decision-making.

Trails also create an informal, relaxed zone for meeting people with whom you would not interact in the urban setting. And, sometimes, trails are the incentive to restore damaged ecosystems.

I view trails as part of the strategy to preserve the natural environment. More importantly, I view them as a tool for educating the entire population to work together to preserve the foundation of our very existence.

I believe that you cannot keep a good thing a secret for long. Therefore, if trails are to be publicized, let this be in an informative and comprehensive manner which conveys responsibility to the user for his conduct, for others' enjoyment and safety, and for the environment itself.

No trail, however well designed, can take an unlimited number of hikers without some damage to the environment. The *ecological carrying capacity* is the maximum level of use that an area or ecosystem can take before there is unacceptable or irreversible decline in ecological value. This capacity, in terms of numbers and activities, is fixed and cannot be manipulated.

The *social carrying capacity* is related to hikers' perceptions and feelings and to the type of outdoor experience sought on a trail. As soon as hikers feel that there are too many people on the trail, the social capacity has been exceeded. Nature conservationists try to pay special attention to this

aspect in order to preserve the very quality that attracts hikers in the first place. Unless numbers are controlled, quiet trails can become human highways and overnight stops can turn into bustling hives instead of places of peace and contemplation.

Overnight facilities are planned according to the ecological and social carrying capacities. Sleeping space, toilets, and so on make up the *physical carrying capacity* of a trail. Naturally, these are also influenced by the extent of funds available at the planning stage.

TRAIL TYPES

The trails in this book are aimed at the outdoor enthusiast and cover the whole of the southern African sub-continent, from South Africa to Namibia, Botswana and Zimbabwe, Zambia and Malawi. The majority of the trails fall under the jurisdiction of South Africa's Department of Environment Affairs, National Botanical Institute, the National Parks Board, the four provincial nature conservation departments, local authorities (regional councils and municipalities), the Wildlife Society of Southern Africa, and other independent organizations. However, there has been a marked increase in the number of trails laid out on private land, usually by farmers who are keen to share the pristine beauty of their environment with hikers. In some areas private landowners have combined resources to form a conservancy in order to preserve their land and the indigenous flora and fauna as a unit. In Namibia, the Ministry of Wildlife Conservation and Tourism is the controlling body, as are parallel government departments in Botswana, Swaziland, Lesotho, Ciskei, Transkei, Bophuthatswana, Zimbabwe, Zambia and Malawi.

Walking trails can be grouped into types, based on factors such as length, level of experience and type of equipment needed, and educational value. Trails created for other 'sports' have recently emerged, as have trails for nature enthusiasts who have a physical disability, and these form additional categories.

1. BACKPACKING OR HIKING TRAILS

These are continuous footpaths through natural environments. As these trails are two or more days long, the hiker must carry essential overnight equipment and food in a backpack or rucksack. Overnight camp sites or huts, remote from built-up areas, are provided. Such trails are essentially 'do-it-yourself' adventures, and do not have trails officers. Detailed brochures and maps are available, however. The National Hiking Way System's overnight trails fall into this category. Trails vary widely in their levels of difficulty, and many have stages that are demanding. For example, the hiker can expect to ascend and descend ravines, ford rivers and hike for long stretches over rugged terrain. The aspirant trailist must be prepared, mentally and physically, to meet these challenges.

2. WILDERNESS TREKKING

Trailing is defined as following or walking on a footpath, nature walk or hiking trail. The wilderness trekker differs from the trailist in that he or she sets off into a mountainous area such as a water catchment zone or wild coastal region where no designated footpaths exist and no overnight accommodation is provided. Rough shelters, caves or rock overhangs offer the only protection from inclement weather. Wilderness trekkers are allowed to sleep under the stars or to pitch a tent wherever they choose. They should be experienced in outdoor survival and first aid, have a basic knowledge of map-reading and make provision for extreme weather conditions. This type of venture requires a great deal of planning, and must be approached with responsibility and care.

3. GUIDED WILDERNESS TRAILS

The term 'wilderness trail' is special to Africa, for here it has grown to imply a walk guided by a game ranger or conservation officer – usually carrying a rifle – through an area rich in big-game animals, some potentially 'dangerous'. *En route* the guide explains the ecology and management of the area, emphasizing conservation principles and ethics. These trails are physically less demanding than hiking trails, but their value in terms of environmental education is unsurpassable. They usually extend over several days, although some are shorter.

Those trails that do not go through big game country, but are led by a reserve officer, knowledgeable ecologist, game scout, or river rafter, are also referred to as guided trails.

4. DAY WALKS

These are reasonably short walks, in scenic areas, that are completed in less than a day. Generally, they are not too strenuous and are ideal for family groups or casual walkers. A daypack is essential for carrying waterproof clothing, food for the trail, emergency rations and water.

In some areas, self-guided interpretive trails have been laid out with a specific educational objective. Trailists are provided with educational aids, usually a written brochure, describing ecological and/or historical features *en route*. Nature trails through botanical gardens and bird sanctuaries also fall into this category.

5. URBAN TRAILS

Only trails which are laid out through green belts in towns and cities, and which emphasize features of natural, geological, historical and architectural interest have been included in this book.

6. SPECIAL INTEREST TRAILS

These trails are becoming more popular as hikers and other outdoor enthusiasts look for new ways of exploring the expanses of southern Africa.
Mountain-biking trails: These are trails completed on fat-tyre (all terrain) cycles or mountain bikes. There are many places suitable for this type of trailing and more and more national parks, state forests and private farms are allowing mountain biking on gravel roads with the proviso that cyclists behave in a responsible manner towards the other users and the environment.
Canoeing trails: Often guided, canoeing or kayaking trails can extend over a few hours or a few days. They include white-water rafting trails.
Horseback and camel trails and pony-treks: Both experienced riders and novices are welcome on these trails, which offer opportunities to view the countryside from a different elevation!
Underwater trail: A trail where interpretation is provided and the participant, wearing a snorkel and mask, 'swims' the trail.

Their guide points out an old grinding stone to trailists on the Umfolozi Wilderness Trail.

7. TRAILS FOR THE HANDICAPPED

These trails are designed specifically for those confined to wheelchairs, or who have some other physical disability, such as blindness.

THE NATIONAL HIKING WAY SYSTEM

'NHWS' stands for the National Hiking Way System, a complex of hiking trails and nature walks in South Africa, each accompanied by a comprehensive information brochure and map.

Before 1975, most mountain catchment areas, plantations and private farms were inaccessible to the public, as authorities and landowners were reluctant to allow general access to their land. A change came in the mid '70s, however, when the Forestry Branch initiated a trail project – a system of hiking and nature trails which, at first, was modelled on the popular Appalachian Trail in the eastern United States, and the European hiking trails. The South African trails evolved a distinctive character and today enjoy unpredicted popularity.

The National Hiking Way System was established on 30 April 1975, following its statutory recognition in the Forest Amendment Act of 1975. It is co-ordinated and managed by the National Hiking Way Board, an autonomous body representing State Departments, Provincial Administrations, National Parks Boards, mountain and other outdoor clubs, as well as influential private citizens.

At one time it was envisaged that a continuous footpath would stretch for thousands of kilometres from the Soutpansberg in the north, along the whole length of the Escarpment, to the Cedarberg in the western Cape. However, experience taught the National Hiking Way Board two important lessons: circular trails (those which begin and end at the same point, thereby obviating complicated transport arrangements) are most popular; and trails in prime country, with attractive scenery, wildlife and other natural or historical assets, are used more frequently that those developed solely to link up the prime trails. For this reason, the NHWB has concentrated on developing trails with the trailist and natural attributes of a region in mind. The continuous footpath is no longer a priority goal.

The Fanie Botha Hiking Trail, the first hiking way, was opened in 1973. Since then over a thousand kilometres of the system have been developed. With heavy usage, a trail's environment can be threatened by erosion and pollution. To prevent this, hikers must abide by certain rules.

Along the entire length of each trail, white footprints painted on tree trunks and rocks mark the route to be followed. Nature trails are sometimes marked with theme pictograms, for example, the elephant on the Elephant Walk near Knysna. Hikers must remain on the trail and hike in the direction indicated only. They must stay overnight at hiking huts or camps – located about 3 to 8 walking hours (or 10 to 22 km) apart, depending on the terrain. Every hut is different in structure and provision, ranging from simple shelters to converted farmhouses and foresters' houses. Most have fireplaces, firewood, water, toilet facilities and sleeping bunks.

The trail brochure is essential, however, to learn exactly what is provided at each site; the length of each trail stretch; beginning, end and parking places; climatic data; specific rules and regulations; precautions; closures; fees; etc.

The NHWS brochures also contain information on natural and cultural history as well as maps of excellent environmental educational value. Despite its comprehensiveness, the information in this book is by no means a substitute for any of the NHWS brochures and/or maps.

Further information can be obtained from the National Hiking Way Board, Private Bag X93, Pretoria 0001, South Africa; tel. (012) 3103839; fax (012) 3200949.

FEES FOR TRAILS

A fee is charged for most hiking trails. Trailists on day walks or self-guided trails may require permits, but access is usually free or at a nominal tariff.

I do not indicate fees for any facilities or amenities, huts, accompanied trails, entry into wilderness areas, trail booklets, or entrance to reserves, because these change frequently. However, the trailist can assume that a charge will be levied on most trails and that this charge will be much higher for privately run trails and guided trails than for those organized by government authorities or run by societies and clubs.

HIKING CLUBS AND TRAIL ORGANIZERS

Hiking is a social activity best undertaken in groups. If you wish to explore new areas with experienced hikers, expand your circle of friends sharing similar outdoor interests, or learn more about the environment from someone knowledgeable, then join a hiking club. There are numerous clubs throughout South Africa, and, in most cases, the Hiking Federation of South Africa will be able to supply you with the names and contact addresses of those nearest to you. They will also be able to assist hikers with queries about many of the trails available in South Africa. Further information can be obtained from the Hiking Federation of South Africa, PO Box 1420, Randburg 2125; tel. (011) 8866507.

If there are no hiking clubs in your area, join the mountain club, bird-watching club, or botanical or wildlife societies, as they all arrange outdoor activities that include some kind of hiking.

For those who prefer to take part in more specialized or adventurous groups, there are commercial companies who organize hikes or special interest trails and provide participants with transport, food, any necessary equipment, and an experienced guide. To join such a hike, contact one of the following or see the Special Interest section at the back of the book.

Drifters PO Box 48434, Roosevelt Park 2129, South Africa; tel. (011) 8881160; fax (011) 88102.
Ventures for Africa PO Box 3005, Cresta 2118, South Africa; tel. (011) 4761517; fax (011) 4761437.
Wilderness Safaris PO Box 651171, Benmore 2010, South Africa; tel. (011) 8841458; fax (011) 8836255.

BEFORE SETTING OUT

THE PRACTICAL ASPECTS OF PREPARATION

Wouldn't it be idyllic to venture onto the trail clad in nothing more than a T-shirt and shorts, with no paraphernalia on our backs or hanging from our necks or shoulders? Idyllic – but impractical – and virtually impossible, for this would imply 'living off the land' to survive. Not only are we ill-equipped for such adventuring, but also destroying wild plants and animals for both food and shelter are 'luxuries' that modern man can no longer afford. Whether we like it or not we are products of twentieth century society – seeking recreation on a shrinking planet. When we leave the security of our homes to go trailing, whether on foot, horseback, in a canoe or on a mountain bike, we must cater constantly for our needs – hunger, thirst, protection from heat or cold, sleep, cleanliness and safety – and, of course, our curiosity. Since we can no longer live off the land, or interfere with it, we must prepare ourselves like an astronaut does for a journey in a spaceship. We must venture into the wilds carrying all our creature comforts in a backpack, taking care to leave as little trace of our passage as possible. This is the new wilderness ethic. Fortunately, the technology of our space-probing era has produced an array of food, equipment, clothing and first aid items that are astonishingly compact, lightweight, efficient and simple to use. (See also page 331.)

PHYSICAL AND MENTAL FITNESS

A basic fact is that the fitter you are, the more you will enjoy trailing. Physical fitness is twofold: fitness of the heart, and muscle fitness (especially important for backpacking, in the legs and knees, lower back and arms, and upper body). Fitness of the heart, or cardiovascular fitness, is simply how efficiently your heart-lung machine can use oxygen to supply energy to working muscles. You inherit 90 per cent of your fitness potential, while the remainder can be developed by endurance exercises such as jogging, bicycling and swimming. However, the best sport to get your heart tuned for hiking *is* hiking. The best way to strengthen muscles used to carry packs *is* backpacking.

Another type of fitness develops from trail use – mental fitness. A hike should be both a mental and physical challenge – you ought to feel a sense of achievement on reaching your destination, a 'Wow, I made it!' To many hikers the feeling of complete independence, self-reliance and solitude is as exhilarating as the breathtaking scenic beauty experienced on most trails.

To those who have never hiked, the trail can be many things – wonderful, pleasant, unpleasant, harrowing or disastrous. Some hikers emerge from the mountains with the scent of bushes and ferns on their clothing and dust on their boots – enriched physically and mentally. Others stumble out exhausted, footsore, sunburnt, dehydrated or soaked to the skin – sadder but wiser for their ordeal. Others are even less fortunate, but basically the outcome of these ventures depends largely on the

The physical and mental demands of a hike are invariably rewarded by the sheer beauty of the setting.

hiker: proper preparation, clothing and equipment, good physical condition and common sense.

The question often asked is, 'How far can I walk?' Here are some guidelines:
• 33 km a day if you are in top shape and don't want to see anything more than a blur.
• 25 km a day if you are in pretty good shape and don't dawdle.
• 20 km a day if you are in poor shape and are intent on suffering.
• 10 to 15 km a day if you are in fair shape and want to enjoy yourself.
• 5 km a day if your companion is an attractive person and you both enjoy flowers!

Remember that the trail is not a suitable place for anyone who considers it a loss of face should he decide to turn back when conditions require it; and it is no place for backbiting or sensitivity over small slights. Most of the fun you have from backpacking depends on mental attitude. I quote the American Harold Allen:

'A trail is
remote for detachment
narrow for chosen company
winding for leisure
lonely for contemplation.
The trail leads not merely North or South,
but upward to the body, mind and soul of man.'

This is the beauty of the trail and what backpacking is all about.

EXPERIENCE AND KNOWLEDGE

Don't do what I did on my first hiking trip. I flew into a remote section of Alaska, shoddily equipped with a pack, no experience and little knowledge of the area. The pilot was three days late in returning, during which time I ran out of food and spent miserably sleepless nights uncomfortably clad in all my clothes, as my sleeping bag was of poor quality and I didn't have a foam pad. I wandered aimlessly without a map and narrowly escaped grizzly bears because I was ignorant of their habits. Good weather, an abundance of non-poisonous berries and fat-filled migrating fish – caught in my hat as they jumped rapids – helped me to survive. Other hikers aren't so lucky – and only have themselves to blame.

Each type of trail demands different degrees of fitness, experience and knowledge. Realize your limitations, choose dependable and experienced trail leaders and gain your experience by trailing with them.

1. Hiking trails: The main difference between nature rambles, day walks and hiking or backpacking is one of degree – hikers go further, stay out for one or more nights and carry more need-satisfying items. The hiker must be familiar with various skills such as basic first aid, recognizing the symptoms of hypothermia, heat exhaustion and mountain altitude sickness; using a compass and map-reading; using equipment and knowing its limitations and – most important – being environmentally 'literate'. When hiking you should be able to use all your senses to 'read' nature – wind direction, vegetation, bird species, wildlife habits, insects flying about, sounds and smells all provide clues for understanding your surroundings.

Environmental literacy and hiking skills develop slowly and with experience; by starting to hike with qualified and reputable members of mountain clubs or organized expeditions, you will be pointed in the right direction.

2. Guided wilderness trails: The fortunate novice will begin trailing on a guided wilderness trail, such as those run by the Wilderness Leadership School, Educational Wildlife Expeditions, National Parks Board or Natal Parks Board. The degree of fitness required is that of any healthy, keen individual and distances covered each day are relatively short. Because the trail is led by an experienced ranger, he will modify its length, route and strenuousness, taking into consideration the weather and his party. You carry a minimum of items, as most of your essentials are transported by porters, mules or jeep. Having an experienced trails officer with you, you will be warned of sudden dangers (such as puff adders in the path or lightning storms), and first aid will be readily available.

Much time is taken up with discussions and observations in the veld – a most important aspect. The trails officer will help you achieve the right orientation towards trailing – to become aware of what you are 'looking at' – by imparting his knowledge of the region, its plants and animals as well as the archaeology and bush lore.

3. Wilderness trekking: Unlike the hiker, the wilderness trekker must carry everything he needs (including his shelter) into an environment in which he must be able to navigate and survive.

4. Self-guided nature trails: Self-guided trails (and here I emphasize trails for which trail guide booklets are available and which have visitor centres with interpretive displays) lead to an awareness of nature which we have lost because we have become city oriented. The self-guided nature trail is where you can start learning about your environment as, unburdened by sleeping bags and tents, you can walk slowly and explore, observe and record, using binoculars and field guides to aid your senses and expand their potential. For many people, rambling, bird-watching, photographing nature or

just reaching a point and taking in sounds, scents and movements is an incomparable 'high'. Try it, but beware ... self-guided nature trails are addictive and lead you towards the longer and more challenging hiking trails.

HIKING WITH CHILDREN

To share with your children a walk in the woods, the flight of a lourie, or the crimson sunset over the high peaks is a wonderful experience, but is it practical, possible and realistic to hike with the whole family? How many times has the old story been repeated: the keen varsity hiker graduates to a job, joins a hiking club, finds a spouse, then has a family. Suddenly he feels trapped – the forests and mountains are no longer his domain, and his fitness and spirit fade. And all the backpacking gear just gathers dust...

This doesn't have to happen. In fact, the thrill of hiking and camping can be enhanced by sharing it with your children. However, there are changes, compromises and new methods to adapt for successful family outings. These are largely dependent on the ages of your children.

Parents who take children less than three years old on a hike must be prepared to carry not only their own loads but also those of their children, and the toddlers as well! Infants take to front and back carriers very well. Front carriers allow the parent to attend to a baby's needs while hiking. Toddlers enjoy negotiating the trail on their own, with an occasional free ride in the backpack from Mom or Dad. Child carriers are now being manufactured in greater varieties and quantities.

Women should not carry children high up, but rather centre the weight lower down on the body to take advantage of their own distinctive weight distribution and musculature.

School-going children (five to six years old) can begin to help carry some of the load in a daypack,

Hiking is an activity that families can enjoy together.

even if this is only a book, snack, water bottle or a whistle to blow if they get lost. From seven years and older, children will enjoy participating in longer, overnight hikes and should be able to carry their own sleeping bags, clothes and a little food in a small backpack. To reduce weight, parents must trim some of their packs to allow for the children's food, sleeping bags, nappies, clothes, and also those special little extras such as story books or stuffed animals, which make a camp more like home and add to a child's feeling of security. It is also a wise idea to camp in one large dome-type tent with a lantern – children younger than eight or 10 years can become frightened in a tent by themselves or alone with other children. Before the hike, let the kids camp in the tent in the back yard. If you pack 2-person tents, have a parent sleep in each tent.

If your child is likely to urinate in the sleeping bag, I suggest using only synthetic-fill bags which wash easily and remain warm when wet.

To feed babies and small children on the trail, take along bagged bottles, which can be prefilled with powdered formulas and reconstituted along the way. Children often don't perceive dehydration, so it is sometimes a problem to get your child to drink enough water. Try filling water bottles with lemonade or orange juice and freezing the bottle before you set out. Alternatively, buy small cartons of fruit juice and stop regularly to drink. To make the trip pleasant, carry foods children enjoy and let them nibble high-energy snacks along the way.

Dress your child properly in bright colours (so he can be seen if he gets lost), and in wools and tough fabric blends which are able to withstand the vigours of outdoor wear. Layering for warmth, although time-consuming, is necessary. Boots in children's sizes are scarce, so sturdy running shoes, preferably with high tops for ankle support, are the best alternative. Children's daypacks are easily purchased whereas sleeping bags are not.

Children are born nature enthusiasts. Small children love large animals and older children favour small animals. Most children hate 'slimy and dirty' snakes and 'hairy and creepy' spiders. All children exhibit an exploratory behaviour and display intense curiosity about their surroundings. Parents should be prepared to stop frequently on a walk, giving their children lots of time to explore, and to explore with them. You will be astonished how your children will open up new worlds for you through their eyes. Try to take with you simple identification picture books and magnifying glasses to make the hike a learning experience.

Children must be kept busy on a hike. Give them responsibilities such as reading a map, taking the lead, determining the route or finding the next trail marker. Let the fittest and fastest carry a heavier weight as you must always walk at the pace of the slowest child. After the hike your children will remember the special moments, so plan something unusual – a braai, flying kites, exploring a cave, etc. And when you get home, sew a patch on their daypacks for a small memento of the experience.

First hikes should be short to avoid boredom. A day hike should be no more than fours hours, with a long rest stop, while an overnight hike for 2 to 3 nights is sufficient. For the first overnight hike, go to a place from which you can return home fast if necessary. Setting up camp in a pleasant area and doing day walks should be considered.

Camping with another family has its advantages. Although logistics are more difficult, the children will enjoy the company of others their age, and parents will also have a diversion. Besides, it will lessen your children's demands for constant parental attention and coaching.

To hike with your family is to bridge the generation gap. It is one of the few activities which is fairly inexpensive to do *en masse*, and where all members can share in the fun and chores, with each having a function and responsibility. Hiking with your children will undoubtedly bring the family closer together.

EQUIPMENT

Look through the checklist provided on page 19 – but don't despair. Believe it or not, a well-equipped hiker can carry everything he needs in a backpack with a mass of between one quarter to one third of that of his body. The secret is the 'light-style'. The lighter your gear, the longer and further you can walk. Buy only quality equipment to prevent frustration and unnecessary replacements.

You will need three important basic items for overnight hiking: a pair of good hiking boots, a comfortable backpack and a warm sleeping bag.

BOOTS

Boots are the foundation of a comfortable hike. Buy carefully! Trail boots are always recommended, although on short walks a pair of well-cushioned velskoens or tennis or jogging shoes may be sufficient if your ankles are strong.
Synthetic hiking boots: In recent years, several new kinds of hiking boots have been developed. Improving on all the features of the classic European mountaineer's boot, the synthetic hiking boots weigh little more than a pair of running shoes. Although they seldom last as long as the classic boots and cost the same, I highly recommend them for any trail described in this book. They are painless to break in, thus eliminating the discouraging 'blister' period. Other special features include their abrasion-resistant uppers, in-soles offering superb cushioning and arch-supports, and engineered soles that claim not only to eliminate slipping (and mud clogging, which also decreases gripping power), but also to reduce damage to ground cover, the first stage of the erosion process.
Leather boots: Look for full-grain leather uppers that are foam-padded at the ankles and have a padded 'scree guard' around the top for comfort. The toe and heel should be hard. The tongue should be sewn to the uppers to keep out dirt and water. Before using leather boots on the trail, treat the leather parts with boot polish, Neatsfoot oil or a similar product. Wear them at home, in town and on short walks to break them in, so that the leather moulds to your feet. A good pair of leather boots needs at least 75 kilometres of walking to wear them in properly.

If you participate in a variety of different trails, you will find it worthwhile to own more than one pair of boots, each of different mass and quality, saving the best boots for the rugged expeditions.

The midsole (layers of leather or rubber between the boot upper and the bottom sole) determines the stiffness of the boot. Climbers need very rigid boots for support, whereas those for walkers and hikers need not be so heavy. Remember, a kilogram of boot when worn is the equivalent of four kilograms carried on your back. The most popular sole is the black, knobby, lugged sole, its high carbon content ensuring long life. Its major drawback is that the rugged, deep-patterned sole forms a reverse imprint in the soil, thus making it susceptible to erosion. Tyre-sole boots are sufficient for nature trails and summer hiking.

The fit of the boot is critical. A poorly made or badly fitting pair not only leads to painful blisters but also causes the feet to tire much more quickly than a well-fitting boot with good support. Take your own socks with you when trying on boots. A heavy wool outer sock should be fitted over a light cotton or light, woollen sock. Push your foot forward in the unlaced boot until your toes touch the front. There should be room to insert your index finger between the back of the boot and your heel. Your toes should never reach the end of the boot, as this will cause extreme discomfort on any downhill stretches.

A final point: even when hiking boots get very wet – which happens frequently – never dry them next to a fire or in direct heat. It cooks the life out of the leather. Rather allow them to air dry, stuffed with newspaper to retain their shape.

BACKPACKS

Today most hiking backpacks have internal frames, although external frame packs still have their devotees amongst experienced hikers. Each has advantages and disadvantages.

External frame packs are stable, able to carry heavy weights or odd-shaped loads, and are cool – the frame allows some air to flow between the back and the pack. Internal frame packs are firm, flex to allow freedom of movement, and the better models can be finely adjusted to fit the shape of your body perfectly.

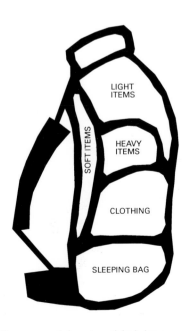

The recommended way to pack for balance and comfort.

I own both an external frame pack for hiking trails, and an internal frame, softpack for mountaineering and kloofing trips. I prefer to travel with the latter as it is more acceptable to airlines and can be squeezed more easily into the boot of a car.

Whether you choose a soft pack or an external frame model, buy one which has a firm, foam-padded hip belt and adjustable shoulder straps. The hip belt takes much of the load from your shoulders and the padding is essential to prevent sore, bruised muscles and bones.

To keep the top of the pack from falling over backwards, look for the new suspension system which uses the shoulder harness. Better packs have 'load-lifter' straps that can be adjusted to lift the top of the shoulder straps right off your shoulders. The only contact then is against the front of your upper chest.

As with boots, fit your backpack in the store before buying it. Make sure that the hip belt wraps around your hips and not your waist or torso. Do not buy a pack that rides more than five centimetres above your head.

Women should be aware that most packs are designed for longer-bodied men, although very recently 'women-only' packs have been manufactured. These take into consideration a woman's lower centre of gravity, wider hips, narrower shoulders and shorter torso.

The bag itself comprises one, two or three compartments, often with two to four pockets. Be sure these zipped or buckled pockets are large enough for items you want handy – water bottle, bird guide, first aid kit, camera, etc. A top-loading bag is best for oversized and protruding loads – make certain the storm flap that covers the top is large enough to cover the bulkiest load you will carry. Front-loading bags with large, zipped flaps are most accessible and easiest for keeping your gear organized. No matter how waterproof your pack is supposed to be, always wrap everything in plastic.

Check nylon coil and plastic-toothed zip fasteners for clean stitching, reinforced at stress points. Also, look for the new, quick-release plastic buckles which are not only more convenient, but safer in some situations, such as when crossing streams. Lift tabs are also useful as they make tightening or loosening your shoulder straps easier, which in turn makes it easier to get a proper adjustment. This lessens back strain, prevents blisters and gives the legs more freedom.

When loading your bag, pack the densest items closest to your centre of gravity. In other words, place the heaviest items on top and to the back of your pack, with the smaller equipment in the lower side pockets; the water bottle should be placed in an upper side pocket.

Women should realize that they often suffer from weight packed too high because they do not have the upper body strength of men. This weight can interfere with arm movement and breathing. Therefore, a good suspension system and hip belt are essential. A 'moonbag' worn around the waist is handy for small items you are likely to need along the way – lip salve, tissues, snacks, camera, permit and the like – and avoids unnecessary stops to offload and open your backpack along the trail.

Although colour choice is personal, remember that bright colours aid identification in dense bush, heavy mist or snow and low light intensities.

Few backpacks are as neatly packed as this one!

DAYPACKS

On short walks or guided wilderness trails, you will need only a daypack. Some daypacks have padded backs, which come in handy as you don't have to concern yourself with packing the bag too carefully. To be inconspicuous near large game, wilderness trail participants should avoid brightly coloured (orange, red or yellow) packs. Daypacks should have one or two easily accessible side pockets and should be large enough to contain all your cold-weather needs and interpretive equipment (guide books, camera, binoculars, etc.).

Another consideration when buying a daypack is that it should fit comfortably into your larger backpack. Many hiking trails allow you to reach the hut by lunch time, leaving you the afternoon to ramble or climb to a nearby peak, carrying only your daypack. Many people on mountaineering trips camp in an area and then make day trips from their base. Daypacks are also useful as hand baggage on airlines. Some backpacks are now made with a removable, zippered compartment that, when detached, can be worn as a small daypack.

Kloofing trips require fully waterproofed packs. Such a pack can be dropped in a river or pool and will float freely downstream over and under rapids, without any of its contents getting wet. The best way to waterproof a pack is to place all critical items (ones that must be kept dry) in a heavy-duty, double-seamed plastic bag, twisting the opening and tying it securely with a shoelace. A second bag over the first provides extra protection. Garbage bags, shopping bags and even some sports bags are not strong enough for waterproofing packs. The most reliable bags can be purchased at camping stores. Place the bag inside the major compartment of your backpack. Non-critical items (water bottle, plates, tinned food, etc.) are carried in side pockets. For ordinary hikes, place all your gear in a waterproof bag inside your pack and simply fold over the opening. This will ensure dry gear at the end of a rainy trek. I use a brand new, heavy-duty bag for each kloofing expedition to ensure that there are no small holes, and then put the 'used' bags in my pack for more usual mountaineering or hiking trips.

Bearing all this in mind, if you should ask for a porter to assist you on Malawi's Mount Mulanje, in the Drakensberg, or elsewhere in Africa, do not be too surprised if he empties the contents of your smartly styled pack into a duffel bag and then proceeds up the mountain carrying it on his head!

SLEEPING GEAR

The major consideration when buying a sleeping bag should be warmth. If you plan to hike during winter or in regions with sharp nocturnal drops in temperature, a natural down filling is highly recommended. Down is not only light and warm but also soft, easily compressible and capable of complete recovery after being stuffed into a carrying sack for long periods. Duck (as opposed to goose) down is slightly less efficient, but cheaper. Some manufacturers combine the two to produce a more economical bag. The biggest drawback of any down is that it will not keep you warm if it gets soaked. It is also allergenic and is becoming increasingly expensive.

The highest quality man-made fibre fills, however, have none of these drawbacks and, most importantly, they will keep you warm even when wet. They dry quickly and are easily washed at home and, being less compressible, insulate you better from the ground. On the minus side, they are not as light or compact as down. However, new fillings, such as Hollofil, have narrowed the gap between synthetics and down considerably in recent years.

Whichever you choose, make sure your zip fastener is nylon, backed by a 'draught tube' filled with down or fibre to keep out the cold. Unless your sleeping bag is used only in warm temperatures, you should avoid sewn-through constructions, which cause cold spots along stitch lines. If you buy a bag for cold weather but also plan to use it in warm weather, make sure that it has a double zipper so that you can vent the lower end to keep cool.

Never buy a sleeping bag made of waterproof material. When you sleep you perspire and the resultant condensation will soak you and your bag if it cannot evaporate. I find the ideal combination to be a cotton inner lining with a water-repellent but breathable nylon material used for the outside.

The shape of the bag is also important. Mummy bags (form-fitting and with a hood) give maximum warmth, and are more compact than standard rectangular bags.

Mattresses are only really necessary for camping in wilderness areas. Most huts in southern Africa supply them and they are usually provided on guided trails. Some people carry an air mattress that can double as a lilo, but these are very heavy and puncture easily. If a mattress is required, a thin, closed-cell foam mattress is ideal, being both waterproof and very light.

A reasonably comfortable pillow can be made by stuffing clothes into the bag used to carry your sleeping bag during the day.

If you intend hiking in an area where malaria is prevalent you should invest in a lightweight mosquito net. With the current upsurge of multiple drug-resistant strains of malaria in African countries, it makes sense to avoid being bitten by malaria-bearing mosquitoes.

TENTS

When selecting a tent, look for one with a waterproof floor and roof and a 'breathing' ceiling. Until recently, all quality tents were double-skinned, with a ceiling of breathing nylon, having a few centimetres or more below a waterproof flysheet. Body moisture passes through the ceiling, condenses on

Lightweight dome tents are ideal for backpacking trips in wilderness areas.

the impermeable fly and drips off harmlessly on the outside.

There are new waterproof materials available which let out body moisture yet repel rain. These materials are patented as Goretex, Ventex, etc. Single-layer tents are constructed from these fabrics, the 1-person tents having proved most successful.

Today's lightweight tents come in a multitude of shapes – tepee, A-frame, dome, 'half-dome', tunnel or hoop, and star. Any one of these is satisfactory if it has the specifications I have mentioned. However, dome or half-dome designs will stand without pegs or guy ropes, which makes them particularly useful where staking is difficult – on beaches or riverbanks, on frozen ground or in snow. Dome designs have flexible poles which tense inside fabric sleeves, pushing outwards on the walls so as to support the tent.

Other features to look for when buying a tent are tight, preferably double- and triple-row stitching; reinforced stress points; mosquito netting for doors, windows and vent openings; and nylon zips. A 2-person backpacker's tent should weigh less than 3 kg. Good tents are expensive but can last a lifetime, so don't compromise on quality.

Portable camp-stoves have replaced the roaring and potentially dangerous campfire on most overnight trails.

STOVES

It is virtually impossible to go trailing today without a camp-stove if you want to cook food or have hot fluids. The camp-stove is the symbol of the environmentally conscious trailist. In many areas fires are prohibited – either because of depletion of natural wood supplies, fire danger or simply to prevent unsightly camp fire remains from spoiling the environment. Hence, with the exception of organized (guided) trail safaris, camp-stoves are necessary for all trail users and mountaineers.

Like tents, there is a wide range of stoves from which to choose and although selection is largely a matter of personal preference, it is important to know what to look for. Among the aspects to be considered are type of fuel needed, its availability and price; the stove's mass; accessories included, such as pots; ease of packing; safety, stability and reliability; boiling speed; cold weather performance; starting and running ease; cleaning; noise; and environmental concerns such as disposing of fuel cartridges.

Fuel, especially its availability in rural areas, is a very important consideration. There are three main types of backpacking stoves which can be classified according to the fuel they use: liquid fuel (benzine and paraffin), gas (butane and propane) and alcohol (methylated spirits).

Benzine stoves (such as the Coleman and Swedish Optimus models) rate high on efficiency and fuel economy and work well in low temperatures. Their main disadvantages are the delicate task of refuelling and the preheating, which results in a dangerous flare being created. In Africa generally, benzine is not readily available except in some of the larger towns.

Paraffin stoves such as Optimus 45 and 111 are safer and burn hotter than those that run on benzine. Another 'pro' of paraffin is that it is relatively cheap and readily available in most African countries, making it an excellent choice for groups and expeditions. The 'cons' include its smokiness,

smell and starting difficulty. A popular stove is the multi-fuel Coleman, which burns either paraffin or benzine and does not need to be primed, even in cold weather or at high altitudes.

Butane fuel (such as Camping Gaz) and propane fuel come in disposable pressurized steel cylinders. These fuels are popular with beginners because they are convenient, refuelling is simple (either push or screw in a new cylinder) and they start easily. The problems are possible leakage of gas between the stove and the canister, the sheer bulk and mass of the cylinders, and what to do with the 'empties'. Butane is a poor cold weather fuel because it will not vaporize below 0° C; in addition, the heat output decreases as the amount of fuel in the cartridge decreases. Propane, popular in Europe and America because it is a better fuel for cold weather and at high altitudes, is not readily available in southern Africa.

Alcohol (methylated spirits) stoves include my favourite, the Optimus storm-cooker. It weighs only 0,68 kg and includes two large saucepans, a frying pan, wind-shield and a pot grip. The main disadvantage of an alcohol stove is that more fuel is needed to produce as much heat as paraffin stoves. However, unlike most other stove fuels, it is not a petroleum product. The storm-cooker is quiet, stable, reliable and poses no problems in starting or

No member of a hiking party should be without a waterbottle.

refuelling. Alcohol spirit is readily available throughout Africa.

Solid fuel stoves are best kept for emergencies – they have low heating power and less delicate simmering control, but they are safe and relatively impervious to cold.

Compatibility is critical. Observe your friends' stoves, know the conditions in which you will be trailing and then decide what to buy. *Warning*: Never use a camp-stove in your tent. They have been known to cause carbon monoxide poisoning, and they can flare up and turn all your petroleum-based synthetic equipment into a blazing inferno.

CLOTHES

High, exposed windy summits; warm, sun-heated valleys; hot midday sun; and cold nights – these may all be experienced in a 24-hour hiking day. Always be prepared for a wide range of temperatures, as well as humidity and rain. Two important principles to keep in mind are that several light layers are more adaptable than a single, heavy garment, and that wool is the only fabric that retains its warmth even when wet. Wearing wet cotton clothing actually makes you feel colder than walking naked.

Warm clothing: Adopt the layered look and be as warm or as cool as you like. Here are suggestions, starting with extremities: light wool or synthetic socks under heavy woollen ones (avoid cotton socks inside boots as cotton holds moisture next to the skin, promoting soft skin and blisters); thin leather glove liners and wool or fibrefill insulated mittens; a brimmed cotton hat for sunshine and a woollen hat or balaclava for the cold; cotton shorts or long pants for daytime; warm underwear, long woollen pants for winter or high altitudes; water repellent, breathable nylon, wind-resistant pants; a thin, cotton, long-sleeved shirt for summer, a woollen one for cold weather or high altitudes; a woollen jersey or a down or fibrefill sleeveless jacket; a down or fibrefill hooded parka; and a waterproof/breathable hooded parka and long pants for rain. Do not take denim jeans on a hike; lightweight tracksuit pants are more comfortable and not as bulky or heavy.

Choose versatile clothes. For example, a long-sleeved cotton shirt can be worn buttoned or unbuttoned, sleeves rolled up or down, and it has pockets for handkerchief, glucose sweets or tissues. A T-shirt has none of these.

A small but useful hint for day hikers – leave a change of warm clothes at your base camp. It is a most encouraging prospect to look forward to if you become cold and wet in the course of a strenuous outing.

Rainwear: The biggest clothing dilemma hikers face is choosing between waterproof and water repellent outerwear. If, when trailing, you walk wearing a waterproof jacket and pants, you keep out the rain but keep in body moisture. Water-repellent clothes allow body moisture to escape but, as the waterprof coating wears off, will eventually prove useless in keeping out rain. If you do not have a Goretex or Ventex rain suit, it is inevitable that in prolonged rain you will get wet. Waterproof rain gear has the advantage, however, of keeping out wind associated with rain and thereby allowing your body to warm its trapped moisture. In this way, the waterproof jacket and/or pants work like a diving wetsuit.

An alternative to Goretex or Ventex rain suits is the waterproof gear with new design features such as fuller cut or zipped underarm vents, a hood with a rain visor to keep water out of your face, and few seams, with none over the top of the shoulders.

Some people have expressed dissatisfaction with Goretex or Ventex and similar fabrics that claim to be windproof and waterproof while allowing condensation to evaporate. This is because these fabrics work well only if the rate of perspiration is low, there are significant temperature and relative humidity differences between the outside and the inside of the material, and the outer surface is not coated with a layer of water, such as during a torrential downpour. These are also the reasons why the large dome Goretex tents have failed while the tiny, one-person Goretex tents work well. In pouring rain you will get damp no matter what you wear. How wet you get will depend on how ingeniously you arrange your clothing layers.

Underwear and pyjamas: Select your underwear by taking into consideration the weather conditions you are likely to encounter. The coolest types of underwear are those made from pure cotton or cotton and nylon wash-and-wear combinations. I prefer the quicker-drying synthetic fabrics on long trips when washing must be done. Cold weather underclothing requires more thought. Longjohns made of cotton in a conventional weave or net construction are warm, but woven wool and silk combinations are even warmer. In really cold conditions wear 2- or 3-ply thermals – which usually consist of a wool outer layer, with silk or cotton next to the skin.

For winter nightwear, I use long wool underwear – either for lounging in a tent or as pyjamas. In the summer, a cotton track suit or clean, light underwear is all that is necessary.

Never wear your walking clothes in your sleeping bag. Apart from reasons of hygiene, the fibres of your walking clothes compress and fill with dirt and moisture so that they are no longer able to trap and hold warm air.

SMALL ITEMS

Included here are some hard-learned hints about some small items I suggest in the checklist.

Space blanket (sportsman's blanket): This is a true space-age product and has rapidly become indispensable. Incredibly light (340 g), it consists of a centre fibre net with an aluminium film laminated in a different colour on either side of the fibre. The silver side reflects heat while the red serves as an emergency signal. I have used my space blanket as a groundsheet, blanket, rain poncho, tent, heat reflector, signal to a lost companion, waterproofer in my pack and even as a 'tablecloth'.

Survival bag: A large plastic bag which can be used in extreme weather conditions to prevent you getting cold and wet. It can also be used as a groundsheet or to waterproof your pack.

Mug or cup: Metal ones burn your lips when you are drinking hot fluid and can freeze your lips when the mercury drops, so the heat-resistant, strong plastic type is preferable.

Wristwatch: I never concerned myself with time until I started leading hikes and realized how important a watch is. Days are not endless – darkness does fall and most of us are not particularly good judges of sun-time. Watches are essential in emergencies – to arrange meeting or search times. Some reserves close their gates at certain times, especially in day-use areas. At low altitudes (below about 3 000 m), the average hiker can climb 300 m in an hour or hike between 2,5 and 3,5 km an hour on a trail. Watches, in conjunction with maps, can give you an idea of how to pace yourself and how long your meal and swim breaks can be.

Torch (flashlight): Headlamps, such as those worn by miners are most convenient and leave your hands (and mouth) free for other things. However, small, bright hand-torches weigh less. Always use long-life, alkaline batteries and carry spares, plus an extra bulb. To prevent accidental switch-on and draining, invert the batteries and place a piece of paper between them and the contact.

Binoculars: When hikers think of binoculars they immediately think of watching birds. However, binoculars on the trail have much broader uses – identifying wildlife, picking out landmarks for a compass bearing, searching for lost souls, sighting distant beacons and structures, studying a cliff face or rough terrain, or just generally taking in the 'big picture'. In the past their bulky size and heavy weight made binoculars an item sure to be left behind. However, the new generation of compact, lightweight binoculars allows for more magnifying power and brightness, and can weigh as little as 200 g. The 'roof prism' models, in which the prisms are inside the straight barrel of the instrument, are among the lightest and trimmest of all.

FOOD

Everyone's favourite subject and the hardest to agree on. I find it enormously amusing to hike with a group of people and watch the various foods produced from their packs – everything from smoked oysters to hard, fishmeal squares, commonly referred to as 'dog biscuits'. Many factors govern what foods to take: length of trip, number of people, distance to be travelled, demands of the terrain, time of year and nature of overnight facilities – quite apart from personal preference.

In general, hiking food should be nutritious, lightweight, low in bulk, and prepared with a minimum of fuss and fuel. I divide food into five categories: fresh, tinned, dried, dehydrated and freeze-dried.

Fresh foods, such as oranges, apples, cold meats, tomatoes, bread and eggs, spoil easily with exposure to the sun, and are heavy and bulky. They are great for day walks, but for mountaineering and hiking only the strongest members of the party will feast on them. I find, however, that the enjoyment of one item of fresh fruit a day on any type of hike is worth the extra muscle strain!

Tinned foods should generally be avoided as the tins and the opener add extra mass, and once the

The packed lunch supplied on a guided wilderness trail provides balanced nutrition.

TRAILING CHECKLIST

N Necessary **S** Suggested **D** Dependent on season **A** Dependent on ecotype **O** Optional – not needed
UP Usually Provided (check information sheet from company operating the trail, or trail brochures
I Inquire when and if needed (necessary when crossing political boundaries)

	SELF-GUIDED NATURE TRAILS AND DAY WALKS	WILDERNESS (Guided trails)	HIKING (with huts)	WILDERNESS TREKKING AND MOUNTAINEERING	MOUNTAIN BIKING (overnight)
Camping/sleeping					
Overnight backpack	—	—	N	N	—
Daypack	N	S	S	S	—
Moonbag	S	S	S	O	S
Tent, poles, pegs	—	UP	—	N	N
Spare cord	O	—	O	S	S
Sleeping bag and stuffsack	—	UP	N	N	N
Survival bag	—	—	S	S	O
Foam pad or air mattress	—	UP	UP	N	N
Ground sheet or space blanket	S	S	S	N	N
Pillow	—	O	O	O	O
Mosquito nets	—	UP	SA	SA	SA
Bike panniers	—	—	—	—	N
Eating					
Camp-stove	O	UP	S	N	O
Pots	O	UP	N	N	O
Pot gripper	O	UP	S	N	O
Dishes	O	UP	N	N	O
Fuel container/spare canister	O	UP	N	N	O
Fuel	O	UP	N	N	O
Water bottle (1 litre capacity)	N	UP	N	N	N
Mug/cup	S	UP	N	N	O
Can opener	O	UP	O	O	O
Matches (waterproofed)	S	UP	N	N	N
Plastic rubbish bags	N	UP	N	N	N
Biodegradable washing-up liquid	O	UP	N	N	O
Scouring pad	O	UP	N	N	O
Dishcloths	N	UP	N	N	O
Knife, fork, spoon set	O	UP	N	N	O
Water purification tablets	S	UP	S	S	S
Fresh foods	S	UP	O	O	O
Dried foods	O	UP	S	S	S
Dehydrated foods	O	UP	S	S	O
Emergency rations	N	UP	N	N	N
Tea/coffee	N	UP	N	N	O
Isotonic powders	O	UP	S	S	O
Toiletries					
Toilet paper	N	N	N	N	N
Toilet trowel	S	UP	N	N	S
Toothbrush/toothpaste	—	N	N	N	N
Biodegradable body soap	—	N	N	N	N
Towel	O	N	N	N	O
Moisturizing cream	S	S	S	S	S
Insect repellent	DA	SA	DA	DA	DA
Sun-screen cream	N	N	N	N	N
Lip salve	N	N	N	N	N
Tissues	N	N	N	N	N
Facecloth	N	N	N	N	N
Shaving kit	—	O	O	O	O
Mirror (also for emergency signalling)	N	O	N	N	S
Foot powder	O	N	N	N	O
Hair brush/comb	O	S	S	S	O
Emergency					
First aid kit (see page 21)	N	N	N	N	N
Snakebite kit	O	UP	O	O	O

	SELF-GUIDED NATURE TRAILS AND DAY WALKS	WILDERNESS (Guided trails)	HIKING (with huts)	WILDERNESS TREKKING AND MOUNTAINEERING	MOUNTAIN BIKING (overnight)
Emergency fire starter	O	UP	N	N	N
Whistle	N	N	N	N	N
Pocket knife	N	N	N	N	N
Compass	N	O	N	N	N
Candle	O	UP	N	N	O
Safety pins	OS	O	N	N	N
Rubber bands	OS	O	N	N	O
Small change (20c, 50c pieces)	N	O	N	N	O
Spare spectacles/contact lenses	O	N	N	N	N
Sunglasses	N	N	N	N	N
Needle and thread	O	UPS	S	S	O
Spare bootlaces	N	N	N	N	O
Pen/pencil/paper	N	S	N	N	O
Wristwatch	N	S	N	N	N
Torch with spare batteries and bulb	N	N	N	N	O
Bike lights (headlight and reflector)	—	—	—	—	N
Bike repair kit	—	—	—	—	N
Clothing					
Woollen Socks	N	N	N	N	O
Cotton Socks	N	N	N	N	N
Spare socks	OS	N	N	N	O
Underwear	N	N	N	N	N
Thermal underwear	OD	D	D	D	D
Tracksuit	—	S	O	O	O
Sunhat or cap	N	N	N	N	O
Woollen hat/balaclava	D	D	N	N	D
Waterproof rain jacket/poncho	N	N	N	N	N
Waterproof rain pants	D	D	N	N	N
Boots	N	N	N	N	O
Spare footwear	O	N	N	N	O
Gloves/mittens	D	D	N	N	N
Long pants	N	N	N	N	S
Shorts	S	S	N	N	S
Bathing costume	S	S	S	S	O
T-shirt	S	O	S	S	O
Long-sleeved shirt	N	N	N	N	S
Woollen sweater	N	N	N	N	S
Windjacket	S	S	S	S	N
Padded jacket/vest	D	D	D	D	D
Helmet	—	—	—	—	N
Gaiters long (for snow)	D	D	D	D	—
Gaiters short (for vegetation)	S	S	S	S	—
Down booties/mukluks	—	O	DO	DO	—
Handkerchief	S	S	S	S	S
Miscellaneous					
Maps	N	S	N	N	N
Personal identification	N	N	N	N	N
Passport/visas	I	I	I	I	I
Vaccination certificate	I	I	I	I	I
Permit	N	UP	N	N	N
Brochure/trail guide	N	S	N	N	N
Camera/film	O	O	O	O	O
Binoculars	S	N	S	S	O
Walking stick	O	O	O	O	—
Field guides	S	S	S	S	O
Waterproof bags	N	UP	N	N	N

contents have been eaten you must put the smelly tin with its rough edges back in your pack and carry dead weight. No, you cannot bury the tin. Exceptions to carrying tins can be made on canoeing or kloofing trips when waterproofing is essential and space for waterproofed items is dear.

Dried foods (figs, raisins, crispbreads, sweets, nuts, health bars and energy bars) will form your diet's bulk, make great trail snacks and are usually packed with energy-giving kilojoules.

Dehydrated foods such as dried soup mixes, isotonic drinks, non-fat milk powders, instant potatoes, some breakfast cereals, and certain brand meats or soya, or ready-made meals such as Toppers or Wonderfood, are important hiking foods. They need little storage space, have a long storage life and a higher long-term nutritive value than any other type of food. Their only disadvantage is that preparation takes a little longer. Dehydrating removes 98 per cent of moisture, making the food shrink in size. Dehydrated foods are usually less costly than dried or off-season fresh foods, and are certainly less expensive than those which are freeze-dried. (Note: in some African countries dehydrated foods are not cheap, but can easily be airfreighted for expeditions or carried in your baggage.)

Freeze-dried foods (Mountain House and other specialized brands) are sliced or processed, immersed or sprayed with a preserving agent, and frozen. The moisture content in the food turns to ice. The food is then placed in a vacuum chamber and subjected to microwaves. As a result of this, the ice is evaporated, leaving the cellular structure of the food essentially the same. The food is lightweight and porous and, when immersed in water, rapidly soaks it up to become reconstituted and ready to use. The convenient and extremely lightweight nature of freeze-dried foods makes them indispensable for strenuous hiking trips. However, they are hard to find in Africa, are very expensive and within six months their nutritional value is lower and deteriorates faster than dehydrated products. Two of the more unusual freeze-dried foods that are my favourites are freeze-dried pizza and ice-cream!

When planning meals remember the following guidelines:
1. Energy: Kilojoules required by the average hiker walking with a moderate load during a cool summer's day vary between 14 700 and 16 800 a day. Hard, mountain walking in winter, such as in the Drakensberg, can increase needs to between 25 200 and 33 600 kj a day.
2. Properly planned meals, including snacks, need not exceed 1 kg per person per day.
3. Seasonings are important and give a necessary sparkle to the trail traveller's meal.
4. Always carry extra, high-energy and quickly digestible food, some of which can be eaten cold, in a separate re-sealable plastic bag. Suggestions include glucose tablets, nuts, dried fruit, chocolate, instant soup and 'health' bars (for example, Noogy bars, PVM bars and Muesli bars). Always carry more tea than you think you will need; not coffee or alcohol, both of which if drunk in excess can cause hypothermia.

For more detailed information, read Ursula Steven's *The South African Backpacker's Cookbook* (Struik).

EMERGENCIES ON THE TRAIL

I hesitate to write this section and hope you never need it. I hesitate because it is not a substitute for a proper first aid course or mountain survival training. Statistically, besides common blisters, burns, insect bites, scratches and sprains, most of you will never be affected by mountain altitude sickness (the trails included in this guide book are all under 3 700 m), hypo- or hyperthermia, malaria or bilharzia. However, you will not be affected only if you are aware of how to avoid the dangers.

Analysis of survival cases has proved that mental stress associated with emergencies – especially with being lost and alone – produces fear and anxiety. In turn, these psychological stresses detrimentally affect judgment and attitudes. The prepared hiker can certainly curb, if not eliminate, such stresses. Before embarking on a hike or trail:
1. Obtain adequate information about your route by reading this guide and the relevant hiking pamphlet thoroughly.
2. Each member of the group should carry a map. If the trail authorities don't issue enough to go around, make more copies.
3. Know how to use your equipment. Be familiar with the use of a compass, reading a map, lighting a camp-stove, setting up a tent, fixing a broken pack frame, preparing powdered foods, using a first aid kit, treating snake-bites and using water purification tablets. It is beyond the scope of this guide to provide instructions on all these aspects; however, it is the responsibility of the hiker to prepare himself with such knowledge before setting off.
4. Build into your schedule ample time between overnight points. Taking into consideration stops *en route* for rest, nature study, food and water, the hiker should average at least 2 to 3 km an hour. Remember, however, that more time will be needed for steep climbs.
5. Discuss plans of action for all foreseeable emergencies with members of your party. Make sure that each member carries his own water, trail snacks, emergency rations and first aid kit.
6. Never hike alone.

In an emergency, stop immediately. Review your situation thoroughly, consider possible solutions by analyzing the weather, terrain, available resources and time of day, and only then plan a course of action which best suits your available energy, health and resources.

Above all, stay calm (remember that, nowadays, a crisis is generally short-term, lasting less than 72 hours) and stay together. The following are suggestions which will help you to cope with common outdoor problems.

GETTING LOST

If you lose your way on a hiking trail, retrace your route, returning to some clear indication of the path. Make certain that you have not overlooked a change in trail direction. If you find yourself completely lost, stay put. Usually if the hiker does not wander aimlessly, he will not be far from the trail. Signal for help audibly and visibly – blow three times on your whistle, or flash a mirror three times to the sun.

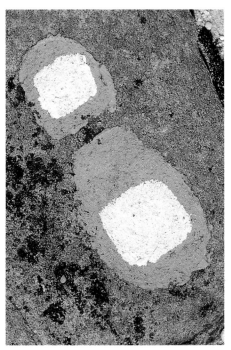

Watch for the signboards or bright motifs that usually demarcate the trail and indicate a change of direction.

Dense smoke, produced by placing green leaves or grass in a fire, will generally be seen from lookout towers. Don't start a veld fire! Repeat your distress signal regularly. If you have not wandered far from the trail, there is a good chance of other hikers or officials responding. Air searches can be assisted by placing a large, bright object, such as your space blanket, in a conspicuous place.

AIR, WATER, SHELTER AND FOOD

Air, water, shelter and food are essentials for survival. You can live for three weeks or more without food, three days without water, three hours without protection in hostile weather and three to five minutes without air. It is, therefore, imperative that the hiker be familiar with techniques to provide these essentials if faced with a survival situation.
Water If you become lost without sufficient water, conserve body fluids by moving only in the cool of the day, talking as little as possible and keeping your mouth closed.

Study the immediate terrain, searching for clues to water sources, such as dense reeds or thickly marked, converging game trails. Large movements of animals (including doves and game birds) during sunset and sunrise usually indicate the directions in which water can be found. Dig beneath the surface of dry riverbeds, especially near the base of big rocks and cliffs where an abnormal amount of vegetation is growing, or at the base of large sand dunes on the shady or steep sides.

Many of the water-securing techniques of the Bushmen can teach modern man how to survive. For example, if you find water by digging, preserve the hole with a bark lining and bury a grass bundle with two reeds projecting. The bundle acts as a sieve, and the reeds (one thoroughly perforated) act as a straw. Dew or moisture from rocks and plants can be gathered, using a cloth to gently mop up moisture and and then wringing it into a container. During the rainy season, collect water by digging a hole and lining it with a groundsheet or poncho.

The probability of having to resort to the extremes described above in order to find water while trailing is very slight. However, the possibility that water on the trail is contaminated with diarrhoea-causing bacteria or disease-causing viruses (for example, hepatitis) or protozoa (for example, amoeba) is increasing. All water not originating from high mountain areas should be sterilized by boiling for at least 3 minutes; by adding water purification tablets; or by using one of the lightweight filters now on the market to filter out harmful organisms: be sure to follow the instructions provided carefully.

The use of tincture of iodine is one of the simplest, safest, most rapid and effective methods of water sterilization. Add 5 drops to one litre of clean water or 10 drops to one litre of cloudy water (strained or filtered if necessary) allowing 30 minutes before drinking. The water will be sterilized of entero-viruses, bacteria and their spores, algae and protozoans and their cysts.

The tincture of iodine method is superior to other common chemicals used to sterilize water, such as commercial tincture (alcohol solution alone) or chlorine solution or tablets. Chlorination does not kill cysts causing amoebic dysentery nor some other parasites causing infective diarrhoea.

Water contaminated with bilharzia must be boiled, as cercariae (the snail parasites) can pass through a simple sand filter or strainer.

Shelter When building a shelter, avoid expending excess energy. A cave or natural depression is far superior to a complicated wooden structure. Your shelter must minimize body heat loss and maximize body protection. Choose an area protected from the wind. Avoid valleys, streambeds or areas close to rivers. Avoid camping near anthills as snakes are often prevalent here. Also avoid fig trees, as the figs are often infested with flies and insects teem around them. Urine on paths leading into your camp site helps to discourage wildlife visitors.

Food In an emergency, food is your least important worry and excess energy should not be expended searching for edible plants and animals. Many plants in southern Africa are toxic and should not be eaten unless you are absolutely sure of their identification and edibility.

FLOODED RIVERS

In 1978 I was caught with 40 children on the Transkei's Wild Coast in a flood reputed to be the worst in that country's history. In 1981 I was on the Springbok Hiking Trail during the infamous Laingsburg Floods which took many lives and virtually destroyed several Karoo towns. I have experienced numerous occasions where a flooded river presented a major obstacle between myself and the hiking hut or another destination. Because of these experiences I have learned to respect the tremendous force of rushing water and its potential hazards – and to act accordingly.

If you are confronted by a flooded watercourse *do not attempt to cross it*. If mountaineering, set up camp on high ground well away from the river. A swollen river usually returns to normal flow almost as quickly as it rises. Wait until the waters subside.

HIKER'S FIRST AID KIT

Crêpe bandage
Sterile wound dressings
Gauze bandages
Triangular bandage
Cotton wool
Adhesive first aid tape
Elastoplast
Moleskin (for blisters)
Scissors
Pain killer (e.g. aspirin, or Panado)
Antiseptic ointment
Antihistamine cream
Anti-diarrhoea pills
Anti-nausea and vomiting tablets
Oral rehydration fluid sachets
Water purification tablets
Tweezers
Needle and thread
Knee and ankle guards
Personal medication prescription pills
Malaria tablets

FIRST AID EXTRAS

The following are additional aids suggested for more comprehensive or group kits.
Disposable plastic chemical cold pack The cold pack consists of chemicals in a double-walled plastic bag. When the inner pouch is squeezed the chemicals mix, and in three seconds the temperature of the pack drops to approximately 0 °C, at which it stays for about 30 minutes. Cold packs can be applied to injuries in order to slow bleeding and lessen pain and muscle spasm; reduce temperature; lessen swelling resulting from burns, insect bites and other causes; and help in the management of heat exhaustion and heatstroke.
Disposable plastic instant heat pack The heat pack works on the same principle as the cold pack, producing a source of immediate heat for therapy where needed, such as for hypothermia or superficial frostbite, or as a 'hot water bottle' in your sleeping bag.

If hiking on a trail, return to the last accessible shelter or examine the route map for emergency exits. In either case, do not feel you are 'losing face' or failing by turning back. Rather sleep safe and dry than be mentioned in Monday morning's newspaper headlines.

AILMENTS, INJURY AND ILLNESS

The wise trailist has a thorough knowledge of basic first aid. All outdoors people should be prepared for emergencies – by taking a course run by the Red Cross, St. John Ambulance or an equivalent first aid society and by carrying a comprehensive first aid kit including a first aid manual, such as the small, lightweight, concise booklet issued by the Red Cross Society.

If a hiker suffers from any condition such as asthma, diabetes or a life-threatening allergy, or is

---

taking any medication, the group should be informed, in case of an emergency.

Most trailists will experience at least one of the following problems (listed here alphabetically). I have encountered most, either personally or as a mishap to a companion:

Animal bites
All animals carry potentially harmful germs on their teeth and any bite breaking the skin should be cleaned with an antiseptic. Medical attention should be sought, as tetanus and rabies could cause complications.

Artificial respiration
(Cardiopulmonary resuscitation) Hikers may need to administer CPR if a victim is struck by lightning, drowns, is crushed by ice, snow or rocks, chokes, falls or suffers a head blow, or is suffering from inadequate ventilation in his tent. If an individual has difficulty breathing, artificial respiration must be applied within minutes or death will occur. Ideally, CPR should be administered by someone who has had the basic training; failing this, try to remember the following steps.

Lie the victim on his back. Remove all foreign matter from his mouth and open the air passage by pulling the chin upwards until the head is fully tipped back. Form a tight seal by placing your mouth over the victim's mouth (with a small child, place your mouth over both nose and mouth) while exhaling. If there is no pulse at the wrist or neck, place hands one on top of the other on the victim's left chest and compress every second. For small children, exhale shallow breaths every three seconds and compress the left chest by placing both thumbs on the chest and your fingers around the child's sides and back. For every breath, compress the chest five times. If at all possible, don't give up until medical assistance arrives.

Bilharzia
This potentially dangerous disease is endemic to many areas of southern and central Africa including Zambia, Malawi, Botswana and Zimbabwe, as well as the northern and eastern part of South Africa including much of the Transvaal, Natal, Ciskei and Transkei. It is contracted by contact with water contaminated by freshwater snails.

When in a bilharzia area, avoid drinking, swimming or washing in water along the edges of quiet pools, dams, streams or irrigation canals, especially those near human habitation. If you do enter such streams or pools, the risk of infection is reduced if you dry yourself well immediately after swimming or washing.

Unless you are trailing for a very long time, bilharzia will not be noticed until you return home. Signs of blood in your urine or faeces, or painful or frequent urination should be reported immediately to a doctor. A word of caution: bilharzia is on the increase in southern Africa.

Bites and sting
Bees, wasps and spiders If a person is not allergic, then bee and wasp stings and spider bites produce only local irritation and swelling which can be treated by cold compresses and aspirin. Calamine lotion applied to the area is soothing and relieves itching. Remove the sting, being careful not to

irritate the affected area in doing so. Allergic reactions to bees and wasps are uncommon but dangerous, and include shortness of breath, shock and unconsciousness. All allergic persons should carry a special anti-allergy kit at all times. Poisonous spider bites will produce similar reactions to the bites of scorpions.

Scorpions All scorpion stings cause local burning pain, but only some species are harmful. The reactions to harmful species depend on the type of scorpion, and include swelling and redness at the bite site, restlessness and agitation, sweating and salivation, confusion, nausea or vomiting, muscular twitching, numbness, impaired visual acuity, difficulty with breathing and convulsions.

An icepack, if available, should be applied as soon as possible to relieve the pain and retard the onset of systematic signs. Immobilize the limb involved with tight crêpe bandages and splints, to prevent spread of the venom. The scorpion should be preserved intact for identification. Specific antivenoms should be administered only by doctors when there are obvious systematic signs.

Snakes Snake bites are uncommon in southern Africa and fewer than one in 10 species are dangerous to man. Because snake venom differs widely from species to species, there is no place for anti-snake venom serum in a hiker's first aid kit. Antiserum should only be administered by a doctor.

In all cases of snake bite, keep the victim as still as possible, elevate the affected part, keeping the area of the bite cold (but not ice-cold), apply a broad crêpe bandage over the wound and along the limb and take the victim to a doctor or hospital without delay. Do not apply a tourniquet or make incisions over the fang marks.

Ticks Tick bites are characterized by local redness and itching, and can result in tick bite fever. All ticks that have burrowed into the skin should be gently pulled off; do not crush them. The more patient hiker can remove a small tick by covering it with oil, vaseline or antiseptic ointment to close its breathing pores. If the entire tick does not back out within a few minutes, and steady pulling does not succeed, the area must be cleansed and covered.

To prevent ticks attaching themselves, hikers should apply insect repellent around their ankles and below their knees, and wear socks. This method is effective in discouraging most ticks, in particular the tiny red 'pepper' ticks that cause severe itching and skin irritation.

Ticks are most active in spring and early summer and are found wherever cattle or game are plentiful. If you have been walking in a tick-infested area, inspect your clothing and body for these elusive creatures at the first opportunity.

Blisters

Blisters will probably be your most common hiking injury and are caused mainly by friction from ill-fitting boots or pack straps. As soon as you feel discomfort, cover the tender area with moleskin or an adhesive tape such as 'Elastoplast'. If a blister has already formed, cut a hole in the moleskin which is equal to the size of the blister and place the moleskin around the blister – the purpose being to reduce rubbing on the tender area. Contrary to popular belief, placing plasters on blisters serves only to increase friction, not reduce it. Broken blisters should be kept clean to prevent infection.

Burns

Never apply a lotion to a second degree burn (a deep burn with blistering). Instead, immerse the burn in cold water, blot dry and cover with a dry, sterile dressing. Third degree burns (those causing underlying tissue damage, charring and cell destruction) should be treated with sterile dressings and then wrapped in plastic to exclude air and possible infection. Ice packs can be applied over the plastic for pain relief. Treat the victim for shock and seek medical attention without delay. If the burn is very deep, then a tetanus toxoid booster is recommended for anyone who has not had a booster for 5 years.

Choking

In the event of a companion choking, remove any objects from the mouth but do not attempt to prise out anything lodged in the throat.

If this does not dislodge the object, do the 'Heimlich manoeuvre'. Stand behind the victim with his back against you, and encircle his waist with your arms. Make a fist with one hand and clasp it with your other. Then push your fist sharply upwards into the diaphragm (in the middle of the body below the ribs). The object should be expelled with the air in the windpipe. Repeat the manoeuvre if necessary. If the victim is not breathing, begin artificial respiration immediately.

Dehydration

In extreme heat dehydration can lead to heat exhaustion. Symptoms are a headache, dizziness, fatigue, weakness, rapid heart rate, nausea, vomiting, muscle and abdominal cramps, confusion and unconsciousness. Death can occur if timely action is not taken.

At the first signs of dehydration or heat exhaustion, seek shade if possible. If no shade is available, a space blanket can be used as a sun guard. Remember to place the silver side facing the sun. Strip the victim, sprinkle him with cool water and fan him to create an artificial sweat.

To prevent dehydration, make sure that you have enough to drink in hot weather, and carry extra water in dry areas or during summer.

If a hiker becomes dehydrated, he should ideally drink quantities of a diluted hypotonic commercial solution, or a mixture of 1 teaspoon of salt plus 8 teaspoons of glucose or sugar (sucrose) in 1 litre of water, until he passes urine. If these are not available, water or other cold beverages should be taken.

Dislocations

Injuries in which the normal relationship of a joint is disrupted are indicated by pain aggravated by motion, tenderness, swelling, discoloration, limitation of motion and deformity of the joint.

Correction of dislocation is dangerous if attempted by amateurs. Therefore, treat dislocations as fractures – immobilize by splinting. Dislocation of a finger, however, can be corrected by gently pulling on the injured digit, and then splinting by taping to an adjacent, uninjured finger.

Eyes

Tree sap in the eye can cause inflammation. Bathe the eye with milk or water. If foreign particles get into the eye and are not quickly washed away, gently lift particles with a moist corner of a sterile gauze pad. If an object becomes lodged in the eye, prevent further harm by placing a doughnut bandage over the eye (encircle the orbit), and bandage both eyes. To prevent further harm the victim must be carried so there is absolutely no temptation to use the injured eye.

Fainting

Simple fainting occurs as a result of reduced blood supply to the brain. The symptoms of fainting can be alleviated by making the victim sit with his head between his knees, or, if he has fainted, by lying him down and elevating his feet. Should the victim not regain consciousness within minutes, fainting may be a symptom of a more serious problem (such as heat exhaustion or low blood sugar).

Food poisoning

Meat and other foodstuffs that have been contaminated by bacteria can make a person ill. Symptoms such as vomiting, diarrhoea and stomach cramps are the most common signs of food poisoning. Give frequent sips of electrolyte solution, or a glucose-salt solution as described earlier (see Dehydration), but if this is impossible, give Coca-Cola or plain water, which may prevent dehydration in an emergency if the vomiting and diarrhoea are severe.

Fractures and related injuries

The first aid treatment for fractures is immobilization – splints above and below the fracture, and keeping adjacent joints as still as possible. Signs of a fracture include severe pain and tenderness, swelling and discoloration, deformity and/or shortness of the limb, abnormal mobility, shock and the inability or disinclination of the patient to move the broken limb. If a patient has a neck or back injury do not move him/her until medical assistance arrives. Incorrect handling may cause spinal cord injury and paralysis.

Not all fractures are easily detected. I hiked on a stress fracture for 5 weeks before the pain and discomfort drove me to an orthopaedic surgeon who put me in a cast for 3 months. A stress fracture is not a sharp break and you do not feel sudden pain. Rather, it is many micro-fractures caused by continual strain, such as carrying too heavy a backpack. If you feel localized pain and cannot understand why, see your doctor. X-rays are the only means of identifying a stress fracture, but such a fracture may appear on film only 3 to 4 weeks after the onset of symptoms.

Frostbite

Southern Africa is not always warm and sunny, and many mountainous regions, especially in the Drakensberg and western Cape, are regularly snow-capped in winter. In such conditions frostbite is a real danger. It occurs when water in the cells and between the skin and capillaries freezes, thus injuring tissues both physically and chemically.

There are two types of frostbite, and each is treated differently. Superficial frostbite occurs when the skin is a pale, greyish-white colour, and is cold or numb. This occurs because the skin and adjacent subcutaneous tissues are frozen. Treatment includes covering the area with a dry, insulating windproof material, placing a warm body next to it, and applying firm, steady pressure. In no case should the affected area be rubbed! Immerse the limb in water with a temperature of 42 to 44° C and administer warm food and non-alcoholic drinks to the patient.

In contrast, deep frostbite occurs when tissue muscle, bone and tendons are frozen and the patient does not feel pain but the tissues are hard. Deep frostbite cases should never be thawed if in danger of refreezing. When properly sheltered, immerse the affected area in a large waterbath of 42 to 44 °C under sterile conditions for no longer than 20 minutes at a time. After rewarming, clean the affected area gently with disinfectants and apply antibiotic creams to the broken skin. Elevate the affected area to reduce swelling and seek medical assistance as soon as possible.

Hypothermia
Southern African hiking trails have been the stage of avoidable and unnecessary deaths from hypothermia. This can easily be avoided with the correct equipment, the right attitude and basic knowledge.

What causes hypothermia? Hypothermia occurs when heat is lost from the body because of cold weather injuries; dampness from sweating, rain, mist, snow or wind; fatigue from over-extending yourself; and excessive drinking of alcohol or coffee. Eventually, the body's core temperature plummets and if not halted, death occurs in 2 hours.

How to avoid hypothermia Wear woollen clothes which insulate when wet; avoid heavy cotton clothing such as denim jeans. Dress in layers and adjust heat by taking off or putting on clothing as desired. Carry top-quality rainwear. Protect your head and neck with a balaclava, hat or scarf. Carry warm mittens with a waterproof outer covering. Eat regularly when hiking, including energy-rich foods like nuts, chocolate, sweets, raisins and dried fruit. Drink sweet, hot fluids like soup, tea with honey, or hot chocolate; avoid coffee and alcohol. Seek shelter in extreme conditions rather than push on regardlessly, especially if one of the party develops symptoms of hypothermia. Act to restore warmth.

What can I do if my body loses heat faster than it produces it? Stay dry by getting out of the elements. Find protection from the wind. Put on dry clothes and a woollen hat. Eat high-energy foods. Drink hot, energy-rich fluids. Rest, set up camp, give up your goal – tomorrow is another day!

Malaria
Malaria, which was almost wiped out in Africa through strict control measures but has once again reached epidemic proportions and become the continent's most deadly disease, is endemic to northern Namibia, Zimbabwe, Malawi, Botswana, the northern and eastern Transvaal, Swaziland and northern Natal. It is transmitted by infected *Anopheles* mosquitoes and in many areas in Africa there are multiple, drug-resistant strains. In spite of taking their malaria tablets, hikers in northern Natal, Zimbabwe and Malawi have contracted malaria. Standard malarial drugs prevent many, but not all cases of malaria, although they may reduce its clinical severity. Before entering a malaria zone, take prophylactic tablets according to instructions. Consult your doctor or local pharmacist for advice on the correct prophylactic to take for the area you intend visiting.

The main clinical manifestations are severe flu-like symptoms such as chills, headache, light-sensitive eyes and muscle pains with a persistent fever. Any person who has severe flu-like symptoms with fever and weakness as early as 7 to 14 days, and up to six months, after returning from an endemic malaria area should inform their doctor that they have been in these areas, even if they have taken their preventative medication as prescribed. Note that very young children and pregnant women are particularly vulnerable to malaria.

To reduce the chances of contracting malaria: Visit endemic malarial areas only during winter when mosquitoes are absent or less active – September to April are times of greatest risk, while May and August are the months of lowest transmission in Zululand; apply insect repellents at regular intervals (every 2 to 3 hours) and wear long pants and sleeves from sunset to sunrise; sleep under mosquito nets.

Mountain altitude sickness
It is generally believed that altitude sickness occurs only above 4 250 m. However, it can affect any mountain traveller who attains altitude too quickly – even at 2 500 m. Therefore it is a potential problem for two areas described in this guide: the Mulanje Massif in Malawi, and the Drakensberg in Natal and Lesotho.

People affected by altitude sickness display some of the following symptoms: loss of appetite, sleeping difficulty, severe headaches and nausea. More serious cases are characterized by vomiting, irrational behaviour, loss of energy or unconsciousness. Although the most severe forms of mountain altitude sickness are possible at altitudes as low as 2 500 to 3 500 m, they are usually associated with climbers at higher elevations.

When mountaineering at high altitudes, allow your body time to acclimatize. In other words, by climbing slowly (at a rate at which you feel comfortable) and resting between climbs, your body will gradually adapt. If symptoms persist, stay put or descend until you feel better. If you have a cold, influenza, a cough, asthma or are feeling unwell, do not proceed to high altitudes as these conditions will become exaggerated above 2 500 m.

An individual's bodily response to altitude change is difficult to predict and although pre-trip physical conditioning will make your trip easier, it does not guarantee prevention of altitude sickness. I have witnessed the finest and keenest member of a climbing party become afflicted with severe altitude sickness because of over-exertion and refusal to walk slowly and rest frequently.

Nosebleeds
Minor nosebleeds can be stopped by applying direct pressure against the nostril or by clamping the tip of the nose. The patient should sit with the head tilted slightly forward, so that blood does not drain back into the throat. Cold applications to the nose should also aid coagulation.

Shock
Shock can be caused by fractures, loss of fluids (either blood, plasma or perspiration) or any significant injury combined with cold and/or pain. When a person is suffering from shock he feels cold and

---

SYMPTOMS AND TREATMENT OF HYPOTHERMIA

Symptoms	Treatment
Shivering	Stop immediately
Difficulty in manual movements	Drink hot, sweet liquids
Unusual responses	Eat high-energy foods
Loss of clothing goes unnoticed	Protect against the elements
Stumbling	Rewarm with dry clothes
Intense shivering	
Difficulty in speech	
Sluggish thinking	
Loss of memory	
Increased shivering	Drink fluids as hot as possible
Muscle rigidity and jerky movements	Eat only quickly digested foods such as soup,
Frequent stumbling	sweet liquids and candy bars
Sluggish responses	Get out of wind and wet into a sheltered location
Skin blue and puffy	Get into sleeping bag after stripping off wet clothes
Loss of memory	Continue drinking hot liquids
Irrational behaviour	Build fire to warm the camp
Drowsiness	
Pulse and respiration slows	DO NOT FALL ASLEEP
Unconscious	All of the above plus:
No response to the spoken word	Apply skin to skin reheat with two naked,
No reflexes	warm donors, in the same sleeping bag
Erratic heartbeat	Keep victim awake; sleep means death
Respiratory and cardiac failure	All of the above plus:
Oedema and haemorrhage in lungs	Seek professional medical treatment
Death	

REMEMBER: If you are tired, wet and cold, hypothermia can still strike – even at 10 °C!

These hikers on the strenuous Genadendal Mountain Trail appear inadequately prepared for the midday sun.

clammy to the touch, the pulse is weak and rapid and he may feel faint.

If shock is suspected:

1. The person should lie down with his/her feet raised (except in cases of head injury, breathing difficulty, an unsplinted fractured lower extremity, or pain). In the case of deep cuts or wounds, control bleeding if possible.

2. Maintain body heat but *do not overheat!* Insulate the patient from the ground and keep him/her dry and covered (especially head and neck); protect the patient from the weather, and provide external warmth. Placing him/her in a warm sleeping bag with another person is a fast and effective method of providing external warmth.

3. Give no food or fluid by mouth.

4. Obtain medical help immediately.

Sprains

Torn or stretched soft tissue surrounding joints results in local haemorrhaging and painful swelling. Elevate the injury and apply cold compresses locally to the affected joints. Sprained ankles should be supported by a figure-of-eight bandage put on over the hiking boot. If you forget these tips, remember 'PRICE': Principles of Rest, Ice (if possible), Compression and Elevation for sprains.

Strains

Stretched muscles are accompanied by minor haemorrhaging and should be treated with warm compresses to aid circulation.

More common injuries, bursitis, tendinitis and shin splints are caused by inflammation of the tendons or the fluid lubricating them. Hikers unaccustomed to the use of certain muscles for an extended length of time may initially feel stiff. Apply moist heat and take aspirin for relief. If it is necessary to continue using the affected area, the application of an ice bandage may relieve pain.

Sunburn

In southern Africa, and, in fact, internationally, the incidence of skin cancer from exposure to sunlight, and ultraviolet radiation in particular, has been firmly established. Ultraviolet rays cause irreversible damage to the skin and are at their most intense at high altitudes and between 10.00 am and 2.00 pm during the day.

It makes sense to avoid the harmful effects of the sun by wearing a hat and long-sleeved shirt with a collar, and by using a protective sunscreen cream on all exposed areas, including ears and feet.

Unconsciousness

Shock, a blow to the head, heat and numerous other factors may cause unconsciousness. The most immediate action is to keep the air passages open. If the neck is not broken, lie the victim on his side (so his tongue falls forward), tilting his head back. If the victim vomits, keep his head lower than his chest and turned to the side. Never administer food, fluids or medication by mouth to an unconscious person. If the victim has false teeth or contact lenses, remove them.

Wounds

A major wound, accompanied by severe bleeding, is best treated by applying direct pressure on the wound, or major arm and leg arteries, and elevating the wounded limb and applying a cold compress. The use of a tourniquet can be dangerous and such a bandage should be applied only as a last resort. If used, a tourniquet should be wide so that it does not cause further injury.

Minor wounds (abrasions and punctures) should be cleaned and dressed under sterile conditions. If further injury or bleeding could result from removal of foreign objects embedded in the wound, leave them.

Lacerations or incisions must be cleaned thoroughly and then an antiseptic ointment applied. Open wounds should be closed with adhesive tape or dressing. Cover with a sterile dressing and bandage (preferably roller gauze covered with a triangular bandage).

'THE CARRY'

Evacuation of a victim should be attempted only if the accident takes place near the trail, if the injuries are not major, if the distance to reach help is no longer than 8 to 12 km and if the victim is strong enough to be moved.

The following carries are used in an emergency when a rope is unavailable: when two men are present, a 2-man carry chair can be made by grasping one of your own wrists and one of the other carrier's. Over rough terrain, you should 'back-pack' the victim out. A 1-man carry involves tying the patient's wrists to his ankles with strips of cloth, then carrying him like a pack. An unconscious person can be carried out in this fashion.

A stretcher can be made from two poles and a blanket (or sleeping bag, if necessary).

TRAILING AND THE ENVIRONMENT

Perhaps it is ironic that an American should write a book on how to see southern Africa on foot. My Capetonian hiking companions often joke, 'Meet an American, see the Cape'. In 1975 when I was 'imported' by the then-Department of Forestry, there existed only a handful of trails for the public and an overriding reluctance among many government authorities to permit the public access to natural areas under their control.

As I write, the entire scene has changed – the trails era has hit southern Africa. Suddenly it appears as if everyone has taken up trailing in one or more of its many forms: hiking, rambling, back-packing, snorkelling, jogging, canoeing, caving, horse-riding … and with government authorities planning and constructing trails and private entrepreneurs organizing expeditions, would-be trailists are inundated with fascinating, yet sometimes confusing, new opportunities. This guide has been compiled to put these trails into perspective, and to provide background and a detailed directory of what exists and 'what's coming'. So whether you are a resident wanting to explore your surroundings as the trailblazers of earlier times did (well, almost), a teacher/youth leader wanting to capture the attention and interest of your students, a traveller seeking the adventure approach to touring, or an amateur naturalist, this book will serve as your companion while discovering the wonderful diversity of southern Africa's natural environment.

In *Everyone's Guide to Trailing & Mountaineering in Southern Africa*, I grouped the trails into broad ecologically based regions. My reasoning was that when you decide to go trailing or mountaineering, you are, consciously or otherwise, making a decision to travel to a specific environment because it promises the climate, scenery, wildlife, terrain and type of atmosphere or mood you wish to experience. Hence, an ecological directory seemed better able to allow you to choose your travels and prepare yourself for the natural elements you were likely to encounter.

However, feedback from many users of the first edition indicated that grouping trails in traditional geo-political boundaries better facilitated their trip planning. Ecological groupings are educationally expedient, but regional groupings are more practical. Therefore, although I still emphasize 'ecotrail zones' throughout the text, readers of this edition will find that all trails are grouped in close proximity to each other; that is, either in one of South Africa's four provinces or its independent states, or in other countries of southern Africa.

'Ecology', 'ecosystems' and many other 'conservation orientated' terms are much bandied about, and in the process, very often misused. Each has its specific meaning. Ecology is the study of relationships between animals and plants and the environment in which they live, while an ecosystem is the whole community of organisms interacting within a particular environment, for example, a pond or a forest. Major ecological regions with distinct groups of plants and animals extending over large natural areas such as the savannah, coastal forest or desert, incorporate a

number of ecosystems and are known as biomes. In compiling this guide I have adopted the following 10 major biomes: fynbos; semi-desert and karoo; acacia savannah (Kalahari); coastal desert; eastern evergreen temperate forests; coastal bush and subtropical forests; eastern grasslands; Drakensberg; highveld; and dry woodlands. Malawi, which is the only region dominated by the Rift Valley system, has been considered separately as the eleventh major ecoregion.

The limits of these regions lack the rigidity of man-devised boundaries. Nevertheless, each biome is, by virtue of its living and non-living components, distinct. These include physical factors such as soil type; climatic factors such as temperature, rainfall, wind, light intensity, air pressure and humidity; physiographic factors such as the general topography, altitude, slope of the land, drainage and presence of water; and finally, biotic factors, which are the plant and animal communities interacting in the region.

When the biomes meet, the transition from one to the next is seldom abrupt. More typically, the changeover is gradual, providing an 'in-between' region referred to by ecologists as an edge or ecotone. Ecotones are often richer in species diversity that either of the adjacent biomes because they harbour species from both. An intertidal rocky coast is such an edge, the meeting of the sea and the land creating a unique habitat for a profusion of plants and animals: birds, fish, invertebrates, seaweeds – the myriad forms of intertidal life.

FYNBOS

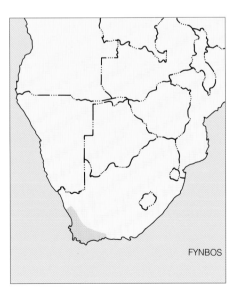

FYNBOS

From the Olifants River in the west and tailing out beyond the Cedarberg to the north, the fynbos extends southwards to the sea and then eastwards to Port Elizabeth along two mountain chains, the inland ranges of Swartberg-Baviaanskloof and the coastal Langeberg-Outeniqua-Tsitsikamma ranges. Traversed by numerous nature and hiking trails, and offering many opportunities for mountaineering,

this irregular, L-shaped region is one of southern Africa's most popular trailing zones. It is a region of striking contrasts. Sweeps of unspoilt beach, interrupted by rocky promontories where mountains slide into the sea, encourage countless hours of rambling. But it is inland that real adventure and challenge await the addicted outdoorsman, for the narrow coastal plain rapidly gives way to a rugged mass of high peaks that tower over fertile, river-veined valleys.

Hiking through these magnificent folded mountains inevitably leads to questions concerning their origins. During the Upper Silurian to Lower Carboniferous times (the Paleozoic pre-Karoo Era), the Cape formations – known technically as Table Mountain quartzitic sandstones and shales, Bokkeveld shales and Witteberg shales, sandstones and quartzites – were deposited under water. In Karoo times (Permo-Triassic), geological forces of unimaginable power heaved and buckled these sediments into the tortured convolutions and folds of the Cape mountains. Today, the Witteberg rocks are scarce, brutally weathered and eroded through time, and the Bokkeveld shales form the economically important basin and valley soils. It is, therefore, the more resilient Table Mountain sandstone outcrops with their intricate mass of knobs and pinnacles, which are responsible for the spectacular mountaineering challenges.

The 'variegated' cliff faces always attract the hiker's attention – worn to an overall whitish-grey, but gashed with reddish-brown or broken surfaces where deposits of iron oxides have formed. The rough surface of the weather-beaten sandstones is frequently hollowed out into shallow depressions which hold water for some time after rains – a welcome refreshment for tired, parched hikers when no other source of water is available.

This rugged terrain is tough on hikers' boots: durable soles are essential. I recommend investing in a pair of boots with the closely spaced, lugged soles which pick up less debris and therefore cause less damage to the environment.

As breathtaking and spectacular as the contorted landscape undoubtedly is, however, the true wonder of the region surely lies in its dense and shrubby vegetation. The mountain complex yields a nutrient-deficient sandy soil which, ironically, supports the most diverse and puzzling plant kingdom in the world. Known as fynbos – an Afrikaans term meaning 'fine bush', alluding to the fine-leaved form of many of the shrubs and their bushy habit – this remarkable vegetation type occupies less than one thousandth of the total area covered by the earth's six floral kingdoms. Yet it contains more species per square metre than anywhere else in the world. Furthermore, a great number of these plants have a very limited distribution range; for example, the snow protea, *Protea cryophila*, is seen in nature only on the high peaks of the Cedarberg, where winter snowfalls are common.

The fynbos, therefore, is a zone to be enjoyed by trailists with a sensitive botanical eye; although at first the sheer number of different plants is bewildering, once aware of the three main 'elements',

Fynbos of the Cape forms one of the world's six floral kingdoms.

you will have a framework for identifying individual plants. The dominant element – the restioids – comprises the 'Cape reeds', which many people confuse with grasses. On closer inspection, however, these are distinguished by their tufted, near-leafless, tubular or wiry stems. The ericoids – sometimes referred to as heaths, which so often paint mountain slopes in bright colours – are small shrubs with narrow, rolled leaves. It is the proteoid element, however, which although not always present, is so characteristic of the Cape. The most easily recognized member of the Proteaceae family is the genus *Protea* as many produce large, showy flowerheads.

The fynbos is threatened on many fronts. Already 60 per cent has been destroyed by indiscriminate use of fire and other human actions, agriculture, careless urban sprawl and alien plant species. These 'exotic' invaders were introduced, deliberately or inadvertently, from overseas and now seriously threaten indigenous flora. Hakea, rooikrans and wattle are some of the more than 50 alien plants that are rapidly changing the veld and, in the process, endangering the many animals reliant on the fynbos for their survival. Endemic birds such as the Cape sugarbird, the protea seedeater and the orangebreasted sunbird, are vulnerable to diminution of the fynbos, but it is the mammals which are particularly at risk. Many have been ruthlessly exterminated or have had their habitats destroyed. Species such as klipspringer, grey rhebok, baboon and dassie are still readily seen by hikers, but others such as the bontebok exist only in reserves or on farms.

When trailing in the fynbos, always keep a wary eye on the sky as, of all 11 trailing zones, the weather patterns in this region are the most unpredictable. This is very largely because of the Cape's diverse topography, and is further complicated by the marine temperature differences between the cold west coast and warmer southern waters. Long-term forecasting for mountaineers is particularly difficult as temperature, visibility and precipitation often vary, not only from range to range but also with altitude.

I love the fynbos for its unbelievable diversity – in winter when softly hued light reflects off rain-laden clouds, in spring (September and October) when the veld explodes with floral colour unequalled elsewhere on earth, and during the long, hot, lazy days of summer which invite boulder-hopping and swimming in the clear, refreshing waters of the kloofs. Whenever you choose to hike, however, respect the mountains and their latent power. Be prepared – always carry warm clothes, emergency rations and waterproof bags – and you will be able to appreciate fully the Cape's many-faceted character.

SEMI-DESERT AND KAROO

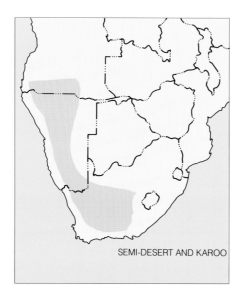

SEMI-DESERT AND KAROO

I once drove a young man from Johannesburg to Cape Town who insisted that 'nothing' existed between these two cities. Obviously he had never hiked in the Karoo for if he had, he would have come to know and appreciate the great natural wealth of these seemingly endless scrubby plains, punctuated occasionally by rocky outcrops and rondavel-shaped koppies.

Perhaps, though, my companion had a point, for certainly the region is very different from what it

must have been like in early times. The great herds that once roamed the plains have been hunted almost out of existence and replaced with flocks of merino sheep, regimented into camps whose barbed wire perimeters line kilometre after kilometre of the national highway. Such farming has also placed great pressure on the natural vegetation and, despite advanced farming practices, erosion is extensive in some places.

There are parts, although often remote, where the trailist can enjoy glimpses of the Karoo's past. Also, a renewed interest in preserving the Great Karoo's natural heritage has motivated the creation of many new reserves, such as the Karoo National Park in Beaufort West and the Karoo Nature Reserve in Graaff-Reinet, where the aim is to re-create a balanced Karoo ecosystem. Hiking trails designed to encourage people to discover the Karoo are an integral part of these programmes.

The semi-desert and Karoo, one of the larger trailing and mountaineering regions discussed in this book, is a vast tract of land that sweeps down diagonally from the north-west to the barrier of mountains along the Cape coast. It encompasses the Kaokoveld in northern Namibia; the Damaraland Plain, between the Otavi and Khomas highlands; Great Namaqualand and Bushmanland, a very dry area which extends southwards from Damaraland and the Kalahari to the Orange River; Little Namaqualand, from the Atlantic coast to the hilly escarpment edge; the Little Karoo, the dry plains lying to the north of the southern Cape folded mountains; and the Great Karoo, the large basin, 600 to 900 m above sea level, between the highveld escarpment and the Little Karoo.

Geologically, the region is very young. It comprises mostly the Karoo System which was laid down only some 280 to 180 million years ago. Despite its comparatively short history, the region has passed through many developmental stages.

The story of the Karoo begins in the humid heat of 'Dwyka times', about 250 million years ago, when most of southern Africa was a low-lying basin, a natural sump in which sediments – accumulated from riverborne sand, mud and silt – settled to form shales. Vleis and swamps with primitive vegetation evolved. But then the earth froze and huge rivers of ice deposited rocks and mud into the basin. This material hardened into what is termed Dwyka tillite.

As the earth again grew warmer, the glaciers retreated and mud and coarse sand were carried into the swampy Karoo basin to form the Ecca Series. A temperate climate prevailed and diversified plant life evolved. Early conifers, club-mosses, horsetails, ferns and large trees flourished in the congenial conditions, and these were eventually to fossilize into the great coal deposits that underline the Karoo veld. Then temperatures and rainfall rose, and animals dependent on the verdant vegetation evolved. Reptiles populated the swamps in great abundance.

The next series laid down, the Stormberg, comprises sediments deposited in desert conditions and capped by lava which poured through fissures. Less susceptible to the effects of weathering than the shales and sandstones into which they intruded, these Stormberg lavas formed the dolerite ridges, koppies and cliffs so characteristic of the Karoo landscape of today.

The parts of Namibia falling within the semi-desert and Karoo ecological zone have an older geological history. Namibia is composed of pre-Cambrian rocks (more than 500 million years old), which originated when life on earth barely existed. Predominant are the Damara System of the Late pre-Cambrian era, and the even older Nosib System. These series contain limestones, shales and sands which were deposited in a deep sea and then metamorphosed into marble, schist, gneiss, granite and sandstone. The Damara and Nosib systems have produced copper, lead, zinc, iron and vanadium deposits – all of which are important to the country's economy.

The popular mountaineering area of the Waterberg is formed from the Karoo system, while the Brandberg, Spitzkoppe and Erongo mountains are the granitic cores remaining from intense volcanic activity that metamorphosed triassic sandstones of the Stormberg Series. The canyons of the Kuiseb, Swakop, Kunene and Fish rivers, also of particular interest to the mountaineer, were formed by vigorous erosion in a humid climate that coincided with the Pleistocene ice-age in the northern hemisphere.

In the north-west the Karoo's contact with the highveld, grassveld and savannah is abrupt, but in the south, transition with the fynbos is gradual and suggests that Karoo vegetation is an environmental modification of fynbos. Plants of the Karoo are basically of two types – succulents and woody shrubs. Succulents, except for some outlying populations in the Little Karoo, occupy the driest, western parts of the Karoo area, and the drier the region, the shorter the bushes. Low succulent bushes, those less than 20 cm tall, include ericoid shrublets and fleshy-leaved mesembryanthemums. Kraalbos and yellow milkbush are common. In the western winter rainfall area, geophytes – plants that survive the harsh winters by storing food in subterranean buds – provide the rich spring flower displays for which Namaqualand is so justly famed. Tall succulent bushes, those over a metre high, include euphorbias, cotyledons, aloes, crassulas and portulacas.

Along river courses, even though many are dry for much of the year, trees grow abundantly; common species include sweet thorn, white karoo (a willow-like bush), and kunibush.

Woody shrubs thrive in the more easterly parts of the Karoo where conditions are less harsh. They comprise the taller mountain plants growing along ridges and on koppies, and the smaller Karoo bushes, covering the flat plateau area. These smaller shrubs are well adapted to conserving moisture – they are spaced apart to reduce competition, their leaves are small to reduce transpiration and they have spreading root systems with the main roots penetrating very deeply into the soil. Common Karoo bushes include pentzias, daisies, the sweet resin bush and bitter Karoo bush, the 'gannas' and the saltbushes.

Karoo animals, too, are well attuned to their dry habitats. Once the plains thronged with large herds of antelope such as springbok, eland, gemsbok and hartebeest. Although their numbers were huge, reports by early travellers indicate that the game was never uniformly scattered, but was concentrated in massive, migrating herds. These animals were subsequently decimated by indiscriminate hunting during the 1700s and 1800s but even today, animals abound in the more remote areas. For example, the

The wild flowers of Namaqualand are well adapted to their dry environment.

Namibian plateau still supports kudu, duiker, steenbok, zebra, warthog and leopard, as well as smaller mammals such as the wildcat, meercat, fieldmouse, skunk, hare, dassie, bat and the scaly anteater. The *Agama planiceps* is a commonly seen, brightly coloured rock lizard, while mountain tortoises and leguaans are also present.

The central plateau of Namibia, studded with prominent termite mounds, hosts land snails, unusual for such a dry region, long stick insects and many centipedes, giant millipedes, solifuges and spiders, including the large baboon, or trap-door, spider. The totally red sand lizard, *Eremias undata rubens*, well camouflaged in its red sandstone habitat, is also occasionally spotted by the alert hiker.

Trailists with an interest in bird-watching will not be disappointed as, considering the overall aridity of South Africa's semi-desert and Karoo, birdlife is surprisingly plentiful. My personal favourite is the rosyfaced lovebird. Some of the region's 'specials' are, in Damaraland, the Monteiro's and Bradfield's hornbills, Rüppell's parrot and the whitetailed shrike; in Great Namaqualand and Bushmanland, the Scaler's and red lark and the sociable weaver; and in the Karoo, the rufouseared warbler, Layard's titbabbler, the Karoo green warbler and the Namaqua prinia.

Climatic variations in the semi-desert and Karoo zone are extreme. In the Karoo, the main rainy season is March and April, while for the rest of the region, the rain (250 mm annually) is distributed fairly evenly throughout the year. Thunderstorms are common. Temperature fluctuations, both diurnal and seasonal, are extreme, so much so that even after the hottest of summer days – the average for January is 32 °C – the hottest temperature can drop sharply when the sun sets and reduce trailists to a huddle around a campfire. Such fluctuations are even more drastic during winter, and although daytime temperatures may be pleasantly cool to warm – the average for July is 18 °C – temperatures regularly plummet well below freezing under the crystal-clear night skies. From June to August,

frosts are common, as are snowfalls on the mountain peaks. Backpackers in the semi-desert and Karoo region must be well equipped, therefore, to ensure daytime comfort and warmth at night.

In Namibia, although rainfall is low and droughts can be prolonged, flash floods are not uncommon. Such spates can be extremely hazardous for the unwary hiker and camp sites must be chosen with care. Never pitch your tent in a dry watercourse – this is asking for trouble. Sudden floods are not restricted to Namibia, and, as evidenced by the devastating 1981 floods of Laingsburg, are possible throughout the region.

ACACIA SAVANNAH OR KALAHARI

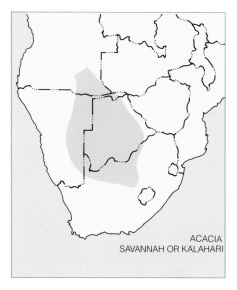

ACACIA SAVANNAH OR KALAHARI

Sprawling across the centre of southern Africa, embracing much of Botswana and encroaching into Namibia, Zimbabwe and the northern Cape, is a vast sea of undeveloped sand and swampland ideal for rambling and wilderness exploration. Ecologically, this huge basin, lying 915 to 1 067 m above sea level, is known as acacia savannah, but more commonly it is referred to as the Kalahari, thornveld or simply 'bush'.

Basically, the Kalahari is two contiguous regions. In the north-east, the predominantly summer rainfall exceeds 500 mm a year and feeds the swamplands formed by the Okavango, Linyanti and Zambezi rivers. Apart from these 'oases', however, the northern parts are characterized by sand, scrub, a few trees and grassland. By contrast, the drier south-western Kalahari, which reaches southwards from Ovamboland to the Orange River where it merges with the semi-desert and Karoo ecological zone, is a region of sparsely vegetated red sandveld, dissected by corridors of 'dry forest' along waterless riverbeds.

But for the occasional rocky projection providing some relief, the entire Kalahari basin is mantled with sand. In places it is fluvial in origin, but mostly it derives from the Stormberg Series of the Karoo System. Whatever its origins, however, its distribution results from wind action under desert conditions. It is this sand, not the meagre annual rainfall, which contributes largely to the region's 'dehydrated' appearance, as the loosely packed particles allow water to drain away too rapidly to benefit plant life.

Synonymous with the stark Kalahari landscape is the camelthorn, *Acacia erioloba*. This tall tree, with its spreading branches, sparsely leaved and wickedly armed with long, needle-like thorns, is welcomed by animals and hikers alike, for it provides all-too-scarce shade from the relentless sun. Other trees include the deciduous commiphoras, burkeas and terminalias, which vary in density from fairly close cover, through scattered parkland to almost pure grassland. Even where the savannah is thickest, however, the covering of short and tall Bushman grasses is interrupted by bald patches of all-pervading dry red sands.

Surface water is very seldom available and trailists must always carry sufficient liquid for their needs. In a few localities, calcification has sealed the porous sand and here, in pans and depressions, water collects during infrequent downpours. The few Bushmen who still subsist in the Kalahari make their homes near these pans which are crisscrossed with tracks of cattle and wildlife in search of water.

Animals of the acacia savannah, especially the beetles, are closely allied to those of the Namib (see Coastal Desert ecological zone). Gemsbok, hartebeest, springbok, lion and ostrich are as much part of the Kalahari as the thornveld and sand, but perhaps the most evocative image is that of huge sociable weaver nests which often envelop the crowns of tall trees. These unmistakable 'condominiums' represent highly integrated nest chambers. They are used continuously for many, many years and extend beyond the housing needs of the weaver birds themselves: rosyfaced lovebirds, pygmy falcons, and scalyfeathered and redheaded finches are some of the 'uninvited guests', while giant eagle owls often nest atop the communes. These intruders cause little direct harm to the weavers, unlike the Cape cobra which raids the nest for eggs and the honey badger which will claw it to shreds in search of chicks.

Other birds commonly seen in the Kalahari are the chat flycatcher, sandgrouse, pied babbler and many lark species. The dry riverine forests throng with Cape and Burchell's glossy starlings and yellowbilled hornbills. Trailists camping near water are likely to be woken by turtle and Namaqua doves which fly in for their daily drink, and on cloudy or dewy mornings, harvester termites emerge from their sandy retreats, unwittingly providing a handsome feast for a variety of birds from warblers to vultures.

Throughout the Kalahari, beware of puff adders and scorpions. Solifuges, or sun-spiders, should also be treated with respect, for although their bite is not poisonous, they can deliver nasty wounds. They are extremely savage hunters and will devour any arthropod they can conquer.

Hiking in this region is most comfortable in winter. Mosquito netting during the night is recommended for those sensitive to biting insects; and although uncomfortable in the heat of the day, thick clothing helps guard against the bite of the tsetse fly that infests the northern swamps.

If you are a novice to the Kalahari, including its northernmost wilderness, the Okavango swamps, I strongly recommend experiencing this area under the guidance of a reputable organization. The Wilderness Leadership School, Educational Wildlife Expeditions and Wildlife Safaris, for example, run fantastic adventures into the remotest areas. Although more expensive than a do-it-yourself safari, these organizations not only transport you by light aircraft and canoe into the heart of the primeval setting, but also have as their objective interpreting its ecological intricacies for their trailists. In comparison, self-generated treks require thorough and judicious planning. A rugged vehicle – a four-wheel drive is recommended – fully equipped with spare parts, extra petrol and water tanks, and a mechanically minded trailist, are minimum prerequisites for exploration off the 'tourist track'.

COASTAL DESERT

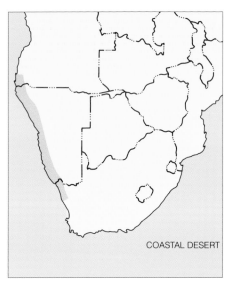

COASTAL DESERT

Steep, shifting sand dunes, rocks laid bare by wind and the ceaseless pounding of the sea, great time-worn canyons, sliced through the earth's crust ... all are part of the beautiful but forbidding landscape of the Namib, a 50 to 80 km-wide coastal belt which stretches northwards from the Orange River to southern Angola – a distance of some 1 600 km.

There is irony in the Hottentot name, as although *namib* means 'large plain' or 'desert', it can also be interpreted as 'place where there is nothing'. Admittedly, vegetation is sparse or non-existent and wildlife often less than obvious, but within the gravels of raised beaches from Conception Bay in Namibia, southwards to Doringbaai near the mouth of the Olifants River, lies the unimaginable wealth of one of the world's greatest deposits of alluvial diamonds. The region is a gem collector's paradise, with beryl, agate and amethyst being just a few of the many semi-precious stones that occur in great abundance there.

For the trailist, the Namib is a fascinating region, a fascination enhanced by the inherent dangers of hiking in an environment of such extreme aridity. Unfortunately, however, much of it is inaccessible. The southern parts form the *Sperrgebiet*, the restricted diamond fields, while the northern areas, including Kaokoland and Caprivi, are relatively undeveloped. A further impediment to hiking is the almost total lack of amenities for hundreds of kilometres on end – enough to deter all but the most stouthearted adventurer. Trailing and mountaineering experiences, therefore, are virtually confined to a few areas, of which the Fish River Canyon, Waterberg Plateau and Naukluft Park are the most accessible and popular.

From the Kunene River, the boundary between Namibia and Angola, to just north of Lüderitz, the coast is geologically fairly homogeneous, low-lying and sandy. Occasionally, low rock platforms protrude; these were formed by the same Stormberg lavas responsible for the Drakensberg escarpment. Some of the rivers along this coastal stretch (the Swakop, Ugab, Omaruru and Hoarusib) are

Seemingly hostile, this coastal desert is home to myriad forms of life.

susceptible to flash-flooding in summer – a very important factor for campers to bear in mind.

The southern Namib from Lüderitz to Chamais Bay is rugged, a precipitous and rocky coastline formed from ancient eroded crystalline rocks, Nama quartzites, and dolomites with softer intervening shales.

Although the Karoo and Kalahari are also often referred to as deserts, only the Namib, with a rainfall of less than 150 mm per year, is truly so. Plant life is most prolific in the south, where two of the more unusual plants are the 'halfmens' or 'elephant's trunk' and the kokerboom, which forms fascinating, forest-like stands. To the north, the cover of low succulents gradually thins until, on the Namib sand dunes, there is little or no plant growth, and only scanty desert grass and acacia trees in the valleys.

Northwards from the Kuiseb River near Walvis Bay, grows the unique *Welwitschia mirabilis*. This prehistoric plant has adapted well to its hostile habitat; it even helps support desert life, as many plant-eating animals are partial to its long, sprawling evergreen leaves. Also in this area, river courses support a good growth of trees such as camelthorn, ana, African ebony, tamarisk and the leadwood.

For the greater extent of the Namib, the Great Escarpment limits its sprawl into the interior and forms a distinct border between the coastal desert and the semi-desert and Karoo. North of the Swakop River and north of the dune area, however, the escarpment is ill-defined and the desert gives way more gradually to a landscape softened by sparse grass and thornveld.

Within this harsh yet beautiful Namib landscape of ancient bare rock, high dunes and cliffs, and weird plants, a fascinating animal life thrives. A large number of the smaller desert dwellers are nocturnal and escape the heat of the day in deep burrows. The Namib gerbil, when it does emerge, is seen scurrying across the parched sand on wide, furry feet. Gemsbok, springbok and ostrich are among the larger animals adapted to the scarcity of water. Birds special to the area include pallid larks, Layard's chat and Rüppell's korhaan, all ground birds whose pale plumage blends well with the desert sands. Birds of prey include the lappetfaced vulture, pygmy falcon and martial eagle.

As with other coastal deserts of the world (for example, the Atacama in South America), the Namib, despite its extreme aridity, is relatively cool. These low temperatures are attributed to the Benguela current which originates in the Antarctic and sweeps up the west coast of Africa. Thick fog frequently gathers above these icy waters and, propelled by onshore winds, rolls in over the land. This misty blanket not only shields the desert from the fierce sun but also supplies life-giving moisture to a number of superbly adapted smaller desert animals, particularly the dune beetles such as *Lepidochora* species which dig trenches in the sand to trap condensing fog. The story of *Onymacris unguicularis*, however, is without parallel. This tenebrionid beetle senses the fog rolling in and climbs to a ridge where it points its abdomen upright to the wind. Moisture condenses on its raised body and runs down to its mouth. These and many other small desert creatures obtain their nourishment

Lush and abundant undergrowth is typical of eastern evergreen forests.

from wind-blown organic debris that settles on the dunes.

The desert is also snake territory and some of these animals have developed unusual ways and means of coping with their environment. For instance, Peringuey's desert or side-winding adder, a small reptile confined to the sandy Namib, has evolved a sideways-on mode of locomotion which facilitates maximum traction over the loosely compacted sands while keeping to a minimum contact with the often hot surface. The grooves of its 'spoor' are most distinctive. Many of the most venomous scorpions are found in the desert and one species, *Parabuthus villosus*, can squirt venom – as toxic as that of a cobra – with such force that it can reach a person's eyes.

Hiking in the drought-wracked Namib holds obvious dangers and common sense at all times is paramount. Never venture far from your base without carrying plenty of water; protect yourself from the sun; and avoid camping in dry riverbeds during summer, especially between January and March, when sudden floods are more likely. As in many arid regions, differences between day and night temperatures can be dramatic, so be prepared. Contracting rocks 'exploding' in the cool night air can be disquieting for the uninitiated. May through to August are the preferred hiking months, as though the winter nights can be bitter, any discomfort is compensated for by the pleasant, warm days.

EASTERN EVERGREEN TEMPERATE FORESTS

When I arrived in southern Africa I was frequently asked: 'Why would a foreigner educated in forestry come here to work?' This was a valid question in many respects, as natural forest covers only about 0,25 per cent of South Africa and, except for Malawi, the proportion is even less for the rest of the subcontinent. What people do not always realize is that forestry embraces a number of related disciplines and its students naturally develop a very broad

interest in the ecology of the land. However, this ecological region does concentrate on trees.

Perhaps my formal forestry training prejudiced me towards favouring forest trails as the idyllic hiking environment. They offer a soothing escape into a microcosm of peace and tranquillity. On closer inspection, however, a struggle is constantly being waged for life's necessities – space, light and water – among the earth's largest and longest living giants. The outcome of this struggle determines the character of the forest – a character which is everchanging through the seasons and decades of time. To familiarize yourself with a forest trail is to know and understand its scents, sounds and textures, individual trees, fungi, flowering herbs and rotting logs. Forests provide man with many products (oxygen, food, drugs, shelter, building material) and services (weather modification, pollution filtration, erosion control and soil fertilization). Yet to the trailist they offer shade and refreshing water and, most importantly, rejuvenation and inspiration.

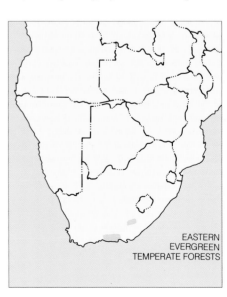

EASTERN EVERGREEN TEMPERATE FORESTS

Forests have several basic requirements, a constant supply of adequate soil nutrients, as well as year-round moisture and sunlight being the most important. Forests also flourish best where diurnal and seasonal temperature variations are small. These conditions are fulfilled in only a few localities in South Africa: the eastern parts of the southern continuous rainfall area; the narrow eastern coastal zone; parts of the Great Escarpment in the eastern midlands and further north; and parts of the high central plateau facing the rain-bearing winds blowing in from the low Moçambique plain.

In southern Africa, the three principal forest types are temperate, subtropical and montane. The largest and best-known temperate forest blankets the landscape from Mossel Bay westwards to the Wit Els River. Within this area the broad mountain belt of the Outeniqua range supports the famous 'Knysna Forest'. Known as the Cape Fold, these mountains and their sub-parallel chains form an impenetrable barrier to humid air moving in off the sea. Rain-heavy clouds gather and eventually discharge themselves over the south-facing slopes which form a sharp divide between the moist coastal belt and the dry Karoo plains to the north.

In the eastern Cape interior, conditions are similar and the sea-facing escarpment, formed by the Winterberg and Hogsback Amatola ranges, is heavily forested.

Coastal forests with their milkwoods, white stinkwoods, erythrinas and wild figs are slightly different in character from those inland which comprise mostly yellowwoods, assegais, black stinkwoods and Cape chestnuts. Other valuable inland forest species include black ironwood, Cape beech, sneezewood and white ironwood. Where rainfall is heaviest, trees grow 18 to 30 m tall, the dense foliage of their upper limbs forming a closed canopy. Trailists with an interest in photography will need fast film and probably a flash as well, if they are to enjoy any success in these dark woods.

Many trees along the trail are conveniently labelled with their national tree list numbers. A list of trees corresponding to these numbers is usually provided in the trail's brochure. If it is not available, purchase the *National List of Indigenous Trees*, an inexpensive and very useful publication compiled by F. von Breitenbach. Forests are more than just trees however, and other plant life abounds, especially climbers, mosses, ferns, fungi, lichens, grasses and many herbs.

Unfortunately, as with so many of South Africa's indigenous plant communities, exotic invader plants pose a threat to the survival of natural forests that is even more serious than previously uncontrolled exploitation for valuable timber. Southern forests are invaded by Australian myrtle, black wattle, blackwood and other aliens, while the predominant enemies of eastern Cape forests are black and golden wattle, jointed cactus and the Port Jackson willow.

The two other principal forest types occurring in South Africa are Coastal Bush and Subtropical Forest, which is discussed separately, and montane forests – located on the high east- and south-facing aspects of the Great Escarpment in the Transvaal, Zimbabwe and Malawi – which are found in isolated patches only, and are therefore described as part of the broader ecological zones within which they fall.

Forest birdlife is plentiful, but trailists intent on bird-watching must be prepared for frustrations, as individual birds are difficult to pick out in the thick tangle of branches and leaves. Crashing through the forest and chatting loudly to your fellow hikers is no way to see forest birds. If, however, you take the trouble to wait quietly in the clearing or shady glade, you will soon be rewarded by the arrival of a surprising variety of birds. Choose a fruiting tree as your post and you may even witness a 'mixed flock', a loose gathering of many species working their way through the forest in search of food. Some of the larger colourful birds characteristic of temperate forests are the Knysna lourie, Narina trogon, rameron pigeon, gymnogene, redbilled hoopoe, blackheaded oriole and Knysna woodpecker.

Mammals of the forest are also shy; footprints and droppings are often the only evidence of their presence. Spoor you are most likely to come across are those of bushbuck, grysbok, blue duiker, bushpig and leopard. Baboons and vervet monkeys, like the birds, are more often heard than seen.

Be alert for the well-camouflaged boomslang (usually bright green, but many varieties occur). Its venom can prove fatal, but these back-fanged reptiles seldom strike at humans and are only aggressive when cornered. Many other snakes, frogs and lizards, woodlice, millipedes, centipedes, spiders, flatworms and scorpions live in the trees or on the litter-strewn floor, all interacting within the intricate web of forest life. Most common among these forest dwellers is the peripatus. This biological curiosity – restricted to environments with a high humidity – has characteristics of both worms and insects and is thought to be the evolutionary link between the two. It looks like a squat velvet worm with fifteen pairs of stumpy legs and its eyes are situated at the base of soft, filamentous antennae. The weather in temperate forests is usually mild, with rain and mist possible year-round. Snow can fall in June, July and August. Because trails in these forests (such as the Outeniqua and Tsitsikamma hiking trails) usually traverse other ecosystems (such as fynbos or grassland) as well, trailists are advised to study the climatic patterns of the entire region in which they intend walking.

All trailing environments hold dangers of one kind or another and forests are no exception, for within these often dark surroundings it is easy to lose your bearings. If for any reason you do lose your companions or stray far from the trail, do not bash through thick undergrowth. Stay in one spot, signal and wait for help. Never walk through dense forest after dark; with the meagre, dappled light of day gone you are liable to miss your footing on the excessively slippery forest floor and the chances of losing your sense of direction are even greater.

COASTAL BUSH AND SUBTROPICAL FORESTS

Tangled bush and dense evergreen forests mantling river-dissected, steeply rolling ridges, coastal plains, swamps, dunes, estuaries, beaches and mudflats … these are the challenging environments awaiting trailists within a narrow belt extending along southern Africa's eastern seaboard from the Gamtoos River, near Port Elizabeth, northwards through Transkei, Natal and Maputaland to northern Moçambique.

COASTAL BUSH AND SUBTROPICAL FORESTS

In the past, most of the region, from sea level to an altitude of some 300 to 400 m, was forested, but here, as with southern Africa's all-too-few other natural forests, over-exploitation has taken its toll. Today, valuable timber trees such as Cape box, Cape mahogany and Cape ebony, and their lianes, have been largely replaced by plantations of sugar cane and other agricultural crops.

The natural areas remaining embrace several forest types; the following summary is extracted from *Veld Types of South Africa* by Acocks (1975):
Typical Coast-belt Forest occurs in small patches on steeply rolling terrain where the soil is stable. Today, these forests, in which umzimbeet, red beech and Natal strelitzia are common, are being invaded by scrubby thornveld.
Zululand Palm-veld – a short, jungle-like tangle of lianes, palms and wild bananas within patches of scrubby thornveld.
Transitional Coastal Forest blankets the region between the Kei and Keiskamma rivers, respectively north and south of East London. It is similar to the drier parts of the 'typical forest', but its species composition is slightly different.
Mangrove Forests thrive on the eastern coast in salty, shallow waters, an environment hostile to all other trees. Mangrove trees actually help to create land, as they send out underwater roots which trap sediments and debris, thereby building up the soil. A rare animal community depends on the perpetuation of mangrove swamps. This unique ecosystem is described in greater detail in the Transkei Hiking Trail – Wild Coast (see page 126).
Alexandria Forest occurs south and west of Port Elizabeth to the Gamtoos River and northwards from Alexandria to just east of Port Alfred. The plants of these parts, such as the principal trees – Cape plane, white pear and kooboo-berry (the latter bearing edible fruit) – and the numerous scrambling shrubs such as cat-thorn, are more drought resistant than those of the coastal forest to the north. Walking through the relatively short Alexandria Forest is difficult, as it grows very thickly. However, in a number of the recognized trailing and rambling areas, paths have been cleared.

One of the most fascinating features of the vegetation within the coastal area between the Gamtoos and Fish rivers is that it comprises four main floral types. Topography, which plays a significant role

Dense coastal bush thrives along Natal's north coast.

in determining local climatic conditions in this transitional area, is responsible for the varied vegetation. Hence, it is not unusual for the trailist to hike through subtropical flora in sheltered kloofs, fynbos on coastal plains, succulent thorny scrub in wide river valleys, and then ascend grassy hills or mountain peaks.

Where protected, coastal forest and bush generally support diverse plant and animal communities. Some of the birds endemic to this ecological zone are the pinkthroated longclaw which inhabits the grasses of marshy areas, the blackbellied glossy starling, the grey waxbill and the olive sunbird.

If you intend hiking in this region in summer you must be prepared to endure hot, humid and rainy weather. As you move inland, however, the climate becomes refreshingly cooler and in the dry winters, frost is possible but uncommon.

EASTERN GRASSLANDS

Transcending the boundaries of many ecoregions, grasslands occur over great areas of southern Africa and together form what is regarded as one of the most vital of all ecosystems. A renowned botanist once assessed the value of grasses in no uncertain terms: 'Whether civilization in South Africa survives or not will be determined by the way we manage our grasslands.' Although the statement may sound a little melodramatic, it has the ring of truth, for wildlife and domesticated stock and, indirectly, humans as well, depend on grass for food, and seldom does an ecological discussion not elaborate on grassland management for our survival.

Although improved agricultural know-how and conservation practices have benefited the state of grasslands, the ravages of mismanagement are still evident. Under particular stress are the eastern grasslands blanketing the plateau which sweeps up between the Great Escarpment foothills and the coastal bush, from the eastern Cape through to northern Natal.

However, despite the poor state of ecology in many parts, there are pockets – the Ntendeka Wilderness Area, Umgeni Valley and Bosberg nature reserves, and the Umfolozi Game Reserve to name a few – where the trailist can experience to the full the beauty of unspoilt grasslands.

This zone is not a challenge to the physically-orientated mountaineer (the close proximity to the Drakensberg fills that niche) but, rather, an excellent area for naturalists and scholars to experience and observe the intricacies of a life-supporting environment. Therefore, many of the trails in this region have education as their principal objective. To participate in a guided wilderness trail is to become involved, physically and spiritually, in the primeval drama of life and to understand that man's future is dependent on the continued existence of these wild areas.

The eastern grasslands of today, as with much of inland southern Africa, were once a huge shallow sea which, hundreds of millions of years ago, thronged with reptilian life. Fossils of these prehistoric lizards lie locked in the sediments –

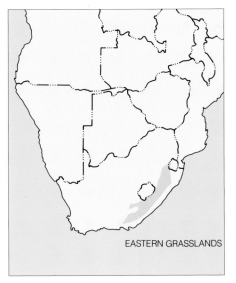

EASTERN GRASSLANDS

mainly the Beaufort Series of the Karoo beds – deposited through time, while the plants of the steamy swamplands formed the vast coalfields of the Natal Midlands.

Rivers have carved broad valleys through the easily eroded sandstones of the Beaufort Series: the remaining spurs or interfluvial ridges, as well as the 'table mountain' and koppie structures which characterize the landscape of the western parts, are monuments to the harder dolerite intrusions which capped the softer sedimentary sandstones. Jointed cliffs in northern Natal, such as those of Ntendeka, were formed from these doleritic dykes and sills.

Grasslands divide naturally into 'sweet' and 'sour' types. Sweet veld grasses remain nutritious throughout the year, even in winter when they are dry, while sourveld species are nutritious only in the early stages of growth; after approximately three months their protein and mineral content decrease rapidly and they become unpalatable and indigestible to animals.

Examples of the two grassveld types occur in the northern and eastern grasslands of the Cape Province. Here the sweet veld grows in dry areas south of the Kalahari thornveld and is characterized by genera such as *Eragrostis* and *Stigagrostis*. The sourveld occurs in higher rainfall, more mountainous areas where *Eylyonurus argentus* and *Harpochloa falx* are dominant.

Within the ecoregion, grassland is more or less 'pure' to altitude of about 1 220 m. Below, and ranging down to the coastal evergreen bush, short and tall grasses carpet the uplands while mixed grass and bush thrive on the deeper valley floors. In the moister regions, temperate forests have developed but the majority have fallen to agricultural expansion and have regressed to poor, unproductive veld. In the lower-lying part of the region, where Table Mountain sandstone and granite formations occur, soils are sandy and infertile. This veld, a mixture of acacia thornbush and *Aristida* grass, makes poor pasture.

Irwin's *Field Guide to the Natal Drakensberg* is a useful handbook for the naturalist wishing to identify the many grass species.

The great migrating herds of animals which once roamed the African grasslands have been severely reduced and today exist only in protected areas. According to Roberts' *Birds of Southern Africa*, the eastern grasslands do not have any birds endemic to the area. The birds are allied to both the highveld and eastern lowveld species. To blend in with their habitat, most grassland bird species are well camouflaged and fly less than those found in an arboreal environment. Some of the birds common to open veld include the secretarybird, blue crane, blackheaded heron, cattle egret, bustards and korhaans.

Hikers in this region can expect warmer and drier weather than in the Drakensberg, with snow in winter occurring only on mountain tops. Rainfall in summer is frequently accompanied by very violent thunderstorms.

In the Usutu-Pongola flood plain and other northern parts, malaria is a constant threat, especially in hotter months. Also in these more tropical areas, rivers are the domain of the crocodile and hippo, so take care when hiking along riverbanks. Swimming or wading in any of these bilharzia-infested waters should, in any case, be avoided.

DRAKENSBERG

DRAKENSBERG

Quathlamba, a barrier of upward-pointing spears, is the Zulu name for the craggy pinnacles that form the most spectacular and scenically dramatic section of the Great Escarpment, southern Africa's watershed; and no less apt is the Dutch-derived epithet meaning 'mountain dragon', for the forbidding, jagged peaks seem a natural domain for these fabled creatures. In its fullest extent, the Drakensberg range describes a great arc from the northern Transvaal through Natal and Transkei, eventually petering out in the eastern Cape. For the purposes of this book, however, I have limited the discussion of this range to the 200-km stretch from Mont-aux-Sources in the Royal Natal National Park, southwards to Bushman's Nek in Lesotho's beautiful Sehlaba-thebe National Park. The region spans an altitude of some 1 500 m from Thaba Ntlenyana (3 482 m) in Lesotho, its highest point – also the

highest point south of Kilimanjaro – to the Little 'Berg, its eastern foothills.

The Drakensberg is an invigorating experience for the rambler, hiker or mountaineer: the scenery is superb, the air crystal clear and the plant and animal life fascinating. But it is, perhaps, the all-pervading sense of great age, the awesome primordial forces that moulded these mountains, that leaves the most indelible impressions. I well recall my own response: a sudden realization that, after several days of hard climbing, I was standing on a remnant of Gondwana, the super-continent that existed more than 140 million years ago.

Three hundred million years ago a shallow sea existed where the Drakensberg is today, and in these waters sedimentary layers of the Karoo System were deposited. Then Gondwanaland, the vast landmass that gave birth to present-day southern Africa, India, Australia, South America and Antarctica, began to break apart. Unimaginable stresses opened great fissures in the earth's crust, and through them poured lava which reached from present-day Lesotho to the coastline of Natal. During the following 140 million years, at an average of one centimetre every 6 to 7 years, wind and water eroded the hardened lava, the Stormberg basalts, which receded 200 km to form the steep descent to the Natal Midlands of today.

The Little 'Berg's underlying sedimentary rocks, moulded into large, rounded foothills and at places protectively capped by Stormberg basalts, were rapidly eroded, giving rise to the many caves, deep valleys and gorges. Appropriately named the 'cave sandstones', these less durable rocks are now known as the Clarens formation, which spans an altitude of approximately 1 700 to 2 000 m.

Crystals of great beauty await discovery in the Drakensberg. Amygdales, originally veins in basalt, are most common, while others include amethyst, a semi-precious purple or blue-violet quartz; clear quartz; chalcedony, a quartz and opal mixture; and chert, a white to grey, opaque stone. With luck, you

may find agate, which is chert in variegated concentric layers. In fact, chert may be responsible for the original settlement of the 'Berg by Bushmen, as it is the only rock in this region suitable for making arrowheads and spear tips.

'Berg vegetation grows in characteristic belts, each influenced by the parent rock, sharp altitude differences and aspect – north-facing slopes are warm and gradients more gentle, those that are south-facing are cold and steep. The 'montane belt' is the lowest and, ranging from 1 280 to 1 829 m, occurs in the river valleys of the Little 'Berg up to the cave sandstone. The 'sub-alpine belt', 1 829 to 2 865 m, extends from the base of the cave sandstone to the foot of the basalt cliffs on the main escarpment, and the highest, the 'alpine belt', ranges from the basalt cliffs up to and including the summit plateau.

Grasses dominate the three belts and are largely responsible for the carpet of summer green and the yellow-russet brown hues of winter. The principal species, 'red grass', makes excellent pasture, but mismanagement and over-burning have unfortunately led to its replacement by hardier, more xerophytic, deeper-rooted members of the genus *Eragrostis* and *Aristida*, the 'needle grass'. In places *Protea roupelliae* or *P. caffra* invade the grasslands to form protea savannah. Indigenous tree growth above the cave sandstone cliffs is absent, probably because of the severely cold, dry winters, and only kloofs and sheltered ridge slopes are forest-clad.

Fynbos is one of the typical plant communities occurring around 2 000 m but, unlike the Cape fynbos, that of the Drakensberg is dominated by small, hard-leaved plants, and not restios and proteas. Two unusual species found in this fynbos (which I will never forget after being sunburnt and trapped in a tangle on a steep slope) are the mountain cedar and the berg cycad. The mountain cedar, *Widdringtonia nodiflora*, closely related to the Clanwilliam cedar, *Widdringtonia cedarbergensis*, has scratchy, dry branches while the berg cycad, a living fossil of Mesozoic times, has narrow-leaved, prickly fronds.

Alpine vegetation characterizes the harsh plateau environment, with evergreen dwarf woody shrubs – predominantly ericas and everlastings – scattered among temperate grasses.

In total, some 1 200 species clothe the Drakensberg and form the basis of a food web which embraces more than 43 large and small mammal species, 24 snake species, 4 to 6 lizard families, and a myriad other creatures. Irwin's *Field Guide to the Natal Drakensberg* gives excellent coverage of these animals as well as aids to their identification. Throughout the Drakensberg, weather patterns are fairly cyclic. Winter (April or May to September) is favoured for mountaineering. During these months, days are usually sunny and temperatures can climb as high as 22° C, but at night they can rapidly drop to below freezing. Heavy frosts are the norm and although snow can be expected at any time of the year, it is obviously most common during the winter months. As a result of temperature inversions, the river valleys are colder than the mountain slopes. For this reason, camping under the shelter of a tent or in a cave to prevent radiant heat loss is recommended. Temperatures on the summit plateau are much lower than on the slopes and range from 10° C during the day to 8° C at night. Dry, warm

The majestic and impressive Drakensberg are a remnant of Gondwanaland.

'Berg winds, at their fiercest in late July or August, often indicate an approaching cold front.

In view of the extreme weather in the Drakensberg, hikers must be wise and remember to take basic precautions against exposure (cold exhaustion) and hypothermia (severe, accidental lowering of the body's temperature). Most important, be aware that even a healthy and physically fit adult can succumb to exposure or hypothermia if over-fatigued by exercise and anxiety – conditions not uncommon to mountaineers who lose their way in wind and snow or rain. Watch your party carefully for any of these symptoms: slow physical or mental responses, stumbling, cramps and shivering, slurred speech, vision impairment, irritability or other unusual behaviour. React immediately by seeking shelter or erecting a tent within which the victim can rest and sip warm drinks. If at all possible, the victim should change into dry clothing or lie in a warm sleeping bag.

To treat frostbite, which usually occurs on the ears, nose, chin, fingers and/or toes, the victim must again be sheltered, given warm drinks and all constrictive clothing should be removed. Never rub or apply direct heat to frostbite; rather thaw the affected part gradually – but never do this if there is a possibility that it will refreeze. A frostbitten victim complains that the affected part is cold, painful or numb and stiff, with no power of movement. Severe cases of frostbite require prompt medical attention; therefore, the victim should be helped down the mountain and treated as soon as possible.

Summer (October to March) is the least popular hiking season because of the prevalence of violent, late afternoon thunderstorms which produce a deluge of water and cold, swollen rivers which should not be forded. Summers can also bring many hot sunny days – but, just as readily, fog that envelopes the mountains, reducing visibility to no more than a few paces. Air temperatures range from 15 °C to 33 °C and nights are cool to warm. Summer hiking has one compensation, though – the 'Berg flowers are at their best.

HIGHVELD

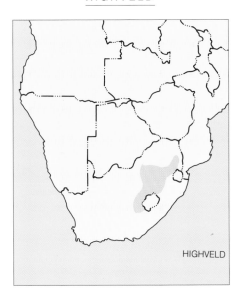

To be honest, the Highveld (with the exceptions of the Magaliesberg and the Witwatersrand) is not a

Vast rolling plains are characteristic of the Highveld.

mountaineer's delight. Although bird-watchers and nature ramblers have endless opportunities to study natural history, the recreation potential of this area is not faring well against competition from farming, mining, industry and urban development.

However, due to the recent commendable efforts of the local municipal authorities, a system of urban walks, available not only to ramblers but also to joggers, horse-riders and canoeists, leads trailists along scenic spruits within and on the outskirts of the Highveld's bustling metropolitan centres. This 'linear park system' links valleys, ridges, gardens, zoos and bird sanctuaries, and historical and archaeological features in a complex of long and short circular walks. In an age where petrol is dear, and distances to the wilder, pristine areas of the Transvaal and bushveld are far, the urban park system is a welcome alternative to the fully fledged wilderness experience.

Very simply, the Highveld is an elevated grassland region. The large part of the Highveld lies between 1 200 and 1 829 m above sea level. From the Great Escarpment it extends inland, terminating in the north at the popular Magaliesberg range, beyond which sprawls the bushveld. In the northwest, the Langeberg and Korannaberg ranges of the Waterberg system separate the Highveld from the Kalahari, while in the south and east, the boundaries coincide roughly with the plateau's edge. The character of Lesotho's landscape differs so drastically from the true Highveld, however, that I have included it with the Drakensberg ecological zone (see page 32).

Some 280 to 180 million years ago (mid-Carboniferous to Triassic periods), in Karoo times, the Highveld lay buried under thick, horizontally arranged layers of shales and sandstones. These were later intruded by dolerite dykes and sills and capped by basaltic lava. By early Cretaceous times, however, erosion had done its work and the high central plateau must have looked very much as it does today, a flat plain, occasionally relieved by koppies capped with resistant sandstone or dolerite.

In the northern Orange Free State and southern Transvaal – an area of tremendous mineral wealth – the geomorphology is far more complex, for here the Karoo cover has been uplifted and so severely eroded that ancient ridges of the Transvaal and Witwatersrand quartzites are exposed.

Plant life varies from locality to locality. The vegetation of the Magaliesberg and Witwatersrand, the prime hiking areas, is discussed in the relevant entries. South of the Magaliesberg, the vegetation is generally referred to as 'Bankenveld', open tree savannah giving way to dense scrub on koppies and stony areas. Important tree species include many of those common to the bushveld: highveld protea, common hook-thorn and white stinkwood. The rolling hills are covered with grass, marking the transition to true highveld grassveld. In the grassveld, woody species are confined to the protected mountain slopes and river banks. Dominant grasses are represented by the genera *Themeda* and *Cymbopogon*, with many other species intermingled.

Large mammals which are indigenous to the Highveld include black wildebeest, red hartebeest, blesbok, eland, duiker, steenbok, gemsbok, zebra and cheetah.

Grassveld birds are usually inconspicuous in colouring and habit and the majority are ground-living species such as larks, pipits, ostriches, secretary-birds, blue cranes, herons, cattle egrets, bustards, coursers, plovers, dikkops, guineafowl, quails, grass owls and marsh owls, not to mention 'LBJ's' (little brown jobs) such as the cisticolas and grass warblers. Many Highveld birds are, in fact, migrants and during their summer sojourns in southern Africa's grasslands, they lack the colourful nuptial plumage reserved for their breeding habitats in the northern hemisphere. Seed-eaters such as waxbills, weavers and parasitic whydahs feed on grass seeds in late summer, but otherwise prefer to feed in bush, vlei or reedbeds.

The intricately woven grass and reed oval nests of the spottedbacked, Cape and masked weavers, as well as those of the smaller and unmistakably coloured red bishop, golden bishop and Cape widow birds, provide a distinctive feature to hanging branches, upright reeds and exotic gum trees that line marshes, rivers and vleis. To observe a weaver bird build these fascinating structures (each species possessing its characteristic technique and design) is one of the highlights of rambling along the various spruits incorporated in the network of urban Highveld walks. In addition, waterbirds are abundant in artificial dams and vleis – mainly egrets, herons and sacred ibises.

Generally, the Highveld is characterized by moderate rainfall, cloudless skies, and moderate day/night and seasonal changes in temperature. Summers are warm and rainy with hot winds blowing from the north-west, common also in spring. Summer days in the western Highveld are markedly warmer. Winters, on the other hand, are dry and cloudless, usually with cool to warm days and colder, sometimes bitterly cold, nights. Daytime temperatures during mid to late winter can, however, be unpleasantly cold, especially when the bone-chilling south winds roar across the plateau from the snow-clad Drakensberg and Malutis. Heavy frosts are not uncommon.

Although frequently dramatic and visually stimulating, the often violent thunderstorms, common from November to March, can be hazardous for those caught in the open. The sudden deluges can turn shallow streams and spruits into raging torrents literally within minutes, while vicious bolts of lightning stab randomly at the veld. Keep an eye on the weather, therefore, and if you see that a storm is imminent, keep away from any potential river race, and avoid high, exposed ground where the chances of a lightning strike are always greater. January and February are the hottest months.

DRY WOODLANDS

'The African bush', bushveld, lowveld, savannah, tree veld, dry woodlands – all refer to the vast tract of land stretching both westwards and northwards from Mozambique through Zimbabwe and Zambia into Malawi; southwards through the northern and western Transvaal, including most of Swaziland, Lebowa and Zululand; and westwards to the acacia savannah or the Kalahari.

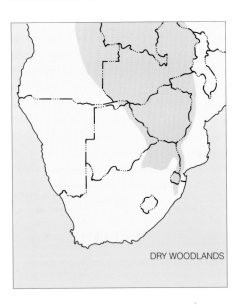

DRY WOODLANDS

The bushveld is largely the 'classical' African ecosystem, the one vividly portrayed in so many epics about Africa and the one where wilderness-type trails gained their popularity. The areas near Lake Kariba and the Tuli Block have always held a special appeal for all big-game lovers, as do the popular wilderness trails in the Kruger National Park and the contiguous private reserves.

But wilderness trails are only a part of the plethora of trailing opportunities in this vast area: the eastern and northern Transvaal, particularly, with its numerous lengthy and dramatic hiking stretches, is a backpacker's paradise. It is also a region of hiking 'firsts': the first NHWS trail (the Fanie Botha Hiking Trail, see page 268), the first hiking trail to incorporate a train-ride en route (the Elandskrans Hiking Trail, see page 271), and the first trail through gold prospecting areas which saw their heyday last century.

Some private hotels and safari lodges in the eastern Transvaal and Swaziland have grounds which present rambling opportunities, while many Zimbabwean towns offer peaceful walks through pleasant urban green areas. Zimbabwe also boasts the world's most sensational nature trail alongside the Victoria Falls. The ancient mountains of Chimanimani in eastern Zimbabwe and the Wolkberg in the northern Transvaal beckon the fittest outdoorsmen to the African bush.

From the air, the bushveld appears endlessly brown, with occasional muddy, green-margined rivers where the thornbushes, acacias, baobabs and yellow-barked fever trees, so evocative of Africa, grow more thickly. These – as well as patches of dense Afro-montane forest and high plateau and floodplain grassland – although providing some of the finest trailing environments on the subcontinent, are no more than local interruptions in an otherwise continuous woodland association.

The aerial impression is misleading, however, as the uniform rusty-grey vista belies a diversity in altitude (the region varies between 150 and 1 375 m), climate, geomorphology and soil conditions which give rise to a number of woodland types, each supporting a wealth of animal life.

Very ancient rocks underlie most of southern Africa and, known broadly as the Basement Complex, they comprise highly metamorphosed sediments as well as igneous rocks – schists, slates, quartzites, granites and gneisses. Further sediments and the sands of time have largely hidden the subcontinent's foundation, but here and there throughout the bushveld, outcrops occur, adding interest to the landscape and providing fine challenges for the mountaineer and serious backpacker. Examples of these primitive outcrops include the Murchison range and Barberton Mountain land in the eastern Transvaal and Swaziland, the Gold Belt in Zimbabwe and the Basement schists, quartzites and volcanic rocks of the Malawi plateaux.

Towards the close of the pre-Cambrian Era, a great intrusion of igneous rock, the Bushveld igneous complex, occurred in the eastern Transvaal. This is the base of the lowveld plateau which abuts the Highveld, and here the Waterberg plateau, Pietersburg plateau and the Soutpansberg, all in the north of the basin, also present their weathered krantzes and kloofs to test the climber's skills. Further north, old granites underlie much of the woodlands plain, with dolerites and quartzites

giving rise to the eastern highlands of Zimbabwe. Savannah divides naturally into three basic vegetation types – mixed woodlands, Brachystegia-Julbernardia veld, and mopane veld.

In mixed savannah the balance of trees to grass varies; either a forest-type association or an open parkland in which grasses dominate, is formed. Both evergreen and deciduous trees occur and most have adapted to long periods without water, their small leaves, deep roots, water-storing organs, and thorns in place of leaves all helping to conserve liquid. In South Africa, mixed savannah occurs principally in the northern and eastern Transvaal and Zululand, and to the south it is transitional with the eastern grasslands, karoo or fynbos. Acacias and baobabs are common in the eastern Transvaal and Zululand, while in the drier areas aloes and euphorbias dot the landscape. Most regions host deciduous broad-leaved trees such as the marula, a highly valued fruiting tree, species of Sterculia (chestnuts), and pod mahogany. Hyphaene and Borassus palms occur in river valleys. Mahogany logs are used by local tribesmen for their dug-out canoes, while the palms are also popular, as a potent liquor is made from their sap.

Brachystegia-Julbernardia woodland is basically parkland but can vary from open grassland to almost closed forest. Dominant among the intermingling trees are Brachstegia spiciformis and Julbernardia globiflora. Often referred to as miombo woodland, this deciduous association sprawls across a large part of Zimbabwe. The red hues of young brachystegia foliage mantle the woodlands in spring and, together with the soft pinks and fawns of J. globiflora leaves, make an attractive and colourful display.

Frost-free situations – the warm valleys around the Limpopo and Zambezi rivers and the continental basin of the interior – are the domain of the mopane tree. Its butterfly-shaped leaves turn their edges to the sun during the heat of the day to reduce dehydration. Even in full leaf, therefore, a mopane forest provides little shade. The leaves and pods are a popular food source for both wild and domesticated animals, while the leaf-eating mopane worms, the caterpillars of a large brownish-grey moth species, are roasted and eaten by locals for their protein content. Stands of baobab are often found within the mopane woodland, and other associated trees include members of Sterculia, Acacia, Combretum, Euphorbia and Terminalia, all well-known bushveld genera.

When summer rains come late to the bushveld and grass is scarce, many animals – all of which leave before the first downpours – feed on the foliage of trees and shrubs. Because of the great numbers of trees, dry woodlands are home to many browsers and some of the mammals that live off savannah trees, either partially or entirely, are elephants, black rhino, giraffe, steenbok, suni and forest dwellers such as the blue and common duiker. Many – for example impala, sable antelope and hartebeest – are both browsers and grazers, while white rhino, zebra, warthog, hippo and oribi are chiefly grazers. Among the predators of the region are lion, leopard, cheetah, jackal, hyena, caracal and serval.

Birdlife is always fascinating in these woodlands. According to Ken Newman in Bird Life in Southern Africa, of the 833 species recorded in southern Africa (excluding Malawi), 711 are recorded within bushveld and thornveld (Kalahari). The reasons for this disproportionately large number of species are, firstly, the great diversity of habitats available in wooded areas, which provide a myriad niches to be filled, and secondly, that the whole northern limit of southern Africa is woodland and so the many tropical birds penetrating just south into this region are also included. Species typical of all vegetation associations and easily identified are the beautifully coloured lilacbreasted roller, yellowbilled hornbill, redbilled hoopoe, long-tailed shrike, brown-headed parrot and purplecrested lourie.

Smaller vertebrates and invertebrates, especially insects and spiders, thrive in the trees, shrubs, creepers and grass. Snakes and lizards also abound, while the Nile crocodile, living mainly in the dry woodland areas, is confined to rivers, lakes and swamps. Because of its man-eating proclivities, hikers must be careful when travelling in these areas, especially while crossing rivers. Another large reptile found mainly in savannah and open bush is the rock or tree leguaan.

Woodland seasons are well defined: wet and dry. The wet season occurs from October to the end of March, with October often being referred to as 'suicide month' because it is the hottest period before the rains break. To the trailist, the advantage of wet-season hiking is the sight of the veld when the trees are fruiting and in leaf, the herbs blooming and the birds breeding. The disadvantages are that insects such as mosquitoes (which carry malaria) and tsetse flies (carriers of sleeping-sickness) are more plentiful too, the game is dispersed because water is readily available, and transport is hindered by wet, muddy road conditions. During the dry season, wildlife concentrates at waterholes, so the chances of spotting game through the dry, dead grass are much improved.

MALAWI

Geologically, Malawi is part of the East African Rift Valley system – a 6 500 km-long graben (or trough) created by land subsiding between two roughly parallel fault lines, and the uplifting of the valley's shoulders. The central and very prominent feature of the valley is the lake which forms the greater part of Malawi's eastern boundary. In the north, the basin of this long, narrow stretch of water is strongly faulted, evidenced by the impressive escarpment. The southern part of the basin and the Shire River Valley, however, are folded and therefore relatively shallow.

Rising from the valley floor of softer schists and gneisses, metamorphosed intrusive rocks form inselbergs and extensive highlands such as the Michiru, Ndirande, Soche and Thyolo in the south and, in the central and northern areas, the Dedza and Chongoni peaks. These formations also underlie the Nyika plateau. In the post-Karoo (or late Jurassic) period, a large portion of present-day Malawi lay beneath Karoo sediments and, intruding into these, a grey crystalline igneous rock, syenite, formed the spectacular massifs of Mulanje and Zomba, as well as other mountains of the south.

Technically, Malawi – spanning altitudes from 220 m below sea level (the lake floor) to 3 300 m on Mount Mulanje – embraces a number of

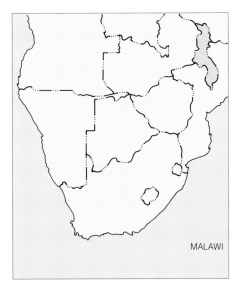

MALAWI

ecological zones. The three major regions are the Shire Valley and Lake Malawi – including cataracts, bird-rich marshes and lake-shore plains; the medium plateau of the Shire highland, Central and Northern provinces – between 762 and 1 372 m; and the highlands of Mulanje, Zomba, Kirk, Dedza, Dowa, Mafingi, Misuku, Viphya and Nyika – averaging 1 372 to 2 934 m, but with higher peaks.

Plant life reflects this topography and geology. Most widespread are montane forests and grasslands and *Brachystegia-Julbernadia* woodlands, but also covering large tracts are *Combretum-Acacia-Piliostigma* woodlands and mixed savannah woodlands.

On the Viphya, Nyika and Zomba plateaux as well as on the isolated Mulanje massif, Mangochi and Thyolo mountains, heavy rains and frequent mists carried by easterly winds combine with the deep soils of gentle slopes to produce conditions well suited to forest growth. Evergreen trees dominate, their trunks clad in a profusion of mosses and

ferns and other epiphytes, which find in these more elevated situations the essential moisture and light, unavailable on the ground because of the dense forest canopy. The montane forests of Mulanje are unique and harbour such valuable endemics as the Mulanje cedar, found either in pure stands or as isolated individuals, and the yellowwood, *Podocarpus milanjiana*. The mighty cedars grow as tall as 42,5 m and are exploited for building timber (the huts on Mulanje are constructed from their timber).

Blanketing the peaks and highlands above the tree line are grasslands interspersed with a variety of flowering plants such as buttercups, orchids and everlastings, and proteas. These grasslands probably owe their origin to destruction of the original forest by fire.

Other major vegetation types include *Brachystegia-Julbernadia* woodland which covers the greater part of Malawi (see page 34 for its description). The lower slopes of Nyika provide a fine example of such woodland, while on the plateau montane grassland predominates. Also characteristic of highlands are the dambos, broad shallow depressions that soak up the rains in much the same way as the bogs of the northern hemisphere. These sponge-like reservoirs are the lifeblood of plateau streams, often providing them with water throughout the year. Short grassland covers the dambos, and geophytes as well as other herbs abound.

Because of Malawi's large rural population, larger mammals are scarce and mostly restricted to reserves. But birds are everywhere, and to aid identification of the more than 600 species – an impressive diversity for such a small country – keen birders should purchase *Birds of Malawi* by Ken Newman. Snakes, lizards, frogs, butterflies and other invertebrates are also well represented, but the most special aspect of Malawi's animal life is probably the strikingly beautiful fishes waiting to delight the snorkeller in Lake Malawi. Over 450 species – most of which are endemic – thrive in these waters.

Mount Mulanje, home to a variety of plant and bird life, forms part of Malawi's highlands.

TRAILS DIRECTORY

KEY

DW = Day walk
GDW = Guided day walk
GHT = Guided hiking trail
GWT = Guided wilderness trail
HT = Hiking trail
K = Kloofing
M = Mountaineering (requires experience, mountaineering skills)
SDW = Self-guided day walk/interpretive trail
UT = Urban trail
WT = Wilderness trekking

(For explanations of the above terms, see pages 12 and 14.)

C = Canoeing/River-rafting
H = Horseback or camel trail, or pony-trek
MB = Mountain biking
TD = Trails for the disabled
UW = Underwater trail

* In the planning stage; check on status.

WESTERN CAPE

1. Verlorenvlei Hiking Trails, Redelinghuys (DW; HT*)
2. Sevilla Bushman Painting Trail and Lorraine Hiking Trail, northern Cedarberg (DW)
3. Cedarberg Wilderness and adjoining area, Citrusdal/Clanwilliam (WT; DW; M; H)
4. Groot Winterhoek Wilderness Area, Porterville (WT)
5. SAS Saldanha Hiking Trail, Saldanha (DW)
6. Postberg Hiking Trail, West Coast National Park (HT; C)
7. Strandveld Educational Trail, West Coast National Park, Langebaan (GHT; GDW; DW)
8. Sandveld Trails, Yzerfontein (DW)
9. Kasteelberg Trail, Riebeeck West (DW)
10. Toll House and Van Stadensrus Trails, Ceres (HT; DW)
11. Hex River Mountains, near Worcester (WT; M; K)
12. Karoo National Botanical Garden, Worcester (SDW)
13. Bain's Kloof walks, Hawequas Conservation Area (DW)
14. Limietberg Hiking Trail, Du Toit's Kloof Pass/Bain's Kloof Pass (HT)
15. Du Toits Kloof Pass walks, Hawequas Conservation Area (DW)
16. Klipkershout Trail, Paarl Mountain Nature Reserve (DW; M)
17. Tygerberg Nature Reserve, Bellville (DW)
18. Kirstenbosch Forest Trails, Kirstenbosch National Botanical Garden (DW; GDW; TD)
19. Table Mountain, Cape Town (DW; M; MB)
20. Elephant's Eye Cave, Tokai State Forest (DW)
21. Silvermine Nature Reserve, Cape Peninsula (DW; MB)
22. Hout Bay walks, Cape Peninsula (DW)
23. Cape of Good Hope Nature Reserve, Cape Peninsula (DW; MB)
24. The Vineyard Trail, Stellenbosch (DW)
25. Eerste River/Coetzenburg Trail, Stellenbosch (DW)
26. Assegaaibosch Trail, Jonkershoek (DW)
27. Jonkershoek State Forest, near Stellenbosch (DW; M; MB)
28. Mont Rochelle, Franschhoek Pass (DW)
29. Helderberg Nature Reserve, Somerset West (DW; M)
30. Helderberg Farm Trail, Somerset West (DW)
31. Harold Porter National Botanical Garden walks, Betty's Bay (DW)
32. Highlands Trail, Kleinmond (HT)
33. Kogelberg Trail, Kogelberg Nature Reserve (DW)
34. Perdeberg Walk, Kleinmond (HT)
35. Three Sisters Walk, Kleinmond (DW)
36. Boland Trail, Hottentots Holland Nature Reserve (HT)
37. Hottentots Holland day walks (DW; MB)
38. Riviersonderend Canyon and Suicide Gorge kloofing trips, Hottentots Holland Nature Reserve (K)
39. Kleinmond Coastal and Mountain Nature Reserve (DW)
40. Kommissiekraal Trail, Villiersdorp Wild Flower Garden and Nature Reserve, Villiersdorp (DW)
41. Klein Houwhoek Peak Trails, Houwhoek (DW)
42. Steenbras Nature Reserve, Gordon's Bay (DW)
43. Caledon Nature Reserve and Wild Flower Garden (DW; MB)
44. Fernkloof Nature Reserve, Hermanus (DW)
45. Vogelgat Private Nature Reserve, Kleinrivier Mountains (DW)
46. Salmonsdam Nature Reserve, Stanford (DW; MB)
47. Genadendal Mountain Trail, Genadendal (HT)
48. Boesmanskloof Traverse, Greyton-McGregor (DW; HT)
49. Whipstock Farm Guided Walks, McGregor (GDW)
50. Boerbok Hiking Trail, Robertson (DW; HT)
51. Rooikat Trail, near Robertson (DW)
52. Dassieshoek Nature Reserve Trail, Robertson (HT)
53. Arangieskop Hiking Trail, Robertson (HT)
54. Pat Busch Private Nature Reserve, near Robertson (DW)
55. Bloupunt and Cogman's Kloof hiking trails, Montagu Mountain Nature Reserve (DW; HT)
56. Bredasdorp Mountain Reserve (DW)
57. De Hoop Nature Reserve, near Bredasdorp (SDW; HT*; MB)
58. Swellendam Hiking Trail, Marloth Nature Reserve (HT; DW; M)
59. Bushbuck Hiking Trail, near Heidelberg (SDW)
60. Boosmansbos Wilderness Area, north of Heidelberg (WT)
61. Klapperbos Trail, Ladismith-Klein Karoo Nature Reserve (SDW)
62. Elandsberg Trail, near Ladismith (SDW)
63. Besemfontein Trails, near Ladismith (HT; SDW)
64. Sleeping Beauty Hiking Trail, Riversdale (DW)
65. Kristalkloof Hiking Trail, Riversdale (HT)
66. Rooiwaterspruit Trail, Riversdale (DW)

SOUTHERN CAPE

1. St Blaize Trail, Mossel Bay (DW)
2. Ruitersbos Forest and Protea Hill walks, Mossel Bay (DW)
3. Attaquaskloof Hiking Trail, Robinson Pass (HT)
4. Koumashoek Circuit, Robinson Pass (DW)
5. Gamka Mountain Nature Reserve (DW; GDW)
6. Groenfontein Farm, Calitzdorp (DW)
7. Swartberg Hiking Trail, Swartberg Pass/Cango Caves/De Hoek/Scholtzkloof (HT; DW; MB)
8. Ou Tol Circuit, Swartberg Pass (DW)
9. De Hoek Circuit, near the Cango Caves (DW)
10. Mons Ruber Walk, near De Rust (DW)
11. Steve H. Landman Trail, Glentana (DW)
12. Doringrivier Wilderness Area, Waboomskraal/Robinson Pass (DW; WT*)
13. Cradock Pass Trail, George (DW)
14. Pass-to-Pass Trail, George (DW)
15. Cradock and George Peaks Trail, George (DW)
16. Tierkop Hiking Trail, George (HT)
17. Garden Route Dam and Waterfall Hike, George (DW)
18. Groenweide Forest Walk, near George (DW)
19. Melville Peak Trail, near George (DW)
20. Kingfisher Trails, Wilderness (DW)
21. Cape Dune Molerat Trail, Rondevlei (DW)
22. Outeniqua Hiking Trail, Beervlei/Diepwalle (HT)
23. Millwood Circuit, near Knysna (DW)
24. Jubilee Creek Walk, near Knysna (DW)
25. Goukamma Nature Reserve, Sedgefield/Buffel's Bay (DW; H; C)
26. Bushbuck Trail, Knysna (GDW)
27. Terblans Nature Walk, near Knysna (DW)
28. The Elephant Walk, near Knysna (DW; MB)
29. Langkloof Nature Reserve, north-west of Uniondale (WT; DW*; HT*; MB)
30. Harkerville Coast Hiking Trail, near Plettenberg Bay (HT; MB)
31. Kranshoek Walk, near Plettenberg Bay (DW)
32. Robberg Nature Reserve, Plettenberg Bay (DW)
33. Wittedrift Nature Trail, Wittedrift (DW; HT)
34. Nature's Valley walks, Tsitsikamma National Park (DW)
35. Grootkloof Forest Trail, Tsitsikamma National Park (DW)
36. Stinkhoutkloof Forest Trail, Bloukrans State Forest (DW)
37. Tsitsikamma Hiking Trail, Nature's Valley/Storms River (HT)
38. Ratel Forest Trail, Storms River Bridge (DW)
39. Storms River Mouth walks, Tsitsikamma National Park (DW; UWT)
40. Otter Trail, Storms River Mouth/Nature's Valley (HT)
41. Fourcade Trail, Witelsbos State Forest (HT)
42. Captain Harison's Trail, Witelsbos State Forest (DW)
43. Formosa Conservation Area, Joubertina (WT; DW)

EASTERN CAPE, CISKEI AND TRANSKEI

1. Le Ferox Paradis Trails, near Joubertina (DW; GDW; WT)

36

2. Cockscomb and Baviaanskloof State Forests, Patensie to Willowmore (WT; M; HT*)
3. Gonaqua Trail, Loerie (HT)
4. Groendal Wilderness Area, near Uitenhage (WT; DW; M)
5. Uitenhage Nature Reserve (DW; H)
6. Van Stadens Wildflower Reserve, Port Elizabeth (DW)
7. Sir Peregrine Maitland & De Stades trails, Maitland Nature Reserve (DW)
8. Bosbok Walk, Island Conservation Area (DW)
9. Settler's Park, Port Elizabeth (DW)
10. Zuurberg National Park walks (DW; M)
11. Spekboom Trail, Addo Elephant National Park (DW)
12. The Alexandria Trail (HT)
13. Oribi Nature Trails, Port Alfred (GDW)
14. Kowie Hiking/Canoe Trail, Port Alfred (C/DW)
15. The Shipwreck Trail, Great Fish River to Chalumna River (HT)
16. Fort Fordyce Nature Reserve, Fort Beaufort (DW; HT)
17. Bosberg Nature Trail, Somerset East (HT)
18. Commando Drift Nature Reserve, Tarkastad/Cradock District (HT; DW; GHT; GDW; MB)
19. Tarka Toorberg, Tarkastad (HT)
20. The Tsolwana Trail, Whittlesea (GDW; GHT)
21. Katberg Loop Trail, Katberg Plantation (HT; H; MB)
22. Katberg Hiking Trail, Mpofu Game Reserve to Benholm Forest Station (HT; H)
23. Double Drift Hiking Trail (GHT)
24. Hogsback Walks (DW; HT; M)
25. Hogsback Hiking Trail (HT)
26. Kologha Hiking Trail, Stutterheim (HT)
27. The Amatola Hiking Trail, Amatola Mountains (HT)
28. Evelyn Loop Hiking Trail, Maden Dam (HT)
29. Zingcuka Loop Hiking Trail, near Hogsback (HT)
30. The Pirie and Sandile day walks, Maden Dam (DW)
31. Ocean View Guest Farm Trails, Komga (DW; GDW)
32. The Strandloper Trail, East London (HT; GHT)
33. Bridledrift Nature Reserve, East London (DW)
34. Umtiza Trails, East London (DW)
35. Madeira Guided Trails, Queenstown (GDW)
36. Rotary Aloe Trails, Queenstown (DW)
37. Lammergeyer Hiking Trail, Lady Grey (HT)
38. Sethunzini Hiking Trail, Lady Grey (GHT; MB; H)
39. Ecowa Hiking Trail, Elliot (HT)
40. Mountain Shadows Walks, Barkly Pass (DW)
41. Prentjiesberg Trails, Ugie (HT)
42. Woodcliffe Cave Trails, Maclear (HT; GHT*)
43. Pitlochrie walks, Barkly East (DW)
44. Ben MacDhui Hiking Trail, Rhodes (HT)
45. Transkei Hiking Trail, Wild Coast (HT)

NAMAQUALAND, KAROO AND NORTHERN CAPE

1. Gifberg Rusoord, south of Vanrhynsdorp (DW)
2. Klipkloppies Trail, Nieuwoudtville Nature Reserve (DW)
3. Oorlogskloof Nature Reserve, Nieuwoudtville (HT; DW)
4. De Hoop Trail, south of Nieuwoudtville (HT)
5. Akkerendam Nature Reserve, near Calvinia (DW)
6. Rooiberg Trails, near Garies (DW*; HT*)
7. Ian Myers Nature Walks, Goegap Nature Reserve (DW)
8. Richtersveld National Park, bordering the Orange River (GWT*; DW; C)
9. Pofadder Hiking Trail, Onseepkans (HT)
10. Klipspringer Hiking Trail, Augrabies Falls National Park (HT; DW)
11. Kokerboom Trail, the Brandvlei Road (DW)
12. Orange View Hiking Trail, north-west of Prieska (HT)
13. T'Keikamspoort Hiking Trail, near Prieska (DW)
14. Springbok Hiking Trail, Karoo National Park (HT; GDW; TD; MB)
15. Dries le Roux Nature Reserve, Touws River (DW)
16. Driekoppe Hiking Trail, Karoo Nature Reserve, Graaff-Reinet (HT/ WT)
17. Eerstefontein day walks, Karoo Nature Reserve, Graaff-Reinet (DW)
18. Mountain Zebra National Park, Cradock (HT; DW)
19. Transkaroo Hiking Trail, north of Middelburg (HT)
20. Pied Barbet Trail, PK le Roux Dam (DW)

ORANGE FREE STATE AND QWAQWA

1. Bethulie Dam Walks, Bethulie (HT; DW)
2. Tussen Die Riviere Game Reserve, Bethulie (DW; HT)
3. Aasvoëlberg Hiking Trail, Zastron (HT)
4. Stokstert Hiking Trail, Smithfield (HT)
5. Orange Free State National Botanical Garden, Bloemfontein (DW; GDW)
6. Maria Moroka National Park trails, Thaba Nchu, (DW; GDW; H)
7. Virginia Nature Trails, Virginia (DW)
8. Steve Visser Nature Walk, Ladybrand (DW; HT)
9. Evening Star Walk, Clocolan (DW)
10. Koranna Hiking Trail, near Excelsior (HT; MB; H)
11. Merriemetsi Hiking Trails, near Excelsior (DW; HT)
12. Kameelkop Hiking Trail, near Marquard (HT)
13. Christmaskrans Hiking Trail, Marquard (DW; HT*)
14. De Hoek Trails, near Marquard (DW)
15. Imperani Hiking Trail, Ficksburg (HT)
16. Porcupine Hiking Trail, Ficksburg (HT)
17. Waterkloof Hiking Trail, near Ficksburg (HT)
18. Sphinx Hiking Trail, near Ficksburg (HT)
19. Kututsa Hiking Trail, near Ficksburg (HT)
20. Vingerpol Hiking Trail, near Paul Roux (HT)
21. Tepelkop Hiking Trail, Slabberts (DW; HT)
22. Dikitla Hiking Trail, near Fouriesburg (HT)
23. Mountain Fern Trail, Biddulphsberg, east of Senekal (DW)
24. Wolhuterskop Hiking Trail, Bethlehem (HT)
25. Wyndford Holiday Farm, Fouriesburg (DW; GDW)

26. Bushman Cave Hiking Trail, Fouriesburg (DW)
27. Rhebok Hiking Trail, Golden Gate Highlands National Park (HT; DW; GDW; H)
28. Lesoba Hiking Trail, near Clarens (HT)
29. Clarens Hiking Trail, Clarens (DW; HT; H)
30. Bokpoort Hiking Trail, near Clarens (DW; HT)
31. Sterretjies Hiking Trail, near Harrismith (HT)
32. Platberg Hiking Trail, Harrismith (HT)
33. Mount Everest Holiday Game Reserve, Harrismith (DW)
34. Sentinel Hiking Trail, QwaQwa (DW)
35. Metsi Matsho Hiking Trail, QwaQwa (HT)
36. Fika Patso Hiking Trail, QwaQwa (HT; DW)

DRAKENSBERG AND LESOTHO

1. Spioenkop Nature Reserve, Winterton (SDW/GDW)
2. The Royal Natal National Park, Bergville (SDW; DW; M; H)
3. Upper Tugela Location, northern Drakensberg (HT; M)
4. Mont-aux-Sources to Cathedral Peak Hike, Lesotho/Natal (WT; GWT)
5. Cathedral Peak and Mlambonja Wilderness Area, near Winterton (DW; WT; M; MB; H)
6. Cathedral Peak Two Passes Hike, Cathedral Peak/Mlambonja Wilderness Area (WT)
7. Cathkin Peak and Mdedelelo Wilderness Area, near Winterton (DW; WT; M; MB; H)
8. Organ Pipes Pass to Gray's Pass Hike, near Winterton (WT; GWT)
9. Inkosana Lodge Trails, Champagne Castle (GWT; SDW; MB)
10. Giant's Castle Area, near Estcourt (SDW; DW; M; H)
11. Giant's Castle Two Huts Hike, near Estcourt (HT)
12. Mkhomazi Wilderness Area: southern/central Drakensberg (DW; WT; TD)
13. Burnera Trail, Himeville (GWT)
14. Mzimkulu Wilderness Area and Mzimkulwana Nature Reserve, southern Drakensberg (WT; DW)
15. Giant's Cup Trail, southern Drakensberg, near Himeville (HT)
16. Sehlaba-Thebe National Park, Lesotho (WT; DW)
17. Coleford Nature Reserve, Underberg (DW)
18. Mount Currie Nature Reserve, Kokstad (DW)
19. Malealea Lodge Trails, Makhakhe, Lesotho (DW; H)

NATAL AND KWAZULU

1. Weenen Game Reserve, Weenen (SDW)
2. Old Furrow Trail, Moor Park Nature Reserve, Estcourt (SDW)
3. Mhlopeni Nature Reserve, Muden (DW; HT; GDW)
4. Mooifalls Hiking Trail, Mooirivier (HT)
5. Nyoni Trail, Albert Falls Nature Reserve, near Cramond (DW)
6. Dargle River Trail, near Howick (DW)
7. Umgeni Valley Nature Reserve, Howick (DW)
8. Cedara Forest Trail, near Hilton (SDW)

9. Idube Trail, Queen Elizabeth Park, Pietermaritzburg (SDW)
10. Natal National Botanic Garden, Pietermaritzburg (SDW)
11. Ferncliffe Nature Reserve, Pietermaritzburg (DW)
12. Green Belt Trails, Pietermaritzburg (UT)
13. Bisley Nature Reserve, Pietermaritzburg (DW)
14. Ingweni Hiking Trail, Durban (GHT)
15. Krantzkloof Nature Reserve, Kloof (DW)
16. Paradise Valley Nature Reserve, Pinetown, Durban (DW)
17. Durban's Self-guided Trails, Durban Municipal Area (SDW/UT)
18. Palmiet Nature Reserve, Westville, Durban (SDW; GDW; TD)
19. Kenneth Stainbank Nature Reserve, Durban (SDW; TD)
20. Ngele Hiking Trails, near Harding (HT/GHT)
21. Lorna Doone Forest Hostel trails, near Harding (SDW)
22. Umtamvuna Nature Reserve, Port Edward (DW/GDW)
23. Oribi Gorge Nature Reserve, Port Shepstone (DW/GDW)
24. Vernon Crookes Nature Reserve, Umzinto (DW/GDW)
25. Empisini Nature Reserve, Umkomaas (DW)
26. Hawaan Forest Nature Reserve, Umhlanga Rocks (GDW)
27. Harold Johnson Nature Reserve, Darnall (SDW)
28. Amatikulu Nature Reserve, Amatikulu (DW)
29. Dhlinza Forest Nature Reserve, Eshowe (DW)
30. Entumeni Nature Reserve, Eshowe (DW)
31. Umlalazi Nature Reserve, Mtunzini (SDW)
32. Nyala Game Ranch, Empangeni (GDW)
33. Enseleni Nature Reserve, Empangeni (GDW)
34. Matatane Trail, near Melmoth (SDW)
35. Game Park trails, St Lucia Estuary (SDW)
36. Lake St Lucia Wilderness Trail, St Lucia Game Reserve (GWT)
37. Umvube Trail, Cape Vidal, Greater St Lucia Wetland Park (SDW; GDW)
38. Mapelane Nature Reserve, Greater St Lucia Wetland Park (SDW)
39. Dugandlovu and Mpophomeni trails, False Bay Park, Greater St Lucia Wetland Park (SDW)
40. Mziki Trail, Eastern Shores Nature Reserve, Greater St Lucia Wetland Park (HT; SDW)
41. Lake Trail, Eastern Shores Nature Reserve, Greater St Lucia Wetland Park (GWT)
42. Isikhova and Umkhumbe Trails, Charter's Creek, Greater St Lucia Wetland Park (SDW)
43. Umkhiwane Trail, Fanie's Island, Greater St Lucia Wetland Park (SDW)
44. Umfolozi Wilderness and Primitive Trails (GWT)
45. White Rhino Trail, Umfolozi Game Reserve (GWT)
46. Hluhluwe Game Reserve, Hluhluwe (GDW)
47. Ubizane Game Reserve, Hluhluwe (GDW)
48. Mkuzi Game Reserve, Mkuze (SDW; GDW)
49. Mkuze Bushveld Trail, Mkuzi Game Reserve (GWT)

50. Thaba Ye Zulu Hiking Trail, Hluhluwe (HT)
51. Sodwana Bay National Park, Mbazwana, northern Zululand (SDW)
52. Lake Sibaya Nature Reserve, Baya Camp, near Mbazwana (DW; GDW)
53. Amanzimnyama Trail, Kosi Bay Nature Reserve (GWT; GDW)
54. Ndumu Game Reserve, Jozini (GDW)
55. Ngwenyama Trail, Magudu (HT)
56. Mkhaya Trail, Pongola (HT)
57. Itala Game Reserve, Louwsburg (GDW; GWT)
58. Ntendeka Wilderness Area, near Vryheid (DW; HT)
59. Lancaster Hiking Trail, Vryheid Nature Reserve (DW; HT*)
60. Balele Hiking Trail, Utrecht (HT)
61. Bushman Krans Hiking Trails, Newcastle (SDW)
62. Geelhout Trail, Newcastle (HT)
63. Mpati Hill Hiking Trail, Dundee (DW; HT)
64. Talana Trail, Dundee (DW/SDW)
65. Oribi Hiking Trail, Biggarsberg Conservancy (GHT)
66. Monks Trail, Biggarsberg Conservancy (GHT)

SWAZILAND

1. Meikles Mount, Mhlambanyati (SDW; H)
2. Mlilwane Wildlife Sanctuary, Mbabane (SDW; GDW; M; H)
3. Malolotja Nature Reserve, Mbabane (SDW; H)
4. Hlane National Park, Simunye (GDW)
5. Mlawula Nature Reserve, Mhlume (SDW; GDW)
6. Mkhaya Nature Reserve, Phuzumoya (GDW)

NORTHERN AND EASTERN TRANSVAAL

1. Diepdrift Hiking Trails, near Warmbaths (HT; DW)
2. Kransberg Hiking Trails, near Thabazimbi (DW)
3. Taaibos Hiking Trail, near Vaalwater (HT; DW)
4. The Rhino Trail, Lapalala Wilderness (GWT)
5. Sable Valley Hiking Trail, near Naboomspruit (HT)
6. Sterkstroom Tent Trail, Doorndraai Dam Nature Reserve (HT)
7. Mapulaneng Hiking Trails, Bushbuck Ridge (DW)
8. Rhino Hiking Trail, Pietersburg Game Reserve (DW; HT)
9. Bakoni Trail, Pietersburg (SDW)
10. Masebe Trails, Masebe Nature Reserve (DW)
11. Limpopo Wilderness Hiking Trail, Alldays (HT)
12. Soutpansberg Hiking Trail: Entabeni Section, near Louis Trichardt (HT)
13. Soutpansberg Hiking Trail: Hanglip Section, Louis Trichardt (HT; DW)
14. Mabuda-Shango Hiking Trail, Soutpansberg (HT)
15. Ben Lavin Nature Reserve Trails, near Louis Trichardt (DW)
16. Kruger National Park Wilderness Trails, eastern Transvaal (GWT)
17. Leopard Trail, Duiwelskloof (HT; DW)
18. Modjadji Nature Reserve Trail, Bolobedu (DW)
19. Magoebaskloof Hiking Trail: Dokolewa Section, near Tzaneen (HT)
20. Magoebaskloof Hiking Trail: Grootbosch Section, near Tzaneen (HT)
21. Rooikat Nature Trail, New Agatha State Forest (DW)
22. Hans Merensky Nature Reserve trails (SDW; DW)
23. Giraffe Hiking Trail, Hans Merensky Nature Reserve (HT)
24. Wolkberg Wilderness Area, Haenertsburg (WT; M)
25. Lekgalameetse Hiking Trail, Trichardtsdal (HT)
26. Potlake Nature Reserve Walks (DW)
27. Jock of the Bushveld Trails, Timbavati Game Reserve (GWT)
28. Protea and Yellowwood trails, Blyderivierspoort Nature Reserve (HT)
29. Blyderivierspoort Hiking Trail, (HT)
30. Swadini Nature Trails, Blyderivierspoort Nature Reserve (SDW)
31. Prospector's Hiking Trail, Pilgrim's Rest (HT)
32. Morgenzon Hiking Trail, Pilgrim's Rest (HT)
33. Mount Sheba Nature Trails, Pilgrim's Rest (DW)
34. Boschhoek Trail, Ohrigstad (HT; DW)
35. Vlakvark Hiking Trail, near Lydenburg (HT)
36. Dinkwanyane Hiking Trail, Ohrigstad (HT)
37. Fanie Botha Hiking Trails, Sabie (HT; DW)
38. Gustav Klingbiel Nature Reserve, Lydenburg (HT; DW)
39. Sterkspruit Hiking Trail, Lydenburg (HT)
40. Steenkampsberg Hiking Trail, Dullstroom (HT)
41. Crane Creek Trail, near Waterval Boven (DW)
42. Elandskrans Hiking Trail, near Waterval Boven (HT; DW)
43. Uitsoek Hiking Trails, Waterval Boven/Lydenburg (HT; DW)
44. Wathaba Wilderness Trails, near Machadodorp (DW; WT)
45. Kaapschehoop Hiking Trails, near Nelspruit (HT)
46. Riverside Trail, Nelspruit (SDW)
47. Pioneer Trail, Barberton (HT)
48. Umvoti Trail, Barberton (HT)
49. Gold Nugget Trail, Barberton (HT)
50. Songimvelo Wilderness Experience, Kangwane near Badplaas (GWT)
51. The Brook Hiking Trail, near Carolina (HT)
52. Cycad Hiking Trails, near Middelburg (HT; DW)
53. Botshabelo Trails, Middelburg (DW; HT)
54. Ngodwana Trail, Ngodwana Dam (DW)
55. Mashonamien Forest Trails, near Ngodwana (DW)
56. Kalkoenkrans Trails, near Badplaas (GDW; GHT; H)

HIGHVELD

1. Rustenburg Nature Reserve Trails, Magaliesberg (HT; SDW)
2. Magaliesberg, south-central Transvaal (WT; K; M)
3. Moreleta Spruit Hiking Trail, Pretoria (UT)
4. Pretoria National Botanical Garden, Pretoria (SDW; GDW)
5. Faan and Neels van Wyk Trail, Zemvelo Game Park (HT)
6. Krugersdorp Game Reserve (GDW)
7. Abe Bailey Nature Reserve, Carletonville (SDW; GDW)
8. Witwatersrand National Botanical Garden, Roodepoort (DW; GDW)
9. Kloofendal Nature Reserve, Roodepoort (DW)
10. Braamfontein Spruit Trail, Johannesburg (UT)
11. Sandspruit Trail, Johannesburg (SDW/UT)
12. Mervyn King Ridge Trail, Johannesburg (SDW/UT)
13. Jukskei Trail and Randlords Heritage Walk, Johannesburg (SDW/UT)
14. Bloubosspruit Trail, Johannesburg (SDW/UT)
15. Suikerbosrand Hiking and Nature Trail Complex, Heidelberg (DW; HT)
16. Klipkraal Hiking Trail, near Heidelberg (HT)
17. Three Rivers Nature Trail, Vereeniging (DW)
18. Likkewaan Hiking Trails, Parys-on-Vaal (DW; HT)
19. The Rooihaas Hiking Trail, near Venterskroon (HT)
20. Barberspan Nature Reserve (GDW)
21. Marico Hiking Trail, Bronkhorstfontein (HT; DW)
22. Botsalano Game Reserve, north of Mmabatho (GDW)
23. Pilanesberg National Park, Bophuthatswana (GDW; GWT)
24. Borakalalo National Park, Jericho, north-west of Pretoria (GWT; DW)

ZIMBABWE

1. Matobo National Park, near Bulawayo (DW; MB; H)
2. Mushandike Sanctuary, Masvingo (DW)
3. Great Zimbabwe Park and National Monument, Masvingo (DW)
4. Lake Mutirikwe Recreational Park, south of Masvingo (DW; H)
5. Gonarezhou National Park, south-east Zimbabwe (GWT)
6. Chirinda Forest Botanical Reserve, eastern Highlands (DW)
7. Chimanimani National Park, eastern Highlands (WT; M)
8. Bunga Forest and Vumba Botanical reserves, south-east of Mutare (DW)
9. Cecil Kop Nature Reserve, Mutare (DW; GWT; H)
10. M'Tarazi Falls National Park, Nyanga National Park (DW)
11. Nyanga National Park, eastern Highlands (DW; M; H)
12. Robert McIlwaine Recreational Park, south-west of Harare (DW; H)
13. Ewanrigg Botanical Gardens, near Harare (DW)
14. Chinhoyi Caves National Park, Chinhoyi (DW)
15. Mufure Recreational Park, Zimbabwe Midlands (GWT)
16. Mana Pools National Park, Zambezi River (GWT)
17. Charara Safari Area, Lake Kariba (DW)
18. Matusadona National Park, Lake Kariba (GDW; GWT; C)
19. Chizarira National Park, south of Lake Kariba (GWT)
20. Hwange National Park, north-west Zimbabwe (GWT)
21. Kazuma Pan National Park, north-west Zimbabwe (GWT)
22. The Victoria Falls and Zambezi national parks, Zambezi River (DW; GDW; H; C)

BOTSWANA

1. Mashatu Game Reserve, eastern Botswana (GDW)
2. The Rhino and Elephant Trail, Lapalala Wilderness/Mashatu Game Reserve (GWT)
3. Kalahari Bushman Hiking Trail, north-west of Gaborone (GWT)
4. The Fish Eagle Trail, Okavango Swamps/Chobe National Park or Linyanti (GWT)

NAMIBIA

1. West Caprivi Game Reserve, Caprivi (GWT; C)
2. Madumu National Park, Caprivi (GWT)
3. Mamili National Park, Linyanti Swamps, Caprivi (GWT)
4. Waterberg Plateau Park, near Otjiwarongo (GWT; HT)
5. Ugab Hiking Trail, Skeleton Coast Park (GWT)
6. The Brandberg, north-western Namibia (DW; M)
7. Spitzkoppe, near Usakos (DW; M)
8. Tsaobis-Leopard Nature Park, near Karibib (DW; WT)
9. Daan Viljoen Game Park, near Windhoek (DW)
10. Hochland Venture Trails, near Windhoek (DW; HT; H)
11. Namib-Naukluft Park, Namib Section, west-central Namibia (DW)
12. Namib-Naukluft Park, Naukluft Section, west-central Namibia (HT; DW)
13. Hardap Resort and Game Park, near Mariental (DW)
14. Oas Hiking Trail, Oas Holiday Farm, southern Namibia (HT; H)
15. Fish River Canyon, southern Namibia (HT; H)

ZAMBIA

1. Lunga-Luswishi Game Management Area, western Zambia (GDW)
2. Kafue National Park, western Zambia (GDW; GWT)
3. Tongabezi Camp, Zambezi River (GDW; C)
4. Kota Kota Hills Game Reserve, Victoria Falls region (GDW; GWT; C)
5. Lochinvar National Park, Kafue Flats (GDW)
6. Lilayi Lodge, near Lusaka (GDW)
7. Chiawa Camp, Lower Zambezi National Park (GDW)
8. Kasanka National Park, eastern Zambia (GDW)
9. Bangweulu Game Management Area, eastern Zambia (GDW)
10. South Luangwa National Park and Luangwa Valley, eastern Zambia (GDW)
11. Walking Safaris, South Luangwa National Park (GWT)
12. North Luangwa National Park, eastern Zambia (GWT)
13. Nyika Plateau National Park, eastern Zambia (GWT)
14. Nsumbu National Park and Kasaba Bay, Lake Tanganyika (GDW)

MALAWI

1. Mwabvi Wildlife Reserve, southern region (GDW)
2. Lengwe National Park, southern Malawi (SDW; GDW)

3. Majete Wildlife Reserve and Shire River, Chikwawa (GDW: DW)
4. Thyolo Mountain, south of Blantyre (DW)
5. Mulanje Mountain, southern region (HT; MB; M)
6. Soche Mountain, Blantyre (DW)
7. Michiru Mountain Conservation Area, Blantyre (DW; GDW)
8. Zomba Plateau, southern region (SDW; M)
9. Liwonde National Park, Liwonde (GDW)
10. Lake Malawi National Park, Cape Maclear (DW)
11. Dedza Mountain, Dedza (DW)
12. Lilongwe Nature Sanctuary, Lilongwe (SDW)
13. Kasungu National Park, central region (GDW)
14. Nkhota-kota Wildlife Reserve, Nkota-kota (GDW)
15. Viphya Plateau, Mzuzu (DW)
16. Vwaza Marsh Wildlife Reserve, Katumbi (SDW; GDW)
17. Nyika National Park, near Rumphi (GWT; DW; GDW; H)

SPECIAL INTEREST TRAILS

Mountain-biking trails
1. Jonkershoek State Forest, near Stellenbosch
2. Table Mountain, Cape Town
3. Silvermine Nature Reserve, Cape Peninsula
4. Cape of Good Hope Nature Reserve, Cape Peninsula
5. Grabouw State Forest, south-western Cape
6. Caledon Nature Reserve, Caledon
7. Salmonsdam Nature Reserve, near Stanford
8. De Hoop Nature Reserve, near Bredasdorp
9. Anysberg Trail, south-western Cape
10. Hoopoe Trails, Breede River Valley, near Bonnievale
11. Karoo National Park, near Beaufort West
12. Rooiheuwel Farm, near Beaufort West
13. Swartberg Trail, near Prince Albert, southern Cape
14. Rock Jumper and Kammanassie Trails, near Uniondale
15. Knysna Forest Trail, Knysna
16. Knysna Wilderness Trail, Sedgefield/Knysna area
17. Harkerville State Forest, Knysna/Plettenberg Bay
18. Commando Drift Nature Reserve, near Cradock
19. Sethunzini Mountain Bike Challenge, near Lady Grey
20. Katberg Mountain Biking Trails, Balfour, Ciskei
21. Flora Ride, Koranna Conservancy, eastern Orange Free State
22. Koranna Two Mountain Bike Trails, eastern Orange Free State
23. Cherry Trail Challenge, near Marquard, eastern Orange Free State
24. Rietfontein Ride, Rietfontein Conservancy, near Marquard
25. Wolwerand Ride (Red Trail), Rietfontein Conservancy, near Marquard
26. Sparrowfarm Trails, north-eastern Orange Free State
27. The Drifters Inn Trails, Bergville/Harrismith, north-eastern Orange Free State

Trails are not dust and pebbles on a hill,

Nor even grass and wild buds by a lake;

Trails are adventure and a hand to still

The restless pulse of life when men would break

Their minds with weight of thinking. Trails are peace,

The call to dreams, the challenge to ascent;

Trails are the brisk unfolding of release

From bitterness and from discouragement.

Trails are the random writing on the wall

That tells how every man, grown tired at heart

Of things correct and ordered, comes to scrawl

His happy hour down – then goes to start

Life over with new eagerness and zest.

Who builds a trail finds labor that is rest!

Trails
HELEN FRAZEE-BOWER

28. Blanerne Game-viewing Trails, Newcastle, northern Natal
29. Cathedral Peak, Natal Drakensberg Park
30. Champagne Valley, Champagne Castle, Drakensberg
31. Mountain Bike Adventures, Lesotho
32. Mariepskop Forestry Area, near Graskop, eastern Transvaal
33. Matobo National Park, near Bulawayo, Zimbabwe
34. Chambe Path, Mulanje Mountain, near Blantyre, Malawi

Canoeing and River-rafting trails
1. Orange River, Cape/Namibian border
2. Orange Gorge, Orange River, Cape/Namibian border
3. Orange River (near Augrabies), north-western Cape
4. Two Ships Trail, Orange River and Bushmanland, near Augrabies Falls
5. Doring River, northern Cedarberg, western Cape
6. Langebaan Lagoon, Cape West Coast
7. Breede River, near Swellendam, south-western Cape
8. The Wine Route Canoeing and Rafting Adventure, Breede River, south-western Cape
9. Bushmans River Canoe Trail, eastern Cape
10. Kowie Canoe Trail, Port Alfred, eastern Cape
11. Tugela River, northern Natal
12. Vaal River, near Parys, Transvaal

13. Hadeda Creek Trail, Vaal River, Parys, Transvaal
14. Chobe River, Caprivi, Namibia
15. Upper Zambezi River, Kazungula to Victoria Falls
16. Zambezi River, below the Victoria Falls to Lake Kariba
17. Lake Kariba, northern Zimbabwe
18. Lower Zambezi River, from Lake Kariba to Kanyemba

Horseback, Pony-trekking and Camel trails
1. Kalahari Gemsbok National Park, near Upington
2. Kameeldoring Trail, Bushmanland, near Augrabies Falls
3. Two Ships Trail, Orange River and Bushmanland, near Augrabies Falls
4. Cedarberg Wilderness Trail, western Cape
5. K'Taaibos Horse Trails, western Cape
6. West Coast Wilderness Trail, Verlorenvlei Bird Sanctuary
7. Novice Trails, Ottery, near Cape Town
8. Noordhoek Beach, Cape Peninsula
9. Montagu to De Doorns, western Cape
10. Worcester Game Trail, western Cape
11. Knysna Wilderness Trail, Sedgefield/Knysna area
12. Benghoil Horse and Hiking Trails, near Cathcart, eastern Cape
13. Sethunzini Horse Trail, near Lady Grey, southern Drakensberg
14. Katberg Mountain Horse Trails, Balfour, Ciskei
15. Mpofu Game Park, Balfour, Ciskei

16. Maria Moroka National Park, Thaba Nchu, Bophuthatswana
17. Golden Gate Highlands National Park, near Clarens
18. Sparrowfarm Trails, north-eastern Orange Free State
19. Bokpoort Horse Safaris, north-eastern Orange Free State
20. Rietfontein Horse Ride, eastern Orange Free State
21. Franshoek Mountain Horse Trail, eastern Orange Free State
22. Qwibi Horse Trail, near Melmoth, northern Natal
23. Ndanyaan Mountain Trails, near Newcastle, northern Natal
24. Royal Natal National Park, northern Drakensberg
25. Cathedral Peak Hotel Horse Rides, Drakensberg
26. Dragon Peak Horse Rides, Champagne Castle area, Drakensberg
27. Champagne Castle Hotel Horse Rides, Drakensberg
28. Hillside, Giant's Castle Reserve, Natal Drakensberg Park
29. Gateshead Lodge, southern Drakensberg
30. Frasers Lodge, Semonkong, Lesotho
31. Matelile Pony-Trekking Tours, Mafeteng District, Lesotho
32. Malealea Lodge, near Makhakhe, Lesotho
33. Basotho Pony-Trekking, Molimo Nthuse Pass, Lesotho
34. Meikles Mount, Mbabane, Swaziland
35. Malolotja Nature Reserve, near Mbabane, Swaziland
36. Equus Trails, Waterberg Mountains, northern Transvaal
37. Kalkoenkrantz Horse Trails, near Carolina, eastern Transvaal
38. Namib Desert Horse Riding, Khomas Hochland/Swakopmund, Namibia
39. Dusternbrook Horse Trails, Khomas Hochland, Namibia
40. Oas Guest Farm, near Keetmanshoop, Namibia
41. Fish River Canyon Horse Trails, southern Namibia
42. Zambezi Horse Trails, north-western Zimbabwe
43. Matobo National Park, near Bulawayo, Zimbabwe
44. Lake Mutirikwe Recreational Park, near Masvingo, Zimbabwe
45. Cecil Kop Nature Reserve, near Mutare, eastern Zimbabwe
46. Nyanga National Park, near Mutare, eastern Zimbabwe
47. Robert McIlwaine Recreational Park, near Harare, Zimbabwe
48. Horseback Safaris, Nyika National Park, Malawi

Trails for the Disabled
1. Kirstenbosch National Botanical Garden, Cape Town
2. Karoo National Park, near Beaufort West
3. Kenneth Stainbank Trail, Durban, Natal
4. Durban Botanic Gardens, Durban, Natal
5. Palmiet Nature Reserve, Durban, Natal
6. Glenholme Trail for disabled and blind persons, Kloof, Natal
7. Kamberg Nature Reserve, Natal Drakensberg Park
8. Bonnet Herbs Farm, Graskop, eastern Transvaal

Underwater trail
1. Storms River Mouth, Tsitsikamma National Park

THE WESTERN CAPE

The area commonly referred to as the Western Cape comprises the southern-most part of Africa and the adjacent interior. Its coastline stretches from the Gouritz River mouth westwards past the tip of the continent – Cape Agulhas – to Cape Town, and curves north to Lambert's Bay. Running parallel to the southern and western coasts respectively are two mighty series of mountain ranges which meet at the Worcester fault. The eastern series includes the Langeberg and the Riviersonderend Mountains and, inland, the Klein Swartberg. There are isolated low ridges such as Potberg, together with the coastal ranges – the Bredasdorp and Kleinrivier mountains. Concentrated in the south-west corner of the area is an extensive complex of contiguous mountains: the Hottentots Holland, Franschhoek, Slanghoek, Du Toit's, Wemmershoek, Jonkershoek and Bain's Kloof mountains. Stretching northwards from these are the Ceres, Hex River and Groot Winterhoek, Kouebokkeveld and Cedarberg mountain ranges.

Although it stands apart, Table Mountain and the Cape Peninsula are a constituent of this geological system. Between the mountains and the sea is a more-or-less flat area of land of varying width, except near Gordon's Bay, where the mountains drop straight into the sea. Inland the mountains meet the Karoo.

These, then, are the mountains that give the shape to what is recognized as one of the most scenically dramatic regions of the world. Add to this a flora which is unique, diverse and beautiful and it is easy to understand why the Western Cape is a hiker's paradise. As the entire region has been settled for a long time, it offers the hiker a myriad hiking routes. More people tramp the paths on Table Mountain than on any other mountain in southern Africa.

The Western Cape has a Mediterranean climate which means cold, wet winters and dry, windy summers. Beware of the summer south-easter, which often reaches gale force, and can quickly envelop mountains in heavy, moist clouds; the 'table cloth' which sometimes covers Table Mountain is a well-known example. In winter, cold fronts drive cloud and rain over the land; sometimes they even bring snow to the high peaks. When it blows for long periods, its desiccating effect increases the fire hazard.

Rugged sandstone peaks and extensive fynbos-covered ranges cut by deep kloofs harbouring crystal rushing streams, form the interior of this area.

This coastal berg interface is considered to be one of the most dramatic in the world. Hikers, ramblers and mountaineers need no encouragement to explore the Western Cape's plentiful and scenic wilderness areas, hiking trails, nature and forest reserves, and botanical gardens. The main population centre, Cape Town, boasts Table Mountain, the most-climbed massif in the world.

LEFT: *Chapman's Peak Drive winds above the indigo waters of Hout Bay.*

1. VERLORENVLEI HIKING TRAILS
REDELINGHUYS

Trail details: 1. Spoonbill Route: 18 km/1 day
return (duration depending on time taken watching
birds); there are plans to extend the route, possibly
all the way to Elands Bay, to make a total distance
of 30 km (one way). 2. Wheel Cliff Route: 18 km/
8 hours (circular). 3. Kruisfontein Route: 14 km/
6 hours return, although this may be extended to a
2-day trail.

Permits/bookings: Must be obtained from Mr J
Conradie, Hostel, tel. (0263) 604; PO Box 6,
Redelinghuys 8105.

Maps/information: For further information, contact
the Verlorenvlei Hiking Trail Committee, tel. (021)
5918658; PO Box 676, Goodwood 7460.

Facilities/amenities: Accommodation available in
the hostel at Redelinghuys, or you can camp or
caravan there. Wheel Cliff Route has braai
facilities; an overnight hut may be available at
Picnic Koppies in the course of 1994. On the
Spoonbill Route there are bird-watching towers.

Main attractions: Wheel Cliff Route: Wheel Cliff
cave, Picnic Koppies, spring flowers, rock
formations, panoramic views. Spoonbill Route: a
birder's paradise.

Pertinent information: Carry at least 2 litres of
water per person.

Verlorenvlei is a permanent pan, stretching for
30 km west to east and emptying into the sea at
Elands Bay. August to October is regarded as the
best time for a visit, as it is then that the veld is in
all its floral glory; the pink afrikander or sandveld
lily, *Gladiolus caryophyllaceus*, is endemic to the
area. Since their opening in 1992 these trails have
quickly gained year-round popularity, however.
1. The Spoonbill Route makes for easy walking on
the flat, along the southern side of the vlei. Among
the 200 species of birds that have been recorded
here are pelicans, spoonbills, darters, gallinules,
kingfishers, sacred ibises and bee-eaters. For news
on the progress of the 30-km route, consult the
Velorenvlei Hiking Trail Committee.
2. Wheel Cliff Route You need to be reasonably
fit to undertake this one, which offers plenty of
challenges and variety. The trail, which is marked
with arrows, begins and ends at Redelinghuys. The
first 3 km are on the level alongside the vlei, but
the gradient becomes gradually steeper over the
next 6 km. The eventual reward for your effort is a
magnificent panorama stretching from Redelinghuys to Verlorenvlei, down to the sea and across

to the Piketberg. There are braai facilities among
the wind- and sandweathered rocks of Picnic
Koppies. A further descent and ascent lie in wait,
ahead of the final 4 km downhill. Look out for the
optional short cut if you wish to reduce the distance
by about 4 km.

Appropriately named Red Embankments, Wheel
Cliff and its cave, Houthoek Valley and Mierberg
are all memorable features of this trail, on which
several antelope species, baboons and a variety of
birds may be seen.
3. Kruisfontein Route An easy route that heads
north from Redelinghuys along one of the smaller
vleis and through farmlands where potatoes are a
major crop. There are plans to extend the route to
make it a 2-day trail.

2. SEVILLA BUSHMAN PAINTING
TRAIL AND LORRAINE HIKING TRAIL
NORTHERN CEDARBERG NEAR CLANWILLIAM

Trail details: 1. Lorraine Trail: 14 km/7 hours.
2. Sevilla Trail: 10 km/5 hours. Both are circular
day walks. A shorter walk, known as Salmanslaagte,
can be done to view Bushman paintings.

Permits/bookings: Reservations at a small fee can
be made with Land Trek, Pinelands, tel. (021)
5318441 or 5318939; fax (021) 5316508;
PO Box 383, Howard Place 7450.

Maps/information: Mrs H. Strauss, tel. (02682)
2203 (evenings only); PO Box 209, Clanwilliam
8135. Detailed maps available on request.

Facilities/amenities: 3 overnight/holiday cottages,
each sleeping 6 on Sevilla; fully equipped
farmhouse, sleeping 5, on Lorraine.

Main attractions: Bushman paintings; magnificent
views of the Cedarberg; wildlife includes jackal,
brown hyaena and even leopard.

Pertinent information: Group size is restricted to
20 people.

These trails, which are marked with white footprints, have been laid out on two separate farms
(both belonging to Mrs H. Strauss) in close
proximity to each other, in the northern Cedarberg.
Both farms lie roughly 36 km from Clanwilliam on
the road to Calvinia, and each trail takes the name
of the farm on which it has been laid out. The trails
were opened in 1991.

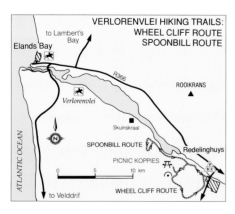

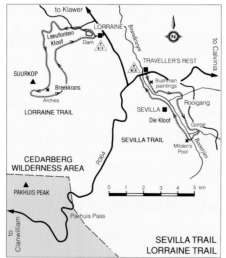

The Maltese Cross, a Cedarberg landmark.

1. Lorraine Trail Beginning near the Lorraine
homestead, the path leads around the dam, over a
stile, and up into Leeufontein Kloof. Dense stands
of restios are prominent on the first ridge, while the
rocky sandstone ledges feature vygies and stone
plants (*Lithops* spp.) adapted to the harsh conditions. After using another stile over a fence, trailists
cross the jeep track and ascend a rocky ridge,
which necessitates some rock clambering through
the kloofs. The stillness here is broken only by the
honk of Egyptian geese or the barking of baboons.
Felicia, the medicinal buchu and the tortoise berry
bush, whose lilac flowers are followed by edible
berries in summer, grow here. On top of the plateau
the acid sandy soil supports a prolific mountain fynbos community which includes blombos (*Metalasia
muricata*) and the broom-like bergriet (*Brachycar-
paea juncea*), which bears a mass of mauve flowers
in early spring.

Near Breekkrans there are natural arches in the
sandstone rock, formed by weathering. When they
are in flower, everlastings (*Helichrysum* spp.) may
be noticed beside the path. After descending
Breekkrans and passing through a dense stand of
proteas, the full-day trail leads back, via a jeep
track and a stile, to the Lorraine homestead.
2. Sevilla Trail Bushman paintings can be found
beneath the rocky ledges along this trail. The circular route crosses the Brandewyn River and leads up
a valley past the caves and overhangs used as shelters by the nomadic Bushmen. Ancient wild olive
trees grow at the base of the rocky cliffs and wild
almonds occur closer to the stream. The veld in the
Rooigang area is particularly colourful in spring.
As one climbs to the dry, stony plateau above Rooigang, the change in vegetation is marked; aloes and
succulents make their appearance. A steep descent
across a picturesque gorge, past a weir and to the
Boontjies River below it brings one to Milden's
Pool, into which a spectacular waterfall cascades
after good rains. It is an easy stroll back along the
jeep track to the start.

3. CEDARBERG WILDERNESS AND ADJOINING AREA
CITRUSDAL/CLANWILLIAM

Trail details: An extensive network (254 km) of unmarked, well-maintained footpaths, and excellent rock climbing. The length of your hike is limited only by the weight of the provisions you can carry on your back. The Wolfberg Cracks and Arch, the Maltese Cross and Sneeuberg are each the subject of a separate popular day walk from the private farms adjoining the wilderness area in the south. Other day walks on the farms in or to the south of the wilderness are described below. A new day walk has been laid out on the farm Dwarsrivier (distinct from the farm of the same name in the south) on the far northern edge of the Cedarberg Wilderness Area.

Permits/bookings: A permit to enter one of the three 'blocks' of wilderness area must be obtained from Cape Nature Conservation, Cedarberg Wilderness Area, tel. (02682) ask for 3440; Private Bag X1, Citrusdal, 7340. (Valid permits must be carried at all times.) Map, available on request, is essential. As the southern approach to the Wolfberg Cracks, Wolfberg Arch and Maltese Cross is through private farmland, hikers must request a permit to enter the area from Mrs H Nieuwoudt, Dwarsrivier; tel. (02682) ask for 1521. Permits are obtainable from the office during working hours and Saturday mornings.

Facilities/amenities: Book through Cape Nature Conservation at above address, for: Algeria camping and caravanning area with modern ablution blocks, located near the forest station (book at least three months ahead for peak times/seasons); Kliphuis camp site on Pakhuis Pass; Waenhuis, accommodating eight people, with shower, toilet and bunkbeds, and Uitkyk forest refuge, accommodating 16 people in four rooms, with kitchen, bath, toilet and bunkbeds. There are patrol shelters within the wilderness area at Sleeppad, Sneeukop, Crystal Pool, Middelberg, Sneeuberg and Boontjieskloof. Accommodation on private farms in the area (at least some of which is for whites only) includes: Sanddrif (whites-only camp site and cottages on the farm Dwarsrivier), enquiries to E. and H. Nieuwoudt, tel. (02682) ask for 1521; Matjiesrivier (guest house and 3 flats), enquiries to Mr W. du Toit, tel. (02682) ask for 1512; Kromrivier (bungalows; shop), enquiries to E. and O. Nieuwoudt, tel. (02682) ask for 1404; Nuwerust (3 cottages), enquiries J de V Esterhuizen, tel. (02682) ask for 1402; Krakadou (chalets on the northern farm Dwarsrivier), enquiries Mrs T. Louw, tel. (02682) ask for 1222.

Main attractions: Impressive rock formations; endemic flora.

Pertinent information: Beyond Algeria camp site, access to the wilderness area is on foot only. Group size is restricted to 12; no fires allowed (take a gas stove) and no washing in streams (although swimming allowed). If you plan to sleep out, take a foam mattress, as the ground is hard; in winter, carry a tent, sleeping bag and warm clothing. Being in the winter rainfall area, the mountains receive north-west winds, precipitation and possible snowfalls mainly between May and September, when you should be prepared for harsh conditions; however, expect rain even in summer. The summers are hot (days reach 35 °C in January and February), but cooled by the prevailing south-east to east winds. Watch out for the berg adder and puff adder, two of the fifteen resident snake species. Note that on-duty forest guards take precedence at patrol shelters.

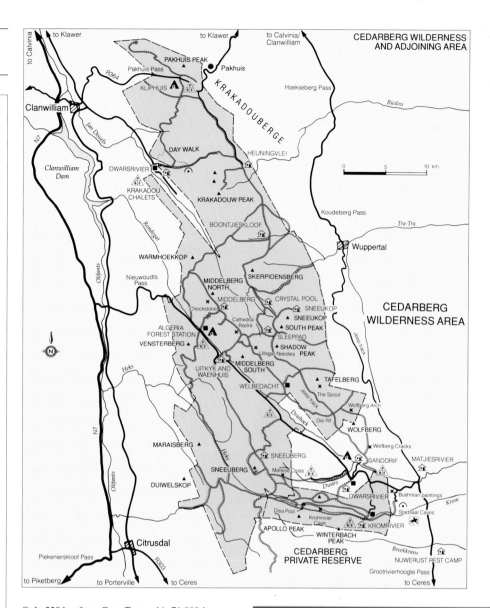

Only 220 km from Cape Town, this 71 000-ha mountain complex is managed by Cape Nature Conservation, principally for conservation of the pure, silt-free water of this catchment area, as a recreation area (one of the few areas in this country where visitors can enjoy the 'wilderness experience') and as a sanctuary for the biodiverse Cape fynbos. The Cedarberg is so diverse in form and structure, so valuable for its plants and animals and so unique in its landscape, that any nature lover, hiker or mountaineer will find its opportunities and challenges difficult to exhaust.

Geological formations can generally be clearly seen in Western Cape mountains, but erosional processes in the Cedarberg appear to have advanced one step further, fashioning a bizarre landscape highlighted by such famous natural rock sculptures as the Maltese Cross and the Wolfberg Arch. The highest peak, Sneeuberg (2 028 m), is one of the few homes of one of the world's rarest plants, *Protea cryophila*, the snow protea. Another unusual species found in the Cedarberg is the Clanwilliam cedar, *Widdringtonia cedarbergensis*, after which the mountain range is named. Over-exploitation and uncontrolled burning threatened the tree with extinction, but today the Clanwilliam cedar is protected in this wilderness area. It is hoped that fewer

Now a protected species – the mountain cedar.

From beneath the natural portal of the Wolfberg Arch the all-round views are quite magnificent.

The Middelberg Falls in full spate.

fires and careful management will foster its growth. Two plants of considerable economic importance – rooibos tea (*Aspalathus linearis*) and round-leaved buchu (*Agathosma betulma*) – are also present.

Animal life is diverse in species but not high in numbers, as a result of the low breeding rate, the reasons for which are not yet clear. Mammals commonly seen include baboon, dassie, grey rhebok and klipspringer. Cape leopard are present, and are protected within an area which extends beyond the wilderness area, but hikers are unlikely to see them. Bird diversity is not great (81 species) but the fynbos specials – sugarbirds, orangebreasted sunbirds, ground woodpeckers, Cape rockjumpers, and others – are present, in addition to the frequently sighted black eagles, rock kestrels and jackal buzzards. Geckos, lizards and agamas are commonly seen on the rocks.

Mountaineers and environmentalists almost lost the Cedarberg to the National Parks Board in 1984, when that organization planned to develop a recreational complex in the wilderness. At the time, the concerted efforts of an outraged public who preferred to see the Cedarberg and its surrounding private land survive as an example of an unspoilt environment, won a tense political battle. However, it seems the area is destined to remain controversial.

Ideally, wilderness areas are supposed to be devoid of modern human artefacts, but there does exist a network of established 'management paths', and simple, rustic forestry patrol huts (see 'Facilities/amenities' p. 43), providing nothing more than shelter, were left standing when this area was proclaimed. Those who have hiked the area on blizzardy, snowy winter nights will appreciate why.

It is these humble dwellings that appear to be at the centre of two opposing schools of thought. On the one hand are those – including the authorities – who would prefer to see visitor numbers more tightly controlled in an effort to maintain the Cedarberg environment in a pristine, balanced condition; who itch to tear down even the basic, ill-maintained huts which, they believe, invite 'visitor pressure' and concomitant refuse and environment degradation. They are happy, they say, for responsible visitors to explore the area and camp anywhere – at their own risk. On the other hand are the keen hikers who feel that a more realistic approach is needed, that facilities should be upgraded to reflect the popularity of the area and to reduce the number of deaths resulting from hikers' overnight exposure.

Whatever your own feelings on the matter, make sure you have a forestry map before you set out: all paths (and there are plenty of them) and huts are clearly marked on this and are easy to find.

The only other hiking amenity lacking in the Cedarberg is large swimming holes; however, drinking water and 'cooling off' pools are adequate.

The wilderness area has been zoned into three blocks; to protect the environment there is a daily limit of 50 hikers in each block. Block A, the northern area, extends southwards from north of the

Pakhuis Pass to Skerpioensberg; Block B, the central area, extends to Wolfberg; and Block C in the south incorporates popular Sneeuberg and the Maltese Cross – features which can also be accessed via private farms, provided you have obtained the necessary permit.

1. Block A The Krakadouw range forms the backbone of most trails in this section. A triangular three-day route begins and ends at **Kliphuis** camp site on the Pakhuis Pass and offers overnight stops at the stable at Heuningvlei and at a cave near the old Dwarsrivier blockhouse (distinct from the farm of the same name further south). The triple-peaked **Krakadouw** offers a challenge to rock-climbers; the highest is at an altitude of 1 745 m. In winter the pools on its summit are frozen over and icicles hang from the rock!

2. Block B The main gravel road provides easy access to camp sites and accommodation at Algeria, Sanddrif and Kromrivier, with the result that this block is heavily used. One of the best-known routes is that to **Crystal Pool**, a demanding 2-day/15-hour hike for the fit, which begins and ends at the Algeria Forest Station. Most would agree that a short detour to the waterfall above Algeria makes a welcome break on the initial stiff climb up Helsekloof, and is the highlight of the day's hike. Other landmarks are the Middelberg Huts and Cathedral Rocks, while Crystal Pool itself – a series of small, dark pools – offers a pretty spot to overnight for those who choose not to continue to the basic hut some 15 minutes' walk further on. An early getaway is recommended on the second day, which begins with a steep climb up rugged Engelsmanskloof; at the top rise Sneeukop (1 932 m) and South Peak (1 875 m). A level jeep track leads past the Sleepad Hut, down a ridge and into the valley below. A short ascent to Grootlandsvlakte and long descent to Uitkyk ('lookout') finally brings you to the river which leads back to Algeria.

Wolfberg Cracks and **Arch** are most easily reached in a day-hike from the recreation area at Sanddrif, which lies at the foot of the Wolfberg on the Sand River. The climb to the Cracks – a vertical cleft some 30 m or more high – is undeniably strenuous. The first crack is easy to pass through, but the overweight hiker will be unable to squeeze through the second. Once on top, a walk of less than an hour and a half across a level moonscape will bring you to the Wolfberg Arch, one of the Cedarberg's more spectacular rock formations.

3. Block C Algeria and Sanddrif provide hikers with access to popular **Sneeuberg** and the **Maltese Cross**. The walk to the Cross takes about an hour and a half, and requires a fairly mild climb up the ravine which leads to it. At the top, you are greeted unexpectedly by the 20-m vertical block of weathered sandstone, a salutory fist at the end of an arm. Nearby Sneeuberg towers over it, however; at 2 027 m, it is the highest peak in the Cedarberg, and is frequently snow-covered in winter. The ascent of Sneeuberg is tough and ends in a rock scramble which most hikers would find daunting. The reward at the summit of Sneeuberg Peak is an overview of the entire Cedarberg, and all the way to Table Mountain, 150 km away, on a clear day.

4. Farms to the south of the wilderness area On the farm **Kromrivier** (for enquiries, see box on p. 43), which is a private nature reserve adjoining the wilderness area, there are several walks. A popular destination is **Disa Pool**, at the far end of an 11-km/4-hour circuit which uses a path that climbs 200 m to run along the 1 100-m contour above the river, and returns along the opposite bank, crossing the river twice. A short detour roughly halfway on the return route allows a visit to Kromrivier Cave. It takes 2,5 hours (6,5 km) to reach the lower slopes of **Sugarloaf Peak** on a route that leaves the farm buildings on the northern bank of the river and climbs gently. From there, you can continue to the Maltese Cross, about another 4 km/2 hours away, or return on a path that circles Sugarloaf Peak almost on the level.

On the farm **Nuwerust** (see box on p. 43 for telephone number), which offers unsophisticated self-catering accommodation, there are two short circular trails. The longer, up Rooiberg, takes 3 hours at most. It crosses the Breekkrans River, zigzags up the mountainside at an easy gradient and reaches the top via a gully. Crossing a plateau, the path circles back in the direction of the Breekkrans Valley, where hikers must scramble down the river to the camp. The second trail, to and from a waterfall on the Breekkrans River, takes about 2 hours. Both are best done in spring, when attractive wild flowers dot the landscape.

4. GROOT WINTERHOEK WILDERNESS AREA
PORTERVILLE

Trail details: There are 90 km of footpaths. From the office to Groot Winterhoek and back: 30 km/ 8 hours return. Two-day hike possible, comprising office to Groot Winterhoek on day 1: 15 km/ 4 hours; day 2: Groot Winterhoek to Die Hel: 6 km/ 2 hours return, and back to office via Groot Kliphuis River: 23 km/8 hours.

Permits/bookings: Required in advance and obtainable from Cape Nature Conservation, Porterville office, tel. (02623) 2900/2907; PO Box 26, Porterville 6810.

Facilities/amenities: There are three huts in close proximity to each other at Groot Winterhoek/De Tronk; all are basic and have no beds.

Main attractions: Groot Winterhoek Peak (2 077 m); rugged, dramatic mountain terrain; large swimming pools; fynbos vegetation; red disas bloom in summer.

Pertinent information: Maximum of 12 people per group; 24 people admitted per day, but only 12 per day to Die Hel. Winters are wet (80 per cent of annual rainfall occurs between April and September) and extremely cold, especially at night when the temperature can drop to below freezing-point; frost occurs from April to November; snow is possible. Summer is dry and generally mild, but be prepared for rain, mist, cold weather and snow throughout the year. Take your own stove; as this is a wilderness area, no fires are allowed anywhere. Hikers are not allowed to sleep at Die Hel.

As a forestry officer in the Western Cape, I spent many weeks exploring the Groot Winterhoek Wilderness Area: the Vier-en-Twintig Riviere; Die Hel; Klein Kliphuisrivier; the grounds surrounding the old farms of Groot Kliphuis, Groot Winterhoek, De Tronk and Perdevlei; the Sneeugat terrain near the Tulbagh Valley; and the Klein and Groot Winterhoek peaks.

Disa uniflora *makes a splash of scarlet on the Kliphuisvlakte.*

Many kilometres of bushwhacking through dense kloofs and along old buchu-pickers' paths, scrambling up hills to explore high mountain caves, boulder-hopping through shallow rivers, traversing plateaux of weather-beaten rocks and climbing steep slopes to the summit of the Groot Winterhoek (2 077 m), have left me with deepseated

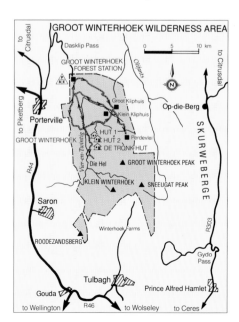

impressions. This is an extremely rugged region, lush with montane fynbos flowers adapted to the leached, acidic soil of the flats (*suurvlakte*); warm in summer and cold in winter, lacking in readily observable wildlife except baboons, klipspringers, snakes, sunbirds and predatory birds, and still satisfyingly wild. It is similar in nature to the Cedarberg, but greener and arguably more beautiful.

Access to the Groot Winterhoek Wilderness Area (now over 30 000 ha in extent) is limited. The entrance point is through Dasklip Pass (an approximately 45-minute drive from Porterville), where a forest station has been constructed.

From the office, access to the wilderness area is on foot only. There are a number of paths wandering off in different directions, providing day walks and longer trails, although hikers are not restricted to these and can spend the night anywhere in the wilderness area. In terms of shelter, there are only the three huts, described on p. 45, and two cave-like shelters: one 15 minutes' walk from the office, the other at Klein Kliphuis. From De Tronk, you can hike to Die Hel, an amazing place where the Vier-en-Twintig Riviere suddenly enters a gorge and drops as a sheer waterfall into a mysterious, cold, dark swimming pool, surrounded by cliffs.

5. SAS SALDANHA HIKING TRAIL
SALDANHA

Trail details: There are four circular day walks, ranging from 4 km/1 hour to 17 km/5 hours.

Permits/bookings: Permit and informative booklet obtainable at the main gate.

Maps/information: Officer Commanding SAS Saldanha, tel. (02281) 42211; PO Milnavair 7396.

Facilities/amenities: Toilets; museum; water at starting point.

Main attractions: A wide variety of flowers and birds; tidal rock pools; caves; geological and historical features of interest.

Pertinent information: Park at the north gate only; camping overnight is not permitted. Guided tours for 40 people (one busload) are available. Ticks can be a problem.

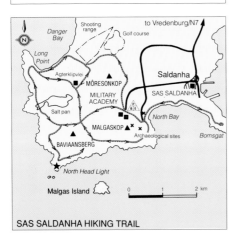

SAS SALDANHA HIKING TRAIL

The SAS Saldanha Hiking Trail in fact comprises a series of walks, laid out in the 1 800-ha Saldanha Military Area on the coast 3 km outside Saldanha. SAS Saldanha is a training base for all permanent force recruits of the South African Navy; it also

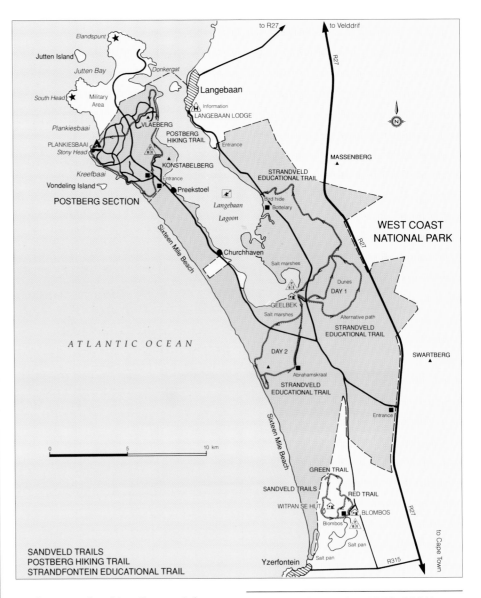

SANDVELD TRAILS
POSTBERG HIKING TRAIL
STRANDFONTEIN EDUCATIONAL TRAIL

sees the conservation of the military area's fauna, flora and history as being among its roles. Springbok and ostrich have been introduced; in addition, steenbok, duiker and bat-eared foxes can be seen among the Strandveld vegetation so typical of the West Coast. Birdlife is rich and includes the Cape gannet and the jackass penguin.

The four well-demarcated interlinking routes were opened to the public in 1990. They incorporate several archaeological sites, geological features and historical sites. Gun batteries and other relics employed in defending the bay and coastline during World War II can still be seen. All of these features are identified in the booklet available at the gate.

Spring in the Postberg area.

6. POSTBERG HIKING TRAIL
WEST COAST NATIONAL PARK, POSTBERG SECTION

Trail details: 24 km/2 days; circular

Permits/bookings: Must be obtained from the West Coast National Park, tel. (02287) 22144; PO Box 25, Langebaan 7357. Note that the trail is open for only August and September (flower season) each year and booking opens on 1 April.

Facilities/amenities: There is an information centre, where a map is obtainable, at the Langebaan Lodge. Within the Postberg section, there is only a camp site with ablution block and braai spots at Plankiesbaai (take a tent and a braai grid) and a shop near the end of the trail.

Main attractions: Flowers, wildlife and birds, all in great profusion and variety; views of Langebaan Lagoon and the Atlantic Ocean.

Pertinent information: To reach the Postberg section of the park, take the Churchaven/West Coast National Park turnoff from the R27 and proceed for 23 km in the direction of Kraalbaai.

The 26 000-ha West Coast National Park stretches from Langebaan to Yzerfontein. This trail, in the

Postberg section of the park, opened in 1989. It is demarcated by white-painted poles, but as parts of it cross private property, and the trail is in use for only two months of each year, the path may not always be distinct. This is not a strenuous trail, but you must carry water.

The Postberg Hiking Trail offers the hiker the opportunity of a close-up view of some of the most beautiful spring flowers on the West Coast. Nine species of antelope inhabit the park, as well as caracal, African wild cat and bat-eared fox. Southern Right whales are often spotted at Plankiesbaai. The trail crosses a section of Sixteen Mile Beach and continues through duneveld where gemsbok are often seen. There are swimming sites, in the sea or lagoon, along most of the route.

7. STRANDVELD EDUCATIONAL TRAIL
WEST COAST NATIONAL PARK, LANGEBAAN

Trail details: 30 km/2 days, 3 nights; guided. Day 2 of the Strandveld Trail is available as a day walk any day of the week. Three short conducted trails form part of a half-day programme and cover a variety of themes. A 'school programme' is run along similar lines; both are followed by lunch.

Permits/bookings: Booking is essential; contact Geelbek Environmental Centre, West Coast National Park, tel. (02287) 22798; PO Box 25, Langebaan 7357.

Facilities/amenities: Geelbek Homestead, a national monument, sleeps 30 trailists on the full Strandveld Educational Trail in relative luxury (traditional West Coast meals in the diningroom, varied lunch packs provided, bar facilities, and double bunks with linen). Briefings and film shows are given at Geelbek prior to each day's hike. An identification booklet is handed out at the start of the trail; keep this with you at all times. The fee for all this is not insubstantial.

Main attractions: Flowers in springtime; strandveld vegetation; educational videos shown at environmental centre; 255 recorded bird species, including migrant waders; whales off the coast if you're lucky.

Pertinent information: Weekday trails leave on Monday or Tuesday evenings at 5.00 pm and weekend trails on Friday evenings; groups are limited to a minimum of six and a maximum of 30 people. Hikers return to Geelbek each evening, to overnight. Take lightweight boots or tackies for travelling easily over sand; a day pack; a water bottle; warm clothes, as the weather is changeable; and an insect repellent, as ticks and horseflies can be a problem. Maximum group size for the half-day programmes is 30 and minimum six.

The West Coast National Park (26 000 ha in extent, excluding the four islands) was established to conserve representative samples of the West Coast ecosystems, together with the cultural and historical characteristics of the region. The lagoon system has been identified as a wetland of international importance: it supports more waterbirds than any other South African wetland.

The Strandveld Education Trail offers the hiker a 'comprehensive self-interpretive ecological experience'. During the two days, hikers are introduced to the strandveld with its amazing diversity of plant life: 24 plant species are identified in the brochure.

A tranquil stretch of the Langebaan Lagoon as seen from Oesterwal.

The brochure also interprets the environment at 30 separate sites along the way. The trail starts and ends at the Geelbek Gold Fields Environmental Centre at the southern end of the Langebaan Lagoon within the West Coast National Park. March to May and August to October are the best times to undertake the trail (May-August is the rainy season). Summers are dry; hot days are windy or begin with mist. The trail is not particularly strenuous, although it is on sand.

The first day traverses 14,4 km of strandveld, dunes and granite landscape, and ends at the bird hide at Bottelary; from here, hikers are transported back to Geelbek to overnight. The second day, comprising 16 km, crosses strandveld to Sixteen Mile Beach, where trailists can take to the beach or elect to walk another 2 km before turning towards Geelbek. Some hikers have been fortunate enough to experience the bizarre sight of ostriches frolicking in the waves off the beach. The return route passes through the strandveld of Abrahamskraal, a vantage point which offers a rewarding view of most aspects of the West Coast National Park: dunes, saltmarsh and lagoon, in addition to strandveld.

Strandveld trailists in discussion.

8. SANDVELD TRAILS
YZERFONTEIN

Trail details: Trail 1: 16,5 km/4 to 5 hours; Trail 2: 8 km/2 to 3 hours. Both trails are circular.

Permits/bookings: Enquiries, and reservations for bungalows/hut, tel. Mrs Wightman (021) 242755; 14 Higgo Crescent, Higgovale, Cape Town 8001. Fee for trails includes use of trail hut.

Facilities/amenities: Two self-contained bungalows for hire near start of trails sleep 6 each, but have no cutlery, bedding or electricity; 'Witpan se hut' has 6 beds, braai area, bush shower and water.

Main attractions: Rich birdlife, buck, small mammals and tortoises; wild flowers in season; coastal scenery and salt pans.

Pertinent information: Carry water. You will need an insect repellent in spring, as a guard against ticks and blind flies.

If you are looking for a day's outing that is not as strenuous as most Western Cape trails but every bit as interesting, then explore the Sandveld Trails near Langebaan Lagoon. While walking conditions are pleasant from March to May, the main attraction of these two nature walks – besides the birdlife – is the plethora of colourful wild flowers which bloom in the spring.

Both trails begin and end on the 703-ha farm Blombos, which borders land that was previously administered by the Forestry Department but now forms the southern end of the West Coast National Park. Note that the Parks Board does not approve of hikers entering the park via Blombos.

The sandveld, with its associated rich indigenous stunted dune bush, large salt pans and coastal environment, ranks as one of the richest bird habitats in the Cape Province. In addition to hundreds of species ranging from European bee-eaters to spoonbills, animals such as duiker, steenbok, grysbok and tortoise are commonly spotted.

Many of the footpaths are actually fourwheel-drive tracks or fence lines.

Because of the soft nature of the terrain, it is best to wear running shoes instead of hiking boots. For trailists who wish to sleep near the bird-rich salt pan, rustic accommodation in 'Witpan se hut' is available. Water is supplied only at the hut and at the bungalows.

9. KASTEELBERG TRAIL
RIEBEECK WEST

Trail details: 6,5 km/4,5 hours, circular; shorter routes into the picturesque kloofs of 1 hour and 4 hours each. (No map available.)

Bookings/Permits: Book in advance through Mr Relihan, tel. (0224) 22050; Spesbona, PO Box 97, Malmesbury 7300.

Facilities/amenities: Accommodation is available in comfortable cottages on the farm. A small kiosk offers souvenirs.

Main attractions: Wonderful views from the top of Kasteelberg; yellowwood forest on mountain; features of historical interest.

Pertinent information: No open fires are allowed on the mountain or the trail.

This trail, designed in conjunction with Cape Nature Conservation, takes its name from the mountain on which it was laid out in 1991. Kasteelberg (946 m), with its remarkable plant and animal life, rises as an island from the undulating wheatfields and the vineyards at its base.

The farm Spesbona is near Riebeek West, and 20 km by road from Malmesbury, at the top of the lush Riebeek River valley. The trail begins on the coastal side of the Kasteelberg, and zigzags up the mountain, traversing private land in the main, although some sections cross Cape Nature Conservation property.

At the top, you will be treated to one of the most breathtaking outlooks in the Western Cape: the West Coast, Cape Town to the south-west, and fold upon fold of mountains – the peaks of the Groot and Klein Drakenstein, the Hawequas, the Limietberg, the Matroosberg and Witzenberg and, finally, the Groot Winterhoek to the north-east. If you diligently follow the signs, you will encounter the site of old gold diggings worked by earlier, optimistic members of the Relihan family.

A bonus is the small forest of yellowwoods on the ridge of Kasteelberg, where ferns rise from moist crannies. From up here, if you are fortunate, you might spot a black eagle gliding silently past the rockface.

Although the ascent and descent are steep, the path is sound and the walk could not be classified as particularly difficult.

The farm itself (which has been in the Relihan family for seven generations) boasts two further features of interest: one of the largest oaks in the country (at the end of the trail), and a fully equipped blacksmith and wagon museum, where one of the family forefathers crafted carriages and wagons. Equipment used in the gold mining episode is also housed in the museum.

10. TOLL HOUSE AND VAN STADENSRUS TRAILS
CERES

Trail details: 1. Van Stadensrus Trail: 25 km/8 to 10 hours; circular day walk or 2-day trail. Shorter route: 12 km/5 hours; return. 2. Toll House Trail: 8 km/2 hours; return.

Permits/bookings: Permits are required for both trails and their variations, obtainable from The Manager, Pine Forest Holiday Resort (administered by Ceres Municipality), tel. (0233) 21177; fax (0233) 21965; PO Box 44, Ceres 6835. Map and brochure available on request.

Facilities/amenities: None.

Main attractions: Views of Ceres Valley with dam; small wildlife including klipspringers and Cape leopard; unusual rock formations; rare indigenous flowers; black eagles. Perennial streams and pools on Van Stadensrus Trail.

Pertinent information: Both trails begin and end at the Pine Forest Holiday Resort run by the Ceres Municipality, and are demarcated with small stone cairns. A maximum of 12 people is allowed per group. For the full Van Stadensrus Trail, you need to be fit! Be prepared for icy weather in winter by taking plenty of warm clothing.

---

1. Van Stadensrus Trail This circular trail starts at the Pine Forest Holiday Resort and follows a fairly difficult route into the Skurweberg mountains which surround the town, with the first three hours being particularly tough. Rock slides resulting from the earthquakes of 1969 and 1970 can be seen at several places. The trail is best undertaken between September and May, as it can be wet and cold during winter. You may consider taking two days and camping overnight under the trees near the stream at Van Stadensrus, once known as Kleinplasie. Note that there is only one other perennial water source beyond this – at Cascade Pools, about 2 km further on. Allow an extra couple of hours if you wish to include an ascent of Ceres Peak which, at 1 204 m, is 118 m higher than Table Mountain.

The last section of the Van Stadensrus Trail, in reverse, makes a popular shorter alternative walk. It

comprises a fairly stiff climb to the viewpoint on the ridge below Ceres Peak, and continues to the grassy plain (ideal for a picnic) on its slopes.

2. Toll House Trail This fairly easy walk follows an old wagon trail for part of its route. The tearoom at the Toll House (a national monument) makes a pleasant halfway stop. Walkers can decide whether to retrace their footsteps to the start or to return to the Pine Forest Holiday Resort via Michell's Pass. Take water in summer, as there are no perennial streams *en route*.

11. HEX RIVER MOUNTAINS
NEAR WORCESTER

Trail details: Jan du Toit's Kloof; various peaks and kloofs (see below).

Permits/bookings: Permits for Jan du Toit's Kloof must be obtained from the Porterville office of Cape Nature Conservation, tel. (02623) 2900; in addition, Mr van Zyl of 'Somarso', tel. (0231) 93746, must be phoned for permission to park on and traverse his farm. Note that large parts of this area are privately owned and farmers must be contacted for permission to cross their land.

Facilities/amenities: Shelters for members of the Mountain Club of South Africa only.

Main attractions: Most rugged and dramatic of all Western Cape mountains.

Pertinent information: This area is for expert hikers and climbers only; it is best to hike with someone who knows the mountains well. Very little water is available on traverses and peak climbs. Group sizes in all conservation areas are restricted in the interests of conservation.

Cradled between the road running from Michell's Pass to Worcester and the Hex River, there lies a complex of the highest and most rugged mountains in the Western Cape.

Rugged rocks in the Hex River Mountains.

[Map]

VAN STADENSRUS TRAIL
to Prince Alfred Hamlet
SKURWEBERG
Koekedou
Modder
R303
to Sutherland
VAN STADENSRUS
Koekedou
WITSENBERGE
Dam
PINE FOREST
VAN STADENSRUS TRAIL
Cascade pools
Nature Reserve R46
Ceres
WITSENBERG STATE FOREST
CERES PEAK
Old wagon trail
TOLL HOUSE TRAIL
Railway
Ou Tol
Michell's Pass
0   1   2 km
TOLL HOUSE TRAIL
VAN STADENSRUS TRAIL
to Wellington

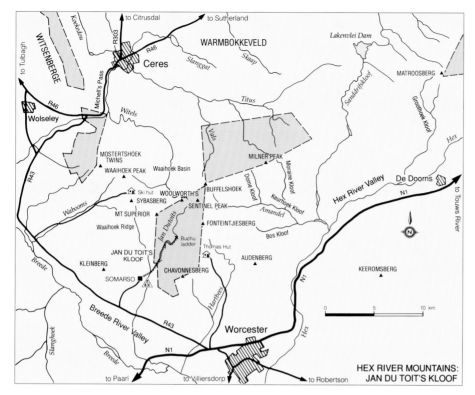

**HEX RIVER MOUNTAINS:
JAN DU TOIT'S KLOOF**

Only the fittest will fully appreciate the Hex's mass of awe-inspiring peaks and pinnacles, sheer exposures, interlaced ridges, gorges and kloofs, dense bush and high waterfalls. Opportunities for long, strenuous traverses, in addition to 'peak-bagging', are endless. Mountains such as Fonteintjiesberg (1 992 m), Sentinel (1 839 m), the Twins (2 034 m), Buffelshoek Peak (2 063 m), Milner Peak (1 996 m) and Matroosberg (2 250 m), and kloofs such as Groothoek, Waaihoek, Boskloof, Dome Kloof, Moraine Kloof and Kleurkloof, conjure up vivid memories for all serious Cape mountain climbers.

Bear in mind that although the Hex River Mountains are an important catchment area, much of the land is in private ownership and access permission must be obtained from the farmer whose land you wish to cross.

There is very little water for hikers on this range, as most rain runs off the steep ridges, slopes, peaks, rock faces and traverses into kloofs and the valley below. The Hex River mountains are most popular during the cooler winter months when skiing is possible on the slopes of the Matroosberg.

Jan du Toit's Kloof, not to be confused with the more southerly Du Toit's Kloof, is one of the Hex's easiest and most popular day kloofing trips. Its entrance lies between Chavonnesberg and Waaihoek Ridge. The huge sandstone structures of Mt. Superior on the left and Fonteintjiesberg on the right provide the runoff which feeds the numerous waterfalls, rock pools and riverine bush of this breathtaking gorge. The variety of scenery while boulder-hopping up the kloof is impressive in both its diversity and massiveness. You need half a day to reach the 'ladder', originally placed in the bed of the kloof by buchu gatherers during World War I to facilitate climbing past an 18-m waterfall. It has since been replaced by a fixed rope. Any further exploration of Jan du Toit's Kloof should be attempted by expert rock climbers only.

12. KAROO NATIONAL BOTANICAL GARDEN
WORCESTER

Trail details: 1. Fairy Glen Hiking Trail: 7 km/5 hours; return. 2. Beacon Hill Trail: 5 km/2 hours; circular. 3. Lookout Trail: 4 km/2 hours; circular. A network of paths in the lower reaches of the Garden provide for shorter rambles.

Permits/bookings: A permit is required to walk the Fairy Glen Hiking Trail, available at the office. The Garden is open from 8.00 am to 5.00 pm. A small entrance fee is payable during the spring flower season only (1 August - 31 October). For more information, a map and a brochure phone the officer at the Garden: Worcester (0231) 70785.

Facilities/amenities: Toilet block; carpark; bird list.

Main attractions: Special collections of plants from the Karoo and arid areas of South Africa and Namibia; rugged Hex River Mountain scenery.

Pertinent information: These gardens fall under the auspices of the National Botanical Institute. The area is subject to great daily and seasonal changes in temperature: 4-42 °C. Hikers on the longer routes should take drinking water with them.

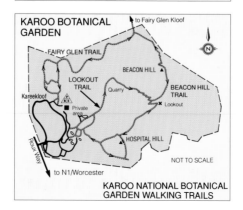

KAROO NATIONAL BOTANICAL GARDEN WALKING TRAILS

Unusual in shape and structure, brilliant in colour and full of predator-evading devices, xerophytic (drought-resistant) plants such as aloes, vygies, spekbome, succulents, buttertrees, lithops and euphorbias attract the attention of even the least botanically minded rambler. The plants are labelled and described in the comprehensive trail guide, and well-constructed footpaths offer easy rambles in the shadow of the formidable Hex River mountains. In addition, there are three fairly undemanding day walks. The entrance to the 154-ha Garden is in Roux Way, Riebeeck Park, off the national road.

1. Fairy Glen Hiking Trail shares the same path as the Beacon Hill Trail as far as the northernmost point of the Garden, where it crosses the boundary onto an adjoining private farm. The path ends in the charming Fairy Glen Kloof, the catchment area of the Hartebeest River, and you return along the same route. Alternatively, if you are just getting into your stride, turn right at the intersection and return to the start along the Beacon Hill Trail.

2. Beacon Hill Trail is a longish route offering superb views from the vantage points of both Beacon Hill and Lookout.

3. Lookout Trail zigzags up the slopes of Lookout, via the old quarry, and returns via the lower hillock of Hospital Hill. A short optional detour leads steeply to the top of the hill and back down and along its slopes to the start.

13. BAIN'S KLOOF WALKS
HAWEQUAS CONSERVATION AREA

Trail details: 1. Bobbejaans River Walk: 4 km each way. 2. Happy Valley Walk: 4 km each way. 3. Wolwekloof Circuit, Tweede Tol (camp site residents only): 9,5 km circuit.

Permits/bookings: A permit and booking are required for each of these walks, from The Manager, Hawequas Nature Conservation office, tel. (02211) 611535; 269 Main Street, Paarl. Booklet available on request.

Facilities/amenities: A picnic site at Tweede Tol (of possible interest to walkers of the Happy Valley and Wolwekloof trails). Note that camp sites, which are not intended for day visitors, need to be booked in advance.

Main attractions: Waterfalls; swimming; fynbos.

Pertinent information: Note that the number of people allowed on each of these walks at any one time is 24; groups are limited to 12 people each. Remember to leave your permit displayed in your vehicle. Take warm clothes, in all seasons; be alert to changes in weather and be ready to leave high ground quickly in worsening conditions.

All the walks from Bain's Kloof Pass fall within the Hawequas Conservation Area (117 000 ha), administered by Cape Nature Conservation.

1. The Bobbejaans River Walk begins near the parking lot in Bain's Kloof at the remains of a hotel which burned down in 1976 – a site known as Eerste Tol. Look for the wooden stile over the fence. Footprint markers lead down into the kloof, to a crossing of the Wit River – note that in winter the river is sometimes too high to be crossed safely. After a short climb up the opposite bank, the path runs along a contour high above the Bobbejaans River, a tributary of the Wit. A detour about 1 km

A cascade on the Bobbejaans River, Bain's Kloof.

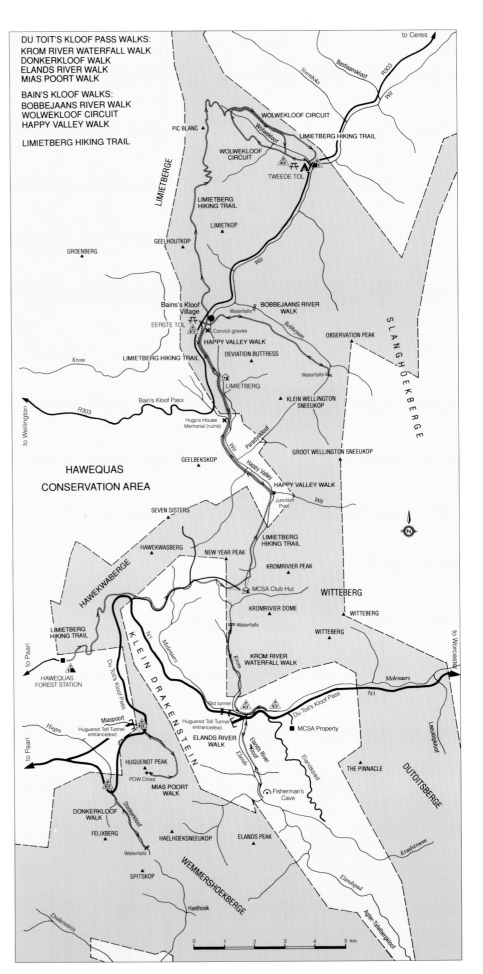

DU TOIT'S KLOOF PASS WALKS:
KROM RIVER WATERFALL WALK
DONKERKLOOF WALK
ELANDS RIVER WALK
MIAS POORT WALK

BAIN'S KLOOF WALKS:
BOBBEJAANS RIVER WALK
WOLWEKLOOF CIRCUIT
HAPPY VALLEY WALK

LIMIETBERG HIKING TRAIL

from the end leads to lovely natural swimming pools. The trail ends dramatically at a three-tiered waterfall cascade.

2. Happy Valley Walk Another trail which begins at the Eerste Tol parking area, this covers the last section (in reverse) of the Limietberg Hiking Trail (see opposite page) and turns back at Junction Pool.

3. Wolwekloof Circuit Unfortunately, this trail is open only to residents of the Tweede Tol camp site at the bottom of Bain's Kloof; to prevent over-crowding, day visitors are not allowed beyond the picnic area. However, for those who wish to tackle more than one day walk in the Bain's Kloof area, this camp site is the obvious spot to overnight and therefore the Wolwekloof Circuit deserves a mention. The trail, which is marked by white footprints and takes approximately three hours to complete, features a long climb, but this is mostly in shade. The stream, which takes its name from the kloof, is always within reach. Walkers could find themselves sharing the descent with weary Limietberg trailists (see Limietberg Trail, opposite page), as this part of the route is common to both walks. Note that Tweede Tol camp is closed during the winter months – May to beginning September.

14. LIMIETBERG HIKING TRAIL
BETWEEN DU TOIT'S KLOOF PASS AND BAIN'S KLOOF PASS

Trail details: 35,5 km/2 days; one way.

Permits/bookings: A permit and booking are required, obtainable in advance from The Manager, Hawequas Nature Conservation office, tel. (02211) 611535; Private Bag X14, Main Street, Paarl 7622; 269 Main Street, Paarl 7622.

Facilities/amenities: Limietberg Hut, in Happy Valley, near a superb swimming hole, contains four bedrooms with six bunks and mattresses in each.

Main attractions: Spectacular mountain scenery; floral wealth; red disas; natural swimming pools.

Pertinent information: Take warm clothes, no matter what the season, as the weather can change rapidly and there is not much shelter *en route*. This is a winter rainfall area. Carry water. The size of a group is limited to 12 people. Open fires are not allowed at the hut, or anywhere else – take a stove. You will need to leave a car, or have someone meet you, at the end of the trail at Tweede Tol picnic area at the foot of Bain's Kloof Pass; an entrance fee is payable and parking is provided, but Tweede Tol is closed in winter.

Brown water and rounded white boulders typify this mountain stream in Du Toit's Kloof.

The Limietberg Trail links two spectacular passes: the Du Toit's Kloof and Bain's Kloof, and leads to picnicking spots such as well-known Junction Pool. Although the trail has its ups and downs, it is easily within the capabilities of the average hiker.

Hikers start at Hawequas Forest Station, near the foot of Du Toit's Kloof Pass. They wind their way for 18,3 km along the Witteberg range between New Year Peak (1 327 m) and Kromrivier Dome (1 457 m), before ending up at Limietberg Hut overlooking the beautiful Happy Valley. Although the distance (17,2 km) is slightly shorter on the second day, the going is rather more demanding: the trail crosses Bain's Kloof Pass (a national monument, completed in 1853), gradually ascends to a height of 1 049 m at Pic Blanc, and finally descends into Wolwekloof. It terminates at the popular Tweede Tol camping and picnic site on Bain's Kloof Pass.

As with most hiking trails in the Western Cape floral kingdom, stupendous views, proteas and swimming pools rival for attention (in winter, keep your eyes open for a rare glimpse of *Protea nana*, the mountain rose, just after the 12-km mark on the second day). Wildlife is difficult to spot; consider yourself fortunate to see klipspringer, grysbok, grey duiker or leopard. Dassies, baboons and red hares are more common, as are rock kestrels, Cape francolins, sunbirds and black eagles.

Transport is a problem as cars must be shuttled between Tweede Tol and Hawequas Forest Station. If you have friends or family meeting you at Tweede Tol, they can arrive early and enjoy a picnic on the lawns provided, but will need to book a camp site if they wish to take advantage of the other facilities, which include a trail (see Wolwekloof Circuit, page 50).

15. DU TOIT'S KLOOF PASS WALKS
HAWEQUAS CONSERVATION AREA

Trail details: 1. Elands River Walk: 3 km each way. 2. Krom River Waterfall Walk: 2,5 km each way. 3. Donkerkloof Walk: 3 km each way. 4. Mias Poort: 4 km each way.

Permits and bookings: Required and obtainable from: The Manager, Hawequas Nature Conservation office, tel. (02211) 611535; 269 Main Street, Paarl/Private Bag X14, Main Street, Paarl 7622. Booklet available on request.

Facilities/amenities: A fenced parking area, reserved for holders of permits for the Elands River and the Krom River Waterfall walks, lies 700 m beyond the mouth of the Huguenot Tunnel, on the Worcester side.

Main attractions: Waterfalls; swimming; spectacular mountain scenery; fynbos.

Pertinent information: Note that the number of people allowed on any one route per day is 24; groups are restricted to 12 people each. Walkers should be on constant guard against changes in weather and should leave the mountain as quickly as possible the moment a deterioration in conditions is noticed. The Krom River Kloof is impassable after heavy rain; the climb between the waterfalls can be dangerous in winter – take a rope.

The Hawequas Conservation Area extends over 117 000 ha and offers a variety of worthwhile walks that can be completed in a couple of hours.
1. Elands River Walk follows the east side of the Elands River Kloof, to Fisherman's Cave, and is particularly popular in summer. Leave your car at the parking area mentioned above and walk back towards the tunnel. You will find a directional signboard beneath the two bridges. Those who plan to 'lay a couple of lines on the water' along the way, in the hope of catching an unwary trout, should remember to obtain a licence beforehand.

From the Limietberg Hut the view south seems neverending.

2. Krom River Waterfall Walk crosses the river about five times, past lovely swimming pools, and leads eventually to two magnificent waterfalls. From the parking area, walk back towards the tunnel, but this time turn right towards the old tunnel (as shown on the signboard there), and walk along the right-hand bank of the Molenaars River, which meets up with the gorge of the Krom River. The rocks on the climb between the two waterfalls can be dangerously slippery in winter, and a rope will be an invaluable aid to both ascent and descent.

3. Donkerkloof Walk starts at the hairpin bend on the Paarl side of the old Du Toit's Kloof Pass; leave your car in the lay-by just before the bend on the Cape Town side and follow the footprint markers. The path continues through the gorge in dense indigenous forest, crossing a stream several times, and finishes at a waterfall. Good walking shoes are essential for negotiating the stony sections. The birdlife on the forest edge is prolific.

4. Mias Poort Walk begins, like the Donkerkloof Walk, from the Paarl side of the pass, and leads to the cross erected in 1945 by the Italian prisoners of war who cut the roadway. Perhaps their choice of site is intended to emphasize their feat: Huguenot Peak, at a height of 1 318 m, offers breathtaking views but the price you pay is a punishing two-hour climb to the ridge below it. Thereafter the path ascends more gradually to the summit.

---

16. KLIPKERSHOUT TRAIL
PAARL MOUNTAIN NATURE RESERVE, PAARL

Trail details: 4,2 km/1 hour; circular. There are many other minor roads and footpaths, and Paarl Rock can be climbed.

Permits/bookings: There is a small entrance fee to the reserve. Fishing in the dams is allowed with a permit, obtainable at the Paarl Municipality/information offices: tel. (02211) 23658; 12 Main Street, Paarl; PO Box 12, Paarl 7622. A detailed and informative map/brochure and a bird list are available.

Facilities/amenities: Toilets and picnic/braai spots (firewood can be purchased at the reserve) are situated adjacent to the wild flower reserve.

Main attractions: Unique geological formations; diversity of flora, including some rare species, representing a form of fynbos that grows on granitic clay; grysbok and caracal; black eagles; inspiring views.

Pertinent information: Watch out for ticks, scorpions and snakes.

The reserve extends over 1 910 ha, and incorporates the Meulwater Wild Flower Reserve as well as Paarl Mountain, a national monument. From the view site on Jan Phillips Mountain Drive (the main road through the reserve), a minor road leads, past the Wild Flower Reserve and Nantes Dam, to the circular drive which comprises the scenically attractive Klipkershout Trail.

From the parking area on the far side of the circle, a path leads to the Afrikaans Language Monument, 1,2 km away, which is actually outside the nature reserve.

The minor roads and one-way dirt drives throughout the area link up with footpaths to offer the walker many more hours of pleasant rambling:

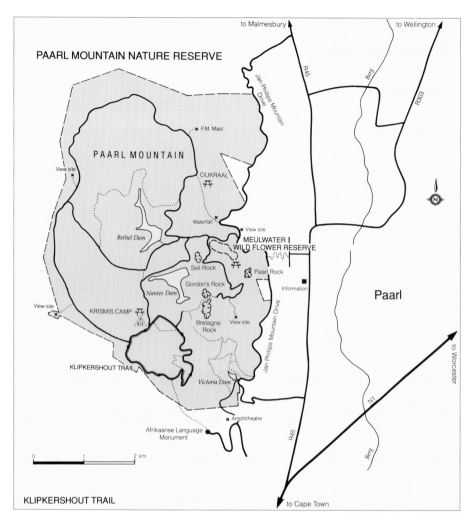

around another two dams which are endowed with black bass; to further view sites, and on the famous granite massif of Paarl Mountain. The town below took its name from Paarl Rock, whose domed summit gleams like a pearl after rain. It is easy to climb, and the old cannon dating from the early days of the Cape Colony can still be seen at its

crown. A sturdy chain helps climbers make it up the final incline of Bretagne Rock, whose summit offers an incredible panorama of the Cape's mountain ranges, vineyards and picturesque towns, as well as False Bay and Table Bay, on a clear day. By contrast, nearby Gordon's Rock should not be attempted by any but the most experienced climber.

The imposing granite domes of Paarl Mountain dominate the Klipkershout Trail.

17. TYGERBERG NATURE RESERVE
BELLVILLE

Trail details: There is a network of mini-trails, together totalling about 9 km/1,5 hours.

Permits/bookings: Permits are issued (free) at the gate. An information sheet with map is obtainable from Bellville Municipality, tel. (021) 9182911.

Facilities/amenities: Picnic area (no open fires allowed); well-constructed footpaths with bird-watching points.

Main attractions: Renosterveld vegetation and its birdlife; wonderful views; peace – in the midst of Cape Town's northern suburbs.

Pertinent information: The reserve is open on weekdays from 8.30 am to 4.30 pm and over weekends and on public holidays from 9.00 am to 6.00 pm. To get there, turn off the N1 between Paarl and Cape Town at the Welgemoed/Bellville West off-ramp, then left into Jip de Jager Street; thereafter the route to the gate is well signposted.

The sculpted beauty of Kirstenbosch attracts thousands of visitors each year.

A 123-ha island surrounded by residential area, Tygerberg Nature Reserve continues to protect a portion of the renosterveld on the slopes of the Tygerberg. (The reserve almost doubled in size in 1993 when a property company presented the municipality with 60 ha of adjoining land.) The name of the reserve stems not from the existence of *tygers*, as is often assumed, but from the spotted pattern made by fallow grass when viewed from afar. It is a fairly exposed spot which tends to be breezy for most months of the year; it is at its best in spring, when most of the flowering plants are in bloom. The fruits of the wild peach and wild olive trees which grow in the kloofs attract a wide variety of birds, including Cape francolins, Cape bulbuls and speckled mousebirds. Grysbok, Cape grey mongoose, porcupines, mole-rat and spotted eagle owl also occur.

A highlight of the reserve is the lookout point on the **Uitkyk walk**, which offers an almost 360° view – from Paarl through Gordon's Bay and False Bay to Table Mountain, Sea Point, and finally the beginning of the West Coast.

18. KIRSTENBOSCH FOREST TRAILS
KIRSTENBOSCH NATIONAL BOTANICAL GARDEN, CAPE PENINSULA

Kirstenbosch, just 11 km from Cape Town and extending for 528 ha along the eastern slopes of Table Mountain, is one of the world's great botanical gardens. Apart from its natural assets, it has a centre fully equipped with environmental education materials and teaching aids. This makes Kirstenbosch the ideal place to initiate a study of Cape fynbos.

Directional signs make the following walks easy to follow; they are physically undemanding.

1. Silvertree Trail Park near and enter via the top gate to Kirstenbosch. The path climbs to the dam and, passing to its left, crosses a stream and veers west to the boundary fence, before turning right to join a contour path. Nursery, Skeleton and Window streams and their wooded banks are crossed along the way. The path makes a wide turn adjacent to

Trail details: 1. Silvertree Trail: 6 km/3 hours.
2. Yellowwood Trail: 2,5 km/1,5 hours; return.
3. Stinkwood Trail: 1,2 km/45 minutes.
Kirstenbosch is also a convenient starting point for walks up Table Mountain, for example via Skeleton Gorge or Nursery Ravine (see 'Table Mountain Walks', page 54).

Permits/bookings: A small entrance fee is payable at the upper and lower gates. For enquiries, contact the National Botanical Institute, Kirstenbosch, tel. (021) 7621166/7613422; Private Bag X7, Claremont 7735.

Facilities/amenities: Conducted and self-guided walks; nature study school run by the Cape Provincial Administration; information office; facilities for disabled visitors, including wheelchairs, the Braille Trail and the Fragrance Garden; labelled display of plants; seasonal exhibitions and flower shows; Sunday sunset concerts in summer; heavily patronized annual sale, in March, of indigenous plants; restaurant, book shop and small nursery open every day except Christmas Day.

Main attractions: Attractively laid-out gardens featuring selected plants from all over South Africa in the magnificent Table Mountain setting; forest walks; mountain streams and plentiful birdlife; historical features, including Van Riebeeck's hedge.

Pertinent information: Open 8.00 am – 6.00 pm April to August and 8.00 am – 7.00 pm September to March. Botanical Society members are admitted free of charge. Dogs allowed, on leash. No picnicking allowed. Public transport available to and from Mowbray and Claremont bus stations.

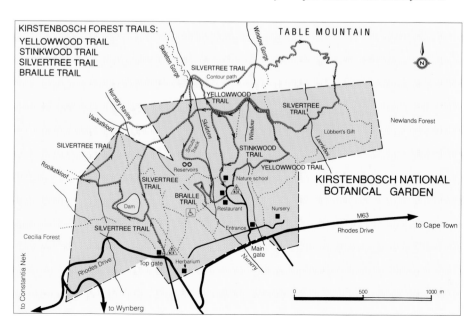

Newlands Forest and returns along a parallel route, lower down the slope. Bypassing the dam, on the eastern side this time, the trail returns to Kirstenbosch's top gate.

2. Yellowwood Trail begins beside the Nature Study School near the shop. The trail turns right and crosses Window Stream, then winds back on itself, recrosses the stream and heads towards Skeleton Gorge. Having climbed the gorge to the waterfall – a particularly pretty sight in winter – it descends along Smuts' Track, on the opposite bank, passing the reservoirs on the way. Most of the trail is in shade.

3. Stinkwood Trail This short stroll, perhaps best suited to the elderly, begins and ends at the garden shop. It makes a short loop that ascends and descends the slope of Table Mountain above the Nature Study School.

19. TABLE MOUNTAIN
CAPE TOWN

Trail details: A network of over 550 walks.

Permits/bookings: None required.

Maps/information: Shirley Brossy's map of Table Mountain; Municipality of Cape Town; Cape Nature Conservation; National Botanical Gardens.

Facilities/amenities: Some well-constructed footpaths; picnic sites; cableway.

Main attractions: Spectacular setting of a mountain amidst a city; easily accessible wild areas; rich flora and indigenous forested kloofs.

Pertinent information: The Table Mountain range has been sorely abused. Walkers have contributed to its gradual degradation (soil erosion, flower picking, vandalism such as mutilation of trees, defacing rocks, arson and littering). Please do not take short cuts; always carry off the mountain all bottles, bags and other litter that you carry up. Restrictions – such as a prohibition on all fires and overnight camping – are strictly enforced and all users of the mountain must obey these rules, but, despite the efforts of forestry officials, the destruction continues. Proof of this are the fires that devastate hundreds of hectares virtually every summer.

Available literature: Mike Lundy's *Best Walks in the Cape Peninsula*; *Table Mountain Walks*, Colin Paterson-Jones; *Table Mountain – A Natural Wonder*, Glen Moll.

In the 96 years to 1987, Table Mountain claimed 94 lives. With increased usage of the mountain over the intervening years, deaths on its rocky faces have topped two a year, and the number of injured who, for one reason or another, have to be rescued when an innocent 'climb' turns into a life-threatening disaster grows by leaps and bounds. To avoid becoming a victim of the famous landmark, bear the following points in mind.
Weather changes rapidly on the mountain and can be very different to that in the city below. No matter how settled the weather appears to be, never venture onto the mountain without a warm jersey, waterproof windcheater, map, compass, torch and spare food. From October to March, gale-force south-east winds can blow the mountain in thick mist. It is very easy to lose your way and become disorientated in mist. Note: the only predictable aspect of Table Mountain's weather is its unpredictability and rapid changes – be prepared!
Until you feel confident about knowing your way, hike with an experienced leader or organized club. *Always* stick to well-defined routes and avoid those that are dangerous, have a particularly bad record or that have been closed; these include Blinkwater Ravine (Pipe Track side) and Donkerkloof (Newlands). New trails are being constructed on the western table, and hikers are expected to use only these marked trails.

Against the backdrop of Table Mountain, hikers skirt sheer cliffs on Lion's Head.

Table Mountain could well be the world's most-climbed mountain. It includes the Table (the large 1 000-m plateau at the northern end of the Cape Peninsula), Lion's Head (669 m), Signal Hill (350 m) and Devil's Peak (1 001 m). The highest point is Maclear's Beacon (1 087 m) on the Table. Southwards, the mountain drops from the upper table to the lower or 'Back Table' (800 m). Five reservoirs are located on the Back Table, behind which lies Orange Kloof, a large open valley bounded by the Twelve Apostles extending south-west along the Atlantic Coast to Hout Bay Corner. To the east of Orange Kloof lies Constantia Nek. The mountain covers an area of 6 500 ha.

One never tires of the contrast between the dramatic beauty of the mountain and the sea and city below. However, this impressive complex of peaks, tables and ridges is, from an ecological point of view, in a sorry state. Table Mountain is home to more than 1 400 plant species (the entire British Isles has 1 750 species); but it is disturbing that 10 species on the mountain have become extinct in recent decades and others are endangered. Alien vegetation is posing a serious problem. Soil erosion and rock slides have taken their toll, partially caused by the ever-increasing use by tourists, walkers, hikers, rock climbers and joggers – incredibly, this mountain complex can boast over 550 walks and climbs. Large mammal life is rare today and one seldom sees buck, but dassies and grey mongoose are common. Baboons have reached the 'cheeky' stage in parts of the mountain and can present a threat to hikers. Birdlife is reasonable – redwinged starlings, rock pigeons, bokmakieries, sunbirds and sugarbirds are usually seen and black eagles occasionally soar overhead.

Only the Drakensberg can equal the amount of literature available in the form of printed guides and maps. To avoid duplicating too much information, therefore, the following sets out only some of

the more popular nature rambles and includes a few of my favourites.

The Pipe Track and its radiating ascents
The Pipe Track, originally a service path for maintaining pipes leading from the high reservoirs, is a beautiful stroll in itself, and also serves to link the paths leading up to the Twelve Apostles ridge.

Leaving Kloof Nek opposite the toilet facilities, the track passes the red-brick water-filtration plant, crosses the gully known as Diepsloot, where an alien vegetation removal programme is in progress, and winds around several bends, offering wonderful views over Camps Bay, and through thick bush for about 7 km before reaching a point below the exit of the disused Woodhead Tunnel in Slangolie Ravine. Along the way, there are several exciting routes up the mountain from the Pipe Track, and even one beyond Slangolie Ravine:

1. Diagonal Route Pass the metal signs marking Blinkwater (a steep ravine which is closed), and take the Diagonal path. This is a particularly interesting ascent because it crosses three buttresses (Porcupine, Jubilee and Barrier) and two ravines, ending in an ascent of Barrier Ravine to the Valley of the Red Gods.

2. Kasteelspoort Path Barrier Buttress is followed by Valken and Kasteel buttresses, beyond which one of the most popular ascents of the mountain, via the ravine of Kasteelspoort, is signposted. This is a well-worn path, scheduled for upgrading; do keep to the stone treads, where these are provided. The remains of the cableway which carried materials for the construction of the Woodhead Reservoir can be seen at the top.

3. Corridor Ravine Do not waste time climbing partway up Slangolie Ravine, as the final section, below the tunnel, has been closed off. The reason for this is that loose scree has made the route highly dangerous. Instead, continue along the path which

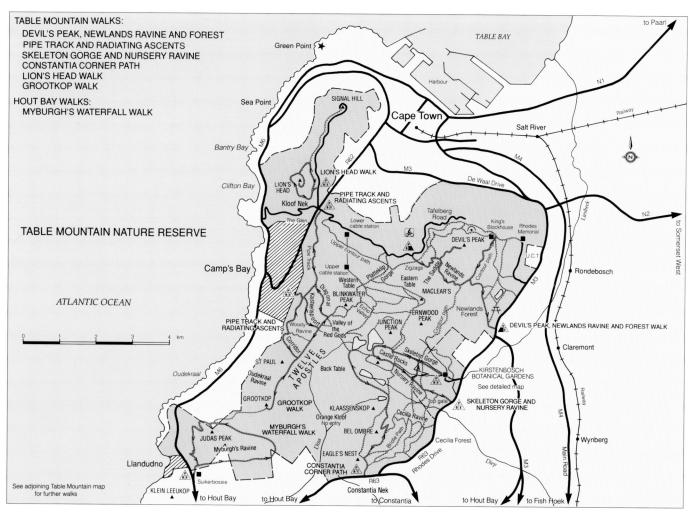

TABLE MOUNTAIN WALKS:
 DEVIL'S PEAK, NEWLANDS RAVINE AND FOREST
 PIPE TRACK AND RADIATING ASCENTS
 SKELETON GORGE AND NURSERY RAVINE
 CONSTANTIA CORNER PATH
 LION'S HEAD WALK
 GROOTKOP WALK

HOUT BAY WALKS:
 MYBURGH'S WATERFALL WALK

TABLE MOUNTAIN NATURE RESERVE

is a continuation of the Pipe Track and which skirts Slangolie Buttress, and leads to the top of the mountain via Corridor Ravine.

These routes are subjected to tremendous erosional pressures from hikers, which is why the authorities have cut zigzags and reconstructed the treads with stone – please keep to these.

Grootkop

The excursion to Grootkop is my favourite – probably because so few people go there and the view from the summit is one of the best on the whole range. If you start from Theresa Drive in Camps Bay and climb the mountain via Kasteelspoort – the shortest route to Grootkop – and return the same way after a lunch stop on the summit, you will need about six hours. Once you reach the Back Table, take the well-worn southern path along the ridge of the Twelve Apostles. It leads you to Grootkop. The ascent is more tricky than difficult, although marked with beacons. Beware of snakes on Grootkop – I've seen my share!

Lion's Head

The one-hour climb to the summit of Lion's Head (669 m) provides the best scenery for the least amount of effort in the whole fynbos region. At dusk, dawn and full moon, the city, sea and Table Mountain are mantled with soft light, a particularly beautiful sight from Lion's Head. The path begins at the dirt road (which has a chain across it) opposite the parking area off the tarred road running from

Kloof Nek to the long ridge of Signal Hill. Follow the path right the way around Lion's Head until the steep cliffs near the top are reached. Here there are alternative routes to the summit: one uses two sets of chains, the other two steel ladders; both routes are perfectly safe provided you keep to the constructed paths.

Skeleton Gorge and Nursery Ravine

One of my first tasks when I arrived as a forestry officer in the Western Cape was to help re-route and mark the extremely eroded and loose paths up Skeleton and Nursery gorges, both of which are shaded by indigenous forest. I also added tree identification tags (small yellow squares); sadly, few of these remain.

Skeleton Gorge (the beginning of a route known as Smuts Track) ascends from the 310-m contour path above Kirstenbosch Gardens. Ladders have been provided in a couple of places to help climbers over the worst of the rocks and there are a few short sections left which necessitate scrambling. Once you reach the top, near the Hely-Hutchinson Dam, I suggest you follow the southern leg of the intersection (working your way left, past the dam), to the top of Nursery Ravine. The descent of the ravine – whose gradient is steeper than that of Skeleton Gorge – will bring you back to the 310-m contour path. From here, it is a gentle downhill walk to Kirstenbosch Gardens. The total circuit takes about 3,5 hours.

A permanent ladder in Skeleton Gorge.

55

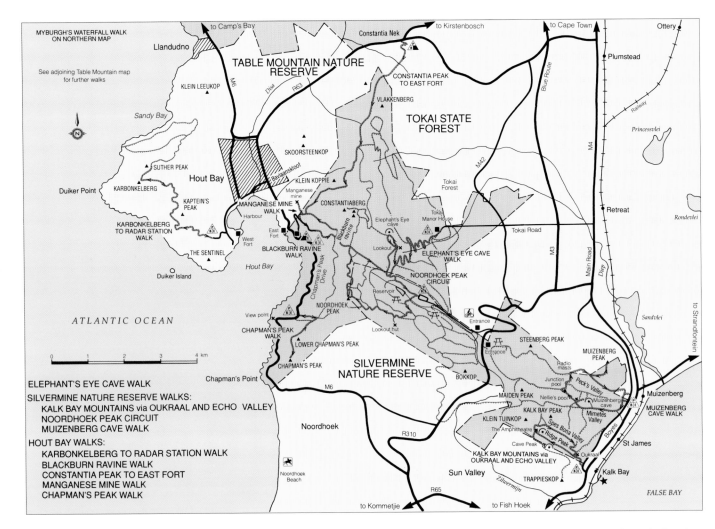

Muizenberg beach seen from Silvermine Nature Reserve.

Devil's Peak, Newlands Ravine and Forest

There are many routes up Devil's Peak. I have included only one – the most direct route to the top which is really a long, steep slog. Once you have conquered this route, surveyed the topography, read maps and guide book information, you can explore the other ascents.

About 2 km beyond the lower cableway station on Tafelberg Road (400 m), you come to some well-constructed zigzags known as the Saddle Path. Follow these – without being tempted to short-cut – and they will eventually level out at 650 m. Continue on the main track northwards to Breakfast Rock and thence to the Saddle. From here, turn left to ascend the steep (eroded) firebreak from 700 m to the top of Devil's Peak at 1 000 m.

If you do not mind ending up on the other side of the mountain from your car, return to the Saddle and follow the south-westerly path which crosses the Saddle diagonally and gradually winds to the top of 'Newlands Ravine Footpath'. Be sure to avoid the first ravine you encounter, Dark Gorge: it looks innocent enough but is in fact an extremely dangerous way down, which has claimed several lives. Newlands Ravine should be challenge enough; it descends first via rock steps, then zigzags across scree before reaching the shade of trees. Upon reaching the 360-m contour path, turn right and ten minutes later you will find the descent into the very popular and beautiful Newlands Forest. If you have time, however, turn left and follow the contour path all around the northern side of the

mountain, past the King's Blockhouse, back to the original zigzag path. This round trip requires approximately five hours.

Peninsula Trail

Starting at Kloof Nek between the city bowl and Camps Bay and ending at Kalk Bay railway station, this new trail takes 2 days to complete and covers 38 km. Saturday-night accommodation can be arranged at either Houtkapperspoort (tel. (021) 7945216) or Silvermist (tel. (021) 7947601), both at Constantia Nek. Booking for the trail is not necessary, as permits can be obtained at a small charge on arrival at the eastern section of the Silvermine Nature Reserve. For further information and a detailed route description, refer to *Weekend Trails in the Western Cape* by Mike Lundy.

Constantia Corner Path

I like the Constantia Corner Path because of its distant views, its winding and undulating pattern and the rock formations near the top. Starting at Constantia Nek, walk up the east side of the picnic area opposite the restaurant and into Cecilia State Forest. About 30 m beyond the gate, the path leads off to the left from the dirt road. Although it is obscure in places, you can follow the path up the crest of Constantia Ridge to the service road linking Constantia Nek to Cecilia Plantation and the Woodhead Reservoir. The distance to this point is only 2,5 km; including the return along the same route, the walk takes about 3,5 hours.

The view south from the Tokai Forest lookout, towards the cloud-covered Muizenberg mountain.

20. ELEPHANT'S EYE CAVE
TOKAI STATE FOREST

Trail details: 6 km/3 hours, return (direct route to Elephant's Eye); the gravel zigzag is an easy, but longer, alternative. There is a short, circular walk (1,2 km) through the arboretum.

Permits/bookings: The forested section falls under the jurisdiction of the Department of Forestry (Western Cape Region), tel. (021) 727471; Cape Nature Conservation administer the area beyond this.

Facilities/amenities: An interesting 'museum' (open every day: key available from office) furnished with interpretive, forestry-orientated educational displays, at the trail base; picnic site in pine plantation; horse-riding allowed; a network of forestry tracks used by joggers.

Main attractions: Tokai arboretum; Elephant's Eye Cave and lookout; montane fynbos and American redwoods; mountain scenery.

Pertinent information: The route is marked with elephant motifs. Mushroom-picking is allowed in Tokai Forest in autumn provided you obtain a permit from the gatekeeper.

Although the Elephant's Eye Cave can be reached from the Silvermine Nature Reserve, the route through Tokai State Forest is more varied. From Elephant's Eye, paths radiate to link up with those from Silvermine, Hout Bay, Constantia Peak and Noordhoek Peak.

Make your way to Tokai Manor House, turn left and follow the road until you reach the forest gates at the Tokai arboretum, an interesting collection of early-1900s trial plantings. Beyond the arboretum the path leads into a shady *Pinus radiata* plantation with patches of indigenous forest in moist ravines. The old Californian redwoods can be seen about 2 km from the start, to the left of the path. Emerging from the plantation, on the upper slopes of the Constantiaberg, the trail enters the world of Cape montane fynbos, and zigzags steeply up the mountain. Not far from the top is a fire monitoring

station, manned 24 hours a day, which offers an impressive vista over the Cape Flats. Elephant's Eye Cave is a large, open cave with a lovely view; it is reputed to have been the stronghold of a woman-led tribe of Khoikhoi. Having visited it, you can descend the trail to return to your car, or take any of a number of alternative routes (see Silvermine Nature Reserve, below).

21. SILVERMINE NATURE RESERVE
CAPE PENINSULA

Trail details: Network of tracks and paths; walks include 1. Noordhoek Peak circuit: 7 km/3 hours. 2. Kalk Bay mountains and Echo Valley: 4 km/2 hours, one way. See map p. 56.

Permits/bookings: Permit obtainable at gate.

Further information: The Forester, Silvermine, tel. (021) 753040/1/2/3, or Parks and Forests Branch, City Engineers Department, tel. (021) 4003269. See also Shirley Brossy's map *Hout Bay to Simonstown Mountains.*

Facilities/amenities: Picnic and braai sites; water and litter bins; toilets.

Main attractions: Cape Peninsula mountain scenery; indigenous forest and montane fynbos.

Pertinent information: The reserve can be reached on foot by ascending Elephant's Eye Trail in Tokai State Forest, or by car via Ou Kaapseweg. The area is subject to strong winds.

The Silvermine Nature Reserve, which is 2 151 ha in extent, extends from Muizenberg and Kalk Bay in the east to Noordhoek Peak in the west and forms part of the Cape Peninsula mountain chain. The reserve is bisected by Ou Kaapse Weg which effectively divides it into the western section where picnicking is allowed near an attractive reservoir and an eastern section which extends down to the Kalk Bay mountains and Muizenberg Peak overlooking False Bay. Within the reserve are numerous caves, mountain peaks, extensive plateaux and valleys. Small patches of evergreen forest may be encountered but most of the area is

covered by montane fynbos. Several small mammals and reptiles inhabit the reserve, but hikers should consider themselves lucky to glimpse Cape grysbok, steenbok or grey rhebok.

Most of the reserve's many features are explored by walks; these range from easy to moderate, and in duration from half an hour to half a day.

1. Noordhoek Peak circuit Because it is a relatively easy walk and one of the most scenic in the Peninsula, this 7-km/3-hour circular route is probably the most popular within the reserve. Begin below the reservoir near the parking area, sticking to the gravel road, and keeping right whenever there is a choice – except when you are close to Noordhoek Peak, when you make the ascent via a path to the left of the road. On the return leg, follow the road as it zigzags downwards and take the road closest to the dam. (For a more detailed description of this circuit, and the detour to Elephant's Eye, see Mike Lundy's *Best Walks in the Cape Peninsula*.)

2. Kalk Bay mountains via Oukraal and Echo Valley (4 km/2 hours one way). On the eastern side of the reserve, this contrasting trail offers excellent views, the opportunity to wander through indigenous forest and to take a peep into caves (exploration is only for the experienced). Steps lead up the mountain from Boyes Drive in line with Kalk Bay harbour. At the clearing called Weary Willy's, turn right and cross the stream to Oukraal, then left onto the gravel road. Leave the road where the second zigzag straightens out, to enter the forested depths of Spes Bona Valley. At its head is the Amphitheatre, a blind canyon. After the path rounds Ridge Peak, two short detours to the left lead, respectively, to Robin Hood Cave and Ronan's Well. Echo Valley literally speaks for

The erosion-proof path up Steenberg.

A sweeping view of the Sentinel, Karbonkelberg and Hout Bay from the path to Silvermine Nek.

Trail details: Numerous walks. See map p. 56.

Permits/bookings: None required.

Further information: Parks and Forests Branch, City Engineers Department, tel. (021) 4003269. See also Shirley Brossy's map *Hout Bay to Simonstown Mountains.*

Facilities/amenities: None.

Main attractions: Cape Peninsula mountain scenery; indigenous forest and montane fynbos.

Pertinent information: Guided walks are often arranged by Hout Bay Museum, tel. (021) 7903270.

1. Myburgh's Waterfall (2,5 hours; return) To get to the start of this walk requires some initiative, as ongoing development at the head of Hout Bay valley makes access to the mountain behind it increasingly difficult. However, some 200 m along the turn-off to Suikerbossie are two white pillars that mark the entrance to what was a large estate. Walk through these and follow the fence upwards, as it skirts a reservoir, and you will reach a firebreak. Follow this, and the path which merges with it, as it leads east below Geelklip Buttress to Myburgh's Ravine, where there are some magnificent indigenous trees. I would not recommend climbing up the waterfall, even in summer, when red disas flower in the ravine and around the waterfall.

2. Karbonkelberg to Radar Station (3,5 hours return; one-hour optional detour) Starts from the top of Bay View Road, where there is a gravel track that zigzags up the mountain. On the damp, shady side of the track, ferns grow from the rock face in winter. As you climb, the sea on the Sandy Bay side of the Sentinel becomes visible in the nek between it and Karbonkelberg. This is just the first of a kaleidoscope of unique views, which include Sentinel Peak (below) with Chapman's Peak and Noordhoek beach in the background, and the entire length of Table Mountain – from the back.

The derelict buildings once occupied by radar personnel at the summit are a little depressing, but the view from the rocks behind them is simply stunning. The mountainside drops with dizzying precipitousness to the coastal road below. While we sat contemplating the sea between Clifton and Kommetjie, two black eagles glided soundlessly by, just a few metres away.

About 200 m from the radar station a stone beacon marks the detour to Suther Peak, which is richly rewarding, if you have an hour to spare. The path leads across a marshy plateau, at times through head-high fynbos, and up through gnarled old milkwood and yellowwood trees, to another wonderful view. This one is over Sandy Bay and Klein Leeukoppie.

3. Manganese Mine (2,5 hours; return) This walk starts from just beyond the East Fort on Chapman's Peak Drive. Having studied the fort, proceed up the gravel track and leave it after the hairpin bend to take a path to the left. Soon this path crosses the track which marks the course of the 750-m iron chute laid in 1909 to transport the ore mined here to the jetty below, near Flora Bay. Zigzag up the hill and take the left fork, which leads to the large

itself, but its name gives no hint of the lovely forest at its head. Unless you have several hours to spare, pass up the path to Cave Peak: this mountain is riddled with caves that take time to explore. Cavern Rocks (or Hungry Harry's) is a suitable spot to rest before continuing back to Weary Willy's, and thence down to Boyes Drive.

3. Muizenberg Cave (4,5 km/3 hours; circular) Remember to take a torch with you on this walk, or you will miss half the fun. Muizenberg Cave lies on St James' Peak above Muizenberg station. The path to it begins on a bend on Boyes Drive, roughly opposite the station below. A short climb brings you to a T-junction, where you turn left. Keep right and take the steps up Bailey's Kloof. Below, on the sea edge, lies the cottage that once belonged to the mining magnate of old, Abe Bailey.

The views of False Bay from up here are wonderful. The path runs beside a small stream for a while, climbing all the way. Eventually it meets a gravel road, where you turn right. Keep an eye open for

the path to the right, a little further on, that leads to the Muizenberg cave; it doubles back from this road.

To the right of the cave's main chamber are two smaller entrances; the nearer and larger one leads to a deep well, which you can investigate with the help of your torch. Take care, however, as the rocks can be slippery. A left turn will bring you to a T-junction. Turn left to return to the main chamber; turn right if you are prepared to crawl 40 m through the mountain before emerging out in the open.

When you have completed your exploration of the cave, climb back up to the gravel road and turn right. Nellie's Pool appears on the right. Further on, the path descends to Junction Pool, the ideal picnic spot. Cross the river and turn right. Past the next landmark, a Defence Force mast, turn right again. The gravel road is replaced first by a track and then by well-laid steps down Peck's Valley. From here it is easy to find the way you went up, and you can relax and enjoy the view of Muizenberg below.

mouth of one of the more obvious mine shafts; there are about six others, but few are safe to explore. Here you can pick up black ore and rejoice that its poor quality led to the abandoning of mining activities on this mountain after only two years.

4. Blackburn Ravine to Silvermine Nek (3 hours; return) The route begins on Chapman's Peak Drive 1,6 km from the turn-off to the beach from the main road in Hout Bay. Follow the gravel path until you meet the stream which sometimes runs dry in summer in Blackburn Ravine. A strenuous zigzag climb alongside the stream takes you through an attractive wooded kloof until the contour path is reached. Take the right-hand path and after another steep ascent to Silvermine Nek, you will be rewarded with panoramic views of Hout Bay on one side and False Bay and the Hottentots Holland on the other.

5. Chapman's Peak (3,5 hours; return) Park at the picnic spot on the last major bend on the Hout Bay side of Chapman's Peak Drive before it reaches Chapman's Peak. A stiff climb via a sheltered and hot (especially in summer) ravine brings you to a plateau which is the ideal spot to rest. Turn right and begin the steady and easy climb up on the path which runs below the ridge, through tall protea bushes and other thriving fynbos. From about halfway you can see around the Sentinel on the other side of the bay. A short scramble from the saddle below Chapman's Peak brings you, surprisingly easily, to the summit of the peak itself. The view is bound to give your spirits a lift: to the right, the pretty bay and settlement of Hout Bay; to the left Noordhoek valley, Fish Hoek and beyond – right across False Bay on a clear day.

6. Constantia Peak to East Fort (5 hours, but allow a full day for maximum enjoyment of the scenery) Begins near Constantia Nek Restaurant, where you can park your car in the shade. Proceed down the road towards Hout Bay; after about 150 m you will see a sign on the left pointing to the Vlakkenberg Hiking Trail. After a fairly steep climb, the path levels out to cross Vlakkenberg and Skoorsteenberg, and gradually descends Constantiaberg to emerge below it at the East Fort on Chapman's Peak Drive (at the start of the Manganese Mine walk described earlier), where you should have a car waiting for you. This is a long walk but its rewards are glorious, constantly changing views of valley, mountains and sea around Hout Bay.

23. CAPE OF GOOD HOPE NATURE RESERVE
CAPE PENINSULA

Trail details: 1. Kanonkop Trail: 1 hour; return.
2. False Bay Scenic Walk: 70 minutes; return.
3. Thomas T. Tucker Shipwreck Trail: 80 minutes; return. 4. Cape of Good Hope Scenic Walk: 1,5 hours; return. 5. Phyllisia Circuit: 2,5 hours.
6. Sirkelsvlei Trail: 2-3 hours; circular.
7. Gifkommetjie/Good Hope Coastal Walk: 3-4 hours; one way.

Permits/bookings: None required; an entrance fee is payable at the gate.

Maps/information: The map supplied at the entrance shows all formal trails, and these are signposted. There is an ongoing programme of providing demarcated walks and trails; to enquire about the current status, contact the information centre in the reserve.

Facilities/amenities: Walking, fishing, skin-diving and snorkelling are allowed in most sections of the reserve; braai sites; boat-launching ramp; refreshment kiosk and curio shop; restaurant; bus service from the carpark to the lookout point.

Main attractions: Cape Point and Cape of Good Hope; coastal scenery; rare fynbos vegetation.

Pertinent information: The west coast of the reserve is a marine reserve; the catching of any fish or marine animals between Schuster's Bay, Scarborough and Cape Point is prohibited, with the exception of the daily quota of five crayfish per person between Hoek van Bobbejaan and Cape Point; the eastern coastline of the reserve is open for rock angling.

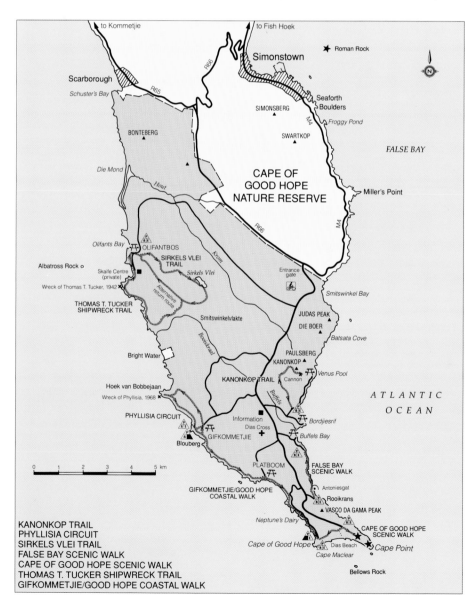

KANONKOP TRAIL
PHYLLISIA CIRCUIT
SIRKELS VLEI TRAIL
FALSE BAY SCENIC WALK
CAPE OF GOOD HOPE SCENIC WALK
THOMAS T. TUCKER SHIPWRECK TRAIL
GIFKOMMETJIE/GOOD HOPE COASTAL WALK

Dias Beach as seen from lofty Cape Point.

The wreck of the World War II liberty ship Thomas T Tucker *is a familiar sight to hikers.*

A number of trails have been constructed in the 7 765-ha Cape of Good Hope Nature Reserve, offering an unlimited potential for day walks. Most of these are easy, and few take longer than three hours to complete.

A surprising number of animals such as baboon, bontebok, zebra, springbok, grey rhebok, eland, Cape grysbok, steenbok and grey mongoose, and over 150 species of birds, including the black oystercatcher, black eagle and ostrich, are seen more easily by hikers than by motorists.

1. Kanonkop Trail, leading up to the Paulsberg and a historic signalling cannon.

2. False Bay Scenic Walk, from Rooikrantz to Buffels Bay (or vice versa) and return. Affords lovely views of the Rooikrantz angling ledges, Antoniesgat Cave and False Bay, where whales cavort in whale season.

3. Thomas T Tucker Shipwreck Trail takes you past lovely rock pools, leading eventually to the wreck of the *Thomas T Tucker*. You can return along the escarpment if you prefer.

4. Cape of Good Hope Scenic Walk A popular walk from Cape of Good Hope to Cape Point (fairly strenuous) and back (easy, offering excellent views of Cape Point, Cape Maclear and Cape of Good Hope). Dias Beach can be reached by a steep wooden stairway.

5. Phyllisia Circuit begins at Gifkommetjie carpark, leads parallel to the coast, then down to the wreck of the *Phyllisia* (1963) off the Hoek van Bobbejaan. The return route follows the coast, making a loop back to the carpark, although there is a short cut back through the bush if you prefer.

6. Sirkelsvlei Trail Begin from Olifantsbos parking area and walk to Sirkelsvlei through assorted fynbos; return along the same route.

7. Gifkommetjie or **Good Hope Coastal Walk**, affords beautiful coastal scenery, and fynbos that is prettiest in spring. Park one car at Gifkommetjie off Circular Drive and a second car at the Cape of Good Hope or Cape Point parking area. For a shorter version of this walk, start from Platboom or Pegrims Point.

24. THE VINEYARD TRAIL
STELLENBOSCH

Trail details: 24 km/1 day (shorter variations of 16 km or 12 km possible).

Permits/bookings:: Permits required from the Stellenbosch Publicity Association; tel. (02231) 833584; fax (02231) 833993; 30 Plein Street, Stellenbosch 7600.

Facilities/amenities: Parking at Oude Libertas Centre.

Main attractions: Vineyards; rolling hills; coastal renosterveld; old tin mine; views of the Cape.

Pertinent information: Trains can be used to return from Kuils River to Stellenbosch; check the train schedule before you begin the trail so you can return easily to Stellenbosch. The trail is open every day of the week but is closed during the grape harvesting season: mid-January to mid-April. Carry drinking water, as there is none available on the trail, which runs on exposed hillsides, and can be hot.

The Vineyard Trail, a full day's ramble best undertaken in autumn or spring, is unusual in that it follows a route almost entirely above privately owned wine estates. It starts at the Oude Libertas Centre near the cemetery in which historical figures, such as Dr D.F. Malan, a former Prime Minister of South Africa, have been laid to rest. The trail meanders through farm vineyards, cultivated land, plantations, along gravel tracks and over large hills, until it reaches a minor tarred road leading into Kuils River, from where you can catch a train back to Stellenbosch. (Each of the shorter routes is identified by markers of a separate colour.)

Note the coastal renosterveld on Ribbokkop, near the 14-km mark. Bottelaryberg (476 m) is worth climbing as it is the highest point on the trail and the 360° view of the Cape Peninsula and the inland mountains is superb.

25. EERSTE RIVER/ COETZENBURG TRAIL
STELLENBOSCH

Trail details: 10 km (4 km along river; 6 km on Coetzenburg)/2 to 3 hours; one way.

Permits/bookings: None required.

Maps/information: Available from Stellenbosch Publicity Association, tel. (02231) 833584; fax (02231) 833993; 30 Plein Street, Stellenbosch 7600

Facilities/amenities: None.

Main attractions: River; panoramic view of the historic town of Stellenbosch.

Pertinent information: Trail is open all year but is most pleasant in spring and autumn. Walking surface is mainly soil, except where route follows tarred roads.

This fairly easy trail starts at Aan de Wagenweg, near the Volkskombuis Restaurant. It follows the

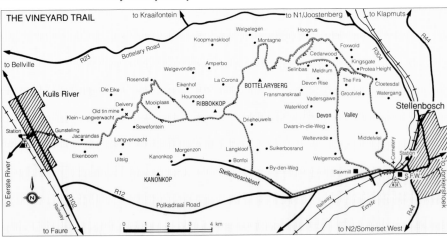

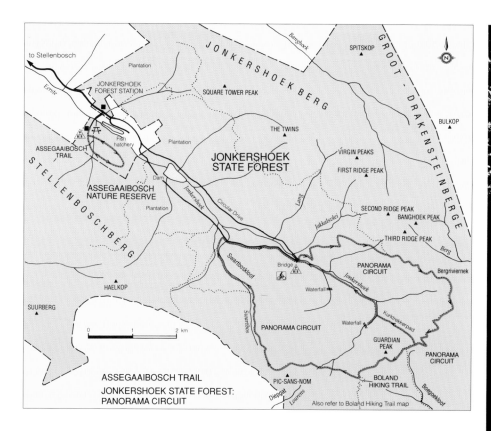

ASSEGAAIBOSCH TRAIL
JONKERSHOEK STATE FOREST:
PANORAMA CIRCUIT

Dappled sunlight in the Jonkershoek State Forest.

tree-shaded southern and northern banks of the Eerste River to Brummer Park, where it crosses the river, and then traces the fynbos-covered northern slopes of the Stellenbosch Mountain (Stellenbosch-berg). Walkers can choose whether to continue along the mountain in the direction of Brandwacht township or to keep right and finish at the Coetzen-burg sports grounds. (A third option is to retrace the early stage of the route, back along the river to Aan de Wagenweg, which will take a little longer than the three hours allocated.)

Look out for small buck and various bird species.

26. ASSEGAAIBOSCH TRAIL
ASSEGAAIBOSCH NATURE RESERVE, JONKERSHOEK

Trail details: 2-km/half-hour nature trail; there are also footpaths on the northern slopes of Stellenbosch Mountain (Stellenboschberg).

Permits/bookings: Arrange a permit by telephoning in advance (weekdays only): (02331) 70111; Private Bag 5024, Stellenbosch 7599. Visitor numbers are restricted owing to the small size of the reserve.

Facilities/amenities: Picnic/braai facilities; toilets.

Main attractions: Wild flower garden; spectacular mountain scenery.

Pertinent information: In summer, the reserve is open every day from 7.00 am to 6.00 pm; in winter, it opens an hour later. The historic Jonkershoek Fish Hatchery, with its information centre and freshwater aquarium, is situated directly opposite the nature reserve, on the Jonkershoek Road. Conducted tours of the hatchery can be arranged for groups on weekdays, by prior arrangement with the officer in charge, tel. (02231) 70111.

From Stellenbosch, follow the Jonkershoek Road for 8 km into the Jonkershoek Valley, and you will find the Assegaaibosch Nature Reserve to your right. This 204-ha reserve extends up the northern slopes of Stellenbosch Mountain, its upper reaches adjoining the Hottentots Holland Nature Reserve. The land was originally a farm and the Cape Dutch farmhouse, which dates from 1790, still stands. Pockets of forest occur on the banks of the streams and the sides of the Eerste River, which forms one of its boundaries, but mountain fynbos is the pre-dominant vegetation.

The walk is easy; it begins in a wild-flower garden, leads up the mountain and continues along a contour, from where one can enjoy a panoramic view of the Jonkershoek Valley below. Birdlife is surprisingly rich; forest buzzards, paradise flycatchers, kingfishers and waterfowl can be spotted here. The resident steenbok, caracal and leopard are unlikely to be seen.

Morning mist rises from the Jonkershoek valley.

27. JONKERSHOEK STATE FOREST
NEAR STELLENBOSCH

Trail details: Panorama Trail: 20 km/6-7 hours; shorter Kurktrekker option of 9 km/3-4 hours (both return); a network of other footpaths in the plantation and Hottentots Holland Nature Reserve; several peaks suitable for mountaineers only.

Permits/bookings: Permits necessary for the plantation area, obtainable at the gate. Open 7.30 am – 5.00 pm weekends and public holidays, except during fire danger season (September to end March). For further information about the forestry area, tel. (02231) 5715. For permits to walk into the Hottentot Holland Nature Reserve, tel. Nuweberg (0225) 4301.

Facilities/amenities: Numerous footpaths; horse-riding is allowed; mountaineering; picnic sites; angling, with permit (obtainable from Forestry).

Main attractions: Mountain scenery and wooded ravines; indigenous montane fynbos.

Pertinent information: Lower section of the valley is dammed. Be prepared for abrupt changes in weather. Park in shade at the wooden bridge on Circular Drive.

Jonkershoek State Forest, which extends over 730 ha, is surrounded on three sides by the Hotten-tot Holland Nature Reserve and lies in one of the most beautiful valleys in southern Africa. A number of footpaths meander through stands of pine plantation and into diverse and attractive montane fynbos. These offer a variety of day hikes, of which the Panorama Trail is the best known. Many of these footpaths provide mountaineers with access to the Jonkershoek Twins (1 504 m), First, Second and Third Ridge peaks (1 517 m, 1 515 m and 1 516 m respectively), Banghoek Peak (1 526 m), Haelkop (1 384 m), and other summits. The footpaths vary in difficulty, with most being easy to follow, but the peaks should be ascended only by mountaineers guided by a competent leader.

To undertake the Panorama Circuit, which is fairly long and comprises some testing ascents, you need to be moderately fit. The trail begins a few metres back along the road, using a firebreak on the northern side of the river, which soon joins a path zigzagging to the base of the cliffs that form one arm of the valley. The path levels out where it joins the 1 000-m contour. A short, steep climb brings you to Bergriviernek, a wonderful viewpoint overlooking the Jonkershoek Valley, La Motte State Forest, and six well-known peaks. At the base of a grassy embankment about 5 km beyond the nek, a shorter option, the Kurktrekker ('corkscrew'), drops to the right. This option crosses two streams below waterfalls on its way back to the parking area. There is usually no shortage of water on the longer circuit either, which, after passing stone cairns marking the route to Boegoekloof (see Hottentots Holland Day Walks p. 68), crosses several streams. It then meanders past Diepgat, source of the Lourens River, at which point False Bay comes into view. This is replaced by a panorama of the Jonkershoek Valley before the long descent beside the thickly wooded Swartboskloof stream begins. When you turn right onto Circular Drive you will be 3 km from your parking spot.

The kloofs are cool and shady; they generally boast abundant birdlife and large specimens of indigenous trees such as Breede River yellowwood, red alder, Cape beech, ironwood and wild olive.

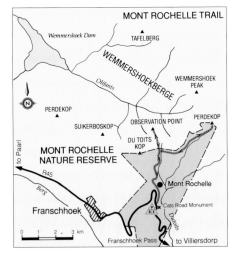

The Panorama Circuit passes beneath a waterfall.

Tadpoles of the ghost frog, *Heleophyne purcelli*, are found in all the mountain streams and can be identified by their relatively large, pale bodies, and flat heads with sucker-like undersides. The sucker helps them cling to underwater vegetation and rocks, thereby aiding survival in fast-flowing waters. Large mammals present in the valley include baboon, klipspringer, grey rhebok, grysbok and the introduced eland.

A world-renowned, long-term catchment research programme, emphasizing the influence of plant cover on water supplies and on the ecology, is in progress at Jonkershoek. The reserve is also concerned with the conservation of montane fynbos. Be particularly careful not to pollute.

28. MONT ROCHELLE NATURE RESERVE
FRANSCHHOEK

Trail details: 15 km/6 hours; return.

Permits/bookings: Permits are required from the Franschhoek Municipality, tel. (02212) 2055; 27 Huguenot Road, and over weekends, from the Museum annex, Lambrecht Street (Sat. 9.00 am-1.00 pm and 2.00 pm – 5.00 pm and Sun. 2.00 pm-5.00 pm; tel. (02212) 2532.

Facilities/amenities: None.

Main attractions: Beautiful fynbos; magnificent vistas, dams and valleys.

Pertinent information: The only available drinking water is at the start. No fires and no dogs allowed. The maximum number of people permitted on the walk per day is 20.

The entrance to the Mont Rochelle Nature Reserve lies above the second hairpin bend in the Franschhoek Pass, near the Cats road monument. The trail begins at the settlement of Mont Rochelle and ascends Du Toits Kop to a contour high above the river. On the way to Observation Point (1 056 m), the hiker can look back over Theewaterskloof Dam and the Villiersdorp Valley, and there is a lovely view from Observation Point itself of the Wemmershoek Valley and Dam. The path to Perdekop leaves the main path at a junction well marked by a beacon. At first it climbs steeply and deep kloofs fall away to the left. It is quite a relief to reach the plateau, which provides level access to Perdekop.

MONT ROCHELLE TRAIL

Wemmershoek Dam · TAFELBERG · WEMMERSHOEKBERGE · Olifants · WEMMERSHOEK PEAK · to Paarl · PERDEKOP · SUIKERBOSKOP · OBSERVATION POINT · PERDEKOP · DU TOITS KOP · MONT ROCHELLE NATURE RESERVE · R45 · Berg · Mont Rochelle · Cats Road Monument · Franschhoek · 0 1 2 3 km · Franschhoek Pass · Duitots · to Villiersdorp · N

29. HELDERBERG NATURE RESERVE
SOMERSET WEST

Trail details: Circular nature walks ranging from 2,5 km/35 minutes to 11 km/4 hours.

Permits/bookings: Entrance is free for residents of Somerset West; non-residents are charged a fee.

Maps/information: Municipality of Somerset West, tel. (024) 8522421; fax (024) 516207; PO Box 19, Somerset West 7129.

Facilities/amenities: Information centre; herbarium; arboretum; duck pond; buck camp; tea kiosk, open at weekends and on public holidays.

Main attractions: Spectacular views; reintroduced large mammals; endemic birdlife; gardens and natural fynbos.

Pertinent information: Day-use area only. Open 7.00 am – 6.00 pm May-October; for the rest of the year, closes at 8.00 pm. No fires and no dogs allowed; as this is a fire problem area, visitors are requested not to smoke. Ticks are common. In winter, be prepared for rapid changes in weather.

Nature walks at Helderberg Nature Reserve (385 ha) offer mountain views, glimpses of wildlife such as springbok, bontebok, steenbok, grysbok and duiker, and a rich endemic birdlife whose existence depends upon the lush, flowering fynbos. There have even been rare sightings of caracal, leopard and honey badger. Not surprisingly, the reserve is extremely popular, especially among the local residents of Somerset West. It is just 4,5 km outside the town (follow the signs from Main Street).

The four colour-coded walks on the lower reaches of the mountain are designed as consecutive loops, allowing the user to circle back to the starting point at the herbarium at a number of points. Together these traverse half the length of the Helderberg.

Woodies Walk, at the far end of the reserve, provides the most exacting loop, along the upper reaches of the mountain. It uses an old forestry track which leads right up to the cliff face at Disa Gorge, named for the disa orchids which bloom here from December to February. From this point, only mountaineers should try to ascend the Helderberg Peak by following Disa Gorge – or via Porcupine Buttress, which avoids all the difficult parts of Disa Gorge. The view from the summit is a sensational 360° sweep, taking in the Cape Peninsula, its bays, the Hottentots Holland mountains and other Western Cape ranges.

The Lourens Trail is the reserve's newest – a short stroll of about half an hour along the river of the same name, between Main Road and Reitz Park.

Hakea, one of the serious invader plants in the fynbos, is prevalent on the higher slopes of Helderberg Nature Reserve. The winged seeds are released from their cones after a fire, so uncontrolled burns spread hakea plants. The reserve has been chosen by the Department of Agricultural Technical Services as one of the experimental zones for testing the biological control of the invader – by hakea seed-eating beetles.

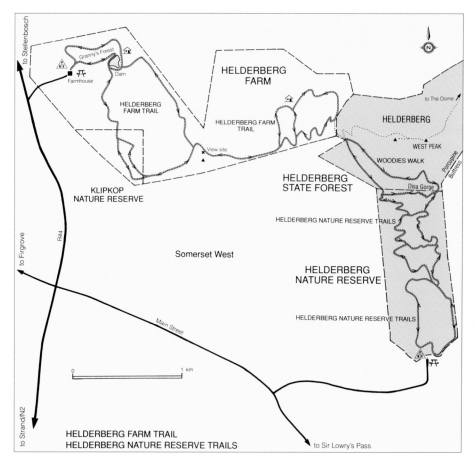

30. HELDERBERG FARM TRAIL
SOMERSET WEST

Trail details: 19 km/2 days, return; many shorter options.

Permits/bookings: Braai facilities and the overnight hut must be booked in advance with Mr W Obermeyer, Helderberg Farm, tel. (024) 554308; PO Box 507, Somerset West 7130. Day-hikers each pay an admission fee.

Facilities/amenities: Base hut near parking area, with 6 beds, inside and outside fireplaces, toilets and braai facilities. A second overnight hut at the far end of the trail sleeps 6 and has a spring supplying fresh water; no fires are allowed here. Dam in which swimming is possible.

Main attractions: Granny's Forest, with 17 fern species; the viewpoint, from which the entire Cape Peninsula can be seen; proteas.

Pertinent information: Carry water, as there is very little on the trail. Take sleeping bags on the 2-day trail, as well as spare toilet paper and candles. No swimming allowed in ponds or streams.

Helderberg Farm lies in the foothills of the Helderberg, on land granted by Simon van der Stel in 1692. From Cape Town, turn off the N2 onto the R44 towards Somerset West; 3,7 km beyond the town's main street, turn right into Klein Helderberg Road. The farm is signposted 1 km further on.

The paths offer anything from a short ramble of under 2 km in Granny's Forest, to a two-day hike.

A splash of pink watsonias brightens a mountain slope on the Helderberg Farm Trail.

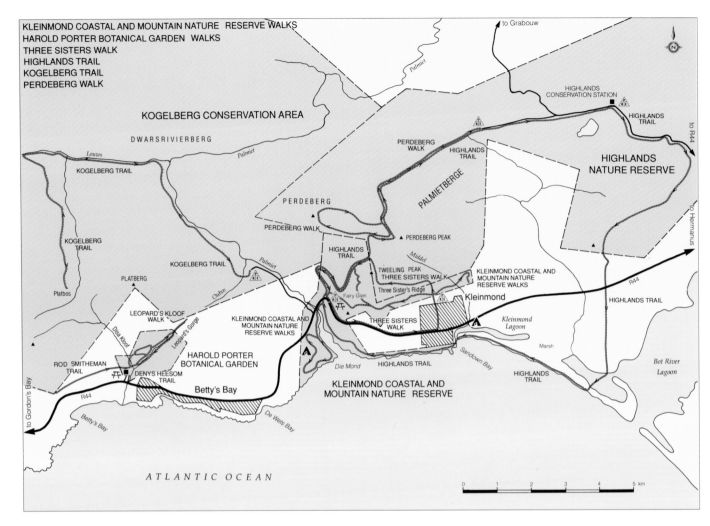

KLEINMOND COASTAL AND MOUNTAIN NATURE RESERVE WALKS
HAROLD PORTER BOTANICAL GARDEN WALKS
THREE SISTERS WALK
HIGHLANDS TRAIL
KOGELBERG TRAIL
PERDEBERG WALK

KOGELBERG CONSERVATION AREA

DWARSRIVIERBERG

Louws

KOGELBERG TRAIL

KOGELBERG TRAIL

KOGELBERG TRAIL

PLATBERG

Platbos

LEOPARD'S KLOOF WALK

ROD SMITHEMAN TRAIL

HAROLD PORTER BOTANICAL GARDEN

DENYS HEESOM TRAIL

Betty's Bay

R44

to Gordon's Bay

Betty's Bay

De Wets Bay

ATLANTIC OCEAN

Palmiet

to Grabouw

HIGHLANDS CONSERVATION STATION

HIGHLANDS TRAIL

to R44

HIGHLANDS NATURE RESERVE

PERDEBERG WALK

HIGHLANDS TRAIL

PALMIETBERGE

PERDEBERG

PERDEBERG WALK

Perdeberg Peak

Palmiet

KLEINMOND COASTAL AND MOUNTAIN NATURE RESERVE WALKS

HIGHLANDS TRAIL

to Hermanus

HIGHLANDS TRAIL

Oubos

HIGHLANDS TRAIL

TWEELING PEAK
THREE SISTERS WALK

Three Sister's Ridge

Fairy Glen

Middel

Kleinmond

Kleinmond Lagoon

R44

THREE SISTERS WALK

KLEINMOND COASTAL AND MOUNTAIN NATURE RESERVE WALKS

Marsh

Bot River Lagoon

Disa Kloof

Leopard's Gorge

KLEINMOND COASTAL AND MOUNTAIN NATURE RESERVE WALKS

Die Mond

HIGHLANDS TRAIL

Sandown Bay

KLEINMOND COASTAL AND MOUNTAIN NATURE RESERVE

HIGHLANDS TRAIL

0 1 2 3 4 5 km

Part of the 4,5 km 'Red route' takes the walker into the Klipkop Nature Reserve, a small area which the farmer has set aside for conservation of its fynbos. Although the 2-day trail involves a steady climb to the lower slopes of West Peak – you will have climbed over 500 m by the time you reach the overnight hut – it is not particularly taxing, which makes it suitable for beginners. The viewpoint, roughly halfway between the start of the trail and the mountain, commands a spectacular vista over False Bay, Stellenbosch, Table Mountain and the Cape Peninsula. Among the animals hikers may be fortunate enough to glimpse along the way are grysbok, duiker, silver and blackbacked jackal, honeybadger and porcupine. There are said to be close to 100 bird species in the fynbos and indigenous forest on the farm.

Disa Kloof, Harold Porter National Botanical Garden.

31. HAROLD PORTER NATIONAL BOTANICAL GARDEN WALKS
BETTY'S BAY

Trail details: 1. Leopard's Kloof Walk: 3 km/ 2 hours, circular; 2. Zigzag Trail: 2-3 hours, return; 3. Robert Smitheman Trail: 3 km/1,5 hours; 4. Denys Heesom Trail: 1 hour.

Permits/bookings: For the Leopard's Kloof walk a permit and gate-key, which carries a deposit, is required from the office. A brochure with map of the garden, as well as pamphlets on the Rod Smitheman and Denys Heesom trails, are available on request.

Facilities/amenities: Picnic site; toilets; labelled display of plants; garden shop and plant sales; tea garden.

Main attractions: Coastal and mountain fynbos.

Pertinent information: Rapidly changeable weather in winter. The garden is open daily from 8.00 am to 5.00 pm. There is a small entrance fee except for members of the Botanical Society.

The Harold Porter National Botanical Garden is a scenic, well-maintained sanctuary for mountain and coastal fynbos and the setting for many gentle walks. It extends for 200 ha from the mountains above Betty's Bay, through marshlands down to the coastal dunes. Flowers are the main attraction; the red disa blooms in January and the nerine lily in March. Look out for the sunbird, sugarbird and other endemic birdlife attracted to these colourful displays; 78 bird species have been recorded in the garden. Small antelope, baboon and possibly even leopard are also present.

The network of walks caters for all levels of interest and fitness. There are plans to link part of the garden's existing trail system to a longer hiking trail in the Kogelberg area.

1. Leopard's Kloof Trail A walk that leads through beautiful forest to pools and a waterfall. The access path is fairly rough.

2. Zigzag Trail This leads up the mountain to a contour path affording spectacular views over Betty's Bay. Hikers must return on the same route.

3. Rod Smitheman Trail Hikers on this interpretive trail are able to identify plants and ecological features with the aid of a pamphlet available at the office. The trail begins in the garden but crosses onto municipal commonage maintained by Betty's Bay municipality.

4. Denys Heesom Trail Another interpretive trail best enjoyed with the self-guide pamphlet available at the office. It is an easy route, which meanders along the coastal river plain.

32. HIGHLANDS TRAIL
KLEINMOND

Trail details: 36,5 km/2 days; circular. Day 1: 16 km/6-8 hours (to Kleinmond); day 2: 20,5 km/ 8-10 hours.

Permits/bookings: Must be obtained from Cape Nature Conservation, tel. (0225) 4301; Private Bag X27, Elgin 7180.

Facilities/amenities: There is no hut on the trail, although one is being planned, and hikers should book accommodation at Kleinmond or Palmiet camp site, at the holiday cottages or the hotel in the town.

Main attractions: Fynbos; views of mountains and sea; rock formations.

Pertinent information: Rapidly changeable weather all year round; in winter the lagoon is chest-deep; hikers should carry their own water and, if planning to use one of the camp sites, take their own tents. There is a limit of 12 people on the trail at a time. There are plans to provide an overnight hut for trailists at one of the caravan sites.

From parts of the Perdeberg Walk one can catch a glimpse of the Palmiet River mouth far below.

This trail is the namesake of the Highlands Forest Station (behind Kleinmond), where it begins and ends. Although the trail is most pleasant during summer, a bonus for those who brave the winter squalls is the possibility of seeing whales out to sea. Carry water, and a swimming costume for the lagoon crossing.

The first day leads for 16 km down to the Kleinmond lagoon. Hikers can pitch their tents at the local camp site, proceed to accommodation in the town, or continue for 4,5 km along the beach to Palmiet camp site for the night. The second day, which is a little more strenuous than the first, takes hikers back to the forest station via Perdeberg (see Perdeberg Walk below).The trail is well marked.

33. KOGELBERG TRAIL
KOGELBERG NATURE RESERVE

Trail details: 12-20 km/4-6 hours; return.

Permits/bookings: Book (up to 2 months) in advance with Hottentots Holland Nature Reserve at Nuweberg; tel (0225) 4301, between 8.00 am and 4.30 pm (closed 1.00-2.00 pm); bookings are provisional until payment is made to: Cape Nature Conservation, Private Bag X27, Elgin 7180. Map supplied with permit.

Facilities/amenities: Carpark at Oudebosch.

Main attractions: The Palmiet Valley; great diversity of fynbos.

Pertinent information: There is a limit of 12 people per permit and one group per day. The gate is open from 7.30 am to 5.30 pm.

The Kogelberg Nature Reserve extends for 16 537 ha between Kleinmond, Rooiels and Steenbras, across deep valleys and high peaks. The entrance is off the main road from Betty's Bay, 3 km west of Kleinmond.

It is a delight to walk among fynbos that is as exquisite as it is remarkable: it contains many species endemic to the area, and the diversity of the plant species is among the highest in the world. The beautiful, unspoiled valley of the Palmiet River must rate as the highlight of the Kogelberg Trail, which uses the jeep track leading to the reserve.

Kogelberg supports a variety of game, including grey rhebok, grysbok, klipspringer and secretive leopard. Sharp-eyed hikers may be rewarded with sightings of black eagle, fish eagle, kingfishers, any number of waterbirds, and sunbirds.

34. PERDEBERG WALK
KLEINMOND

Trail details: 16 km/8,5 hours; return.

Permits/bookings: Must be obtained from Hottentots Holland Nature Reserve at Nuweberg, tel. (0225) 4301, between 8.00 am and 4.30 pm (closed 1.00 – 2.00 pm); bookings are provisional until payment is made to: Cape Nature Conservation, Private Bag X27, Elgin 7180.

Facilities/amenities: Parking at start.

Main attractions: Montane fynbos; memorable views of mountains, sea and surrounding towns.

Pertinent information: There is a limit of 12 people per group.

The Perdeberg Walk shares part of its route with the 2-day Highlands Trail (see above) and, like the latter, it begins and ends at the Highlands Forest Station. This is a fairly stiff trail, but the walking conditions are pleasant throughout the year. Walkers pass through well-managed montane fynbos where there are wild flowers in bloom in every season. A level access path from the parking area leads for 5 km to and from a 6-km circuit on the slopes of Perdeberg, whose highest point is 498 m.

Critical junctions on the walk are indicated by yellow and white footprint markers. On a clear day Kleinmond, Betty's Bay, False Bay and the Kogelberg are visible.

35. THREE SISTERS WALK
(KLEINMOND TRIPLETS)
KLEINMOND

Trail details: 8 km/3,5 hours; circular.

Permits/bookings: Must be obtained from the Kleinmond Municipality, tel. (02823) 4010; Private Bag X3, Kleinmond 7195.

Facilities/amenities: None.

Main attractions: Montane fynbos; mountain and sea views.

Pertinent information: No more than 12 people per day are allowed on this walk.

The highest part of this pleasant trail is situated in Kogelberg Nature Reserve. The path begins directly behind Kleinmond with a very steep ascent to the Three Sisters Ridge. From the beacon at 634 m, the path descends to join the trail from Fairy Glen to Perdeberg, passes through lush protea growth and circles back to town past two quarries, or down to Fairy Glen.

There are magnificent views along the coastline from Danger Point (past Hermanus) in the east to Cape Hangklip in the west, including the Palmiet River and its spectacular valley, and the Bot River vlei. The rich natural display of delicate blooms such as painted ladies and China flowers is another highlight of this walk, as are the easily spotted rock kestrels, orangebreasted sunbirds and klipspringer.

Restios or Cape reeds, such as this stand of Cannemois virgata, *are a feature of the fynbos vegetation at Nuweberg on the Boland Trail.*

36. BOLAND TRAIL
HOTTENTOTS HOLLAND NATURE RESERVE

Trail details: 1. Full Circuit: 41,5 km/3 days;
2. Landdroskop Route: 18 km/2 days;
3. Boesmanskloof Route: 30 km/2 days;
4. Jonkershoek Traverse: 27,5 km/2 days. All are circular except for the Jonkershoek Traverse, which is one way. (For day walks in this reserve see page 68; and for the Riviersonderend kloofing trip see page 68.)

Permits/bookings: Book in advance with the booking office, Hottentots Holland Nature Reserve at Nuweberg; tel. (0225) 4301, between 8.00 am and 4.30 pm (closed 1.00-2.00 pm); bookings are provisional until payment is made to: Cape Nature Conservation, Private Bag X27, Elgin 7180. Overnight trails can be booked 12 months in advance. Map is supplied with permit.

Facilities/amenities: There are 4 overnight huts on the trail, each with bunks and mattresses; no accommodation at the starting point.

Main attractions: Mountain scenery; wild flowers; natural pools for swimming; breathtaking views.

Pertinent information: Closed every year in July and August, the most severe winter months, to reduce the risk to hikers, and for hut and trail maintenance. The area is subject to sudden weather changes; in particularly bad conditions the Boland Trail is closed at short notice. At such times there will be a recorded message on (0225) 4301. There is a maximum of 12 people per permit for all sections. Be aware that offences such as illegal entry, departure from marked routes, littering and picking of wild flowers result in large spot fines.

'The Boland Hiking Trail, Hottentots Holland Section' as originally devised by the National Hiking Way Board has undergone a number of changes to keep pace with such considerations as the security, safety and convenience of hikers. No doubt the new-look Boland Trail that has evolved is not a static fixture, and will continue to change as the need arises. For the moment, however, this well-loved hiking system begins and ends at Nuweberg (where there is safe parking) in the Hottentots Holland Nature Reserve, 83 km from Cape Town and 11 km from Grabouw on the Villiersdorp road. Note that the access points on Sir Lowry's Pass and from the country club 2 km from Grabouw were closed in September 1991; Eikenhof is no longer in use as an overnight stop.

While the basis of the trail is a 'clover-leaf' system of loops beginning and ending at Nuweberg and allowing hikes of 2 or 3 days' duration, other permitted exit points are Eikenhof; through Jonkershoek State Forest; and at Jan Joubertsgat Bridge on the Franschhoek Pass.

The Hottentots Holland Nature Reserve comprises 26 000 ha of rugged terrain in the mountains of the same name, between Sir Lowry's and Franschhoek passes. It is crossed by narrow gorges, where the Steenbras, Palmiet and Riviersonderend rivers rise. The vegetation is primarily mountain fynbos, including many endemic species. Some of the floral rarities found include the endangered marsh rose *(Orothamnus zeyheri)* and blushing bride *(Serruria florida)*. Antelope such as klipspringer and grey rhebok and other smaller mammals inhabit the reserve, and it is thought that there are a few leopard left in the kloofs. The bird-

life along these walks is unexpectedly abundant for a mountain fynbos area, ranging from sunbirds and seedeaters, such as Cape buntings, siskins, neddickies, Victorin's warblers, grassbirds and greybacked and Levaillant's cisticolas, to ground woodpeckers, and raptors such as kestrels, harriers, black eagles and jackal buzzards.

The many people who venture onto the Boland Trail do so with varying motives. Some enjoy its

High adventure in Boesmanskloof.

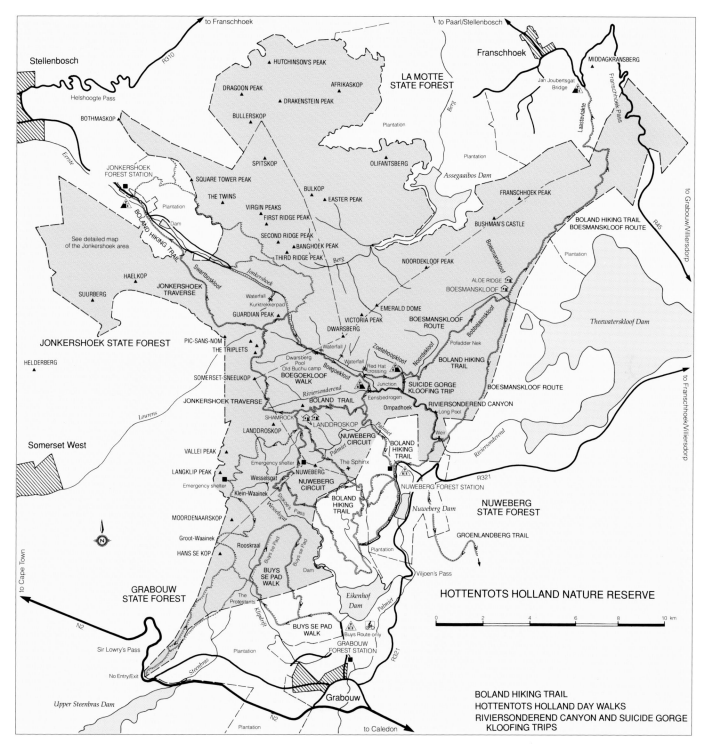

BOLAND HIKING TRAIL
HOTTENTOTS HOLLAND DAY WALKS
RIVIERSONDEREND CANYON AND SUICIDE GORGE
KLOOFING TRIPS

physical challenge; others appreciate the opportunity to walk in a botanic and wildlife reserve. Views into the indigenous forest-clad kloofs (such as Wesselsgat) and the views of the coast (such as False Bay from Pic Sans Nom) are superb. Being only an hour and a half's drive from Cape Town contributes to the trail's popularity, so if you seek peace and solitude, avoid this trail over holiday periods and weekends.

Field rangers patrol the reserve, checking that each hiker has a permit for the trail.

1. Full Circuit A 3-day hike with two overnight stops: from Nuweberg to Landdroskop, to Boesmanskloof, and back to Nuweberg. On the first night, after hiking 11,5 km, hikers sleep in the

Landdroskop hut or the Shamrock Lodge. Day 2 comprises a hike of 18 km to the overnight huts at Boesmanskloof and Aloe Ridge. The third day is a relatively easy walk back to Nuweberg, 12 km away.

2. Landdroskop Route This is the least strenuous of the four 2-day walks, although by no means easy. The first day of 11,5 km to Landdroskop is not too physically demanding. Hikers overnight at either Landdroskop or Shamrock Lodge. The second day, 7 km long, is particularly scenic, with diverse fynbos. By making a short detour left to the Riviersonderend River, hikers can lunch and relax at the wonderful Eensbedrogen swimming spot before returning to the start at Nuweberg. (Those who

have the energy can cross the river and explore part of Boegoekloof but must return the same way.)

3. Boesmanskloof Route The first day, 18 km long, is very strenuous, although there are swimming holes along the way to ease the pain! Hikers overnight at the Boesmanskloof or Aloe Ridge huts. The second day (12 km), which is much easier than Day 1, overlooks beautiful orchard-filled farmlands. A special feature of this route is the new footbridge over the swirling Riviersonderend River, 4 km from the end.

4. Jonkershoek Traverse, starting at the reserve and finishing at Jonkershoek, is open in April, May, June and September only. The first day is the same as that of the Landdroskop route. The second day

67

Fynbos and mountains feature strongly in this striking view of the Riviersonderend Valley.

(16 km) begins with a taxing 2-hour ascent, followed by a brief level respite, before the steep descent towards the end. Hikers must arrange to have transport waiting at Jonkershoek State Forest.

37. HOTTENTOTS HOLLAND DAY WALKS
HOTTENTOTS HOLLAND NATURE RESERVE

Trail details: 1. Boegoekloof: 17 km/7 hours, return; 2. Buys se Pad: 20 km/6 hours, circular; 3. Groenlandberg: 24 km/8 hours, return, and the Riviersonderend kloofing trip (see opposite). See also Boland Trail, p. 66.

Permits/bookings: Book (up to 2 months) in advance at the Hottentots Holland Nature Reserve, tel. (0225) 4301. Booking is provisional until payment is made. Simple map provided with permit. Permits/bookings for Buys se Pad Walk also available from Forestry Office, Worcester Street, Grabouw, tel. (024) 592606, during office hours only.

Facilities/amenities: Carpark, toilets and change room at Nuweberg.

Main attractions: Mountain scenery; wild flowers; natural pools for swimming; breathtaking views.

Pertinent information: There is a limit of 12 people per permit for all overnight and day trails. The weather is unpredictable; cloud, mist, strong gusty winds and rain can occur at any time of the year; hikers must always be prepared for extreme conditions. Boegoekloof is closed from May to end September, when the high river level blocks the route. During poor weather other trails may be closed at short notice. At such times there will be a recorded message on (0225) 4301. In summer water may be scarce. Illegal entry, departure from the marked routes, littering and picking of wild flowers are offences and can result in large spot fines.

To reach the Hottentots Holland Nature Reserve, which is 83 km from Cape Town, drive through Grabouw and turn left to Villiersdorp; continue for 11 km along the Viljoens Pass road, when you will

see the sign to the Hottentots Holland Nature Reserve. All the trails are clearly marked.

1. Boegoekloof Walk begins on the route of the Boesmanskloof trail. Hikers can choose how far they wish to walk. The first kilometre follows a jeep track beneath pines, then leads through fynbos, across the Palmiet River (no swimming allowed). From the ridge 1,5 km further on, the Dwarsberg and the Riviersonderend Valley are a lovely sight. Turn right, down the jeep track and into the valley of the Riviersonderend River, where you will find Eensbedrogen pool, a wonderful swimming spot. Having crossed the river, take the path straight up the valley – which crosses the river a few times – to the exquisite Dwarsberg pool. Return the same way.

2. Buys se Pad Walk The route starts at the forestry gate near the country club outside Grabouw.

The Franschhoek Mountains dwarf this hiker in the Hottentots Holland Nature Reserve.

It proceeds through the plantation and makes a clockwise loop in the Hottentots Holland Nature Reserve, past the ridge known as The Protestants, across a pleasant stream of the Klipdrift River, joins Buys se Pad, rounds two unnamed peaks, and returns to the start through pines. Wear hiking boots, as the going is stony underfoot.

3. Groenlandberg Trail offers breathtaking views over the Theewaterskloof Dam to the north and the verdant Elgin Valley to the south. Follow the jeep track over the Groenlandberg for a distance of 12 km (or more if you wish), returning the same way. As there are no significant streams along the route, carry ample water, especially in summer.

38. RIVIERSONDEREND CANYON AND SUICIDE GORGE KLOOFING TRIPS
HOTTENTOTS HOLLAND NATURE RESERVE

Trail details: 1. Riviersonderend Canyon: 17 km/8,5 hours; 2. Suicide Gorge: 18 km/9 hours. Both are circular.

Permits/bookings: Book (up to a month) in advance with Hottentots Holland Nature Reserve at Nuweberg; tel. (0225) 4301, between 8.00 am and 4.30 pm (closed 1.00-2.00 pm); bookings are provisional until payment is made to: Cape Nature Conservation, Private Bag X27, Elgin 7180. Map supplied with permit.

Facilities/amenities: Change rooms, toilets and carpark at the reserve.

Main attractions: Spectacular canyon scenery; jumps over waterfalls.

Pertinent information: Open only from November to the end of April because the river level is dangerously high in winter. There is a limit of 30 people per day (a minimum of 4 at all times, and a maximum of 6 per group over weekends and public holidays and 12 per group on weekdays). Each group **must** include someone who knows the route.

Any hiker who is afraid of heights, unfit or not a strong swimmer should not attempt this trip, as it entails jumping off high rockfaces into inky black pools and swimming. Take with you: lightweight hiking boots, a wetsuit, a change of clothes in a sealed plastic bag; valuables in sealed containers; basic first aid items, lunch and high energy snacks in sealed bags. Fires and braais are strictly forbidden because of the high risk of veld fires. Follow religiously the guidelines that are issued to you with your permit. Hikers must complete the full circuit and exit at Nuweberg: it is no longer permitted to leave a car on the tar road at Viljoens Pass, and escape routes should be used in emergencies only. Remember to sign the safety register at the start before setting out and again on your return.

There are many lovely rivers in the Cape, but few offer the opportunity for such action-packed adventure as a trip down the Riviersonderend. Overhangs and cave-like formations, compulsory leaps into long, dark rockpools as well as swims, all contribute to the challenge and popularity of this trip. Access to both the canyon and to Suicide Gorge is from the Hottentots Holland Nature Reserve at Nuweberg.

1. Riviersonderend Kloofing Trip Take to the Boesmanskloof Trail and, after 5 km, take a side trail to the right that leads to the Riviersonderend

Suicide Gorge near Nuweberg.

Canyon. Once in the canyon, which is in shade for most of the day, you have no choice but to follow the eccentricities of the river for the next 8 km and 5,5 hours. Clamshell Cavern is just a foretaste; several long swims lie ahead. At the 7-m high Big Jump I have seen some tough guys shiver in their wet tackies at the prospect of a jump into a very dark, round rock pool. Next stop is Junction Pool. You should try to reach this point by 12.00 pm, to allow you enough time to get to the finish by at least 5.00 pm.

Before leaping into a pool, make sure that the centre is free of obstructions and, after careful negotiation, jump!

Leave the river at the weir and head up the hill, following the signs and footprint markers back to the station at Nuweberg.

This is not an easy trip, and it should only be done in warm weather.

2. Suicide Gorge Only those who have graduated with honours from Riviersonderend Canyon should consider coming back to try this one. In fact, this alternative route is only for those who thrive on physical challenges.

From Nuweberg, proceed along the path towards Riviersonderend Canyon, but pass the turnoff to the kloof, and continue to the bridge named Red Hat Crossing, following the path for 2,5 km to the sign at Pootjiesglypoel. This is the start of the ominously named Suicide Kloof, which is a tributary of the Riviersonderend Canyon. (You will have walked 8 km from Nuweberg, which should have taken you about 2 hours, by the time you reach the start at Pootjiesglypoel.) Three daunting leaps (1,5 hours) lie in wait, but the climax of the trip is the notorious Highest Jump at 14 m. Beyond lies Junction Pool in Riviersonderend Canyon, which you should try to reach by 12.00 pm. The rest of the route down the kloof (3 hours) will probably seem tame to those who have made it thus far. This part and the return route are common to the Riviersonderend Kloofing Trip described earlier.

39. KLEINMOND COASTAL AND MOUNTAIN NATURE RESERVE
KLEINMOND

Trail details: Various walks, ranging from one hour to one day/14 km. These are circular and open-ended. See map p. 64.

Permits/bookings: Not required.

Maps/information: A comprehensive booklet *Where to Walk in Kleinmond* is available on request from the Kleinmond Nature Conservation Society, PO Box 2, Kleinmond 7195. Further information available from the Kleinmond Municipality, tel. (02823) 3030/4010; Private Bag X3, Kleinmond 7195.

Facilities/amenities: Picnic sites.

Main attractions: Coastal and mountain fynbos; views of the Kogelberg's sandstone cliffs; Palmiet River lagoon and Kleinriviersvlei; rocky tidal pools.

Pertinent information: Unpredictable weather; ticks are prevalent. A limit of 12 people per hiking group.

There are various walks in the Kleinmond Coastal and Mountain Nature Reserve, those along the rocky coast being fairly easy, and others, in the mountains, requiring a higher level of fitness. Baboon, klipspringer, grysbok and other smaller mammals can be seen throughout the area, along with a rich diversity of sea birds and waterfowl. There is also an abundance of reptiles: tortoises, snakes, and lizards. Sea mammals such as southern right and humpback whales are often sighted during winter. All walks are well marked.

40. KOMMISSIEKRAAL TRAIL
VILLIERSDORP WILD FLOWER GARDEN AND NATURE RESERVE, VILLIERSDORP

Trail details: 10 km/4 hours, circular, with plans for extensions. There are shorter paths through the wild flower garden.

Permits/bookings: Key is issued with permit at the control gate to the neighbouring caravan park. The reserve is open from 8.00 am (9.00 am at weekends) to 5.30 pm daily.

Maps/information: The curatrix: (0225) 31130 (am); (0225) 32244 (pm); PO Box 23, Villiersdorp 7170.

Facilities/amenities: Lecture/conference hall and herbarium; system of paths; 'summer houses' and benches. Accommodation is available in a caravan park and 7 chalets adjacent to the reserve.

Main attractions: Rich montane fynbos; Kommissiekraal River; lovely views over valley and Theewaterskloof Dam.

Pertinent information: An annual Wild Flower Show is held over the last weekend in September in the Botanical Society Hall adjacent to the garden.

Tortoises, hares, baboon and klipspringer are occasionally seen in this 536-ha reserve 1 km north-west of Villiersdorp. It is also home to at least five species of snakes, and 70 species of birds. However, the reserve's strong point is its wealth of fynbos species: it boasts 25 species of proteas, some of them rare, as well as ericas, watsonias, orchids and spring annuals. This abundance is explained in part by the fact that the reserve is the meeting place of several veld types: renoster and rûnsveld, mountain fynbos, mistbelt and snowline vegetation.

There are five open, thatched shelters distributed across the reserve, which provide welcome shade in the heat of the day, and benches where weary hikers can rest *en route*. The trail, which begins and ends in the botanical garden, and is walked in a clockwise direction, has recently been extended to include a loop on the upper slopes behind Blokkop, which, being the highest peak in the Aasvoëlberg range, is often snow-capped in winter.

The river halfway along the route flows year-round, but hikers should carry water in summer, when the streams are dry.

41. KLEIN HOUWHOEK PEAK TRAILS
HOUWHOEK INN, HOUWHOEK

Trail details: 1. Old Pass Trail: 4 km/2 hours; return. 2. Klein Houwhoek Peak Trail: 16 km/ 7 hours; return.

Permits/bookings: Must be obtained from Hottentots Holland Nature Reserve at Nuweberg, tel. (0225) 4301; Private Bag X27, Villiersdorp 7180. Bookings are provisional until payment is made to: Cape Nature Conservation, Private Bag X27, Elgin 7180.

Facilities/amenities: None.

Main attractions: Fynbos vegetation; impressive sea and mountain views.

Pertinent information: Groups are limited to 12 people each.

1. The Old Pass Trail leads from the Houwhoek Inn, down the old road to the Bot River.

2. The Klein Houwhoek Peak Trail begins at the Inn, and leads up the jeep track to the summit.

Both trails require a medium level of fitness, although in very hot weather more endurance may be required on the Peak Trail in particular. They are both clearly marked.

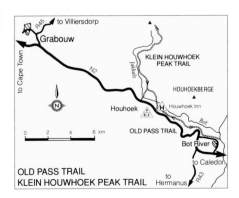

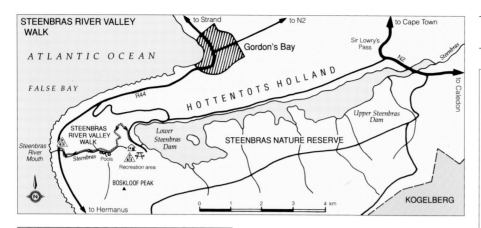

STEENBRAS RIVER VALLEY WALK

ATLANTIC OCEAN

FALSE BAY

to Strand   to N2   to Cape Town

Gordon's Bay

Sir Lowry's Pass

HOTTENTOTS HOLLAND

R44

Upper Steenbras Dam

Lower Steenbras Dam

STEENBRAS RIVER VALLEY WALK

Steenbras River Mouth

Steenbras Pools

Recreation area

BOSKLOOF PEAK

to Hermanus

STEENBRAS NATURE RESERVE

to Caledon

KOGELBERG

0 1 2 3 4 km

42. STEENBRAS NATURE RESERVE
GORDON'S BAY

Trail details: Steenbras River Valley Walk : 6,6 km/3 hours.

Permits/bookings: Applications for permits for the hike should be made 3 days in advance to the Parks and Forests Dept, Cape Town City Council, tel. (021) 4003269/4003823; 12th floor, Civic Centre, Cape Town. A brochure/map is available on request. Permits for the dam area, also chalet bookings: Booking office, Waterworks, tel. 4002507; 2nd floor, Civic Centre, Cape Town or purchasable at any of the following municipal offices during office hours: Stellenbosch, Parow, Somerset West, Strand, Gordon's Bay and Grabouw; swimming baths at Long Street, Cape Town, and Newlands.

Facilities/amenities: 14 chalets, sleeping from 4-6 people, at the Steenbras Dam recreation area.

Main attractions: Views of the Steenbras Valley; 3 natural rock pools; a variety of mountain fynbos.

Pertinent information: Hiking groups are limited to 12 people each. Be careful when climbing over wet boulders.

The catchment area of the Steenbras River, the mountains and pine plantations surrounding the Steenbras Dam, and the gorge through which the river runs down to the coast are all part of this 8 400-ha reserve. Access to the reserve area is strictly controlled by permit, and consequently remains peaceful and largely unspoilt.

The trail begins about 5 km east of Gordon's Bay, on the western side of the river mouth, opposite a tea garden, where you can park.

Admittedly, the first 500 m or so of the trail are through invasive alien trees, but these soon diminish and are replaced by indigenous riverine scrub, as the path winds down to the river, over a wooden bridge, and through a gate in a fence. The first rock pool is reached about 1 km further on; here the trail crosses the river and takes a course through mountain fynbos. A 10-minute walk brings you to a fork leading to the second rock pool, the largest of the three. The path to it should be negotiated with care. The small waterfall above this pool can also be reached on a side-path. The last pool is about 600 m further on, on a path just beyond a small overhang. A scramble up a steep rock face to the left of the path will reward you with a panoramic view over the Steenbras Valley, a highlight of the trail. The gravel road that leads to the dam about 1,2 km away is just across the stream.

The area around the dam and chalets is very popular – and populous – over weekends and other holidays. Picnicking is the chief pastime, and there are no set walks here.

43. CALEDON NATURE RESERVE AND WILD FLOWER GARDEN
CALEDON

Trail details: 10 km/3,5-4,5 hours; circular. There are other short rambles.

Permits/bookings: Must be obtained at the reserve gate.

Maps/information: Available on request from the authority in charge: Caledon Municipality, tel. (0281) 21090; PO Box 24, Caledon 7230.

Facilities/amenities: Water and toilets at the start; tearoom; camping facilities are available at the nearby hot mineral springs.

Main attractions: Rich indigenous fynbos vegetation; prolific birdlife; interesting rock formations.

Pertinent information: Hikers should carry their own water during the hike. Rare and threatened species of indigenous flora, as well as more common varieties, are propogated in the nursery. Plants and seeds are offered for sale.

The Caledon Nature Reserve and Wild Flower Garden, which comprises an area of 214 ha, lies against the Swartberg on the northern outskirts of Caledon. It features many species of indigenous trees and fynbos under cultivation, and the garden is a delight in spring, when a Wild Flower Show is held, as it has been every year since 1895.

The 10-km trail, which was founded in 1977, starts at the nursery, just beyond the tearoom, and ascends to the crest of the mountain, from where there are panoramic views of the surrounding areas.

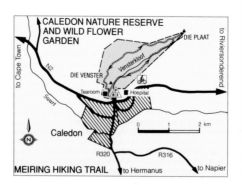

CALEDON NATURE RESERVE AND WILD FLOWER GARDEN

to Cape Town

DIE PLAAT

to Riviersonderend

Vensterkloof

DIE VENSTER

N2

Tearoom

Hospital

Stuart

Caledon

R320   R316

MEIRING HIKING TRAIL

to Hermanus   to Napier

0 1 2 km

44. FERNKLOOF NATURE RESERVE
HERMANUS

Trail details: There are 40 km of footpaths including a 4,5-km/90-minute, circular nature trail, and a 2-hour Red Route.

Permits/bookings: Must be obtained from the Hermanus Municipality, tel. (0283) 21122; PO Box 20, Hermanus 7200.

Facilities/amenities: Visitors' centre offering botanical displays and trail guide booklet; interpretive centre (botanical lectures, shows and displays); herbarium (open on Monday and Friday mornings only); guided trails for organized groups on request. There is one hut (which is being upgraded), with sleeping arrangements for 4 people, but if you wish to sleep over you will need to become a member of the Hermanus Botanical Society beforehand.

Main attractions: Coastal montane fynbos; 92 species of birds; views of Kleinrivier mountains, Hemel-en-Aarde Valley, lagoon, Walker Bay, and coastal towns.

Pertinent information: Do not deviate from the paths, which would cause soil erosion. No fires allowed; camp-stoves only. Take binoculars, especially in spring, so that you can study the whales off the coast. The Walker Bay path is in shadow in the morning.

Fernkloof Nature Reserve is dedicated to the preservation of unspoilt montane coastal fynbos. The 4,5 km nature trail starts and ends from the interpretive centre. The footpaths sprawl over 50 km, on gradients that vary from very slight to steep, requiring corresponding degrees of effort. Zigzag paths lead to the mountain peaks.

Situated in an open kloof in the western region of the Kleinrivier mountains above Hermanus, the reserve occupies 1 446 ha (and is due to expand),

Coastal fynbos in the Fernkloof Nature Reserve.

and spans an elevation from 63 m above sea level to 842 m on Aasvoëlkop, its highest point.

The views of the mountains, Hermanus and the sweep of Walker Bay are impressive. The lovely floral composition of the reserve attracts endemic bird species such as the orangebreasted sunbird, Cape sugarbird and rock thrush. Baboon, klipspringer and other mammals are present, but not readily seen.

The hut, which accommodates four (at a squeeze), is reached after a relatively strenuous 2-hour walk that follows a well-signposted route from the parking lot via Galpin's Kop. Fires are not allowed, so you must carry a camp-stove with you to the hut and, since no toilets are provided, you are expected to display proper outdoor toilet etiquette by burying all human waste.

45. VOGELGAT PRIVATE NATURE RESERVE
KLEINRIVIER MOUNTAINS

Trail details: A network of footpaths totalling approximately 30 km.

Permits/bookings: Must be obtained from Vogelgat Nature Reserve (Pty) Ltd, tel. (0283) 771411; PO Box 115, Voëlklip 7203.

Facilities/amenities: Three overnight huts, for use by permit holders only; access to the reserve's herbarium on request.

Main attractions: Rich montane fynbos; deep pools fed by perennial streams; superb mountain scenery; abundant birdlife; well-graded footpaths.

Pertinent information: Entry to the reserve is strictly limited to permit holders and their immediate families, and trespassers are prosecuted. Permits are issued at a considerable fee and there is a waiting list. Permit holders receive a map, details of nature walks, lists of plant and bird species to be seen in the reserve, and an annual newsletter. The reserve is prone to mists.

Dr Ion Williams, who purchased Vogelgat in 1969, deserves credit for turning it into one of the finest privately run ecosystem reserves in southern Africa. Spanning an elevation from just above sea level to 800 m, well-constructed footpaths lead through the reserve up to its highest points. Apart from the beauty of the kloofs, rock pools and mountain slopes, unsurpassed views can be enjoyed of Walker Bay, coastal towns and Kleinriviersvlei. The fynbos in this 602-ha reserve adjoining Fernkloof is lush, and constant vigilance has prevented invasive alien vegetation from gaining a hold.

About 700 species of plants, many of them rare, endangered or endemic to the area, have been found in the reserve so far. For this reason, Vogelgat was declared a National Heritage Site in 1985. The rich birdlife includes the black eagle.

One of the more unusual plants found in Vogelgat is the sundew-related *Roridula gorgonias*, more commonly known as vlieëbos. Once insects are trapped by this plant, a small beetle feeds among them without itself being caught.

Although not often seen, grysbok, klipspringer and rhebok live in these mountains, as do baboon, otter, snake-like whip lizards, frogs and toads.

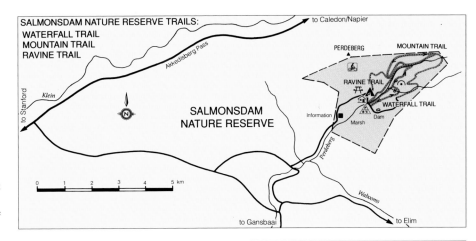

46. SALMONSDAM NATURE RESERVE
STANFORD

Trail details: 1. Mountain Trail: 8 km/3,5 hours; 2. Ravine Trail: 5 km/2,5 hours; 3. Waterfall Trail: 3 km/2 hours. All are circular.

Permits/bookings: Must be obtained from the Manager, Salmonsdam Nature Reserve, PO Box 1, Voëlklip 7203.

Further information: Cape Nature Conservation, Walker Bay: tel. (0238) 770062. A bird list is available on request.

Facilities/amenities: Three huts (two 4-bed and one 8-bed); caravan and camp site; ablution block; picnic and braai facilities provided.

Main attractions: Fynbos reserve with reintroduced mammals; attractive kloof with waterfall; 124 bird species; picturesque valley.

Pertinent information: Keep to the paths. Fires are allowed only in the designated fire-places. No swimming in rivers and dams.

Salmonsdam Nature Reserve is not well known and most people seem unaware of the lovely, gentle nature trails following paths and dirt roads radiating from the camping area along both sides of the Keeromskloof. The reserve, which lies 45 km east of Hermanus and covers an area of 846 ha, comprises an open valley surrounded by a semi-circle of mountains, and a vlei area.

1. Mountain Trail begins on an old jeep track and proceeds along the mountain ridge to the radio mast at the top, from which there is an excellent view of the Kleinrivier mountains and surrounding area. Hikers return via a deep ravine, first along the river and then along the bank, to rejoin the jeep track.

2. Ravine Trail leads through a river bed and then onto the side of the ravine. It traverses the ravine and leads into the indigenous forest alongside the river, before crossing the water. Hikers then travel past caves and interesting rock formations and ultimately join the outgoing trail at the camping area.

3. Waterfall Trail leads through dense bush before starting a steep climb to the top of a waterfall, then down the opposite bank. Hikers return to the camping area via an old jeep track. The waterfall is at its most impressive during winter.

On all these trails mammals such as grysbok, springbok, steenbok and klipspringer are often seen. More than 124 bird species have been recorded in the reserve, which is recommended for fynbos studies and bird-watching.

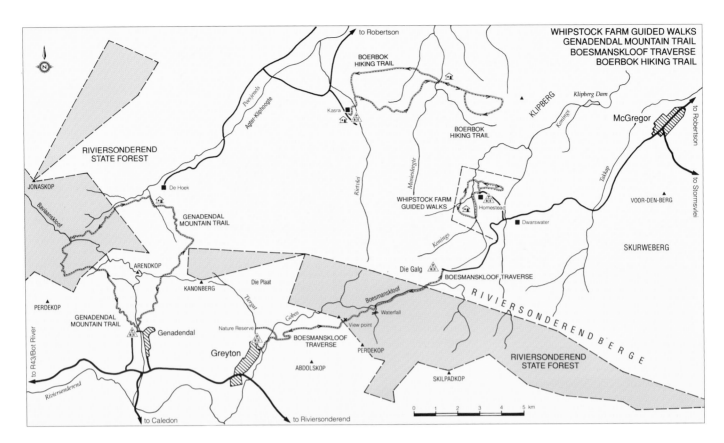

In 1737 the Rev. Georg Schmidt established a Moravian mission in the rugged Baviaanskloof, setting for the Genadendal Mountain Trail.

47. GENADENDAL MOUNTAIN TRAIL
GENADENDAL

Trail details: 25,3 km/2 days; circular.

Permits/bookings: It is essential to book with Vrolijkheid Nature Reserve office, tel. (02353) 621/671; Private Bag X614, Robertson 6705. A permit must be carried. Map and brochures in the process of being designed.

Facilities/amenities: Hikers can overnight at the private farm 'De Hoek'. Contact the owner on (02351) 2176 to enquire.

Main attractions: Swimming; fynbos; birds of prey.

Pertinent information: Rapidly changeable weather; the trail passes through private land in parts; there is no water for most of Day 2. There is a limit of 12 people per permit and 20 per day on this trail. No fires allowed except at overnight accommodation.

A high level of fitness is required for this new hike. Situated in the Riviersonderend mountains, the trail starts and ends at the historic Moravian Mission Church (built in 1738) in Genadendal, and traverses the Sonderend Conservation Area (a catchment area) as well as private land. Recommended periods are March to June and September to December, when hiking conditions are excellent. Klipspringer, duiker, grey rhebok, caracal and leopard inhabit the area, along with black eagles, sunbirds and sugarbirds. Hikers spend the first day walking 13,7 km up to De Hoek farm where they may overnight. The path crosses a stream several times, and hikers can look forward to cooling down in two natural swimming pools. The first 2 km of the second day's hike are fairly tough, but the rest of the trail is an easy stroll through lovely mountain fynbos back to the start.

48. BOESMANSKLOOF TRAVERSE
GREYTON-MCGREGOR

Trail details: Approximately 16 km/4 to 5 hours; one way. Some hikers walk there and back, making arrangements to overnight at either Greyton or McGregor.

Permits/bookings: Must be obtained from the Nature Conservator at the Vrolijkheid Nature Reserve office, which lies 15 km south of Robertson; tel. (02353) 621/671; Private Bag X614, Robertson 6705. Map and brochure are available on request.

Facilities/amenities: None, but there are overnight cottages at the end of the trail, equipped with fridge, stove and beds; tel. (02353) 735 for details.

Main attractions: Spectacular, rugged mountain scenery; Cape wild flowers; large rock pools and year-round waterfalls.

Once an old track, now upgraded to a fine hiking trail, this walk winds through the only gap in the rugged Riviersonderend mountain range. Now known as the Boesmanskloof Traverse, this route between McGregor and Greyton has become one of the most popular trails in the Western Cape. Highlights of the walk include views of the majestic Riviersonderend mountains, their steep gorges and the Greyton and McGregor valleys; the scenic Oak

After the demands of the Boesmanskloof Traverse, mountain pools offer refreshing relief.

Falls, comprising a series of waterfalls and pools; and the lovely mountain fynbos. Over 50 species have been recorded in these mountains, as well as the rare *Erica galgebergensis* and *Erica parvulisepala*. Water is abundant in large rock pools.

Physically the trail requires a reasonable degree of fitness, as there is a lot of 'up-and-downing' on the slopes of Boesmanskloof.

A delightful way to do the trail is to begin from 'Die Galg' outside McGregor (where there is now accommodation), walk to Greyton, stay the night at one of the many quaint guest houses, and return to McGregor the following day. Hikers should be aware that the trail at McGregor ends at a dirt road, 14 km from the town.

49. WHIPSTOCK FARM GUIDED WALKS
MCGREGOR

Trail details: Two guided walks, both approximately 10 km/5 hours; circular.

Permits/bookings: Must be obtained in advance from the owners of Whipstock Farm, tel. (02353) 733; PO Box 79, McGregor 6708. Brochure available on request.

Facilities/amenities: Holiday cottages on Whipstock Farm; converted barn for hikers.

Main attractions: Fabulous mountain views; fynbos; prolific birdlife; swimming in summer.

Pertinent information: Minimum group is 8 people.

Just a 2-hour drive from Cape Town, Whipstock Farm, situated 8 km outside McGregor, is the perfect country getaway. The guided Whipstock Walks take hikers through rugged kloofs in the Riviersonderend mountains, thick with greenery and tinkling pools. The views are spectacular, as is the birdlife and abundant fynbos. Lunch is provided

on both trails, and swimming in the mountain pools is popular in summer. The trails do not require a particularly high level of fitness, and are pleasant all year round.

50. BOERBOK HIKING TRAIL
ROBERTSON

Trail details: 15 km/1 day; circular. An optional loop from the halfway point extends the trail by about 3 km.

Permits/bookings: Must be obtained from Mr and Mrs A. Rabie, tel. (02351) 2165; 'Kasra', PO Box 559, Robertson 6705. Map and brochure available on request.

Facilities/amenities: Two huts – one at the start and another at the overnight stop – with bedding, gas stoves and lamps, cold running water, toilets, fridges, crockery and cutlery, fire-place. Each hut sleeps 10 people.

Main attractions: Prolific birdlife; tranquil, pastoral atmosphere.

Pertinent information: Hikers must carry their own water on the trail.

This pleasant walk through a fruit- and wine-producing area 28 km from Robertson is not particularly demanding and is perfectly suited to the beginner hiker. The trail can be covered in one day, or hikers can slow down a little and spend the night in the overnight hut.

The path leads through karoo veld and tranquil farmland, and walking conditions are pleasant throughout the year. In winter, bare fruit trees and vines present a stark and tranquil scene; the apricot blossom and abundance of flowering vygies are a delight in spring; and in summer there is the activity of the harvest. Two especially spectacular lookouts along the way provide views over the Breede River and Le Chasseur.

A reflective moment on the Rooikat Trail.

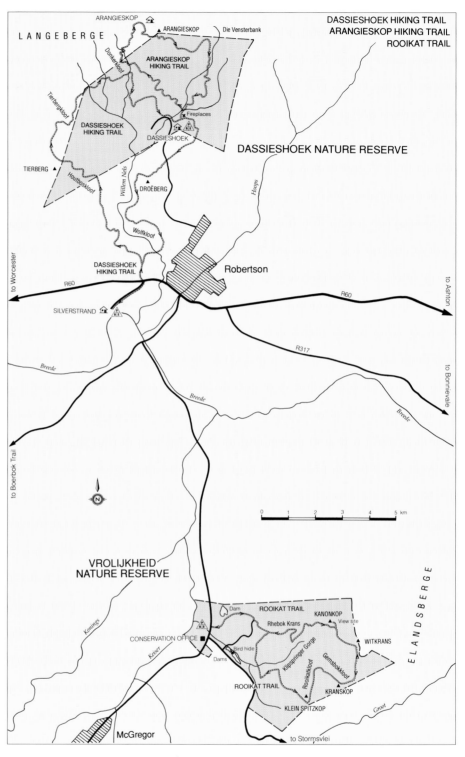

51. ROOIKAT TRAIL
VROLIJKHEID NATURE RESERVE
NEAR ROBERTSON

Trail details: 18 km/6 to 8 hours; circular.

Permits/bookings: Telephonic bookings are taken: tel. (02353) 621/671, and permits obtainable from the officer in charge at the conservation station, or from Private Bag X614, Robertson 6705. Map/brochure and species list available on request.

Facilities/amenities: A bird-watching hide at one of the dams; 11 km of roads.

Main attractions: Monumental rock wall; arid undulating veld; Bokkeveld shale geology.

Pertinent information: Ticks; rapidly changeable weather; very cold winters and high temperatures in summer. In fact, no hikes are allowed to begin after 9.00 am between November and March. There is no water on this trail, and hikers must carry their own drinking water. Sturdy hiking boots are essential. There is a limit of 12 people for this trail.

This fairly demanding trail starts and finishes at the Vrolijkheid Nature Conservation Station, 15 km from Robertson. A quagga breeding programme is being conducted at the conservation station, and visitors are welcome to view these animals.

July offers especially pleasant conditions for walking the Rooikat Trail, which is clearly marked, though fairly rough going underfoot. It traverses the reserve, winding through the Elandsberg in the process. The vegetation is described as arid Robertson karoo, although it is very different from that in the neighbouring Great Karoo. The reserve is home to the rare *Chasmanthe bicolor*, a lily-like plant with an orange flower. The terrain comprises hills covered with mountain renosterveld, low-lying flats of broken veld, with sweet-thorn along the seasonal watercourses. Erosion has created interesting rock formations, and the higher points offer views of the Robertson area.

About 40 mammal species, including klip-springer, grysbok, springbok, grey rhebok and ant bear, as well as 26 reptile species, including the rare Robertson dwarf chameleon, inhabit the reserve. Black eagle, fish eagle and jackal buzzard are common, and a variety of waterbirds can be observed from the bird-hide.

The curious Robertson chameleon.

52. DASSIESHOEK NATURE RESERVE TRAIL
ROBERTSON

Trail details: 38 km/2 days; circular.

Permits/bookings: Must be obtained from the Robertson Municipality, tel. (02351) 3112; PO Box 52, Robertson 6705. Map and brochure available on request.

Facilities/amenities: Hut sleeping 23, with bunks and mattresses, hot water, braai facilities and electricity; picnic areas in the reserve.

Main attractions: Prolific birdlife at the picnic site; tranquil atmosphere and waterfalls on the trail.

Pertinent information: Hikers must carry their own water on the first day. Take the necessary precautions against ticks. There is a limit of 35 people per day on this trail.

Located in the Dassieshoek Nature Reserve 6 km north of Robertson, this trail requires a medium to high level of fitness. Hiking is especially pleasant between March and May, and in spring: September and October.

Vegetation is mainly mountain renosterveld, with fynbos in the kloofs and on the Langeberg. Hikers may come across dassies, baboon and even leopard along the way. The first day leads for 23 km from Silwerstrand along the Langeberg to Dassieshoek overnight hut. The second day leads for 15 km along the Wilhelm Nels River gorge back to Silwerstrand.

53. ARANGIESKOP HIKING TRAIL
ROBERTSON

Trail details: Approximately 21 km/2 days; circular.

Permits/bookings: Must be obtained from the Robertson Municipality, tel. (02351) 3112; PO Box 52, Robertson 6705.

Facilities/amenities: Two overnight huts, one at the start and one in the mountains, each with 23 beds and mattresses, hot water, braai facilities and wood.

Main attractions: Fabulous view from the overnight hut; interesting rock formations.

Pertinent information: During winter this trail may be inaccessible, due to heavy rains and snow. There is a limit of 23 people per day on this trail.

This is the second trail situated in the Dassieshoek Nature Reserve 15 km north of Robertson. A fairly demanding route, which requires an above-average level of fitness, the Arangieskop Hiking Trail is especially pleasant between March and June, and in September and October.

The fynbos vegetation is rich in proteas, disas and nerines. Hikers may see dassies, baboon and even leopard, and there is an abundance of small birds, many of which are attracted to the picnic site.

The first day leads for 9,6 km up to the overnight hut via the beautiful Langeberg. From here you can look down on the Koo Valley and back to Dassieshoek. On the second day hikers walk via Arangieskop, the highest part of the Langeberg, and down to the start, a distance of 11,4 km. Swimming spots along the way add to the attraction of this trail, which is clearly marked.

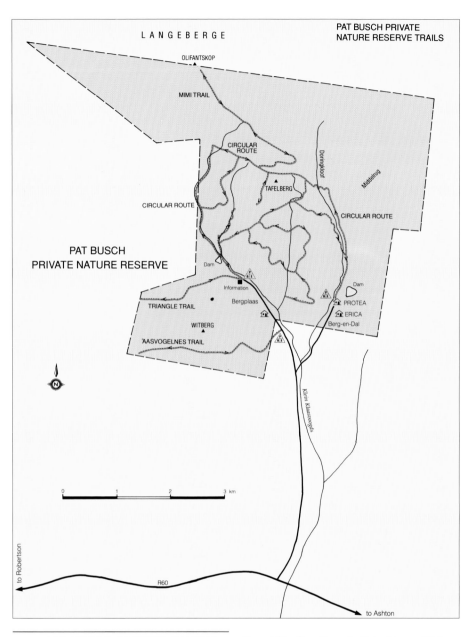

54. PAT BUSCH PRIVATE NATURE RESERVE
NEAR ROBERTSON

Trail details: Network of trails, totalling about 40 km. Circular Trail: 12 km/5 hours, with shorter and longer options.

Permits/bookings: Book with Mrs Busch, tel. (02351) 2033; PO Box 579, Robertson 6705.

Maps/information: Detailed map/brochure provided on request.

Facilities/amenities: Accommodation available in fully equipped, self-catering cottages.

Main attractions: Attractive scenery; birdlife; dams stocked with bass; wine-tasting; wooded streams and rock pools.

Pertinent information: Day hikers permitted only when nature reserve accommodation not booked to capacity.

Some 15 km from the pretty Boland town of Robertson in the foothills of the Langeberg lies this 2 000-ha nature reserve on the wine-producing farms Bergplaas and Berg-en-Dal. As these names suggest, the area is dominated by a series of hills, the highest being Tafelberg at 742 m. The trails comprise a series of interlinking loops in the kloofs between these hills, and along the banks of two streams which feature rock pools and waterfalls. A detour off the Circular Trail leads the energetic to the top of the Langeberg. Tafelberg can also be climbed.

Local vegetation varies from renosterveld to montane fynbos, displaying a variety of protea species and many ericas; lilies and ferns grow along the water courses.

The area is heavily patronized by birds such as the orangebreasted sunbird, Cape sugarbird and black and martial eagles. Indigenous game is being reintroduced and patient and vigilant hikers may see several types of small antelope, which include grysbok, grey rhebok, klipspringer and duiker. Leopard, the rare water mongoose, caracal and serval also occur.

Part of the historic town of Montagu is visible from this stretch of the Bloupunt Hiking Trail.

55. BLOUPUNT AND COGMAN'S KLOOF HIKING TRAILS
MONTAGU MOUNTAIN NATURE RESERVE

Trail details: 1. Bloupunt Hiking Trail: 15,6 km/ 6-9 hours; circular. 2. Cogman's Kloof Trail: 12,1 km/3-6 hours; circular. 3. Lover's Walk: 2,2 km/1 hour; one way.

Permits/bookings: Must be obtained from the Montagu Municipality, tel. (0234) 42471; Bath Street, PO Box 24, Montagu 6720. Map available on request.

Facilities/amenities: Accommodation is available in cabins: the Klipspringer cabins sleep 12 in total and the Dassie cabin sleeps 4. Showers, toilets and cooking facilities are provided. There is also a small camp site, the only place where camping is allowed in the reserve.

Main attractions: Narrow gorges formed by coastward-flowing streams; weird rock formations; wild flowers; waterfalls; caves.

Situated in the Montagu Mountain Nature Reserve, all these hikes begin from the Old Mill near the car-park at the top of Montagu's Tanner Street. The best months to book for these routes are March through to November. The mountains, a transitional zone between Cape fynbos and Karoo vegetation, are aglow with colour in October, the flowering season. Birdlife, baboon, klipspringer and dassies abound on the steep, cave-dotted mountain slopes.

1. Bloupunt Hiking Trail requires a reasonable level of fitness. From the Old Mill the path climbs Bloupunt via Rietkloof (the last water source for quite a while), before descending via Donkerkloof. The scenery varies from ravines through which run perennial mountain streams to craggy cliffs featuring awe-inspiring rock formations. Similarly, vegetation ranges from watsonias and orchids to ericas and vygies. Indigenous trees are plentiful and some are identified by nameplates. Klipspringer,

dassies and black eagle are common on this route. From the summit of Bloupunt at 1 000 m, hikers are treated to a breathtaking panoramic view; the towns of Montagu and Ashton can be seen, as well as Robertson, McGregor and Bonnievale in the distance. Small pools in Donkerkloof, passed on the descent, provide relief from the heat. Three small waterfalls can be reached via short detours from the main trail.

2. Cogman's Kloof Trail explores Droëkloof and Cogman's Kloof. Only the first 2 km are fairly strenuous, as the climb from the overnight hut is steep. From the top of the mountain, where there are fascinating rock formations and pretty wild flowers, there is a rewarding view of Montagu, ravines and mountains.

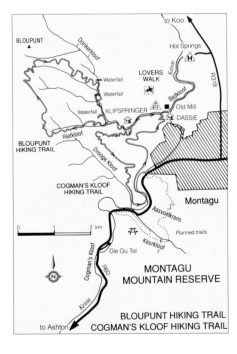

3. Lover's Walk provides a lovely short stroll, through Badkloof, to the hot mineral springs and hotel resort.

More trails, into Keurkloof and over Aasvoël-krans, are planned.

56. BREDASDORP MOUNTAIN RESERVE
BREDASDORP

Trail details: 20 km of nature trails.

Permits/bookings: Not required.

Facilities/amenities: Footpaths; resting shelters; ablution blocks.

Main attractions: Wild flower garden containing, among other flowering plants endemic to this area, the Bredasdorp lily; views from Bredasdorp to the Indian Ocean; coastal renosterveld and fynbos.

Pertinent information: Hikers should carry their own water.

This reserve covers 800 ha and extends up a low hill which overlooks Bredasdorp to the north-east. Examples of coastal bush and montane fynbos are protected in an 86-ha cultivated area within the Bredasdorp Mountain Reserve.

The trails are clearly marked and require a medium level of fitness. Hikers may spot monkeys or one of the three species of mongoose that inhabit the reserve. At dusk listen for the 'screaming' call of the tree hyrax, a relative of the dassie, which has nocturnal and arboreal habits.

Snowy dunes in the De Hoop Nature Reserve.

57. DE HOOP NATURE RESERVE
NEAR BREDASDORP

Trail details: At the Potberg end: 1. Potberg Trail: 10 km/4 hours, circular; 2. Klipspringer Trail: 5 km/2 hours, circular. At De Hoop end: 3. Vlei Trail: 10 km/4 hours, circular; shorter loops available. A 5-day Whale Trail is still in the planning stages.

Permits/bookings: Entry permits may be purchased at the gate. Education centres and accommodation must be reserved in advance with The Manager, Cape Nature Conservation, tel. (02922) 782; Private Bag X16, Bredasdorp 7280.

Facilities/amenities: Environmental education centre accommodating 60 students at Potberg; 7 cottages: 6 accommodate 4 people in each and the seventh accommodates 10 people; camp sites.

Main attractions: De Hoop Vlei with its excellent birdlife; Potberg, with eroded limestone cliff formations and treed kloofs; coastal environment (rich intertidal life; high dunes); southern right whales; the restored farm buildings, which are a national monument; interpretive centre; boardwalk.

Pertinent information: Hikers must carry their own water; boots should be worn at all times for protection against poisonous snakes. Carry binoculars. No fishing or collecting is allowed along the coastline, which is part of the reserve.

De Hoop, which lies 50 km east of Bredasdorp and covers 40 000 ha (excluding the marine reserve), embraces widely varying terrains: a large fresh-water vlei; 13 km of sandy and rocky coastline with diverse intertidal pools and shifting sand dunes reaching 90 m in height; unspoilt strandveld; calcareous ridges and kloofs. These varying habitats support a wealth of wildlife including bontebok, Cape mountain zebra, eland, grey duiker, steenbok, baboon, blackbacked jackal, marsh mongoose, mice, snakes (especially puff adder, cobra and skaapsteker), angulate tortoises, mountain agamas, scorpions, and large dung beetles. The birdlife is spectacular: there are over 200 species in the reserve, including masses of waterbirds and ostriches, as well as 25 pairs of Cape vultures, representing the last breeding colony of these birds in the Cape. The intertidal community is also very diverse and the beachcomber or snorkeller is likely to encounter octopuses, sea urchins, sea anemones, rock-pool fishes, snails and whelks, to name but a few of the more common life forms. Southern right whales breach offshore for six months of the year in far greater numbers than anywhere else along the southern African coast (including Hermanus!); dolphins, too, are sometimes seen close inshore.

The self-guided nature trails (maps available at the gate), all physically undemanding, are located in each major ecosystem in the reserve. To reach the Potberg end of the reserve, you must drive 26 km and park in the area provided.
1. Potberg Trail ascends the mountain of the same name, from the top of which there is a magnificent view of the Breede River.
2. Klipspringer Trail takes you to a small cave and offers the chance to see a rare Cape vulture.
3. Vlei Trail As its name suggest, this trail runs alongside De Hoop Vlei – in fact for its full length, returning inland along a roughly parallel path. Two loops provide short cuts.

One of the delights along the De Hoop Nature Reserve coastline is this impressive arch.

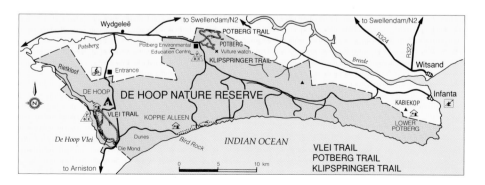

The six-day Swellendam Hiking Trail traverses the slopes of the Langeberg.

58. SWELLENDAM HIKING TRAIL
MARLOTH NATURE RESERVE

Trail details: 74 km/6 days (shorter variations are possible); circular. There are also day hikes in the reserve, varying from 1-5 hours in duration.

Permits/bookings: Must be obtained from The Manager, Marloth Nature Reserve, tel. (0291) 41410; PO Box 28, Swellendam 6740. Climbers must apply to the manager of the reserve for permits to ascend peaks which do not form part of the hiking trail. Map available on request.

Facilities/amenities: Six overnight huts with bunks, mattresses and lanterns; firewood at two huts only (Koloniesbos and Wolfkloof); safe parking at the forest station; picnic site at Hermitage.

Main attractions: Mountain scenery and fynbos; ravines with indigenous forest.

Pertinent information: The trail should be avoided in rain, strong winds and mist, and by those afraid of heights.

Located in and around the Marloth Nature Reserve (which lies 2 km north of Swellendam), this hiking trail is often said to be one of the most beautiful in the Cape. It was the first National Hiking Way System trail to follow a 360° route, thereby returning hikers to the starting point on the final day of the trail. There are numerous shorter routes if six days of hiking is too long for you and, as an inevitable result, the trail has become very popular on weekends and public holidays.

Kruispad, near Proteavallei Hut, and the Vensterbank route provide short cuts over the mountain, thereby eliminating the western section. These options provide impressive views but are recommended only to shorten your hike.

On each day of the trail, stretches of shadeless fynbos alternate with cool, indigenous forest in the kloofs. The southern and northern Langeberg slopes offer far-reaching views of the Swellendam Valley, including the Bontebok National Park and the Robertson Valley respectively. Other sec-

tions provide the sensation of being in a peaceful and secluded wilderness.

The trail demands a medium to high level of fitness; the third day's walk is particularly strenuous.

Middelrivierberg, Leeurivierberg, Misty Point (1 710 m), Twelve o'clock, One o'clock and Ten o'clock peaks, as well as others, are encircled by the trail and are popular with mountaineers. Misty Point is a particularly treacherous ascent because, as its name indicates, it often becomes rapidly shrouded in mist.

There are numerous paths into some of the densely forested kloofs such as Wolfkloof, Duiwelsbos, Koloniesbos and Wamakersbos. These paths also make fascinating day excursions, especially in hot, sunny summer weather.

59. BUSHBUCK HIKING TRAIL
GROOTVADERSBOSCH NATURE RESERVE, NEAR HEIDELBERG

Trail details: The Bushbuck Hiking Trail is 10 km/ 6 hours in length and circular, but there are other, shorter options.

Permits/bookings: Are necessary to hike the Bushbuck Trail, and can be obtained from the officer on duty at Grootvadersbosch Nature Reserve, tel. (02692) 1812. Map and brochure available on request.

Facilities/amenities: An interpretation centre provides visitors with information about the area.

Main attractions: Beautiful forest scenery; 35 indigenous trees present.

Pertinent information: Hiking groups of more than 12 people are permitted only by prior arrangement. Berg wind conditions occur during May to July. Beware of tree-felling and timber-hauling operations in the pine plantation on weekdays.

The Grootvadersbosch Nature Reserve contains the largest remnant of indigenous forest in the Langeberg. It lies in the foothills of the range, between Swellendam and Heidelberg, and adjoins the Boosmansbos Wilderness Area (see opposite). The northern boundary of the forest runs along the Worcester fault.

The Bushbuck Hiking Trail provides an easy hike through tangled and lush vegetation known as Knysna high forest. Ironwood is one of many typ-

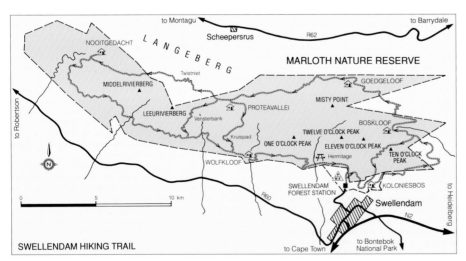

SWELLENDAM HIKING TRAIL

A frosty welcome in Grootvadersbosch.

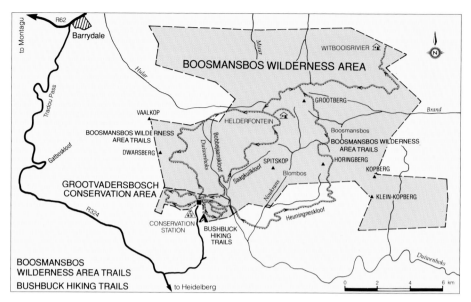

BOOSMANSBOS WILDERNESS AREA TRAILS
BUSHBUCK HIKING TRAILS

ical forest trees present. A variety of shorter routes provides other easy options.

A paradise for bird lovers, this 250-ha area is the westernmost point of distribution of a variety of bird species; some 180 species are known to occur in this area. Bushbuck, grysbok, baboon and leopard are also present, and a sub-species of ghost frog occurs exclusively in the Grootvadersbosch indigenous forest.

Adjacent to Grootvadersbosch forest is a 200-ha pine plantation, established around the turn of the century in an attempt to cover the areas earlier denuded by woodcutters; it includes a hectare of rather lovely Californian redwoods.

60. BOOSMANSBOS WILDERNESS AREA
NORTH OF HEIDELBERG

Trail details: 70 km of footpaths and gravel roads.

Permits/bookings: Must be obtained from the Manager, Boosmansbos Wilderness Area, tel. (02962) 1812; PO Box 109, Heidelberg 6760.

Facilities/amenities: The overnight huts are simple shelters with no facilities except for water from a nearby stream. Alternatively, hikers may sleep in the open. There is also accommodation available on a neighbouring farm.

Main attractions: Indigenous kloof forest; Cape fynbos in dramatic mountain terrain.

Pertinent information: The maximum allowable size of a hiking group is 12 and the minimum 2. Boosmansbos borders on the winter and all-year rainfall areas.

Approximately 267 km east of Cape Town, between Swellendam and Heidelberg in the Langeberg range, exists a large (14 200 ha), rugged forest reserve that is not very well known to the general public.

Boosmansbos Wilderness Area is an excellent place for hikers to clamber up peaks with far-reaching views, explore one of the larger remaining indigenous Cape forest patches in the fynbos ecological zone (it has never been exploited on a large scale), and enjoy the many flowering species which blanket the mountain slopes.

Hikers can walk to Helderfontein hut, an old stone 'management' hut, ascending via Bobbejaanskloof (14 km), and can descend via Saagkuilkloof (13 km) *en route*. For a longer and more fascinating alternative to the Saagkuilkloof path described, try the Grootberg-Horingberg path, probably one of the most scenically dramatic in the Cape folded mountains. Approximately 30 km long, it ascends from Helderfontein hut on the north-facing slope of Grootberg, whose highest point is at 1 637 m, traverses the mountains in a southerly direction, affording views of rich kloof forests below, and descends the south-facing slope of Horingberg in a series of zigzags. Not often used, the path is indistinct and steep in places. Hikers should be prepared to sleep in the open.

The actual forest of Boosmansbos is one of the larger relics of indigenous kloof forest within Cape montane fynbos. Located on the slopes of Grootberg, it contains impressive specimens of stinkwood, yellowwood, Cape holly, white alder

(witels), red alder (rooiels), beech and candlewood. A patch of mountain cypress (one of the few indigenous softwoods in South Africa) grows on an adjoining ridge. The descent into the deep ravines is steep but worthwhile. Once under the forest canopy, you are enveloped by a completely different atmosphere to that on the fynbos-covered slopes. The forests are dark, cool and moist, providing ideal cover for bushbuck. Two uncommon birds recently recorded here are the Knysna woodpecker and the martial eagle.

On the slopes of the reserve, proteas abound and *Leucadendron pubibracteolatum* occurs in the vleis. Baboon and dassies are frequently seen, and keen observers may also spot grey rhebok, klipspringer and grysbok. This is the habitat of birds such as the Cape bulbul, doublecollared sunbird and redwinged starling.

The existing footpaths and tracks were originally constructed for patrol purposes; be prepared to leave the main routes and walk in the veld to reach some of the interesting peaks, forests and kloofs.

61. KLAPPERBOS TRAIL
LADISMITH-KLEIN KAROO NATURE RESERVE

Trail details: 12,6 km/5 hours; circular.

Permits/bookings: Permit/booking required, must be obtained from the Municipality of Ladismith, tel. (02942) 20. PO Box 30, Ladismith 6885.

Facilities/amenities: None.

Main attractions: Views; Karoo spekboom.

Pertinent information: Hikers must carry their own water. It is advisable to get an early start in summer, so as to avoid the fierce midday heat.

The 2 800-ha Ladismith-Klein Karoo Nature Reserve is situated south-west of Ladismith on the road to Barrydale. This trail, with its stunning views of the apricot and peach orchards in the valley below Elandsberg, starts and ends near the

Cape folded mountains form a conspicuous spine through the Boosmansbos Wilderness Area.

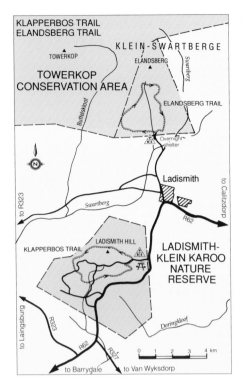

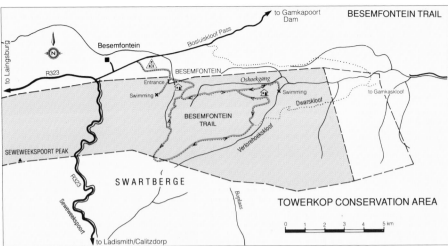

picnic site below the reservoir in the reserve. Hikers can spot herds of eland, springbok and steenbok. The vegetation in the nature reserve is typical succulent mountain scrub of the arid Klein Karoo region with a scattering of low bushes including guarri, karee, taaibos and Karoo num-num. Klapperbos, *Nymania capensis,* after which the trail is named, is a drought-resistant shrub with decorative, inflated rose-pink seedpods which are borne in great profusion in spring. Its common name is Chinese lantern.

The hilly terrain requires a medium level of fitness, and is climatically pleasant all year round, although in summer it can be very hot. This area has a very low annual rainfall.

62. ELANDSBERG TRAIL
TOWERKOP NATURE RESERVE, NEAR LADISMITH

Trail details: 12,2 km/5 to 7 hours; circular.

Permits/bookings: Must be obtained at the entrance of the Towerkop Nature Reserve. Map and brochure available on request.

Facilities/amenities: Base camp at start/end point; overnight shelter.

Main attractions: Karoo scenery; high krantzes.

Pertinent information: Hikers should carry their own water and take along warm clothes, as the mountain becomes very misty quickly, with the appropriate drop in temperature.

Situated 3 km north of Ladismith, but still within the Towerkop Nature Reserve, this trail requires a high level of fitness; it is very steep in parts. October, November, April and May are the best months for hiking. The trail follows the firebreak at the foot of the mountain for the first 1,5 km before it starts to ascend. The highest point of the trail is 1 430 m above sea level. The peak of Elandsberg is

2 126 m. The difference between the top and bottom of the trail is 792 m, which makes it a stiff climb. The trail is clearly marked.

63. BESEMFONTEIN TRAILS
TOWERKOP NATURE RESERVE, NEAR LADISMITH

Trail details: 1. Klipkraal Trail: 22,5 km/2 days; circular. 2. Verlorenhoek Trail: 15,6 km; return route. 3. Longer option: 29,6 km/2 days; circular (combining both trails).

Permits/bookings: Must be obtained from Cape Nature Conservation, tel. (028) 5511077; 9 Nissen Street, Ladismith 6885. Map and brochure available on request.

Facilities/amenities: Base camp at start/end point; overnight shelter.

Main attractions: Panoramic views of the Karoo; high krantzes; deep pools; Bushman paintings.

Pertinent information: Hikers should carry their own water; the weather is extreme. There is a limit of 10 people for the trail.

Mimetes cucullatus flourishes in the Langeberg.

Situated in the Towerkop Nature Reserve, 49 km north-west of Ladismith, this trail should not be undertaken by the unfit. Spring and autumn are especially good times for hiking, and swimming in the deep pools is very pleasant.

1. The first day of the **Klipkraal Trail** is a steep, strenuous hike to the summit of the Klein Swartberg range, where hikers overnight in the shelter. From here there are spectacular views into the Karoo and Gamkaskloof.

2. The shorter **Verlorenhoek Trail** follows some of the Klipkraal Trail for a time, then leads on to a beautiful pool situated at the bottom of a series of waterfalls.

3. Both these trails can be combined into one longer hike, the first day covering 19,4 km to the overnight shelter. Day 2 route passes the Verlorenhoek pools before returning to the base camp. The trail is clearly marked along the way.

64. SLEEPING BEAUTY HIKING TRAIL
RIVERSDALE

Trail details: 13 km/4 hours; return.

Permits/bookings: Must be obtained from the Riversdale Municipality, tel. (02933) 32418; PO Box 29, Riversdale 6770.

Maps/further information: To ascertain weather conditions on the trail, consult the officer in charge, Garcia Forest, tel. (02933) 32558.

Facilities/amenities: None.

Main attractions: Magnificent views over the Langeberg; beautiful fynbos.

Pertinent information: Watch out for the aggressive bees in the yellowwood forest. This area is subject to strong berg winds from mid-May to August. Do not climb Sleeping Beauty Peak if there is any danger of mist.

The Sleeping Beauty Hiking Trail, a walk which features many streams *en route,* currently runs from the Toll House on Garcia Pass some 8 km north of Riversdale to the crest of Sleeping Beauty in the Langeberg and back.

Hikers should fill their waterbottles in the yellowwood forest at the top of the first kloof, while keeping a lookout for bees. From here a long, steep, zigzag path leads to the nek behind Sleeping Beauty. The final 1,5 km to the summit at 1 200 m

The slopes of Sleeping Beauty rise from Garcia Pass.

is a stiff climb, which is rewarded with one of the loveliest views that the Langeberg has to offer.

Birdlife is concentrated around the streams and in the indigenous forests of the area, which include such tree species as rooiels, boekenhout, yellowwood, hard pear, ironwood, candlewood and keurboom. Two pairs of black eagles inhabit the area. The mountain slopes are home to three rare erica species; flowering ericas are responsible for the pink appearance of the mountain from late winter into early summer. Animal life includes dassies, baboon, grysbok and klipspringer. Grey rhebok are limited to the foothills, and there is evidence of one or two leopard in the kloofs.

The Sleeping beauty Hiking Trail can be combined with the newer Rooiwaterspruit Trail (see opposite) for a longer hike ending at the Koerentevette River Dam.

65. KRISTALKLOOF HIKING TRAIL
RIVERSDALE

Trail details: 20,9 km/2 days; one way.

Permits/bookings: Must be obtained from the Riversdale Municipality, tel. (02933) 32418; PO Box 29, Riversdale 6770.

Maps/further information: To ascertain weather conditions on the trail, consult the officer in charge, Garcia Forest, tel. (02933) 32558.

Facilities/amenities: Overnight hut sleeping 8 people; camping spot for small tents.

Main attractions: Wide variety of fynbos species, as well as bulbs, orchids, tree and mountain ferns.

Pertinent information: Leave a car at the end of the trail, or allow time to walk the extra 4,5 km back along the pass to the start. Take full camping gear, and carry water from the halfway mark at Kruisrivierkloof, particularly in summer. This area is subject to strong berg winds from mid-May through August.

Although a fit hiker could complete this hike in about nine hours, this would not be a particularly pleasant way to do it, especially during the winter

months. Besides, it would not allow time to enjoy the amazing diversity of the fynbos along the way.

The first day takes hikers from the Garcia Pass (part of the road which links Riversdale and Ladismith) in Kristalkloof to the overnight camping spot. Situated next to the upper Kruis River, it is within reach of some lovely swimming pools. Two tiny leucospermums endemic to Riversdale, *Leucospermum mundii* and *L. winterii*, occur in Kristalkloof and the Kruis River kloof respectively.

The trail passes briefly through plantation in the northern end of the Garcia State Forest. The forest, which lies on a plateau between the Kruis and Meul rivers, is not developed for visitors.

On the southern face of Kampscheberg the path crosses four mountain streams where graceful ferns, including treeferns, grow. The trail returns to the pass, for the most part along a contour, at a point about 4,5 km from the start.

From September to November a variety of bulbs and ground orchids are in flower along the route. Dassies and baboon are continually seen and heard. Grysbok and klipspringer occur throughout the area, and may be spotted. Grey rhebok keep to the foothills, and the odd leopard inhabits the kloofs.

66. ROOIWATERSPRUIT TRAIL
RIVERSDALE

Trail details: 13 km/5 hours, with a longer option via Oom Boet se Pad; circular.

Permits/bookings: Required from the Riversdale Municipality, tel. (02933) 32418; PO Box 29, Riversdale.

Facilities/amenities: Overnight hut with mattresses. stove and firewood.

Main attractions: Great variety of fynbos, including some rare species; magnificent views.

Pertinent information: Be alert to changes in the weather. Strong berg winds are common from May until August. Watch out for snakes.

This new trail starts at the parking area by the Korentevette River Dam. The route leads between the plantation and the dam then continues in a north-westerly direction for some 9 km to the overnight hut. Follow the path up to the beautiful Stinkhoutbos. From this point, you can either head south to join up with your original path or continue along Oom Boet se Pad for an additional 6,5 km stretch before turning around and heading back to the dam.

As a third option, from Oom Boet se Pad you could keep going for another 5 km, past Sleeping Beauty and through Geelhoutbos, to Garcia Pass (The Sleeping Beauty Hiking Trail – described on opposite page – in reverse), where you would need to have transport waiting.

This area has a wide variety of fynbos. There are few exotic species and these are kept well under control. Erica is particularly prolific here and 3 rare species can be found in this region – *Erica inclusa*, *E. blenna* and *E. papyracea*. Their pink blooms can be seen from late winter through to early summer. Indigenous trees are found mainly in the ravines and include Cape beech, ironwood, yellowwood and keurboom.

Birdlife is concentrated around the forests and close to the mountain streams. A great variety of sugarbirds can be observed in this area.

Klipspringer and grey rhebok are among the animals making their homes here. Rock hyrax and baboon are often heard while leopard, although present in small numbers, are very seldom seen.

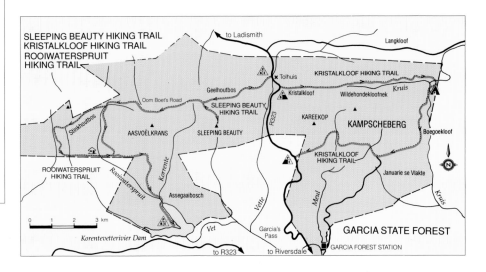

THE SOUTHERN CAPE

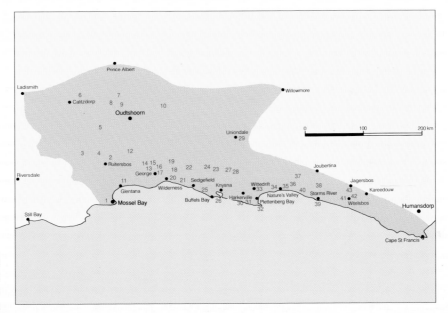

Bounded in the west by the Gamka and Gouritz rivers and by the Langkloof, the southern Cape borders the dry Great Karoo in the east. The mountains are cut by dramatic passes and contain several long-distance hiking trails as well as many shorter day walks and nature trails, as does the exceptionally beautiful coastline. The southern Cape's beaches are famous, and the many broad sweeps of sand provide opportunities for walking. Before setting off check the tides as headlands can cut off the beaches for several hours at high tides.

The coastal temperate forests of the southern Cape owe their existence to the Outeniqua/Tsitsikamma range of mountains and the southern Cape's year-round rainfall. The southernmost of three parallel ranges of Cape fold mountains, this range forms a barrier to humid air moving in off the sea. Rain clouds pushed inland by the prevailing southerly winds precipitate mainly on the south-facing slopes.

In general, forests are classified according to canopy height, species, ground cover and undergrowth, in addition to other technical characteristics. Each type is adapted to its respective moisture regime: Hikers on steep northern and north-western slopes will encounter 'dry' forest, where the trees have a scrub-like appearance. Much of the forest growing next to the sea is also dry, and thorny bushes such as the numnum, *Carissa bispinosa,* are common. The 'high forests' of the coastal plateau and foothills contain many species such as stinkwood, Outeniqua yellowwood, real yellowwood, white pear, candlewood and ironwood, and, where conditions are right, a dense undergrowth of witchhazel. In deep, perennially damp kloofs and gorges, 'wet' forest predominates. Trees such as red and white alder, stinkwood, tree-fuchsia and Cape holly reach heights of about 15 m, above a dense undergrowth of ferns.

Although the southern Cape's rainfall is all year round, varying from 700 to 800 mm per year at the coast, to 1 100 to 1 300 mm in the Outeniquas, to as little as 400 mm on the inland mountain ranges and 200 mm in the Little Karoo, the highest falls occur from September to April. There is an appreciable drop in temperature with increasing altitude from the coast to the coastal mountain peaks. The average daily minimum temperature along the coast in July is 7,4°C, the average daily maximum, 24,5°C in January. Inland temperatures are far more extreme. At the foot of Gamka mountain in the Little Karoo, frost is frequent in winter and temperatures of 35°C and above, common in summer. A special warning to hikers is necessary about the Swartberg mountains; night temperatures high up in winter are well below freezing point, and day temperatures are high in summer. The weather is also extremely changeable. Be warned and be prepared!

Snow falls sporadically on the mountains between June and August. Occasionally, a hot, dry berg wind blows in winter, severely increasing the fire hazard.

LEFT: *Brooding black rocks are distinctive of the coastline of the Tsitsikamma National Park.*

Traversing a rocky shoreline, the St Blaize Trail heads for distant Pinnacle Point.

The green Outeniqua foothills of Ruitersbos.

1. ST BLAIZE TRAIL
MOSSEL BAY

Trail details: 13,5 km/5 hours; one way.

Permits/bookings: Not required.

Maps/information: Map and brochure available from the Mossel Bay Municipality and Publicity Association, tel. (0444) 912215; 101 Marsh Street, Mossel Bay. There are interesting brochures of environmental and historical information available at a nominal cost from the Publicity Bureau at the Bartolomeu Dias Museum.

Facilities/amenities: None.

Main attractions: Rugged coastal scenery; caves; rock formations; interesting plant life.

Pertinent information: Do not walk this trail in strong winds; if you visit the caves or coastal rocks beware of high waves; there are some steep falls away from the path in places. Arrange transport from Dana Bay back to Mossel Bay.

The scruffy condition of the St Blaize cave at the start of the trail is a poor introduction to this interesting walk along the rugged and rocky coast between Mossel Bay and Dana Bay. If you follow the white trail marker of a bird in flight you will discover 13,5 km of wonderfully scenic coastline with a fascinating variety of plant life – a patchwork of dune fynbos and strandveld – on the rock formations and the stabilized dunes.

If you wish to leave the trail early, you can get off just before Pinnacle Point. Otherwise, walk on until you see the houses of Dana Bay alongside the path and up through them to the road.

2. RUITERSBOS FOREST AND PROTEA HILL WALKS
ROBINSON PASS

Trail details: 1. Ruitersbos Forest Walk: 10,3 km/ 4 hours, circular; 2. Protea Hill Walk: 5 km/2 hours, circular; other shorter walks available.

Permits/bookings: Permits for the Ruitersbos Forest Walk must be obtained from Ruitersbos Forest Station, tel. (0444) 952788, or from the management of the Eight Bells Mountain Inn, tel. (0444) 951544. There is a rough map printed on the permit. Permits for the Protea Hill Walk from the Inn only.

Facilities/amenities: The Eight Bells Mountain Inn owns the land adjoining the forest and is a convenient place to stay while walking in the area; trees on the Ruitersbos Forest Walk are labelled with their national tree list numbers.

Main attractions: Indigenous forest along the Perdeberg River; a profusion of ferns; proteas.

Pertinent information: The path can be very muddy after rain; after heavy rain the height of the Perdeberg River may make the most attractive stage of the walk impassable.

1. The Ruitersbos Forest Walk comprises two connected loops. The outward leg of the first loop which leads in natural forest along the course of the Perdeberg River is particularly beautiful. The return leg of this first loop goes through a pine plantation and can be avoided by returning via the Perdeberg River to the start. The second loop affords a glimpse of the fynbos on the mountain slopes behind; it returns along a small stream.

2. The walk up aptly named **Protea Hill** begins at Eight Bells Mountain Inn. From the summit there is a panoramic view of the coast and mountains of the southern Cape. Descend the same way or steeply via a pine forest where buck shelter.

Various shorter walks explore the farmland surrounding the Inn.

3. ATTAQUASKLOOF HIKING TRAIL
ROBINSON PASS

Trail details: 36 km/3 days (plus 3 km/30 minutes to walk back down the pass to the start); the second day's 10-km circuit is optional.

Permits/bookings: Must be obtained from Cape Nature Conservation, tel. (0441) 742671/747934; Outeniqua Nature Reserve (Witfontein Forest), Oudtshoorn Road, George. Map available on request.

Facilities/amenities: Overnight hut with 12 bunks.

Main attractions: Beautiful fynbos in a pristine state; spectacular mountain scenery; the historic Attaquaskloof Pass.

Pertinent information: Parts of the trail are strenuous; cloud descends rapidly on the mountains.

The Attaquaskloof Hiking Trail was established in 1991. On the first day the route of 14 km/8 hours takes the hiker from the southern side of the Robinson Pass westwards to the overnight hut. The second day's circular route of 10 km is optional. The last day's walk leads along part of the historic

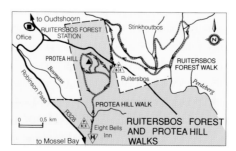

Attaquaskloof Pass before swinging away from the pass on the southern slopes of the Skurweberg to the top of the Robinson Pass.

Attaquaskloof was a route once used by elephant to cross the Outeniquas from the coastal plains to the Little Karoo. It was well known to the Khoi-Khoi herdsmen who also used it. In fact, it was the Khoi-Khoi who guided the first crossing of the Outeniquas by the early Dutch settlers, an exploratory expedition led by Ensign Isaac Schrijver in 1689.

The magnificent fynbos along this clearly marked trail harbours many beautiful and unusual plants such as the local variant of the Riversdale bluebell and a black orchid.

In the future hikers may be able to walk this trail in conjunction with the Doringrivier Wilderness Trail (planned but not yet completed), with which it will link up.

At the end of the trail hikers have to walk approximately 3 km (30 minutes) over the Robinson Pass back to their cars.

A wealth of flowering fynbos clothes the rolling slopes of Koumashoek valley.

---

4. KOUMASHOEK CIRCUIT
ROBINSON PASS

Trail details: 14,7 km/6 hours (plus 3 km/ 30 minutes to walk back down the pass to the start); circular if the pass is included.

Permits/bookings: Self-issue permit must be obtained at the start of the circuit. A rough map is also available.

Facilities/amenities: None.

Main attractions: Magnificient mountain scenery and fynbos.

Pertinent information: This trail is very strenuous and must not be undertaken by the unfit; hikers must carry their own water; mist sometimes occurs without warning.

This spectacular circular walk uses a recently cut path to link the first part of the outward leg and last part of the return leg of the new Attaquaskloof Hiking Trail (see previous entry). To keep on the correct path follow the klipspringer-motif trail markers. The Kouma River, which you cross early on in the walk, is the last source of water before a long, stiff climb; fill your water bottles here. If you have left a car at the top of the pass where the trail meets the road (3 km from the starting point), you can drive back; otherwise, walk back down the pass.

5. GAMKA MOUNTAIN NATURE RESERVE
GAMKABERG

Trail details: Pied Barbet Trail: 4 km/1,5- hour circuit; Tierkloof Trail: 15 km/5,5 hours; return.

Permits/bookings: Booking required if overnighting in the reserve, obtained from The Officer-in-charge, Gamka Mountain Nature Reserve, tel. (04437) 33367; Private Bag X21, Oudtshoorn 6620; day walkers obtain a self-issue permit at the start. Rough map of the Pied Barbet Trail available at the start, but there is no map of the Tierkloof Trail.

Facilities/amenities: Information centre; guided trails; water supply at cave in Tierkloof and overnight accommodation is planned; bush camp.

Main attractions: Prolific birdlife; arid vegetation; spectacular rock formations.

Pertinent information: Hikers must carry their own water; the trails are very hot in summer; hikers overnighting in the cave will need camping gear.

The Gamkaberg is part of a broken range of mountains which lies between the Outeniqua and the Swartberg ranges. Gamkaberg is arid; the plateau area on top of the mountain receives an average of 400 mm of rainfall per year, while just over half of this is normal at the foot of the mountain where the short walks occur and the longer trail begins. (The turnoff to the reserve leaves the old Warmbad road 25 km west of Oudtshoorn.)

Four arid veld types occur in the reserve. Succulent karoo vegetation just penetrates the reserve's northern boundary. Dry mountain fynbos occurs in the higher areas, spekboom veld on the lower northern shale slopes and renosterveld on the moister shale slopes. The fynbos contains several rare and

Aloe comptonii thrive in the stern, rocky landscape of the Tierkloof Trail.

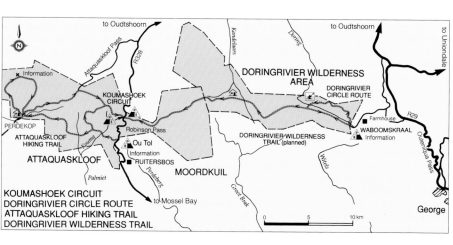

KOUMASHOEK CIRCUIT
DORINGRIVIER CIRCLE ROUTE
ATTAQUASKLOOF HIKING TRAIL
DORINGRIVIER WILDERNESS TRAIL

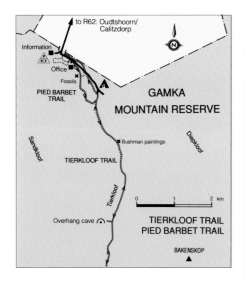

At a height of 1 585 m the summit of the Swartberg Pass offers panoramic views.

localized species; the most spectacular of these is the recently discovered golden mimetes *(Mimetes chrysanthus)*, a member of the protea family.

There is a wealth of birdlife in the reserve, mainly concentrated at the foot of the mountain and in the kloofs. The Cape mountain zebra, eland and grey rhebok keep mostly to the plateau region and these animals are seldom seen by hikers. Grysbok, steenbok and klipspringer are commonly seen, as are baboons.

Several short walks start at the information centre. The longest of these, the circular **Pied Barbet Trail**, leads through spekboom veld to the start of Tierkloof and back through *Acacia karroo* along the dry riverbed. The **Tierkloof Trail** leads up one of the deeply incised kloofs of Gamkaberg with spectacular rocky sides. Some primitive facilities are planned at the overhang cave in Tierkloof, so hikers can overnight here and explore further up the kloof. More sophisticated overnight accommodation – the bush camp – has been established at the entrance to Tierkloof.

6. GROENFONTEIN FARM
CALITZDORP

Trail details: Aloe Route: 20 km /6 hours, circular; Klaasrivier Route: 12 km/4 hours, circular; Lucifer se Kop Route: 19 km/5 hours, circular.

Permits/bookings: Must be obtained from the owner, Mr E. Potgieter, tel. (04437) 762; PO Box 30, Calitzdorp 6660.

Facilities/amenities: The owner can provide accommodation at the Groenfontein Victorian farmstead, or at an old farmstead nearby.

Main attractions: Aloe Route: aloes flowering in winter, mountain views; Klaasrivier Route: succulent karoo and renosterveld vegetation, mountain scenery; Lucifer se Kop Route: strange rock formations of the Rooikoppe.

Pertinent information: Extremely hot in summer; hikers must carry their own water.

The farm Groenfontein lies 20 km north of Calitzdorp on the Matjiesrivier road which joins up with the southern end of the Swartberg Pass. This is a scenically beautiful area with views of ravines, mountain peaks and, on the floor of the Little Karoo, the strange chocolate-coloured hills of the

Rooikoppe. The plant cover varies from succulent karoo vegetation in the valley to renosterveld and arid fynbos on the slopes. There is a network of paths on the farm which includes the three trails mentioned above. These may eventually link up with the planned Nature Conservation trail in Die Hel, which lies over the mountains.

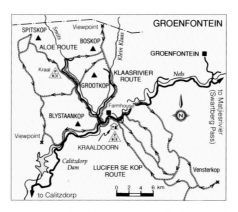

7. SWARTBERG HIKING TRAIL
SWARTBERG PASS/CANGO CAVES/ DE HOEK/SCHOLTZKLOOF

Trail details: 60 km/5 days, one way; many shorter variations of this route are possible.

Permits/bookings: Must be obtained from Cape Nature Conservation, tel.(0443) 291829/291739; Private Bag X658, Oudtshoorn 6620. Map with information available on request.

Facilities/amenities: Overnight huts at Gouekrans, Bothashoek and Ou Tol, each with 30 bunks, outdoor toilets, showers, braai facilities and wood.

Main attractions: Magnificent mountain scenery; pristine mountain fynbos; spectacular rock formations; birds and animals.

Pertinent information: Hikers must carry their own water between huts; temperatures on the mountain are extreme; the weather is very changeable; be prepared for cloud, rain and even snow any time of the year. There is a limit of 30 people for the trail.

The Swartberg Hiking Trail consists of a web of interlinking loops east of the Swartberg Pass with entry and exit points at the Cango Caves, De Hoek, the top of the Swartberg Pass and the north side of the pass, together with a route up Scholtzkloof to the top of the pass.

A large number of 1 to 5-day routes can be selected. Hikers should plan their route beforehand, using the Hiking Trail map. A special warning to prospective hikers on the Swartberg: you must be prepared and properly equipped for rapid and extreme changes in the weather.

The trail, a spectacular, twisted and contorted mass of Table Mountain sandstone, was opened to the hiking public in 1987. Lying mostly between 2 000 and 3 000 m above sea level, it traverses rocks that are 250 million years old, formed during the Cretaceous Period. Since then nature's forces – rain, wind and earth movements – have sculpted these once flat-lying sediments into a landscape not easily rivalled by those on other trails.

The impressive diversity and richness of the varied fynbos and Karoo flora on these slopes are equally magnificent. The soil is poor in nutrients and also shallow, and the slopes themselves are steep. Yet proteas, leucadendrons, ericas, watsonias, gladioli, disas, *Haemanthus* species and many lesser known, rare plants abound.

The animal life is also interesting. Colourful lizards delight the trailist, while 11 species of snake keep you alert for these sunbathers on rocks and paths. The rarer birds include the booted eagle, martial eagle, Cape eagle owl, Victorin's warbler and protea seedeater. Sunbirds and sugarbirds, rock jumpers and black eagles are often spotted. Mammals most likely to be seen by hikers include the dassie, klipspringer and baboon, although leopard, otters, jackal, aardvark, kudu, steenbok, grysbok and grey rhebok are also present.

A new trail in Gamkaskloof (Die Hel), west of the Swartberg Pass, will be opened in 1993; consult the Oudtshoorn office of Cape Nature Conservation for details.

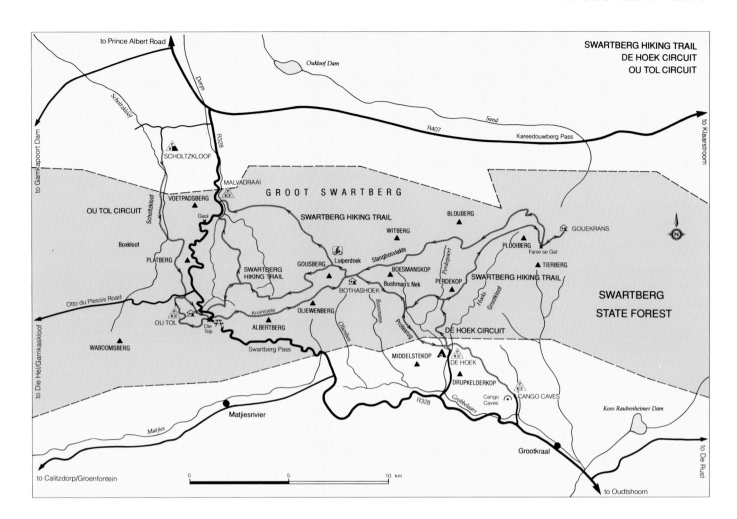

8. OU TOL CIRCUIT
SWARTBERG PASS

Trail details: 8 km/4 hours; circular.

Permits/bookings: Must be obtained from Cape Nature Conservation, tel. (0443) 291829/291739; Private Bag X658, Oudtshoorn 6620.

Facilities/amenities: None; Ou Tol hut in emergencies only.

Main attractions: Unrivalled views of Swartberg, Little and Great Karoo; high alpine vegetation.

Pertinent information: Rapidly changeable weather; cloud, rain and even snow are possible at any time of the year; hikers must carry warm clothing and their own water.

This recently cut, circular route leads high up the summit ridge of the Groot Swartberg from the top of the Swartberg Pass, then drops down the northern slopes to meet the road to Die Hel (Gamkaskloof) next to the arboretum – an old planting of pine tree species to test their adaptability. The views north to the Great Karoo, south to the Little Karoo and the Outeniquas, and east and west along this mighty range of mountains are unparalleled. The prostrate vegetation is characteristic of the high peaks, and sprawls amongst rocks for protection from the harsh climate. Look out for Cape rockjumpers which are regularly seen on the top of the pass. Another fynbos endemic, the Cape siskin, is common higher up.

The road to Die Hel winds along the scrub-covered Swartberg slopes.

9. DE HOEK CIRCUIT
DE HOEK, NEAR THE CANGO CAVES

Trail details: 12 km/6 hours; circular. The trail can be extended by starting from the Cango Caves. See map page 87.

Permits/bookings: Permits must be obtained at the gate to the De Hoek camp.

Maps/information: Swartberg Hiking Trail map available on request from Cape Nature Conservation, tel. (0443) 291829/291739; Private Bag X658, Oudtshoorn 6620. There are orientation maps on boards *en route*.

Facilities/amenities: The walk starts at the privately owned De Hoek camp where there are chalets, a camp site and swimming pools.

Main attractions: Spectacular rugged mountain scenery; rock pools for swimming; fynbos.

Pertinent information: Changeable weather with extremes; hikers must carry their own water.

The serene setting for the new Doringrivier trails.

This circular route is a short but strenuous introduction to the delights of the Swartberg Hiking Trail of which it forms a part. The outgoing and ingoing legs are in fact the first part of the route from De Hoek to the Gouekrans and Bothashoek huts respectively. The scenery of the Swartberg range's high peaks, the Little Karoo and the Perdepoort River kloof is magnificent.

As hikers climb from the renosterveld above the river at the start, the trail traverses first arid then moist fynbos typical of the southern slopes of this range. The most prominent plants are proteas and leucadendrons and, in the damper places, enormously tall restios.

10. MONS RUBER WALK
MONS RUBER WINERY, NEAR DE RUST

Trail details: 2,5 km/1 to 2 hours; circular.

Permits/bookings: A permit must be obtained from Mons Ruber Winery, tel. (04439) 6812.

Facilities/amenities: Toilets and water available at the winery during the week.

Main attractions: Spectacular rock formations; spring flowers.

Pertinent information: Hikers must carry their own water; very hot summers.

Situated near the Mons Ruber Winery 7 km west of De Rust, on the R29 east of Oudtshoorn, this short walk is not too taxing, apart from one short, steep

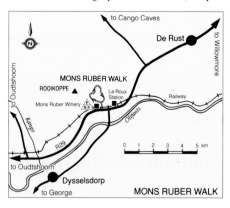

section. It starts 300 m along the main road west of the entrance to the winery. The Rooikoppe, a striking group of low hills with orange-coloured cliffs some 10 km west of De Rust (not to be confused with the Rooikoppe to the west of Oudtshoorn) have been declared a National Heritage Site. In 1992 the walk was laid out by Cape Nature Conservation officials to allow visitors to explore these strange rock formations. In spring, if the rains have been adequate, the wild flowers are abundant and extremely beautiful.

11. STEVE H. LANDMAN TRAIL
GLENTANA

Trail/details: 4 km/1,5 hours; circular.

Permits/bookings: Not required.

Facilities/amenities: None.

Main attractions: Coastal bush; coastal views.

Pertinent information: Hikers should carry insect repellent and drinking water.

Glentana is reached via a turnoff from the N2 roughly halfway between Herold's Bay and Little Brak River. This short, privately owned trail winds through coastal bush up the course of a small stream on the south side of a stabilized dune. Below is Glentana Beach on which hikers can also walk eastward to the wreck of a floating dock and beyond to Cape Windlass. (See map below.)

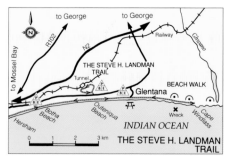

Hikers must check the tides if they choose to walk on the beach, as at high tide the headland is cut off.

12. DORINGRIVIER WILDERNESS AREA
WABOOMSKRAAL/ROBINSON PASS

Trail details: Doringrivier Circle Route: 14 km/6 hours; a 26-km/2-day Doringrivier Wilderness Trail is currently under construction. See map page 85.

Permits/bookings: Must be obtained from Cape Nature Conservation, tel. (0441) 742671/747934; Outeniqua Nature Reserve (Witfontein Forest), Oudtshoorn Road, George. A map is available on request.

Facilities/amenities: None.

Main attractions: Beautiful and unique fynbos; mountain scenery; Doring River with rock pools.

Pertinent information: No fires are allowed in the wilderness area; overnight hikers should take their own camping stores.

The Doringrivier Wilderness Area is a recently proclaimed area on the slopes of the Outeniqua mountains stretching from Waboomskraal on the northern side of the Outeniqua Pass westwards to the Robinson Pass. The Doringrivier Circle Route has just been completed, starting at Waboomskraal. A new 2-day trail, with a rustic shelter, which will link this walk with the Attaquaskloof Hiking Trail (see page 84) is under construction.

The fynbos in this area is particularly rich. Recently, two new species of the protea family, one *Leucadendron olens,* the other a pincushion *(Leucospermum hamatum)* have been discovered here. If you are a fynbos fundi, you may spot no fewer than seven different *Leucadendron* species in the space of a few kilometres along the river. Look out for sunbirds and sugarbirds, and for grysbok. There are several rock pools along the Doring River, which make the area an ideal destination in summer when you can swim to cool down after your walk.

13. CRADOCK PASS TRAIL
GEORGE

Trail details: 12,4 km/5 hours; one way.

Permits/bookings: Self-issue permit (with a rough map) at the start of the trail.

Facilities/amenities: None.

Main attractions: Magnificent scenery; extensive views of mountains and passes behind George; montane fynbos.

Pertinent information: Arrange to have transport waiting at the top of Montagu Pass; carry water.

The first part of this strenuous hike leads from the entrance to the old Witfontein forest station through pine plantations on forestry tracks. Soon the Tierkop Trail leads off to the right. Follow the yellow ox-wagon markers and the clear signposts. Once you have crossed Tierkloof (the last place where there is reliable water) and are on the old Cradock Pass (follow the telephone line at first) keep to the series of large stone cairns demarcating the pass. High up on the slopes of Cradockberg you cross the railway line between George and Oudtshoorn.

The final climb up Cradock Kloof to the nek which marks the top of the pass is a sustained, steep and, in wet weather, slippery one, but the increasingly grand views of the mountains more than make up for this. The trail ends near the top of Montagu Pass and if you do not have transport waiting, you will have to walk the 11 km (3 hours) down the pass to the start.

14. PASS-TO-PASS TRAIL
GEORGE

Trail details: 7,3 km (including a 2,6-km detour to Losberg)/3 hours; one way.

Permits/bookings: Self-issue permit, with a rough map, obtained at the start of the trail.

Facilities/amenities: None.

Main attractions: Mountain scenery; rich fynbos; views of George.

Pertinent information: Parts of the trail are steep, and slippery when wet. Arrange transport from the end of the trail.

This newly laid-out trail links the Montagu and Outeniqua passes, and can be walked either way. You may wish to turn around and walk back when you reach the end of the trail, but if you do not you must have transport waiting at the end. The trail begins near the disused quarry at the top of Montagu Pass. Halfway along the trail, which climbs up and down the southern slopes of the Outeniquas, there is an optional detour to the top of Losberg. As its name implies, this koppie stands apart from the main range and provides a unique vantage point to view the town of George below. The trail is particularly lovely in winter, spring and early summer, when many of the fynbos species are in flower. The route is clearly marked. Amongst the birds to be seen and heard on the trail is Victorin's warbler, a secretive fynbos endemic in streamside vegetation.

15. CRADOCK AND GEORGE PEAKS TRAIL
GEORGE

Trail details: Cradock Peak: 19 km/8 hours; George Peak: 17 km/7 hours; both peaks: 21 km/9 hours.

Permits/bookings: Self-issue permit (with a rough map) obtained at the start of the trail.

Facilities/amenities: None.

Main attractions: Spectacular scenery; montane fynbos; beautiful views.

Pertinent information: This is an extremely strenuous trail and should not be undertaken by the unfit; warm, windproof clothing is essential; hikers should carry their own water.

The first part of this trail follows the same route as the Cradock Pass Trail and takes about an hour, passing through pine plantations. Watch out for the signpost directing you to Cradock and George peaks. Once you reach the slopes of George Peak below the railway line, you must be prepared for a stiff and strenuous climb for most of the way. (If you grow too tired or the weather closes in at any point, turn back.) During this second leg of the walk, look out for *Mimetes splendidus*, the only silver mimetes species on the Langeberg/Outeniqua range. Hikers must not approach these plants as their delicate surface roots are easily damaged.

From this point the route follows the top of the ridge in a series of steep climbs. When you reach

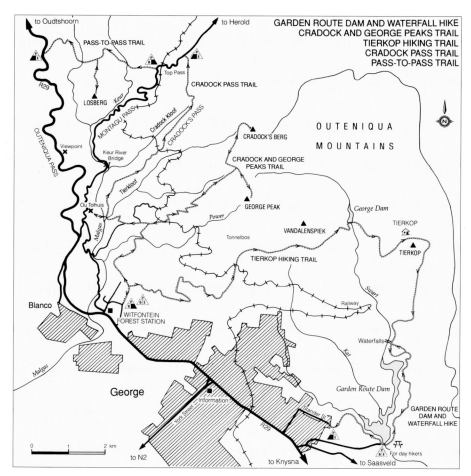

Montagu and Outeniqua passes link the coastal plain to the Little Karoo.

Atop Cradock Peak; the Outeniqua Pass scars the distant slopes.

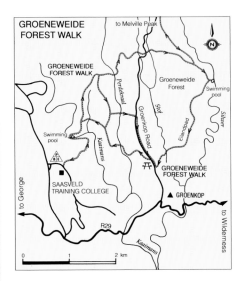

GROENEWEIDE
FOREST WALK

to Melville Peak

N

GROENEWEIDE
FOREST WALK

Groeneweide
Forest

Swimming
pool

Swimming
pool

SAASVELD
TRAINING COLLEGE

GROENEWEIDE
FOREST WALK

GROENKOP

to George

R29

to Wilderness

0   1   2 km

18. GROENEWEIDE FOREST WALK
SAASVELD, NEAR GEORGE

Trail details: 15 km/5,5 hours; circular. Short cuts provide shorter routes of 11 km/4 hours and 7 km/2,5 hours.

Permits/bookings: Self-issue permit obtained at the start of the walk.

Maps/information: Map and brochure available from the Department of Water Affairs and Forestry, tel. (0445) 23037; Demar Centre, Main Road, Knysna.

Facilities/amenities: None.

Main attractions: Indigenous moist and wet forest; natural swimming pools; abundant forest birdlife. Trees labelled with their national tree list numbers.

Pertinent information: The walk can be muddy in wet weather; keep to the path.

The Groeneweide Forest lies just north of the Saasveld Training College (hikers can park their cars here) on the foothills of the Outeniquas. Several rivers – the Kaaimans, Stof and Silwer – and many streams run through the forest. On the Kaaimans and Silwer rivers are two beautiful swimming places. The forest is a favoured habitat of the Knysna lourie, olive woodpecker and many other forest birds.

19. MELVILLE PEAK TRAIL
SAASVELD, NEAR GEORGE

Trail details: 25 km/9 hours; return. See map p.92.

Permits/bookings: Self-issue permit (with a rough map) obtained at the start.

Facilities/amenities: None.

Main attractions: Indigenous forest; montane fynbos; spectacular mountain scenery. Trees labelled with their national tree list numbers.

Pertinent information: Rapidly changeable weather; hikers must carry their own water; strenuous hike not for the unfit.

At 1300 m, Melville Peak is one of the higher peaks in the Outeniquas behind George. Hikers must be prepared for a long and arduous hike. The

the nek at which a signpost marks the point where the paths to George Peak and Cradock Peak diverge (about 3 hours from the start), walk a few steps over the rise to take in the breathtaking vista eastwards, along the Outeniqua mountains and the coast.

From the nek it is an easy 1-km/20-minute walk to George Peak, but it is a more strenuous climb, with a bit of easy rock scrambling, to Cradock Peak (about 1 hour). Retrace the route to the start.

16. TIERKOP HIKING TRAIL
GEORGE

Trail details: 30 km/2 days; one way. See map p.89.

Permits/bookings: Must be obtained from Cape Nature Conservation, tel. (0441) 742671/747934; Outeniqua Nature Reserve (Witfontein forest), Oudtshoorn Road, George. A map is available on request.

Facilities/amenities: Overnight hut with sleeping facilities for 12.

Main attractions: Views of the Outeniquas and the coast; fynbos; waterfalls and pools.

Pertinent information: Rapidly changeable weather; parts of the second day's route can be muddy and slippery when wet. Make arrangements for transport at the end of the hike.

The first leg of this trail was the first day's route of the old Outeniqua Trail (see page 92). The second leg leaves the Tierkop hut and swings down the slope to follow, more or less, the course of the Swart River to the Garden Route Dam.

The first day's route of 17,5 km leads through the pine plantations of the Witfontein State Forest (to reach the entrance to the old forest station, take the Oudtshoorn road, which leads off CJ Langenhoven Road). The path then starts up through the fynbos and natural forest into and out of the kloof surrounding the George Dam. The first day is a strenuous hike; the second day is easy. This trail can be tackled in reverse, starting from the George Dam, but the ascent to Tierkop hut is a tiring one.

17. GARDEN ROUTE DAM AND WATERFALL HIKE
GEORGE

Trail details: 11 km/4 hours; return. See map p.89.

Permits/bookings: Make enquiries with Department of Water Affairs and Forestry regional office, tel. (0445) 23037; Demar Centre, Main Road, Knysna 6570.

Facilities/amenities: Picnic site at the dam.

Main attractions: Waterfalls and pools; wet mountain fynbos.

Pertinent information: The path can be muddy and slippery when wet.

For a long time a favourite with the residents of George and the vicinity, the hike starts at the Garden Route Dam and leads through some beautiful fynbos to the waterfall at Pepsi pools on the Swart River, where hikers can enjoy a swim before returning along the same path to the start.

The route is shared with hikers on the final leg of the 2-day Tierkop Hiking Trail.

first part of the trail leads through the Groeneweide Forest, the remainder leads through fynbos which, at first, is badly infested with pines. The views of the Outeniqua mountains from the peak are quite superb. To get to the start, hikers must return along the same route.

20. KINGFISHER TRAILS
WILDERNESS (WILDERNESS NATIONAL PARK)

Trail details: 1. Pied Kingfisher Trail: 12 km/ 4 hours, circular; 2. Giant Kingfisher Trail: 3 km/1,5 hours, return; 3. Brownhooded Kingfisher Trail: 7 km/3 hours, return; 4. Half-collared Kingfisher Trail: 6 km/3 hours, return.

Permits/bookings: Permits not required for the day trails but bookings required for overnight accommodation at the camps, obtained from National Parks Board offices in Cape Town, tel. (021) 222810; PO Box 7400, Roggebaai 8012, and Pretoria, tel. (012) 3431991; PO Box 787, Pretoria 0001.

Facilities/amenities: Wilderness camp with camp site and chalets; Ebb and Flow camp site; angling and watersports.

Main attractions: Prolific birdlife; waterfalls and pools; lakes; riverine forest.

Pertinent information: Do not walk in very wet weather as the river may suddenly flood.

The Wilderness National Park stretches from the Touw River mouth in the west to Swartvlei and the Sedgefield Lagoon in the east. The lakes, one of the major attractions of the southern Cape, form a uniquely beautiful wetlands area, conserved as a functioning ecosystem and recreational area. Here there is a series of four Kingfisher Trails and the Cape Dune Molerat Trail (see next entry) which together cover the park's various aspects.

1. The Pied Kingfisher Trail takes hikers from the Wilderness camp across the flood plains of the Serpentine, along the road west of the railway line, past the Wilderness Lagoon to the Touw River mouth. The return leg of the circuit leads along the beach and back onto the road from the N2 highway to the camp.

2. The Giant Kingfisher Trail runs from the Ebb and Flow camp site into the forest along the eastern side of the Touw River, to a huge tumble of boulders which marks the end of the trail. There are some lovely pools and waterfalls here. For part of the way the route follows a pipeline that carries water from the upper reaches of the Touw River to the camp site. At one point the only way across an exposed rock face is on the pipeline: if this fazes you, sit down and shuffle across it.

3. The Brownhooded Kingfisher Trail, an easy walk, starts on the Lakes road east of the Hoekwil road and takes you along the Duiwe River, then up a tributary to a rock pool, and back again. Follow the perspex signs carrying the brownhooded kingfisher markers. There are two detours along side-paths that take hikers to good viewpoints.

4. The Half-collared Kingfisher Trail is the shortest of the Kingfisher Trails. It runs along the western side of the Touw River from the Ebb and Flow camp site. It is a beautiful stroll through the forest. Half-collared kingfishers are rare, although the other three species are common in the park.

21. CAPE DUNE MOLERAT TRAIL
RONDEVLEI (WILDERNESS NATIONAL PARK)

Trail details: 6 km/3 hours; circular.

Permits/bookings: Not required, but hikers must register at the start of the trail.

Facilities/amenities: Rondevlei environmental information centre and bird hide; benches *en route*; bird-feeding table.

Main attractions: Prolific birdlife; dune fynbos; views of Swartvlei and Groenvlei.

Pertinent information: Carry water; the dune can be hot in summer. Beware of molerat burrows!

The Cape Dune Molerat Trail starts at the office at Rondevlei, the renowned bird sanctuary. This moderately easy circuit follows the long dune that lies on the northern edge of Rondevlei, and takes walkers up over the dune along the Wolwe River to the edge of Swartvlei, and back over and along the dune to the start. The fynbos on the dune is wonderfully colourful in spring and there are panoramic views east and west of the Lakes area.

Dune fynbos overlooking Swartvlei.

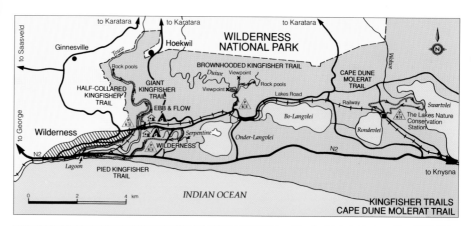

The clear, amber stream of the Duiwe River.

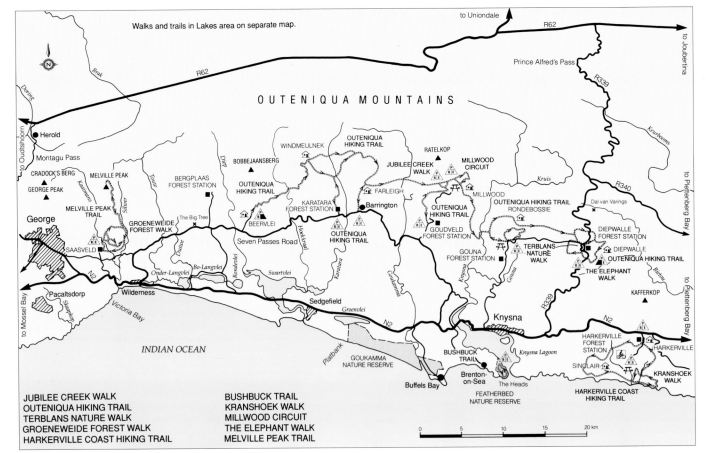

Walks and trails in Lakes area on separate map.

to Uniondale

OUTENIQUA MOUNTAINS

JUBILEE CREEK WALK
OUTENIQUA HIKING TRAIL
TERBLANS NATURE WALK
GROENEWEIDE FOREST WALK
HARKERVILLE COAST HIKING TRAIL

BUSHBUCK TRAIL
KRANSHOEK WALK
MILLWOOD CIRCUIT
THE ELEPHANT WALK
MELVILLE PEAK TRAIL

The Outeniqua Trail near Millwood.

22. OUTENIQUA HIKING TRAIL
BEERVLEI/DIEPWALLE

Trail details: Approximately 90 km/5 days; one way (shorter sections of the trail can be hiked).

Permits/bookings: Must be obtained from the Department of Water Affairs and Forestry regional office, tel. (0445) 23037; Demar Centre, Main Road, Knysna. A detailed map with practical and environmental information is available on request.

Facilities/amenities: Five huts, each accommodating 30 people, with bunks, mattresses, fireplaces and firewood.

Main attractions: Indigenous forest and montane fynbos; mountain scenery and views of the coastal plateau; relics of the gold rush near Millwood; bird and animal life of the forest and fynbos; mountain streams and pools.

Pertinent information: The forest and the wet fynbos depend on high rainfall, so be prepared for rain and mist.

The old Outeniqua Hiking Trail was a strenuous 8-day/140-km route from Witfontein to Diepwalle. In February 1993 the trail was shortened and made less taxing by eliminating the first three days of the old trail. The trail now begins from Beervlei in the Bergplaas State Forest for the first day's hike to the Windmeulnek hut; the trail's last four days to Diepwalle remain unchanged. To get to Beervlei take the Hoekwil road diagonally opposite the Holiday Inn at Wilderness. This will take you across the serpentine railway line and up a steep hill. Follow the signs to Beervlei Forest Station which is beyond the Woodville/Bergplaas turnoff. A new hut is

planned in the Kafferkop area which will extend the trail by two days and which will also link it up with the established and very popular 2-day Harkerville Trail (see page 95).

The first two days of the trail take hikers through extensive areas of montane fynbos. Because of its more recent evolution, the fynbos of the southern Cape has fewer species and is less variable than that of the south-western Cape with its winter rainfall. June to January are the best months to see the fynbos in flower; February to May are perhaps the poorest months. Unfortunately, two plants you are sure to notice are *Hakea sericea* and *Pinus pinaster*, both alien invaders of the fynbos.

The last three days of the trail pass through indigenous forest; many trees are labelled with their national tree list numbers. At the end of the last day, hikers walk to Diepwalle on the outgoing leg of the Elephant II Walk (see page 94). It is on this section of the trail that there is an extremely remote possibility of spotting one of the endangered Knysna elephants. There were once great herds of these animals in this area but their numbers have dwindled to a possible three whose survival is in doubt. However birds are plentiful, and buck which may be seen by hikers include klipspringer, grey rhebok and Cape grysbok in the fynbos areas, and the elusive blue duiker and bushbuck near the forest edge.

23. MILLWOOD CIRCUIT
GOUDVELD STATE FOREST, NEAR KNYSNA

Trail details: 5,6 km/3 hours; circular.

Permits/bookings: Not required; hikers must register at the entrance to the Goudveld Forest Station, where they can also obtain a map.

Facilities/amenities: Picnic site at the start.

Main attractions: Old Millwood town site and cemetery; Millwood goldfield mining restoration project; mountain scenery.

Pertinent information: Enter the old mining shafts at your own risk, and carry a torch; parts of the route can be slippery when wet.

As a result of the discovery of gold in the Outeniquas and the subsequent gold rush, the town of Millwood sprang up in 1885 and prospered briefly; most of the local mines were depleted by 1890. Monk's Store, the only building remaining here, marks the beginning and end of this easy trail. The Millwood Circuit takes hikers through the plantation to the western side of Nol se Kop, where there are good views of the Outeniquas. Here in the fynbos the watsonias flower in profusion during November. There is a side-path to some old adits, before the path returns through the plantation to the old Bendigo mine site and Monk's Store, which is now a small museum with artefacts and pictures of the gold-mining era.

24. JUBILEE CREEK WALK
GOUDVELD STATE FOREST, NEAR KNYSNA

Trail details: 4 km/2 hours; return.

Permits/bookings: Not required; hikers must register at the entrance to the Goudveld Forest Station, where they can also obtain a map.

Facilities/amenities: Picnic site at Jubilee Creek.

Main attractions: Historical interest; natural forest and stream; forest birds.

Pertinent information: Enter old mining shafts at your own risk; take a torch.

This short, easy stroll leads from the popular Jubilee Creek picnic site through natural forest alongside the stream in Jubilee Creek, the scene of gold-mining activity a century ago. On the way to the pool which marks the turning point of the walk, hikers pass some old adits. The route (apart from the last section) is shared by the Outeniqua Trail, but you may not continue up Millwood Creek past

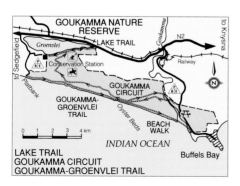

the turn-off to the pool. This walk and the Millwood Circuit (above) can be done on the same day.

25. GOUKAMMA NATURE RESERVE
SEDGEFIELD/BUFFEL'S BAY

Trail details: 1. Goukamma-Groenvlei Trail: 14 km/5 hours, one way; 2. Goukamma Nature Reserve Circuit: 8 km/3,5 hours, circular. 3. Lake Trail: 4 km/1,5 hours, return.

Permits/bookings: Self-issue permit at the start of the trails.

Facilities/amenities: Fireplaces and picnic sites at the camp on the Goukamma River; marine and freshwater angling.

Main attractions: Beautiful sandy and rocky coastline and estuarine scenery; freshwater lake; diverse birdlife and small buck, reintroduced bontebok; dune fynbos; milkwood forest.

Pertinent information: The beach is dangerous for swimming (rip currents); trailists should carry water, be wary of snakes on the dunes, and take insect repellent for mosquitoes in forest areas. The dunes can be extremely hot in summer.

Goukamma is a lovely coastal sand dune and freshwater lake complex lying between Knysna and Sedgefield. The tranquillity of the 13-km stretch of sandy beach with occasional rocky outcrops is most

Lazy shores of the Indian Ocean come into view along the Goukamma-Groenvlei Trail.

appealing, and the sand dunes, clothed in dune fynbos and scrub forest containing milkwood trees, a welcome retreat from the crowded beaches in the Knysna region.

1. The Goukamma-Groenvlei Trail leads hikers from the start just across the Goukamma River in the east of the reserve, up over the dunes, and down to Groenvlei. Hikers will need transport at the end of the trail, at the Groenvlei Conservation Station. Groenvlei, originally an estuary, is now cut off from the sea by high dunes and is fed by rainwater and freshwater springs. Almost completely fringed with reedbeds, it provides an ideal habitat for a great many of the 75 bird species which make the reserve their home.

2. The Goukamma Nature Reserve Circuit follows the first 2 km or so of the Goukamma-Groenvlei Trail; at a point where a path to the beach and a jeep track meet, the circular trail cuts back in the milkwood forest, towards the Goukamma River again.

3. The Lake Trail leads from the Groenvlei Conservation Station along the edge of Groenvlei (otherwise known as Lake Pleasant) and the milkwood forest. The Groenvlei Conservation Station is reached by driving past the Lake Pleasant Hotel onto the dune and then turning left onto a narrow road which is signposted.

The vlei and the lower reaches of the Goukamma River are pleasant for canoeing; the beach is unspoilt and ideal for walking.

26. BUSHBUCK TRAIL
FEATHERBED NATURE RESERVE, KNYSNA

Trail details: A guided circular walk of 5 km/
2 hours (2,5 km can be ridden on a motorized
trailer); a fee is payable for the walk. See map p.92.

Permits/bookings: Contact The Trail Organiser,
tel. (0445) 21233; PO Box 1261, Knysna 6570.

Facilities/amenities: Teas and meals are provided;
group tours are arranged on request; swimming is
pleasant off the reserve's beaches; restaurant;
conference centre.

Main attractions: Spectacular views of coastal
environment; wildlife and flora, including
milkwood trees; beachcomber caves.

The easy gradients of the Terblans Nature Walk lead through dense fern and forest.

The guided Bushbuck Trail is situated in the
Featherbed Nature Reserve in Knysna, which can
be reached by water only. Small and large parties
can be catered for, and educational walks for children can be arranged. The trail is for tourists rather
than mountaineers. The scenic south-east corner of
Knysna's Western Head is the venue of this small
private reserve.

You can reach the trailhead, the Featherbed Bay
Beach, via a private boat or on one of the ferries
operating on the Knysna Lagoon. These ferries
leave from the jetty next to the Knysna Railway
Station (in the near future they may leave from the
eastern head itself).

Visitors are given a choice whether to walk the
first 2,5 km, rising 120 m from sea level, or ride a
motorized trailer. The second 2,5 km, a descent
along the coast, is for walking only. Here, on the
Bushbuck and Old Rocket paths, the trail leader ex-
pounds on the ecology and history of the
surrounding area.

About 100 species of birds are present as well as
small game such as Cape bushbuck, blue duiker
and klipspringer.

At an extra charge, hikers can enjoy a fish braai
or a traditional meat braai on their return.

27. TERBLANS NATURE WALK
GOUNA STATE FOREST, NEAR KNYSNA

Trail details: 6,5 km/2 to 3 hours; circular.
See map page 92.

Permits/bookings: Not required, but hikers must
register at the start of the walk (there is a fee to
enter Gouna State Forest).

Maps/information: Map and brochure available
from the authority in charge: the Department of
Water Affairs and Forestry, tel. (0445) 23037;
Demar Centre, Main Road, Knysna 6570.

Facilities/amenities: Picnic site; swimming hole.

Main attractions: Indigenous moist forest; trees
labelled with their national tree list numbers; forest
birds and bracket fungi.

The Terblans Nature Walk, located just north of
Gouna Forest Station, meanders through the heart
of the southern Cape's spectacular indigenous
forest. (The Gouna Forest, reached via the Old
Cape Road, is signposted on the N2 along the
Knysna Lagoon, on the western outskirts of the

town.) Looping away from the Grootdraai picnic
site and then back, this walk is not strenuous and is
therefore ideal for families with small children as
well as reasonably fit, elderly people.

The forests blanketing these lower mountain
slopes lie 250–350 m above sea level and, classified as moist and medium moist types, contain tall,
densely growing indigenous trees such as Outeniqua yellowwoods, real yellowwoods, ironwoods,
stinkwoods and boekenhouts. Pine plantations also
occur along the trail.

Although the southern Cape forests contain
fewer than 50 typical forest-dwelling bird species,
hikers may see the crowned eagle which preys on
monkeys and small antelope, or the African goshawk, the main predator of forest birds. More
easily heard than seen are the olive thrush and
chorister, Cape and starred robins. The beautiful
Rameron pigeon and Knysna lourie are also present.

28. THE ELEPHANT WALK
DIEPWALLE STATE FOREST, NEAR KNYSNA

Trail details: Whole walk: 19,6 km/8 hours,
circular; there are three shorter circular options:
Route I: 9 km/3,5 hours; Route II: 8 km/3 hours;
Route III: 6 km/3 hours.

Permits/bookings: Not required; hikers must sign
the register at the forest station.

Maps/information: Colour map with historical and
environmental information is available from the
authority in charge: the Department of Water
Affairs and Forestry, tel. (0445) 23037; Demar
Centre, Main Road, Knysna 6570.

Facilities/amenities: Picnic sites.

Main attractions: Indigenous forest; eight 'Big
Trees' (Outeniqua yellowwoods); prolific birdlife;
forest ferns, fungi and streams. Trees marked with
their national tree list numbers.

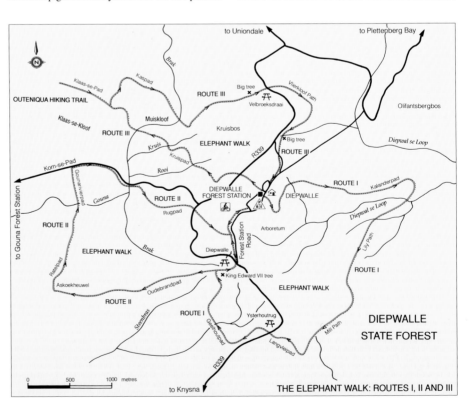

Although the Diepwalle State Forest (reached via a turnoff on the Uniondale road, R339) through which this walk runs, is part of Knysna elephant terrain, hikers are far more likely to see bushbuck, baboons and vervet monkeys, a large variety of birdlife including the narina trogon, crowned eagle and gymnogene, and possibly the boomslang, the most common snake in the area. You cannot help but notice some very fine specimens of stinkwood, yellowwood, red and white alder, Cape beech and other indigenous forest trees.

The Elephant Walk comprises three interlinking loops, Routes I, II and III, which can be walked separately or in combination. The complete route takes a full day; a hike which leaves you with little time to enjoy the great beauty of this environment.

29. LANGKLOOF NATURE RESERVE
NORTH-WEST OF UNIONDALE

Trail details: There is no formal trail, but one is currently being planned.

Permits/bookings: Must be obtained from the Langkloof Nature Reserve office, tel.(04462) 110; PO Box 48, Uniondale 6460. There is a map available on request.

Facilities/amenities: None at the moment, but facilities are planned (see text below).

Main attractions: Magnificent mountain scenery; mountain fynbos; relic forest patches in the kloofs.

Pertinent information: The area is well known for its rapidly changeable weather and extreme variations in temperature.

The Langkloof Nature Reserve, situated approximately 25 km north-west of Uniondale, includes the Kammanassie range of mountains which lies between and parallel to the Outeniquas and the Swartberg range further inland. This is a magnificent range with its highest peak, Mannetjiesberg, rising to 1955 m and deep kloofs on both the north and south slopes. The mountain fynbos is rich and attractive and includes several rare and endemic species such as *Leucadendron singulare*, *Leucadendron rourkei* and *Bobartia paniculata*. There is an endemic population of Cape mountain zebra in the reserve as well as grey rhebok, klipspringer, grysbok and baboons.

Up until now, the reserve has been managed as a wilderness area in which hikers can walk, although there are no facilities. At present there are plans for the establishment of two bush camps; one in the east and one in the west of the Kammanassies, from each of which there will be two day walks and a 2-day walk with overnight accommodation on the northern slopes of the reserve.

Access to the bush camps will be along existing tracks on which visitors can use fourwheel-drive vehicles and mountain bikes.

30. HARKERVILLE COAST HIKING TRAIL
HARKERVILLE STATE FOREST, NEAR PLETTENBERG BAY

Trail details: 27 km/2 days; circular. See map p. 92.

Permits/bookings: Must be obtained from the Department of Water Affairs and Forestry, tel. (0445) 23037; Demar Centre, Main Road, Knysna 6570. A detailed map is available.

Facilities/amenities: Hut at start/end; overnight hut; ladders and chains placed at difficult sections of the coastal route.

Main attractions: Magnificent rocky coastline; indigenous forest; occasional sightings of whales, otters and dolphins.

Pertinent information: The coastal section of this route involves rock scrambling and negotiating narrow, exposed ledges; the rocks may be slippery when wet; unfit hikers or those with a fear of heights should not attempt this trail. Groups should have at least one member experienced and competent in this type of terrain; it can rain here at any time of the year. There is a limit of 12 people per day for this trail.

To get to Harkerville State Forest, take the turnoff from the N2 20 km east of Knysna (12 km west of Plettenberg Bay), which is signposted.

Since being opened in 1990 this trail has rapidly gained popularity, mainly due to the scenic splendour of the coastline. The trail runs through natural forest, fynbos and rugged coastal terrain. Vervet monkeys and baboons are commonly seen along the way, as are fish eagles. Lucky hikers may catch glimpses of bushbuck and grey duiker.

31. KRANSHOEK WALK
HARKERVILLE STATE FOREST, NEAR PLETTENBERG BAY

Trail details: 9,4 km/3 to 4 hours; circular. See map page 92.

Permits/bookings: Not required, but hikers must register at the start of the walk; a charge is levied to enter the forest.

Maps/information: Map and brochure available from the authority in charge: the Department of Water Affairs and Forestry, tel. (0445) 23037; Demar Centre, Main Road, Knysna 6570.

Facilities/amenities: Kranshoek picnic and viewing site; swimming; Harkerville Youth Group Centre nearby for school or university students; ecologically instructive information boards along the route.

Main attractions: Coastal cliff scenery; fynbos and coastal scrub forest; varied birdlife.

Pertinent information: Parts of the trail are slippery when wet; hikers must carry drinking water.

This lovely walk in the Harkerville State Forest takes you from the Kranshoek picnic site down to the mouth of the Kranshoek River and along the rugged coastline to the Crook's River mouth and back along the coastal plateau. It was designed not only to reward hikers but to provide information about the local environment. There are eight information boards along the way providing fascinating information about a range of natural points of interest. These enrich an already beautiful outing along the coast. There are two swimming spots along the way. For directions to Harkerville State Forest, see the previous entry, Harkerville Coast Hiking Trail.

Coastal scrub-covered dunes and stern, rocky outcrops fringe the ocean along the Kranshoek Walk.

Viewed through the Robberg Gap, Die Eiland is joined by a spit of sand to the main peninsula.

Opened in December 1983, this trail was made by the boarders of the Wittedrift High School at the small settlement of Wittedrift north of Plettenberg Bay. The route follows the course of the Bitou River and it is this watercourse with its associated birdlife which is the main attraction of the trail.

A series of interconnected loops allows longer and shorter variations to be chosen. The trail runs across private land, and dogs and horses are welcome. Walkers can spend the night at the hut.

34. NATURE'S VALLEY WALKS
TSITSIKAMMA NATIONAL PARK, DE VASSELOT SECTION

Trail details: There is a network of paths, providing walks that range in length from 3 km/1 hour (Kalanderpad circuit) to 18 km/7 hours (Forest Hall-Rugpad circuit) and longer.

Permits/bookings: Permits must be obtained for day walks at the De Vasselot camp gate. For camp bookings contact the National Parks Board offices in Cape Town, tel. (021) 222810; PO Box 7400, Roggebaai 8012, or Pretoria, tel. (012) 3431991; PO Box 787, Pretoria 0001.

Facilities/amenities: Groot River camp site for both youth groups and the general public; angling and swimming in the lagoon and sea.

Main attractions: Indigenous forest; coastal plateau; magnificent coastline; Groot and Salt river estuaries; unspoilt natural environment.

The De Vasselot section of the Tsitsikamma National Park incorporates a large area of fynbos-covered coastal plateau surrounding the deep kloofs of the Groot and Salt rivers as well as a large section of coastline. The park is a refuge for coastal fynbos, elsewhere threatened and modified by forestry, agricultural and residential development, as well as some beautiful forest ranging from high forest types in the kloofs to scrub forest along the coast, which is in exceptionally good condition.

A network of interleading paths has been laid out west of the Groot River. The paths lead through the fynbos, the forest, along the coast and through the Salt River estuary. Hikers can follow the routes suggested in the Parks Board brochure or choose their own. In the eastern part of the park, apart from the short walk along the Groot River lagoon to the mouth and up to a view site, and back, there is the Grootkloof Trail (see following entry).

The delightful, unspoilt Salt River estuary lies west of Nature's Valley and can be reached either by a path over the intervening ridge or by a path along the shoreline. The latter is not safe at high tide. The park's birdlife is rich and includes forest species such as Knysna lourie, paradise flycatcher and olive woodpecker, amongst others. The animals present in the park are shy and seldom seen, although fortunate hikers may spot a Cape clawless otter in the Salt River estuary.

32. ROBBERG NATURE RESERVE
PLETTENBERG BAY

Trail details: 11 km/4 hours, circular; short cuts provide two shorter circuits of 2 km and 5 km.

Permits/bookings: Permit must be obtained at the reserve entrance or from the Cape Nature Conservation office, tel. (04457) 32125/32185; 7 Zenon Street, Plettenberg Bay 6600. Maps available on request at both places.

Facilities/amenities: Information centre, picnic and braai facilities at the parking area.

Main attractions: Diverse coastal scenery; varied plant and littoral life; excellent angling and bird-watching area.

Pertinent information: Drinking-water sources along the trails are unreliable; freak waves can wash the unsuspecting off the rocks; hikers must not attempt to climb to the top of the sand dune above Witsand as it is unstable; there are two places along the way where exposed ledges must be negotiated, the second with the help of a chain.

33. WITTEDRIFT NATURE TRAIL
WITTEDRIFT

Trail details: Up to 12 km/6 hours; circular (shorter routes are available).

Permits/bookings: Not required for day hikers; for overnight stays book through the Wittedrift Butchery; tel. (04457) 9760.

Facilities/amenities: Overnight hut.

Main attractions: Prolific birdlife; swimming; the Bitou River.

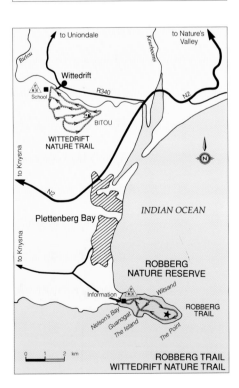

Robberg, 'mountain of seals', has always been popular with anglers for its fine fishing and intertidal life. As a result, there is a network of old fishermen's paths from the present carpark to the Point, a distance of about 4,5 km. These form the basis of the circular Robberg Trail which takes hikers along the steep northern slopes of the peninsula to the Point and back along the lovely southern shoreline and past the Gap.

The Nelson Bay cave, rich in artefacts and fossils from early Upper Pleistocene times, is proof that prehistoric man lived on the peninsula. Hikers have a good chance of spotting crowned eagle, black oystercatcher, Cape dikkop, swift tern, spotted eagle owl, giant kingfisher, ground woodpecker, tchagra shrike and black sunbird. Dassies and Cape grey mongoose are also present.

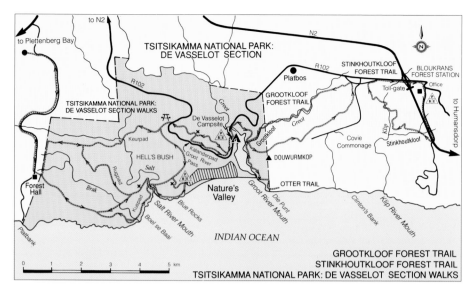

GROOTKLOOF FOREST TRAIL
STINKHOUTKLOOF FOREST TRAIL
TSITSIKAMMA NATIONAL PARK: DE VASSELOT SECTION WALKS

35. GROOTKLOOF FOREST TRAIL
TSITSIKAMMA NATIONAL PARK, DE VASSELOT SECTION

Trail details: 15,5 km/6 hours; circular.

Permits/bookings: Permit must be obtained at the De Vasselot camp office or gate; a good sketch map available on request here.

Facilities/amenities: Parking available at De Vasselot camp.

Main attractions: Indigenous forest; montane fynbos of the coastal plateau; Grootkloof stream.

Pertinent information: The return leg down Grootkloof may be slippery when wet; in or after heavy rains the 21 river crossings are difficult and even dangerous.

The outward leg of the Grootkloof Forest Trail follows the beginning of the Tsitsikamma Hiking Trail from the De Vasselot camp, along the side of the Groot River lagoon, and then steeply up through scrub forest to the fynbos of the coastal plateau. The path then leaves the national park and enters indigenous forest in the Bloukrans State Forest, where there are large stands of alien blackwood trees. The trail leaves the Tsitsikamma Trail in the forest, to return down Grootkloof next to the stream, which the trail crosses 21 times. Depending on the tide, and if the lagoon is open, you may have to paddle through the last crossing.

This is a fairly strenuous but rewarding walk. In spring the fynbos is bright with colour and Grootkloof is always enchanting. The birdlife in the fynbos and in the forest is prolific.

36. STINKHOUTKLOOF FOREST TRAIL
BLOUKRANS STATE FOREST

Trail details: 8,4 km/3 hours; circular.

Permits/bookings: Not required; hikers must register at the start of the trail, where they can also pick up a map.

Facilities/amenities: None.

Main attractions: Magnificent natural forest; streams and rock pools.

Pertinent information: The path through the forest can be slippery when wet.

To get to Bloukrans State Forest, turn east off the N2 just before or just after the toll exchange (depending on your direction of travel) between Storms River and Nature's Valley. Hikers should not be discouraged by the first 2 km of this trail; it is worth enduring the noise of the passing traffic on the national highway to reach the natural forest, where the peace is absolute. In Stinkhoutkloof itself the trail traverses only a few hundred metres of natural forest before reaching pine plantations, from which there are glimpses of the Klip River Valley and the sea below. The path crosses a small patch of fynbos before re-entering the natural forest. The stream crossings here are exceptionally lovely with tree ferns lining the banks, and moss-covered rocks contrasting with the brown peaty water. Apart from the last few hundred metres along the R102 and back to the forest station, the rest of this walk is in natural forest. Ferns are a prominent feature of the forest sections of the trail. Seven weeks ferns are harvested here in a strictly controlled operation.

Misty cliffs extend to the skyline beyond the rock-bound mouth of the Groot River.

The Tsitsikamma trail graced by watsonias.

37. TSITSIKAMMA HIKING TRAIL
NATURE'S VALLEY/STORMS RIVER

Trail details: 61 km/5 days; open-ended. Shorter routes are possible, with access to the trail from the Boskor sawmill and the Bloukrans, Lottering and Storms River forest stations.

Permits/bookings: Must be obtained from the Tsitsikamma Forest Region office of the Department of Water Affairs and Forestry, tel. (0423) 51180; Private Bag X537, Humansdorp 6300. Map available on request.

Facilities/amenities: Five huts, each accommodating 30 people, with bunks, mattresses and fireplaces.

Main attractions: Tsitsikamma mountain scenery; indigenous forest; fynbos; mountain streams.

Pertinent information: Beware of flash floods while crossing rivers, and carry waterproof bags; rapidly changeable weather; ticks are prevalent. The Tsitsikamma Trail is one of South Africa's most popular trails, and early booking is essential in peak seasons.

Beginning at Kalander hut on the Groot River at Nature's Valley and terminating at the suspension bridge over the Storms River, the Tsitsikamma Hiking Trail winds in and out of high, moist, wet and very wet types of forest, alternating with fynbos and plantations. The trail runs over the low and high plateaux below the Tsitsikamma mountains

inland from the Otter Trail. Fast-running, clean rivers, subject to rapid flooding, flow over the plateaux to the sea.

The Tsitsikamma Hiking Trail is an easily negotiated hike; no day's stretch is longer than 17 km, thus allowing leisurely walking and plenty of time to enjoy and appreciate the environment.

The indigenous forests, reaching a height of 18 to 30 m, grow on shale formations; trees are labelled with their national tree list numbers. The fynbos on the sandstone and quartzite soils is most colourful in spring and early summer. This vegetation is the typical tall-growing montane fynbos of the southern Cape mountains' wet southern slopes.

38. RATEL FOREST TRAIL
STORMS RIVER (PAUL SAUER) BRIDGE

Trail details: 4,2 km/1,5 hours; circular. There is a shorter 2,6 km variation of the same route.

Permits/bookings: Not required; hikers must register at the Big Tree at the start of the trail.

Maps/information: A map and brochure are available from the Tsitsikamma Forest Region of the Department of Water Affairs and Forestry, tel. (0423) 51180; Private Bag X537, Humansdorp 6300.

Facilities/amenities: None.

Main attractions: Indigenous forest; birdlife.

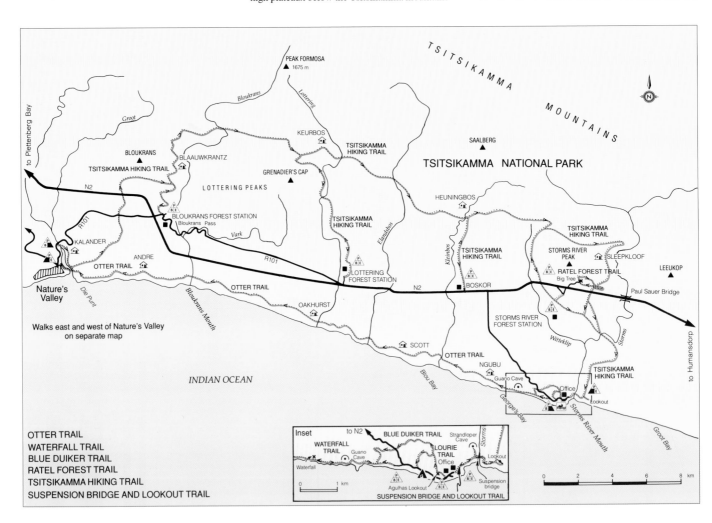

OTTER TRAIL
WATERFALL TRAIL
BLUE DUIKER TRAIL
RATEL FOREST TRAIL
TSITSIKAMMA HIKING TRAIL
SUSPENSION BRIDGE AND LOOKOUT TRAIL

The Ratel Forest Trail starts at the Big Tree next to the N2 national road, 2 km west of the Paul Sauer bridge over the Storms River. It is an easy, disappointingly short walk through a particularly beautiful stretch of the moist and wet forest just west of the bridge. Hikers can expect to see many forest birds here.

39. STORMS RIVER MOUTH WALKS
TSITSIKAMMA NATIONAL PARK, STORMS RIVER MOUTH SECTION

Trail details: 1. Suspension Bridge and Lookout Trail: 4 km/2,5 hours, return; 2. Waterfall Trail: 5,3 km/3 hours, return; 3. Blue Duiker Trail: 6 km/3 hours, circular.

Permits/bookings: Not required, although a fee is charged to enter the park. Maps and brochure available from the information centre in the park.

Facilities/amenities: Restaurant; shop; chalets, camp site and caravan park; information centre; Agulhas lookout platform; trees marked with their national tree list numbers; underwater trails.

Main attractions: Waterfall; Guano Cave; views of coastline; Storms River mouth; scrub and dry forest types; birdlife; intertidal zone sea life.

Pertinent information: The first part of the route can be slippery when wet.

The Storms River camp has been a firm favourite of visitors to the southern Cape for decades. The reason is the wild beauty of the coastline and the restless, often stormy sea. The Otter Trail starts here and the National Parks Board has laid out several short trails for day visitors.

1. The Suspension Bridge and Lookout Trail is an easy stroll that leads along the western side of the river mouth, past the Strandloper Cave to the suspension bridge across the mouth. On the other side of the bridge there is a short but very steep climb to a lookout point from which there are fine views of the mouth and the camp.

2. The Waterfall Trail is an undemanding hike which follows the first 2,65 km of the Otter Trail (see the following entry); hikers may not walk beyond the waterfall unless hiking the Otter Trail.

3. The Blue Duiker Trail starts just west of the information centre and leads through scrub forest up to the Agulhas lookout from where whales and dolphins can often be spotted in winter. After crossing a short section of fynbos, the trail takes hikers into the dry forest with some fine Outeniqua yellowwoods evident. A short cut, the Lourie Trail, branches to the left here.

The Blue Duiker Trail continues through the forest, crossing a stream below a delightful waterfall. Several more streams and a cavernous tree bole mark the route. After crossing the road to the camp, the path drops to the coast just west of the start of the Waterfall/Otter trails and returns past the camp site and chalets.

The birdlife in the forest west of the road is quite exceptional, making this trail a great favourite with bird-watchers.

A suspension bridge crosses the mouth of the Storms River.

40. OTTER TRAIL
STORMS RIVER MOUTH/NATURE'S VALLEY

Trail details: 41 km/5 days; one way.

Permits/bookings: Must be obtained from National Parks Board offices in Cape Town, tel. (021) 222810; PO Box 7400, Roggebaai 8012, and Pretoria, tel. (012) 3431991/9; PO Box 787, Pretoria 0001; book well in advance. Map and brochure available on confirmation of booking.

Facilities/amenities: Log huts with toilets, fireplaces and firewood; 2 huts per site, each hut accommodating 6 people, in bunks with mattresses.

Main attractions: Coastal scenery with tidal pools rich in marine life; indigenous forest and fynbos; Elandsbos; Lottering and Bloukrans river mouths.

Pertinent information: The Bloukrans River must be crossed by wading or swimming; waterproof your backpack and check the tide table to determine low water; the first part of the hike can be slippery when wet.

South Africa's first organized hiking trail and a perennial favourite, the Otter Trail winds from the Storms River mouth along the coast to the Groot River estuary at Nature's Valley on the park's western boundary. Its popularity stems from its unbeatable coastal scenery, indigenous forest, and the short daily stretches which make hiking possible for backpackers of limited ability and experience, including families, although the unfit will find the going tough.

The Otter Trail, built and run by the National Parks Board, is clearly marked with the otter emblem painted yellow in rocky areas, instead of the more usual white footprints. The route follows the shore, and ascends 200 m to the coastal plateau where necessary. It funnels through thick canopy forest and crosses streams and rivers. Although the stretches between overnight shelters are short (the longest day's hike is only 14 km), some of the slopes are steep. However, there is enough time to walk slowly, enjoy the flowers, snorkel in the tidal pools and observe birds and other wildlife. The

Trails of water cascade down to a still pool near the start of the Otter Trail.

Oakhurst overnight huts on the Otter Trail overlook the surging sea.

This clearly marked trail gives hikers a glimpse of a little-known wilderness area. Witelsbos lies in a region of all-year rainfall. To reach the Witelsbos Forest Station, turn off the N2 11 km east of the Storms River bridge.

42. CAPTAIN HARISON'S TRAIL
WITELSBOS STATE FOREST

Trail details: 9 km/3,5 hours; circular.

Permits/bookings: Permits must be obtained from the Witelsbos State Forest station, tel. (04230) 777; PO Witelsbos 6304.

Facilities/amenities: Picnic and braai area.

Main attractions: Natural forest; streams; ferns; forest birds.

Captain Christopher Harison, whose headquarters were at Witelsbos, was the first Conservator of Forests of the Tsitsikamma area. (The Forest Station is 11 km east of the Storms River bridge.) The trail that borrows his name runs at first through a uniquely lovely remnant patch of forest, before swinging up and back along the slopes of Witelskop. The trail is clearly marked, and does not require a particularly high level of fitness. The large number of witels trees growing in the forest, and the tree ferns lining the many streamlets that cross the trail, together characterize the environment as wet forest. This small patch survives in stark contrast with the slopes of Witelskop above, which are heavily infested with alien pines and acacias. Despite its limited size, Witelbos still harbours bushpig as well as a healthy complement of forest birds.

National Parks Board insists that hikers sleep at every hut, to prevent bookings becoming confused.

Some of the features of the trail include cave middens left by Strandlopers, the Guano Cave, and waterfalls; coastal forest with a wealth of Outeniqua yellowwood, stinkwood, saffronwood, elder, Cape beech and white milkwood; large marine mammals such as dolphins, seals and whales; dassies (on the cliffs); bushbuck, grysbok, blue duiker, baboon and vervet monkeys in the forest; and spoor of bushpig, leopard, the Cape clawless otter and klipspringer. A total of 210 species of birds has been recorded – these include 35 seabirds such as the black oystercatcher, sooty shearwater and the Arctic skua.

41. FOURCADE TRAIL
WITELSBOS STATE FOREST

Trail details: 24 km/2 days; circular.

Permits/bookings: Must be obtained from the Witelsbos State Forest Station, tel. (04230) 777; PO Witelsbos 6304.

Facilities/amenities: None, but several overnight resting places situated next to water are suggested.

Main attractions: A wilderness experience; fynbos; mountain streams; riverine forest.

The Fourcade Trail was opened in 1991. Intended to provide a wilderness experience, it leaves the depot next to the natural forest below Witelskop and makes a complete circle around the mountain. The northern side of Witelskop and the mountains to the north are covered with fynbos; there are patches of natural forest in the kloofs.

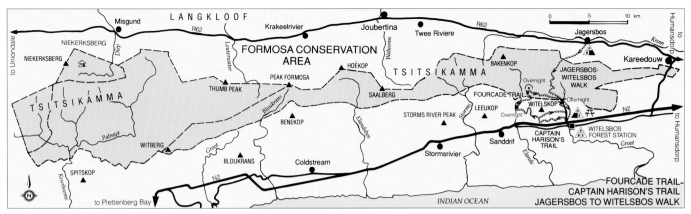

43. FORMOSA CONSERVATION AREA
JOUBERTINA

Trail details: Jagersbos to Witelsbos walk: approximately 10 km/5 hours; one way.

Permits/bookings: For day walk and overnight hikes, must be obtained from Cape Nature Conservation office at Formosa Conservation Area, tel. (0427) 31530; PO Box 117, Joubertina 6410. There is an entrance charge for the wilderness area.

Facilities/amenities: Overnight hut.

Main attractions: Mountain scenery; fynbos.

Pertinent information: Hikers must arrange their own transport at Witelsbos at the end of the day walk; cloud is common on the peaks.

The Formosa Conservation Area includes not only the Kouga mountains to the north of Langkloof, but the catchment areas of the Tsitsikammas to the south as well. Although there are no formal, demarcated trails, hikers can walk in the area and make use of the overnight hut at Niekerksberg. This area, in the Tsitsikammas south of Misgund, is currently being developed by the National Parks Board as an extension of the Tsitsikamma National Park, where trails and overnight facilities may be established some time in the future.

Formosa Peak, the highest peak in the area at 1675 m, looms high over the Tsitsikamma Trail. The climb up to Peak Formosa is very stiff, but hikers are rewarded for their efforts with spectacular views of the coast.

The strenuous Jagersbos to Witelsbos walk starts at the farm Jagersbos, which is approximately 5,5 km east of Joubertina on the R62. The walk takes the hiker over the Tsitsikamma range through a little-known and wild area. The scenery is spectacular. There is fynbos on the mountain slopes, and patches of forest in the rocky kloofs. This is an area of high rainfall; cloud can come up quickly on these mountains, and hikers should be alert to a deterioration in the weather.

One of the shallow streams in Witelsbos forest.

THE EASTERN CAPE, CISKEI AND TRANSKEI

In the west, the eastern Cape is bounded by the Langkloof, Uniondale and Willowmore; it includes the Kouga and Baviaanskloof mountain ranges. Inland it grades into the Great Karoo all the way to the Orange River, which forms part of its northern boundary. The eastern Cape coast runs from Cape St Francis in the south, to the Kei River mouth.

This is an area of extraordinarily diverse landscape and vegetation types, the reason being that it is the meeting place not only of an all-year round rainfall climate in the south and a summer rainfall region further north and east, but also of a variety of geological formations. The high peaks of the western mountain ranges support mesic and arid mountain fynbos, their mid slopes a fynbos type in which grasses replace restios as a dominant component, and their lower slopes two veld types: succulent vegetation and a dense, high, shrubby vegetation known as valley bushveld. Nowhere is the conjunction of the essentially Mediterranean-type vegetation, fynbos, and summer rainfall grassland more vividly demonstrated than in the Zuurberg range.

The grass thornveld of the hills inland from Port Elizabeth to the Kei River mouth grades steadily into Nama karoo vegetation further from the coast as rainfall decreases. The dry inland areas are subject to devastating drought.

Further north, the Amatola, Katberg and Stormberg ranges carry, in addition to grassland, extensive stretches of temperate forest. Climate is more extreme the further inland one goes: the area around Barkly East is renowned for its sub-zero winter temperatures and snow can be heavy in the surrounding mountains. In all the mountains, hikers should always be prepared for cold, wet conditions.

The eastern Cape and Ciskei offer hikes in wilderness areas, nature reserves, national parks and along rivers, lagoons and the coast, to suit anyone from the nature rambler to the adventurous backpacker.

At the eastern Cape's northern boundary lies the Xhosa republic of Transkei. Most rain falls during the summer, when skies can be cloudy to overcast. The country's highlands with their deep valleys and great ridges offer trailing potential for the explorer, but only the coast has thus far been developed for trailing. This magnificent, 280-km stretch of Wild Coast, with its rugged cliff-faces, breathtaking estuarine valleys edged by dense, tangled forests and grassy fields, wide, bleached-white beaches, and rich tidal marine life has been a retreat for family holidays for decades. It is also one the world's few ideal coastal hiking venues.

LEFT: *Paintings in the caves above the idyllic Baviaanskloof River are evidence that Bushmen once inhabited what is now the Baviaanskloof Wilderness Area.*

1. LE FEROX PARADIS TRAILS
LE FEROX PARADIS PRIVATE NATURE RESERVE, NEAR JOUBERTINA

Trail details: 1. Aloe-fynbos Trail: 14 km/6 hours, circular; 2. Gorge Walk: 6 km/4 hours, circular; 3. Skrikkerivier Wilderness Trail: open-ended.

Permits/bookings: Must be obtained from the owners of the Le Ferox Paradis Private Nature Reserve, tel. (0427) 32079; PO Box 218, Joubertina 6410. Brochure available on request.

Facilities/amenities: Hikers can be accommodated in the owners' farmhouse with full board, or they may pitch their tents and sleep out in the open. Overnight huts are planned.

Main attractions: Indigenous forest; prolific birdlife; interesting rock formations; Bushman paintings; swimming in the farm dam; traditional farm fare.

Pertinent information: Rapidly changeable weather. There is a limit of 12 people on the trails at any one time. No open fires allowed.

Tilted strata and flourishing clumps of succulents surround a quiet pool in Baviaanskloof State Forest.

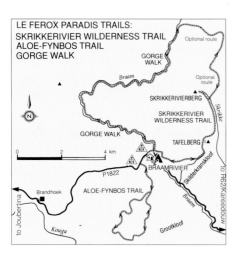

To reach this private nature reserve in the heart of the Kouga mountains, follow the P1822 from Joubertina for 31 km to the farm Braamrivier, where there is a signpost to the reserve. The area is home to a wide variety of animals, including bushbuck, bushpig, otter, steenbok, mountain reedbuck, duiker, klipspringer, civet cat, leopard, caracal, jackal, honey badger and mongoose. The birdlife in the reserve is prolific; Knysna lourie, black eagle (nesting along the Skrikkerivier Wilderness Trail), blue crane and sunbirds can be seen.

The owners of this 800-ha farm and reserve are happy to act as guides for the **Gorge Walk** and **Aloe-fynbos Trail**. These two walks are both clearly marked (the Aloe-fynbos Trail follows fourwheel-drive tracks for part of the way) and are not particularly arduous; the Gorge Walk in particular is suitable for children.

Hikers preferring a more strenuous walk should do the **Skrikkerivier Wilderness Trail**, which is an unmarked route through the open wilderness of the reserve; parts of this trail border the Baviaanskloof mountain range.

The best time for hiking in the area is from March to November, although the trails are open all year. The summers tend to be very hot.

2. COCKSCOMB AND BAVIAANSKLOOF STATE FORESTS
PATENSIE TO WILLOWMORE

Trail details: A number of trails are in the process of being designed.

Permits/bookings: Must be obtained from the officer-in-charge, Cape Nature Conservation: Cockscomb State Forest, tel. (04232) 30270; Baviaanskloof State Forest, tel. (04942) 6102. PO Box 218, Patensie 6335 for both.

Facilities/amenities: Footpaths; 5 Geelhoutbos huts, each equipped with 6 beds and all amenities.

Main attractions: Vast, dramatic wilderness; deep kloofs; large specimens of Willowmore (Baviaanskloof) cedar, *Widdringtonia schwarzii*; rock pools; wildlife; Bushman paintings.

Pertinent information: This area is for experienced hikers only; always carry maps, a compass, and plenty of water. The summers are extremely hot.

The Baviaanskloof and Kouga mountains merge into a tough, vast and wild region which is similar to, but not as dramatic as, the Cedarberg in the Western Cape. Of all the southern and eastern Cape mountains, these are the most challenging and scenically rewarding, with their deep kloofs and bathing pools, impressive rock faces, high peaks and endless traverses.

It is up to mountaineers to plan their adventure carefully, using topographic maps and conferring with the nature conservators for advice. Private land is usually crossed to reach the mountain catchment, therefore it is important to make arrangements with the relevant farmers (the nature conservators will have their details). Careful investigation of krantzes, ponds and vegetation reveals birds such as the black cuckooshrike, black crake, Cape reed warbler, African sedge warbler, blue-billed firefinch, redbreasted sparrowhawk, peregrine falcon and black eagle. Duiker, klipspringer and baboon are plentiful.

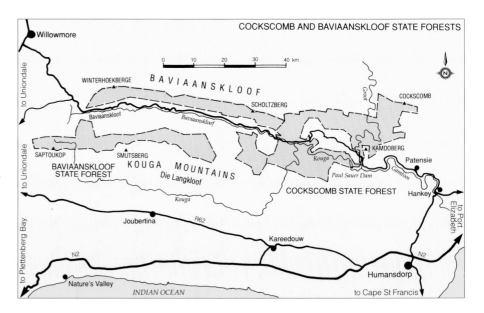

Access to the southern slopes of this area is via Langkloof, the apple-growing heartland of the area, while the northern slopes can be reached from the Patensie-Willowmore road, itself a spectacular scenic drive through a fertile valley where citrus and other crops grow under irrigation.

3. GONAQUA TRAIL
LOERIE

Trail details: 30 km/2 days; circular.

Permits/bookings: Must be obtained from the Regional Director, Tsitsikamma Forest Region, tel. (0423) 51180; Private Bag X537, Humansdorp.

Facilities/amenities: Robinson hut at the start, and an overnight hut accommodating 18 hikers; hot-water showers.

Main attractions: Fynbos; abundant birdlife.

Pertinent information: This area is extremely hot in summer, and the trail is fairly exposed. There is a limit of 18 people per day on the trail.

The Gonaqua Trail begins in the Loerie Dam Nature Reserve, just outside the village of Loerie, approximately 65 km west of Port Elizabeth. The mountainous terrain requires a high level of fitness. Hikers walk 20 km on the first day (although an optional loop reduces this by 8 km, if necessary) and 10 km on the second.

The hike leads through the adjoining Otterford State Forest, towards the Baviaanskloof mountains. The route then descends to Grootkloof, across a riverbed, and begins the 300-m ascent to Windnek. Along this part of the route is an indigenous forest containing numerous tree orchids. After crossing the river hikers can stop at Lily Pond for a swim, which should be appreciated before the steep walk to Hazyview. Along Protea and Euphorbia ridges there are some lovely views over river, pools and waterfalls. The route then climbs through the indigenous forest and makes a slight detour to the overnight hut.

The second day of the hike begins with a stiff climb to the old lookout, before descending to the river and arriving at Long Ridge and Robinson hut at the start.

This trail offers the chance of seeing bushbuck and grysbok, as well as baboon. Birds of interest include the Knysna lourie and narina trogon. The winter months offer the most pleasant hiking conditions; the summers are extremely hot.

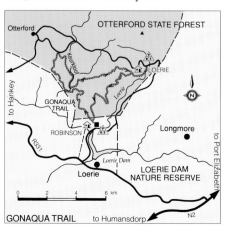

4. GROENDAL WILDERNESS AREA
NEAR UITENHAGE

Trail details: Blindekloof: 14 km/6 hours; Upper Blindekloof: 36 km/2 days; Dam Route: 38 km/ 2 days; Emerald Pool: 32 km/2 days; all are circular.

Permits/bookings: Must be obtained from the Nature Conservator of the Groendal Wilderness Area, Cape Nature Conservation, tel. (041) 9925418; PO Box 445, Uitenhage 6230.

Facilities/amenities: There are no overnight huts – patrol paths and footpaths only; labelled tree specimens; caves available for shelter.

Main attractions: Deep forested ravines; Emerald Pool and other rock pools; fynbos-type vegetation and valley bushveld; prolific antelope and forest bird species; Bushman paintings in natural rock shelters. There is a limit of 12 people per walk at any one time.

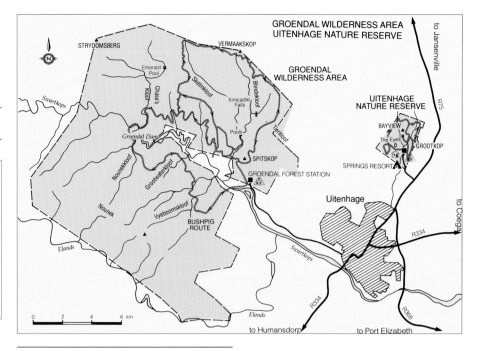

The south-eastern Cape is not as richly endowed with unexploited rugged mountain terrain as some other regions of South Africa. However, 8 km from Uitenhage, in the Groot Winterhoek range, lies a stretch of almost inaccessible ravines, vertical rock faces, natural cave shelters, impenetrable valley bushveld, fynbos and indigenous forest where leopards are, on occasion, still seen. This mountainous area, known to mountaineers for the 1 180-m Strydomsberg Peak, was given wilderness conservation status in 1976.

All the walks start and end at the Groendal office. Apart from the Blindekloof Walk, all the walks are strenuous. The Groendal Wilderness Area (21 793 ha) has numerous well-marked footpaths and patrol tracks which mountaineers may use, but you are not restricted to them. However, at the lower elevations (314-630 m) the dense form of valley bushveld vegetation makes hiking on routes other than prepared trails almost impossible.

The still waters of Groendal's Emerald Pool mirror stern rock and lush green foliage.

One of the traditionally popular destinations for hikers was Emerald Pool, a strenuous 32-km/2-day hike. Unfortunately, this route had to be closed in 1987 to allow the veld to recover from excessive trampling which had caused serious erosion. Heat exhaustion is a possible hazard in summer, especially if the berg wind blows.

Among the bushveld, fynbos and forested kloofs live grey duiker, grysbok, bushbuck, blue duiker, baboon, bushpig and the Knysna lourie. Other animals and birds which hikers may be fortunate to see are the yellowbilled duck, black duck, grey rhebok and mountain reedbuck.

The entire wilderness area is a catchment for the Swartkops River whose tributaries have cut impressive, deep ravines in the consolidated river gravel sands and mud, and higher folded and fractured quartzitic formations. The Groendal Dam, which supplies Uitenhage's industrial and domestic water, and some small private properties are also situated within the wilderness area.

This area is believed to have been the last refuge of the Bushmen between the Gamtoos and Kei rivers. Some of their fascinating paintings can still be seen here.

5. UITENHAGE NATURE RESERVE
UITENHAGE

> **Trail details:** Various walks from 40 minutes to 3 hours; approximately 24 km in total (circular). See map p. 105.
>
> **Permits/bookings:** Must be obtained from the supervisor of the Springs Holiday Resort, tel. (041) 9926011; Uitenhage 6230. Map and brochure available on request.
>
> **Facilities/amenities:** Footpaths; the Springs resort has bungalows and caravan sites, and horses are available for hire.
>
> **Main attractions:** Tropical and temperate plant and animal life; cycads; freshwater springs.
>
> **Pertinent information:** Walkers must carry water.

The 900-ha Uitenhage Nature Reserve is situated just 7 km outside Uitenhage. Emphasizing indigenous vegetation and its associated bird and small mammal life, the walks in the Uitenhage Nature Reserve offer gentle, pleasant strolls over a variety of undulating terrain. Three wide, circular paths, requiring from 40 minutes to three hours to complete, lead the rambler through thick valley bushveld and karroid shrub and grassland. These plant communities, noted for their inclusion of both tropical and temperate species, support small antelope such as bushbuck, grysbok, steenbok and duiker. The veld is also home to bushpig, porcupine and more than 100 bird species, including a number of waterfowl which are attracted to an old concrete dam converted into a 'pan'.

Plant-lovers will enjoy the variety of angiosperms, including many representatives of the Compositae, Liliaceae and Crassulaceae families. June to the end of August, the blooming season for aloes, is recommended for visits. Interesting trees such as white milkwood, sneezewood, wild olive and the Karoo boer-bean are also present in this reserve. The north- and west-facing slopes, being drier and warmer, naturally support the

more succulent-type plants such as spekboom and euphorbia.

In addition to following the footpaths, a visit to 'The Eyes' freshwater springs is worthwhile. Here, approximately 3,6 million litres of water bubble out of the ground each day, attracting many birds and small animals to the resultant lush 'oasis' vegetation. Uitenhage is able to use the natural fountains for part of its water supply as the reserve is located only 7 km from the town.

6. VAN STADENS WILDFLOWER RESERVE
PORT ELIZABETH

> **Trail details:** 1. River Walk: 3 km/1,5 hours, return; 2. Forest Walk: 2 km/1 hour, circular.
>
> **Permits/bookings:** Not required, although if a party of more than 10 people plan to walk, arrangements should be made beforehand with the Reserve manager; tel. (041) 9555649.
>
> **Facilities/amenities:** Information centre; picnic sites; toilets.
>
> **Main attractions:** Forested riverine slopes; mountain views; protea plantings; indigenous flowering plants.
>
> **Pertinent information:** Walkers must take their own water.

Situated 35 km west of Port Elizabeth on the east bank of the Van Stadens River, this area conserves Alexandria forest and eastern Cape fynbos, and also has as its aim the protection and propagation of proteas and other indigenous flora. The reserve offers a number of expansive views of ravine and forest scenery.

Neither of the trails is particularly strenuous, although some may find the end of the Forest Walk demanding in hot weather.

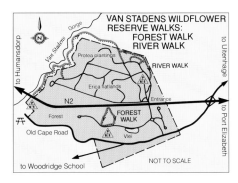

1. The River Walk begins opposite the main picnic area near the nursery. The path follows a contour between the river and the plateau, eventually descending to river level. Walkers return over the same route.

2. The Forest Walk starts at the manager's house within the reserve, and descends through fynbos into a lovely shady kloof. Hikers cross a stream and enter the forest along a path more-or-less alongside the twisting Van Stadens Pass. The route makes a circuit back to the stream and fynbos path.

Attractive chiefly to the botanically and ornithologically orientated rambler, tracks on level to gently sloping terrain crisscross erica flatlands and plantings of protea, and lead to vantage points overlooking forested gorges. Table Mountain sandstone soils support ground orchids, succulents and annuals in addition to cultivated and forest species. The forests along the southern slopes and river are transitional between the more western Knysna flora and the more tropical vegetation to the east. February to August is the main flowering season.

Birdlife flourishes within the forests and the vleis; the sombre bulbul, narina trogon and paradise flycatcher are just some of the 102 recorded species to be seen. The reserve also hosts colourful butterflies and a population of small mammals which includes grysbok, blue and grey duiker and bushbuck.

Van Staden's Flower Reserve is renowned for its proteas, but it also has a wealth of rare indigenous tree species.

7. SIR PEREGRINE MAITLAND AND DE STADES TRAILS
MAITLAND NATURE RESERVE

Trail details: 1. Sir Peregrine Maitland Trail: 3,2 km/2 hours; 2. De Stades Trail: 9,4 km/3,5 hours. Both are circular.

Permits/bookings: Must be obtained from the Algoa Regional Services Council: Nature Conservation Division, tel. (041) 561000; PO Box 318, Port Elizabeth 6000.

Facilities/amenities: Picnic sites; trees along the trail labelled with their national tree list numbers; angling; Maitland camp site at the Maitland River mouth; information boxes at regular intervals.

Main attractions: Coastal forest and bush; birdlife.

Pertinent information: Hikers should take their own water, as the stream water in the reserve is not suitable for drinking.

Both these trails are situated in the Maitland Nature Reserve, which is approximately 35 km west of Port Elizabeth.

1. The Sir Peregrine Maitland Trail starts and ends at the entrance to the reserve. It cuts through the forest and leads along the old wagon road. Part of this road is steep, although a moderate level of fitness is sufficient. The route is clearly marked. Named after the governor of the Cape in 1846, the Sir Peregrine Maitland Trail is used by the Nature Conservation Division of the Algoa Regional Services Council to introduce children to the wonders of nature.

2. The De Stades Trail starts in the De Stades Valley and has the De Stades Stream at its foot. The first part of the walk provides hikers with open views across coastal countryside, passing through high bush and big trees. Then it drops into the De Stades Valley's low bush and small trees. Again it climbs out of the valley onto a ridge of forested dune with a wonderful view of the bigger Maitland River Valley, near the mouth of the river. The route is well-marked.

A group of vervet monkeys bask in the morning sun.

A feature of these trails is the information boxes dotted along the way, which provide data on the natural cycle, succession, soil and soil erosion, aesthetical values, animals and territorial behaviour, habitats and niches, forest and canopy levels, and bird observation. The birdlife in the reserve includes the emeraldspotted wood dove, African hoopoe, paradise flycatcher, forest canary and Knysna lourie. The reserve is home to many small mammals including bushbuck, blue duiker, porcupine, antbear and mongoose.

8. BOSBOK WALK
ISLAND CONSERVATION AREA

Trail details: 16 km/6 hours (variations possible); circular route.

Permits/bookings: Must be obtained from the manager, Island Conservation Area, tel. (041) 741634; PO Box 19061, Linton Grange 6015. Map available on request.

Facilities/amenities: Picnic sites with fireplaces; trees labelled with their national tree list numbers.

Main attractions: Alexandria-type forest; birdlife (120 species recorded to date); small mammals; spectacular sea views.

Pertinent information: Ticks are a big problem in the forest. It is easy to take the wrong route; get a map at the start.

The Bosbok Walk starts from the forester's house at the Island Conservation Area near Sea View, 25 km from Port Elizabeth, and winds through and around indigenous forest on an ancient vegetated 282 m-high dune. Forty-nine tree specimens, including hard pear, white Cape beech, Cape cherry and Outeniqua yellowwood, are marked with their national tree list numbers to facilitate identification. The region provides a fine example of what is known botanically as Alexandria forest, a xerophytic form of the more verdant tropical coastal forest to the north-east and the coastal bush of Natal and the Transkei. Within this forest, you have an excellent chance of seeing bushbuck and the Knysna lourie, both secretive species, and possibly vervet monkey, grey duiker, the black cuckoo and scalythroated honeyguide as well.

MAITLAND MINE ✕
MAITLAND NATURE RESERVE
SIR PEREGRINE MAITLAND TRAIL
DE STADES TRAIL
to N2/Port Elizabeth
to N2/Port Elizabeth
Gate
BOSBOK WALK
Eucalyptus
Lookout tower
Lookout tower
Forester's House
Maitland Beach
Maitland Camping Site
Indigenous forest
to Port Elizabeth
to Port Elizabeth
Maitland River Mouth
Lookout tower
Beach View
THE ISLAND STATE FOREST
ST FRANCIS BAY
Sea View
INDIAN OCEAN
Kini Bay
BOSBOK WALK
DE STADES TRAIL
SIR PEREGRINE MAITLAND TRAIL
0   1   2   3 km

The Bosbok Walk takes the hiker through stands of *Pinus radiata* and crosses a number of old plantation roads, all of which provide easy exits to terminate your walk if necessary.

The entire trail is on gently undulating terrain and physically is not too demanding, although in hot weather it may require some endurance.

9. SETTLER'S PARK
PORT ELIZABETH

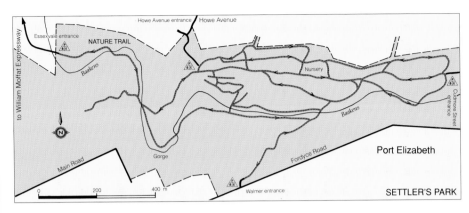

Trail details: 2 km/1 hour to 7,5 km/3,5 hours; one way trail.

Permits/bookings: Not required; guided tours can be arranged by contacting the curator of the park; tel. (041) 336794.

Facilities/amenities: Footpaths with benches; display centre featuring flowers in bloom; toilets and tap water.

Main attractions: Indigenous vegetation and botanical displays; excellent birdlife;

Pertinent information: Note that the numerous river crossings are hazardous after heavy rains. Hikers must carry their own water and should under no circumstances drink from the Baakens River. As the major section of this park is situated in an urban area, walking in groups is suggested.

Settler's Park, a large open kloof framing the Baakens River in Port Elizabeth, is one of South Africa's most interesting urban green areas. Several paths contour the 54-ha reserve and lead walkers around the dams, wide, tree-planted lawns and bright flowers into the Baakens River Gorge. The Port Elizabeth Parks and Recreation Department is in the process of constructing a 7,5 km nature trail from Target Kloof to Mangold Park, at the William Moffatt Expressway. The path follows the valley floor, crossing and recrossing the river by stepping stones or drifts.

Energetic hikers can extend their walk along the Baakens River Valley beyond Settler's Park. The official trail extends from the vicinity of 7th Avenue in Walmer to 'The Dip', the causeway crossing of the river which is an extension of 3rd Avenue in Newton Park. However, the valley can be walked as far as Circular Drive, Walmer, in the vicinity of Frame's Drift.

The principal botanic value of Settler's Park lies in its location as the meeting point of four vegetation types: the subtropical flora of the summer rainfall area, fynbos, grasslands of higher altitudes, and karroid vegetation. This diverse flora attracts a fascinating array of birdlife, especially exciting because of its close proximity to the city centre. Paradise flycatcher, Knysna lourie and malachite kingfisher are a few of the more colourful species.

10. ZUURBERG NATIONAL PARK WALKS
ZUURBERG NATIONAL PARK

Trail details: Two trails: 12 km/4 hours, and 2,5 km/1 hour. Both are circular.

Permits/bookings: Required. Must be obtained from the National Parks Board, tel. (021) 222810; PO Box 7400, Roggebaai 8012; or the Park Warden, tel. (0426) 400581; PO Box 76, Addo 6105. Map and brochure available on request from both these bodies.

Facilities/amenities: Guests may stay at the newly opened Kabouga Guesthouse, under a canopy of spectacular fig and yellowwood trees.

Main attractions: Wild, broken terrain with pleasant kloofs, pools and forested ravines; rare plants (Zuurberg cushionbush and Zuurberg cycad); large game species (to be introduced).

Pertinent information: Hikers must carry their own water at all times. Make enquiries about the new Breakneck Trail.

Local mountaineers have long been familiar with the footpath in the Sundays River catchment area, a wild, broken terrain, previously the Zuurberg State Forest but now under the authority of the National Parks Board. This park is found north of Port Elizabeth and Addo and is open for the exploration of its kloofs, krantzes and the peaks rising 250–970 m above sea level.

The short 1-hour walk passes through a plantation and along the fringe of a kloof, and the longer 4-hour walk leads into the forest and back up an open fynbos ridge. Both walks are extremely well marked and start at the former forester's office at the top of the Suurberg Pass.

Zuurberg National Park is composed of folded quartzites, sandstones and shales of the Witteberg series (Cape system), and tillites and shales of the slightly younger Dwyka series (Karoo system), both belonging to the Palaeozoic Era. Grasses dominate the peaks and their upper slopes, while the valleys are wooded with dry scrub. In these vegetation zones two rare and beautiful plants, the Zuurberg cushionbush and the Zuurberg cycad, were discovered.

Kudu, bushbuck, blue duiker, grysbok, water leguan and Knysna lourie are found in the forest ravines while mountain reedbuck, grey rhebok and baboon can be seen on the broken terrain of the mountain slopes. There are plans to introduce mountain zebra, black rhinoceros, buffalo and Addo elephant into the park.

A home of the hyrax in Settlers' Park is aptly named Dassie Cliff.

Violent intermittent floods have produced the rounded boulders that lie in the gouged-out channel.

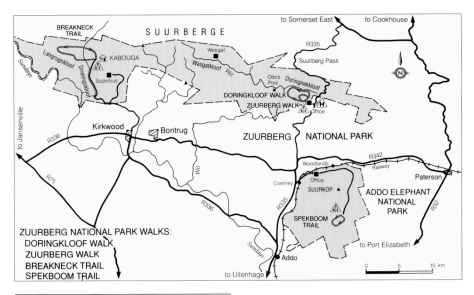

ZUURBERG NATIONAL PARK WALKS:
DORINGKLOOF WALK
ZUURBERG WALK
BREAKNECK TRAIL
SPEKBOOM TRAIL

11. SPEKBOOM TRAIL
ADDO ELEPHANT NATIONAL PARK

Trail details: 6 km/2 to 4 hours; circular.

Permits/bookings: Must be obtained from the Warden, Addo Elephant National Park, tel. (0426) 400556; PO Box 52, Addo 6105. Brochure available on request.

Facilities/amenities: Rest benches along the way.

Main attractions: Lush valley bushveld; prolific birdlife; game; trees labelled with their national tree list numbers.

Pertinent information: Hikers must carry their own water. Be sure to take along a good set of binoculars as well as a bird book.

The Spekboom Trail, situated in a botanical reserve within the Addo Elephant National Park, takes the nature lover through pristine vegetation, where the trees and succulents are labelled. There is an abundance of trees, game and birds; it is recommended that hikers take along a good set of binoculars and a bird book. Large mammals such as buffalo, black rhinoceros and elephant have been fenced out of the trail area. Due to the highly palatable 'spekboomveld' the park has one of the largest concentrations of game in Africa in relation to its size and you may come across bushbuck, grey duiker, kudu and a variety of smaller animals and reptiles. The Spekboom Trail is clearly marked and leads up a low hill, giving marvellous views over the surrounding countryside.

12. THE ALEXANDRIA TRAIL
ALEXANDRIA

Trail details: 35,8 km/2 days; circular. See map page 110.

Permits/bookings: Must be obtained from Cape Nature Conservation, tel. (046) 6530601; PO Box 50, Alexandria 6185.

Facilities/amenities: Base hut with cold water, showers, toilets, 12 bunks and mattresses, and braai facilities; overnight hut with 12 bunks and mattresses, rain water must be used, no fires allowed; trees labelled with their national tree list numbers. Hikers must arrange to obtain the key for the hut when booking.

Main attractions: The Alexandria dunefield, one of the largest active coastal dunefields in the world; coastal dune forest (impressive specimens and rich birdlife); Damara tern, the rarest seabird breeding in South Africa.

Pertinent information: Many ticks; rapidly changeable weather (wind in particular). There is a limit of 12 people for this trail at any one time.

This circular coastal forest trail is relatively easy; running shoes can be substituted for heavy boots. A unique feature of the trail is the traverse across the spectacular Alexandria dunefield, which, at 120 km, is one of the largest active coastal dunefields in the world, and the largest in South Africa. Less than 10 000 years old, this field is still expanding. The first day leads for 19,4 km from Langebos through the forest to Wonderboom, and down to the beach and Woody Cape. The second day leads from Woody Cape to the dunefield, up to Langevlakte and home to Langebos.

Sea-eroded rocks form interesting patterns above a shingled shoreline on the Alexandria Trail.

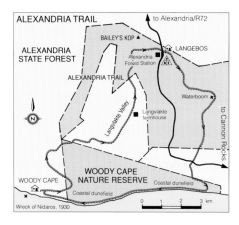

The largest tree specimens on this trail can be found in the impressive dune forest, and comprise such species as common wild (Natal) fig, coast coral tree, yellowwood and white ironwood. You will also pass through the lush Langevlakte Valley, with its green, rolling farmlands. Binoculars are strongly recommended for this trail, to enable you to view the schools of dolphins and flocks of gannets along the coast. You may also encounter a kangaroo-like mouse, the hairy footed gerbil, endemic to these dunes, along the way. The Alexandria Trail is clearly marked.

13. ORIBI NATURE TRAILS
PORT ALFRED

Trail details: Guided walks ranging from 1 km/ 20 min to 20 km/9 hours. All are circular.

Permits/bookings: Booking must be obtained in advance from the owners of Hope Farm, tel. (0464) 43144; PO Box 48, Port Alfred 6170.

Facilities/amenities: None.

Main attractions: Scenic undulating hills extending to beautiful beaches; numerous species of birds, game and flora.

Pertinent information: There is a daily limit of 30 people on the trail. Hikers should carry their own water, as there is only a (brackish) borehole *en route.*

The Oribi Nature Trails begin and end at Hope Farm, an area of 1 276 ha, which lies 3 km from Port Alfred. Ideal for the beginner hiker, these walks do not require a high level of fitness. Whether you decide to try just a short part of the trail or the entire route, the rolling hills and temperate climate of this area ensures pleasant walking conditions all the year round.

The length of the trail depends on you; the guide is willing to take you wherever possible and to show you whatever you wish to see of the area. The coastal bushveld is home to oribi, bushbuck, duiker, blue duiker, bushpig, jackal, caracal and other smaller animals such as monkeys. Many interesting birds can be seen on the trail, including Knysna lourie, African fish eagle, secretarybird and Stanley's bustard.

14. KOWIE HIKING/CANOE TRAIL
PORT ALFRED

Trail details: Hiking Trail: 12 km/4 hours; Canoe Trail: 21 km/3 hours.

Permits/bookings: Must be obtained from Cape Nature Conservation, tel. (0464) 41140; PO Box 13, Port Alfred 6170. Informative brochure and map available on request.

Facilities/amenities: Camp site with toilets, water, and braai area; canoes must be obtained from the Cape Nature Conservation control officer.

Main attractions: The only self-guided hiking/canoe trail in South Africa; birdlife; trees marked with national tree list numbers.

Pertinent information: This is an extremely popular trail; hikers/canoeists must book at least six months in advance; in strong winds this trail can be extremely unpleasant. There is a limit of 14 people for the trail at any one time.

The Kowie Hiking/Canoe Trail is South Africa's only self-guided combination of this kind. There are other organized canoe and walking adventures, guided by conservation officers. Canoes can be rented at the Kowie River mouth, or canoeists can use their own equipment. It is strongly recommended that canoeists travel upstream on an incoming tide and downstream on the outgoing tide.

Visitors may spend a night at the Horseshoe camp site (take your own tent) and spend the afternoon of the first day or the morning of the second day rambling on the pleasant, demarcated forest trail in the Waters Meeting Nature Reserve. Many birds, such as the giant and pied kingfishers, yellow-billed duck, Egyptian goose, sandpiper, greenshank, sacred ibis, whitebreasted and reed cormorants, mousebird, Knysna lourie and fish eagle, can be seen from canoes.

In warm and windless weather the 25-km stretch of river to the forestry camp site is a pleasant, flat-water, 3-hour paddle, negotiable by anybody who is capable of manoeuvring on a lake or dam.

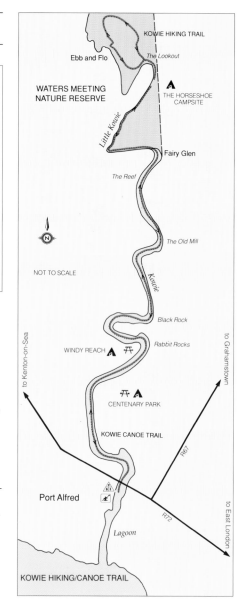

Fortunately for the lover of the outdoors, determined attempts to turn the Kowie River into a commercial waterway did not succeed.

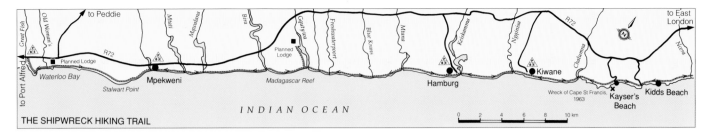

to Peddie · to Port Alfred · Great Fish · Old Woman's · R72 · Waterloo Bay · Planned Lodge · Stalwart Point · Mpekweni · Mtati · Mgwalana · Bira · Gqutywa · Planned Lodge · Freshwaterpoort · Madagascar Reef · Blue Krans · Mtana · Hamburg · Keiskamma · Kiwane · Ngqinisa · Wreck of Cape St Francis 1963 · R72 · Chalumna · Kayser's Beach · Kidds Beach · Ncera · to East London · INDIAN OCEAN · 0 2 4 6 8 10 km

THE SHIPWRECK HIKING TRAIL

15. THE SHIPWRECK TRAIL
GREAT FISH RIVER TO CHALUMNA RIVER

Trail details: Options range from 11 km/1 day to 64 km/4 days.

Permits/bookings: Must be obtained from Contour, tel. (0401) 952115; PO Box 186, Bisho.

Facilities/amenities: Hikers may pitch their tents anywhere along the beach (excluding the demarcated military zone). There are two hotels and a camp site along the way, as well as bungalows at Kiwane.

Main attractions: Hiking; rambling; rock and surf angling; bird-watching; fishing; sea-sports; unspoilt beaches; shipwrecks.

Pertinent information: There is no limit on the maximum number of people per group for this trail. The trail can be walked in either direction.

The Ciskei coast, extending from the Great Fish River mouth beyond the Keiskamma estuary to the Chalumna River, boasts a unique wilderness character. The 64 km of coast can be walked in either direction in 3 or 4 days, or can be tailored to personal choice. Combined with the Transkei Hiking Trail, Strandloper and Alexandria trails, the Shipwreck Trail forms a link in a unique and unspoilt coastal hiking paradise.

Walking distances between major points are given here for planning purposes. Remember that coastal walking is generally faster than on mountainous terrain.

Great Fish River to Chalumna River: 64 km; Great Fish River to Mpekweni: 11,5 km; Mpekweni to Bira River: 11 km; Bira River to Keiskamma River: 20 km; Keiskamma River to Chalumna River: 10,5 km; Chalumna River to Kidds Beach: 15,6 km.

The rock sculptures at the mouth of the Great Fish River are worth exploring. Numerous wave- and wind-eroded tunnels and caves have been carved out of the headland, which played a significant role in Ciskeian history. It served as the port captain's office from 1846 to 1848 when soldiers disembarked and supplies destined for Fort Peddie were offloaded in Waterloo Bay. In order to protect landing operations, Fort Albert was established at Old Woman's River.

The Great Fish River mouth and lagoon between the Boy Retief bridge and the river mouth teem with birdlife. Cape teal and other ducks breed here. Yellowbilled ducks, pochards, and Egyptian and spurwing geese are often seen, while stilts, whimbrels, greenshanks and smaller migratory waders are numerous.

Mpekweni's estuary, once a quiet fisherman's hideaway, is now the site of the new Mpekweni Marine Resort, a very attractive hotel complex offering all sorts of watersports.

Bira Mouth is a place of immense charm. It was here that the *Grosvenor* survivors, trekking to civilization, were confronted by a herd of bathing elephants. On its eastern side is a dangerous ridge of rocks called Madagascar Reef, where the steamer *Madagascar* was wrecked in 1858, and the *Ben Holden* in 1934. The sailing ship *Elizabeth* has the dubious honour of being the first wreck at this spot, in 1839. To get a good view of this reef climb the hill to the east of the settlement.

It is an easy walk from Bira to Gqutywa River mouth, a beautiful unspoilt area, and easily crossed. The coastline is open, with high-forest covered sand dunes set well away from the sea. Both oyster-catchers and whitefronted sandplovers can be seen breeding here in season.

The Keiskamma River estuary is extremely rich in birdlife, as is the adjacent coastal bush. It is also one of the best fishing grounds on the whole coast. The charming little village of Hamburg originated as one of the many German settlements established along the southern bank of the Keiskamma in the 1850s. The wildest area of the Shipwreck Trail lies between the Keiskamma estuary and the Chalumna River. Its forested dunes are being developed as a game reserve and large mammals have been reintroduced. The rocky stretches are rewarding to shell collectors. The size and variety of the mussels found here is legendary.

The Shipwreck Trail is within the capabilities of any reasonably fit person. Hikers can exchange heavy mountain boots for lighter boots, or a sturdy pair of running or walking shoes. Sunglasses, sunhats and sunscreen lotion are essential.

16. FORT FORDYCE NATURE RESERVE
FORT BEAUFORT

Trail details: There are 4 trails varying in length from 5 km to 10 km. In addition, there is a 2-day trail of approximately 25 km. All are circular. See map page 112.

Permits/bookings: Required for overnight hikers only. Must be obtained from the officer-in-charge, Cape Nature Conservation, tel. (046) 6840732; Private Bag X232, Fort Beaufort 5720. Hikers should book well in advance. Map and brochure available on request.

Facilities/amenities: There is an overnight hut accommodating 12 hikers; two picnic areas are provided for day hikers, one situated under a giant oak, the other on the banks of the dam. The hut is equipped with a fridge, oven, hot water, electricity and a fireplace.

Main attractions: Views overlooking the Hogsback mountains; indigenous forest vegetation.

Fort Fordyce is a 2146-ha nature reserve about 13 km from Fort Beaufort on the road to Queenstown. It offers hikers spectacular views of the

The soldiers who garrisoned long-vanished Fort Fordyce had one of the most beautiful environs in the world.

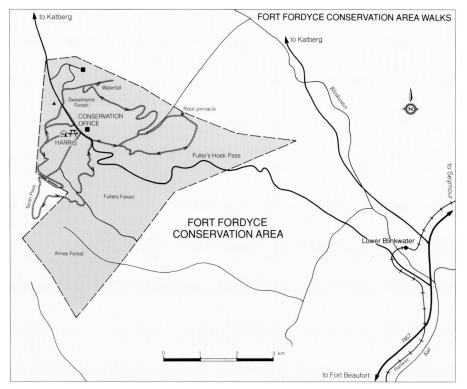

FORT FORDYCE CONSERVATION AREA WALKS

The smooth green plains in the distance are, in fact, the local golf course.

Hogsback mountains, and comprises an extensive central escarpment with steep cliffs and kloofs falling away to valleys and flatter areas. The indigenous forest vegetation in the kloofs and valleys, the false eastern Cape thornveld, and the Dohne grassveld, are home to a wide variety of animals. Wildebeest, red hartebeest, Burchell's zebra, bushpig, blue duiker, kudu, mountain reedbuck, bushbuck, and wildcat all abound. Bird species you are likely to see include hornbills and barbets, sunbirds, flycatchers, Knysna louries and the crowned, longcrested and black eagles.

All the walks are clearly marked.

17. BOSBERG HIKING TRAIL
SOMERSET EAST

Trail details: Approximately 15 km/2 days; circular.

Permits/bookings: Must be obtained from the Municipality of Somerset East, tel (0424) 31333; PO Box 21, Somerset East 5880. Map and brochure available on request.

Facilities/amenities: Information hut; overnight hut with 10 mattresses, gas lamp and candles, braai facilities and wood, water and toilets; game camp; caravan park.

Main attractions: Magnificent views of Somerset East and Karoo landscape; forest relics; birdlife; Kebe's Cave.

Pertinent information: Beware of ticks and rapidly changeable weather. Hikers should carry their own water and a torch. There is a limit of 10 people for the trail at any one time.

The Bosberg Hiking Trail is a magnificent circular walk on the slopes of Bloukop, above Somerset East, in the Bosberg Nature Reserve (2 050 ha). The trail requires a medium level of fitness, and starts and ends at the information hut at the entrance to the reserve. It passes through relic patches

of indigenous forest, rich in yellowwood and wild olive, which provide a valuable habitat for bushbuck and many bush-dwelling birds.

Looking back towards Somerset East from the Bloukop ridge, the views are superb, while the forward landscape suddenly gives way to the waves of flat-topped koppies so typical of the Karoo. The large municipal dam on the flat summit is a good spot for bird-watchers to observe waterfowl. Gymnogenes, jackal buzzards and other raptors soar above the ridge in search of prey, and Stanley's bustard can be seen marching purposefully among grass tussocks.

From the ridge the trail leads to Kebe's Cave, situated near the overnight hut. Kebe's Cave has clear, cold running water to reward hikers willing to crawl into its maw with their torches.

On the second day hikers double back for a short way, and then head west, through sour grasses and fynbos. The highest point on the trail is Bloukop (1 622 m) with a truly spectacular view. From Blou-

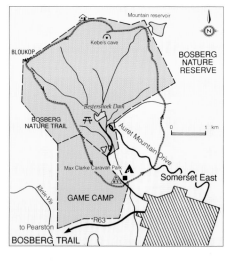

BOSBERG TRAIL

kop the path descends over the first section and follows an even route until reaching the information hut 11 km later. The trail is clearly marked and is especially pleasant in summer.

18. COMMANDO DRIFT NATURE RESERVE
TARKASTAD/CRADOCK DISTRICT

Trail details: 1. Endurance Trail: 28 km/2 days, circular; 2. Aardvark Trail: 6 km/2,5 hours, return.

Permits/bookings: Permits must be obtained at the reserve from the officer-in-charge; accommodation must be booked in advance with Cape Nature Conservation, tel. (0481) 3925; PO Box 459, Cradock 5880. Map available on request.

Facilities/amenities: Guided trails on request; the recreation area has 3 huts with basic accommodation for 4 people each, toilets and cold showers; camping and caravanning are allowed; picnic, braai and toilet facilities; small information centre; overnight hut on Endurance Trail sleeps 6, has cold shower and fireplace.

Main attractions: Commando Drift Dam; karroid plains; sandstone and dolerite krantzes; wooded watercourses and dolerite koppie veld; birdlife; large game.

Pertinent information: Take water, as there are no water points, and insect repellent in summer. Thunderstorms may cause path floods in summer, making the Endurance Trail impossible.

Situated approximately 78 km from Cradock off the Cradock/Tarkastad road, the main feature of this nature reserve, the Commando Drift Dam, is popular with boating enthusiasts and bird-watchers alike. Egyptian goose, South African shelduck, yellowbilled duck, southern pochard, African black duck, redknobbed coot, redbilled teal, and African fish eagle are commonly observed. The waterfowl

Four rivers provide a wonderful habitat for waterfowl in Commando Drift Nature Reserve.

habitat is further enhanced by the four rivers which flow into the dam: the Elands, Tarka, Palingkloof and Vlekpoort.

Indigenous animals are being introduced in small numbers and include Cape mountain zebra, kudu, blesbok, springbok, steenbok, grey duiker and black wildebeest.

1. The Endurance Trail follows the edge of the dam for the most part, and crosses the four rivers that feed this water body. A reservoir adjacent to the overnight hut at the 16,5-km point is the perfect spot for a dip. Dusk and dawn should be spent at the nearby viewing hide.

2. The Aardvark Trail is an easy route that leads from the cabins and up Palingkloof on a management track, returning the same way. The kloof is rich in birdlife, which ranges from kingfishers, honeyguides and mocking chats to owls, hamerkops and ducks.

The reserve is a mountainous landscape which slopes down to the river banks, and includes Karoo flats, sandstone and dolerite cliffs, woodedwatercourses and dolerite koppie veld. The vegetation is false karroid broken veld, with lush acacia thickets along the river courses.

19. TARKA TOORBERG
TARKASTAD

Trail details: 30 km/2 days; circular.

Permits/bookings: Must be obtained from the Tarka Hiking and Adventure Association, tel. (04582) 33; PO Box 21, Tarkastad 5370. Map and brochure available on request.

Facilities/amenities: Overnight accommodation in disused farmhouse with mattresses and running cold water; braai facilities available on request; fireplace in farmhouse.

Main attractions: Open Karoo vistas with panoramic views of the surrounding Winterberg and Stormberg mountain ranges; area is rich in fossil remains.

Pertinent information: This is a very exposed trail, with rapidly changeable weather. There is a daily limit of 12 people on this walk.

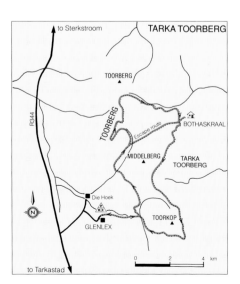

This circular hike is on Glenlex Farm, situated near the turnoff 19 km from Tarkastad on the Tarkastad/Sterkstroom road. It requires a medium to high level of fitness. Starting from the farm, you begin the 2 155 m ascent up the Toorberg, overnighting 16 km later at Bothaskraal. The next morning you circumvent the Toorkop and return down to Glenlex. Along the way you may encounter mountain reedbuck, baboons, jackals, dassies and signs of caracal living here. The grassland vegetation is excellent for viewing the animals, as there is limited bush.

20. THE TSOLWANA TRAIL
WHITTLESEA

Trail details: Varies depending on the group.

Permit/bookings: Must be obtained from the director of the Tsolwana Game Reserve, tel. (0408) 22104; PO Box 1424, Queenstown 5320.

Facilities/amenities: Bush camp accommodation with bunks and mattresses, hot and cold water; there is also accommodation available in fully serviced lodges.

Main attractions: Magnificent mountain scenery; broad vistas and valley plains; abundance of game and birdlife; Bushman cave paintings.

Pertinent information: There is a limit of 10 people at any one time for this trail.

The Tsolwana Trail is not a demarcated trail, but is led by professional game rangers through the Tsolwana Game Reserve in the northern Ciskei.

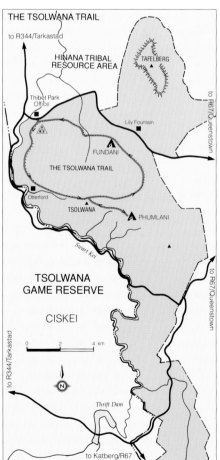

Depending on the requirements of the group, the trail can last from several hours to several days. Rising 1 877 m above sea level is a conically shaped hill named Tsolwana, Xhosa for 'sharp little one', formerly known as Spitzkop. Just north of the Tsolwana range is Tafelberg, the massive flat-topped plateau (1 965 m) edged with dolerite cliffs and visible from many vantage points in Ciskei and the eastern Cape. Between the two peaks lies a plateau teeming with animal life, and riddled with valleys, cliffs, caves, gulleys and wooded hollows. Waterfalls and streams run in numerous lightly wooded kloofs during strong rains.

In this lovely setting, hikers have the opportunity of viewing 48 species of game, including wildebeest herds, red hartebeest, gemsbok, eland, springbok, impala and blesbok. There is also a dassie colony that is unusual in that it inhabits old antbear holes. Species not indigenous to southern Africa (fallow deer, mouflon and barbary sheep and Himalayan tahr) roam freely among the other animals. Of the 117 species of birds in the area, hikers have an excellent chance of seeing woollynecked storks, Cape vultures, martial and fish eagles, Stanley's bustards and giant kingfishers.

Clothing this magnificent topography are three vegetation systems: subdesert (karoo dwarf shrub), temperate (fynbos and grassland) and arid savannah (thornveld). Wild flowers are abundant during the rainy season, creating a colourful spectacle on the green hills and plains.

21. KATBERG LOOP TRAIL
KATBERG PLANTATION

Trail details: 40 km/2 days; circular.

Permits/bookings: Must be obtained from Contour, tel. (0401) 952115; PO Box 186, Bisho 5600. Map and brochure on request.

Facilities/amenities: Diepkloof overnight hut with bunks and mattresses for 12 hikers, braai area, water and toilets; the Katberg Protea Hotel is only a short distance away from the forest station; tel. (04049) ask for Katberg 3.

Main attractions: Beautiful views of the Kat River Valley and beyond; rugged krantzes; lovely forests; streams and waterfalls; interesting rock formations.

Pertinent information: Sudden drops in temperature; berg winds create fire hazards, so smoking and fires made outside of the braai areas are not advised; hikers should carry their own water. There is a limit of 12 people for the trail at any one time.

The Katberg Loop Trail is situated in the mountainous area 8 km north-east of Balfour. The Katberg forms part of the greater Winterberg range, and peaks such as Branderskop (1 531 m), above the forest station, and Didima Peak (1 829 m) to its west are particularly attractive during the infrequent snowstorms.

The trail starts and ends at the Katberg Forest Station. It begins with a steep climb from below Branderskop up to the Katberg Pass and Diepkloof hut with its splendid views. Water is scarce on this first day. The second day leads for 22 km through forest and plantation before arriving back at the forest station.

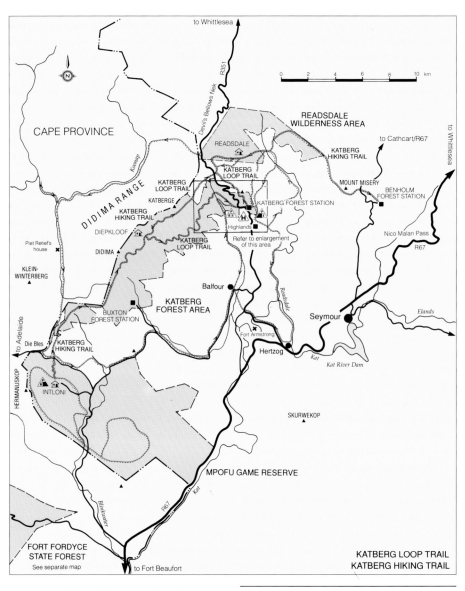

KATBERG LOOP TRAIL
KATBERG HIKING TRAIL

A section of the trail is shared with the 3-day Katberg Hiking Trail, as is the Diepkloof overnight hut. A medium level of fitness is required because of the distance, although the trail is very well laid out. (The blue crane markers are being replaced by yellow footprints.)

Vegetation comprises mountain fynbos, grassland and indigenous forest which flourish on the slopes below the krantzes. Fine examples of white ironwood, assegaai, lemonwood, yellowwood, treefuchsia and many other indigenous trees are present. In addition to the exotic pine plantations, remnants of early experimental plots dating back to 1883 comprise majestic deodars (Himalayan cedar, *Cedrus deodara*), redwoods and oaks.

Within the Katberg Forest, bushbuck are often seen. Vervet and samango monkeys, baboons and duiker are common. The birdlife in this area is also rich: crowned hornbill, Knysna lourie, grey cuckooshrike, yellow canary, chorister robin, blackheaded oriole, jackal buzzard, Cape robin and doublecollared sunbird are just some of the more common sightings.

The trail is situated in a summer rainfall area; thunderstorms and mist are common. Winter days are warm and sunny, the nights cold; snow is possible on the mountains.

22. KATBERG HIKING TRAIL
MPOFU GAME RESERVE TO BENHOLM FOREST STATION

Trail details: 51 km/3 days, open-ended; or 2 days, circular.

Permits/bookings: Must be obtained from Contour, tel. (0401) 952115; PO Box 186, Bisho 5600. Map and brochure available on request.

Facilities/amenities: Overnight huts, each with 12 bunks and mattresses, braaiwood, water and toilets. Intloni hut at the start of the trail in the reserve; Diepkloof and Readsdale overnight huts in the Katberg mountains; each hut sleeps 12 hikers and has toilets, a fireplace and wood. Water is available at each hut (use sparingly).

Main attractions: Beautiful panoramic views; Bushman paintings; wide open spaces.

Pertinent information: Rapidly changeable weather. There is a limit of 12 people for this trail at any one time. Hikers must arrange their own transport at the end of the trail. Hikers should carry their own water; berg winds create a fire hazard; be prepared for sudden drops in temperature and rain or snow; drive carefully along the old Katberg Pass to Benholm, especially in wet conditions.

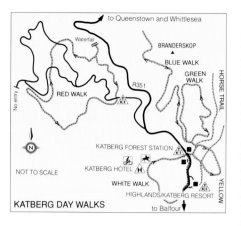

KATBERG DAY WALKS

NOT TO SCALE

to Queenstown and Whittlesea

Waterfall

BRANDERSKOP

BLUE WALK

GREEN WALK

R351

RED WALK

HORSE TRAIL

No entry

N

KATBERG FOREST STATION

KATBERG HOTEL

WHITE WALK

HIGHLANDS/KATBERG RESORT

YELLOW

to Balfour

This open-ended trail starts in the Mpofu Game Reserve (approximately 45 km north of Seymour) and finishes three days later at the Benholm Forest Station (about 16 km south-east of Balfour). It passes through several farms and plantations, taking in dry forest, mountain grassland, fynbos and a pine plantation. (The 2-day, circular alternative begins at the Katberg Forestry Office.)

The 3-day trail climbs from Intloni hut in the reserve, and leads for 17,3 km up to Diepkloof hut past some interesting Bushman paintings. The second day passes just below spectacular rugged krantzes before descending into the beautiful Readsdale wilderness area. The second night is spent at the rustic Readsdale hut (it is planned to upgrade this hut in the near future). The trail passes through what was Piet Retief's farm just before The Great Trek and overlooks the Kat River area, now a thriving citrus-growing region.

The third day's route of 18,7 km takes hikers out of the Readsdale area via some beautiful scenery to the Benholm end point. Along the way hikers may spot black wildebeest, eland, gemsbok, red hartebeest, Cape grysbok and zebra. Crowned eagles and hornbills are also commonly seen. The trail is very well laid out, and is marked with yellow footprint markers. It is open all year round, and requires a medium level of fitness. To avoid the demanding ascent from the Dakota crash site, take the short cut, which bypasses the 'plane.

23. DOUBLE DRIFT HIKING TRAIL
DOUBLE DRIFT GAME RESERVE

Trail details: 64 km/2 days; guided, circular.

Permits/bookings: For bookings and further information, contact Contour, tel. (0401) 952115, fax (04010 92756; PO Box 186, Bisho.

Facilities/amenities; Double Drift Lodge has beds and mattresses, a bathroom, a kitchen with a stove and cooking utensils; firewood is provided. Hikers must provide their own food, bedding and linen.

Main attractions: game animals; site of historical interest; Bushman paintings.

Pertinent information: Day visitors are welcome in the reserve, provided they are in possession of the necessary permit.

Double Drift Game Reserve lies in the south-western Ciskei, and is bordered by the Great Fish and Kat rivers in the west, and the Keiskamma River in the east. Between these rivers is dense thor-

ny valley bushveld which is now home to a wide variety of game including impala, giraffe, zebra, blesbok, hippo, black rhino and Cape buffalo. Numerous bird species are also resident in the reserve.

Hikers can enjoy the Double Drift Hiking Trail in the company of an experienced game guard. Both nights are spent at Double Drift Lodge.

Besides offering visitors the excitement of encountering game in its natural environment, the reserve contains a wealth of interesting historical sites. This area was once the scene of fierce battles between British troops and the local Xhosa people; the ruins of two abandoned forts, Fort Wilshire and Fort Montgomery bear witness to this. In earlier times, the Bushman lived here and fine examples of their rock art can be seen on some cave walls. Evidence of Middle and Late Stone Age peoples living in this area can be found in the form of stone tools at numerous sites around the reserve.

Fishing is permitted in the reserve's rivers, and you could catch yellowtail, carp, barbel or eel, a well known delicacy of the eastern Cape.

24. HOGSBACK WALKS
HOGSBACK STATE FOREST AND AUCKLAND NATURE RESERVE

Trail details: Various walks, ranging in length from 3 km to 20 km. See map p. 116.

Permits/bookings: Must be obtained from the Government Forester, Hogsback Plantation, tel. (0020) 55; PO Box 52, Hogsback 5721. Map and brochure available on request.

Facilities/amenities: Base camp with levelled site suitable for pitching tents; ablution blocks, braai areas, running water; overnight camp similar but with no ablution facilities.

Main attractions: Indigenous forest and waterfalls; birdlife and monkeys; peak climbing; wild berries; rock-climbing; tranquil atmosphere.

Pertinent information: While hiking in spring and summer, be on the alert for puff adder, boomslang and cobra. Thunderstorms are frequent and mist can envelope the peaks and valleys within minutes. Always take a raincoat, jersey, map and water bottle. There is a limit of 50 hikers per day.

I lived in and explored the Hogsback for more than four years, and I recommend this area as prime rambling country. It always frustrates me to see tourists walking only up and down the main gravel road, for Hogsback State Forest, Auckland Nature Reserve and the adjoining Zingcuka Forest offer a myriad of unforgettable day excursions. There are 'piggy walks', 'blue crane walks', peaks to climb and historic sites and waterfalls to visit. The keen hiker can happily combine many short walks into an all-day excursion.

The dense, indigenous evergreen forest, with its primeval atmosphere, is rich in yellowwood, white stinkwood, knobwood, white ironwood, underbush, sneezewood and Cape chestnut. The call of the Knysna lourie and the chattering of the samango monkey echo through the valleys and moist slopes below the Hogsback plateau.

It is essential to obtain the booklet *Exploring Hogsback* which is an excellent orientation to the complex of clearly marked walks in the area. For a

Better known as a place of waterfalls and gentle walks, Hogsback has its more challenging aspects too.

pleasant 3-to 4-hour walk, enter the Auckland Nature Reserve near King's Lodge. Descend through the forest to the Big Tree, a 36-m high Outeniqua yellowwood estimated to be 800 years old. Then continue to the Madonna and Child Waterfall on the Tyume River, accessible from both South Africa and Ciskei. Backtrack to near the Big Tree (perhaps after a side-trip to the Bridal Veil Falls). Return to King's Lodge on Wolfridge Road, and then the main Hogsback road.

Another 'piggy walk' combination, this one lasting about 2 hours and running above the level of the main road, starts at the Oak Avenue picnic site. Proceed down Forest Drive, detour to the Kettlespout Falls, and return along the contour path. Shorter walks include the 'Military Path' (through indigenous forest, stretching from the little library to the Alice-Hogsback road below King's Lodge), and the short excursion from the picnic site to the 39 Steps Waterfall.

Almost everyone is keen to climb Tor Doon (1 565 m), a minor summit overlooking the forest station, where a panoramic view of Hogsback and

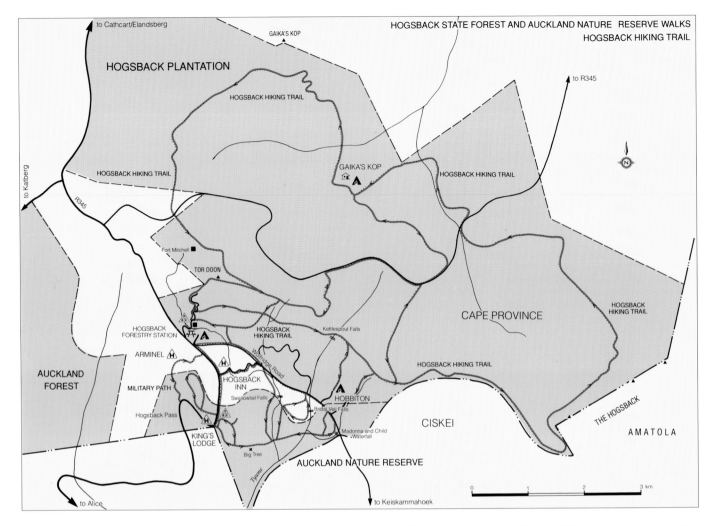

its environs unfolds. Below the peak stands a plaque and traces of the earth embankment of Fort Michell, bearing testimony to the border clashes during the 1800s.

I suggest the following full-day excursion for the ambitious hiker: starting at Gaika Road, enter the state forest plantation area (with a permit) and climb Gaika's Kop (1 963 m). Follow the firebreak to the rocky summit, scrambling to the beacon. Gaika's Kop is Hogsback's most prominent peak, named from the Xhosa *Ntab' egqira* (the doctor's or diviner's mountain), and not for the chief Gaika as is usually assumed. From its flat summit, you can see as far north as Hangklip (above Queenstown), and south over the Hogsback Peaks to the sea. Descend Gaika's Kop via the opposite, less steep side, cross the valley of plantations and ascend Tor Doon. Return following the piggy signs through indigenous forest to either the forest station or the picnic site.

Hiking on the Hogsback grassland plateau and peaks affords far-reaching views, sightings of jackal buzzard, and also a chance to see the Cape rock hyrax (dassie). The wild flowers in season are exquisite, especially the dainty harebells. Between December and February the ubiquitous *Rubus* bramble bears its inexhaustible supply of tasty sweet blackberries.

The other popular hiking peaks include Elandsberg (2 017 m) and the famous Hogsbacks (1 836 m, 1 824 m and 1 937 m). These peaks are responsible for this area's name. The three ridged

summits suggest the bristly-backed wild hogs (pigs) which roam the local forests at night.

25. HOGSBACK HIKING TRAIL
HOGSBACK

Trail details: 32 km/2 days; circular.

Permits/bookings: Safcol, tel. (0423) 51180; Private Bag X537, Humansdorp 6300.

Maps/information: Map and brochure available from the Government Forester, tel. (0020) 55; Hogsback Plantation, PO Box 52, Hogsback 5721.

Facilities/amenities: Overnight hut with mattresses, lapa, braai wood, sleeps 18 people.

Main attractions: Indigenous forest and waterfalls; birdlife and monkeys; peak climbing; wild berries; rock-climbing; tranquil atmosphere.

Pertinent information: Rapidly changeable weather; keep a look out for snakes. There is a limit of 18 hikers for this trail.

The recently opened Hogsback Hiking Trail begins at the Hogsback Forest Station and leads through indigenous forest past the Kettle Spout. On the afternoon of Day 1 the trail traverses the Hogsback mountains in pine plantation; hikers can overnight in the hut at Gaika's Kop. A shorter 'escape route' can be used in an emergency such as bad weather. The second day leads back to the forest station via the mountains above Cathcart. The first day's hike

covers a distance of 19 km and takes approximately 8 hours; it is not overly taxing but due to the distance a medium level of fitness is required. The easier second day's route covers a distance of 13 km and takes approximately 4 hours.

26. KOLOGHA HIKING TRAIL
STUTTERHEIM

Trail details: 34,6 km/2 days; one way.

Permits/bookings: A permit and booking must be obtained from the officer-in-charge, Kubusi State Forest, tel. (0436) 31546; Private Bag X31, Stutterheim 4930.

Facilities/amenities: Hut with accommodation for 30 hikers, verandah, cooking shelter, and ablution block with showers. There is a hotel near the end of the trail.

Main attractions: Gubu Dam and hiking hut; Kubusi Crest view; indigenous forest; De Fin oak tree; waterbirds.

Pertinent information: Hikers must make their own transport arrangements for the end of the trail. The weather is apt to change rapidly, and warm clothing should be carried at all times, even in summer. Groups are limited to a maximum of 30 people at any one time.

This trail, which starts at Isidenge Forest Station near Stutterheim, has truly lovely scenery. Kubusi Crest and Rooikrans (both on the second day)

Kologha Hiking Trail passes close by the blue, trout-stocked waters of the Gubu Dam.

have magnificent views of Gubu Dam, the Keiskammahoek Valley (Ciskei), King William's Town and the Kologha Forest. But the best section of the trail for many is the final descent past several waterfalls, old sawpits and magnificent yellowwoods.

A wide range of wildlife can be found in this area, and a full list is supplied when trail reservations are made.

The first day is 15 km long, and zigzags up through the Barwa indigenous forest. The overnight hut is set among pine and pin oak trees on a steep slope above the Gubu Dam (which, from the verandah, looks like a natural lake because the dam wall is not in view); this weatherboard cabin is reminiscent of an American log house. The ducks and herons on the water and the duiker browsing in the oaks add atmosphere to the setting. Hikers should have a good night's rest before tackling the 19,6 km leg on the second day, which ends at Kologha Forest Station.

The trail requires a medium to high level of fitness, and is extremely well marked.

27. THE AMATOLA HIKING TRAIL
AMATOLA MOUNTAINS

Trail details: 105 km/6 days; open-ended. See map page 118.

Permits/bookings: Must be obtained from Contour, tel. (0401) 952115; PO Box 186, Bisho 5600. Map and brochure available on request.

Facilities/amenities: Overnight huts, each with bunks and mattresses, wood, braai area, toilets and water: Evelyn hut sleeps 30, Dontsa, Cata and Mnyameni 16 each and Zingcuka 20.

Main attractions: Beautiful mountain forests; waterfalls and pools.

Pertinent information: Unpredictable weather; although water is available most of the way, it may be scarce on the first, second and sixth days of the trail, and hikers should be prepared for this. There is a limit of 16 people. Hikers must arrange their own transport at the end of the trail.

The Amatola Trail starts at Maden Dam, approximately 23 km from King William's Town, and ends 3 km from Hogsback. The Amatolas are a deceptive range – hikers must fully immerse themselves in the dense yellowwood forests and spacious plateaux, with the enormous specimens of indigenous trees, spectacular waterfalls, cool, clear bathing pools and rushing trout streams, to fully appreciate their beauty. From the plateaux and forest openings, the views extend from the Karoo to the sea, encompassing the greater part of the Ciskei, Hogsback and beyond.

The trail is strenuous and requires a high level of fitness, although there are optional 'escape' routes along the way: there is parking at Maden Dam, Dontsa, Cata and Zingcuka forest stations, with numerous exit and entrance link paths from the forest stations. This means that the trail can be done in a series of shorter walks or weekend trails, and two loop trails (in the Pirie and Zingcuka forests) located at either end of the trail. The first day is a 15-km hike from Maden Dam to the overnight hut at Evelyn Valley. The second day leads for 22,5 km to Dontsa Forest, where there are stunning rock pools, and traditionally styled Xhosa rondavels. The third day's hike leads to Cata Forest, 19 km from Dontsa. This is a strenuous climb to the plateau grassland with a steep descent to the Eseka Forest which lies below. The overnight huts here have basic amenities.

The fourth day is a 14,4 km climb to Mnyameni Valley and Geju Peak, where the overnight hut has a spectacular view. The fifth day's hike leads for 17,7 km along a contour path, with many pools along the way. It is approximately a 2-hour walk from the last pool to the overnight hut. The final day of the trail leads from Zingcuka hut to the Tyume River, a 16,3-km walk. This last day passes a beautiful forest and an impressive waterfall.

The trail is open all year round, although the waterfalls and pools are best enjoyed in the summer months. Bushbuck, duiker, samango monkey, baboon, bushpig, giant golden mole, giant earthworm, Amatola toad and Hogsback frog are just some of

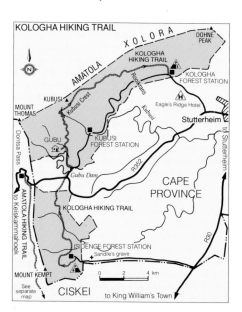

Dainty ferns and trees that are giant forest patriarchs shade countless paths on the Amatola Mountains.

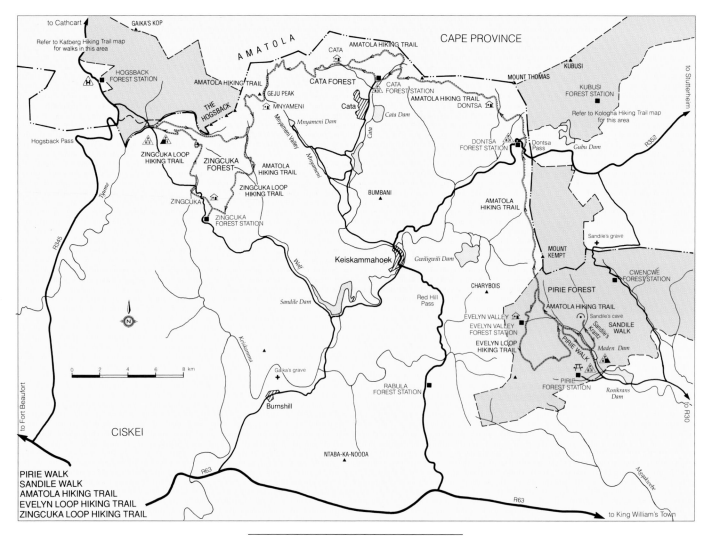

PIRIE WALK
SANDILE WALK
AMATOLA HIKING TRAIL
EVELYN LOOP HIKING TRAIL
ZINGCUKA LOOP HIKING TRAIL

the many creatures you may encounter along the way. The rich birdlife includes Cape parrot, Knysna lourie and a host of other species.

About a third of the trail runs through indigenous, climax-type high forest which has a tall, extensive canopy reaching up to 30 m in height. The canopy and the subcanopy are so dense that they exclude sunlight from the lower levels, resulting in little or no undergrowth. Shrub-like bush and grassland also occur, and fynbos or macchia grows in rocky areas on the mountain peaks.

The Amatolas span an area rich in cultural history. Frontier pioneers were responsible for the many villages, mission stations, graveyards and churches nestling in the shadow of the escarpment. The Xhosa used to graze their livestock here in spring and summer, as did the Hottentots before them. The people who lived in the fertile Keiskammahoek Valley and the slopes above placed heavy demands on the forest until demarcation began in 1883. Evidence of the 19th and early 20th century forest exploitation can still be seen on the Pirie Walk (see following page).

28. EVELYN LOOP HIKING TRAIL
(BEGINNING OF AMATOLA TRAIL)
MADEN DAM

Trail details: 27 km/2 days; circular.

Permits/bookings: Must be obtained from Contour, tel. (0401) 952115; PO Box 186, Bisho 6500. Map and brochure on request.

Facilities/amenities: The refurbished old forester's house serves as a very comfortable overnight hut with mattresses and bunks, wood stove, firewood and braai area, solar-powered lighting.

Main attractions: Indigenous forest in magnificent setting; stunning views and sunrises from the overnight hut.

Pertinent information: Hikers should take care at river crossings after heavy rains; falling branches may occur during strong winds. There is a limit of 30 people for this trail at any one time.

The Evelyn Loop Hiking Trail begins at Maden Dam, 23 km from King William's Town. The Pirie Forest, through which the trail leads, is steeped in history, featuring in the frontier wars of the 19th century. The trail follows an old railway line route into the heart of the Pirie Forest, rising to a height of 1 040 m at the plateau behind McNaughton's Krans, and passing into the Evelyn Valley plantation and finally arriving at the overnight hut high above the forest. The views overlooking the forest

canopy from the overnight hut are breathtaking. The second day takes hikers through another section of the forest and to the end point, 12 km later.

Hikers may come across a variety of wildlife including samango monkey, bushpig, duiker, bushbuck, baboon, tree dassie, golden mole and giant earthworm. The numerous forest birds to be seen include Cape parrots and the Knysna lourie.

29. ZINGCUKA LOOP HIKING TRAIL
(END OF AMATOLA TRAIL)
AMATOLA MOUNTAINS, NEAR HOGSBACK

Trail details: 36 km/2 days; circular.

Permits/bookings: Must be obtained from Contour, tel. (0401) 952115; PO Box 186, Bisho 5600. Map and brochure available on request.

Facilities/amenities: Fully-equipped Zingcuka hut with beds, mattresses, firewood, solar-powered lights, braai area, hot and cold shower facilities.

Main attractions: Lovely rock pools; waterfalls; cool forests; comfortable overnight hut.

Pertinent information: Rapidly changeable weather, especially on the second day; the first day is a long hike, so it is advisable to get an early start. There is a limit of 20 people for this trail.

This circular trail starts and ends at the Tyume River, 3 km from Hogsback. The first day leads for

19,7 km up to the Tyume River, past exquisite
waterfalls, to its source between the Hogsback
Peaks and down to the Wolf River and Schwartz-
wald Forest. The second day leads past several
waterfalls, over Hog 1, and back to the start.
Hikers have an excellent chance of seeing
bushbuck, duiker, samango monkey, baboon, bushpig, giant golden mole, giant earthworm and
Amatola toad. The birds of the area include Cape
parrots and the Knysna lourie. The trail is clearly
marked, and requires a medium to high level of fitness. Although the trail is pleasant all year round,
the pools are particularly enjoyable in summer.

30. THE PIRIE AND SANDILE
DAY WALKS
MADEN DAM

Trail details: 1. Pirie Walk: 9 km/1 day, circular;
2. Sandile Walk: 8 km/1 day, return.

Permits/bookings: Must be obtained from Contour,
tel. (0401) 95 2115; PO Box 186, Bisho 6500. Map
and brochure available on request.

Facilities/amenities: Parking and picnic sites at
Maden Dam; information hut at the beginning of
the walks.

Main attractions: Indigenous evergreen forest, rich
in yellowwoods and birdlife; interesting historical
forestry and Frontier War artefacts; Sandile's Cave
with its spectacular view and intriguing history.

Pertinent information: These walks can be guided
if preferred; contact Contour for details.

Early 19th-century woodcutters and foresters were
quick to realize the great potential of Pirie for commercial timber. As far back as 1819, trees were
felled from this area to build Fort Willshire, on the
banks of the Keiskamma River. Wood was then
taken by settlers for pioneering necessities.

In 1853 the Pirie forests were declared royal
reserves, along with others in the catchments of the
Tyume, Keiskamma and Buffalo rivers. However,
injudicious hunting of game and felling of trees
continued, including cutting and clearing for military operations. During 1897 Mr J E Howse was
granted the sole right to extract wood from the Pirie
Forest. To facilitate exploitation, he built a railway
line and timber chute, using lemonwood *(Xymalos
monospora)* for the sleepers and coffee bitterberry
(Strychnos henningsii) for the construction of the
bridge over Hutchin's River. Howse extracted
40 000 cubic metres of wood from 16 500 trees
from 1910 to 1917.

1. The Pirie Walk follows the route of the railway
from Howse's mill site over the trestle bridge to the
old timber square where the train was loaded. Part
of the trail is shared with the route of the first day
of the Amatola Trail. Only restricted exploitation
of indigenous trees takes place in the forest today.

The Pirie Forest contains the grave and cave of
Sandile, the legendary Ciskeian warrior and Paramount Chief of the amaRharhabe. Sandile
succeeded to the chieftainship of the Rharhabe section of the Xhosa people at the age of nine years,
after his father died in 1829. Chief Sandile led his
tribe in the Frontier Wars of 1846-7, 1850-3 and
1877-8. His shrewd and brave fighting tactics
presented a major problem to the British forces at-

*Settlers regarded the Pirie bush and forest as impenetrable, but delightful and shady paths
lead easily through its foliage.*

tempting to safeguard the ever-expanding colonial
borders. Sandile was shot by a group of Captain
Lonsdale's volunteers in May 1878 in a dense
forest to the east of Mount Kempt.

2. The Sandile Walk leads to Sandile's Krantz.
The name derives from the fact that a few days before his death, while being pursued by the British
and colonial forces, Chief Sandile used the cave at
the base of the krantz as a hideout. Walkers wishing to explore the cave do so at their own risk;
previous caving experience is recommended, and
strong torches and ropes are essential.

Sandile Dam has brought the boon of water, and more stable cultivation patterns, to the area.

31. OCEAN VIEW GUEST FARM TRAILS
KOMGA

Trail details: Various circular trails, adding up to approximately 8 hours of walking time; the longest takes 3 hours.

Permits/bookings: Must be obtained from Mr and Mrs M von Plato, Ocean View Guest Farm, tel. (04372) 2603; PO Box 159, Komga 4950. Map and brochure available on request.

Facilities/amenities: Three fully furnished cottages (two with cooking facilities) accommodating up to 5 people each; firewood for sale; option of eating at the main house or taking your own food.

Main attractions: Indigenous riverine and high forests; coastal views; birdlife (187 species); informal country atmosphere.

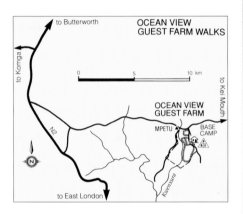

Approximately one hour's drive from King William's Town and East London, Ocean View is conveniently situated for a weekend or relaxing holiday. (Take the Morgan Bay/Kei Mouth turnoff 65 km north of East London.) The clearest weather occurs in winter (May to August); flowers are at their best in late winter and spring, and the birdlife excels from September to November.

Mr and Mrs Von Plato are nature lovers who have opened their 20-ha farm to others who share their interest in natural history and rambling. Not only have they converted three cottages on the farm for public use, they also welcome visitors to dine with their family.

Within the bounds of the farm (declared a Natural Heritage Site in 1989), nature rambles pass through unique high and riverine forests and grassland, beside dams and watercourses. Botanical and ornithological specialists in particular are attracted to the wide diversity of unique species found here; more than 187 bird species alone have been recorded on this farm.

Because the forest captures the mist, its composition contains many tropical elements. On request, Mrs Von Plato will lead trails and point out orchids, cycads, and eagles' nests, as well as describe practical uses for the sneezewood, ironwood, red beech, white gardenia and other indigenous trees growing on the farm.

Some of the animals you may see include bushbuck, blue duiker, samango monkey, tree dassie, Stanley's bustard, crowned and crested eagles, and the ground hornbill. The farm is also home to leguan and the endangered golden mole.

Aerial view of a bush-backed coastal dune shaped by wind and water along the Strandloper Trail.

32. THE STRANDLOPER TRAIL
EAST LONDON

Trail details: 93 km/4 days; shorter 1-day options as well. See map p. 121.

Permits/bookings: Not required for day ramblers, but hikers doing the entire trail must obtain permits from the officer-in-charge, Cape Nature Conservation, tel. (0431) 463532; PO Box 5185, Greenfields 5200.

Facilities/amenities: Various hotels and camp sites *en route*.

Main attractions: Coastal scenery; middens; shipwrecks; forests; dunes; rock formations; abundant birdlife.

Pertinent information: Hikers should obtain the booklet *The Strandloper Trail: Kei Mouth to East London* from the East London Publicity Association: tel. (0431) 26015. It is also advisable to carry a tide table.

The Strandloper Trail can be divided into several short excursions, or serious hikers may wish to tackle the entire 93-km stretch at one time, sleeping at the various hotels and camp sites *en route*. Whichever way you choose, carry the trail booklet at all times as it is an excellent guide to the river crossings, the accommodation, the shipwrecks, birdlife and rock formations that are encountered along the way.

For hikers doing the entire trail, the start is at the Hotel Florence. To get to the hotel, leave East London on the N2 East and 45 km from East London turn right on the road to Kei Mouth, Morgan Bay and Haga Haga. The road is tarred for about 2 km, and the remaining 48 km to Kei Mouth is a well-graded dirt road.

The trail traverses a magnificent stretch of coast, with rugged rocky scenery and a history of wrecks – *Margaret, Nossa Sewhora, Da Atalaia* and *Santo Alberto*, among others.

The hiker is in the constant company of terns, kelp gulls, cormorants and waders, among others. Walking distances between major points are given here for planning purposes. Remember that coastal walking is generally faster than that on mountainous terrain.

Kei Mouth to Haga Haga: 18 km/5 hours; Haga Haga to Glengariff: 23 km/7 hours; Glengariff to East London: 24 km/8 hours.

There are several river mouths – the Quko River at Double Mouth, Kwenxura, Cefane, Cintsa, Bulura and Nahoon – which should be crossed with caution, preferably at low tide, or at the turn or beginning of an incoming tide.

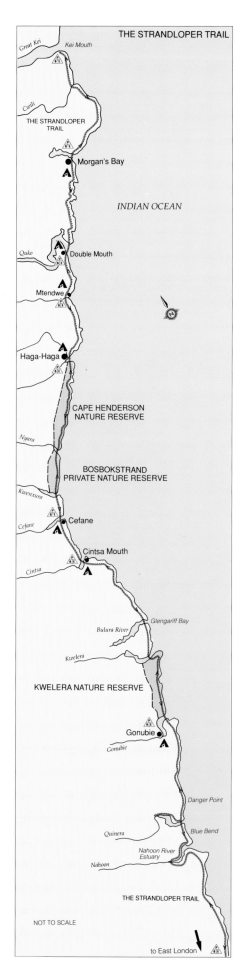

THE STRANDLOPER TRAIL

Great Kei
Kei Mouth

Cwili

THE STRANDLOPER
TRAIL

Morgan's Bay

INDIAN OCEAN

Quko
Double Mouth

Mtendwe

Haga-Haga

CAPE HENDERSON
NATURE RESERVE

Nyara

BOSBOKSTRAND
PRIVATE NATURE RESERVE

Kwenxura

Cefane
Cefane
Cintsa Mouth

Cintsa

Glengariff Bay
Bulura River

Kwelera

KWELERA NATURE RESERVE

Gonubie
Gonubie

Danger Point

Quinera
Blue Bend

Nahoon River
Estuary
Nahoon

THE STRANDLOPER TRAIL

NOT TO SCALE

to East London

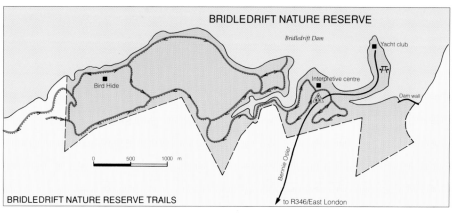

BRIDLEDRIFT NATURE RESERVE

Bridledrift Dam
Yacht club

Bird Hide
Interpretive centre

Bennie Osler

Dam wall

0   500   1000 m

BRIDLEDRIFT NATURE RESERVE TRAILS

to R346/East London

33. BRIDLEDRIFT NATURE RESERVE TRAILS
EAST LONDON

Trail details: Several unmarked trails, varying in length from 1,3 km/30 minutes to 7,5 km/3 hours.

Permits/bookings: Not required.

Facilities/amenities: Bird hide; overnight hut; water; toilets and braai area; yacht club; canoes.

Main attractions: Birdlife; Bridledrift Dam.

Situated 25 km inland from East London, the Bridledrift Nature Reserve is a popular boating and fishing venue for locals. The dam attracts many bird species, and there is a bird-watching hide.

34. UMTIZA TRAILS
EAST LONDON

Trail details: Three trails: 1,5 km/30 minutes; 2,5 km/1 hour; 6 km/2 hours. All are circular.

Permits/bookings: Must be obtained from the officer-in-charge, Cape Nature Conservation, tel. (0431) 463532; PO Box 5185, Greenfields 5200.

Facilities/amenities: Trees labelled with their national tree list numbers; braai areas.

Main attractions: Eastern Cape valley bushveld; eastern Cape cycads.

Pertinent information: A limit of 8 people per trail is recommended.

These easy trails are situated in the Umtiza Nature Reserve, which forms part of the East London Conservation Area, 15 km west of East London. Follow the signposts to Buffalo Pass. The 1-hour trail traverses the plateau surrounding the forest station,

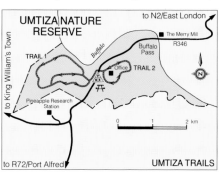

UMTIZA NATURE RESERVE

to N2/East London
The Merry Mill
R346

TRAIL 1
Buffalo
Buffalo Pass
Office
TRAIL 2

to King William's Town

Pineapple Research Station

0   1   2 km

to R72/Port Alfred

UMTIZA TRAILS

and the 2-hour trail runs to the north of the Buffalo Pass road, in indigenous forest. The subtropical climate ensures pleasant walking conditions all year round. Hikers may see blue duiker, samango monkey, tree dassie and bushbuck. The abundant birdlife of the area includes fish eagle, Cape parrot, crowned eagle, narina trogon, dusky flycatcher, red-billed woodhoopoe, a number of kingfisher species and the Knysna lourie. The trails are clearly marked.

35. MADEIRA GUIDED TRAILS
QUEENSTOWN

Trail details: Routes vary according to arrangement. See map overleaf.

Permits/bookings: Must be obtained from the Parks Department, Municipality of Queenstown, tel. (0451) 3131; PO Box 135, Queenstown 5320.

Facilities/amenities: Picnic and camp sites.

Main attractions: Attractive views of Queenstown; large mammals and prolific birdlife; tamboekie thorn (localized endemic); Bushman paintings.

Pertinent information: There is a limit of 10 people per group.

On its journey to the sea at East London, the Buffalo River flows through Umtiza Nature Reserve.

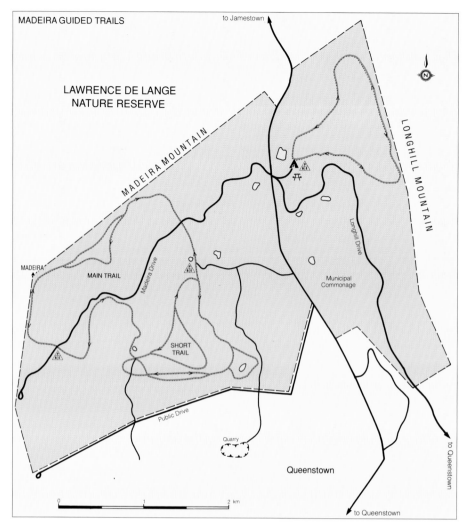

MADEIRA GUIDED TRAILS

LAWRENCE DE LANGE
NATURE RESERVE

to Jamestown

MADEIRA MOUNTAIN

LONGHILL MOUNTAIN

MAIN TRAIL

MADEIRA

Madeira Drive

SHORT
TRAIL

Longhill Drive

Municipal
Commonage

Public Drive

Quarry

Queenstown

to Queenstown

to Queenstown

0   1   2 km

37. LAMMERGEYER HIKING TRAIL
LADY GREY

Trail details: 33 km/3 days; circular.

Permits/bookings: Must be obtained in advance from Lady Grey Municipality or Lammergeyer Conservancy, tel. (05552) 112; PO Box 14, Lady Grey 5540.

Facilities/amenities: Huts and farmhouses along the way; water.

Main attractions: Witteberg range; snowfalls in winter; unique fauna and flora; Bushman paintings; caves.

Pertinent information: Typical Drakensberg weather conditions; unpredictable thunderstorms and snow. There is a daily limit of 20 hikers for this trail.

This circular trail in the Witteberge starts and ends in Lady Grey, 76 km from Barkly East. Requiring a medium to high level of fitness, it can be hiked all year round, although the weather conditions are extreme. The vegetation is typical of the area, with scrub and mountain grassland. You may spot bearded and Cape vultures, black eagle, mountain reedbuck and vaal rhebok, baboon and dassie along the way. The first day is a strenuous 9-km trail, taking approximately 5 hours. You spend the night in bungalows. The second day, less strenuous than the first, will take you 15 km further, in approximately 8 hours, and you will spend your second night in a farmhouse. Finally, the third day sees you through a medium-exertion 9-km walk into Lady Grey. The trail is very well marked.

38. SETHUNZINI HIKING TRAIL
LADY GREY

Trail details: 60 km/3 days; guided, circular.

Permits/bookings: Must be obtained from the trail organizers, tel. (05552) 272; PO Box 64, Lady Grey 5540.

Facilities/amenities: Nights 1 and 4 spent very comfortably at Sethunzini homestead; middle nights spent in comfortable mountain cottage and river camp; hot water and toilets.

Main attractions: Bushman rock art; trout fishing; mountain reedbuck.

Pertinent information: The tariff includes guide, portage and full catering.

Situated 17 km from Lady Grey on the R58 to Barkly East, the guided Sethunzini Hiking Trail requires a medium to high level of fitness. The rolling hills, steep inclines and typical Drakensberg grasslands are home to mountain reedbuck, grey rhebok and duiker, and you have an excellent chance of seeing the Cape vulture, black and martial eagles and even the lammergeier along the way.

The distance travelled on the first day is 25 km, which takes approximately 6 or 7 hours. The second day covers 18 km and the third day 17 km. Breathtaking scenery varies from the beauty of a waterfall plunging to a crystal-clear river, to the panorama from the top of Kammelle Canyon. Horse trails are also offered: see the Special Interest section at the back of this book.

These trails, led by the Parks Department of the Municipality of Queenstown, in the Madeira Nature Reserve, are run according to the interests of the particular group; they are very flexible.

The reserve itself is situated on the slopes of Madeira Mountain, and the vegetation is principally grassveld, incorporating aloes, cycads and acacia. Of special interest is the tamboekie thorn, *Erythrina acanthocarpa*, a dense, thorny shrub whose large prickly seed pods give this plant its name. Endemic in the Queenstown district, the tamboekie thorn is rumoured to be a cure for skin cancer.

A cooling breeze ruffles the waters of a large pool in the Witteberge near Lady Grey.

There is a good chance of spotting giraffe, kudu, mountain reedbuck, zebra, eland, bushbuck, duiker, black wildebeest, gemsbok, red hartebeest, blesbok, springbok, steenbok, impala and ostrich. Because of the high concentration of game, all walks are accompanied by a conservation officer. They begin early in the morning so as to allow the hiker to see as much game as possible.

36. ROTARY ALOE TRAILS
QUEENSTOWN

Trail details: Two trails: 2,5 km/1 hour, and 6 km/2,5 hours; both are circular.

Permits/bookings: Must be obtained from Queenstown Municipality, tel. (0451) 3131; Private Bag X7111, Queenstown 5320.

Facilities/amenities: None.

Main attractions: Wonderful views of Queenstown.

Pertinent information: There is a daily limit of 20 people per trail.

Opened in 1991, these trails, laid out by the Queenstown Rotary Club, require a medium level of fitness. They begin and end at the Berry Dam, and lead along the mountainside, through scattered thorn trees, where mountain reedbuck may be seen. They are well marked with red and white stones, and walking is pleasant all year round.

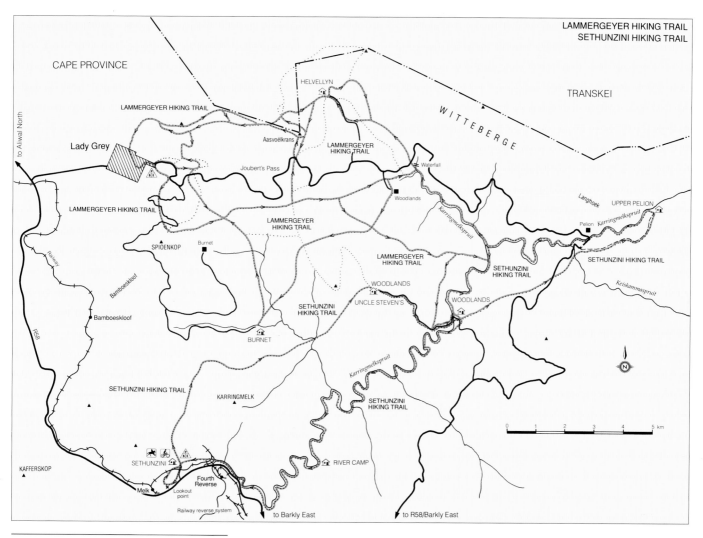

39. ECOWA HIKING TRAIL
ELLIOT

Trail details: 45 km/3 days; open-ended.
See map page 124.

Permits/bookings: Must be obtained from the Elliot Municipality, tel. (045312) 11; PO Box 21, Elliot 5460. Informative map and brochures are available on request.

Facilities/amenities: Môreson farmhouse; Willmore dormitory and Waterkloof cabin, both with bunks and mattresses; plenty of braaiwood.

Main attractions: Scenery of the southern Drakensberg, the Gatberg, and large sandstone caves; ouhout stands; birdlife.

Pertinent information: Ticks; rapidly changeable weather; snakes. A compass is necessary due to very misty conditions. This trail is extremely arduous, and should under no circumstances be attempted by unfit or beginner hikers. There is a limit of 10 hikers for the trail at any one time.

This Ecowa Hiking Trail (Xhosa for 'mushroom') begins on the farm Môreson in sight of the unique Gatberg, 'the mountain with the hole', and ascends to an escarpment from which there are breathtaking views over 30-m high cliffs to the rolling hills below. Falie's Cave is an enormous work of natural art, as are the forest stands of *Leucosidea sericea* (ouhout, oubos or umChiohi), a gnarled tree of

ancient appearance which is common on the lower slopes of the Drakensberg and in the Transvaal Highveld. The first two days are each 16 km long, and the third day is 13 km long, but hikers must not underestimate the difficulty of these routes.

The endless vistas of rock and wind-blown sandstone, black eagles, kestrels and secretarybirds soaring overhead, Xhosa kraals and grass-covered slopes, contribute to the attraction of the relatively unexplored southern Drakensberg midlands.

Gatberg is an obvious (if inelegant) name for this peak within sight of the Ecowa Hiking Trail.

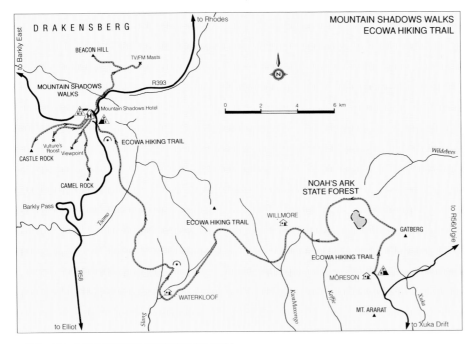

40. MOUNTAIN SHADOWS WALKS
BARKLY PASS

Trail details: Six self-guided day walks, ranging from 1,7 km/30 minutes to 14,8 km/7 hours; return.

Permits/bookings: Not required, but for more information contact the manager of the Mountain Shadows Hotel, tel. (045312) ask for Barkly Pass 3; PO Box 130, Elliot 5460.

Facilities/amenities: All trails are colour-coded. Parking, refreshments, meals and accommodation at Mountain Shadows Hotel.

Main attractions: Spectacular mountain scenery; game-viewing on foot.

Pertinent information: Hikers must carry their own water; extremely cold winters.

The manager of the Mountain Shadows Hotel in Elliot has compiled a detailed and informative brochure on these walks, embracing southern Drakensberg ranges and cave sandstone ramparts, with caves, overhangs and arches; hikers should obtain a copy before setting out.

41. PRENTJIESBERG TRAILS
UGIE

Trail details: 50 km/3 days; circular.

Permits/bookings: Must be obtained from the North East Cape Forests, tel. (045332) 42; Private Bag Ugie 5470. Map and brochure on request.

Facilities/amenities: Hut, bungalow and cave sleep 12 each and have toilets and water.

Main attractions: Protea woodland; indigenous forest; caves with Bushman paintings; magnificent panoramic views overlooking Ugie.

Pertinent information: Rapidly changeable weather and mist occasionally at the top of the mountain. There is a daily limit of 12 hikers for this trail.

This moderately strenuous circular walk begins and ends approximately 6 km north-west of the town of Ugie. The first day begins at Ben Vorlich hut and leads through magnificent woodland forest for 17 km to Fontana hut, where hikers overnight. The second day is a 16-km walk to Craigmore where hikers sleep in a comfortable cave, before setting out for the final stretch home to Ben Vorlich. Along the way blesbok, mountain reedbuck and dassie may be spotted. The birds of interest include crowned and black eagles, bearded vulture and the lanner falcon.

There are stunning rock pools at the top of the mountain, in which a new species of fairy shrimp was recently discovered. The walk is clearly marked with footprints and arrows.

42. WOODCLIFFE CAVE TRAILS
MACLEAR

Trail details: 34 km/4 days; circular. A new, guided 5-day/4-night, one-way trail is being developed. Accurate map unavailable.

Permits/bookings: Must be obtained by contacting Graham and Phyll Sephton, tel. (045322) 1222 or 258; PO Box 65, Maclear 5480. Informative brochure available on request.

Facilities/amenities: Caves and mountain cottages for overnighting en route, all equipped with the basic necessities; one self-catering holiday cottage that sleeps 6. The farmhouse is used as a base camp.

Main attractions: Drakensberg; indigenous forest; waterfalls; Bushman paintings; dinosaur footprints.

Pertinent information: The weather is unpredictable; always be prepared for the worst.

These trails are situated on Woodcliffe, a private farm outside Maclear. The walks are clearly marked and lead through stunning Drakensberg scenery. The first day is a 4-km walk to Tok's Cave. The second day leads for 12 km from the cave to Reed Park, and includes ascending the Drakensberg. The third day is more strenuous than the others, and leads for 12 km along the escarpment to Wide Valley. The fourth day starts at Wide Valley and leads back down to Woodcliffe, 6 km later. The abundant birdlife is currently being identified and classified by Rhodes University. The summer months are hot, with thundershowers, and winter is cold and dry with frost and snow. There are strong winds from May to August. For latest details on the guided trail from Woodcliffe to Rhodes, contact the Sephtons at the telephone number given above.

Double Cave on one of the Mountain Shadows walks has been home to man and beast for thousands of years.

A stratified formation on the Prentjiesberg trail suggests an old-time Crusaders' castle.

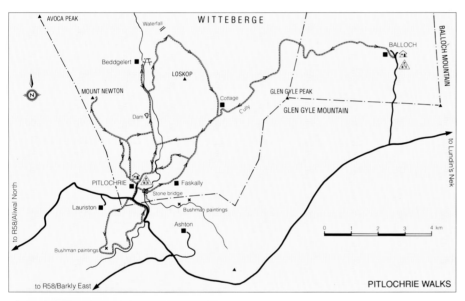

PITLOCHRIE WALKS

These green undulations of the Little Berg are seen near the end of the Woodcliffe Trail.

43. PITLOCHRIE WALKS
BARKLY EAST

Trail details: There are 11 walks varying in duration from 1 to 7 hours.

Permits/bookings: Must be obtained from Paul and Jannis Sephton, Pitlochrie Farm, tel. (04542) 2440; Barkly East 5580. Map and brochure on request.

Main attractions: Stunning Drakensberg scenery; mountainous terrain; Bushman paintings.

Facilities/amenities: None.

Pertinent information: Changeable and extreme weather patterns.

All these walks occur on and around Pitlochrie Farm in the beautiful district of Barkly East.

The farm itself is set against the backdrop of the Witteberg, the range which forms the boundary between the Cape and a small enclave of the Transkei that boasts Lesotho as its northern neighbour. Mount Newton, Avoca Peak (2 769 m), Bushman paintings, streams and a natural swimming pool are

just some of the many features explored by the challenging Pitlochrie routes. The owners have put together a useful brochure on walks in the area.

44. BEN MACDHUI HIKING TRAIL
RHODES

Trail details: 51 km/3 days; circular.

Permits/bookings: Must be obtained from Mr G van Zyl, tel. (04542) 7021; PO Box 299, Barkly East 5580. Brochure available on request.

Facilities/amenities: Farm accommodation on the first night; the hut on the second night (accommodating 12 hikers) is known for being the highest mountain hut above sea level in South Africa; all overnight accommodation is equipped with coal stoves.

Main attractions: Stunning Drakensberg scenery; waterfalls; snow in winter.

Pertinent information: Weather prone to rapid change; hikers must always carry a map, as snow may conceal the markers in winter. There is a limit of 12 people for the trail.

This trail begins and ends in the historic town of Rhodes, 60 km from Barkly East. The first day of the trail is 16 km long; hikers overnight at old Mavis Bank farm. The second day of 18 km leads along the Kloppershoek River. This is a strenuous walk, up Ben MacDhui, which at 3 001,2 m is the highest peak in the Cape Province. The second night is spent in a hut high in the mountains – the southern Drakensberg – with stunning views. The final day of the trail leads for 17 km back down to Rhodes, and has truly spectacular views over the mountainside and overlooking Carlisle's Corner. The trail is clearly marked, but should not be undertaken by beginner hikers or the unfit.

So far, 193 different species of bird have been identified in the area, including the lammergeyer. In spring there is a wide variety of flowers, and their scent fills the air. Summer the evenings are wonderfully cool, and peaceful.

Hikers above Cathedral Rock on the Transkei Wild Coast.

45. TRANSKEI HIKING TRAIL
WILD COAST, TRANSKEI

Trail details: 280 km/approximately 25 days; open-ended. The trail is divided into five 3-6 day sections.

Permits/bookings: Required from the Department of Agriculture and Forestry, Nature Conservation Section, tel. (0471) 312711, fax (0471) 312713; PO Box X5002, Umtata 5100. Bookings are accepted up to 11 months in advance.

Facilities/amenities: Huts accommodating 12 people, with water, bunks and mattresses, tables and benches, and fireplaces; *en route*: hotels, nature reserves with accommodation, hamlets, small trading stores, and clusters of private cottages; fishermen's tracks run from the main road to the coast; cars can be left at the trail heads, and local buses or taxis transport you back to your starting point.

Main attractions: One of Africa's most dramatic and beautiful coastlines: sandy and rocky beaches, coves, lagoons, cliffs, rock formations in the sea, and mangrove swamps; intertidal life and birdlife; fishing.

Pertinent information: All hiking must start at the trail heads and proceed south. Groups are limited to a maximum of 12 people. Always carry your passport, permits and a tide table. Always carry water, and do not drink from rivers and estuaries without first boiling or purifying the water. Roads can be extremely difficult to negotiate after heavy rains. Ticks can be a problem. Theft from campers is not uncommon. Be warned: estuaries host sharks. Never cross an estuary at the mouth during an outgoing tide.

The Wild Coast, riddled with the well-worn footpaths of both livestock and people, is not wild through lack of human settlement – on the contrary, Xhosa villages dot the hillsides all along the coast from Port St Johns southwards. Its reputation stems rather from the numerous ships and lives that have been claimed along the dangerous coastline.

The Wild Coast is the only wilderness trip on which I was able to buy a Coke *en route*; it is also the only wilderness experience during which I was visited by a helicopter, adopted by a stray dog, honoured by the local women for swimming across shark-infested estuaries, saved by two brothers from drowning in mud and befriended by a huge Transkeian sheriff on a beautiful white horse! At the cost of a pair of running shoes and a handful of sweets, his 1,3 m-tall son carried my 1,3 m-tall backpack across the incredible black pebble beach near Brazen Head.

The region explored by coastal hikers lies between the Umtamvuna River (Port Edward) and the Great Kei River, with the most popular stretches being between Port Edward and Port St Johns (approximately 110 km), and between Port St Johns and Hole-in-the-Wall (approximately 170 km). The former area, the less-populated Pondoland Wild Coast, is rugged, with sensational coastal rock formations and deeply incised river gorges. The latter stretch, on the other hand, provides a much gentler terrain, mangrove swamps, lovely scenery and more settlements.

A marked hiking trail runs along the entire stretch of coast, with accommodation in traditional Xhosa-style huts provided at intervals. The 5-day stretch from Port St Johns to Coffee Bay (approxim-

ately 100 km) was completed in 1983. Camps along the route are located at 12-km intervals at Silaka Nature Reserve, Mngazana, Mpande, Hluleka Nature Reserve, Ngcibe and Coffee Bay. The second part, opened in late 1985, runs from Coffee Bay to Cwebe Nature Reserve at the mouth of the Bashee (Mbashe) River (Bomvanaland) with huts at Coffee Bay, Mhlahlane, Manzimnyama (Mbiza), Xora and the Bashee River mouth. It takes 4 days to walk. (Note that 2 sets of huts exist in the caravan park at Coffee Bay; one is for hikers finishing the walk from Port St Johns, the other for those starting the walk to Bashee. There are also huts at Bashee for those who wish to stay over on completion of the latter trail. These are less than a kilometre from the hotel.)

Sections of trail opened subsequently are, from north to south, the 3-day stretch from Mtamvuna near Port Edward to Msikaba River, with camps at Mtentu and Msikaba; a 6-day hike from Msikaba River to Agate Terrace (Port St Johns), with camps at Port Grosvenor, Lupatana, Mbotyi and elsewhere; and 5 days from Nqabara Estuary (the southern border of the Dwesa Nature Reserve) to north of the Great Kei River at Qolora Mouth, with overnight stops at Nqabara Point, Shixini Estuary, Mazeppa Point, Cebe and Kobonqaba.

If you get lost and cannot find the markers on the trail, stay close to the coast and ask the locals for directions to stores, river mouths and beaches. They are very helpful and will lead you on the often perplexing network of paths through the thick indigenous bush.

Some noteworthy features of the coast from Port Edward south to Port St Johns include fossil beds visible at low tide near the Mzamba River; narrow stretches of creamy beaches south of Port Edward; the rare endemic Pondoland palm (also known as Pondoland coconut) on the north banks of the Mtentu and Msikaba rivers; the fishermen's shacks at Lupatana which face huge breakers that easily challenge those of the Tsitsikamma coast; Waterfall Bluff, a sensational waterfall where you can walk between the waters plummeting directly into the sea, and the cliff; the picturesque Mamba Pools, behind Waterfall Bluff; Cathedral Rock and the Castle, two of the most unusual erosional features in the sea that you are likely to come across; and Mfihlelo Falls, an approximately 160-m waterfall flowing directly into the ocean – it is reputed to be the highest of its kind in Africa.

Farther south, between Port St Johns and Hole-in-the-Wall, I found the following quite fascinating: the Table Mountain sandstone cliffs of Port St Johns; the very lovely Mpande Bay; the extensive dolerite intrusion named Brazen Head, south of Mngazana; Hluleka, a nature reserve with plenty of waterfowl on the river; the resort at Coffee Bay; and, just a bit farther south, the famous Hole-in-the-Wall, where a deep rumbling sound is caused by heavy surf further eroding the weathered-out hole.

All along the coast, tidal estuaries are fringed by one of the world's most valuable ecosystems, the mangrove swamps. In Transkei the mangroves reach their southern limit of tolerance, and this is borne out by patchy stands of trees which may be of a single species. Grossly exploited and misunderstood by man, mangrove ecosystems are actually unparalleled as nursery areas for marine fish fry and invertebrates. These swamps are the breeding

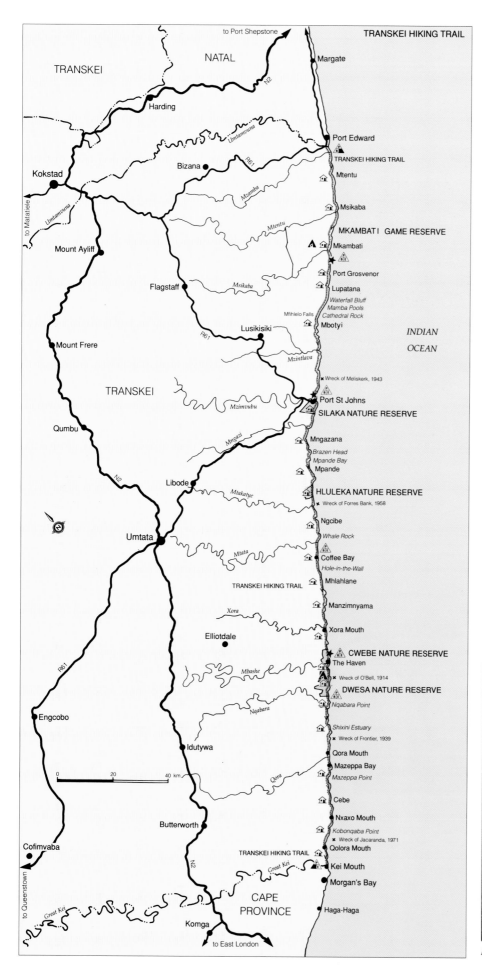

TRANSKEI HIKING TRAIL

to Port Shepstone

NATAL

TRANSKEI

Margate

Harding

Umtamvuna

Port Edward

R61

TRANSKEI HIKING TRAIL

Bizana

Mzamba

Mtentu

Kokstad

to Matatiele

Umtamvuna

Mtentu

Msikaba

Mount Ayliff

MKAMBATI GAME RESERVE

Mkambati

Flagstaff

Msikaba

Port Grosvenor

Lupatana

Waterfall Bluff
Mamba Pools
Mfihlelo Falls *Cathedral Rock*

Mbotyi

INDIAN

OCEAN

Lusikisiki

R61

Mzintlava

Mount Frere

× Wreck of Meliskerk, 1943

TRANSKEI

Port St Johns

Mzimvubu

SILAKA NATURE RESERVE

Qumbu

Mngazana

Brazen Head
Mpande Bay

Mngazi

Mpande

HLULEKA NATURE RESERVE

Libode

Mtakatye

× Wreck of Forres Bank, 1958

Ngcibe

Whale Rock

Mtata

Coffee Bay

Umtata

Hole-in-the-Wall

Mhlahlane

TRANSKEI HIKING TRAIL

Xora

Manzimnyama

Elliotdale

Xora Mouth

CWEBE NATURE RESERVE

Mbashe

The Haven

× Wreck of O'Bell, 1914

DWESA NATURE RESERVE

Nqabara

Nqabara Point

Engcobo

R61

Shixini Estuary

× Wreck of Frontier, 1939

Idutywa

Qora Mouth

Mazeppa Bay

Qora

Mazeppa Point

Cebe

Nxaxo Mouth

Butterworth

Kobonqaba Point
× Wreck of Jacaranda, 1971

TRANSKEI HIKING TRAIL

Qolora Mouth

N2

Great Kei

Kei Mouth

Cofimvaba

Morgan's Bay

to Queenstown

Great Kei

CAPE
PROVINCE

Haga-Haga

Komga

to East London

0   20   40 km

grounds of mullet, grunter, stumpnose, perch, kob, springer, prawns and crabs. Associated with or dependent on the swamps is a diverse bird population: the fish eagle, whitebacked night heron and tiny mangrove kingfisher, to name a few.

Other vegetation zones along the Wild Coast include coastal grasslands which have a lawn-like appearance as a result of heavy grazing by domesticated stock. Valley bushveld occurs in the larger river valleys, along with coastal forest, including dune and swamp forests.

Here are a few suggestions and hints which you may find useful: when you have to cross an estuary, it is advisable to walk upstream first and head directly across the stream. By the time you reach the far shore, the current will have carried you to near the mouth. Always cross during incoming tides. Swimming across estuary mouths while wearing your pack is dangerous and foolish: rather float it in front of you or use the private ferry systems where they are available.

For the less adventurous hiker wishing to overnight where specific facilities exist, there are three nature reserves:

Mkambati (with a lodge, camping areas and a riverside complex sleeping 20, canoeing and horse-riding), north of Port St Johns between the Msikaba and Mtentu rivers, contains the Pondoland palm. Birdlife is plentiful; the rare Cape vulture nests here on the cliffs above the Msikaba River.

Hluleka, 30 km south of Port St Johns, offers fully furnished log cabins, each accommodating 6 to 8 people. Self-guided walks are available through pristine evergreen forest.

At **Dwesa,** south of Coffee Bay, rustic log cabins that blend well with the forest environment can be rented, and hikers can also camp. This is a particularly lovely reserve, comprising a large indigenous forest, rolling coastal grasslands, rivers and estuaries. Mammals that can be seen here include eland, blesbok, buffalo, hartebeest, warthog, blue and grey duiker, bushbuck and rhino. Dwesa is worth visiting even if you terminate your hiking tour at Hole-in-the-Wall, and there are many interesting paths within the reserve for day rambles. Guided walks are provided to the game areas.

Relaxing near Hole-in-the-Wall on the way to Coffee Bay.

127

NAMAQUALAND, KAROO AND NORTHERN CAPE

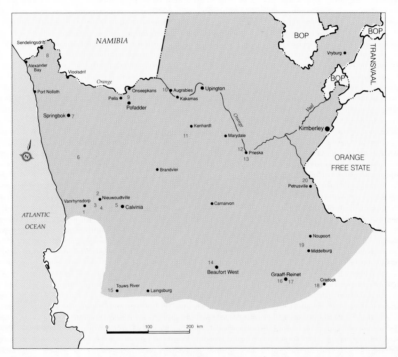

'Karoo' is the Khoi word for 'drynesss' – and dry is the dominant characteristic of this vast region which makes up most of the area of the Cape Province. The Great Karoo is a plateau 600-900 m above sea level, formed during the break-up of the ancient super-continent Gondwana. In the west and south, the Great Escarpment, particularly evident around Calvinia, marks its edge. To the west is Namaqualand. Running from east to west through the Great Karoo is the Orange River which, in the west of the region, marks its northern boundary with Namibia. The river's course is particularly spectacular near Prieska, at Augrabies and near Onseepkans.

In general terms, rainfall over the region decreases as you travel westwards and northwards. The Great Karoo has a summer rainfall pattern as have the grasslands in the north-east of the region and the Kalahari dunes in the north-west. The lower-lying area between the Great Escarpment and the Swartberg mountains in the south has all-year round rainfall (though very sparse!) which merges in the west with the winter-rainfall regions of Namaqualand. These areas have a succulent karoo vegetation while the Great Karoo has a grassy arid vegetation – Nama karoo.

This is a harsh environment but the well-known spring flowering of Namaqualand is one of the world's marvels. Less obvious is the unique beauty of the Great Karoo landscape.

In all of this region, there is a wealth of interest in the rocks, the plant life, and the specially adapted animals, insects and birds. Very recently, one of the most forbidding but beautiful areas in southern Africa – the Richtersveld – has been proclaimed as a national park and is now accessible to the adventurous and properly equipped. The whole region offers the hiker an experience different from the familiar and well trodden trails elsewhere. The prospective hiker must be aware, however, of the extremes of climate that can be experienced here. Inland, the winters can be bitterly cold. On the other hand, at Vioolsdrif on the Orange River, the temperature recently reached 51° C one summer's day. Daily temperature variations are extreme. Always carry sufficient water and dress sensibly.

LEFT: *Forbidding dolerite pillars stand guard over the Valley of Desolation.*

below. Part of the escarpment above the extremely arid Knersvlakte, Gifberg is covered with dry and mesic fynbos and several rare, endemic species are found here. This is a beautiful and little-known area, with clean mountain streams and Table Mountain sandstone rock formations where you can see klipspringer, steenbok and duiker and a variety of birdlife, including black eagles.

2. KLIPKOPPIES TRAIL
NIEUWOUDTVILLE NATURE RESERVE

Trail details: 3 km/1 to 2 hours; circular.

Permits/bookings: No permit or booking required; the reserve is always open.

Facilities/amenities: Information centre; toilets; picnic site; footpaths.

Main attractions: Spring flowers including endemic species; dolerite koppies; views of the Bokkeveld escarpment.

Pertinent information: The spring flower display depends on the previous rainfall. In good years it is marvellous particularly in September.

The 66-ha Nieuwoudtville Nature Reserve, which lies about 2 km east of Nieuwoudtville, was established in 1979 to conserve two ecological habitats – the dolerite koppies in the north of the reserve, and a flat plain area. Each of these carries representative flora. After adequate rains, the show of flowers is magnificent, as are individual flowers of some of the endemic species which are protected here. There is drinking water at the halfway point.

The easy Klipkoppies Trail winds through the dolerite koppies which are always interesting for their plant, animal and birdlife. Observant hikers may spot klipspringer, anteater and barking gecko.

3. OORLOGSKLOOF NATURE RESERVE
NIEUWOUDTVILLE

Trail details: Route I: 46 km/4 days, circular; Route II: 37,5 km/4 days, circular. There are also day walks and weekend routes in the reserve.

Permits/booking: Advance booking required for the routes that are longer than one day; contact the Officer-in-Charge, Oorlogskloof Nature Reserve, tel, (02726) 81052 (office) or 81010 (home); fax (02726) 81346; Nieuwoudtville 8180. Permits for day walks from the Officer-in-Charge at the reserve. A nominal charge is levied to enter the reserve.

Facilities/amenities: Braai area and toilets at the start; long-drop toilets at points along the route; no overnight huts: bring your own tent or sleep under the stars.

Main attractions: Interesting rock formations with cracks and tunnels to negotiate; tree-lined kloofs; Bushman paintings; river and waterfalls. Varied bird and animal life. Breathtaking views of the Knersvlakte and of the Oorlogskloof itself.

Pertinent information: Hikers can plan their own routes. The escarpment is cold and wet in winter, dry and warm in summer. Water must be carried on all routes. A maximum of three groups of 12 people each is allowed in the reserve on any one day.

Wild flowers carpet the Nieuwoudtville Nature Reserve in spring.

1. GIFBERG RUSOORD
SOUTH OF VANRHYNSDORP

Trail details: 1. Gifboom route: 7 km/4 hours; circular. 2. Hamerkop route: 4 km/2 hours; circular; 3. Boesman route: 15 km/6 hours; circular. 4. Spoelgat route: 2 km/1 hour; circular.

Permits/bookings: Bookings to walk the trails or for accommodation on the farm: H A J Huisamen, tel.(02727) 91555; PO Box 126, Vanrhynsdorp 8170.

Facilities/amenities: Overnight accommodation is available in the farmhouse or adjoining chalet.

Main attractions: Fynbos; mountain scenery; rock pools, potholes and waterfalls; Bushman paintings.

Pertinent information: Maximum number of people per group: 18. This is a dry, winter-rainfall area. Summers are moderate but winter nights can be cold.

Gifberg is the flat-topped mountain that dominates the town of Vanrhynsdorp on the plains ('vlakte')

Hikers have a commanding view over Vanrhyns Pass on the Oorlogskloof Trail..

The Nieuwoudtville area is best known for its extravagant displays of spring flowers. The 5 070-ha Oorlogskloof Nature Reserve, 12 km south of the town, offers hikers another dimension. The reserve, on the edge of the escarpment overlooking the Knersvlakte, contains a large stretch of Oorlogskloof and is a rocky area with dry and mesic fynbos, some of the most northerly of this veld type. The plant cover is most colourful in spring. There is also a wealth of animals here – bat-eared foxes, blackbacked jackals, porcupines, baboons, klipspringer, duiker, steenbok and, next to the river, Cape clawless otters. Birdlife includes Namaqua sandgrouse, fish eagles and black eagles.

Two 4-day trails have been laid out in the reserve. Because of the broken terrain, these are strenuous and not for the unfit. Both trails traverse a varied route through magnificent rock formations, kloofs and the Oorlogskloof River. Hikers can also plan their own routes for day, weekend and longer walks in the reserve.

4. DE HOOP TRAIL
SOUTH OF NIEUWOUDTVILLE

Trail details: 11,5 km/5 to 6 hours, circular.

Permits/bookings: Advance booking of accommodation in the De Hoop cottage and permission to walk the trail required – contact Mrs Mariette van Wyk, Papkuilsfontein, tel. (02726) 81246; PO Box 46, Nieuwoudtville 8180.

Facilities/amenities: Overnight accommodation is available for a maximum of 10 people in the historic De Hoop cottage at the start of the trail – there is a charge per person. Hikers must bring their own food and sleeping bags. Hikers may also sleep out in the veld in an overhang cave at a nominal charge and at their own risk.

Main attractions: Historic De Hoop cottage; fynbos; 200 m-high waterfall; rugged scenery around Oorlogskloof.

Pertinent information: Winter nights can be freezing. The best time for the fynbos flowers is spring (September to November). The trail requires average exertion.

The Papkuilsfontein farm 23 km south of Nieuwoudtville borders the Oorlogskloof Nature Reserve and shares the same type of rock formations and plant life as the Oorlogskloof itself. These are characteristic of the Bokkeveld mountains, an extension of the Cedarberg system. The De Hoop Trail runs from the historic De Hoop cottage to a 200 m-high waterfall in the kloof (best seen after rain), along the edge of the kloof and back via a different route. Hikers attempting the C-grade rock climb down the waterfall do so at their own risk.

5. AKKERENDAM NATURE RESERVE
NEAR CALVINIA

Trail details: 1. Sterboom Route: Approximately 12 km/6 to 7 hours; circular. 2. Kareeboom Route: 2 km/1 hour; circular.

Permits/bookings: Permits and information from the Municipality, Calvinia, tel. (0273) 411712; fax (0273) 412750.

Facilities/amenities: Braai area.

Main attractions: Scenery of the Hantamberg; proclaimed bird sanctuary; flowers of the Karoo.

Pertinent information: No water is available on the trail – you must carry your own. This area can be very hot in summer, very cold with occasional snow in winter. The trails in the reserve are being replanned, so contact the Municipality for further updated information.

1. The Sterboom Route climbs the eastern face of Hantamsberg to the summit. This is a fairly strenuous route.

2. Kareeboom Route is an easier, 2-km route on the slopes, which is suitable for the elderly.

The Karee Dam provides an oasis for many migrating birds; the keen birdwatcher could expect to see 65 different species over a 2-day period in the reserve, which is a proclaimed bird sanctuary.

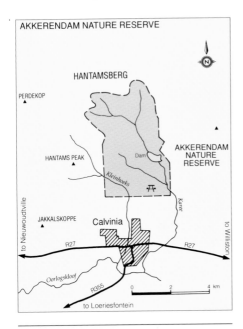

6. ROOIBERG TRAILS
NEAR GARIES

Trail details: Not finalized; 1 to 3 day trails.

Permits/bookings: Permits are required. These and further information available from Garies Municipality, tel. (02792) ask for 14.

Facilities/amenities: None at this stage.

Pertinent information: Hikers must carry water. The Kamiesberg are cold in winter with occasional snow, but hot in summer.

In consultation with officials of Cape Nature Conservation, a new trail is currently being made in the

Succulent karoo vegetation on the Studer's Pass at the beginning of the Rooiberg Trail.

Kamiesberg on private land. The trail, which is planned to allow 1 to 3 day hikes, starts on Studer's Pass east of Garies and runs on the steep slopes of the mountain to Rooiberg, one of the highest peaks in the area. Parts of the trail can already be walked – Garies Municipality will have up to date information. The Kamiesberg are a high, spectacular granite outcropping in Namaqualand with a fascinating flora which is particularly beautiful in late spring. These mountains contain patches of fynbos, the most northerly in the Cape.

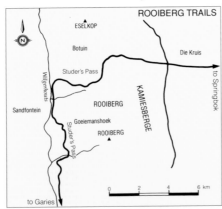

7. IAN MYERS NATURE WALKS
GOEGAP NATURE RESERVE

Trail details 4 km/1 hour; 5,5 km/2 hours and 7 km/3 hours. All are circular.

Permits/bookings: None required.

Maps/information: From The Officer-in-Charge, Goegap Nature Reserve, tel. (0251) 21880; Private Bag X1, Springbok 8240.

Facilities/amenities: 7-km, circular game-viewing drive; picnic and braai facilities at the beginning/end of the circular trails; toilets and water; exhibition of Namaqualand succulents housed at the office complex.

Main attractions: Namaqualand broken veld, famous for its spring display of wild flowers; dome-shaped, rocky granite hills; kokerbooms; Hartmann's zebra, springbok, gemsbok, klipspringer and other antelope.

Pertinent information: The reserve is open for day use only; no overnight accommodation available. Visitors using the hiking trail in summer should walk during the cooler parts of the day.

The Goegap Nature Reserve, 16 km east of Springbok, is noted for its strikingly beautiful but ephemeral spring display of wild flowers. The Na-

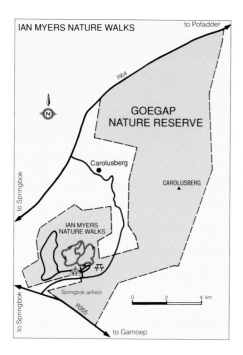

IAN MYERS NATURE WALKS

to Pofadder

GOEGAP
NATURE RESERVE

R64

to Springbok

Carolusberg

CAROLUSBERG

IAN MYERS
NATURE WALKS

Springbok airfield

to Springbok

R355

0   2   4 km

to Gamoep

The recently-proclaimed Richtersveld National Park is characterized by its rugged mountain ranges.

maqualand broken veld is fascinating, however, at
all times of the year. The reserve protects endemic
species such as *Gladiolus salteri* and a *Spiloxene*
species. The kokerboom is common on some of the
hills. Animal life is also plentiful and easily spotted
along the Ian Myers Nature Walks, all of which
begin at the same point. Endangered species include the Hartmann's mountain zebra, aardwolf
and honey badger. Springbok and gemsbok have
been reintroduced but 31 mammal species, including klipspringer, baboon, Cape fox and steenbok,
occur naturally. Of the 47 recorded bird species, the
ostrich, black eagle, Karoo korhaan, spotted dikkop
and ground woodpecker are frequently seen. Smaller animal life such as the armadillo lizard, rock
agama and Namaqualand padloper should not be
overlooked as they are also fascinating.

The nature walks are named in memory of the
late Ian Myers, a keen naturalist who spent 30 years
leading groups in Namaqualand.

8. RICHTERSVELD NATIONAL PARK
BORDERING THE ORANGE RIVER

The proclamation of the 162 445-ha Richtersveld
National Park in 1991 was a landmark in the development of conservation in South Africa. After
lengthy negotiations with the semi-nomadic Nama
inhabitants, it was agreed that the National Parks
Board would manage the park on their behalf while
they would continue to live and graze their stock in
the park. The local communities would benefit directly from job creation in the park and sales of
cultivated plants of species found naturally there.

The park was established to conserve its unique,
wild beauty and its highly adapted flora and reptile
and insect fauna. The flora is largely succulent and

includes the halfmans, *Pachypodium namaquanum*,
the quiver tree *Aloe pillansii*, and maïden's quiver
tree *Aloe ramosissima*. There are small numbers
of Hartmann's zebra, springbok, klipspringer,
steenbok and grey rhebok in the park. Baboons
and vervet monkeys are found in the scrub lining
the Orange River, where most of the birdlife
is found.

Trail details: Hikes accompanied by a Parks Board
official, with donkeys to carry packs, are planned.
Walking is permitted.

Permits/bookings: Bookings: National Parks Board
offices in Cape Town, tel. (021) 222810;
PO Box 7400, Roggebaai 8012 or Pretoria, tel
(012) 3431991; PO Box 787, Pretoria 0001.
Permits from the office at Sendelingsdrif.

Maps/information: From The Warden, Richtersveld
National Park, tel. and fax (0256) 506;
PO Box 406, Alexander Bay 8290.

Facilities/amenities: There is no accommodation in
the park; camping areas are designated but have *no*
facilities; network of rough roads; fishing in the
Orange River; 4x4 trails and canoeing down the
Orange River are planned.

Main attractions: Arid, scenically splendid,
mountainous wilderness; specialized succulent
flora; prolific reptile fauna; Orange River.

Pertinent information: The Richtersveld is an
extremely arid and wild area. For the poorly
equipped or foolhardy, it is potentially hazardous.
You must carry all requirements, including fuel and
water, into the park. The nearest shops and petrol
stations are at Alexander Bay and Port Nolloth.
Visitors to the park should be aware of the extreme
heat possible during the days, bitter cold at nights
and the very strong winds which are characteristic
of the area. The park gates are open during daylight
hours – no movement is allowed in the park after
dark. The park's roads are very rough and suitable
only for high clearance pick-ups or 4x4 vehicles.

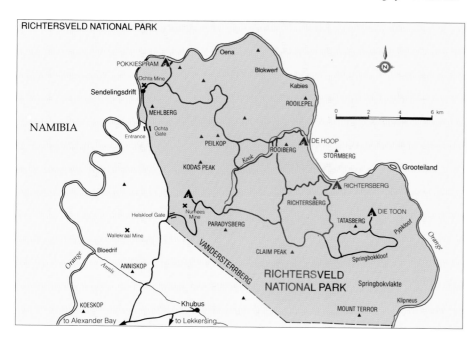

RICHTERSVELD NATIONAL PARK

Oena

POKKIESPRAM

Blokwerf

Ochta Mine

Sendelingsdrift

Kabies

MEHLBERG

ROOILEPEL

NAMIBIA

Ochta
Gate

Entrance

PEILKOP

ROOIBERG

DE HOOP

Kook

STORMBERG

KODAS PEAK

Grooteiland

RICHTERSBERG

RICHTERSBERG

Helskloof Gate

Nurhees
Mine

DIE TOON

TATASBERG

Wallekraal Mine

PARADYSBERG

Orange

Pypkloof

Bloedrif

Annis

ANNISKOP

VANDERSTERRBERG

CLAIM PEAK

Springbokkloof

RICHTERSVELD
NATIONAL PARK

Springbokvlakte

KOESKOP

Khubus

Klipneus

MOUNT TERROR

to Alexander Bay

to Lekkersing

0   2   4   6 km

9. POFADDER HIKING TRAIL
ONSEEPKANS ON THE ORANGE RIVER

Trail details: 72 km/4 days; one way. Shorter variations of 2 or 3 days are possible.

Permits/bookings: Permits and advance booking required. For these as well as maps and information, contact Pofadder Municipality, tel. (02532) ask for 46; fax (02532) ask for 232; PO Box 108, Pofadder 8890. There is a nominal fee charged per person per day.

Facilities/amenities: None.

Main attractions: Spectacular scenery along the Orange River; Groot Pellaberg mountains.

Pertinent information: The trail is closed from 1 October to 30 April. Even out of summer, the days can be hot. Hikers must carry sufficient water. Watch out for snakes. The trail should only be tackled in the company of an experienced hiker. Groups should consist of at least three. Transport to the start and end points can be arranged at a cost. No pets may be taken.

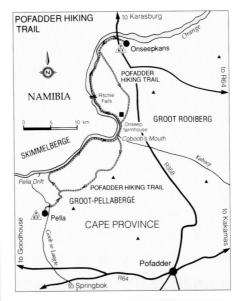

The Pofadder Hiking Trail runs along a little-known part of the Orange River north of Pofadder. The full trail consists of two connected loops, each of which comprises a leg along the river and a leg in the mountainous terrain overlooking its course. The trail can be started either at Onseepkans, a small village on the river, or from Pella, an old mission settlement.

The scenery along this stretch of the Orange River rivals that of the well-known, well-trodden Fish River Canyon in Namibia on the Klipspringer Hiking Trail in the Augrabies Falls National Park.

This is a relatively wild, unpopulated area and hikers should ensure that they are self-sufficient and properly equipped.

10. KLIPSPRINGER HIKING TRAIL
AUGRABIES FALLS NATIONAL PARK

Trail details: 37 km/3 days; circular. Short rambles are also possible in the park.

Permits/bookings: National Parks Board offices in Cape Town, tel. (021) 222810; PO Box 7400, Roggebaai 8012. or Pretoria, tel. (012) 3431991; PO Box 787, Pretoria 0001.

Maps/information: Sketch map and information available with confirmation of booking. There is a fee to enter the park.

Facilities/amenities: 2 overnight huts with bunks, mattresses, toilets, braai facilities, firewood and water; (maximum of 12 people per night); general park facilities: interpretive centre; rest camp with fully equipped chalets, caravan site with ablution facilities, shop and restaurant.

Main attractions: Augrabies Falls and gorge; river landscape; arid area flora and wildlife; birdlife along the river.

Pertinent information: The trail is open only from 1 April to 30 September. Despite this, days can be very hot in the gorge and sun hat and water bottle are vital. Night temperatures in winter can drop below freezing. Beware of snakes. Hikers must report to the camp office before setting out and after completing the trail. Groups must be of between 2 and 12 persons. Hikers are warned against swimming in the river, which can be dangerous with strong currents.

The klipspringer favours a rocky habitat.

Undoubtedly the falls themselves are the main attraction of the Augrabies Falls National Park and its walks and trails. For here, set against the dramatically barren landscape west of Kakamas, the tumbling, muddy-brown waters of the Orange River have eroded the solid granite bedrock into a deep ravine, sculpting in the process a remarkable

Arid, rocky terrain typical of the area traversed by the Pofadder Trail. RIGHT: *Augrabies Falls, one of the world's six largest waterfalls.*

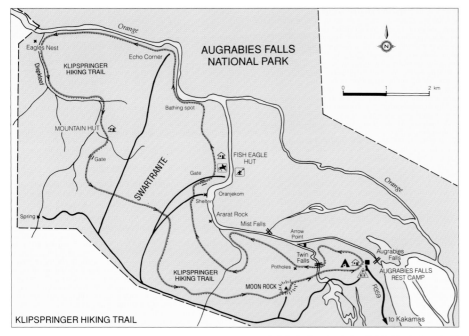

KLIPSPRINGER HIKING TRAIL

Stark granite cliffs of the Augrabies Canyon tower over the Orange River.

array of rock formations and potholes. The main falls are 56 m high, but in total the river drops 191 m, placing it among the largest cataract-type waterfalls in the world. The entire gorge is 18 km long, and the roaring of water plunging, whirling and swirling over such a great distance lends credence to the name Augrabies, a corruption of a Bushman phrase meaning 'place of great noise'.

Ramblers with limited time can take the very easy 2,5 km path to view the gorge, Twin Falls and Arrow Point. To reach Moon Rock takes about an hour and to the potholes about 1,5 hours.

The Klipspringer Hiking Trail also passes the falls but includes sections of the river gorge downstream as well. Other rewards are colourful Cape flat rock lizards basking on the sunbaked rocks, in addition to klipspringer, monkeys, baboons, steen-

bok, and wild cats – or their spoor. The trail is moderately strenuous. There is a stretch of loose sand and boulders to negotiate on the second day's route which can be tiresome.

In sharp contrast with the arid veld dotted with tree aloes surrounding the river, its banks are wooded with bush willows, olives, karee and sweet thorns. Within both vegetation types, birdlife is plentiful, including fish eagles, kingfishers, bustards, dikkops, plovers, finches, wagtails, swifts and many bush-dwelling birds. Nowhere in South Africa have I seen as many rock hyrax (dassies) as on the granite rocks of Augrabies. It is best to plan your hiking times for early morning and later afternoon in order to maximize both comfort and the chances of spotting wildlife. The days' stages allow ample time for enjoying the environment.

11. KOKERBOOM TRAIL
THE BRANDVLEI ROAD

Trail details: 4 km/1,5 hours; circular. See regional map p. 129.

Permits/bookings: No permit or booking required.

Maps/information: Contact the municipality of Kenhardt for further information of the trail, tel.(05462) ask for 25 or 231; Kenhardt 8900.

Facilities/amenities: Parking is available at the start.

Main attractions: Kokerbooms; sociable weaver nests; dolerite koppies.

Pertinent information: Most of the trail is situated on a private farm. There is no water, so carry your own. The area can be very hot in summer.

The Kokerboom Trail, which is 8 km south of Kenhardt on the Brandvlei road, provides the opportunity to walk through a forest of these plants, *Aloe dichotoma* on the slopes of a dolerite koppie. The kokerboom flowers in July. The trail is not strenuous.

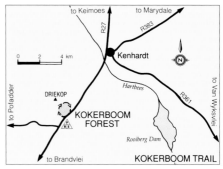

KOKERBOOM TRAIL

12. ORANGE VIEW HIKING TRAIL
NORTH-WEST OF PRIESKA

Trail details: 31,5 km/2 days; return. Two sideshoots (4 km and 6 km) into kloofs are optional on the first day's route.

Permits/bookings: No permit or booking required.

Maps/information: Map and information including directions to the start from Municipality of Prieska, tel. (0594) 61002; PO Box 16, Prieska 8940.

Facilities/amenities: None.

Main attractions: View of Orange River; beautiful gorges; interesting geological formations.

Pertinent information: This area is arid. No water is available along the trail and you must carry sufficient for the whole trail. Summers are very hot, winters very cold. Strong winds blow in August. The trail is moderately strenuous. Groups must consist of at least 2 but no more than 10 persons. The trail runs over private land.

The main attraction of the Orange View Hiking Trail, 27 km north-west of Prieska, is the magnificent view of the river at the turning point, a spur 250 m high next to the river bank. Eight km from the start, on the outward leg along the eastern slopes of a ridge, is an overnight site at an overhang cave but there are no facilities here. On the way, on the left of the trail, are two deep gorges which can be explored – these add 4 km and 6 km respectively to the distance. The return route is 15,5 km, the last

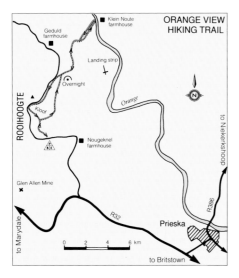

part along an alternative route on the western slopes of the ridge.

13. T'KEIKAMSPOORT HIKING TRAIL
NEAR PRIESKA

Trail details: Approximately 18 to 20 km/5 to 8 hours; one way.

Permits/bookings: None required.

Maps/information: Including directions to the start and end, are available from Municipality of Prieska, tel (0594) 61002; PO Box 16, Prieska 8940.

Facilities/amenities: None.

Main attractions: Panoramic views; interesting geological formations; plant, bird and animal life characteristic of the Great Karoo.

Pertinent information: This area is arid. You must carry water, as this is not available on the trail. You will need transport waiting at the end of the trail; alternatively, make arrangements with the Municipality. Summers are very hot, winters can be bitterly cold. Strong winds blow in August. Groups must comprise between 2 and 10 persons. The trail runs over private land.

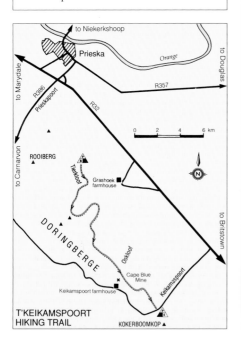

The fairly strenuous T'Keikamspoort Trail begins 15 km south-east of Prieska. It runs up onto and along a ridge of flat-topped Karoo koppies. This area has been mined for asbestos and there are several mines along the ridge. Apart from their interesting geological formations, the koppies are home to springbok, duiker, steenbok, klipspringer, kudu and grey rhebok together with blackbacked jackal, bat-eared foxes, baboons and vervet monkeys. The birdlife includes black eagles and fish eagles.

14. SPRINGBOK HIKING TRAIL
KAROO NATIONAL PARK

The 33 000-ha Karoo National Park, located 7 km from Beaufort West in the Great Karoo, was established to conserve a representative area of the Great Karoo. It includes a plains area at an altitude of 900 m and the Nuweveld mountains with a middle plateau at about 1 200 m and their summit plateau at over 1 800 m. The plant cover reflects this altitudinal variation, with typical Nama karoo vegetation on the plains changing, with increased altitude, to the high mountain vegetation which includes some fynbos elements. There are 2 information centres in the park. The one at the Ou Skuur is mainly used for environmental education of groups of school children. After an introductory talk in the openair-classroom, a maximum of 10 children are taken on the Potlekkertjie Children's walk to observe some of the plant and animal life of the area. The most obvious animals in the park – the springbok, mountain zebra, red hartebeest and

Trail details: 36 km/2,5 days; circular. There are also three shorter day walks: the Fossil Trail the Bossie Trail and the Fonteintjies Kloof Trail.

Permits/bookings: Advance booking required at National Parks Board offices in Cape Town, tel (021) 222810; PO Box 7400, Roggebaai 8012 or Pretoria, tel (012) 3431991; PO Box 787, Pretoria 0001. Permit required – issued by Karoo National Park office at the start of the trail.

Maps/information: Trail maps with information issued by Cape Town and Pretoria Parks Board offices also available at Karoo National Park, tel. (0201) 52828/9; PO Beaufort West 6970.

Facilities/amenities: Kortkloof hut (first night) has 2 rooms, each with 6 bunks and mattresses, kitchen with fireplace, braai area with wood, showers and baths with hot and cold water, and a chemical toilet; the Mountain View camp (second night) has rondavels, each with 4 bunks and mattresses, braai area with wood, bathroom; living room and kitchen with stove and fridge. Main camp has 20 chalets, a restaurant and shop; camping is allowed.

Main attractions: The Nuweveld mountains; karoo flora; animals including, grey rhebok, kudu, civet and honey badger and a wealth of reptiles; spectacular scenery of the Karoo from the top of the mountains; prolific birdlife; black eagles.

Pertinent information: The trail is closed from 1 November to the end of February. This area experiences climatic extremes – summer days can be very hot even at altitude; winters, especially at altitude, very cold with snow and high winds possible. No water is available except at overnight huts – sufficient water (2 litres) must be carried. No fires are allowed along the trail.

Karoo National Park was proclaimed to preserve a typical section of the Great Karoo.

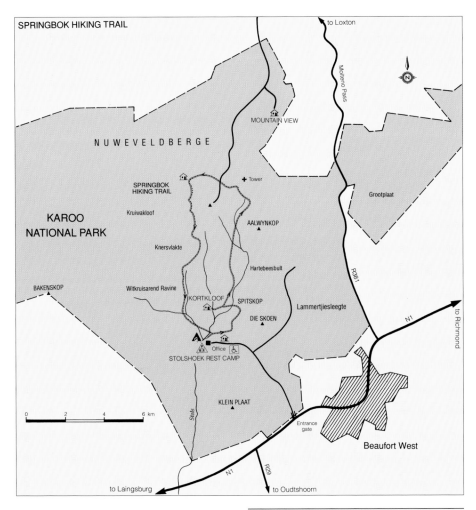

SPRINGBOK HIKING TRAIL

NUWEVELDBERGE

KAROO NATIONAL PARK

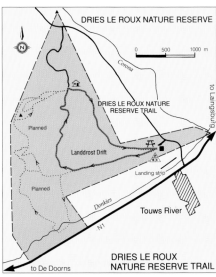

DRIES LE ROUX NATURE RESERVE

DRIES LE ROUX NATURE RESERVE TRAIL

Touws River

DRIES LE ROUX NATURE RESERVE TRAIL

gemsbok – have been reintroduced but it is the wealth of smaller animals which is more interesting. The park has, for example, 66 species of reptiles and amphibians, including five tortoises. There are plans to reintroduce the critically rare riverine rabbit. The park's birdlife is prolific (174 species in all) and includes, together with the surrounding area, the greatest concentration of black eagles south of the Zambezi River.

Despite the fact that it is strenuous, with sustained climbs and very steep gradients in places, the Springbok Hiking Trail allows the hiker opportunities to enjoy all that the park offers. The first day's route of 5 km involves a short climb but leaves a lot of time for exploring. The 14-km route of the second day involves sustained climbing, with steep gradients in places, to the top of the Nuwekloof mountains. The third day's 17 km is easier but includes some very steep descents. The Fossil Trail is adapted for the blind and for people in wheelchairs.

The tent tortoise, psammobates tentorius trimeni.

15. DRIES LE ROUX NATURE RESERVE
TOUWS RIVER

Trial details: 10 km/4 hours; circular. Two longer walks planned.

Permits/bookings: The Town Clerk, Touws River Municipality, tel. (02382) ask for 191; Private Bag X1124, Touws River 6880. A map is available.

Facilities/amenities: Picnic area; pathways.

Main attractions: Diverse vegetation; unusual springbok.

Pertinent information: Take your own water, as this area can be extremely hot in summer.

One of the attractions of this reserve in the Little Karoo north-west of Touws River (its entrance is just 2 km north of the town, off the N1) is the remarkable diversity of vegetation found within its 2 700 ha. There are four different vegetation types: mountain renosterveld, western mountain karoo, succulent Karoo and fynbos. The birdlife is correspondingly diverse, and many tortoises have made their home here.

The reserve's other notable feature is its population of dark-coloured (melanistic) springbok, which has developed naturally as the result of a genetic aberration.

The trail, opened in mid-1993, begins 500 m from the entrance and takes the hiker up rocky out-

crops onto a ridge, from which there is a panoramic view over the reserve and its wildlife. The ridge area has revealed fascinating fossil. The path makes a right-angled turn at the hut, and returns to the start via a fairly flat Karoo plain.

This walk is particularly enjoyable after autumn rains, when the veld produces an abundance of wild flowers.

16. DRIEKOPPE HIKING TRAIL
KAROO NATURE RESERVE, GRAAFF-REINET

Trail details: The trail is intended as an unstructured 2- or 3-day trail – hikers can choose their own way from the start (3/4 km inside the Loodfontein gate to the hut) or there is a marked 12-km (one-way) trail for those who want to follow it to the hut. See map p. 138.

Permits/booking: Advance booking of the trail required. Contact the Cape Nature Conservation office, tel. (0491)23453; fax (0491)23862; PO Box 349, Graaff-Reinet 6280. Special arrangements must be made to enter the eastern wilderness section.

Maps/information: A map of the trail is available from the Cape Nature Conservation office, tel. (0491) 23453; Petrus de Klerk Building, Bourke Street, Graaff-Reinet, is a map of the trail area including the marked trail.

Facilities/amenities: Waaihoek overnight rondavel with 6 bunks and mattresses can accommodate a maximum of 12 people - the rondavel has gas lighting, water and wood for braaiing outside - no fires, candles or stoves are allowed inside the hut, which is thatched; The start, where there is a fireplace and water, may be used as a base camp; by prior arrangement, the reserve's Camdeboo Environmental Education Centre offers environmental programmes for organized groups.

Main attractions: Karoo landscape and vegetation; animal life including Cape buffalo, red hartebeest, mountain zebra, black wildebeest, eland and springbok; birdlife.

Pertinent information: Prior arrangements must be made with reserve officials to collect and return the keys to the overnight hut, which may be booked for a maximum of 2 consecutive nights. There is a cost to stay overnight in the reserve. Water must be carried along the trail, which can be very hot in summer. Be aware that potentially dangerous animals inhabit the area.

A panoramic view including Spandaukop, as seen from the Valley of Desolation.

The 16 000-ha Karoo Nature Reserve surrounds the historic town of Graaff-Reinet. The reserve spans an altitude from 784 m to 1 565 m and includes the unique dolerite pillars of the Valley of Desolation (a national monument); here there is a short 1,5 hour trail along which plants are identified, and an informative display. There are other impressive peaks and cliffs – Spandaukop, Hangklip and the Driekoppe – deep kloofs and natural springs; Vanrhyneveld's Pass Dam, a bird-watcher's paradise; as well as rare and endangered plants and animals. Fossil remains bear testimony to the dinosaurs that tramped through the long-gone swamps of prehistory, while artefacts and, more recently, history books speak of man's involvement in the area from the Early Stone Age to the present day.

The trail runs through rugged terrain and is strenuous. Although often hot and seemingly barren, the sere Karoo veld is in fact alive with creatures, both large and small. Look for hunting spiders, dung beetles, cicadas, mountain and angulate tortoises, and rock leguans, but be cautious, as scorpions, Cape cobras, puff adders and other snakes are also present. Some of the more conspicuous grassland birds are the crowned guineafowl, redwing francolin, secretarybird, ostrich, kori bustard and Karoo korhaan. The raptors to be seen here include chanting goshawks flying low and martial and black eagles soaring overhead may also occasionally be seen .

The mountain vegetation cover of the Karoo Nature Reserve contains large areas of spekboom veld, characteristically bright green. Spekboom is a major food for browsing animals. The three other major vegetation types found in the reserve are the succulent veld of the plains, where plants such as composites, aromatic bushes, thorny succulent shrubs and aloes thrive; the high-altitude grasslands favoured by klipspringer and mountain reedbuck, and the medium-altitude, bush clump savannah, a community of wild olives, karee and white stinkwood interspersed with grasses, which is favoured by the Cape mountain zebra. There is now a large herd of these animals in the reserve.

The Driekoppe Trail is in the eastern section of the reserve and is intended to give hikers a wilderness experience by allowing them to find their own route to the overnight hut. Hikers can spend a second night at the hut, using the day to explore the surrounding countryside.

17. EERSTEFONTEIN DAY WALKS
KAROO NATURE RESERVE, GRAAFF-REINET

Trail details: Three independent circular routes of 5 km, 11 km and 14 km respectively.

Permits/bookings: No booking required; self-issue permit at gate.

Maps/information: The three routes are displayed on an information board at the Spandaukop gate. Karoo Nature Reserve pamphlet with map available from the Nature Conservation Office, tel. (0491)23453; Petrus de Klerk Building, Bourke Street, Graaff-Reinet.

Facilities/amenities: Three picnic spots *en route*.

Main attractions: Rocky, dolerite hills; karoo vegetation; variety of ecological habitats for birds and animals.

Pertinent information: Plants along the trail are identified. This is rugged terrain and the trail is strenuous. There are two normally reliable springs *en route*, where water is available. This area can be very hot in summer. No fires may be made on the route.

The trails begin and end at the Spandaukop gate, which is reached via the suburb of Berg en Dal. This part of the reserve has plenty of large shrubs and trees. The first part of the route up into the dolerite koppies is steep. Black wildebeest, kudu, springbok, duiker and steenbok can be seen in this area of the nature reserve.

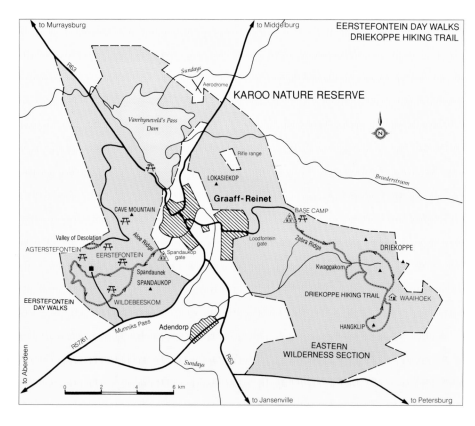

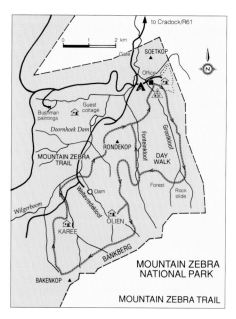

MOUNTAIN ZEBRA
NATIONAL PARK

MOUNTAIN ZEBRA TRAIL

Once endangered, the mountain zebra now thrives at the national park of the same name.

18. MOUNTAIN ZEBRA
NATIONAL PARK
CRADOCK

Trail details: 25,6 km/3 days; circular. There are several shorter trails that each take an hour or more to complete.

Permits/bookings: Obtainable from National Parks Board offices around the country.

Facilities/amenities: The Olien hut and Karee hut built of stone each with 12 bunk beds, firewood, chemical toilets, and showers when water is available.

Main attractions: Large animals, including the Cape mountain zebra; rugged scenery; mountain drives; Karoo vegetation; Bushman paintings.

Pertinent information: There is no guarantee of water along the way, and therefore hikers must carry their own (at least 2 litres per person per day is recommended). The number of people allowed on the trail at any one time is limited to 12.

Situated in the Mountain Zebra National Park 30 km or so west of Cradock, this trail passes through typical Karoo midland vegetation – a transitional zone between the succulent-dominated veld of the arid Great Karoo to the west and the wetter grasslands to the east. The National Parks Board has declared that its management policy for this reserve is to conserve a viable, genetically pure and representative population of Cape mountain zebra as well as a representative range of the fauna and flora characteristic of this environment. When the park was set aside in 1937, only five stallions and one mare lived in the area. Today that number has grown to about 200 mountain zebras.

The trail begins at the park office, where guide books and cooldrinks can be purchased and cars left in the shade. On the first day (9,2 km) the trail ascends the slopes of Grootkloof. One of the highlights of this first leg is the forest near the rockslide, which rings with birdsong. The day ends

with a descent into Fonteinkloof to the Olien hut. It is wise to start out early on the second day (9,2 km) in order to ascend the slopes of the Bankberg while conditions are cool. You will reach the highest point on the trail - 1 885 m - during the course of the day's hike. The night is spent at the Karee hut.

The final day of the hike (7,2 km) is a short walk along the Wilgerboom River, past the Doornhoek Dam and the old homestead to the park's office. This homeward stretch has been altered so that, instead of following the game-viewing road, it leads through the veld. In addition to Cape mountain zebra, hikers have an excellent chance of seeing a variety of antelope, blesbok, kudu, duiker, steenbok, red hartebeest, eland, mountain reedbuck, springbok, black wildebeest – as well as baboon and ostrich. Carnivores in the park include aardwolf, African wild cat, black-footed cat, blackbacked jackal, bat-eared fox, Cape fox and caracal.

Lack of water and the summer heat are the only factors which make the Mountain Zebra Trail physically demanding. Spring and autumn are recommended as the most enjoyable times to hike this trail.

Mountain Zebra National Park is known as a fine wilderness area with magnificent views.

19. TRANSKAROO HIKING TRAIL
NORTH OF MIDDELBURG

Trail details: 42 km/3 days; circular.
25 km/2 days; circular.

Permits/bookings: Book through Elmarie van der Merwe, tel. (04924) 22112 or 21506; PO Box 105, Noupoort 5950. Map and brochure on request.

Facilities/amenities: Overnight accommodation for 12 hikers is provided in two-person tents complemented, on the first night, by a converted barn and on the second by an old farmhouse – both have stretchers (take own sleeping bags), hot shower, toilet, kitchen, fireplace, braai grid and wood – gas and paraffin take the place of electricity; accommodation in the attractive cottages at the base camp is extra and must be reserved separately; farm kiosk, selling a variety of fresh and tinned goods, open on request.

Main attractions: Kloofs; rivers; unusual Bushman paintings; interesting rock formations.

Pertinent information: Watch out for snakes such as the puff adder, Cape cobra, skaapsteker and rinkhals. It is recommended that each hiker carry 3 litres of water on the trail.

The Transkaroo Hiking Trail, which opened to the public in February 1993, in fact comprises two separate loops. Both trails have been cut on the farm Rietpoort, which lies 53 km from Middelburg and 26 km from Noupoort.

The 3-day trail is not difficult, although the owners admit that it is fairly strenuous. Even so, it has to date proved the more popular of the two trails, and many of the hiking parties that have signed the register have included children.

The area is subject to erratic rainfall but in a normal year there is no shortage of water, which may account for the wealth of flora and fauna which makes this trail, with its undulating Karoo landscape, all the more inviting to hikers. Summer rains also create numerous natural swimming pools.

April, May and September through to November are pleasant months for walking in this part of the Karoo; temperatures plummet in July and mid-summer days are scorching.

Birdlife abounds; one of the kloofs even boasts a breeding pair of black eagles. Alert hikers may also glimpse antelope such as mountain reedbuck, grey rhebok, blesbok and springbok, while baboon, Cape

hare and dassies are commonplace. The caracal, which is the motif of the trail, is protected on the farm.

The first day of the 3-day circuit comprises a walk of 15 km, the second day 19 km, and the third and final day 8 km. The 2-day trail, which fits conveniently into a weekend, is made up of 15 km on the first day and a shorter 10 km on the second.

An offshoot of the trail leads to an overhang protecting fascinating Bushman rock art, including an unusual image of an eland in white. According to an expert, this finger-painting, which is estimated to be approximately 500 years old, is in particularly fine condition.

20. PIED BARBET TRAIL
ROLFONTEIN NATURE RESERVE,
P K LE ROUX DAM

Trail details: 4 km/2 hours; circular.

Permits/bookings: No booking of the trail is required; permits can be obtained from the information centre in the reserve. Use of the tented camp must be booked in advance.

Maps/information: Information from The Officer-in-Charge, Rolfontein Nature Reserve, tel. (0536622) ask for 160; PO Box 231, Vanderkloofdam 8771.

Facilities/amenities: Camp with 4 tents, each accommodating 6 adults or 10 children, with basic cooking, toilet and washing facilities; picnic area; limited vehicle routes with viewing points; Douglas Hey Limnological Research Station and small public display of reserve's ecology; angling for yellowfish, catfish and carp; watersports are permitted; the Vanderkloof Municipal Caravan Park is nearby.

Main attractions: Windswept grassy plains with dolerite koppies and wooded kloofs; large and small game; P K le Roux Dam is host to an abundance of waterfowl when it is full.

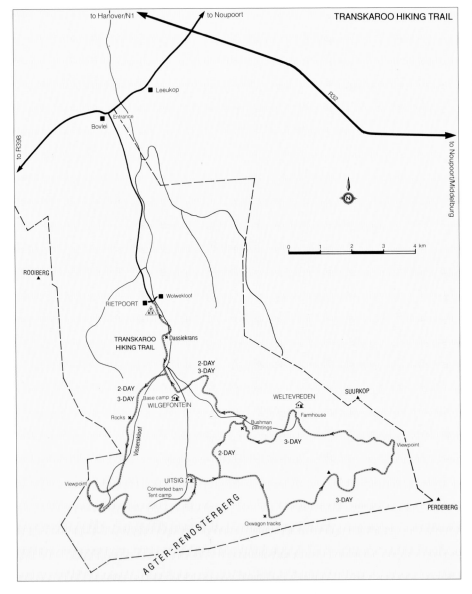

TRANSKAROO HIKING TRAIL

As a result of its remote location on the western banks of the P K le Roux Dam on the Orange River, 13 km from Petrusville and 189 km from Kimberley, the 6 250-ha Rolfontein is one of the least-known Cape Nature Conservation reserves. Yet it is one of the most valuable, for its windswept grassy plains, interspersed with rugged dolerite koppies and heavily bushed river courses, support growing herds of game species such as eland, red hartebeest, black wildebeest, gemsbok, blesbok, kudu and Burchell's zebra. In addition, smaller mammals such as mountain reedbuck, springbok, steenbok, grey duiker, bat-eared fox, vervet monkey and baboon make their home in the reserve. Cheetah, brown hyaena and white rhino have also been introduced in an attempt to recreate the original ecosystem.

The vegetation is the typical grassveld of the Orange River mountainous region, but also includes false upper karoo veld. The latter poses a serious ecological threat; because of past mismanagement of the veld, such as overstocking and soil erosion, the hardier but less productive Karoo species have invaded and replaced the pure grassveld. Sweet thorn, swarthaak, bluebush and camphor bush are some of the more common

Although seemingly inhospitable, the Rolfontein Nature Reserve supports a wealth of plant and animal life.

flowering trees and shrubs that are to be found in this srea.

Within this stark, rugged landscape, the man-made P K le Roux Dam has created a habitat for hundreds of waterbirds. Many quiet inlets and bays are now inhabited by South African Shelduck, yellowbilled duck, spurwinged and Egyptian geese and fish eagles. In the reserve, 200 bird species have been identified to date. Other animals include cobras and puff adders, rock and water leguans, the dainty frog and two toad species.

Hikers may come across flint tools from the Early Stone Age. Samples are displayed at the Douglas Hey Limnological Research Station.

By prior arrangement, hikers may walk anywhere in the reserve. The easy, self-guided Pied Barbet educational trail leads trailists to points of ecological interest, each marked along the path and explained in a pamphlet. Trees along the route are also labelled.

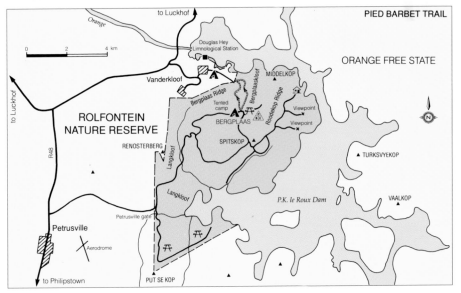

ORANGE FREE STATE
AND QWAQWA

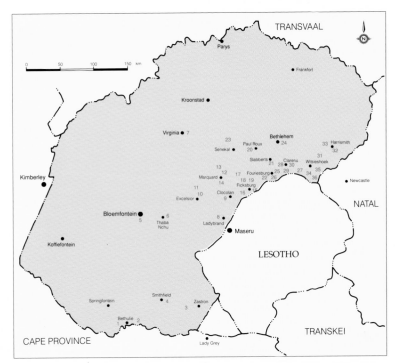

The Orange Free State, situated in the highveld of the central plateau, is one of South Africa's four provinces. Although today the Free State comprises largely farmland, it was known in the past for its vast scenarios of waving grasslands teeming with huge herds of game.

While there has been a general increase in trails in the Orange Free State as authorities and resort owners realize the magnetic potential of their province, the greatest area of expansion has been the formation of conservancies, whereby groups of farmers have set aside tracts of unused land in scenically beautiful countryside for conservation and for recreational purposes, including hiking, horse-riding and mountain biking. Many of these fall in the mountainous eastern section bordering on Lesotho and often referred to as the 'Little Switzerland' of the Republic. The southern area along the Orange River near Bethulie is also attractive to trailists.

The Free State has a temperate climate similar to that of the Transvaal Highveld; cloudless summer mornings followed by afternoon thunderstorms, and cool, dry winters with very cold nights.

QwaQwa, a small homeland belonging to the South Sotho people, is situated on land which was once part of the Orange Free State. Bordered by Lesotho and the Maluti mountains on its south-west, the Royal Natal National Park and Natal on its south-east, and the eastern Orange Free State on its north, it is an attractive mountainous area where the Basotho pony is the national means of conveyance. Mountaineering, wilderness trekking and skiing attract trailists to QwaQwa. (See map page 164.) The Witsieshoek Mountain Resort, situated close to the Royal Natal National Park, is a well-known hiking base.

There are no border formalities for entrance into QwaQwa at present, but trailists planning extensive hikes should get permission from the Secretary for the Interior, QwaQwa Government, Private Bag, Witsieshoek 9870.

The climate is similar to the rest of the Drakensberg region: summer rainfall, mostly in the form of thunderstorms, and dry, sunny but very cold winters when snow is possible.

LEFT: *A dramatic sandstone rock formation in the Maluti foothills which dominate the Golden Gate Highlands National Park.*

Eroded ridges and koppies mark the Free State plains on the Kiepersol Hiking Trail.

1. BETHULIE DAM WALKS
BETHULIE

Trail details: 1. Kiepersol Hiking Trail: 28 km/ 2 days; 2. Hamerkop Trail: 12 km/1 day. Both these routes are circular.

Permits/bookings: Required at least 3 weeks in advance from the Bethulie Municipality, tel. (051762) 2; PO Box 7, Bethulie 9992.

Facilities/amenities: Self-contained cottages at the start of the trail. Overnight huts with mattresses, running water, braai facilities and bush toilet; take your own torches or lamps.

Main attractions: Wildlife; vegetation; interesting rock formations.

Pertinent information: The terrain is very rocky and rather strenuous; strong hiking boots are recommended. Groups are limited to a maximum of 10 people. Fires are permitted only at the overnight camp. Carry water and refill wherever possible.

1. The Kiepersol Hiking Trail Commencing at the Bethulie Dam Resort, follow the marked footpath in a north-easterly direction up into Klipkloof and up Maroccokop for a fine view out over the plain and Hendrik Verwoerd Dam. Continue up a gorge to the top of Verkykersrand; here you can enjoy the vista of steep hills covered in dense vegetation. It is wise to take extra care on the cliffs and more difficult sections of the trail. Descending along an ox wagon trail, the route leads to the overnight camp, set among wild olive trees.

Day 2's walk of 16 km is longer but not as arduous as the previous day and leads through a dry riverbed to the top of the Broekspoort mountains, rich in plant, bird and animal life. If you are lucky, you may see blesbok, rhebok, meerkats, vultures and shadow birds, to name a few of the species that make their home here. From Heel-bo the trail goes downhill along the Hasepad and across a flatter section towards a rocky ridge, where there is a

spectacular view of the Sleutelpoort Canyon. Then its downhill all the way back to the dam.

2. The Hamerkop Trail offers an alternative as a shorter day walk over a distance of 12 km.

As a courtesy to the farmers who allow the route to run through their properties, please use only the stiles to cross fences, even if there is a gate nearby. It has been arranged with the owners that gates will remain shut at all times.

2. TUSSEN DIE RIVIERE GAME RESERVE
BETHULIE

Trail details: 1. Middelpunt Hiking Trail: 7-km circuit. 2. Klipstapel Hiking Trail: 12-km circuit. 3. Orange River Hiking Trail: 16-km circuit.

Permits/bookings: Entrance permits are issued at the gate. Walking permits are not required.

Facilities/amenities: Accommodation is in 6 self-contained cottages, each sleeping 2 people. The Hunter's Camp at the start of the Middelpunt Trail comprises 5 shelters with reed 'bomas' and braais, and a central ablution block. At Spes Bona, starting point for the Klipstapel and Orange River trails, there is an old barn sleeping 40 people on a veranda. Toilets, showers and braai area provided, but no hot water. Hikers can leave their cars and equipment at the shelter, provided they carry sufficient water with them.

Main attractions: Large variety of game such as kudu, zebra, eland, blesbok, steenbok, impala and springbok; confluence of Orange and Caledon rivers; rock formations.

Pertinent information: The reserve is closed for hikers during the hunting season (May to August), so the trails are open only in the summer. Walkers are advised to carry water, and to wear gaiters to protect their legs from grass seeds. Summer rainfall area, mostly in the form of thunderstorms. Strong winds and cold nights are possible year-round, so be prepared for the worst. Hikers should carry binoculars and water.

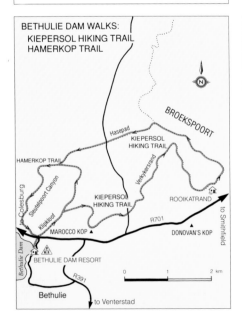

Freaks of erosion are these natural, balancing rock piles to be seen in Tussen die Riviere Game Ranch.

Although the 22 000-ha Tussen die Riviere Game Reserve was developed to cater for the South African hunter, three valuable nature trails have been laid out for hikers visiting the reserve during the summer (non-hunting season). Although relatively unknown, each of these trails has exciting attributes and is well worth walking.

Because of its large size, scenic Karoo splendour and development for hunting, Tussen die Riviere supports large populations of diverse and readily observable game species: hikers can expect to see springbok, blesbok, red hartebeest, black wildebeest and blue wildebeest, steenbok, impala, mountain reedbuck, gemsbok, kudu, zebra, eland and white rhino. Spotting these majestic herds or spooking a solitary antelope while walking can be a unique and thrilling experience.

1. Middelpunt Hiking Trail on the reserve's well-watered western boundary is physically easy as it meanders along the banks of the Caledon River, and offers the trailist the opportunity to spot waders and larger waterbirds including the blue crane, grey heron, white-bellied stork and African shelduck.

2. Klipstapel Hiking Trail, situated in the middle of the reserve's vast 22 000 ha, has a unique attraction: in an approximately 2 km^2 area lies a field of eroded dolerite pillars, each block precariously balanced on its base. This natural phenomenon strongly resembles the stone cairns of the Matopos in Zimbabwe.

3. Orange River Hiking Trail crosses some open plains, but the longest part of this trail follows the course of the Orange River as it makes its way through mountainous terrain, which provides the hiker with some very beautiful views of the river and the hills beyond.

Several species of long grass and thorny annuals possessing seeds with sharply pointed dispersal mechanisms are common in the reserve; gaiters with boots are highly recommended footwear for all hikers.

3. AASVOËLBERG HIKING TRAIL
ZASTRON

Trail details: 35 km/2 days; circular. Shorter variations are possible on both days.

Permits/bookings: Bookings must be made in advance by contacting Paul Botha, Maluti Hotel, tel. (05542) ask for 107, fax (05542) ask for 379; PO Box 2, Zastron 9950. Permits, as well as the key for the overnight huts, are available on arrival at the hotel.

Facilities/amenities: At the start, accommodation is available at the Municipal Caravan Park or in chalets at the dam, at the Maluti Hotel, or at the Outdoor School. At the mid-point there are two overnight huts, each sleeping 6 people on bunks with mattresses, and with fresh water, a braai area, a shower and toilet facilities.

Main attractions: Scenic mountains; a wide variety of interesting rock formations; waterfalls; a large variety of wildlife.

Pertinent information: Groups are limited to a maximum of 12 people.

This hike starts and finishes at the Municipal Caravan Park. It is fairly difficult and an interesting trail for fit and experienced hikers. Follow the white markers. Trailists must start walking before 7.00 am on Day 1 as the route covers some steep terrain. Fill your water bottles whenever you get to a stream. There is a short cut, signposted with yellow markers; however, if red flags are out on the shooting range (used on some Saturdays), this route cannot be used.

The first day's walk is through rough mountain terrain and commences with a steady climb for some 2 hours towards a large boulder on the horizon. From here, you can see the top of Mushroom Rock. The path continues through dense undergrowth and between rock crevices to a sandstone cave, then ascends a small cliff to Bakenkrans. If

This eroded hole, called De Winnaar's Eye (The Oog), has probably been celebrated in folklore since prehistoric man first saw it.

you manage to reach this point before 10.30 am and have energy to spare, you can walk to the top of Bakenkrans, but do stay on the marked path as this is the only way to the top. Moving on, a steep descent brings you to a very narrow ledge, where a chain handrail makes negotiating this section a lot easier. Descending past Face Rock into a steep gully, you find Holkrans. Look for blue footprint markers, as these lead to a cement trough with fresh water; replenish here as there is no more water for quite a distance. The trail's next highlight is The Tunnel.

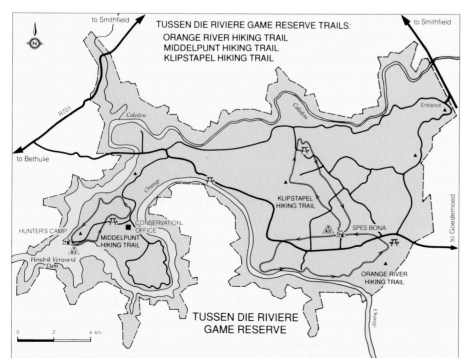

TUSSEN DIE RIVIERE GAME RESERVE TRAILS:
ORANGE RIVER HIKING TRAIL
MIDDELPUNT HIKING TRAIL
KLIPSTAPEL HIKING TRAIL

to Smithfield

to Smithfield

to Bethulie

R701

Caledon

Caledon

Entrance

to Goedemoed

Orange

KLIPSTAPEL HIKING TRAIL

SPES BONA

HUNTER'S CAMP

CONSERVATION OFFICE

MIDDELPUNT HIKING TRAIL

Hendrik Verwoerd Dam

ORANGE RIVER HIKING TRAIL

Orange

TUSSEN DIE RIVIERE GAME RESERVE

0   2   4 km

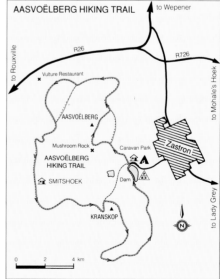

AASVOËLBERG HIKING TRAIL

to Wepener

to Rouxville

R26

R726

to Mohale's Hoek

Vulture Restaurant

AASVOËLBERG

AASVOËLBERG HIKING TRAIL

Mushroom Rock

Caravan Park

Zastron

Dam

SMITSHOEK

to Lady Grey

KRANSKOP

0   2   4 km

The Caledon River makes its lazy way close by the Thaba Total overnight hut on the Stokstert Hiking Trail.

This trail, located in the Caledon River Conservancy, takes its name from the 'stokstert-meerkat' or suricate (*Suricata suricatta*), which is common in the local area. The trail passes through a variety of interesting landscapes including ravines, cliffs, and ridges covered in vegetation. Birdlife is abundant and the fortunate hiker may see martial eagles, African fish eagles and black storks.

The first day's walk takes the hiker to the highest point in the area, Burnetskop, where magnificent views of the area can be enjoyed. Hikers should reach the overnight by lunchtime. From here, an optional circular route of some 6 km can be walked in the afternoon. It is well worth the effort as it leads to the banks of the Caledon River, through a deep kloof and past some very interesting features, such as a natural rock bridge.

Day 2's walk of 12 km passes the ruins of old mission station settlements and hikers also have a good view of the old missionary homestead, Beersheba, which is a national monument. The route follows the winding Arendkloof, with high cliffs, a deep swimming hole and lush vegetation. Freshwater mussels are found in the waters of this kloof.

5. ORANGE FREE STATE NATIONAL BOTANICAL GARDEN
BLOEMFONTEIN

Trail details: 4 km/1,5 hour; circular.

Facilities/amenities: Nursery; plants available for sale on weekdays; plant sales monthly; picnic and braai sites; teas on Sunday afternoons.

Main attractions: Peaceful setting; display of Orange Free State flora; collection of South African karees (*Rhus* spp.); 55 tree species; 110 recorded bird species; Iron Age Sotho dwelling site.

Pertinent information: Open daily 8.00 am to 6.00 pm. Dogs allowed on leash. Groups must be kept to a maximum of 25 people. Conducted trails for school children are available on request.

The main attraction of the Orange Free State National Botanical Garden is the complex of short, easily negotiated, self-guided nature walks. The duration of the complete walk around the 3 koppies is approximately 1,5 hours.

The Garden is situated in typical central Orange Free State terrain: dolerite koppies separated by valleys and dry watercourses. Distinct vegetation types grow in the valleys and kloofs, on grassed plains and on Karoo koppies and their wooded slopes. A useful feature of the Garden is that some of the koppie flora, in addition to that in the cultivated garden, is labelled for easy identification. Visit during spring if you want to see the seasonal blooms at their spectacular best. A visit to trails such as these can enhance trailists' appreciation and understanding of nature when hiking in wilder environments.

Two routes lead through it; the yellow one goes in deeper and comes out via a small hole back on the trail. After ascending another cliff and enjoying splendid views of the surrounding countryside, there is a steep drop to The Oog. You should reach this point no later than 1.30 pm. There is a very dangerous ledge leading into the cave, but this is unmarked and you attempt it at your own risk. The path then gradually heads down to the top of a dry waterfall and splits into 2 paths. The route marked with yellow footprints is the easier option, but remember that it is out of bounds if the shooting range is in use. Both paths lead to the overnight huts at Smitshoek.

Day 2's hike is not as difficult, though reasonably strenuous. It passes several waterfalls, one of which only flows during the wet season, and involves a considerable amount of climbing. There are several streams and some panoramic views along the way.

4. STOKSTERT HIKING TRAIL
SMITHFIELD

Trail details: 26 km/2 days; circular.

Permits/bookings: A permit and booking are required from Mrs. Pretorius, tel. (05562) 2411/234; PO Box 67, Smithfield 9966.

Facilities/amenities: Base camp consists of a restored farmhouse with beds and mattresses, running water, toilet, showers, braai facilities and firewood; overnight hut has beds and mattresses, bush toilet, showers, running water, electric lighting, firewood and braai facilities.

Main attractions: Birdlife; deep ravines; Caledon River; splendid views; old mission station.

Pertinent information: The maximum number of hikers permitted is 24.

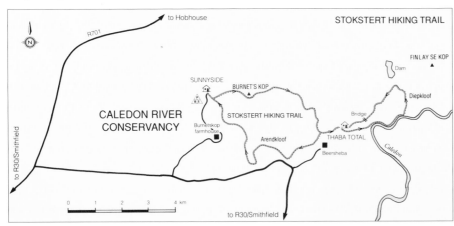

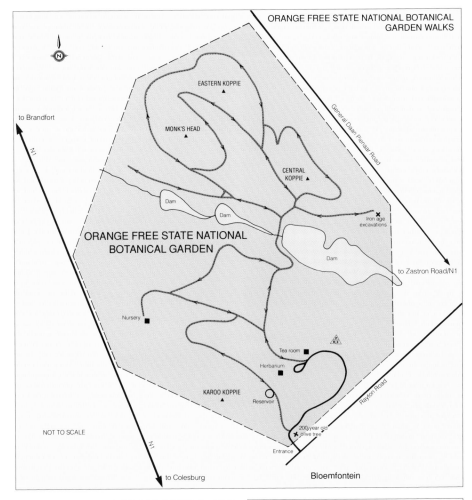

ORANGE FREE STATE NATIONAL BOTANICAL GARDEN WALKS

to Brandfort

EASTERN KOPPIE ▲

MONK'S HEAD ▲

CENTRAL KOPPIE ▲

Dam

Dam

ORANGE FREE STATE NATIONAL
BOTANICAL GARDEN

Dam

to Zastron Road/N1

Iron age
excavations ✗

Nursery ■

Tea room ■

Herbarium ■

KAROO KOPPIE ▲

Reservoir

NOT TO SCALE

200-year old
olive tree ✗

Entrance

to Colesburg

Bloemfontein

General Daan Pienaar Road

Rayton Road

out on the hilltops. The route winds back downhill, then returns to the start along the banks of the Groothoek Dam.

2. The Ostrich Trail also starts from the braai site and climbs up a wooded gorge to the top of the hills, but leads off alongside the dam and back to the start.

Both these trails are clearly marked and are not unduly strenuous. They each offer superb views of the game-rich plains and interesting birdlife. Hikers are ferried to the northern shore of the dam by motorboat and returned to the hotel after they have completed the walk. Horse-riding is also offered in the park (for further details, see Special Interest section).

7. VIRGINIA NATURE TRAILS
VIRGINIA

Trail details: 1. Hamerkop Route: 4 km/1,5 hours. 2. Paradise Flycatcher Route: 6 km/3,5 hours. Both trails are circular.

Permits/bookings: Not required.

Maps/information: A booklet including a map and information about the area is available from either the Public Library in Virginia Gardens or from the Municipality of Virginia, Private Bag X7, Virginia 9430.

Facilities/amenities: Braai area located at the start of the walks.

Main attractions: Plentiful birdlife, the Sand River.

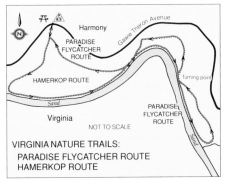

VIRGINIA NATURE TRAILS:
PARADISE FLYCATCHER ROUTE
HAMERKOP ROUTE

These two trails, located beside the Sand River in Virginia, are suitable for the whole family and offer walkers the chance to see indigenous plantlife and the great diversity of the area's birdlife. Trees along the trails are named, and include the wild olive, mountain cabbage tree, and Cape willow and mountain karee. A total of 214 species of birds has been recorded, including the crimsonbreasted shrike, forktailed drongo, whitefronted bee-eater, malachite kingfisher and spotted eagle owl. When the river is in flood, you may even be fortunate enough to see a few fish eagles.

Follow the footprint markers, yellow for the **Hamerkop Route** and white for the **Paradise Flycatcher Route**. Keep to the paths; taking short cuts causes erosion and you may lose your way. Fires are only permitted in the braai area at the start of the walks and you must provide your own wood or charcoal.

6. MARIA MOROKA NATIONAL PARK TRAILS
THABA NCHU, BOPHUTHATSWANA

Trail details: 1. Eland Trail: 8 km/4 to 4,5 hours; 2. Ostrich Trail: 2 km/1 to 1,5 hours. Both are circular. Guided trails can be arranged.

Permits/bookings: Must be obtained from Thaba Safaris, c/o Thaba Nchu Sun Hotel, tel. (05265) 2161, ask for 878 or 825; PO Box 114, Thaba Nchu, Bophuthatswana 9870.

Facilities/amenities: Braai area; toilets; accommodation at the Thaba Nchu Sun hotel.

Main attractions: Scenic landscapes; open plains and Thaba Nchu (Black Mountain); Groothoek Dam; game; birdlife.

Pertinent information: Guided walks can be arranged according to the requirements of the group. There is a limit of 10 hikers for each trail at any one time. For further information contact the PR Office, Bophuthatswana National Parks Board, tel. (0140) 895156/9; fax (0140) 21468; Private Bag X2078, Mmabatho 8670.

The Maria Moroka National Park, situated on farms which once belonged to members of the Barolong Chieftainship, is located in the southernmost section of Bophuthatswana, approximately 80 km east of Bloemfontein.

On the open plains of sweet grassveld thrive the large mammals that in days gone by inhabited the land – springbok, blesbok, Burchell's zebra, red har-

THABA NCHU ▲

MARIA MOROKA
NATIONAL PARK

ELAND
TRAIL

Kgabanyane

ELAND TRAIL

OSTRICH TRAIL

Groothoek
Dam

to R64/Thaba Nchu

Thaba Nchu
Sun Hotel

NOT TO SCALE

MARIA MOROKA NATIONAL PARK TRAILS:
OSTRICH TRAIL
ELAND TRAIL

tebeest and eland. The Groothoek Dam and Kgabanyane River attract waterfowl and the Cymbopogon-Themeda veld swarms with grassland birds, while raptors are also common. The rare and endemic blue korhaan is a speciality due to its restricted distribution in the Orange Free State/southern Bophuthatswana region. The Cymbopogon-Themeda veld type is a sweet grassveld, low shrub savannah. Its grasses are palatable, but the dominant shrubs, *Euclea crispa* and *Rhus erosa*, are unpalatable to browsing animals.

1. The Eland Trail starts at the braai site, and makes a slow ascent for 1 660 m before levelling

The overnight house in Mauershoek on the Steve Visser Walk is set among the wide horizons of plain and koppie.

scented heath, *Erica caffra*; white stinkwood, *Celtis africana*; wild olive, *Olea africana*; wag-'n-bietjie or buffalo thorn, *Ziziphus mucronata*; and the very distinctive fine-leaved karee, *Rhus erosa*.

The trail is marked with painted white arrows on rocks. Because the soil is shallow and rocky, no well-defined path has been constructed. Views over Ladybrand and beyond are excellent. However, the trail does not lend itself to seclusion: motor cars, fences, wires, towers and whistles are fairly often seen or heard.

There is no potable water *en route* so I suggest you carry at least 1 litre.

9. EVENING STAR WALK
CLOCOLAN

Trail details: 6 km/3 hours; circular.

Permits/bookings: These are not necessary, but further information is available from Mr. Cloete, tel. (051931) 3240; PO Box 155, Clocolan 9735.

Main attractions: An old monastery; views of the area; indigenous bush.

Pertinent information: Unsuitable for young children under school-going age, unless they are to be carried. Groups are limited to a maximum of 20 people.

This walk, located near Clocolan on the road to Excelsior, is in a mountainous setting and offers the hiker scenery that is typical of this area. Although it is not difficult, it is in mountainous terrain and therefore is not really suited to young children. An interesting feature at the starting point is an old sandstone monastery, and a cowshed that has been converted into a pottery workshop. The pottery produced here is on display at the monastery.

8. STEVE VISSER NATURE WALK
LADYBRAND

Trail details: 15 km/1 or 2 days; circular. Shorter walks are possible.

Permits/bookings: Reservations must be made for the overnight hut. Contact Municipality of Ladybrand, tel. (05191) 40656; PO Box 64, Ladybrand 9745.

Facilities/amenities: Mountain hut with 40 beds, a gas stove and cold water showers, accessible by motor car; Leliehoek Pleasure Resort (start of trail) with chalets, camping and caravanning, and modern facilities.

Main attractions: Maluti Mountain scenery; Bushman caves; indigenous trees and shrubs; historical sites.

Pertinent information: Carry water.

Ladybrand is located in the shadows of the Platberg, near the Lesotho border. Informal nature rambles, bridle paths, and the 15-km Steve Visser Trail radiate from Leliehoek Pleasure Resort. The overnight house in Mauershoek (near Nursery's Hoek), provided by the municipality for hikers, is most popular with large groups. The trail can easily be walked in a day, and hikers can enjoy the amenities of Leliehoek Pleasure Resort or the stone house before or after their walk. Several historic sites, which lend interest to this walk, are passed on Platberg's slopes. Mauershoek itself was the first inhabited settlement of Ladybrand, and Jacob Mauer was the first person to live here. The second part of the trail passes 'The Stables', a giant crevice against the mountain slope in which the Boers hid their horses during the Basuto War of 1858.

Birdlife is rich: rock kestrels play among the cliffs and rock thrushes and redfaced mousebirds feed on the slopes below. Some of the common plants include ouhout, *Leucosidea sericea*; a sweet-

Suggesting a candelabra, flowers of the 'kopseerblom' (Amaryllis family) spread their bright petals.

10. KORANNA HIKING TRAIL
NEAR EXCELSIOR

Trail details: 32 km/2 days; circular.

Permits/bookings: A permit and booking are required from Jacana Country Homes and Trails, tel. (012) 3463550, fax (012) 3462499; PO Box 95212, Waterkloof 0145.

Facilities/amenities: Base hut with 15 beds plus mattresses, shower, bath, toilet, and limited firewood; overnight camp site at a cave with bush toilet and spring water; bring a gas stove.

Main attractions: Variety of landscapes; weathered sandstone caves with Bushman paintings; intriguing rock formations; waterfall; approximately 150 species of birds; vistas of the Orange Free State; wild flowers.

Pertinent information: The trail overall is fairly stiff and is unsuitable for the very young or very old. Carry water. Mist and thunderstorms are common in summer, particularly in the afternoon. Winters can be very cold.

The Koranna Hiking Trail is the product of an enthusiastic group of Wildlife Society members belonging to the local Marquard Branch. They deserve congratulations for their efforts in laying out an unusual trail, providing both a variety of scenery and physically challenging terrain. The

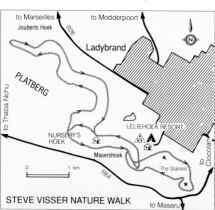

to Marseilles
Jouberts Hoek
to Modderpoort
Ladybrand
R26
PLATBERG
to Thaba Nchu
NURSERY'S HOEK
LELIEHOEK RESORT
Mauershoek
The Stables
to Clocolan
R64
to Maseru

0   1 km

STEVE VISSER NATURE WALK

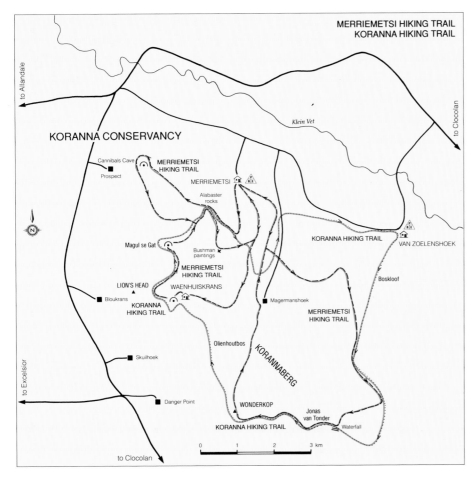

MERRIEMETSI HIKING TRAIL
KORANNA HIKING TRAIL

to Allandale

Klein Vet

to Clocolan

KORANNA CONSERVANCY

N

Cannibals Cave
Prospect

MERRIEMETSI
HIKING TRAIL

MERRIEMETSI

Alabaster
rocks

Magul se Gat

KORANNA HIKING TRAIL
VAN ZOELENSHOEK

Bushman
paintings

MERRIEMETSI
HIKING TRAIL

LION'S HEAD

WAENHUISKRANS

Boskloof

Bloukrans

KORANNA
HIKING TRAIL

Magermanshoek

MERRIEMETSI
HIKING TRAIL

to Excelsior

Olienhoutbos

KORANNABERG

Skuilhoek

Danger Point

WONDERKOP

Jonas
van Tonder

KORANNA HIKING TRAIL

Waterfall

0   1   2   3 km

to Clocolan

trail, located in the Korannaberg Conservancy which is privately owned by a number of farmers, was founded in 1985.

The starting point, 30 km from Excelsior and 48 km from Marquard, is difficult to find in the dark, so obtain the sketch map in advance and plan to arrive before sunset. The base hut is a comfortable farmhouse with a pleasant view.

The first day's 17-km walk is the more difficult of the two days and includes flat bushy areas rich in birdlife, steep ascents necessitating boulder scrambling in a ravine well endowed with streams and waterfalls, and plateau trekking among interesting koppies, over farmland and past stone overhangs. The overnight site is a magnificent cave consisting of two large 'rooms' separated by a stone pillar and sheltered behind natural bush.

The shorter second day (15 km) leads the hiker through fields of wild flowers, past koppies and Bushman paintings to Magul se Gat. Do not forget your torch if you wish to explore this unique rock tunnel and cave.

The Korannaberg is located in a transitional zone between a dry and a wet climate, which results in a wide variety of plantlife: grassland on the mountain plateau, riverine forest, and fynbos. Birdlife includes endangered species such as the black eagle, martial eagle and Cape vulture.

11. MERRIEMETSI HIKING TRAILS
NEAR EXCELSIOR

Trail details: Two circular 1-day trails of 10,5 km. One circular trail of 15 km, which can be done over 1 or 2 days.

Permits/bookings: A permit and booking are required from Jacana Country Homes and Trails, tel. (012) 3463550, fax (012) 3462499; PO Box 95212, Waterkloof 0145.

Facilities/amenities: Merriemetsi barn, with 1 large room, a separate kitchen and diningroom; hot showers, toilets and a gas cooker. Merriemetsi Lodge, a Victorian sandstone homestead, which is fully equipped and sleeps 8. For overnighting on the 2-day trail, there is a cave with water and a bush toilet.

Main attractions: Korannaberg; Magul se Gat; interesting rock formations; Bushman paintings; prolific birdlife.

Pertinent information: Group size is restricted to 20. Fires are not allowed, so take a gas stove if overnighting at the cave. Always carry water. If walking the 2-day trail, you must start by 7.00 am at the latest. The overnight stop for this walk is on a private farm which is not part of the conservancy, so check with Jacana Country Homes and Trails that permission has been granted for you to use this facility. Be alert to changes in weather; thunderstorms are fairly common in summer.

These trails are located in the Koranna Conservancy and, in some instances, share the same route as the Koranna Trail. They are probably best tackled in September and October before the heat of summer or from February to May, as winters in the region can be extremely cold.

The first of the 1-day walks should be commenced before 8.00 am. To see the Bushman paintings, you must hire a guide for a small fee, payable directly to him. You need only carry a day

Cascading waters sparkle in the sunlight on the Koranna Hiking Trail, situated in an interesting transitional climatic zone.

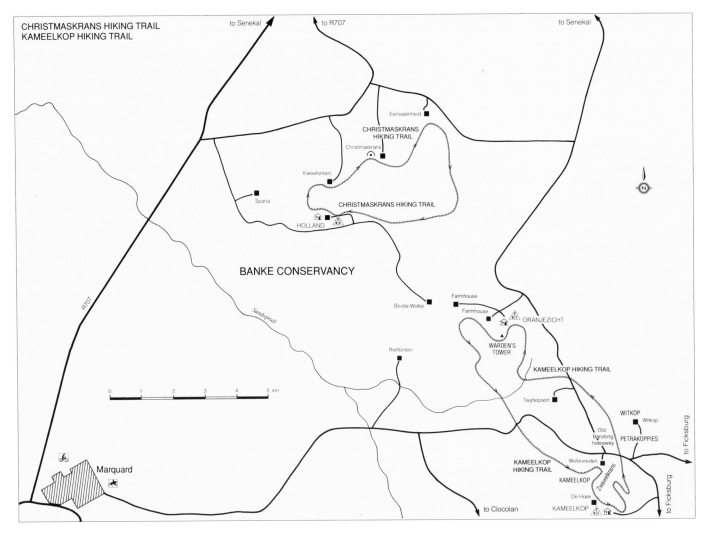

CHRISTMASKRANS HIKING TRAIL
KAMEELKOP HIKING TRAIL

BANKE CONSERVANCY

A martial eagle perches secure and high with its prey of ground squirrel.

pack and an adequate supply of water. The path starts with an energetic climb up Lion's Head, but from here on is fairly flat. The paintings are not marked, as they have been vandalized in the past. From here you join up with the Koranna Trail for a time and walk to the Waenhuis cave, a good spot for lunch, and then proceed to Magul se Gat. A torch is essential if you want to explore this fascinating cave. Shortly after this point, you leave the

Koranna Trail and pass the Alabaster balancing rock formation, then head down back to base camp.

The other 1-day trail must also be started with a guide. Going parallel to the base of the Korannaberg, the path leads up to the point where you go through a gap in the mountain. The Cannibals Cave nearby is large and open, so torches are not necessary. A further ascent of the mountain leads to a spectacular overhang, then joins up with the other 1-day trail to the Alabaster rocks and down a steep incline back to Merriemetsi barn.

The longest of the 3 trails can be done on either 1 or 2 days. For a 1-day excursion, start before 7.00 am. Note that as a day-trail, this is not suitable for unfit or inexperienced hikers. If being undertaken over 2 days, Day 1 is the more difficult. Hikers must be accompanied by a guide until the trail is marked. After crossing grasslands, this route also joins the Koranna Trail for some time, then leads up to an area where martial eagles nest. Do not disturb these birds. Heading into a valley then ascending the other side, the trail leads towards a junction where those overnighting will make their way to the waterfall. As there are no facilities provided here, refer to the advice on p. 331 (Consider the environment). Fires are prohibited.

For those doing the trail as a day walk, or for the second day of the trail, the path continues over the hill towards the top of the Korannaberg and again merges with the Koranna Trail for a fair distance. On descent there is a stream which is usually flow-

ing, even in very dry times. The route then veers right down the kloof past Magermanshoek Farm; do not bother the owners under any circumstances. Continuing along a road then down a ladder, you finish the trail at Merriemetsi barn.

12. KAMEELKOP HIKING TRAIL
NEAR MARQUARD

Trail details: 26 km/2 days, 2 nights; circular.
Permits/bookings: Required from Jacana Country Homes and Trails, tel. (012) 3463550, fax (012) 3462499; PO Box 95212, Waterkloof 0145.
Facilities/amenities: Two base camps, each with 15 beds plus mattresses, bathroom, toilet, hot water, paraffin lamps, candles and braai facilities.
Main attractions: Riverine forest; exciting geological aspects; Barolong hideaway and ruins; excellent views of the Malutis; Wonderkop, a lava-covered mountain.
Pertinent information: Pack according to the weather: summers can be very hot and bring thunderstorms and lightning, and winters are very cold. The trail can be booked for a maximum of 30; 2 groups of 15 hikers can be accommodated at the 2 base camps.

Day 1 of this trail, located in the Banke Conservancy, takes you up a beautiful kloof through riverine forest. The reward at the top is 'Krans

'Punt', a view site. The route follows the mountain for a time, then descends to grasslands. Petra Koppies is the site of an old Barolong hideaway and offers spectacular views of the Maluti mountains, Visierskerf and Wonderkop. A steel ladder makes easier work of climbing a sandstone krantz, then the route passes through some grassland again towards Warden's Tower, finally reaching Oranjezicht base camp.

The second day takes you to Warden's Tower, which the fitter members of your group can cross over while the others pass around it. The trail then runs the full length of the conservancy up to Kameelkop where, once again, there are superb views of the area. From here, the path leads down towards De Hoek cottage; at this point the profile of Kameelkop is very clear and it is easy to see why it acquired its name. Follow the trail past Zwawelkrans, an imposing stone overhang, back to Kameelkop base camp.

Note that you can also commence at Oranjezicht camp, starting the trail past Warden's Tower, spending the second night at Kameelkop hut and returning to Oranjezicht the following day.

13. CHRISTMASKRANS HIKING TRAIL
MARQUARD

Trail details: 13 km/1 day; circular.

Permits/bookings: A permit and booking are required from Jacana Country Homes and Trails, tel. (012) 3463550, fax (012) 346 2499; PO Box 95212, Waterkloof 0145.

Facilities/amenities: Renovated sandstone school building sleeping 8, with mattresses, a woodstove (which also provides hot water for showers), cold water and a bush toilet.

Main attractions: Cave; Bushman paintings (which can be viewed by arrangement); weathered sandstone formations.

Pertinent information: The trail can be booked for a maximum of 8 people. Carry water.

During the Anglo-Boer War a group of local women and children hid from the English soldiers in a cave. It is not known exactly how long they were there; some people say 8 days and others 3 weeks. Their presence went undetected by the nearby soldiers until, on Christmas morning, the women lit a fire to make a warming cup of coffee. The soldiers noticed the smoke and the group was discovered and taken prisoner. The cave has been known as Christmaskrans ever since, and this walk will take you to it.

The trail is in the 12 000-ha Banke Conservancy, located 18 km from Marquard. From base camp the route, shown with black and white footprint markers, leads to the top of a koppie and follows a ridge, giving good views out over Sparta, a huge cattle feedlot. Descending, the path traces an old oxwagon route until it passes the Kareefontein household spring. From here you have a lovely view out over the gum trees to Christmaskrans farm. Keeping on this route you soon reach the 'Christmaskrans' and can stop to ponder the history that gave the cave its name.

Follow the trail down below the ridge and past a freshwater spring and Eensaamheid farmhouse. From here you can enjoy superb views to the east-

ern mountains. From here, you can visit the nearby Bushman paintings, if you have made advance arrangements. The final stretches of the route are past cultivated fields of maize or wheat.

As this is not a very strenuous trail and one that is suitable for families, there is plenty of time to look out for some of the mammals that make their home in the area, including impala, zebra, gemsbok and black and brown springbok.

An extended 2-day trail with facilities for overnighting is currently being planned, and may be in operation in 1994.

14. DE HOEK TRAILS
NEAR MARQUARD

Trail details: 1. 5 km/2-3 hours; 2. 12 km/5-6 hours. Both trails are circular. (Map unavailable.)

Permits/bookings: A permit and booking are required and can be obtained from Jacana Country Homes and Trails, tel. (012) 3463550, fax (012) 3462499; PO Box 95212, Waterkloof 0145.

Facilities/amenities: Fully equipped house sleeping 8 people.

Main attractions: Ericas in profusion; interesting Barolong ruins.

Pertinent information: Carry water on both trails. Trails may be booked for a maximum of 8 people.

Both of these walks are in the Banke Conservancy, located 25 km from Marquard. Neither is strenuous.

Follow the red and white markers for trail 1, and the blue and white markers for trail 2. September through to April is recommended as the best time to enjoy these walks, as winter in the area can be very cold and dry.

15. IMPERANI HIKING TRAIL
FICKSBURG

Trail details: 25 km/2 days, 1 night; circular. See map page 152.

Permits/bookings: Bookings must be made in advance and a deposit paid at least 14 days before you begin the trail. Contact the Municipality of Ficksburg, tel. (05192) 2122; PO Box 116, Ficksburg 9730.

Facilities/amenities: Overnight hut accommodating 16 people; Meulspruit Pleasure Resort can be used as a base camp (camping and caravanning, ablution block, and thatched shelter); there is also a youth centre next to the resort.

Main attractions: Sandstone overhangs; krantzes; a wide variety of plantlife; magnificent views of the distant Malutis; birdlife; rock paintings.

Pertinent information: The terrain is rough in parts, so boots are recommended. Be alert to the presence of snakes, especially puff adders. Famous Cherry Festival in November; cherry blossom season from September to October.

The Municipality of Ficksburg, in conjunction with the Department of Education and Culture, has developed a scenic hiking trail covering the entire circumference of Imperani Mountain, with a loop on Camel Ridge.

The Imperani Hiking Trail is an exciting and invigorating way to experience Ficksburg's scenic grandeur. 'Imperani' is a Basotho word meaning 'mountain of many', and for the hiker it does offer many attractions.

The circular trail starts and ends at the Meulspruit Pleasure Resort, where a steep ascent takes the hiker past Bushman paintings to the grand sand-

On the Imperani Trail, distant flat-topped koppies are erosion features typical of the Karoo-type landscape.

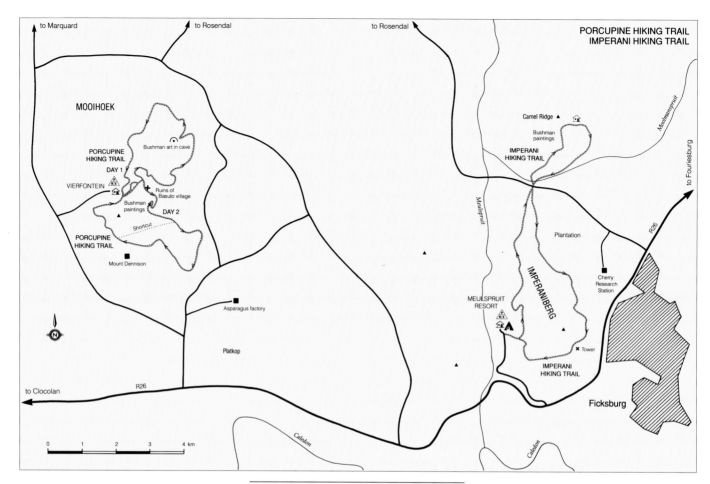

stone overhangs of Imperani. (The scenery in this area reminds me greatly of the Golden Gate Highlands National Park.)

Continuing in a northerly direction on Imperani's west-facing slopes, the trail winds below krantz level over some rough terrain. As you approach the old government plantation on the plateau, now used as grazing commonage, the tread is much easier. Some time is spent walking in a mixed exotic conifer forest.

The trail then descends the mountain, crosses a tarred road and ascends Camel Ridge. Impressive caves, far-reaching views and lovely poplar- and willow-lined streams make this section well worth the effort. Views of the Maluti mountains are magnificent. The overnight hut is rather rustic, but in beautiful surroundings.

On the second day a steep descent into a kloof adds interest before the trail winds back under majestic weathered sandstone krantzes. Wildlife is scarce although dassie, red rockrabbit, grey rhebok, wild cat, porcupine, jackal and meerkat make their home on Imperani. Big-game introductions are planned. Birds are a constant companion: rock pigeon, redwing francolin, guineafowl and orange-breasted rockjumper. Vegetation in the area is plentiful and includes aloes, kiepersol, wild camphor and dogwood.

Although water is available I recommend carrying some, as the sources are far apart. When I walked the trail in June, the snow-capped Malutis were magnificent in the crisp, clear air. However, the town clerk reminded me to return in spring to experience the unique and very beautiful cherry blossom season.

16. PORCUPINE HIKING TRAIL
FICKSBURG

Trail details: 24 km/2 days; figure-of-eight. Shorter routes are possible.

Permits/bookings: A booking is required from Jill Moffett, tel. (05192) 3959; 'Kirklington', PO Box 25, Gumtree 9731.

Facilities/amenities: Fully equipped overnight house with education centre. House has electricity, hot and cold running water and braai facilities.

Main attractions: Prolific birdlife; views of the Maluti Mountains; rock formations; variety of plantlife; old Boer fort.

Pertinent information: The weather can be very changeable and is always cool at night, so be prepared. Ticks are common. The maximum number of people permitted per group is 25. Carry water at all times.

This trail is located in the 5 000-ha Gumtree Conservancy, which lies between Ficksburg, Clocolan and Marquard. It was established to both preserve and promote this beautiful area.

The trail circles two mountains and forms a figure-of-eight, with the accommodation at the centre. It is suitable for inexperienced hikers and intends to educate as well as entertain. There is a rich and varied flora population in the conservancy and the more common trees and shrubs on the trail are labelled for easy identification.

Some 50 different types of grasses grow here, from highveld sourveld to the less common Rooigras. Small forests flourish in the valleys, and

well-adapted indigenous vegetation thrives on the hill slopes.

Follow the metal signboards, markers and arrows. Porcupines are nocturnal so may not be seen, but look out for other small animal life resident here such as mongoose, squirrels and spring hares. The most pleasant months to hike this trail are September through to May. The local cherry orchards are in blossom in September, and the Pompon trees *Dais cotinifolia*, which flower in November/December, provide a breath-taking display of pink blooms.

The first day's trail begins with a steep climb to the top of Mooihoek Mountain, then follows the sandstone cliffs. Perched on top of a ridge, an old Boer fort once used as a lookout post makes a good spot for a tea break, and offers wonderful views out over the Malutis, the cherry orchards and cultivated fields of the area. Descending quite steeply, the path leads through a basin rich in indigenous vegetation then heads back up Mooihoek Mountain. Further along the trail, there are Bushman paintings sheltered by a magnificent rock overhang, but unfortunately these have been vandalized. Heading along the plateau then down a kloof, the trail crosses farmland for some time to return to the overnight house.

Day 2's trail focuses on exploring Mount Dennison, close to base camp. Highlights are the superb views of the Maluti mountains and fantastic rock formations.

Another enjoyable feature of this trail, but one of a different nature, is the fresh organically grown fruit and vegetables, including asparagus, cherries, figs, peaches and apricots, which are available for sale to hikers.

17. WATERKLOOF HIKING TRAIL
NEAR FICKSBURG

Trail details: 23 km/2 days or 33 km/3 days; both are circular.

Permits/bookings: A permit and booking are required from Jacana Country Homes and Trails, tel. (012) 3463550, fax (012) 3462499; PO Box 95212, Waterkloof 0145.

Facilities/amenities: Base camp in an old farmhouse with 30 beds and mattresses, 2 bathrooms with hot water, fridge, cooker and braai facilities; 2 overnight camps, each with mattresses, toilets, firewood and water.

Main attractions: Visierskerf and Sinkoijellahoed mountains; several swimming holes in beautiful kloofs; eastern Free State mountain scenery.

Pertinent information: The trail can be booked for a maximum of 30 people. Summers are very hot; winters are extremely cold and snow on the mountains is common, so be prepared.

Starting from Waterkloof Farm in the 2 950-ha Moolmanshoek Conservancy east of Ficksburg, both the shorter and longer trails share a common route for the first day's walk, taking the hiker through an old fruit orchard, cultivated land and along the stream of a riverine valley to the first gorge. This is a lovely spot for a swim in the rock pools, before climbing ladders to the top of the kloof. Follow the contour path under the cliffs; if you are fit and energetic you can climb to the summit of the Sinkoijellahoed (2 316 m) before arriving at the second 'waterkloof', a good place to enjoy lunch and a refreshing swim in the mountain pools. The trail then descends to Barolong overnight camp, where hikers have the choice of sleeping in the open under a sandstone overhang or in traditional wattle-and-daub rooms.

The second day starts off along the cliffs, past Porcupine Lookout, and those on the 2-day hike can climb Visierskerf Mountain (2 410 m). The trail passes the final gorge where you can choose from seven pools for a cooling dip. At this point the trail splits. Hikers on the shorter trail walk past the pools and across the veld back to base camp. Don't be surprised to see springbok grazing alongside the sheep and cattle. Other mammals you can expect to see include duiker, steenbok, mountain reedbuck and fallow deer.

Those on the longer hike also have the opportunity to climb the Visierskerf, as well as following the trail to the Jacobsberg where black eagles nest.

There is abundant vegetation here; it is a good idea to use the tree guide that is part of the map brochure to identify the marked trees. After descending a ladder and walking for a further kilometre through dense bush, you will come to Sphinx Mountain Hut, with its lovely views across the valley. A swim in the rock pool next to the hut or the nearby dam is the ideal way to finish an energetic day.

A highlight of the third day's walk along the two Pyramid mountains is the swimming pool and waterhole, where reed hides have been built. These provide the ideal spot for watching the many waterbirds of the area at close quarters. The trail then crosses farmland and veld to return to base camp.

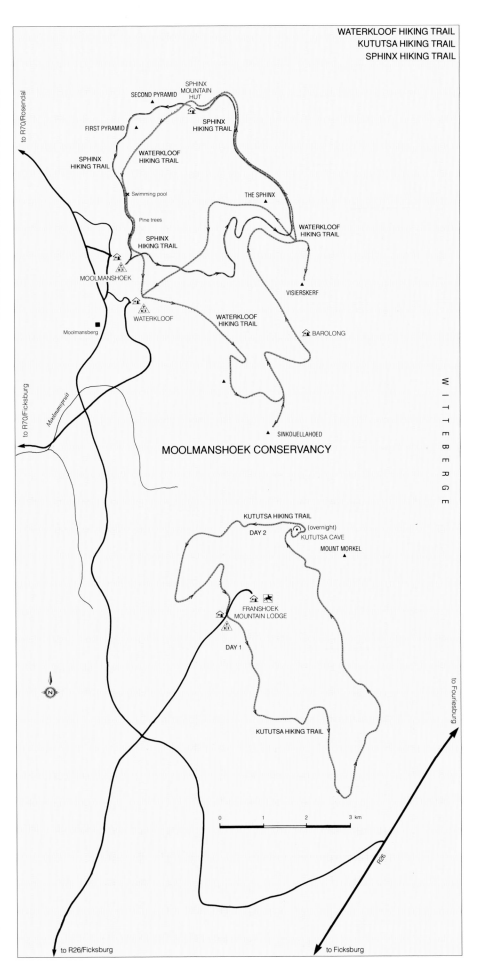

This is the tranquil view that greets hikers looking out from the overnight cave on Kututsa Hiking Trail.

18. SPHINX HIKING TRAIL
NEAR FICKSBURG

Trail details: 19 km/2 days; circular.
See map page 153.

Permits/bookings: Required from Jacana Country Homes and Trails, tel. (012) 3463550, fax (012) 3462499; PO Box 95212, Waterkloof 0145.

Facilities/amenities: Base camp at Moolmanshoek farmhouse can accommodate 22 hikers and has electricity, a fridge, two-plate stove, showers and toilet, wood and braai area. Farmstall sells rusks, milk, jams and fresh produce. Overnight camp has 22 beds and mattresses, pit toilets, cold showers, braai area and wood supplied. Braai packs can be ordered in advance.

Main attractions: Swimming holes; abundant birdlife; Visierskerf Mountain.

Pertinent information: The trail can be booked for a maximum of 22 hikers.

This trail is also located in the Moolmanshoek Conservancy and follows a similar route to that of the 2-day Waterkloof Hiking Trail. However, on the second day the path branches off following a different route along contour paths beneath the two Pyramid mountains and past a huge cave which was once used as a kraal for 1 000 goats, then later was the site of an arsenal during the Anglo-Boer War. The path descends to a grove of willow trees and a large swimming hole, which offers the chance for a last refreshing dip before heading back to base camp. For those keen on bird-watching, there is a reed hide at a waterhole close to the swimming hole.

The trail is not unduly strenuous and is suitable for anyone of average fitness.

A variety of game can be found in the conservancy including springbok, mountain reedbuck, fallow deer, duiker and steenbok. Birdlife is also abundant; fortunate hikers may see black eagles, which nest in the cliffs of the mountain.

19. KUTUTSA HIKING TRAIL
NEAR FICKSBURG

Trail details: 26 km/2 days, 2 nights; circular.
See map page 153.

Permits/bookings: A permit and booking are required from Jacana Country Homes and Trails, tel. (012) 3463550, fax (012) 3462499; PO Box 95212, Waterkloof 0145.

Facilities/amenities: 'Shearing shed' on the first night, with hay beds, shower, pit toilet and braai grid (bring your own wood or buy it there) but no electricity. Accommodation is also available at Franshoek Lodge for the first night. Kututsa cave on the second night, with toilets, braai facilities and wood, drinking water and a swimming hole.

Main attractions: Prolific animal and birdlife; historic interest, including old wagon trails and villages; huge cave; dinosaur fossils.

Pertinent information: A maximum of 30 hikers is allowed. Carry your own water during dry periods. Evenings can be cold all year round, so be prepared.

This new trail takes its name from the Sotho word meaning 'cave', as the overnight stop on the trail is a large sandstone cave, while other caves on the route are said to be some of the most interesting in the area. A booklet of very comprehensive instructions is available from the owner of the farm, Mr C Findlay, who will take backpacks up to the overnight cave on request.

Day 1's walk begins at Franshoek Lodge and is approximately 17 km. Remember to take water with you in the dry seasons; during the rainy season the mountain streams have potable water. Follow the red trail markers. The route is designed to lead through a variety of landscapes including a sandstone gorge, beautiful ravines, and a hidden valley. The area supports a wide variety of game including springbok, mountain reedbuck and blesbok. A good selection of birdlife may be seen; watch out for the black eagles in the cliffs near the Kututsa cave.

There are spectacular views of the eastern Free State and the Maluti mountains.

The second day's hike is a shorter 9 km. The path, which is indicated by yellow and white markers, leads through beautiful indigenous bush with a great range of local flora. Winding up to a plateau, the route passes a scattering of semi-precious stones (these are not to be removed), then proceeds back to base camp.

20. VINGERPOL HIKING TRAIL
NEAR PAUL ROUX

Trail details: 27 km/2 days; circular.

Permits/bookings: A permit and booking is required from Mrs C de Beer, tel. (01432) 230/231 weekdays between 8.00 am and 4.00 pm; PO Box 6, Paul Roux 9800. You may book the whole trail for your party's private use if you do not wish to share with another group; however, you will have to pay accordingly.

Facilities/amenities: Base camp has hot and cold water, shower, toilet and firewood; overnight camp is the same, but has no lighting.

Main attractions: Plantlife including the Vingerpol or lions' spoor; views of the Witteberg; sites of historical interest.

Pertinent information: Groups are limited to a maximum of 15 people. Summer is the rainy season; pack accordingly. The trail is not recommended for children under 10. Take a torch.

The Vingerpol or lions' spoor succulent (*Euphorbia clavarioides*), after which the trail is named, flourishes in this area. When you are walking make sure that these unusual plants are not disturbed or removed.

The trail starts and finishes on Waterskraal Farm, 18 kilometres south of Paul Roux. Cars can be safely left at the base camp. Follow the footprint markers for a steep climb up to the plateau. Although this section can be quite exhausting, it is the most difficult part of the walk and from here on the going is considerably easier. Your reward is a com-

*Vingerpol or lions' spoor (*Euphorbia clavarioides*) has given its name to the trail.*

manding view out over the surrounding country-side, and toward the south is an excellent vista of the Brandwater basin. Further on, the route passes a cave which once sheltered women in hiding during the Anglo-Boer War. The overnight hut is located on Witnek Farm, the site of battle during the 1914 rebellion. Your own gas lamp or torch is a necessity here.

Indigenous animal and birdlife is abundant, so be alert for sightings of grey rhebok, springbok, bles-bok, black eagles and secretary birds.

The second day is less exhausting, covering 12 km with no steep ascents involved, until the route leads back to the base camp.

21. TEPELKOP HIKING TRAIL
SLABBERTS, SOUTH OF BETHLEHEM

Trail details: Two 1-day circular trails of 18 km and 10 km respectively.

Permits/bookings: Through Jacana Country Homes and Trails, tel. (012) 3463550, fax (012) 3462499; PO Box 95212, Waterkloof 0145.

Facilities/amenities: Five-bedroomed house with beds and mattresses, kitchen equipment, gas cooker, and ablution and braai facilities.

Main attractions: Mapieta's cave; eastern Free State mountain scenery.

Pertinent information: Climate is hot in summer, with thunderstorms, and very cold in winter; pack accordingly. Be alert to sudden changes in the weather. Ticks can be a problem. Carry water. The trail can be booked for a maximum of 16 people.

Using Willowdene farmhouse (approximately 25 km south of Bethlehem on the road to Fouries-burg) as an overnight base, this trail offers hikers one-day walks on private farmland along the south-eastern slopes of the Witteberg. The routes, shown with footprint markers, are suitable for hikers of all levels of experience and fitness.

The first walk of 18 km starts roughly 4 km from Willowdene farmhouse at the farm Tepelkop. Drive to the main homestead; cars can safely be left there. The trail ascends Tepelkop Mountain then follows the contours below a sandstone ridge, covered in in-digenous ferns and grass, to Mapieta's Cave. The present owner's grandmother spent the Anglo-Boer War in hiding in this cave with her family. The cave is called by her Sotho-given name meaning 'the wife of Piet.'

The second day-trail (14 km) leads up the moun-tain behind the Willowdene farmhouse to a plateau. The first 3 km of the route are steep but the mag-nificent views across the Maluti mountains, the kingdom of Lesotho and the surrounding Free State make the climb well worth the effort.

Ideal times to walk these trails are in spring and autumn, when you can enjoy the spectacle of wild flowers in bloom and avoid the extremes of weather that can make walking less enjoyable at other times of the year.

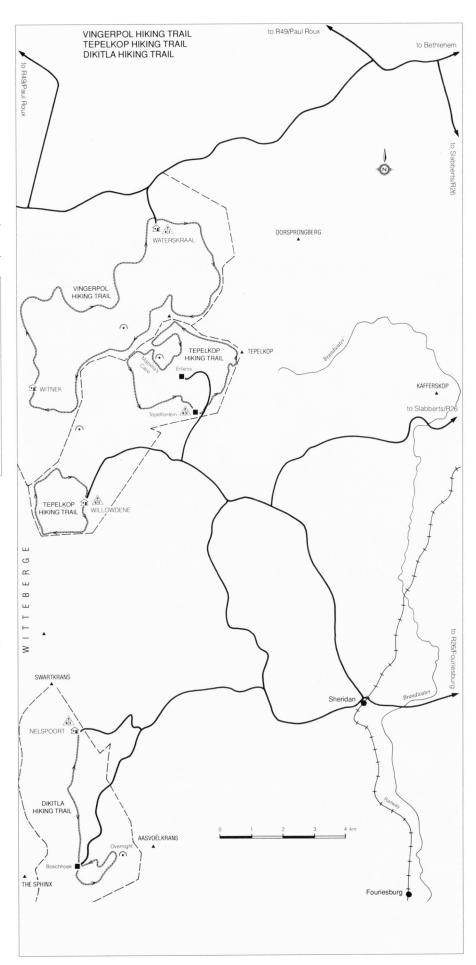

Swirling, water-borne sand has created this interesting erosion feature.

22. DIKITLA HIKING TRAIL
NEAR FOURIESBURG

Trail details: 21 km/2 days; circular.
See map p. 155.

Permits/bookings: Required from A Scheepers, tel. (014332) 2240, fax (014332) 131; 'Gezina', PO Sheridan 9704.

Facilities/amenities: Base camp comprises a garage with hot and cold water, toilet and shower, wood and braai facilities. Cave for overnighting, with toilet and water. Dam for swimming.

Main attractions: Bird and animal life; interesting plants; sandstone formations including caves; views of the Witteberg.

Pertinent information: Groups are limited to a maximum of 25 people. Good hiking boots are recommended.

This trail is located on the farm Nelspoort, 27 km from Fouriesburg.

The first day is a 10-km walk, taking between 4 and 5 hours. Follow the markers and yellow signs. Fill your water bottle from streams along the way. A dam close to the overnight cave provides the opportunity for a refreshing swim, especially during the hotter months of summer.

Day 2 of the trail is slightly longer (11 km) and more strenuous, with a hard climb to the top of a mountain which is part of the Witteberg range. This is not an easy trail and should not be undertaken by the unfit.

As this walk is on a private farm of some 2 000 ha, you will be able to see stud cattle, Merino sheep and Angora goats, as well as smaller buck and a wide variety of birdlife. Vegetation is typical of the eastern Free State and reminiscent of the plantlife in the nearby Golden Gate Highlands National Park.

23. MOUNTAIN FERN TRAIL
BIDDULPHSBERG, EAST OF SENEKAL

Trail details: A day walk of 12 km; circular.

Permits/bookings: These are not required.

Maps/information: For further information, contact Mrs Erasmus, tel. (014351) 2302; PO Box 327, Senekal 9600.

Facilities/amenities: Accommodation is available at Biddulphs Mountain Resort.

Main attractions: A large variety of game; Biddulphs Mountain; historical interest.

Pertinent information: Groups are restricted to a maximum of 15 people.

Starting at the Biddulphs Mountain Resort east of Senekal, this day-trail runs through an area with a great diversity of vegetation, beautiful cliffs and many places of historical interest. As part of the route is through a large game farm, a wide variety of animal life can be seen, including gemsbok and black springbok.

Biddulphs Mountain was the scene of a battle during the Anglo-Boer War in 1900. Remains of entrenchments can still be seen on the slopes of the mountain. A large version of the Ossewa Brandwag movement's insignia was painted on a nearby cliff in 1942. It was later restored and is still a distinct feature of the area.

24. WOLHUTERSKOP HIKING TRAIL
BETHLEHEM

Trail details: 20 km/2 days; circular.

Permits/bookings: For reservations and further information contact The Resort Manager, Loch Athlone Pleasure Resort, tel. (01431) 35732, ext. 171; PO Box 551, Bethlehem 9700.

Facilities/amenities: Fully equipped overnight house sleeping 14 people; waterpoint and toilets 5 km from starting point.

Main attractions: Beautiful scenery; abundant bird and animal life.

Pertinent information: A maximum of 14 people is permitted at any one time. The keys for the overnight hut must be collected from the Loch Athlone Resort office.

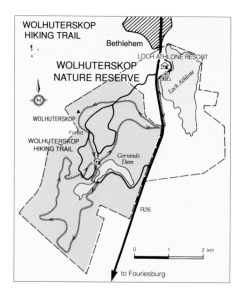

This trail starts and finishes at the Loch Athlone Pleasure Resort, and passes through the 1 200-ha Wolhuterskop Nature Reserve, established by the Free State branch of the Wildlife Society of Southern Africa and the Bethlehem Town Council. Loch Athlone itself was created when the Jordaan River which flows through Bethlehem was dammed. Day 1 covers 14 km, leading the hiker through a variety of landscapes including fields and plains, along the side of Loch Athlone and Gerrands Dam, up the rather steep Wolhuterskop with lovely views of the surrounding area, and through pine forest to the overnight house.

Game is prolific here, so don't be surprised to see herds of kudu, blesbok, impala, zebra, eland and hartebeest. On the banks of the Gerrands Dam, a wide variety of waterbirds, such as waterfowl, can be seen. Plantlife in the area includes proteas and wild flowers.

The second day's walk is an easy 6 km through pine forest again, across the plains and hills back to the resort.

This trail is very popular, as it is ideal for families and the less fit while offering an interesting range of scenery, so it is advisable to book well in advance. Keep in mind that winters in the area can be extremely cold, with the best months to do this hike being September through to May.

Wolhuterskop Hiking Trail offers the double attractions of Loch Athlone and Gerrands Dam with their prolific birdlife.

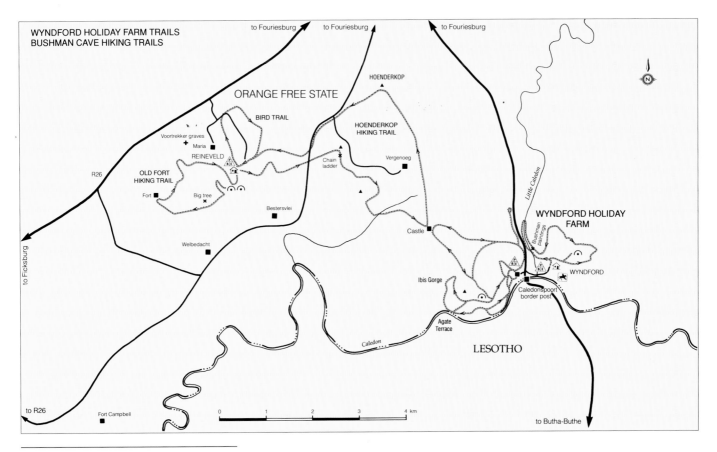

WYNDFORD HOLIDAY FARM TRAILS
BUSHMAN CAVE HIKING TRAILS

25. WYNDFORD HOLIDAY FARM
FOURIESBURG

Trail details: A variety of trails, the longest being a 3-hour walk.

Permits/bookings: Bookings are required. Contact Wyndford Holiday Farm, tel. 014332, ask for 1803; Private Bag, Fouriesburg 9725.

Facilities/amenities: Guided or self-guided walks; horses for hire (guided or self-guided rides); resort facilities including tennis courts, swimming pool, bowling green, cottages and dining room.

Main attractions: Bald ibis breeding colony; a variety of rock cave adventures; sandstone krantz 'sculptures'; Caledon River strolls; Agate Terrace; Bushman paintings (dolphins); the Castle; views of Basotho village.

Pertinent information: The terrain is rugged, so sturdy boots are recommended. For rock cave adventures, wear old clothes.

Wyndford Holiday Farm offers the adventurer and fun-seeker an exciting variety of trails, rock cave scrambles and natural wonders within its 200 ha. I was astonished during my visit to see the many fascinating areas discovered by Roy Langford, the energetic and friendly host. Roy leads trails for guests to all his discoveries on a regular but not scheduled basis. With the trail guide or directions from the Langfords, the hiker can also explore on his own. Self-guide markers are planned for many of the routes.

The most unusual of Roy's trails are the rock cave adventures which have intriguing names such as Cleft Rock Crawl, Rock Rabbit Ramble, The Tunnel, Micky Mouse House, Monkey Jol and Slippery Slide. Each requires a sense of humour, a

Soaring sandstone and a fine mix of vegetation engage a hiker's attention along one of the trails on Wyndford Holiday Farm.

daring personality and agility, and holds the prospect of getting muddy and dirty or wearing out your clothes, so old clothes that don't inhibit your movements are essential. These unusual adventures, competently guided by Roy Langford, are for both the young and the old (even if the old just listen and watch).

The longer trails lead to fascinating sites such as the Castle (a real but uncompleted castle in the midst of the grasslands above the sandstone krantz (see next entry), Ibis Gorge (the bald ibis breeding colony), Rock Pigeon Cave and Bat Cave, Rainbow Rock and Red Cliff Ravine (where towering red cliffs curve over your head). Tranquil, easy strolls along the poplar-lined Caledon River, the border between the Orange Free State and Lesotho, are also popular. These offer views of a Basotho village on the opposite bank, and Agate Terrace. Near the resort's entrance is an unusual Bushman painting depicting several dolphins.

The sandstone krantzes above the resort have been carved by wind and water into sculptures resembling a tortoise, a lizard, a frog and a camel. Walks to each are possible.

Autumn foliage turns to gold near the balancing rock on Bushman Cave Trail.

26. BUSHMAN CAVE HIKING TRAIL
FOURIESBURG

Trail details: 1. Hoenderkop Hiking Trail: 16,5-km circuit; 2. Old Fort Hiking Trail: 6-km circuit; 3. Bird Trail: 3-km circuit. (See map p. 157.)

Permits/bookings: A permit and booking are required from Mr. Venter, tel. (014332) 1702; PO Box 29, Fouriesburg 9725. Route directions and a map, available from the owner, are essential.

Facilities/amenities: A variety of rondavels and huts, showers, a bath and flush toilet, and a central cooking area with 4 gas burners and a sink. Other facilities include a youth camp and an obstacle course. For details, contact Mr. Venter.

Main attractions: Bushman paintings; historical features, including an unfinished castle and English fort; panoramic views over Lesotho; prolific birdlife; magnificent cliffs.

Pertinent information: Groups are restricted to a maximum of 30 people. When making your booking, check that all facilities are still available. According to latest reports, the overnight facilities are in a very bad state of repair; as an alternative, take your own tent and mattresses. If using the base camp, you must collect keys at the farmhouse. From here to the camp, the road is very rough and is not suited to vehicles with a low clearance. With the exception of the Old Fort Trail, the routes are not clearly marked. Ladders and stiles are not well maintained. Summer days can be very hot and may bring thunderstorms, while winter nights are usually extremely cold.

This entry has been included in the interests of making this book as comprehensive as possible. However recent reports suggest that the trail and its facilities are not well maintained; see *Getaway*, (April 1993). Consequently it will probably not appeal to anyone who is fastidious about the standard of their accommodation.

Set among typical eastern Free State mountain scenery, this trail lives up to its name and leads hikers past a large number of Bushman paintings, some of which are well preserved.

Its attractive location and the range of activities offered make this trail a popular venue with church groups; the natural amphitheatre above base camp has been set up as a 'church' with some seating and a pulpit.

1. The Hoenderkop Hiking Trail leads across a plateau, through gulleys and along ridges to the castle. The dream of a certain Mr. Hill, this Normandy-style castle of sandstone and cement stands on top of a sheer cliff. Construction was halted in 1976 due to lack of funds and this incomplete shell is now a prominent landmark. From here there are uninterrupted views of Lesotho. The path then winds back to base camp past a windmill and the Hoenderkop.

2. The Old Fort Hiking Trail is shorter and follows an easy route to a cave with Bushman paintings. After a short climb up to the ridge, the path stays with this contour for some time until it reaches the ruins of an old fort, which dates back to the Anglo-Boer War. The walk to base camp is through some lovely forested areas and passes a lookout spot and more Bushman art.

3. The Bird Trail is a short walk to a valley near the overnight camp. Birdlife is abundant here with 103 species having been identified, including the relatively rare bald ibis.

Game animals such as these are a common subject of Bushman rock art.

27. RHEBOK HIKING TRAIL
GOLDEN GATE HIGHLANDS NATIONAL PARK

Trail details: 31 km/2 days; circular. Day walks and guided walks within the park.

Permits/bookings: A booking can be made up to 1 year in advance through the Chief Director, National Parks Board, tel. (012) 3431991; PO Box 787, Pretoria 0001. Or contact the Cape Regional Office, tel. (021) 222810, fax (021) 246211; PO Box 7400, Roggebaai 8012.

Facilities/amenities: Rhebok Hut, accommodating 18 people, with lamps, stove, cooking utensils and washing facilities, a protective reed 'boma' with braai facilities and firewood, 2 flush toilets, shower and running water; Glen Reenen and Brandwag rest camps at the start with camping, caravanning, huts, a lodge and horses for hire, including a 2-day trail to the Lesotho border; environmental education centre and youth hostel.

Main attractions: Mountain scenery (situated 1 500-2 830 metres above sea level); reintroduced wildlife; birdlife; fresh mountain air; interesting geological formations.

Pertinent information: Hikers must be older than 10 years. The latest time to start walking the trail from Glen Reenen is 8 am and during summer walking should start before 7 am. Sleet, snow and thick mist occur often in winter, thunderstorms in summer; pack accordingly. Puff adders and rinkhals are common so wear ankle-high boots and be alert. For further information, contact the park staff at Golden Gate Highlands National Park, tel. (0143) 256 1471; P O Golden Gate 9708.

The Rhebok Hiking Trail climbs Generaalskop (2 757 m), and provides a panoramic view of Lesotho and the Orange Free State. This rugged, mountainous area is well-endowed with streams, kloofs and waterfalls, traversed by the hiking trail. Walkers must be fit to undertake this hike.

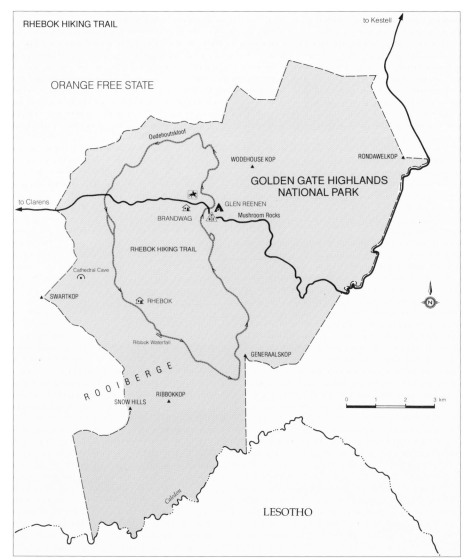

RHEBOK HIKING TRAIL

ORANGE FREE STATE

to Kestell

Oudehoutskloof

WODEHOUSE KOP

RONDAWELKOP

GOLDEN GATE HIGHLANDS
NATIONAL PARK

to Clarens

GLEN REENEN

BRANDWAG

Mushroom Rocks

RHEBOK HIKING TRAIL

Cathedral Cave

SWARTKOP

RHEBOK

Ribbok Waterfall

R O O I B E R G E

GENERAALSKOP

SNOW HILLS

RIBBOKKOP

N

0   1   2   3 km

Caledon

LESOTHO

The grey rhebok has a distinctive white-tipped tail.

Starting at the Glen Reenen Rest Camp, the first leg of the trail winds 16 km (7 hours) to Oudehouts Kloof, and then on to the overnight hut which is scenically situated next to a stream. The climb up Generaalskop on the second day is strenuous; the 1 000-m ascent takes about 3,5 hours, followed by a 2-hour return to the base.

Indigenous wildlife, which includes eland, black wildebeest, blesbok, springbok and zebra, was once prolific in this north-eastern highland region of the Orange Free State and has been reintroduced to the park. Hikers may also spot grey rhebok, mountain reedbuck and oribi. Birdlife is plentiful – the black eagle, jackal buzzard and various waterfowl species can readily be seen, while the rare lammergeyer (bearded vulture) may occasionally be seen.

For those who are not keen on such an energetic trail, there are also shorter walks on marked paths in the Golden Gate Highlands National Park (a map is available from the entrance gate). Guided walks are available on Saturday mornings and, during peak holiday times, every day. During early 1993 more than 5 000 ha adjoining QwaQwa were added to the park, creating a vast new area waiting to be explored.

28. LESOBA HIKING TRAIL
NEAR CLARENS

Trail details: 28 km/2 days. The trail is laid out in a figure-of-eight.

Permits/bookings: For a permit and booking contact Mrs. A. Viviers, tel. (051) 228659; 62 Nerina Street, Gardenia Park, Bloemfontein 9301.

Facilities/amenities: Accommodation comprises a hut with hot water, toilet, washing facilities, braai and firewood.

Main attractions: Rock formations; views over the Maluti mountains.

Pertinent information: Winter weather can be extremely cold, especially at night, so pack accordingly. Groups are limited to a maximum of 22 people.

Set in one of the more attractive areas of the Orange Free State between Clarens and Fouriesburg, this new trail is laid out in a figure-of-eight with overnight facilities in the middle. The name of the walk means 'hole in the mountain' and is reflected by the many interesting rock formations along the trail, including 'Queen Victoria' and 'Church door'. Plant and animal life is abundant and varied. Proteas and bulbous plants are a common sight. As well as spectacular views over the Maluti mountains, other features of interest include Bushman paintings and fossils.

Mushroom-hills of sandstone are to be seen in Golden Gate National Park, along the Rhebok Trail.

29. CLARENS HIKING TRAIL
CLARENS

Trail details: 1. Sunnyside to Ouma's Kraal: 2,5 to 3 hours, one way; 2. De Rots base camp to Ouma's Kraal: 4 km, one way; 3. Angel's Wing: 6-8 hours, circular; 4. Cheche Bush Traverse: 5 hours, circular.

Permits/bookings: A permit and booking are required from Jacana Country Homes and Trails, tel. (012) 3463550, fax (012) 3462499; PO Box 95212, Waterkloof 0145.

Facilities/amenities: De Rots base camp has hut, tank water, bush toilet, gas stove, braai area and firewood. Camping is also permitted. Ouma's Kraal overnight camp has 16 beds, cooking facilities, fireplace, braai area, firewood and hot water.

Main attractions: Panoramic view over the Caledon basin, from one of the highest points in the Orange Free State.

Pertinent information: Summers can be very hot, and thunder- and lightning-storms do occur; winters can be very cold, and may bring snow. Carry water. Groups are limited to a maximum of 16 people.

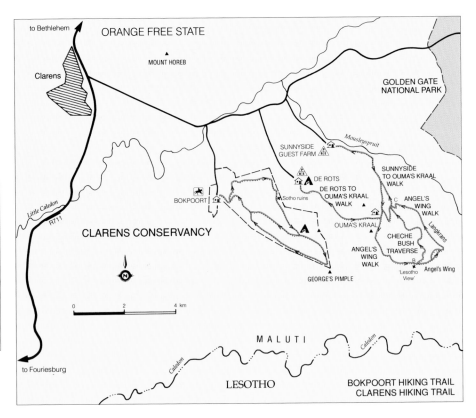

The Clarens Hiking Trail is in fact a number of walks, all of which are located in the Clarens Conservancy. The area, on the northern edge of the Maluti mountains, is particularly scenic, with the four highest peaks in the Free State being on or near the trail. Plantlife found in the region includes wild sage, *Buddleja salviifolia*; wild peach, *Kiggelaria africana*; Cape myrtle, *Myrsine africana* and traveller's joy, *Clematis brachiata*.

There are two different routes up to Ouma's Kraal overnight camp, one starting from Sunnyside Guest Farm and the other leading from De Rots base camp.

1. The Sunnyside to Ouma's Kraal Walk If you want to start your walk from Sunnyside Farm (a private concern not connected with the trail), leave your car in the area provided. Follow the yellow markers until you find a rock on the left-hand side of the road; here two yellow markers show the path changing direction and leading up towards the hill. Keep following the markers all the way to the overnight hut at Ouma's Kraal. To return back to

Sunnyside Farm by a different path, find the white markers at the monolith, just east of the hut.

2. De Rots base camp to Ouma's Kraal Follow the white markers from the camp, where the path leads up behind George's Pimple and along the skyline to join the Angel's Wing route. For inexperienced hikers or parents walking with children, there is a short cut shown with yellow arrows heading up to Ouma's Kraal (these start a short distance from base camp).

From Ouma's Kraal overnight camp there are two day walks, both with variations.

3. Angel's Wing This is a fairly difficult walk; there need to be some experienced hikers in your group. It is definitely not suitable for children. Look for yellow markers on the monolith, leading through indigenous bush. The trail climbs 400 m before continuing above the cliffs to Point B (marked on the map). Follow yellow markers up to 'Lesotho View' then continue until the trail splits. If you head right, the path leads up to the top of Angel's Wing, giving a superb view out over the local area. Taking the other path you traverse back to a point where the two routes meet. The descent from here is fairly steep; take care as you go down the gully, around Langkrans and down a steep ridge back to base camp. It is unwise to attempt this descent in wet weather.

4. Cheche Bush Traverse Less difficult than Angel's Wing, this walk shares the same path as far as Point B. White markers lead along the western side of Langkrans above a large cheche bush. It is worth stopping here for a while to observe the birdlife. Species found in the area include the bald ibis, ground woodpecker and rock thrush. Follow white markers leading down to Point C (see map). There are two options here for returning to Ouma's Kraal, the shorter one shown with white markers, while the longer 1,5 hour option meets up with the return route of the Angel's Wing path.

A winding road amid peaceful pastures near Clarens, on the northern fringe of the Maluti Mountains.

30. BOKPOORT HIKING TRAIL
NEAR CLARENS

Trail details: 15 km/1 or 2 days, circular; a short cut of 11 km/1 day.

Permits/bookings: A permit and booking are required from Jacana Country Homes and Trails, tel. (012) 3463550, fax (012) 3462499; PO Box 95212, Waterkloof 0145.

Facilities/amenities: Restored sandstone barn with three rooms containing 24 beds and mattresses; clear spring water, hot showers and a flush toilet; braai facilities. Overnight shelter with a toilet is available for those wanting to sleep out on the longer walk.

Main attractions: Sandstone hills and rugged mountains, including George's Pimple and a wind-carved tunnel; swimming hole and waterfalls.

Pertinent information: Carry water during dry periods and for the descent. The trail can be booked for a maximum of 24 people at any one time. Braai packs, milk and prepared meals can be ordered when making a booking. Winters are very cold; snow is not uncommon.

This walk is in the 20 000-ha Clarens Conservancy and leads through Bokpoort farm, some 8 km from the town of Clarens. For a time, the trail follows a mountain stream along sandstone cliffs. Tyre ladders have been provided to facilitate the ascent of the steeper sandstone sections. The trail crosses nine streams before reaching an old sandstone kraal, a popular spot for tea. The path continues along the contours and past some ruins of a Sesotho kraal to the halfway point. A large ghwarrie tree close to a waterfall makes this a pleasant place to have lunch. Fill your waterbottle as there is no water available on the descent. There is an overnight shelter here for those who want to make the walk a 2-day trip.

The route splits here with hikers who have selected the short cut returning to base camp via a swimming hole, while those continuing the trail ascend George's Pimple (2 540 m) to enjoy spectacular views of Lesotho and the Malutis. This route is only recommended for the experienced hiker. The descent from the top follows an old horse trail then rejoins the main path past the swimming hole back to base camp.

These trails will be a delight to those who enjoy mountainous terrain and bird-watching; local species include the black eagle, rock kestrel, jackal buzzard and blackshouldered kite.

The edges of Sterkfontein Dam have all the features of an ocean's shore.

The immense blue expanse of Sterkfontein Dam can be seen from many points along Sterretjies Hiking Trail.

31. STERRETJIES HIKING TRAIL
STERKFONTEIN DAM NATURE RESERVE, NEAR HARRISMITH

Trail details: 28 km/2 days; circular. Shorter options available on both days.

Permits/bookings: A permit is required from The Principal Nature Conservator, Sterkfontein Dam Nature Reserve, tel. (01436) 23520 or 30501; PO Box 24, Harrismith 9880.

Facilities/amenities: An empty farmhouse is available at the start of the trail. Overnight facilities will be completed by the end of 1993. Hikers must take their own tents and necessary equipment. Fires are not allowed on any part of the trail or at the overnight stop.

Main attractions: Sterkfontein Dam; eastern Free State scenery; interesting vegetation; deep wooded ravines; magnificent sandstone cliffs and caves.

Pertinent information: The weather can change unexpectedly; always be prepared for the worst. During the summer, biting flies and mosquitoes can be a nuisance so take an insect repellent. A maximum of 20 people is permitted. Hiking boots are recommended. The terrain is quite rough and not suitable for small children.

Roughly 16 km from Harrismith on the Harrismith to QwaQwa road, on the left, is the Qwantani turn-off. Follow this road for 14 km to find the start of the trail, located in the 17 770-ha Sterkfontein Dam Nature Reserve. The route, marked by metal footprints, runs through wooded kloofs to the escarpment of the Drakensberg. The Sterkfontein Dam, visible for most of the trail, is a storage reservoir for the Tugela-Vaal Scheme and has a total surface area of approximately 10 000 ha. Watch out for grey rhebok, mountain reedbuck and oribi, and for Cape and bearded vultures. The trail takes its name from the *Hypoxis* species; its many varieties

of delicate yellow flowers cover the veld druing the summer months. Proteas, tree ferns, ouhout and Natal bottlebrush are among the abundant plantlife of the area.

The second day of the hike reveals some of the most beautiful scenery in the eastern Free State, including imposing sandstone cliffs, a huge cave, indigenous forest and the dam shore.

The trail is probably most enjoyable from October to March, as winters in the area can be extremely cold.

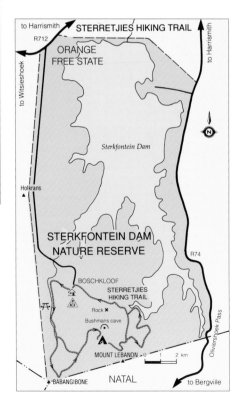

32. PLATBERG HIKING TRAIL
HARRISMITH

Trail details: 27 km/2 days; circular. Shorter walks are possible.

Permits/bookings: A booking is required from Mr. van Zyl, tel. (01436) 30895; PO Box 43, Harrismith 9880.

Facilities/amenities: Base camp accommodation comprises 2 huts sleeping a total of 18 people, and has hot and cold water, gas lighting, firewood and braai facilities. Overnight hut is equipped except for bedding.

Main attractions: wildlife; excellent views of the surrounding area.

Pertinent information: Winters in the area are very cold; snow on the mountain is not uncommon. On weekdays during the winter, the reserve is used for hunting and is not accessible to hikers.

This new trail runs through the Platberg Nature Reserve, a 4 000-ha area of open grasslands and natural forests, just outside Harrismith, surrounding the Platberg Mountain. Day 1 leads up to the top of the mountain, where you will find Gibson Dam, built by English soldiers in 1890 and which is fed by springs. It is an ideal place for a rest while you enjoy the views and fill your waterbottle, before you descend the other side to the overnight hut. There are 17 species of game in the reserve so be alert for a variety of animals including blesbok, eland and wildebeest.

The second day's walk of 15 km is back over the mountain but via a different route.

The most pleasant time of year to tackle this trail is spring, when the days are neither too hot nor too cold and the wild flowers are spectacular.

33. MOUNT EVEREST HOLIDAY GAME RESERVE
HARRISMITH

Trail details: 1. Ouhout Trail: 2 hours, return; 2. Kudu Trail: 2 hours, circular; 3. Hartebees Trail: 3 hours, circular; 4. Rhebok Trail: 6 hours, circular.

Permits/bookings: Not required. Route maps are available from reception.

Facilities/amenities: Fully equipped chalets; 2 caravan parks; conference centre; swimming pool; curio shop; fast-food outlet; picnic sites; horse riding and fishing.

Main attractions: Game-viewing; beautiful mountain scenery; prolific birdlife; a 'vulture restaurant'.

Pertinent information: Winters can be very cold, so pack accordingly. When walking in the reserve, always be alert to the presence of rhino and ostrich; these animals should be regarded as dangerous.

North-east of Harrismith, this game reserve incorporates the mountains Everest, Mooihoek and Glen Paul. As well as a range of sporting facilities, there are four walking trails located within its boundaries. None is difficult and they are well suited to families. Car parks are provided at the start of each trail. The paths are all clearly marked with reflectors.

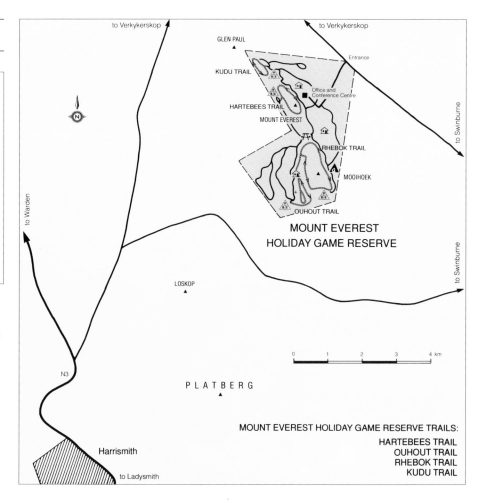

A variety of indigenous and exotic animals make their home in the reserve. You can expect to see mountain reedbuck, black wildebeest, eland, mountain zebra, white rhinoceros, fallow deer and camel. Over 130 species of birds have been recorded here.

The relatively rare black eagle breeds in the mountains; if you are fortunate, you may see one of these magnificent raptors catching a dassie. The 'vulture restaurant' aims to help conserve the Cape vulture by providing these birds with regular food.

From close up, Platberg is anything but flat, and flower and tree alternate with steep open slopes.

Winter snowfalls are frequent on the Sentinel Trail, and the bright dusting lends a new enchantment to the surroundings.

34. SENTINEL HIKING TRAIL
QWAQWA

Trail details: 8 km/4 hours; circular/return. See map p. 164.

Permits/bookings: These are required from QwaQwa Tourism and Nature Conservation Corporation, tel. (01438) 34444 or 30576 changing to (058) 7134444 or 7135076, fax (01438) 34342 changing to (058) 7134342; Private Bag X826, Witsieshoek 9870.

Facilities/amenities: Overnight hut at the start of the trail accommodates 24 people, has wood stove, bush toilet, cold water and braai facilities.

Main attractions: Mont-aux-Sources plateau; spectacular views; interesting birdlife.

Pertinent information: Hikers can camp overnight on the Mont-aux-Sources plateau, but must take their own tents and equipment as there are no facilities. The weather can change rapidly and unexpectedly. Hiking boots are recommended. The wind can blow very strongly in this area. Snow is common in winter. A maximum of 50 day visitors and 50 overnight visitors are permitted.

Located in the QwaQwa Conservation Area, this trail starts at the Sentinel carpark and climbs to the Drakensberg plateau at an average altitude of 3 000 m, with the help of a chain ladder. The thin air and steep climb may tire unfit hikers. For those not wanting to use the chain ladder, there is an alternative route via The Gully to the top of Beacon Buttress and the start of the Tugela River, which forms a waterfall. The path continues to the base of Mont-aux-Sources, the highest peak in the area at 3 282 m, which falls within the boundaries of neighbouring Lesotho.

As well as breathtaking vistas of the mountains, you can expect to see a wide variety of birdlife including the jackal buzzard, black harrier, bearded and Cape vultures and the bald ibis. Although wildlife is scarce in these harsh conditions, mountain reedbuck, baboons, grey rhebok and rock dassie are fairly common sights.

Walkers can camp overnight on the plateau but must carry in their own tents and all other necessary equipment. The guard hut (not available to hikers) has a guard and radio contact with Phuthaditjhaba, from where a rescue operation can be mounted in an emergency.

A chain ladder provides a relatively easy way up.

*A stream has been frozen into silver immobility
by an overnight gale.*

35. METSI MATSHO HIKING TRAIL
QWAQWA

Trail details: 30 km/2 days; circular/return.

Permits/bookings: A permit and booking are
required from the QwaQwa Tourism and Nature
Conservation Corporation, tel. (01438) 34444 or
30576 changing to (058) 7134444 or 7130576, fax
(01438) 34342 changing to (058) 7134342; Private
Bag X826, Witsieshoek 9870.

Facilities/amenities: Base camp comprises hut
sleeping 24 people, and has hot and cold water,
toilet facilities and gas lighting but no stove. Two
thatched stone huts at the overnight point, with
toilets, beds to sleep 24, and spring water. Take
your own gas cooker. Collect key for the huts from
the Witsieshoek Mountain Resort, which is 60 m
from base camp. Accommmodation is also
available at the resort, tel. (014382) and ask for
Ha mota 5, or call toll free (0800) 123000;
PO Box 17311, Witsieshoek 9870.

Main attractions: Drakensberg scenery; beautiful
sandstone formations; caves; protea forests; Metsi
Matsho Dam.

Pertinent information: The weather is
unpredictable and can change very suddenly, so be
prepared for the worst. Hikers should always check
the weather forecast before setting out. Mist,
thunder and lightning are common in summer;
snowfalls in winter are not unusual. Groups are
limited to a maximum of 10 people; 2 groups can
walk the trail at the same time.

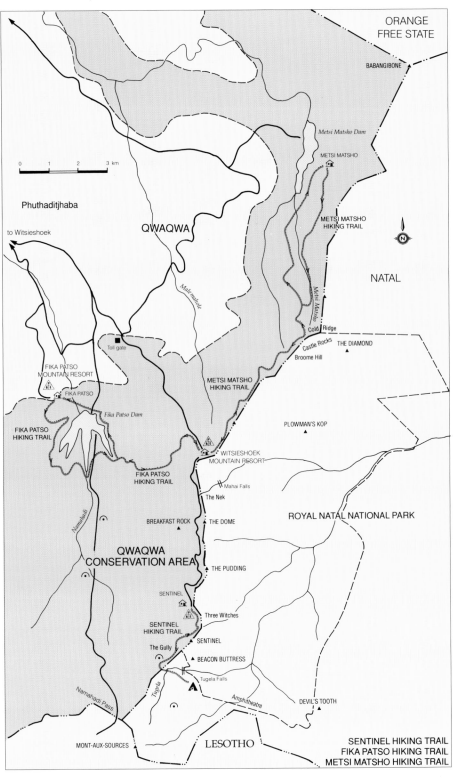

This walk is situated in the QwaQwa Conservation
Area, which although still used for commercial purposes such as farming, is managed on conservation
principles and covers an area of roughly 30 000 ha.
Starting at the Witsieshoek Mountain Resort, the
first day of this hike follows the Natal/QwaQwa
border, then turns downhill onto the floodplain of
the Metsi Matsho River, which flows into the dam
of the same name. Here anglers can enjoy trout-
fishing in beautiful surroundings; permits can be
obtained at the Tourist Information Centre in
Phuthaditjhaba. The path passes through many
interesting landforms, including sandstone formations, kloofs and hills.

The return journey follows a different route for
the first 3 km, and then rejoins the outward leg, so
that much of the walk back to the starting point is
an uphill climb.

This is the high road to the mountains, from Witsieshoek to Mont-aux-Sources.

36. FIKA PATSO HIKING TRAIL
QWAQWA

Trail details: 30 km/2 days; circular; A shorter day walk of 15 km/8 hours.

Permits/bookings: A permit and booking are required from the QwaQwa Tourism and Nature Conservation Corporation, tel. (01438) 3444 or 30576 changing to (058) 7134444 or 7130576, fax (01438) 34342 changing to (058) 7134342; Private Bag X826, Witsieshoek 9870.

Facilities/amenities: Hut at base camp sleeps 24 people and has toilet, water and lighting but no stove. Overnight accommodation is at the Witsieshoek hut (see Metsi Matsho Hiking Trail for facilities available).

Main attractions: Protea forest; rock pools; waterfall; Fika Patso Dam.

Pertinent information: Sturdy hiking boots are essential. Always be prepared for adverse weather conditions. Snow falls often in winter.

An extension of a shorter trail, this new route starts and ends at the Fika Patso Mountain Resort. The path generally leads around the Fika Patso Dam, but branches off at various points to incorporate scenic or interesting spots. The first day's walk is through beautiful scenery past Bushman paintings, and rock pools where a refreshing swim can be enjoyed. A highlight of the trail is a walk through a protea forest, particularly beautiful when in bloom.

Day 2 leads back to base camp via a magnificent waterfall, not marked on any maps, and so an especially welcome discovery.

Be prepared for some steep climbs, but otherwise this hike is suitable for anyone who is reasonably fit. For safety, wear sturdy hiking boots, and always be aware of changes in the weather. It is open throughout the year, although snowfalls occur regularly in winter. The area is especially attractive in spring when the mountains are carpeted in a mass of wild flowers. Due to the harsh climate, much of this region is covered in short grassland, but some small patches of forest do occur in sheltered ravines. Tree ferns grow along some streams and proteas dominate the open areas.

Wildlife includes the rhebok, mountain reedbuck, baboon and rock hyrax.

Forests of protea flourish in the decomposed sandstone along the Metsi Matsho Trail in QwaQwa.

NATAL AND KWAZULU

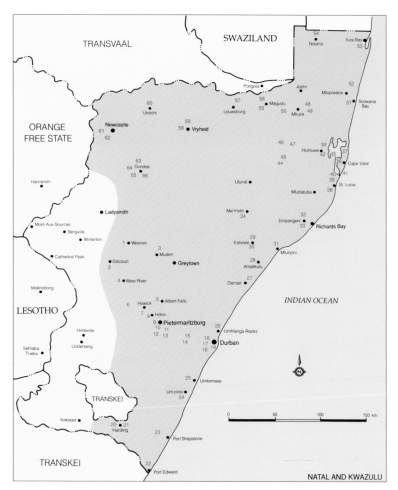

NATAL AND KWAZULU

Natal, or the Garden Province, which also incorporates the territory under the government of the Kwazulu homeland, stretches from the northern border of Transkei to the southern border of Swaziland and Mozambique, bounded on the west by Lesotho, the Orange Free State and the Transvaal and on the east by the Indian Ocean.

Although Natal is South Africa's smallest province, its diversity of trailing opportunities is immense, and the quality of environmental education-type trails and interpretive centres is commendable. This province attracts mountaineers to the high Drakensberg; naturalists who concentrate on wilderness trails in game reserves and self-guided trails and historic routes in the Natal midlands; and seaside ramblers who love roaming the coast and its estuaries with their forested sand dunes and prolific waterbird populations. (No visas are required for entry into KwaZulu).

Climate varies dramatically with altitude and terrain throughout Natal. In general, Natal and KwaZulu are subtropical. The coast in summer is hot and humid, but tempered by cooling sea breezes. The inland summer heat is tempered by altitude. During the winter months, the coast is mild to warm which contrasts with the very cold and often snow-capped 3 000 metre-high Drakensberg.

LEFT: *Hikers enjoy spectacular vistas over the Oribi Gorge, with the Umzimkulwana River some 300 metres below them.*

Weenen Nature Reserve, where big game flourishes today, was a barren and dreary area 30 years ago.

1. WEENEN GAME RESERVE
WEENEN

Trail details: Beacon View Trail: 3,5 hours; self-guided, circular. A short 20-minute trail is also available.

Permits/bookings: To book camp and caravan sites, contact The Officer in Charge, Weenen Nature Reserve, tel. (0363) 41809; PO Box 122, Weenen 3325. Permits obtainable at the gate. A brochure with map is available at the reserve.

Facilities/amenities: 12 caravan and camp sites that can accommodate up to 16 caravans; ablution block with hot and cold water; curio shop; 3 picnic sites with braais; tourist roads in reserve.

Main attractions: Large game; anti-erosion work and damaged veld reclamation.

Pertinent information: Summer rainfall area. Visitors must provide their own grills, charcoal and firewood. An indemnity form must be completed before you can walk the trails. Groups are limited to a maximum of 20 people.

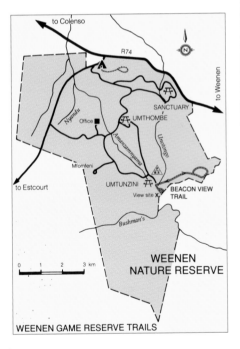

WEENEN GAME RESERVE TRAILS

Located in the Natal Midlands, off the R74 from Colenso to Weenen, the undulating, 4 909-ha Weenen Game Reserve is covered in thornveld, excellent habitat for the larger introduced game species such as white and black rhino, red hartebeest, giraffe, kudu, eland, common and mountain reedbuck, zebra, bushbuck, grey duiker, steenbok, roan antelope and Cape buffalo. Over 130 species of birds have been recorded in the reserve.

The Bushman's River flows through a valley in the south of the reserve. The dense thickets in this area are favoured by kudu and black rhino.

Two of the picnic sites – Umthombe and Umtunzini – are at view sites in the reserve, and the Sanctuary picnic site offers a rustic toilet

and tank water, which does need to be boiled before consumption.

The trails, clearly marked by cement cairns with footprints on them, are educational walks which concentrate on anti-erosion work and damaged veld reclamation. Considering that 30 years ago the whole reserve was barren, and that it now supports a healthy big-game population, you can appreciate the hard labour and time devoted to this remarkable veld recovery programme.

The Umtunzini picnic site is the starting point of the Beacon View Trail, and the route leads to the beacon, from where there is a spectacular view of the reserve and farmland in the Weenen Valley.

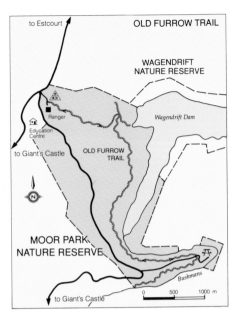

2. OLD FURROW TRAIL
MOOR PARK NATURE RESERVE, ESTCOURT

Trail details: 6 km/2 to 3 hours; self-guided, return route.

Permits/bookings: To make a booking for the education centre and to arrange educational talks, contact the Natal Parks Board, tel. (0331) 471981; PO Box 662, Pietermaritzburg 3200. For the caravan and camp site, you can contact The Officer in Charge, Wagendrift Public Resort, tel. (0363) 22550; PO Box 316, Estcourt 3310 to make a booking.

Maps/information: Booklet describing the trail available at the reserve.

Facilities/amenities: Picnic site with braai facilities and parking area at Moor Park; education centre with 80 beds, caravan and camp site at adjacent Wagendrift Public Resort Nature Reserve.

Main attractions: Acacia thornveld; angling, especially for scaly fish; reintroduced large antelope and other game animals; Wagendrift Dam; talks by Natal Parks Board officials.

Pertinent information: Summer rainfall area. No bookings are required to walk the trail, and groups of up to 80 people can be accommodated.

Moor Park Nature Reserve is situated at the head of the Wagendrift Dam and slopes down to the Bushman's River. To get to the reserve, take the Ntabamhlope Road towards Wagendrift Dam from Estcourt for 12 km, following signposts.

The Old Furrow Trail is a short 6-km, easy walk that is particularly suited to school groups. The ramble starts at the entrance gate to Moor Park and runs parallel to an old furrow irrigation system laid over a century ago by the Moor family, who also donated these lands to the Natal Parks Board for preservation as a nature reserve. It ends at the Bushman's River.

Interpretive displays are strategically placed along the route, while the trail booklet describes aspects of the park's environment and history, emphasizing the range of vegetation, tree types and the ecology of the Bushman's River. A variety of game species has been introduced.

3. MHLOPENI NATURE RESERVE
MUDEN

Trail details: A number of circular trails varying in duration from 3 hours to 2 days.

Permits/bookings: Bookings should be made with Mr R Alcock, Mhlopeni Nature Reserve, tel. (03346) 722; PO Box 386, Greytown 3500. Two brochures available on request. Advance notice for day walks is preferred.

Facilities/amenities: 4 rustic bush camps, with hot water, showers, toilets, fully equipped kitchens and 'bomas' with braai areas; open camp site also available; picnic sites for day visitors; education centre for up to 40 people; trail guides by prior arrangement; special interest groups catered for; hunting and fishing in season.

Main attractions: Historical sites; variety of game and birdlife; museum.

Pertinent information: Rain falls in the summer. All months, except February, are good for walking. Ticks are a problem, and lightning storms in summer can be a danger. Groups are limited to a minimum of 4 and a maximum of 40.

This 1 325-ha, privately owned reserve is situated off the R74 from Weenen to Greytown. In the early seventies Mhlopeni was a desolate valley eroded to red sands. A project to save the region and return it to the 'peaceful valley of white rocks' of its Zulu name was undertaken by SACCAP (the South African Council for Conservation and Anti-Pollution) with the encouragement of the Natal Parks Board. Schemes such as grass habitat management, a reservoir complex, wildlife reintroductions, and the installation of an anti-poacher unit have transformed the valley into a valuable natural area and educational facility.

There are marked trails all over the reserve, and visitors can wander at will enjoying game-viewing, bird-watching and the fauna and flora of the rugged terrain. The trails include a variety of shorter walks, and a 2-day hike where a stay overnight in a hut on a neighbouring farm can be arranged.

The reserve is home to zebra, blesbok, impala, bushbuck, mountain reedbuck and oribi. More than 230 bird species have been recorded in the reserve, including the bald ibis, black, martial and crowned eagles, peregrine falcon and ground hornbill.

People from all walks of life and of all ages visit Mhlopeni; school and university groups are offered lectures on conservation, backed by physical participation. In projects such as donga reclamation, erecting fences and eradication of noxious weeds, a trophy is awarded annually to the school that does the most work in the restoration of the environment.

On the mountain trails, activities include game-viewing and swimming in the natural potholes eroded from the solid white rocks.

Flora includes a wealth of aloes, euphorbias, white stinkwood and many varieties of thornbush. If you are vigilant, you may find some Iron and Stone Age artefacts, and watch out for rock art and settlers' graves.

The warden conducts guided tours to various areas of interest, including climbs to the nest of a black eagle (where the hide is a mere 3 m from the nest itself), Iron and Stone Age sites, and the wagon trails.

The lush landscape of Mhlopeni, made up of a rich variety of aloes, euphorbias and thornbushes.

4. MOOIFALLS HIKING TRAIL
MOOIRIVIER

Trail details: 1,5 days; open-ended.

Permits/bookings: Contact Jacana Country Homes and Trails, tel. (012) 3463550/1/2, fax (012) 3462499; PO Box 95212, Waterkloof 0145 for reservations and more information about the trail. A map is also available.

Facilities/amenities: Base camp on Waterhoek farm in thatched cottage with 24 beds and mattresses, braai and cooking facilities, firewood, bathroom with outside shower and flush toilets; overnight camp on Rensburg farm in big farmhouse with 24 beds and mattresses, cooking utensils, electricity and firewood, bathroom and flush toilet.

Main attractions: Mooirivier; waterfalls; prolific game and birdlife.

Pertinent information: Maximum of 24 people in a group. Hikers should make arrangements to have a vehicle waiting at the end of the trail. This is a summer rainfall area with warm to hot summer days. Winter days are mild, and nights can get cold.

About 20 km from Mooirivier is the Mooifalls Hiking Trail which gives you the opportunity to experience the beauty of the Mooirivier and its waterfalls. At the start of the trail, on Waterhoek farm, the nest of a Wahlberg's eagle is found at the top of a small gumtree. Hikers who arrive early on the day before the hike can not only take the time to observe these eagles but also spend time swimming in the river or trying their hand at river rafting.

The trail itself starts on the old oxwagon route between Durban and the Reef and makes its way through natural bush to a spot where you have a breathtaking view of the Mooirivier Valley. After about 2,5 hours of hiking the trail reaches a weir and you can follow the short canal to the bottom of the Harleston Falls and refresh yourself with a

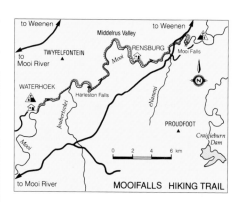

MOOIFALLS HIKING TRAIL

swim beneath the falls, and observe the breeding bald ibis colony that nests here. The falls are spectacular when the river is full – after summer rains. Of further interest here is the mini hydro scheme which the farmer has developed to produce his own electricity.

From the falls, the trail cuts across the river and climbs the ridge, following the contours and keeping the river in sight. Look out for bushbuck, the black eagle, kestrels, rabbits and reedbuck. The trail crosses the river again and descends into the Middelrus Valley, leaving the Midlands highveld behind and entering acacia country with its diversity of landscape and terrain. The overnight camp is on the Rensburg farm and has a lovely view of the valley. The second day's route is only half as long as the first and should take you about 3 hours to walk. It leads you to the majestic Mooi Falls at 84 m. Here you will find the biggest colony of bald ibis, and an adjacent game park gives you the opportunity to spot Cape eland, blesbok, impala, zebra and springbok. Although nocturnal animals such as the serval, caracal, porcupine, antbear and jackal live in the area, these are all shy animals and you are unlikely to spot them. Hikers can enjoy a braai or picnic lunch next to the waterfall before heading for home.

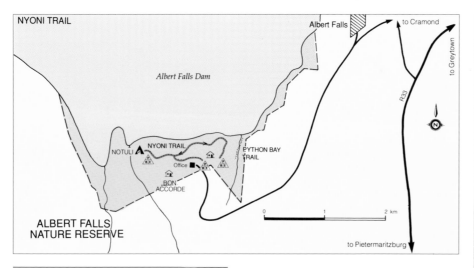

5. NYONI TRAIL
ALBERT FALLS NATURE RESERVE, NEAR CRAMOND

Trail details: 2 km/1 hour; self-guided, open-ended. Shorter walk also possible.

Permits/bookings: Reservations for camp sites may be made through The Camp Superintendent, Albert Falls Nature Reserve, tel. (03393) 202/3; PO Box 31, Cramond 3420. To book hutted accommodation, contact The Natal Parks Board, tel. (0331) 471981, fax (0331) 471980; PO Box 1750, Pietermaritzburg 3200. No permit or booking is required for the walks.

Maps/information: A map is available on request at the reserve.

Facilities/amenities: Two fully equipped hutted camps: Notuli Camp with fifteen 2-bed rondavels and three 6-bed chalets; Bon Accorde Camp with ten 5-bed chalets; Bon Accorde camp site can cater for up to 100 people, while Notuli has 40 stands; many secluded picnic spots; parking and braai facilities are available for day visitors.

Main attractions: Quiet and solitude; game; birdlife.

Pertinent information: Ticks can be a problem and bilharzia is present at places. Climate is generally mild with winters being cold; April to May are the best months. Ideally you should walk in groups of 8-10. Bring your own food and drink.

Albert Falls Nature Reserve is 24 km from Pietermaritzburg along the Greytown road. The game park is about 200 ha of the total 3 090 ha and is home to hartebeest, zebra, blesbok, impala, bushbuck, springbok, oribi, reedbuck and duiker. Vegetation types in the area include the Karoo system, southern tall grass and acacia thorn. Bird-watchers have the opportunity of spotting 266 species on the bird list.

The Nyoni Trail is a gentle 2-km walk along a single gravel contour path, through thorn scrub and grassland, overlooking the lake. Marked by arrows or footprints, the trail starts at Notuli Chalet (an A-frame hut that is to be converted into an information centre) where there is an area for parking, and ends at Notuli camp site. (The trail can also be walked in reverse.) Various options are available along the trail: hikers can start or end the trail from two places at the Bon Accorde Camp. From the end point, hikers can walk back to the parking area along the gravel road.

The Python Bay Trail is a short 300-m walk along a stream where there is a high concentration of tree and bird species. The trail gets its name from the pythons who have taken up residence at one point along the trail, but they are not dangerous as snakes prefer to avoid an encounter with humans. The trail is open-ended and its starting point can be reached via a tar road from Notuli Chalet.

6. DARGLE RIVER TRAIL
DARGLE STATE FOREST, NEAR HOWICK

Trail details: 6 km; circular.

Permits/bookings: Arrangements to walk the trail may be made by telephone with The Forester, tel. (03324) 4322. Permits are obtained from the forest guard on duty at the entrance gate. Information leaflet and map available.

Facilities/amenities: Parking at entrance gate; picnic site with braais, toilets and swimming hole.

Main attractions: Beautiful scenery; birdlife and game; swimming and fishing.

Pertinent information: The forest is in a summer rainfall area. The trail may be closed in winter, when the fire hazard is particularly high. At the time of going to press, all state forests were in the process of being privatized and therefore the future of the trail and who the controlling authority would be was unknown.

The forest is situated off the road from Lions River to Fort Nottingham. Some 2 293 ha of the total area of 2 858 ha have been almost exclusively planted to pine, which is felled and sold. Small indigenous forests are also found on the steep southern slopes of the area. Two prominent trees are the white stinkwood, which is recognizable in early spring by its light green leaves, and the Cape chestnut, which is noted for the mauve flowers that cover the tree before the new leaves emerge.

The trail starts below the parking area and is marked by fish-shaped indicators which lead you along the winding Umgeni River, sometimes on a road. There are numerous pools along the route, as well as a couple of islands in the river. At Krantz Viewpoint, the trail leads you 50 m away from the river onto high ground, where you have a scenic view of the area. A detour from the trail further on will guide you to the Step Falls. At the end of the trail, you have the option of following the river to

The Dargle Trail leads past the trout-stocked Umgeni River .

Stone Pool, or taking the left fork, continuing along the road and walking back along the alternative route, also marked by 'fishprints'. If you take the first option, you will see the devastation caused at Poplar Bend by the floods of September 1987, where trees were uprooted and stacked against standing trees like a picket fence. The alternative route along the roads will take you past newly

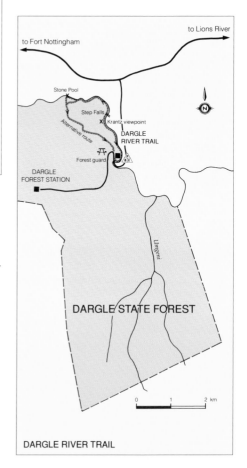

planted areas where roosts have been set up to encourage predators such as hawks and owls in order
to protect the young trees from rodent damage.

The varied habitat provided by the river verge,
veld and pine stands supports a variety of birdlife,
including the jackal buzzard, bulbul, masked
weaver, narina trogon and crested eagle. Game that
may be observed includes reedbuck, bushbuck,
duiker and porcupine. Amongst the different indigenous and exotic herbs and grasses are pests
such as bugweed and the thorny American bramble,
the latter providing the weary hiker with blackberries in the summer months. You can spot many
small, brightly coloured Christmas bell flowers in
the open areas; more noticeable perhaps are the
dwarf coral tree with its brilliant scarlet flowers
and the prehistoric looking cabbage tree with its
large, leathery leaves and rough, corky bark.

7. UMGENI VALLEY NATURE RESERVE
HOWICK

Trail details: 1. Black Eagle Trail: 7 km, circular;
2. Inkonka Trail: 5 km, circular; 3. Dwarfs Dawdle:
5 km, circular; 4. Grasslands Trail: 8 km, circular;
5. Shelter Falls Trail: 3 km, circular. Shorter
1,5-km walk also available.

Permits/bookings: Bookings for accommodation
from Wildlife Society of South Africa,
tel. (0332) 303931; PO Box 394, Howick 3290.

Facilities/amenities: Environmental education
centre open to self-guided groups as well as
individuals; rustic camps consisting of two or more
bungalows, with kitchen, showers, flush toilet and
firewood; guest cottage equipped with beds, linen,
towels, crockery, cutlery, gas, fireplace and
firewood is provided.

Main attractions: Scenic walks through varied
terrain; large and small mammals; over 200 species
of birds.

Pertinent information: Access to hutted camps is
on foot, about 25 minutes' walk from the carpark.
Ticks are prevalent at certain times of the year.

Umgeni Valley Nature Reserve, with its diversity of habitats, also boasts a network of short undemanding trails.

The Umgeni Valley Nature Reserve is important as
it is one of South Africa's few 'outdoor' education
centres where intensive environmental courses are
run by experienced field officers, most of whom
are qualified teachers. Courses offered include
workshops for teachers, courses for adults, school
children and the disabled. Contact the reserve for
details. The setting is ideal – located only 30 km
from Pietermaritzburg and close to Howick, the
reserve borders 10 km of the Umgeni River immediately below the scenic Howick Falls, which
plunge 111 m over dolerite cliffs into the gorge.

Habitats are diverse, ranging from regions of
bushveld harbouring big game such as zebra, wildebeest, giraffe, nyala, impala, eland, bushbuck and
grey duiker, to cliffs topped by grassland plateaux
hosting blesbok, mountain reedbuck and oribi. Birdlife ranges from tiny warblers to magnificent black,
crowned and martial eagles.

A network of trails is available to visitors. None
of the walks is physically demanding.

1. Black Eagle Trail begins at either the Inkonka
or Indulo carpark, passing through a variety of
vegetation from lowland bushveld to grasslands on
the hill tops. Superb views over the valley reveal
the diversity of the geology, as well as the plant
and animal life, of the area.

2. Inkonka Trail is a steep descent and ascent of
the valley through indigenous forest. Expansive
views of the river make this walk worth the effort.
A swimming spot at Fish Jump Waterfall offers the
chance for a refreshing dip; there is a also a picnic
site with a fine view out over the reserve.

3. Dwarfs Dawdle circular walk follows along the
dolerite cliff line which overlooks the eastern part
of the reserve. Again, there are excellent views of
the Umgeni River Valley. The upper path is mainly
along level ground making this an ideal trail for
families, although the lower section of the walk is
slightly more difficult.

4. Grasslands Trail passes through various types
of vegetation, crosses Mhlangweni Stream and
leads past an old Nguni kraal and Cycad Camp.
Diverse vegetation is the predominant feature of
this trail. Watch out for the wild pear, *Dombeya
rotundifolia*, rock-splitting fig, *Ficus ingens* and
cabbage tree, *Cussonia spicata*. The areas of open
bushveld are particularly good for spotting game
such as giraffe, wildebeest and warthog.

5. Shelter Falls Trail splits into two different
routes. Both are short and easy, heading along the
Shelter Falls stream. Some excellent swimming and
picnic spots make this trail a vey pleasant one on a
hot day.

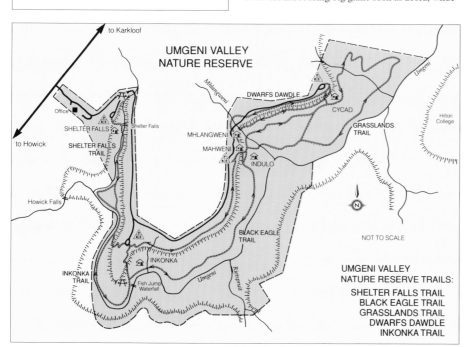

UMGENI VALLEY
NATURE RESERVE

to Karkloof

to Howick

Office

SHELTER FALLS

SHELTER FALLS TRAIL

Howick Falls

INKONKA TRAIL

Shelter Falls

Mhlangweni

DWARFS DAWDLE

MHLANGWENI

MAHWENI

INDULO

INKONKA

Fish Jump Waterfall

BLACK EAGLE TRAIL

Umgeni

Reitspruit

CYCAD

GRASSLANDS TRAIL

Umgeni

Hilton College

NOT TO SCALE

N

UMGENI VALLEY
NATURE RESERVE TRAILS:

SHELTER FALLS TRAIL
BLACK EAGLE TRAIL
GRASSLANDS TRAIL
DWARFS DAWDLE
INKONKA TRAIL

8. CEDARA FOREST TRAIL
CEDARA STATE FOREST, NEAR HILTON

Trail details: 11,5 km; circular with variations.

Permits/bookings: Required from SASCOL, tel. (0331) 431135/39/58; Private Bag X6006, Hilton 3245.

Facilities/amenities: Educational trail with observation points; picnic and braai area; fishing permitted in dams.

Main attractions: Tranquillity of pine plantations; old Voortrekker route; 80-year-old, and older, deodar trees.

Pertinent information: Roads must be crossed with care as they are used by heavy-duty forestry lorries. The forest is closed from the end of May until November. At the time of going to press, the future of this trail was uncertain. It is advisable to telephone in advance, to check that the public still have access to the forest.

Covering an area of 670 ha, the Cedara State Forest contains trees from a variety of countries, including Australia, the Himalayas, Japan, Mexico, the Mediterranean area, Britain, Europe, North Africa, China and the USA. These interesting experimental specimens were planted in 1903, when the plantation was started.

A circular self-guided trail wends its way through the forest and is marked by yellow pointers. Observation points along the way are indicated by black numbers on the pointers, and blue numbers are used for trees. An extension of the trail is an open-ended walk that leads you to a viewpoint at the top of a high ridge. In addition, two linking routes give hikers the option of shorter trails – about 5 km and 9 km.

9. IDUBE TRAIL
QUEEN ELIZABETH PARK, PIETERMARITZBURG

Trail details: 2,5 km/2 hours; circular.

Permits/bookings: Not required; however, groups wishing to visit the resource centre should contact the Natal Parks Board, tel. (0331) 471961; PO Box 662, Pietermaritzburg 3200.

Facilities/amenities: Resource centre for educational groups; picnic sites and braais; headquarters of the Natal Parks Board; curio shop.

Main attractions: Rhino hide with view over white rhino enclosure; bird hide; excellent view over surrounding Pietermaritzburg.

Headquarters of the Natal Parks Board are set in Queen Elizabeth Park.

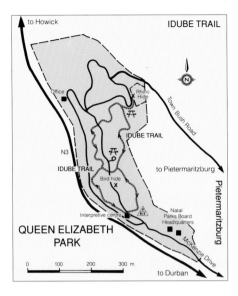

QUEEN ELIZABETH PARK

The Idube Trail is an easy, short educational walk through the 93-ha grounds of the Natal Parks Board's headquarters, located some 7 km from the centre of Pietermaritzburg.

The path winds through riverine forest and grassland to the rhino hide, passing paddocks of game animals such as zebra, impala, blesbok and reedbuck.

Trees are tagged for identification purposes, and a trail booklet and teacher's guide are currently being compiled.

10. NATAL NATIONAL BOTANIC GARDEN
PIETERMARITZBURG

Trail details: A network of paths through the gardens, each lasting not more than one hour.

Permits/bookings: Not required. Small entrance fee charged on weekends and public holidays.

Facilities/amenities: Tearoom; toilets.

Main attractions: The old garden with its exotic tree collection; the indigenous garden which features plants of Natal; flowers bloom year-round; birds (102 species have been recorded).

Pertinent information: Open from 8.00 am until 6.00 pm daily, except Tuesdays.

Situated in a deep bend of the Dorpspruit, on the Swartkops Valley side of Pietermaritzburg, the Natal National Botanic Garden provides a first-class educational introduction to the flora of Natal. Walks of approximately one hour in duration follow constructed paths through an area of mistbelt forest, and provide panoramic views of the Swartkops Valley.

Of special interest is the plane tree avenue, planted in 1908, which is magnificent throughout the year.

The Garden is pleasant to visit year-round; however, summers can be hot and humid with thunderstorms, mist and drizzle. Winters tend to be dry and mild, with occasional frosts.

For further, more detailed information concerning walks in this area, refer to *Day Walks in and around Durban and Pietermaritzburg*, by Geoff Nichols and Monica Fairall.

11. FERNCLIFFE NATURE RESERVE
PIETERMARITZBURG

Trail details: A number of short, interconnecting walks which total 4,5 km/3 hours.

Permits/bookings: Not required.

Facilities/amenities: Parking area with picnic and braai sites, and public toilets nearby.

Main attractions: Urban green pocket; birdlife; waterfalls; views of Pietermaritzburg; bat cave.

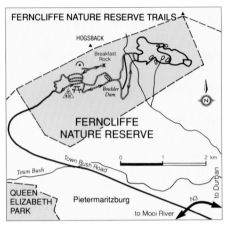

FERNCLIFFE NATURE RESERVE

There are a number of short trails in the 250-ha Ferncliffe Nature Reserve, some of which lead from the picnic site towards Boulder Dam and form a series known as the Ferncliffe Water trails. All the trails are well signposted and lead through plantations of pine, gum and wattle trees. Roughly 100 m beyond Boulder Dam the path forks and you can go either left or right along a circular route known as Town View Walk. Highlights of this trail are Maidenhair Falls, Hadeda Cascade and Fern

Indigenous riverside forest on one of the Ferncliffe Water Trails.

Glen, as well as a series of 6 dams built to store water for fire-fighting purposes.

The reserve hosts a wealth of plant, bird and animal life. Be alert for bushbuck, especially along the streams where indigenous vegetation is still intact. Forest birds that may be seen here include the forest canary, olive woodpecker, starred robin and Barratt's warbler. Despite the strong presence of introduced species, many indigenous plants still thrive here and you may see the forest cabbage tree, and many Streptocarpus plants which flower during the late summer.

12. GREEN BELT TRAILS
PIETERMARITZBURG

Trail details: 1. World's View Trail: 2,4 km/1 hour, return; 2. Teteluku Trail: 7,2 km/2,5 hours, return; 3. Upper Linwood Trail: 2,4 km/1,5 hours, return; 4. Lower Linwood Trail: 4,3 km/1,5 hours, return; 5. Dorpspruit Trail: 2 km/1 hour, return. Shorter walks also possible.

Permits/bookings: Not required. Further information available from The Director, Parks and Recreation, Pietermaritzburg, tel. (0331) 951111; PO Box 31, Pietermaritzburg 3200.

Maps/information: A brochure, map and further information are available from the Pietermaritzburg Publicity Association, tel. (0331) 451348/9; PO Box 25, Pietermaritzburg.

Facilities/amenities: Picnic site and parking at World's View.

Main attractions: Plantations, streams and birdlife; city views; historical significance; abandoned railroad and tunnel.

Pertinent information: Be prepared for sudden thunderstorms in summer. Carry water.

More than 20 km of Green Belt trails, providing scenic natural history and historical interest, have been constructed on Pietermaritzburg's north-eastern escarpment which rises some 350 m above the city. The views from this elevation are excellent.

1. World's View Trail starts from Voortrekker Road and follows the old Voortrekker route to World's View, passing through plantations of pine, black wattle and gum trees. The trees are home to a variety of birds, including the Cape and chorister robins, forest canary and olive thrush.

A bridge halfway along the route marks the intersection of 3 trails: to the right is the Wylie Trail, on the left is the Lower Linwood Trail, while continuing straight ahead will bring you to World's View. This lookout point, 1 000 m above sea-level, deserves its name, as it offers superb views.

2. Teteluku Trail is the longest of the Green Belt trails and starts from the parking area at World's View. Following the World's View road for some time before heading off south-westwards across the top of the plateau, the course ends in a broad circuit which runs north-west and north-east until it reaches Celtis Road, where you turn back. Much of the vegetation comprises plantations, and all the plants except the fig trees and grasses have been introduced.

This is the most difficult of the Green Belt trails to follow as the scenery changes dramatically when the plantations are felled. Therefore it is advisable to contact the Parks and Recreation Department in advance to arrange a guide, or to go in a group led by someone who knows the area well.

3. Upper Linwood Trail is best started at Celtis Road. Look for a trail map mounted on a plinth, which marks the beginning of both the Upper and Lower Linwood trails. Turn right and continue another 300 m to park your car near some forestry houses. Follow the Upper Trail for roughly 1 km until you reach the junction with the Teteluku Trail. From here, the old railway line, built in 1916, forms the route of the trail. The line was closed in 1960 and since then the cuttings have been colonized by many species of ferns. The path disappears into a tunnel which is 100 m long and curved so that you cannot see right through it. It is advisable to take a torch if you want to walk through the tunnel. Otherwise you can scramble up the bank and over the top of it.

4. Lower Linwood Trail can be started either at Celtis Road or Linwood Drive. The trail leads through gum plantations and is an easy walk, but there are a few steep sections. The paths from Linwood Drive and Celtis Road join where they cross a stream and continue until the route meets the World's View Trail. Here you can go right, left or continue straight on to reach Wylie Park about 2 km further on.

5. Dorpspruit Trail starts at the Voortrekker Bridge in Roberts Road. Cross the bridge, turn left and park your car. The path follows the stream after which it was named, crossing it twice by means of small gum-pole bridges. Reaching a disused quarry, the path to the right leads up to Villiers Drive and on to the start of the World's View Trail. The main path at the quarry becomes a vehicle track for 100 m, before crossing the stream again. A right turn brings you to Tomlinson Road which runs between the Dorpspruit and some houses. Here there are some huge specimens of paperbark acacia, Acacia sieberana var. woodii. Alien plants are prolific here but they do attract many birds such as the Cape turtle dove, forktailed drongo, paradise flycatcher and canary. The trail finishes where Tomlinson Road meets up with Mayor's Walk, but you can continue another 200 m to the Natal National Botanic Garden.

13. BISLEY NATURE RESERVE
PIETERMARITZBURG

Trail details: 1. Natal Midlands Bird Club Trail: 2 km/1 hour, circular; 2. John Pringle Trail: 2,5 km/1 hour circular, with a shorter option available.

Permits/bookings: Not required.

Maps/information: A trail guide is being prepared. Contact The Director, Parks and Recreation Department, tel. (0331) 421322; PO Box 31, Pietermaritzburg 3200 for details.

Facilities/amenities: Parking area with braai and picnic areas.

Main attractions: Wide variety of birdlife; thornveld vegetation and wetlands.

Pertinent information: Recommended group size for both these walks is 5 or less. Carry water.

This 250-ha reserve was declared in 1987 with the aim of preserving the atmosphere of the dry parts of Pietermaritzburg.

1. The Natal Midlands Bird Club Trail is a short walk leading to a bird hide. Over 160 species have

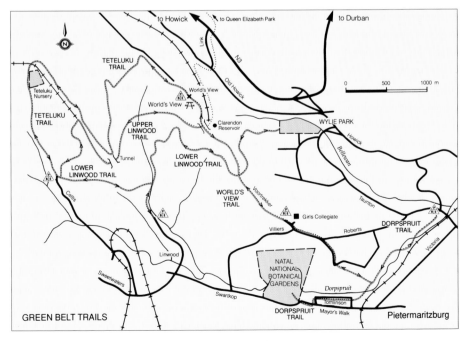

GREEN BELT TRAILS

Pietermaritzburg

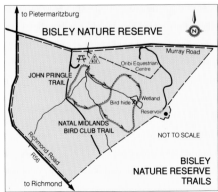

BISLEY NATURE RESERVE TRAILS

been recorded here, including the thickbilled weaver, Burchell's coucal, Shelley's francolin, the white-browed robin and rattling cisticola.

2. The John Pringle Trail, named after a local conservationist, runs through a blend of grassland and thornveld, giving good views of plants and birdlife. The route is marked by red metal squares tacked onto trees, and starts close to the parking area. Following the course of a stream, it leads up to a reservoir then heads south and crosses a marshy patch by means of a boardwalk. Continuing downhill, the path finishes at the car park.

14. INGWENI HIKING TRAIL
DURBAN

Trail details: 30-km/3-day guided trail, laid out in a horseshoe shape. A shorter route can be arranged with your guide.

Permits/bookings: Required from the Wildlife Society of Southern Africa, tel. (031) 213126; 100 Brand Road, Durban 4001.

Facilities/amenities: Three rustic timber cabins, each accommodating 12 people, with bunks and mattresses provided.

Main attractions: Views from the escarpment edge; protea savannah, grassland, cliff communities, forested valleys and waterfalls; wooden ladder; 162 species of birds.

Pertinent information: This trail is normally walked during weekends. Check the availability of guides with the Wildlife Society, if you wish to walk at another time. The trail does not operate from the beginning of December to the beginning of March. Groups are restricted to a maximum of 12 people at any one time. Bilharzia is a hazard.

The Ingweni Hiking Trail is very special. Unlike most South African trails, which are left to government authorities to construct, this trail is a real community development project, the result of the work of enthusiastic students from St. Mary's School, Thomas More School, Pinetown Boys' and Girls' high schools, and Kearsney College, who made themselves responsible for cutting and maintaining sections of the trail, in conjunction with the Wildlife Society and the Lion's Club.

With so much tender loving care being devoted to it, the Ingweni Hiking Trail deserves your support – and you won't be disappointed. This horseshoe-shaped trail runs through the forested river gorges and adjacent grasslands of sandstone formations in the Pinetown/Kloof/Gillitts/Everton subregion of the Greater Metropolitan area of Durban. Following a route of great beauty and natural charm, the trailist passes lovely waterfalls – Everton and Nkutu – and has magnificent views while walking along the edge of the sandstone escarpment on the southern boundary of Kloof, starting at the Cheeseman Nature Reserve. Krantzkloof Nature Reserve, with Nkutu Falls, comprises the last several kilometres of the walk.

Tree ferns and giant *Macaranga* (indigenous wild poplar) trees grow prolifically in the Molweni Valley; the trail even boasts its own species of *Streptocarpus, S. molweniensis*, which grows only on the south-facing bank of the Molweni Stream in the Everton riverine forest. Some hikers may decide that the main attraction of this trail is the

creosoted pole ladder descending 9 m and crossing a metre-wide crevice in an otherwise sheer krantz!

Note that this trail is one of a series in the Durban Metropolitan Open Space System (now known as D'M.O.S.S.), a joint project of the Wildlife Society and the Natal Town and Regional Planning Commission. D'M.O.S.S.'s stated goal is 'to establish and maintain the most efficient open space trail system which will link established and potential conservation areas within metropolitan Durban'.

15. KRANTZKLOOF NATURE RESERVE
KLOOF

Trail details: 1. Nkutu Trail: 4 km/2,5 hours, return; 2. Uve Trail: 8 km/6 hours, return. Shorter options are also possible. The iPithi Falls and Kloof Falls rambles are both under 1 km.

Permits/bookings: Not required.

Facilities/amenities: Toilets, a visitor centre, picnic site and parking area at both the Kloof Falls Road and Valley Road entrance.

Main attractions: Well-forested gorge; Kloof Falls; antelope and birdlife.

Pertinent information: The Ingweni Hiking Trail (see previous entry) runs through the reserve. Sudden thunderstorms are common in summer. The path into and out of the gorge at Kloof Falls is dangerous and has been temporarily closed; check with the authorities as to the current status.

Only 27 km from Durban, the Krantzkloof Nature Reserve (532 ha) serves as a major environmental education centre. A large rondavel-type building

At the top of Kloof Falls on the Molweni River at Krantzkloof.

houses natural history displays and has facilities for film shows. A great number of trees, shrubs and flowers are present, including yellowwoods, cycads and various aloes. Naturally occurring mammals are the bushbuck, grey, red and blue duiker, bush-pig, baboon, vervet monkeys and a number of smaller species such as mongoose, dassie and genet. The reserve has abundant birdlife and is a breeding area for birds such as the crowned and Wahlberg's eagle, and the Knysna and purple-crested lourie.

1. The Nkutu Trail, which starts at the Valley Road picnic area, crosses the stream and follows the escarpment edge through a variety of vegetation, including the wild pomegranate, forest milkberry and flat-crown. The route heads into the forest and winds down to the bottom of the river gorge. Take care on this section as the path is very steep; a walking stick is an excellent aid when negotiating a slippery path in wet weather or a very sandy surface in the drier months. The trail reaches a large pool at the bottom of the gorge. In winter when the river is low, you can scramble downstream over the rocks to enjoy a superb view of the gorge, but this is not recommended in summer when the rocks are likely to be very slippery. Use the same route to return to the picnic site.

2. The Uve Trail starts at Uve Road gate, crosses a ridge and heads down into the Molweni Valley. When you reach the gorge you can turn around and follow the same path back to your starting point, or follow the river up to the Kloof Falls.

16. PARADISE VALLEY NATURE RESERVE
PINETOWN, DURBAN

Trail details: Six short trails that can be combined to make a walk of some 3,5 km/2 hours.

Permits/bookings: Not required; however, organized groups should give advance notice of their visit. Further information available from The Officer in charge, Paradise Valley Nature Reserve, tel. (0331) 723443.

Facilities/amenities: Picnic and braai sites; information centre; toilets.

Main attractions: Coastal forest on the banks of the Umbilo River; waterfall; bushbuck and blue and grey duiker.

Pertinent information: Watch out for snakes, especially the black mamba and boomslang.

This 50-ha river reserve was proclaimed in 1963 and managed by the Natal Parks Board until 1981, when it came under the control of the Pinetown Municipality. There are plans to erect overnight accommodation at Paradise Valley and to connect the trail with Umbilo Park in Umbilo. The proposed route will eventually form part of the D'M.O.S.S. network (see previous page).

Four of the trails in the reserve start from the entrance and take various routes down to the waterfall. The other 2 walks join up with these trails, offering you a range of possible routes.

The rock hyrax, or dassie, is seldom seen in other reserves in the Durban area, but at Paradise Valley signs of their presence are plentiful in rocky areas. Young hyraxes often fall prey to either the black mamba, which also favours this dry, rocky environment, or the crowned eagle.

17. DURBAN'S SELF-GUIDED TRAILS
DURBAN MUNICIPAL AREA

Trail details: A variety of trails in different locations around Durban.

Permits/bookings: Not required. For further information, maps and brochures, contact Durban Municipality, Parks Department, tel. (031) 234466/433608/831333; PO Box 3740, Durban 4000, unless otherwise stated.

Facilities/amenities: Unless otherwise specified, there are public toilets at all the reserves mentioned below. Many also have visitor and/or resource centres, and some have picnic areas.

Main attractions: Abundant plant and birdlife.

Pertinent information: Many of these trails are designed along the principles of D'M.O.S.S. (Durban Metropolitan Open Space System).

Beachwood Mangroves Nature Reserve and Umgeni River Estuary

The 70-ha Beachwood Mangroves Nature Reserve (which is under the control of the Natal Parks Board, tel. (0331) 471980; Officer-in-charge, Elton Place, Congella 4001) has the largest population of mangrove trees in the Durban area; fiddler crabs and mudskippers inhabit the swamp. There are various walks that can be done in the area to take advantage of a bird hide, the high and low tides and the Umgeni River Bird Park.

Burman Bush Nature Reserve

Located in this reserve are the Hadeda Trail (180 m), the Pithi Trail (500 m) and the Umgeni Trail (1 km). The reserve boasts good bird and plant life, trees bearing their national tree list numbers, picnic sites, toilets and a resource centre. It is open from 7.00 am to 4.30 pm (other times by appointment in writing to the Director) and no permits are required. No dogs are allowed in the reserve. The **Umgeni Trail** leaflet and the colour

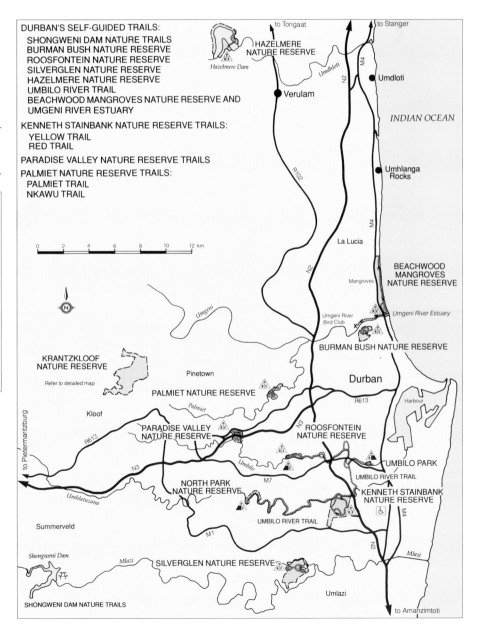

map **Burman Bush: Trail** will be most helpful on the self-guided trails.

Hazelmere Nature Reserve

The nature trail that forms part of the Hazelmere Dam Public Resort runs for 3 km/3 hours through valley bushveld containing interesting tree species that are now rarely seen elsewhere in the area. Watch out for fish eagles among the varied birdlife. You have to cross the dam to get to the start of the trail, and for this you need your own boat. Take drinking water in summer. For further information contact the Natal Parks Board, Hazelmere Resort, tel. (0323) 332315; PO Box 1013, Verulam 4040.

Roosfontein Nature Reserve

There are three trails in this reserve in the Umbilo River Valley, one of 1 km/1 hour, one of 2 km/2 hours and a circular trail of 3 km/2 hours. The reserve contains over 150 species of birds, and a variety of indigenous trees. During the summer months a wonderful display of wild flowers can be seen in the grasslands. For further information contact The Environmental Officer, Westville Parks Department, tel. (031) 861331; PO Box 39, Westville 3630.

Shongweni Dam Nature Trails

The largest single piece of protected natural bush and virtually unspoilt scenery in the metropolitan area of Durban, the Shongweni Dam area provides excellent bird-watching – and a plethora of butterflies. You can walk for about 5 km through the reserve area around the dam. It falls under the control of the Wilderness Leadership School, tel. (031) 7691283; PO Box 2444, Hillcrest 3650.

Silverglen Nature Reserve

The 3,5-4 kilometre Silverglen Trail winds through what are probably the best preserved coastal bush and grasslands in the Durban metropolitan area. The reserve has a resource centre, a picnic site and a nursery for growing medicinal plants. Fishing and wind-powered boating or boardsailing are allowed on the reservoir.

Umbilo River Trail

This 3-5 km trail runs along the banks of the river and canal, and through the fingers of steep land running up the valleys off the river. The trail is to be extended to the borough boundary. The ARC (Awareness, Recreation, Conservation) Trail, which runs for 2,5-3 km, forms the start of the D'M.O.S.S. Umbilo Trail for the greater Durban metropolitan area (see page 175).

---

18. PALMIET NATURE RESERVE
WESTVILLE, DURBAN

Trail details: 1. Palmiet Trail: 2,7 km, return; 2. Nkawu Trail: 2 km, joins the Palmiet Trail. Other shorter walks also available. Trails lead onto one another and can be walked as one longer route of 7 km/4 hours. Three-hour guided trail conducted on the first Sunday of each month. See map p.175.

Permits/bookings: Not required.

Maps/information: A booklet giving detailed descriptions of the trails available from Palmiet Publications, tel. (031) 866191; 111 Jan Hofmeyr Road, Westville 3630, or from the People's Chemist, tel. (031) 865395; 123 Jan Hofmeyr Road, Westville 3630.

Facilities/amenities: picnic site with braai facilities.

Main attractions: Rugged gorge with dense riverine forest and grassy, bush-covered slopes; 145 recorded bird species; over 150 species of indigenous trees.

Pertinent information: Bilharzia in the river.

Although only 90 ha in extent, the Palmiet Nature Reserve, 11 km from Durban, allows an interesting day's exploration for enthusiastic naturalists. Several trails descend the grassy, bush-covered slopes into dense riverine forest along the Palmiet River. These trails, steep in places, give views of the Natal sandstone reddish-brown cliffs, towering 80 to 100 m above the riverbed.

The reserve contains over 150 species of indigenous trees, and 145 bird species have been recorded in the diversified habitat – bush shrikes, sunbirds

and Natal robins are particularly well represented. The booklet on sale from the ranger should be purchased to increase your appreciation of the reserve: it describes the Palmiet's birds, insects, mammals, trees, vegetation communities and geology, and includes a map.

On the first Sunday of every month, the Natal Branch of the Wildlife Society runs a free, half-day guided walk. It is very popular as it caters for all ages and fitness levels.

This reserve is linked to the Durban Metropolitan hiking trail network (see page 175). The Palmiet Trail extends south-west to the Westville Park Trail, north-west to the New Germany Nature Reserve, and east to Durban (the Burman Bush and Beachwood Mangroves nature reserves) via the Umgeni River.

---

19. KENNETH STAINBANK NATURE RESERVE
DURBAN

Trail details: 1. Red Trail: 6 km/3 hours, circular; 2. Yellow Trail: 3 km/1 hour, one-way. There is also a trail for the disabled. See map p. 175.

Permits/bookings: Not required. Brochures with route descriptions available at the gate, where an entrance fee is payable.

Facilities/amenities: Trees labelled with national tree list numbers; picnic and braai sites; parking area; public toilets.

Main attractions: Coastal forest providing habitat for red and blue duiker; other small mammals, and reintroduced zebra, impala and nyala; prolific birdlife; historic Zulu sites.

The Natal Parks Board considers the 214-ha Kenneth Stainbank Nature Reserve to be one of its major educational areas. The land was donated to the Natal Parks Board in 1963 by the Stainbank family, and is now one of the larger reserves within municipal Durban. Located only 9,5 km from the Durban city centre and 6,5 km from the sea, the reserve comprises forest and grassland, and offers students an ideal, easily accessible venue for ecological studies.

1. The Red Trail follows a circular, clockwise route through the reserve. Commencing from the car park, you will pass grassland. Watch out for bushbuck, zebra and impala. The trail winds up to a dam where waterbirds, including purple, grey and greenbacked herons, and kingfishers, are prolific. Past the dam, the trail splits into two different routes. Take the left fork leading into the forest. Follow this path as it crosses the Umhlatuzana River twice and leads back to the parking area.

2. Past the dam, the **Yellow Trail** breaks away from the Red Trail and heads through an area which is rich in birdlife. You may be able to spot the black sparrowhawk, African goshawk, longcrested eagle, goldentailed woodpecker and Cape batis among the many birds that make their home here. The path connects with the Red Trail again, giving you the choice of joining the longer route returning to the car park.

The trail for the disabled, located close to the parking area, was designed especially for the blind, the deaf and people confined to wheelchairs (see Special Interest section for further details).

A distant view of Durban, from one of the trails in the Kenneth Stainbank Nature Reserve.

20. NGELE HIKING TRAILS
WEZA STATE FOREST, NEAR HARDING

Trail details: 1. 40 km/3 days, circular; 2. 2 days/ 36 km, circular; 3. A shorter and longer variation are possible.

Permits/bookings: Bookings are made through The Forester, Weza State Forest, tel. (03942) ask for 24, fax (039452) ask for 74; PO Weza 4685. A comprehensive booklet with a map is available on request.

Facilities/amenities: 5 overnight huts, each accommodating 30 people, with bunks, mattresses, tables, benches, stove, firewood, hot water and toilets; parking at starting points.

Main attractions: Indigenous forest; bushbuck, samango monkeys and birdlife; trout fishing.

Pertinent information: The trails are usually closed during the fire season, from the beginning of August to the end of September. If the trails are open during this time, you must be accompanied by a forest guard. Bookings may be cancelled at short notice due to local conditions. At least one adult must accompany each group of up to 10 persons under the age of 18. Hikers may not hike alone, and the maximum number in a group is 30. Vehicles may only be parked at the following overnight huts: Mackton, Middlebrook and Blackwater. Generally, the climate is cool and subject to change. The area receives summer rainfall, and afternoon thunderstorms and mist are common during November through to March. Frost and snow are common on Ngele Peak in winter. Ticks are prevalent. Hikers must supply their own bedding, food, cooking utensils and lighting.

The Ngele Hiking Trails are physically undemanding walks located within the Weza State Forest near Harding in southern Natal. The forest is situated along the N2 between Kokstad and Port Shepstone.

White painted footsteps mark the trails, and they wind in and out of an indigenous forest boasting yellowwood, lemonwood, knobwood and stinkwood; grasslands with attractive wild flowers; and plantations which are grown to produce timber for veneer logs and softwood timber. The forest sawmill processes some 700 000 m^3 each year.

Birdlife is very good but, as in all dense forests, more easily heard than seen. Some favourites include the black duck, usually found on running waters, and the long-crested eagle, which feeds on rodents. One of the largest populations of bushbuck in South Africa, as well as grey duiker, common reedbuck, grey rhebok and baboon, and samango and vervet monkeys, are easily identified. With the necessary licence, trout fishing is allowed. At the time of going to press, all state forests were in the process of being privatized and therefore the future of the trail and who the controlling authority would be was unknown.

Note that the Lorna Doone Hostel and Forest Trails (see next entry) are also located in the Weza State Forest.

1. The 3-day trail starts at Blackwater, and the first day is a 16-km walk to KwaShwili. The trail follows an old bridle path in the Swartwater cutout (the local name for an open, unplanted ridge), and later an old wagon road. At the beacon on the Weza boundary there are fine views of KwaZulu and the Transkei. The finest stinkwood specimens in Natal are found along this first section of the trail. Before KwaShwili, the trail climbs gradually along a grassy ridge, which provides a fine view over the forest. Day 2 is a 15-km walk from KwaShwili to King's Halt. The Fairview Falls are about 2 km along the route, and from there the trail follows an easy gradient with several streams and small patches of indigenous forest to be found along the way. The third day is a short 9-km walk from King's Halt to Blackwater. Once again there are fine views of KwaZulu and the Transkei. The route follows an easy gradient and should take less than 4 hours to walk.

2. Middlebrook is the starting point of the 2-day trail. The first day is a 20-km hike to Mackton, so hikers should start early and refill water bottles at the Ntunta River crossing. The portion of the trail that traverses the Umsilo cutout offers impressive views over much of Weza. The trail follows a 16-km route back to Middlebrook on the second day. The main feature of this section is a walk through the Ngele indigenous forest along an old bridle path. Beautiful specimens of stinkwood, Cape chestnut and Cape ash can be seen, as well as lemonwood and knobwood.

3. On the 2-day trail, a shorter, 15-km route can be chosen from Middlebrook to Mackton, or you can drive to Mackton and use this as a starting point for a 1-day trail. The overnight hut at Mackton is situated about 500 m from the Ingeli Forest Motel. For those who want to tackle a 5-day hike, you can link the two trails and drive from the finishing point of the one trail to the starting point of the second trail.

21. LORNA DOONE FOREST HOSTEL TRAILS
WEZA STATE FOREST, NEAR HARDING

Trail details: 1. Bushbuck Trail: 10 km/4 hours, circular; 2. Dassie Trail: 5 km/2 hours, circular; 3. Hoopoe Trail: 3,5 km/1,5 hours, circular.

Permits/bookings: Bookings are made by contacting The Forester, Weza State Forest, tel. (03942) ask for 24, fax (039452) ask for 74; PO Weza 4685. A comprehensive booklet, with a map included, is available on request.

Facilities/amenities: Lorna Doone Hostel, accommodating 36 people, with wooden bunks, mattresses, benches, tables, stove and ablution facilities provided.

Main attractions: Forest management practices; indigenous forest; game and birdlife.

Pertinent information: Bring your own food, bedding and cooking utensils. At least one adult must accompany each school or youth group. Rain falls in the summer. In the dry winter, and especially from July to October, the danger of fires is greatest. At the time of going to press, all state forests were being privatized and therefore the future of the trail and who the controlling authority would be was unknown.

The 11 100-ha Weza State Forest is the largest state forest in the country, and is near Harding on the N2 between Kokstad and Port Shepstone.

The three self-guided educational trails laid out in the forest are marked with coloured arrows. They are intended for school, youth and other groups interested in conservation. An informative booklet and leaflets provide valuable and detailed descriptions of forest management practices, trees, ecology, wildlife habitats and species, and activities for scholars. Bushbuck, grey duiker, grey rhebok, reedbuck and troops of baboon, samango monkeys and vervet monkeys can be spotted. Porcupine are more difficult to catch a glimpse of. A number of small predators, such as caracal, otter, serval, mongoose, polecat, wildcat, spotted genet and black

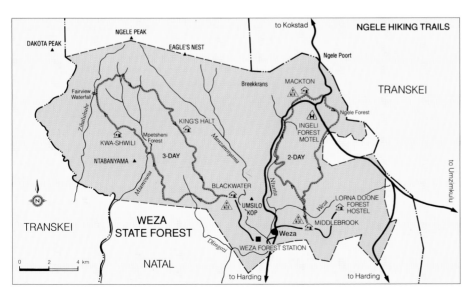

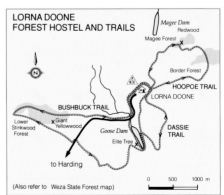

jackal, make the reserve their home, as do a large
variety of birds in the forest, grassland and water
habitats. Exotic trees along the routes are numbered
and marked. The Lorna Doone Forest Hostel Trails
are a valuable and commendable environmental
educational project.

Note that the Ngele Hiking Trail (see page 177)
is also located in the Weza State Forest.

1. The Bushbuck Trail takes you through a stinkwood forest, rich in large yellowwood and wild
quince species.

2. The Dassie Trail traverses the pine plantation,
and visits Goose Dam and an elite tree which has
been selected by forestry tree-breeding specialists
as a specimen showing above-average growth, stem
straightness, wood quality and branch pattern.

3. The short Hoopoe Trail, has trees from California, Japan and Mexico growing in attractive groves.

22. UMTAMVUNA NATURE RESERVE
PORT EDWARD

Trail details: 1. Lourie Trail: 2 km/1 hour, circular;
2. Ingungumbane Trail: 4 km/3 hours, circular; 3.
iMpunzi Trail: 8 km/4 hours, open-ended; 4. Fish
Eagle Trail: 8 km/4 hours, circular; 5. Nkonka
Trail: 8 km/6 hours, open-ended. Shorter 500-m
walk also possible.

Permits/bookings: Bookings a few days in advance
are required if you wish to be accompanied by a
game guard: tel. (03930) 32383.

Maps/information: A map and information about
the reserve are available at the entrance gates. A
bird list is being compiled and will be available in
the future.

Facilities/amenities: Toilet and a boma with braai
facilities available at the northern entrance gate;
access to herbarium on request; parking areas at
entrance gates; research hut available on request;
contact The Officer in Charge, Hebetate Nature
Reserve, tel. (03930) 32383; PO Box 25, Port
Edward 4295.

Main attractions: Steep-sided forested gorge,
botanically rich with many endemic species;
plentiful, clear streams; far-reaching, spacious
views; magnificent sandstone koppies.

Pertinent information: At present, the reserve is
only available for day use. No fishing is permitted.
The river is difficult to cross in rains and hikers
should be wary of bilharzia. Summers are very hot;
winters are generally quite mild in this area.
Groups of approximately 20 people can walk the
trails, and an educational concession for school
groups is available. For an extra fee, you can
arrange for a game guard to accompany you.

On the northern banks of the Umtamvuna River
and its magnificent gorge, which form the border
between Transkei and Natal, lies a developing and
relatively unknown reserve, a paradise for day
hikes. The 3 257-ha Umtamvuna Nature Reserve is
located on the road to Izingolweni, off the R61 to
Port Edward, and is the best example of the eastern
coastal sandstone region in South Africa, and the
only example of Pondoland coastal highland sourveld under coastal management. The fortress-like
koppies and sandstone cliffs, grasslands scattered
with wild flowers and dense riverine rain forest
with numerous pretty waterfalls tumbling into the
gorge have a magical quality.

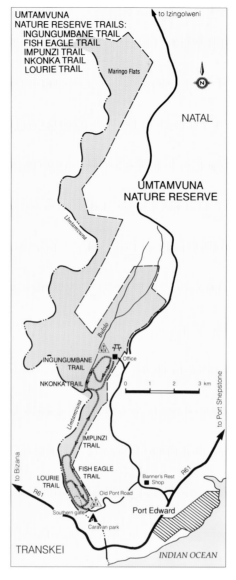

Over 250 bird species, including Gurney's sugarbirds, crowned eagles, peregrine falcons, and
breeding colonies of Cape vultures and fish eagles,
plus more than 100 species of identified plants, contribute to the biological richness of the area. Some
of the protected rarer plants include the wild rubber
fig, *Ficus polita (bizane),* the ironwood *Olea capensis* subsp. *'evervis',* the Natal cycad, *Encephalartos
natalensis, Syzygium cordatum,* waterberry; the
Natal flame bush, *Alberta magna*; and *Manilkara
nicholsonii.* If lucky, hikers can also observe baboons, the southern or common reedbuck, blesbok,
bushbuck, blue and grey duiker, serval and caracal
and many other small mammals.

The Lourie and Fish Eagle trails start and end at
the southern entrance to the reserve, while the other
three trails are located in the northern section of the
reserve. A reasonable level of fitness is required for
the more strenuous Fish Eagle, Nkonka and Ingungumbane trails as these routes involve climbing up
and down the steep rocky cliffs that border the Umtamvuna River.

Enthusiastic hikers can plan a longer walk by
combining two routes, for example, the outgoing
half of the Fish Eagle Trail can be combined with
the iMpunzi trail for a 12 km/6 hour-route that
takes you across the reserve.

23. ORIBI GORGE NATURE RESERVE
PORT SHEPSTONE

Trail details: 1. View Trail; 9 km/4 hours, return;
2. Hoopoe Falls Trail: 7 km/4 hours, return;
3. Nkonka Trail: 5 km/2,5 hours, return. Shorter
walks also available; contact the park staff
for details.

Permits/bookings: Bookings for accommodation
can be made with the Natal Parks Board, tel. (0331)
471981, fax (0331) 471980; PO Box 662,
Pietermaritzburg 3200.

Facilities/amenities: Hutted camp, at edge of gorge,
with six 3-bed fully equipped bungalows, and one
7-bed self-contained cottage; outdoor communal
braai 'boma'; picnic site and toilets along the river;
store selling books, etc., but no food.

Main attractions: Deep, forested gorge; 268 species
of birds.

Pertinent information: Scouts available on request
to lead hikers. Visitors must supply their own food
and drink. Oribi Gorge Hotel at Fairacres provides
spectacular viewing points. Bilharzia may be
present in the main river. The river cannot be
crossed in flood.

Oribi Gorge is a spectacular landscape feature located 21 km west of Port Shepstone near the lower
south coast of Natal. Here the Umzimkulwana
River, a tributary of the Umzimkulu, has carved out
of the Oribi and Murchison falls plateaux a 5 km-
wide and 305 m-deep gorge, through Table
Mountain sandstone right down to granite. The
Umzimkulwana River now rests on a bouldery sub-
strate and has short, shallow rapids with a few low
waterfalls. However, the impressive sandstone cliff
faces bordering the river have dramatic waterfalls
such as the Hoopoe and Samango falls.

Bounded by sugar cane, wattle and cattle farms,
Oribi Gorge protects over 700 plant species, of
which 500 are trees. Coastal forest forms the most
extensive vegetation type; however, the plant communities respond to altitude and the nature reserve
boasts evergreen riverine thickets in the riverbed,
grasslands on the plateau (note that grass owls are
common here), lithophytic flora on cliffs and rocky
areas, and open woodlands with proteas. Of the
many protected animal and bird species, special attention is drawn to the African python, Peringuey's
leaf-toed gecko, the black sparrowhawk, Cape
vulture, bat hawk, water leguaan (nile monitor) and
African broadbill. Ironically, the oribi, a small,
graceful rufous-coloured antelope after which the
gorge is named, is rare.

1. The View Trail deserves its name. Leading from
the hutted camp, it heads up to the escarpment.
About 3 km along the trail, you have the option of
joining the Samango Falls Trail, a short link, via a
waterfall, to the Hoopoe Falls Trail. If you want to
walk back to camp via a different route, follow the
tarred road or join the Nkonka Trail.

2. The Hoopoe Falls Trail starting at the picnic
site, leads along the western bank of the Umzimkulwana River to reach the waterfall. Use the same
route to return to your starting point.

3. The Nkonka Trail joins the longer View
Trail; however, you can walk this trail separately.
Beginning at the picnic site, follow the trail as it
leads eastwards, until it ends at a weir.

24. VERNON CROOKES
NATURE RESERVE
UMZINTO

Trail details: A variety of walks ranging in length from 300 m to 6 km.

Permits/booking: Not required; however, reservations must be made for accommodation; contact The Reservations Officer, tel. (031) 471980; PO Box 662, Pietermaritzburg 3200.

Facilities/amenities: Fully equipped huts at Nyengelezi camp; lecture room also available; bunkhouse which sleeps 10 (bedding not provided); camping facilities, public toilets and picnic areas; fishing is allowed if you have a permit.

Main attractions: Coastal forested valleys; grasslands and grazing animals; sea views; rich birdlife; interesting flora.

The 2 190-ha Vernon Crookes Nature Reserve is prime rambling territory for people with a keen interest in birds and flora. In the surrounding sea of pine, eucalyptus and sugar cane, this lovely little area preserves rolling sourveld grasslands interspersed with coastal forested kloofs and thornveld slopes. The view extends as far as the Indian Ocean, which can be seen in the distance.

Spanning an altitude from 150 to 610 m above sea level, the reserve is dissected by several fast-flowing streams such as the Mhlanga (meaning Egyptian mongoose) and Nyengelezi (or white-naped weasel). Birdlife thrives here: the seeds of the cycads attract louries and hornbills; the grasslands host widow and bishop birds while spurwinged geese and crowned cranes are seen at the dams, along with larger game such as zebra, nyala, blue wildebeest and eland. Bushbuck and blue and grey duiker live in the forests.

The reserve also contains many large specimens of trees representative of the coastal forest, such as the wild date palm, *Phoenix reclinata*; wild banana, *Strelitzia nicolai*; flat-crown, *Albizia adianthifolia*; umzimbeet, *Millettia grandis*; the common coral tree, *Erythrina lysistemon*, and three species of cycad. The honey-scented protea, *Protea welwitschii*, which is not common in Natal, reaches its southernmost point of distribution here.

The Umzimkulwana River coils far below one of the spectacular view sites in Oribi Gorge.

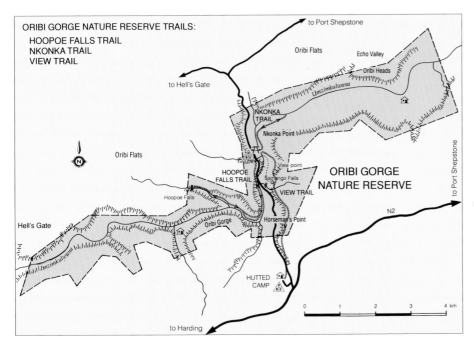

ORIBI GORGE NATURE RESERVE TRAILS:

HOOPOE FALLS TRAIL
NKONKA TRAIL
VIEW TRAIL

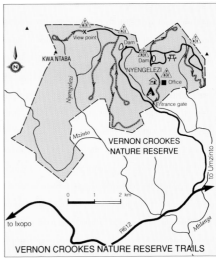

VERNON CROOKES NATURE RESERVE TRAILS

The immensely varied vegetation of Vernon Crookes Nature Reserve is set in a sea of coastal cane-fields.

A number of walking tracks lead off from the gravel roads and cross the grassland, as does the network of paths in the centre of the reserve. In the eastern part of the reserve, a pleasant walk follows the contour for some 3 km and heads up a steep incline to the plateau, and in the western section another path leads to a lookout point through a well-preserved area of coastal grassland. There are also some very localized swamp forests that are worth visiting, if you are keen on botany. None of these areas is visible from the road, so it is recommended that you arrange with the officer in charge for someone to guide you. The swamp forest communities are best visited in mid-January, when the swamp snake lily is blooming.

Early spring is recommended as the ideal time to visit the park, when the wild flowers carpet the veld in a riot of colour. For further information on walks in this area, refer to *Day Walks in and around Durban and Pietermaritzburg*, by Geoff Nichols and Monica Fairall.

25. EMPISINI NATURE RESERVE
UMKOMAAS

Trail details: Three short trails which can be walked in combination, totalling 3 km/3 hours.

Permits/bookings: Not required.

Facilities/amenities: Picnic and parking area; resource centre; toilet and camping facilities.

Main attractions: Birdlife; cascades.

This 300-ha reserve on Natal's South Coast was originally cultivated for sugar cane after World War II. The contour tracks that were cut to allow the cane to be hauled to the nearby sugar mill are now used as pathways for visitors.

This wetland habitat teems with birds and water-loving mammals, such as the water mongoose. You may even see small fish swimming in the stream. Parts of the reserve are very rewarding for bird-watching. The longtailed wagtail, Cape seed warbler and African sedge warbler are all present here.

From the picnic area, two paths lead into the reserve. The **River Trail** on the right follows the main stream, while the left-hand route leads to the resource centre, where it splits again. The right-hand path is the main trail through the reserve, whereas the **Hillside Trail** on the left follows a tributary stream uphill. Both these trails, as well as the **Main Trail**, lead in the direction of the cascades, a beautiful spot where the Dwyka tillite is broken by a band of shale, and the shrinkage cracks appear as straight lines in the rock beneath the clear water. You can then follow the same trail back to the picnic area, or link up with either of the other routes to reach your starting point.

26. HAWAAN FOREST NATURE RESERVE
UMHLANGA ROCKS

Trail details: Guided walks of between 1 and 4 km, lasting 1,5 to 2,5 hours.

Permits/bookings: All visits to the reserve are by appointment only. Contact The Conservation Officer, Hawaan Forest Nature Reserve, tel. (031) 5611101; Private Bag X4, Umhlanga Rocks 4051.

Facilities/amenities: None.

Main attractions: Unique indigenous coastal forest situated close to a main urban centre.

Pertinent information: Access to the forest is permitted only in the company of a guide.

The privately owned Hawaan Forest Nature Reserve, about 16 km north of Durban, on the south bank of the Umhlanga River, is ecologically valuable as it provides a fine example of climax coastal forest. We are indebted to the late Sir Marshall Campbell who had the foresight to set aside and maintain this nature reserve in 1913.

The name 'Hawaan' possibly derives from the language spoken by the Tamil Indian workers in the surrounding canefields, who called the forest

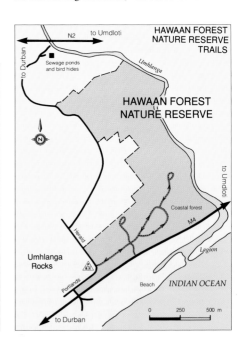

Hawaa, meaning 'light breeze'. (However, it could also be derived from the Zulu name for a dancing shield, *Halwana*.)

Although only 65 ha in extent, the reserve contains tree species rare elsewhere in South Africa and here many trees, birds and small mammals reach their most southerly distribution in Africa. It is the only forest in the Republic known to have *Cola natalensis* and *Cavacoa aurea* as dominant species. *Cola natalensis* (or common cola) is well distributed in other Natal forests, but is not common. *Cavacoa aurea* (Natal hickory) is a rare tropical tree of the euphorbia family, characterized by highly fluted stems and yellow flowers, and known to occur in only two other localities in South Africa. The white stinkwood is also common here. The forest is rich in flowers, and over 30 species of trees and 20 species of liana grow here. The liana contribute to the dense canopy, maintaining the forest micro-climate in an area of high winds and salt spray.

The forest floor is fairly level, so that none of the trails is strenuous. In this unusual forest dwell bushbuck, blue and grey duiker and the rare red duiker, in addition to vervet monkey, bushpig, mongoose and some large specimens of python. The forest also provides the southernmost habitat for the crested guineafowl, yellowbreasted apalis, white-eared barbet, brownthroated golden weaver and purplebanded sunbird.

The lagoon and riverine areas support a variety of waders, waterfowl and seabirds, including the fish eagle and osprey.

27. HAROLD JOHNSON NATURE RESERVE
DARNALL

Trail details: Bushbuck Trail: 5 km/3 hours; self-guided, circular. A shorter walk is also available.

Permits/bookings: To walk the trails and for arrangements for camping, contact The Officer in Charge, Harold Johnson Nature Reserve, tel. (0324) 61574; PO Box 148, Darnall 4480.

Facilities/amenities: Small education centre with reference collection of natural objects; 50 camp and caravan sites with full ablution facilities; picnic sites overlooking river, with braai facilities.

Main attractions: Coastal vegetation; small antelope; historical monuments nearby.

Pertinent information: During the rainy season, in summer, these trails become muddy and slippery. Summers are also very hot, so it is best to start walking early in the morning. Winter days are mild and very pleasant for walking. Carry water with you, and keep a watchful eye out for snakes. Guided tours for groups can be arranged in advance. Two historical sites, Fort Pearson and the Ultimatum Tree, are adjacent to the reserve.

The Harold Johnson Nature Reserve is situated off the N2, between Darnall and Gingindlovu, and is about 100 km from Durban. Although it spans only 104 ha, the reserve encompasses bush-clad slopes of valuable coastal vegetation, which includes such species as epiphytic orchids. Blue, red and grey duiker, bushbuck and impala, as well as the purple-crested lourie, narina trogon and forest weaver, can be seen. The small education centre and the reserve

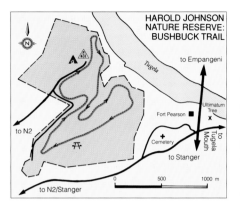

itself are particularly popular with the residents of the nearby town of Stanger.

Both trails are marked with trail indicators and begin and end at the parking area. The **Bushbuck Trail** leads you through dense, bush-clad slopes down into a steep streambed and up out again onto a ridge which overlooks the Tugela River Valley.

There is also the 1,8-km **Remedies and Rituals Trail** which is a short, physically undemanding, educational walk which interprets trees and explains their uses by the Zulus and early Natal settlers, as well as other ecological features such as the geology and fauna in the reserve.

28. AMATIKULU NATURE RESERVE
AMATIKULU

Trail details: Various self-guided day walks.

Permits/bookings: Reservations and permit available from KwaZulu Bureau of Natural Resources, tel. (0354) 74634, fax (0354) 74634/74433; Private Bag X523, Eshowe 3815.

Maps/information: A bird list is available.

Facilities/amenities: 2 tented camps with mattresses, cold shower, bush toilet, gas cookers, pots and pans.

Main attractions: Coastal forest with beautiful large tree specimens; estuary and coast; big game; abundant birdlife; fishing.

Pertinent information: Rain falls in summer, and days tend to be hot and humid, so March to October are the best months for walking. Maximum of 10 people per group, and children under the age of 12 not permitted. Ticks and mosquitoes can be a problem. Due to a lack of drinking water in the reserve, it is not yet open to the public. However, if you wish to visit and walk in the reserve, arrangements can be made with the KwaZulu Bureau of Natural Resources in Eshowe.

This 2 000-ha reserve is situated about 50 km from Mandini – leave the N2 about 12 km from the Mandini turnoff. The typical coastal riverine habitat supports a large number of bird species including the narina trogon. A list of all bird species that have been spotted in the area is available on request. The reserve is also home to big game, such as giraffe, reedbuck, kudu and zebra.

Although Amatikulu is officially not yet open to the public, for those who want to get away from it all and don't mind a very rustic camping experience (bring your own water!), it is worth making arrangements to visit and ramble at your will along the pathways that will lead you through the reserve.

29. DHLINZA FOREST NATURE RESERVE
ESHOWE

Trail details: 2 km/1,5 hours; self-guided, circular.

Permits/bookings: Advance notice that you are going to visit the reserve is preferred. Contact The Officer in Charge, tel. (0354) 42473.

Maps/information: A map of the trail is laid out at the picnic site.

Facilities/amenities: Bishop's Seat, an amphitheatre-like clearing where nativity plays are held; picnic and braai sites.

Main attractions: Indigenous evergreen forest; antelope; interesting birds and insect life; old tracks made by British soldiers.

Pertinent information: There is no accommodation in the reserve, but a caravan park run by the Eshowe Municipality borders the reserve, and there are hotels in Eshowe. Because of the elevation, Eshowe is usually cooler than the rest of Zululand, but January and February can be very hot.

The 200-ha reserve is unusually situated in a large town – Eshowe. Bushbuck, blue and red duiker, vervet monkeys, bushpig and many interesting birds of the indigenous evergreen forest inhabit the reserve. Birds of special interest are the Delegourges pigeon, trumpeter hornbill and crowned eagle, which nests at the reserve.

The marked trail is a pleasant ramble through the forest. Hikers can also wander at will along the dirt track that leads through the reserve.

There are a number of tracks running through the nature reserve. These are thought to have been cut by British soldiers who occupied the area in 1879 after the Anglo-Zulu War.

30. ENTUMENI NATURE RESERVE
ESHOWE

Trail details: 1. 1,5 km/1 hour, self-guided, circular; 2. 5 to 6 km/3 to 4 hours, self-guided, circular trail.

Permits/bookings: Advance notice that you are going to visit the reserve is preferred. Contact The Officer in Charge, tel. (0354) 42473.

Facilities/amenities: Picnic site.

Main attractions: Indigenous evergreen forest; antelope; interesting birds and insect life.

Pertinent information: The area is generally cooler than the rest of Zululand, but January and February can be very hot.

This 700-ha reserve is an island of lush mist-belt forest, surrounded by sugar-cane fields. The birdlife is prolific with the spotted thrush, starred robin, narina trogon and Knysna lourie making their home here. The rich habitat also supports a variety of small mammals including bushbuck, blue and red duiker and bushpig.

The two trails follow pathways in the forest, where there is an abundance of plant and insect life. The longer trail is only for the fit as it involves strenuous climbing to a waterfall and stream.

31. UMLALAZI NATURE RESERVE
MTUNZINI

Trail details: 1. River Mouth Trail: 8 km/2 hours, self-guided, return; 2. Siyayi River Trail: 6 km/1,5 hours, self-guided, return; 3. Mangrove Trail: 4 km/1 hour, self-guided, return.

Permits/bookings: To book camp sites, contact The Officer in Charge, Umlalazi Nature Reserve, tel. (0353) 401836; PO Box 234, Mtunzini 3867. Cabins are to be booked through the Natal Parks Board, tel. (0331) 471981; PO Box 1750, Pietermaritzburg 3200.

Maps/information: A map and brochure are available at the reserve.

Facilities/amenities: Eight 5-bed Swiss-type log cabins, fully equipped; 56 tent and caravan sites with full ablution facilities; nature trails and picnic sites; beach (swimming and surfing); fishing permitted; playground with trampoline; film shows during holiday periods.

Wide beaches, backed by coastal forest and mangroves, are among the attractions of Umlalazi.

Situated on the north coast road, 128 km from Durban, Umlalazi Nature Reserve is the perfect venue for the urbanite who wishes to enjoy the beauty of nature in a peaceful setting. A wide variety of bird species is attracted to the dense coastal vegetation, which includes red and white milkwoods, strangler figs, reeds, rushes and mangroves. Various species of butterflies and spiders also inhabit the reserve.

Each of the three trails offers a different and unique experience.

1. The River Mouth Trail is the longest and most strenuous walk. The path climbs steeply and follows the Umlalazi River from its lagoon, through both dune and mangrove forest, to its mouth – a distance of 4 km. Look out for a variety of birdlife, especially the palmnut vulture, and wild flowers. You will probably spot mudskippers and mudcrabs.

2. The Siyayi River Trail is a 3-km, winding dune forest walk which crosses the Siyayi River via a footbridge and leads onto the beach, where you can see the famous 'walking' dunes that are colonized

by a variety of plant life. Look out for possible glimpses of bushpig, bushbuck, or the red, grey and blue duikers. The route is a winding one with many ups and downs, but the path is clearly defined.

3. The Mangrove Trail is an undemanding walk that meanders for 2 km alongside several species of mangrove. Look out for the comical male fiddler crab, tree-climbing whelks and the amphibious mudskipper fish.

32. NYALA GAME RANCH
EMPANGENI

Trail details: Various guided day and night trails.

Permits/bookings: Reservations must be made through Mr and Mrs Scott-Barnes, Nyala Game Ranch, tel. (0351) 24543/7; Private Bag, Empangeni Station 3910. A variety of informative literature is available on request.

Facilities/amenities: Day and night trails; wildlife can be viewed on foot, from hides and from open vehicles; special education courses for children; education centre; Mbondwe Safari Camp provides rondavels, large lounge, large tents, electric lights, bedding, crockery, cutlery, toilets, hot and cold showers, a resident cook and a swimming pool; Hlati Safari Camp offers the same facilities as Mbondwe but without the lounge and electricity (paraffin and gas lamps supplied); Umvumvu Bush Camp provides rustic huts, tents, beds, bedding, mattresses, utility cooking and eating utensils, water, firewood, a lean-to kitchen, hot and cold showers, bush toilets and a resident cook.

Main attractions: Large game species, including blesbok, waterbuck, wildebeest, zebra, kudu and nyala; diversified wildlife and good birdlife; special educational trails and courses.

Pertinent information: Visitors must provide their own food, unless prior arrangements are made. Maximum of 60 and minimum of 15 schoolchildren per group. Camps are reserved for the sole use of one party, and each camp has its own game guard/cook. Gates open at dawn and close at dusk for day visits. Summers are hot in this area, and winters cooler and generally more pleasant. Anti-malaria precautions are advisable.

Private game ranches, such as the 500-ha Nyala Game Ranch, are able to offer a variety of activities which most government reserves do not. At Nyala, walking safaris at night, in addition to day trails, supply the opportunity to spot aardwolf, caracal, bush baby, porcupine, hare, rabbit and other nocturnal creatures. Lectures on many aspects of conservation can be arranged for organized groups at the interpretive centre near Mbondwe Camp. Conservation-orientated courses for school and youth groups are also available. A typical course for secondary schoolchildren includes day and night trails, practical soil and water conservation, slide and film shows, lectures and discussions on ecology and game ranching, and visits to the adjoining Jabulani Rehabilitation Centre, where physically handicapped Zulu craftsmen make curios from skins and wood.

Nyala Game Ranch also serves as a venue for ACE (African Conservation Education). ACE, once a project of the Natal Branch of the Wildlife Society, is now run jointly by the Natal Parks Board and the KwaZulu Government. The objectives of the environmental education courses are to demonstrate to Zulu teachers the place of man in the environment and the responsibility he has to care for it properly; and teachers are, in turn, expected to impart their knowledge to their students.

The ranch is situated off the R34 between Empangeni and Kwalini.

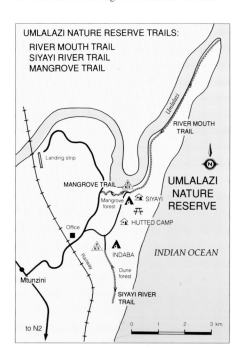

Mangroves flourish in the still waters of estuaries and lagoons.

Supposedly named for its erratic course, the White Umfolozi sweeps past cliff and plateau to the sea.

33. ENSELENI NATURE RESERVE
EMPANGENI

Trail details: Nkonikini Trail: 8 km/3,5 hours; self-guided, circular. A shorter 30-minute trail is also available.

Permits/bookings: Arrangements for guided walks should be made in advance: tel. (0351) 923732.

Maps/information: A map and brochure with information about the reserve are being updated at present.

Facilities/amenities: Picnic sites with braai facilities; ablutions; botanical garden envisaged; education centre being built.

Main attractions: Large mammals have been reintroduced; plant and birdlife.

Pertinent information: Summers are hot and humid in this subtropical region, and winters are mild. Anti-malaria precautions are advisable. Accompanied walks are available on request.

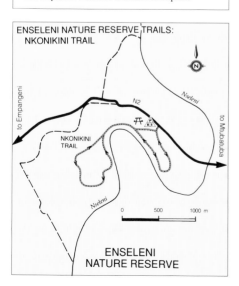

ENSELENI NATURE RESERVE TRAILS:
NKONIKINI TRAIL

to Empangeni

Nseleni

N2

NKONIKINI
TRAIL

to Mtubatuba

Nseleni

Nseleni

0   500   1000 m

ENSELENI
NATURE RESERVE

The 293-ha Enseleni Nature Reserve, located 16 km north-east of Empangeni on the N2 and available for day use only, offers a great deal within a relatively small area.

The reserve offers visitors the opportunity of walking within the 143-ha game paddock to view reintroduced nyala, blue wildebeest, waterbuck, reedbuck, zebra, grey duiker and bushpig. The 8-km Nkonikini Trail takes you through grassland, forest and riverine forest.

34. MATATANE TRAIL
NEAR MELMOTH

Trail details: 1. 14 km/5 hours, self-guided, circular; 2. 4 km/2 hours, self-guided; circular.

Permits/bookings: For bookings contact Mr G Greef, tel. (03545) 2332; PO Box 141, Melmoth, 3835. Brochure available on request.

Facilities/amenities: 2 huts in base camp accommodating 10 people; beds and mattresses provided; camp and caravan sites; toilet and shower; gas lamps and firewood; braai facilities.

Main attractions: Bird-watching and game; fishing; rock climbing; swimming and tubing (in rainy season); historical sites.

Pertinent information: Climate subtropical; summer months best. Maximum of 10 people per group. Ticks are prevalent. Routes are suitable for children over 10 years old, except perhaps the shorter route, which is more strenuous. Bring your own bedding and food.

The trails, marked by footprints, run through a 420-ha privately owned farm, Langewacht, situated next to the 2 500-ha Umfolozi Game Reserve. Look out for eagles, as 80 species have been identified in this area, and you may also spot duiker, rhebok and dassies. Of historic interest are the ruins of the Denny-Dalton gold mine.

The longer route leads from the base camp to the White Umfolozi River and then follows the river, for about 10 km, back to the camp.

The second route wanders alongside the Vatshini River up to rock pools and a waterfall, and then returns to the base camp. The shorter route involves swimming (and tubing when the river is full) and rock climbing.

Two female nyala quench their thirst at a waterhole.

GREATER ST LUCIA WETLAND PARK
CENTRAL ZULULAND

Poised at the edge of the tropical and subtropical climatic zones, the Greater St Lucia Wetland Park teems with plants and animals, all bound within an intricate web of interdependence.

Not surprisingly, St Lucia provides endless hours of discovery and adventure for the outdoor enthusiast. Within the various conservation areas in the Park – such as St Lucia Game Reserve, St Lucia Estuary, False Bay Park, Mapelane, Cape Vidal, Sodwana Bay National Park, Sodwana State Forest and the Eastern Shores Nature Reserve – are hiking trails, self-guided nature trails and rambles, and wilderness trails. None is strenuous but the extreme heat and humidity can, during the hottest months of the year, be most enervating. Launch tours are also available – contact the Natal Parks Board, tel. (035) 5901340; Private Bag X01, St Lucia Estuary 3936, for enquiries and bookings.

To get the most from these trails and amenities, however, some background to the ecology of the complex is essential. Would-be visitors to the region should obtain available literature from the Natal Parks Board.

Often referred to as a lake, St Lucia is in fact a 60-km long estuary lying parallel to the sea. In the north-west, a narrow connection links it to False Bay, while at its southern end the opening to the sea is extremely narrow – one of the main features contributing to its uniqueness.

St Lucia's plants and animals are dependent on numerous dynamic physical, chemical and biological factors which provide fresh water and nutrients to the system. Being relatively shallow, the estuary's water level and salinity fluctuate seasonally. Water levels are dependent on the inflow from four major rivers; prevailing wind directions; the waters of the north-lying papyrus swamps which, fed by the Mkuze River, seep into the lake; and swamps and pans to the east, recharged by an average annual rainfall of 1 000 mm. Plants of the swamps also influence water levels as their huge leaves reduce evaporation by shading the water.

Within this dynamic system food webs are complex. For example, crocodiles, fish eagles and pelicans prey on the large fish population, which feeds on the prawns, which feed on zoo-plankton, which in turn feeds on a thriving plant plankton population. Plankton, the foundation of the food pyramid, thrives in the shallow, warm conditions where nutrients are constantly provided by continuous wind and wave action distributing and circulating bottom sediments. The hippo population also adds to the lake's productivity; by grazing at night on the shore and subsequently fertilizing the lake with their droppings, the hippos bring in humus from the land.

Adjacent to the sea, the 120-m high forested dunes – the world's highest – range along the entire length of the lake. The variety of tropical plants and animals (including birds, insects, malaria-carrying mosquitoes, leeches, tsetse flies and snakes) within these dunes is astonishing. Primarily a hippo reserve, the Greater St Lucia Wetland Park also supports cheetah, nyala, bushbuck, waterbuck, buffalo, red duiker, reedbuck, suni and steenbok.

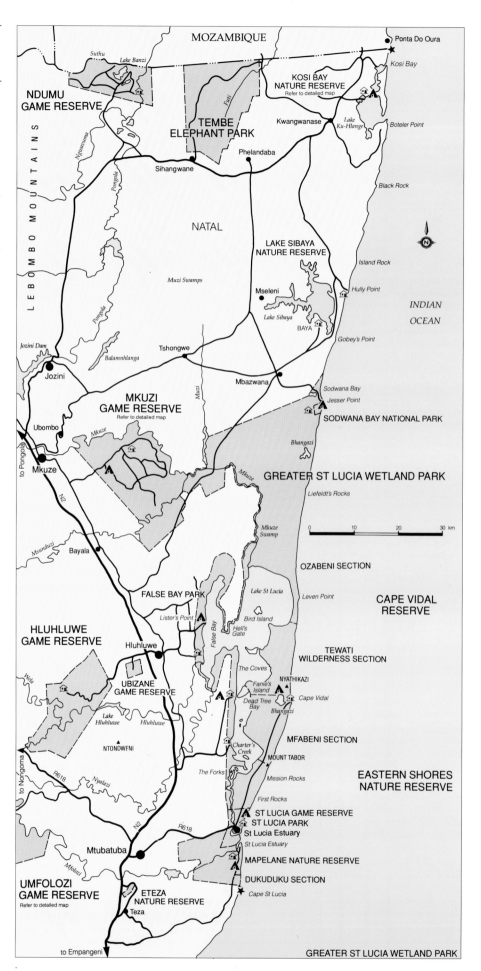

35. GAME PARK TRAILS
ST LUCIA ESTUARY,
GREATER ST LUCIA WETLAND PARK

Trail details: An extensive 12-km trail system for self-guided walks. A shorter walk of 1,5 km is also available.

Permits/bookings: No permit is necessary to walk in the game area. To book accommodation, contact The Officer in Charge, St Lucia Resort, tel. (0355901) 340, fax (0355901) 343; Private Bag, St Lucia Estuary 3936.

Maps/information: Brochures are available from the controlling authority – the Natal Parks Board – at the reserve.

Facilities/amenities: Accommodation for school groups in education centre; 3 camping and caravanning grounds – Sugarloaf, Iphiva and Eden Park – maximum of 6 people per camp site, ablution blocks with hot and cold water, electricity points; swimming pool at Sugarloaf.

Main attractions: Large game; variety of birds; crocodile centre: an interpretive centre featuring an in-depth study of the crocodile; the ecology of the St Lucia area.

Pertinent information: Boat tours are also available. You may not swim or paddle in the estuary because of crocodiles and sharks. Anti-malaria precautions are advisable. Summers are very hot and humid. Trails can become muddy in the rainy season – summer. Beware of crocodiles and hippos.

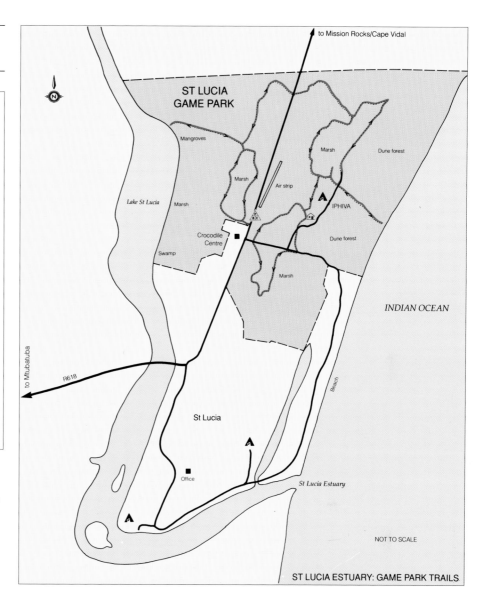

ST LUCIA ESTUARY: GAME PARK TRAILS

This area includes St Lucia Game Reserve, which was proclaimed in 1895 and is the oldest conservation area in the Greater St Lucia Wetland Park. The estuary is off the N2, 25 km from Mtubatuba, and is gateway to the eastern shores of the lake. It contains the highest vegetated dunes in the world, as well as diverse and extensive wetland systems and coastal grasslands, where the world's highest density of common reedbuck can be found. For further information, see the Greater St Lucia Wetland Park, previous page.

Hikers should be wary of hippos: they don't usually come out of the water during the day, but if you should come across one, beat a hasty but quiet retreat, and seek refuge up or behind a large tree if necessary. Hippos are most dangerous if you stand between them and the water.

There is an extensive trail system in the St Lucia Game Reserve along which the visitor can walk unguided. Ensure that you are in possession of a brochure, which gives details on the trail routes. One of the trails meanders down to the estuary bank from where you are very likely to see hippos (about a 2-km, 40-minute walk from the Crocodile Centre). Impala, the side-striped jackal, waterbuck, wildebeest and zebra also make their home here.

The informative brochure available from the Natal Parks Board contains a bird list and a list of trees that can be identified in the area. The reserve is a mosaic of grassland, Umdoni parkland, marsh, reed and sedge beds, and mangrove, swamp and dune forests.

The 1,5-km circular Gwalagwala trail starts and ends from the road at Eden Park and leads you through the coastal and dune forest, close to the estuary shore. A brochure is available that explains the significance of the markers along the trail.

A partly submerged sandbar marks the estuary of the great wetlands of Lake St Lucia.

A setting sun silhouettes canoeists on the St Lucia Wilderness Trail near Eastern Shores.

High dunes on the trail near Cape Vidal.

36. LAKE ST LUCIA WILDERNESS TRAIL
ST LUCIA GAME RESERVE, GREATER ST LUCIA WETLAND PARK

Trail details: 3 days/4 nights; guided, circular.

Permits/bookings: Advance bookings are essential, through the Natal Parks Board, tel. (0331) 471981, fax (0331) 471980; PO Box 1750, Pietermaritzburg 3200. Brochures available on request. For more information about the trail, phone The Warden: tel. (0355901) 233.

Facilities/amenities: Transport to base camp, and all equipment and catering provided; baggage, equipment and food carried by pack-donkeys. Accompanied by trails officer and game guard; accommodation in tented base camp (three 2-man tents with mattresses, pillows, sheets and blankets; fully equipped kitchen, camp cook, shower with hot and cold water, flush toilet) and two tented bush camps (same facilities as base camp except cooking is done over an open fire, hot-water bucket shower, no toilet facilities).

Main attractions: Coastal scenery; game and bird life; canoeing is an option.

Pertinent information: Only available from April to September (as summers are very hot and humid), from Friday to Tuesday. Winter nights tend to be cold. Anti-malaria precautions are essential, and tackies should be worn during the day to wade in pans. A maximum of 6 people is allowed per trail, and children under the age of 14 not permitted. Trailers should be fit enough to walk 10 km per day.

Cape Vidal is about 35 km from St Lucia and the trail starts from the reception office at Mission Rocks. The wilderness area is to the north of Mission Rocks and includes terrestrial and aquatic habitats, plus it offers some beautiful coastal scenery. You may encounter game, such as reed-buck, red duiker, black rhino, and a variety of bird species along the trail.

The first and last nights of the trail are spent at the tented Bhangazi base camp, which is located on the western shore of the picturesque Bhangazi Lake, while Saturday and Sunday nights are spent in tents in the wilderness area – at Swate Camp, next to Lake St Lucia. Canoes are available at Swate Camp for those who wish to explore the lake, and hippos and crocodile can be spotted from the water's edge, where bird-watching is also very rewarding.

The trail follows no set course, and hikers walk about 10 km per day, enjoying the unique experience of the solitude and tranquillity of the wilderness area. You will be led by a trails officer and a game guide. From their experience and knowledge, they will be able to inform you about the environment that you walk through, as well as ensure your safety.

As all your equipment is carried by pack-donkeys, you are left free to carry other items that may enhance your wilderness experience, such as a set of binoculars, a bird identification book, a small day pack and a camera.

For further information, see the Greater St Lucia Wetland Park entry and map, page 184.

37. UMVUBE TRAIL
CAPE VIDAL, GREATER ST LUCIA WETLAND PARK

Trail details: 7 km/3 hours; self-guided, circular.

Permits/bookings: For bookings of camp sites: The Officer in Charge, Cape Vidal, tel. (0355901) 404 or 300; Private Bag, St Lucia 3936. For bookings for other accommodation: Natal Parks Board, tel. (0331) 471981, fax (0331) 471980; PO Box 1750, Pietermaritzburg 3200.

Maps/information: A very informative pamphlet with a map is available from the Natal Parks Board office at Cape Vidal.

Facilities/amenities: 30 Swiss-type log cabins; 6 community angler cabins; camp sites; curio shop; fishing; swimming; large community hall for hire.

Main attractions: Dense coastal forest; shores of Bhangazi Lake; great variety of birds and small mammals.

Pertinent information: Bring your own food and drink. Petrol and firewood are available. Anti-malaria precautions are necessary. Summers are very hot and humid. Beware of crocodiles and hippos in the lake. Wear closed shoes as the trail is littered with Acacia thorns.

Cape Vidal is located in the north of the Mfabeni section of the Greater St Lucia Wetland Park, 35 km north of St Lucia village, and is named after Lt Vidal R N, an officer of the first British hydrographic survey to chart this coast in 1822. The area comprises a continuous belt of sand-dune forest, indigenous forest clumps and open grassland.

The Umvube Trail leads from the road just above the Community Centre across a bridge and up and down dunes through the coastal forest to the shores of the Bhangazi Lake, where it runs along the shores of the lake for a while. The tannin from the leaves of the swamp vegetation has coloured the waters of the lake the colour of tea. The trail then meanders through Acacia woodland and dune forest back to the starting point. This pleasant 7-km walk gives you the opportunity of spotting a great variety of birds and small mammals, like the samango monkey, side-striped jackal and brown hyaena. Black rhino, buffalo, kudu and waterbuck have also been introduced here. The path follows the natural contours of the area to prevent soil erosion, so please remember not to stray from the trail.

Day walks into the wilderness area to the north of Cape Vidal, in the company of a game guard, can also be undertaken by prior arrangement.

38. MAPELANE NATURE RESERVE
GREATER ST LUCIA WETLAND PARK

Trail details: 2 km/1 hour; self-guided, return. A longer trail is being planned. See map p. 184.

Permits/bookings: For booking of camp sites: The Officer in Charge, Mapelane Nature Reserve, tel. (0355901) 407; Private Bag, St Lucia 3936. For booking of cabins: The Natal Parks Board, tel. (0331) 471981, fax (0331) 471980; PO Box 1750, Pietermaritzburg 3200.

Maps/information: Informative literature available from the Natal Parks Board office in St Lucia.

Facilities/amenities: 44 camp and caravan sites with modern ablution blocks; ten 5-bed log cabins, which are fully equipped.

Main attractions: Over 200 species of birds; ski-boat and surf fishing.

Pertinent information: Bring your own food and drink. The Umfolozi River has crocodiles and there may be sharks at the river mouth; no swimming is permitted. Anti-malaria precautions are necessary. Summers are very hot and humid, and winters are generally mild.

This 900-ha forested reserve is situated on the southern bank of the Umfolozi River, in the southern region of the Greater St Lucia Wetland Park. To get to the reserve, turn right off the N2 at the sign for the Kwambonambi lighthouse.

Birdlife is abundant in the reserve, and there are a number of smaller mammals.

The short self-guided trail is a steep walk to the top of the dune. The roads in the reserve can also be used for walking. A longer trail through the dune forest to a viewsite overlooking the Umfolozi River and the St Lucia Estuary is being planned.

For further information, see the Greater St Lucia Wetland Park, page 184.

39. DUGANDLOVU AND MPOPHOMENI TRAILS
FALSE BAY PARK, GREATER ST LUCIA WETLAND PARK

Trail details: 1. Dugandlovu Trail: 8 km/5 to 6 hours, self-guided, open-ended, with variations; 2. Mpophomeni Trail: 10 km/4,5 hours or 7 km/ 3,5 hours, self-guided, circular.

Permits/bookings: Bookings for Dugandlovu Rustic Camp are made through the Natal Parks Board, tel. (0331) 471981, fax (0331) 471980; PO Box 1750, Pietermaritzburg 3200. Camp site bookings are made through The Officer in Charge, False Bay Park, tel. (03562) ask for 2911; PO Box 222, Hluhluwe 3960. Arrangements to walk the trails must be made at the park.

Maps/information: An informative pamphlet with maps is available at the Natal Parks Board office.

Facilities/amenities: Dugandlovu Rustic Camp: 4 huts, equipped with 4 beds, cold water, shower, toilet, 2 small gas cookers, utensils, braai sites and firewood, paraffin lamps and drinking water; False Bay Park: 40 camp and caravan sites along the shoreline; picnic sites for day visitors.

Main attractions: A variety of vegetation; superb setting of Dugandlovu Camp; 160 bird species.

Pertinent information: The huts on the Dugandlovu Trail serve as a base camp, and are reached after an 8,5-km walk, or by road to the camp. Maximum of 16 people admitted per night. Anti-malaria precautions are necessary.

UMVUBE TRAIL
WILDERNESS TRAILS

Lake St Lucia

TEWATI WILDERNESS AREA

Fanie's Island

UMVUBE TRAIL

WILDERNESS TRAILS
BASE CAMP

BHANGAZI BUSH CAMP

Cape
Vidal

Swamp

Bhangazi

ANGLER
CABINS

ST LUCIA WETLAND PARK:
MFABENI SECTION

Swamp

0   2   4 km

MZIKI TRAIL
(Refer to detailed map)

MFABENI SECTION

Charter's Creek

MOUNT TABOR

INDIAN OCEAN

WILDERNESS TRAILS

to St Lucia village

Mission Rocks

The western shores of picturesque Lake Bhangazi, where the base camp for the St Lucia Wilderness Trail is situated.

A Parks Board officer points out a feature of interest where the trail reaches the sea near Cape Vidal .

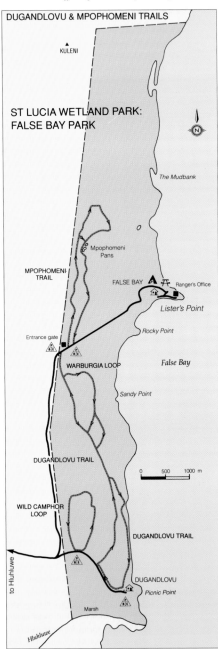

DUGANDLOVU & MPOPHOMENI TRAILS

KULENI

ST LUCIA WETLAND PARK:
FALSE BAY PARK

The Mudbank

MPOPHOMENI
TRAIL

*Mpophomeni
Pans*

FALSE BAY — Ranger's Office

Lister's Point

Entrance gate

Rocky Point

WARBURGIA LOOP

False Bay

Sandy Point

0   500   1000 m

DUGANDLOVU TRAIL

WILD CAMPHOR
LOOP

DUGANDLOVU TRAIL

DUGANDLOVU
Picnic Point

to Hluhluwe

Marsh

Hluhluwe

40. MZIKI TRAIL
EASTERN SHORES STATE FOREST AND NATURE RESERVE, GREATER ST LUCIA WETLAND PARK

Trail details: 1. South Coast Loop: 10 km, self-guided, circular; 2. Lake Trail or Mfazane Pan Loop: 10 km, self-guided, circular; 3. North Coast Loop: 18 km, self-guided; circular.

Permits/bookings: Reservations are to be made through the central office of the Natal Parks Board, tel. (0331) 471981, fax (0331) 471980; PO Box 662, Pietermaritzburg 3200.

Maps/information: Brochures and other literature available from Natal Parks Board office in St Lucia.

Facilities/amenities: Mount Tabor hut is equipped with bunks, mattresses, table and benches, water, gas cooker, gas lamps, bush shower and toilet.

Main attractions: The trail covers many of the components of the St Lucia Complex: open grassland, dune forest, beach, freshwater pans and hippo paths; huge flocks of birds on pans (seasonal); largest population of reedbuck.

Pertinent information: Maximum of 8 and minimum of 4 people per group, and no children under the age of 16. Anti-malaria precautions are necessary. Mosquitoes and ticks are also a nuisance. Carry plenty of water. Summers are very hot and humid with rain falling mainly in squalls, while winters are mild to warm, so April to October are the best months for hiking. Check for high tide before embarking on a walk that will take you along the seashore. You should be wary of hippos, crocodiles and Zambezi sharks in the lake, and the Gaboon adder is a dangerous but shy inhabitant of the dune forests.

False Bay Park is situated on the western shores of Lake St Lucia, about 16 km from Hluhluwe and is 2 247 ha in area. Game-viewing and bird-watching on both trails are good. Game includes hippo, bush-pig, warthog, zebra, reedbuck, nyala, grey and red duiker, suni and crocodile. Common birds of the sand forest include the paradise flycatcher, goldentailed woodpecker and purplecrested lourie. The birds differ in the woodland, where common species are the brownhooded kingfisher, puffback shrike and crested francolin, and also in the thickets, where one is more likely to see the tambourine dove, crested guineafowl and the Natal and white-throated robins.

1. Dugandlovu is Zulu for 'Lost Elephant' and the trail, which is suitable for inexperienced hikers and families, is laid out in the southern section of False Bay Park. Arrows burnt into poles serve as route indicators and lead you from the entrance gate to the park through woodlands and thicket down to the lake shore. The route meanders along the shoreline up to the picnic site and then leads you through bush to the Dugandlovu Rustic Camp, where hikers may spend the night if they wish to walk back to the starting point the next day. The camp, which has a superb setting overlooking the Hluhluwe River and floodplain, is also accessible by vehicle. Near the entrance gate, a shorter, 1,5-hour circular route can be chosen – the Warburgia Loop. Near the rustic camp, there is also the 1,5-hour Wild Camphor Loop that begins and ends at the road that leads to the camp.

2. Mpophomeni is the Zulu word for waterfall, and the trail is situated in the northern part of the False Bay Park. The route is clearly marked by 27 markers which identify points of interest, and passes through woodland, sand forest and thicket, the last-named being the intermediate stage between the other two. The brochure describes the different tree and bird species in each area, emphasizing trees such as the tamboti, marula, black monkey thorn, Zulu podberry, spineless monkey orange, Natal fig, Ilala palm and others. The sand forest, a low-canopy forest which once extended throughout north-eastern Natal, is the home of South Africa's rarest antelope, the suni. Hikers can turn back at the Mpophomeni Pans for a shorter, 7-km walk, or walk the extra 3 km for the complete trail.

Mount Tabor, the base camp for all three routes, is situated about 2 km from Mission Rocks in Cape Vidal and is in an old World War II radar station. The Mziki Trail is part of a trail system planned to link St Lucia Estuary to Cape Vidal and comprises

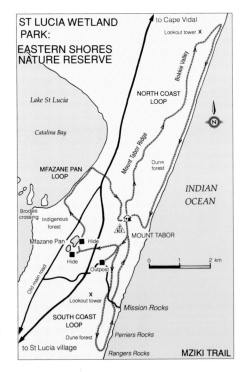

ST LUCIA WETLAND
PARK:
EASTERN SHORES
NATURE RESERVE

to Cape Vidal

Lookout tower X

Lake St Lucia

Bokkie Valley

NORTH COAST
LOOP

Catalina Bay

Mount Tabor Ridge

*Dune
forest*

MFAZANE PAN
LOOP

INDIAN
OCEAN

Brodies
crossing   *Indigenous
forest*

MOUNT TABOR

Mfazane Pan   Hide

Hide

Outpost

Old main road

0   1   2 km

X
Lookout tower

Mission Rocks

SOUTH COAST
LOOP

Dune forest

to St Lucia village

Perriers Rocks

Rangers Rocks

MZIKI TRAIL

three circular routes, which are clearly marked by painted yellow reedbuck spoor.

Animals that you may see are kudu, reedbuck, waterbuck, red duiker, grey duiker, vervet and samango monkeys, hippos, buffalo, crocodile, banded mongoose, bushbuck, bushpig and leopard. Flocks of birds visit the lake during breeding season.

Trees of interest include the common but ornamental coral tree, *Erythrina lysistemon* in the open veld, the long-lived milkwood tree, *Sideroxylon inerme* of the dune forests, the rare forest fig, *Ficus craterostoma*, which is found near the Mfazane Pan, and, of course, the various species of pine in the plantations.

The Natal Parks Board has an informative booklet available that explains the significance of the red trail markers with numbers on the top right-hand corner that you will encounter along the route.
1. The South Coast Loop leads in a southerly direction – the outbound section meanders through open hill sides, indigenous dune forest and pine plantation, and the return journey takes you along rocky coastline, where you can see interesting marine life in tidal pools, to Mission Rocks where you then head back to Mount Tabor through the dune forest.
2. The Lake Trail or **Mfazane Pan Loop** is also a 10-km route, and it heads in a westerly direction through indigenous forest, past the Mfazane freshwater pan, where you can see waterfowl, hippos and crocodile. The trail then leads through open grassland to the shore of the lake, swings north along the shore of the lake for 1,5 km and heads back to Mount Tabor. Part of the route takes you along a hippo highway, so beware. If you are confronted by a hippo and it seems non-aggressive, stand perfectly still and then withdraw quietly. If it appears to be in an aggressive mood, retreat with great haste or seek refuge behind or in a large tree.
3. The third trail is the longest – the 18-km **North Coast Loop**. It heads northwards along the Mount Tabor Ridge, and then drops down to the Bokkie Valley where you will find the reserve's largest concentration of reedbuck. The trail then leads through forested dunes and along 8 km of uninhabited coastline back to Mount Tabor.

41. LAKE TRAIL
EASTERN SHORES NATURE RESERVE, GREATER ST LUCIA WETLAND PARK

Trail details: 5-day guided wilderness trail. See map p. 184.

Permits/bookings: Reservations through the Wilderness Leadership School, tel. (031) 428642, fax (031) 428675; PO Box 53058, Yellowwood Park 4011. Brochure available on request.

Facilities/amenities: All equipment provided, including sleeping bags, backpacks, shelter (when it rains), food and utensils.

Main attractions: Undisturbed habitat; solitude; fantastic birdlife.

Pertinent information: Summers in this area are hot and humid; winters are mild, with August being windy, so March to November are the best months for walking. Anti-malaria precautions are necessary, and ticks and mosquitoes can be a problem. Groups are limited to a minimum of 6 and a maximum of 8. No children under the age of 15.

This area of the Greater St Lucia Wetland Park is a patchwork of grassland, dune forest and riverine vegetation, and is inhabited by black rhino, hippo, buffalo, reedbuck, kudu, waterbuck and wildebeest, as well as an abundance of birds.

Courses begin and end in Durban, and transport to and from St Lucia is provided. The Wilderness Leadership School adopts minimum impact camping techniques, hence the trail does not follow a set route and there are no base camps set up.

42. ISIKHOVA AND UMKHUMBE NATURE TRAILS
CHARTER'S CREEK, GREATER ST LUCIA WETLAND PARK

Trail details: 1. Isikhova Trail: 7 km/3 hours, self-guided, circular; 2. Umkhumbe Trail: 5 km/2 hours; self-guided, circular. See map p. 184.

Permits/bookings: Reservations for accommodation are to be made through the Natal Parks Board, tel. (0331) 471981, fax. (0331) 471980; PO Box 1750, Pietermaritzburg 3200.

Maps/information: Booklet and pamphlet are available at the camp.

Facilities/amenities: Charter's Creek: hutted camp with a 7-bed cottage, fifteen 2- and 3-bed huts, community lounge, kitchen blocks, laundry, ablution block, refrigerator and deep freeze facilities, table tennis, swimming pool and playground, braai and picnic sites; fishing boats for hire; picnic and braai sites; petrol sold at camp; curio shop.

Main attractions: Forest; lake shore; scenery; wildlife; bird-watching.

Pertinent information: Beware of crocodiles. Anti-malaria precautions are necessary. Summers are very hot and humid with rainfall, but winters are mild.

Charter's Creek is situated on the western shore of the lake, about 20 km north of Mtubatuba and overlooks the southern end of the lake. It is a wonderful area for trailing – the area has forest, the scenic lake shore, plentiful bird life and other wildlife, such as warthog, nyala, bushbuck, bushpig, reedbuck and red duiker. It is unlikely that the hiker will encounter a hippo, although there is abundant evidence in the form of dung and hippo paths that they come out of the water to graze at night. On the rare occasion when the hiker does come across a hippo, it is best to move away very quietly. Any sign of restlessness from the hippo means that you should retreat to the safety of a large tree with haste. Make sure that you never place yourself between the hippo and the water.
1. Isikhova is Zulu for 'place of owls', and the 7-km trail traverses coastal forest typical of the western shore of Lake St Lucia. Picnic facilities along the trail consist of logs that have been placed for weary hikers to rest on, but fires are not permitted. The Isikhova Stream is crossed twice and gives the trail its name. Numbered markers indicate items of interest that are explained in the booklet.
2. Umkhumbe means 'red duiker' in Zulu, and the trail is marked by yellow and black route markers depicting buck spoor. It winds through coastal forest and then along the lake shore before leading you back to the starting point. Numbered red and

black signs indicate where interpretive points of some natural feature are explained in the pamphlet. The best time to spot game is early in the morning or late afternoon, but remember to be as unobtrusive as possible.

43. UMKHIWANE TRAIL
FANIE'S ISLAND, GREATER ST LUCIA WETLAND PARK

Trail details: 5 km/2 hours; self-guided, circular.

Permits/bookings: For camp site bookings: The Camp Superintendent, tel. (03550) 1631; PO Box 201, Mtubatuba 3935. For other accommodation: The Natal Parks Board, tel. (0331) 471981, fax (0331) 471980; PO Box 1750, Pietermaritzburg 3200.

Maps/information: A brochure with a map is available at the camp.

Facilities/amenities: Fanie's Island: one 7-bed cottage and twelve 2-bed rondavels, fully equipped, with kitchen, ablution block, refrigerator, and deep freeze facilities; petrol is available; fishing is permitted; boats for hire; camp and caravan site with hot and cold water and 20 camping sites; communal centre and swimming pool.

Main attractions: Coastal forest; birdlife.

Pertinent information: Fanie's Island is a more secluded camp than Charter's Creek. Hippos and crocodiles can be dangerous. Anti-malaria precautions are necessary. Winters are mild, but summers hot and humid with rainfall. Carry water with you.

Fanie's Island is situated on the western shores of Lake St Lucia, approximately 14 km north of Charter's Creek.

The trail meanders through coastal forest that is typical of the western shore of Lake St Lucia, open parkland grassveld and a swamp forest. You can spot birds such as the purplecrested lourie, crested guineafowl, marsh owl and Cape eagle owl. The trail brochure explains marked points of interest, including individual trees.

Wildlife in this area is abundant and includes reedbuck, red duiker, bushbuck and monkeys.

This trail can only be walked in daylight as hippo leave the water to feed in the evening and return in the early morning. It is unlikely that you will meet a hippo while hiking, but should this occur, follow the advice given on page 185.

For further information, see Greater St Lucia Wetland Park, page 184.

44. UMFOLOZI WILDERNESS AND PRIMITIVE TRAILS
UMFOLOZI GAME RESERVE

Trail details: 1. Wilderness Trails: 3 days/4 nights guided trail, 12–15 km per day; 2. Primitive trail also available.

Permits/bookings: Bookings to be made through the Natal Parks Board, tel. (0331) 471981; PO Box 1750, Pietermaritzburg 3200. Informative Wilderness Trail booklet available from the Natal Parks Board.

Facilities/amenities: Transport provided to base camps. For Wilderness Trail: accommodation in tented camps: Mndindini base camp, Ngilandi, Enqabaneni and Dadethu bush camps, mattresses, sheets and blankets, bucket showers and all meals provided, food and equipment carried by donkeys; for Primitive Trail: meals provided and equipment can be hired.

Main attractions: Diverse wildlife, especially big game; 300 species of birds.

Pertinent information: Maximum of 8 and minimum of 4 people per trail; minimum age 14 years, and children under the age of 16 must be accompanied by a parent or guardian. Anti-malaria precautions are necessary; ticks are prevalent. Summers are very hot and humid, so trails are only run between March and November. March to April and October to November are usually best for hiking. Binoculars are a must. Advise trail guide of any allergies that you may have, for example, to bee stings. Note that equipment, tented camps and pack-donkeys are not provided for the Primitive Trail, and only the very fit should attempt this option.

Hikers are led by an experienced game ranger on the Umfolozi Wilderness Trail.

This 47 753-ha reserve lies between, and stretches beyond, the White and Black Umfolozi rivers from which it takes its name. Together with the Corridor and Hluhluwe game reserves it is managed as one reserve, about 96 000 ha in extent. The vegetation, thickest along river courses, is composed largely of tamboti and acacia trees. White and black rhino, waterbuck, wildebeest, nyala, kudu, buffalo, giraffe, cheetah, lion and crocodile, as well as many other smaller animals and a diverse birdlife, can be observed.

Umfolozi is a Zulu word embracing the essential qualities displayed by the leader of a span of oxen – courage, strength and patience. Certainly the name is appropriate for this park as it, too, is a leader in its field. To the ecologist and environmental educationalist the name calls to mind a number of worthwhile ventures in nature conservation, but none could have won as much public sympathy as the determined and successful bid to save the white rhino from extinction.

In conjunction with the nearby St Lucia Game Reserve, Umfolozi is also the birthplace of the first South African wilderness trail, and Ian Player, an erstwhile Natal Parks Board ranger and prominent conservationist, is often credited with the wilderness trail concept: 'I knew in the wilderness areas we had resources that were vital to the well-being of the people of the world. These were like a foundation that they could return to for nourishment; a spiritual recreation, something desperately needed in the twentieth century.'

Player founded the Wilderness Leadership School in 1957, and one of his field officers, Clive Walker, the conservationist and famous wildlife artist, founded Educational Wildlife Expeditions in 1975. Rangers who lead their trails are inspired by their love of nature and the firm belief that the only way man will prevent himself from destroying the fragile web of life of which he is part and on which he is so dependent, is to understand nature's balance and respect it.

The Umfolozi Wilderness Trails are led through the old hunting ground of Shaka, founder and king of the Zulu nation during the nineteenth century. The first night and optional last night are spent in the base camp, while the other two nights are spent under canvas in the wilderness area. An optional 4-day trail includes an overnight stop at Dadethu bush camp. The route is not a fixed one: the trails officer usually chooses a route that allows him to walk into the wind and thus not disturb any game; although the pace is set to suit the slowest in

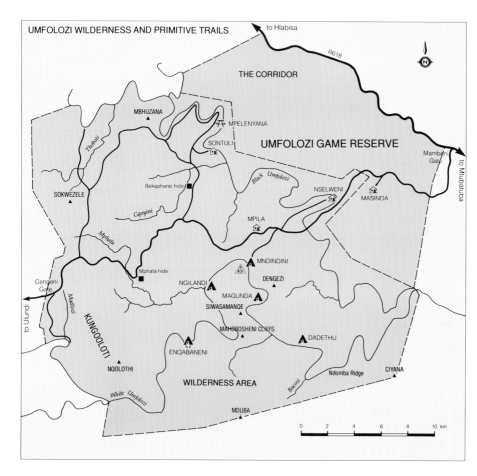

the group, a minimum of 12 km must be walked each day in order to reach the next camp.

The Primitive Trail combines the features of a wilderness trail with a hiking trail; in other words, you carry your backpack with food, clothing and equipment, but the route and overnight stops, in caves or bush enclosures, are not standard and are chosen by the accompanying officer. Novice hikers can rent some equipment from the warden.

---

45. WHITE RHINO TRAIL
UMFOLOZI GAME RESERVE

Trail details: 5-day guided wilderness trail.

Permits/bookings: Wilderness Leadership School, tel. (031) 428642, fax (031) 428675; PO Box 53048, Yellowwood Park 4011. Brochure available on request.

Facilities/amenities: Transport, rucksacks, tents, sleeping bags, groundsheets, meals and utensils are provided by the trail organizers.

Main attractions: Abundant wildlife, including prolific birdlife; historical Zulu traditions; undisturbed habitat and solitude.

Pertinent information: Minimum of 6 and maximum of 8 people per trail (minimum age 15 years). Anti-malaria precautions are recommended. Water must be purified before drinking. Ticks are prevalent. March to November are the best months, as summers are hot and humid with rainfall. Winters are mild, with August being windy.

Operating in the 47 753-ha Umfolozi Game Reserve in Zululand (situated between the White and Black Umfolozi rivers), this well-run and educationally valuable trail incorporates a holistic approach to environmental appreciation with the big game adding excitement to the experience. The reserve is a mosaic of thornveld, grassland and riverine vegetation and is home to white and black rhino, buffalo, lion, leopard, elephant, zebra, wildebeest and giraffe as well as a variety of insects and many bird species. Umfolozi is the cradle of the Zulu empire so the area is rich in history and you can still see the remains of Zulu settlements.

Courses begin and end in Durban, from where trailists are transported to the reserve. There is no set route for the trail as the Wilderness Leadership School adopts minimum impact camping techniques, so no two trails are ever the same.

---

46. HLUHLUWE GAME RESERVE
HLUHLUWE

Trail details: Guided 3-hour walks. Shorter walk also possible. See map page 184.

Permits/bookings: To arrange bookings for accommodation, contact The Natal Parks Board, tel. (0331) 471981; fax (0331) 471980, PO Box 662, Pietermaritzburg 3200.

Maps/information: A general brochure is available at the reserve.

Facilities/amenities: Interpretive programmes, including walks, talks, films and slide shows; game-viewing hide; picnic site where visitors may leave their cars; open-air museum, traditional Zulu homestead; shop for curios, books and film; Hilltop hutted camp: variety of chalets, duplexes, simplexes and rest huts accommodating 710 people (all fully equipped) and restaurant – petrol and oil are available at the camp.

Main attractions: Plentiful and varied wildlife; over 200 species of birds.

Pertinent information: Visitors must provide their own food. Ticks are prevalent. Anti-malaria precautions are advisable. Winter is best for walking as summers are very hot and humid with rainfall. Groups are limited to 8 people.

Located off the N2 (turn off either at Hluhluwe or Mtubatuba), Hluhluwe was established in 1897 and, along with the Umfolozi and St Lucia game reserves, is the oldest existing wildlife sanctuary in South Africa. It is 23 067 ha in area, and along with the Corridor and Umfolozi reserves, forms a 96 000-ha game reserve, making it the third largest game reserve in South Africa. Black and white rhino, elephant, cheetah, nyala, buffalo and giraffe are some of the big game which make their home in this hilly and picturesque reserve.

Giraffe in Hluhluwe, the earliest-established game reserve in South Africa.

Although Hluhluwe is not used as intensively for walking as other Natal game reserves, 3-hour walks in the company of a game guard can be arranged at the reserve. The best time for these walks is in the early morning and late afternoon.

The Mbhombe Forest Trail, a 30-minute walk located at the fringe of the rest camp area, rambles through the semi-deciduous forest.

---

47. UBIZANE GAME RESERVE
HLUHLUWE

Trail details: Various guided 2-hour trails. See map p. 184.

Permits/bookings: Contact Mrs G Christie, tel. (03562) ask for 3602; PO Box 102, Hluhluwe 3960, to book accommodation. Permits available for day visitors, either at the reserve or at Zululand Safari Game Lodge. Brochure available.

Facilities/amenities: Accommodation available in luxurious camp for 12 people, a self-catering bush camp, or Zululand Safari Game Lodge; open-vehicle drives and night drives.

Main attractions: Bushveld; large game; birdlife.

Pertinent information: Anti-malaria precautions are advisable. Summers can be very hot and humid with rainfall.

The 1 700-ha Ubizane Game Reserve is privately owned and located on the road to the Hluhluwe Game Reserve, 1 km from Hluhluwe. The reserve supports game such as white rhino, giraffe, Burchell's zebra, nyala, blue wildebeest, kudu, waterbuck, impala, blesbok and warthog, as well as a variety of smaller mammals and over 400 species of birds. The luxury camp overlooks a fever tree forest.

Guides are available to take visitors on a variety of 2-hour trails through the reserve. The route that the trails take is variable and depends on where game can be spotted on that particular day.

The White Rhino Trail in the Umfolozi Game Reserve is more than just a name.

48. MKUZI GAME RESERVE
MKUZE

Trail details: 1. Fig Forest Trail: 3 km/1,5 hours, self-guided; 2. Several 3-hour guided walks.

Permits/bookings: Reservations for Mantuma Hutted Camp, Rustic Camp, Nhlonhlela Bush Camp and Umkumbi Camp must be made with the Natal Parks Board, tel. (0331) 471981, fax (0331) 471980; PO Box 662, Pietermaritzburg 3200. Reservations for camp and caravan site can be made through The Camp Superintendent, Mkuzi Game Reserve, tel. (0020) ask for 12; Private Bag X550, Mkuze 3965. Permits for day visitors are available at the gate.

Information/maps: Various literature about the reserve is available from the curio shop in the reserve, as well as a comprehensive brochure for the Fig Forest Walk.

Facilities/amenities: Mantuma Hutted Camp with 6 rest huts, 9 bungalows and 2 self-contained cottages: ablution facilities, kitchen and experienced cook available; Rustic Camp with 4 huts: braai facilities; Nhlonhlela Bush Camp with 4 self-contained huts: cook/caretaker in attendance and game guard available for game walks; Umkumbi Camp with 4 self-contained safari tents: cook/caretaker in attendance and game guard available for game walks; camp and caravan site (with ablution block) at entrance gate; petrol sold at entrance gate; curio shop; charcoal and soft drinks can be purchased in reserve.

Main attractions: Diverse and plentiful wildlife typical of northern Zululand; approximately 400 species of birds, including plentiful waterfowl; low-lying thornveld and open, park-like country; 6 permanent game-viewing and birdwatching hides.

Pertinent information: Visitors must provide their own food (camp cooks are available). Anti-malaria precautions are advisable. Summers are hot and humid with rain; winters are pleasantly mild. Hikers could encounter hippos, crocodiles or black rhino and may prefer to be accompanied by a game guard. Accompanied walks must be arranged the day before at the camp.

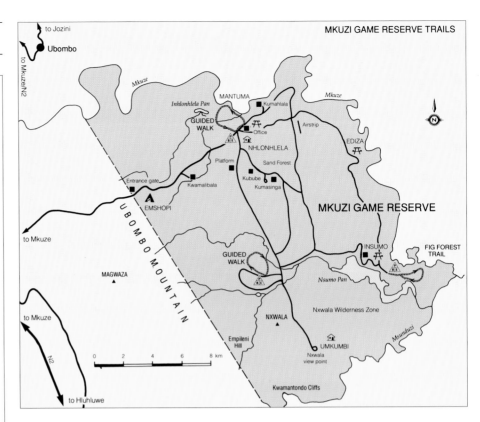

MKUZI GAME RESERVE TRAILS

The 36 000-ha Mkuzi Game Reserve is situated in northern Zululand, off the N2 and about 335 km from Durban. It comprises a variety of bushveld habitats that support black and white rhino, giraffe, nyala, blue wildebeest, warthog, eland, hippo, impala, kudu and other smaller antelope, as well as rare species like cheetah, hyaena, suni and leopard. The four game-viewing hides at Kubube, Kumasinga, Kwamalibala and Kumahlala offer visitors a wonderful opportunity to observe large concentrations of game at waterholes, especially in the dry winter months from June to October. Animals may arrive to drink at the waterholes at any time, however, the largest concentrations of game are usually seen between 9 am and 12 noon. The two bird-watching hides that have been erected next to the Nsumo Pan – Bube and Masinga – are perfect for observing waterfowl in the summer, and for spotting some of the over 400 species of birds found in the reserve. Additional items that may be of use during a stay in the reserve include a torch, a pair of binoculars and a bird identification book.

1. The Fig Forest Trail is a 3-km walk that starts at the car park at Nsumo Pan and is marked by antelope spoor as trail indicators. A short walk through open woodland takes you to the Mkuze River. In winter the river is usually dry enough to walk across, but in summer, when the river may be quite full, there is a suspension bridge that leads you across into the forest of sycamore fig trees. This tree, *Ficus sycomorus,* grows well on the flood plains of the Mkuze River, and the larger trees at Mkuzi have a girth of 12 m and a height of 25 m. Bird-watchers have the opportunity of spotting fruit-eaters like the green pigeon, purplecrested lourie and trumpeter hornbill, as well as Pel's fishing owl, southern banded snake eagle, narina trogon, and insect-eaters like the goldentailed woodpecker and squaretailed drongo. Monkeys and baboons also make their home in the forest and can be seen or heard above in the forest canopy. The trail follows a circular route through the forest and then returns across the Mkuze River flood plain to the car park.

2. Short day walks – about 3 hours in duration – can be arranged in the company of a game guard to various interesting habitats in the reserve.

Game-viewing drives at night can also be arranged one day in advance with the Camp Superintendent. These drives give visitors an excellent opportunity too see nocturnal animals and birdlife.

Viewed from Kumasinga hide in Mkuzi Game Reserve, warthogs take a leisurely drink at the shallow pan.

49. MKUZE BUSHVELD TRAILS
MKUZI GAME RESERVE

Trail details: Guided wilderness trails (number of days flexible).

Permits/bookings: For reservations, contact Mkuze Trails, PO Box 128, Hluhluwe 3960, or phone Ghost Mountain Inn (035662) ask for 18 or 29. You can also book trails through Travel Africa, tel. 080-0112500, fax (011) 8832556; PO Box 781329, Sandton 2146.

Facilities/amenities: Transport to and from base camp provided; Gwala Gwala base camp provides fully equipped tents, cook and all meals, hot and cold water, showers and flush toilet – a vehicle is also available at the camp for game-viewing drives.

Main attractions: Game-viewing; bird-watching; beauty and tranquillity of wilderness.

Pertinent information: The cool, dry winter months are best for walking and game-viewing, while the hot, humid and wet summers are best for bird-watching. You should be fit enough to walk 12–15 km per day. Groups are limited to a maximum of 8 people, and no children are allowed. Anti-malaria precautions are advisable. Cars may be parked at the Ghost Mountain Inn, from where transport will be provided to the base camp.

Emblems of wild Africa, the flattened crowns of umbrella thorn (Acacia tortilis) *stand out against the sunset.*

The Mkuzi Game Reserve is located off the N2 between Hluhluwe and Piet Retief – take the turnoff to Mkuze village – and is 36 000 ha in extent.

Although not as well known as the older Umfolozi Wilderness Trail, the Mkuze Bushveld Trails give participants the opportunity to experience the mood of Africa; to see large herds of mammals such as blue wildebeest and zebra, and also the rare black and white rhino. Birdlife is profuse and includes subtropical visitors and migrant waterfowl that are attracted to the large Nsumo Pan. Some 418 species of birds have been recorded in the reserve. This constitutes roughly 53 per cent of the total number of bird species in South Africa. Binoculars are recommended to enhance both bird-watching and game-viewing.

Walking through Mkuzi, you will notice that it differs from the other nearby game reserves in that it is composed of large, park-like stretches of flat, open country which facilitate game-viewing. Two of the attractive trees in this reserve are the wild wisteria (also known as tree wisteria) and the flame bush. The wild wisteria is deciduous or semi-deciduous and displays beautiful, sweetpea-like, violet-blue flowers among pale green, glossy leaves. In contrast, the flame bush is an evergreen with a crown of shiny green leaves and sprays of tubular scarlet flowers and scarlet fruits. Acacia and marula trees are also prominent.

The trails are flexible and will meet the needs of the particular group. In winter, the day's programme is usually a long walk in the morning and a shorter walk in the afternoon, while in midsummer, walks are shorter and more time is spent bird-watching. A vehicle is available at the camp for night drives and transport to viewing hides.

50. THABA YE ZULU HIKING TRAIL
HLUHLUWE

Trail details: 21 km/1,5 days; self-guided, circular. Longer option available.

Permits/bookings: For bookings and permits, contact Jacana Country Homes and Trails, tel. (012) 3463550/1/2, fax (012) 3462499; PO Box 95212, Waterkloof 0145. Information leaflet available on request.

Facilities/amenities: 16 beds, mattresses, shower and toilet, gas cooker and cooking pots, braais and wood at base camp in old farmhouse; huts with 16 beds and mattresses, donkey boiler, bush toilet, braais and firewood at overnight bush camp; swimming in river.

Main attractions: Cave with old graves; abundant fauna and flora.

Pertinent information: Braai packs can be ordered. Carry plenty of water. High temperatures and humidity in summer with rainfall, so mild winters best for walking. Maximum of 16 people per group.

The trail is on the farms Okalweni and Marcopolo, which form part of the privately owned Msunduzi Conservancy in Zululand. The base camp is located on Okalweni farm, which is 13 km from Hluhluwe off the D464.

Impala, kudu, nyala, duiker, steenbok, reedbuck and baboon can be spotted on the farm, and many species of aloe grow here.

The first day is a 12-km, 6-hour hike from the Okalweni base camp to the overnight bush camp at Marcopolo. The route is marked by white painted rocks and ascends the Thaba Ye Zulu (the mountains of thunder) to a height of 1 788 m. From here you have a superb view of KwaZulu, Zululand and Swaziland and, on a clear day, you can see Nongoma, the Jozini Dam and the Ubombo Mountain range. The trail then descends the mountain into a gorge, past a cave with some interesting relics and

some old graves at the mouth, and follows the Msunduzi River, taking you past cultivated chilli fields, to the overnight camp.

Although Zululand is known for its warm climate, there is ample shade along the route. In summer the river should be full enough to cool off with a swim, or you can have a dip in one of the irrigation dams nearby. For the energetic, there are some sheer cliffs to climb – home to black eagles which nest on the cliffs – and numerous baboons can also be seen in the area.

The second day is an easy 9-km, 3,5- to 4-hour walk through a valley of typical Zululand bushveld and over a smaller hill. The dense vegetation offers the welcome relief of shade on a hot day. After 6 km, the trail splits at a ground dam and you can take the shorter 3-km route across the district road that will lead you back to the base camp, or you can return along a 5-km route. The longer route offers you the opportunity to spot various antelope species that make their home in the conservancy.

Restoration of the coastal dune forest is one of the on-going projects in Sodwana Bay National Park.

51. SODWANA BAY NATIONAL PARK
MBAZWANA, NORTHERN ZULULAND

Trail details: Two dune forest self-guided walks; trail to Ngoboseleni Lake. See map page 184.

Permits/bookings: Booking for camp sites: The Officer in Charge, Sodwana Bay National Park, tel. (035682) 1502; Private Bag 310, Mbazwana 3974. Booking for log cabins: The Natal Parks Board, tel. (0331) 471981, fax (0331) 471980; PO Box 1750, Pietermaritzburg 3200. Information guide available at office in reserve.

Facilities/amenities: Open camping sites (take all your own equipment); 20 log cabins accommodating 130 people; ablution blocks, water and petrol; 15-amp electrical outlets for hire; firewood; freezer space; store on site sells basic food supplies.

Main attractions: Beach with tidal pools; coastal game fishing and scuba diving; small mammals and abundant birdlife; nesting turtles in summer.

Pertinent information: Anti-malaria precautions are necessary; cholera vaccinations are recommended. Summers can be very hot and humid, but winters are pleasantly mild.

Situated 80 km from the N2 after the Ngeni turnoff (from the south) and 120 km from the Jozini/Mbazwana turnoff (from the north), the 413-ha Sodwana Bay National Park is a very popular holiday resort, especially for coastal game fishing and scuba diving; it is also ideal for casual undemanding beach walking. During the summer months of December and January leatherback and loggerhead turtles come onto the beach to nest at night and tours are provided for camp visitors. Bookings can be made at the camp on the afternoon before departure.

Two dune forest routes are interpreted. The bird-life is particularly interesting, with such species as Woodwards' batis and Rudd's apalis being present. Observant walkers can spot a variety of animal life, including suni, red and grey duiker, steenbok, reedbuck, bushpig, the Tonga red squirrel and species of mongoose.

Vehicles with the necessary permit are allowed on beaches, except the swimming beach. However, the stretch of beach between Sodwana Bay and Cape Vidal may not be used as a thoroughfare or alternate route.

The coastal dune forest, the vegetational zone found closest to the shore and lining the estuary, is dominated by Natal strelitzia and wild silver-oak trees. In the early 1950s, in an effort to stabilize the shifting coastal dunes, *Casuarina equisetifolia* trees were planted. These trees, imported from the Far East and Australia, are used for this purpose in many parts of Africa.

Restoration of the mangrove community by methods such as the removal of sediments, re-establishment of the estuarine topography, removal of invasive sedges growing under the existing mangrove trees and planting of black mangrove seedlings, is being implemented. However, it will take many years of work in this area before the delicate natural balance is restored.

52. LAKE SIBAYA NATURE RESERVE
BAYA CAMP, NEAR MBAZWANA

Trail details: 3 km/1,5 hours; self-guided, circular. See map page 184.

Permits/bookings: Reservations for accommodation are to be made through the KwaZulu Bureau of Natural Resources, tel. (0331) 946698, fax (0331) 421984; 367 Loop Street, Pietermaritzburg 3200. Day permits are available at the reserve.

Facilities/amenities: Three 4-bed and four 2-bed units; bedding supplied; cold running water; fully equipped communal kitchen with camp cook; ablution blocks with cold and solar-heated hot water; battery-powered electricity; firewood.

Main attractions: Lake; bird-watching; hides; excellent fishing.

Pertinent information: Summers are hot and humid with rainfall; winters are mild. No swimming is allowed in the lake because of bilharzia and crocodiles. Anti-malaria precautions are necessary.

Baya Camp is situated on the southern shores of Lake Sibaya, South Africa's largest freshwater lake, in the Lake Sibaya Nature Reserve. To get to the camp, follow the Sodwana signs from the N2 to Mbazwana and then follow the signposts to the camp for about 16 km.

Although there is a wide variety of animal life in the reserve including civet, hippo and reedbuck, the area is best known for its birdlife. There are two bird-watching hides situated close to the camp and visitors can observe some of the 279 species of birds that inhabit the lake region, such as cormorants, fish eagles and kingfishers, at their leisure. From the observation platform behind the camp, a 3-km trail leads you through the forest, past the hides and back to the camp again. Arrangements can be made at the reserve to be accompanied by a trail guide.

Its highest levels marked by the barrenness of the sands, a pool near Lake Sibaya gradually shrinks during a dry spell.

53. AMANZIMNYAMA TRAIL
KOSI BAY NATURE RESERVE

Trail details: 34 km/4 days; guided, circular.

Permits/bookings: Reservations should be made through the KwaZulu Bureau of Natural Resources, tel. (0331) 946698, fax (0331) 421984; 367 Loop Street, Pietermaritzburg 3200. Informative leaflets available. Permits for day visitors are available at the reserve.

Facilities/amenities: Accommodation provided at 4 camps: Nhlange base camp, Makawulani tented camp, Bhanga Nek tented camp, and Sihadla hutted camp; beds with mattresses, pots and kettles, gas cooker, ablution facilities and limited drinking water provided.

Main attractions: Kosi Bay lake system, including 247 species of birds; hippos, fish, crocodiles, leatherback and loggerhead turtles; coral reef and mangrove swamps.

Pertinent information: Hikers must supply their own bedding, cutlery, crockery, food, drink and water purification tablets. Anti-malaria precautions should be taken, and mosquitoes can be a problem. Zambezi sharks possible in first lake, and crocodiles and bilharzia make swimming inadvisable. Summers are hot and can be very humid. The minimum age is 8 years, and the maximum number in a group is 10. Short guided walks can also be arranged at the camp.

One of the four freshwater lakes that make up the incomparable feature known as Kosi Bay.

For those willing to venture to the remote north-eastern corner of Zululand, a fascinating experience awaits their arrival. Kosi Bay (not a bay but four interlinked, clear, freshwater lakes in close proximity to the shore, the first of which empties into the sea) is a unique mosaic of interdependent eco-systems. The system stretches over 25 km, therefore the nature reserve on the shore of Nhlange, the third and largest lake, is only a small component. The other lakes include Mpungwini, which is the smallest of the four lakes; Sifungwe, which is four times the size of Mpungwini; and Amanzimnyama, which is located 16 km from the estuary.

Kosi Estuary is the southernmost example of thick mangrove woodlands over large areas. These include all the mangrove species in southern Africa.

The Kosi Bay lake system has 247 species of birds, the most unusual bird of this area being the palmnut vulture which eats, among other things, the husks of the raffia palm and the oil palm. Another inhabitant of the tidal forest is the tiny mudskipper, an amphibious fish which lives on the roots and low branches of mangrove trees. Its fins are shaped so that it can skip over the water's surface, alternating rapidly between swimming and flying. Hippos, fish, crocodiles, leatherback and loggerhead turtles, coral reef and mangrove swamps are other attractions in the area. Tribal customs are also fascinating to observe. With no appropriate soil to use for housing, all huts are built of reeds, and beautiful waterproof basketware is crafted in place of clay utensils.

The Amanzimnyama Trail starts and ends at the Nhlange base camp, which is on the north-western shores of Nhlange Lake. The first day is a short 6-km walk northwards to the Makawulani tented camp. The route passes through scenic coastal forest vegetation and leads to centuries-old traditional fish kraals where the trail guide will demonstrate how they work. Once you reach the camp, an optional further 2-km walk will take you to Kosi Mouth, which is a must for keen snorkellers. The route on the second day takes you 10 km south to Bhanga Nek tented camp and you can choose to walk along the beach or on the dunes passing through the cycad groves. Here, in summer, turtles come up onto the beach at night to nest and you can watch Natal Parks Board guards locate and mark the endangered hatchlings, and then release them into the ocean. The route on the third day is a 7-km walk south to Sihadla hutted camp which takes you through the giant raffia palms. You may spot the Pel's fishing owl or the elusive palmnut vulture. The last day's walk is an 11-km hike back to the base camp through the delicate and fascinating swamp forests.

Shorter guided walks with game scouts have you exploring fig and raffia palm forests, mangrove swamps and marshes and coastal sand dunes with dense bush and milkwood trees. Without a guide, the inexperienced hiker in the bush could just bump into an outraged hippo, and have to struggle through thick, black, glutinous mud in retreat!

To get to the reserve, take the Jozini turnoff from the N2. The entrance is about 13 km from Mangusi.

54. NDUMU GAME RESERVE
JOZINI

Trail details: 5 guided day walks: each about 5 km/2–3 hours. See map p. 184.

Permits/bookings: Reservations for accommodation should be made through the KwaZulu Bureau of Natural Resources, tel. (0331) 946698, fax (0331) 421984; 367 Loop Street, Pietermaritzburg 3200. Book well in advance. Day permits are available at the reserve. Walks should be booked with the Camp Superintendent the day before.

Facilities/amenities: Hutted camp with seven 2-bed huts, ablution facilities, bedding, cutlery and crockery; meals prepared in communal kitchen.

Main attractions: Magnificent birdlife; game; tropical insect species.

Pertinent information: Summers are hot and can be uncomfortably humid. Anti-malaria precautions are advisable. Bilharzia is prevalent. No children under 14 years allowed on walks. Open-vehicle tours also available. Bring your own food and drink.

Ndumu is situated in the far north-eastern part of Zululand, on the Mozambique border, and is 10 117 ha in size. To get to it, take the Jozini turn-off from the N2 and head northwards, following signposts. Ndumu camp is approximately 120 km from Jozini.

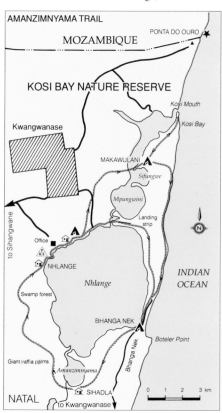

AMANZIMNYAMA TRAIL

MOZAMBIQUE

PONTA DO OURO

KOSI BAY NATURE RESERVE

Kwangwanase

Kosi Mouth

Kosi Bay

MAKAWULANI

Sifungwe

Mpungwini

Landing strip

to Shangwane

Office

N

NHLANGE

Nhlange

INDIAN OCEAN

Swamp forest

BHANGA NEK

Boteler Point

Giant raffia palms

Amanzimnyama

Bhanga Nek

NATAL

SIHADLA

0 1 2 3 km

to Kwangwanase

Visitors to Ndumu Game Reserve cross the Pongola River by this quaint and decidedly rustic suspension bridge.

you can hear the call of the jackal. Look out for eagles soaring above and guineafowl traversing the plains.

The trail is marked by yellow footprints and the first day is an 8-km hike, that will take you 4 to 6 hours, to an overnight hut, Rus-'n-Biekie, which is located next to the Ngwenyama stream. A path leads you past the old homestead up to the present-day residence, where you have a beautiful view of the area. The route then leads you down into a ravine where you can refresh yourself with a swim in the Mathanga waterhole (Mathanga means pumpkin, and the rocks around the waterhole resemble pumpkins). It then climbs to Umkhiwana where you can rest under wild fig trees and admire the view. Another slight climb takes you to Nxala, and the trail is then a level walk to Ingcu-ngcula, where you can climb down to a cave of historical interest. A steep ascent, called Ufudu (tortoise) Pass as you are likely to encounter a tortoise here, then leads you down to where the Hlangana and Ngwenyama streams cross. You can walk through or next to Ngwenyama stream – and enjoy a swim in Uxama and Intini waterholes – until you reach the overnight hut. The second day is an easier 4-km walk that will take you about 3 hours and leads you back to the base camp. The route, which offers a breathtaking view of the area, passes a game farm, so look out for buck and other game, and also visits a fenced-off old mica mine and some old Zulu graves.

56. MKHAYA TRAIL
PONGOLA

Trail details: 27 or 30 km/ 1,5 to 2 days; self-guided, circular. Optional extra 12-km/1-day trail possible.

Permits/bookings: Bookings are to be made through Mrs de Swardt, tel. (03841) 41105/41076; PO Box 734, Pongola 3170. A map is available on request.

Facilities/amenities: Accommodation at base and overnight camps in rondavels and huts; both camps are fully equipped with hot and cold water, but overnight camp does not have electricity.

Main attractions: Interesting trees; historical sites; birds and game.

Pertinent information: Best months for walking are March to November, as summers can be hot and humid with rainfall and late afternoon thunderstorms. Maximum number of people per group is 18.

The Mkhaya Trail is situated on Paradise Farm in the Louwsberg district, 43 km south west of Pongola. The vegetation types are middleveld to bushveld, and the largest *Acacia sieberana* in South Africa is located on the farm. The area is steeped in Zulu history and you will find old Zulu kraals here. Of special interest is the rock where Dingaan slept on his flight to Swaziland, as well as the koppie where his impi slept. A variety of buck, such as kudu and red duiker, as well as numerous species of birds, like the green pigeon, black eagle and secretary bird, also make their homes here.

The trail is marked by footprints painted on rocks and markers on trees, and generally follows an undulating course with a fairly steep climb to Uvundhla Mountain. The first day is an 18-km,

It is the reserve for the avid bird-watcher as here, many bird species from East Africa, such as the African broadbill, yellowspotted nicator and white-eared barbet, reach the southernmost limit of their distribution, thereby making the region unique in South Africa. Largely low-lying and well-watered, with numerous pans and the Pongola-Usutu floodplain, Ndumu is also a haven for water-dependent birds such as the black heron, pygmy goose, fish eagle and fishing owl, as well as numerous waders.

The guided walks are located in different habitats, and are geared for bird-watchers, who can ramble slowly through riverine forests and bush, alert for any moving creature. My game guard was able to 'call up' several species, including the narina trogon and chorister robin.

Ndumu Hill (115 m) is covered with Acacia trees. Mammals inhabiting the semi-evergreen scrub forest and swampy grassland of Ndumu include hippo, nyala, bushbuck, impala, grey and red duiker, reedbuck, zebra, white and black rhino, bushpig and suni.

55. NGWENYAMA TRAIL
MAGUDU

Trail details: 12 km/1,5 days; self-guided, circular.

Permits/bookings: For bookings: N Potgieter, tel. (03841) 41148/41174; PO Box 685, Pongola 3170.

Facilities/amenities: Base camp hut and overnight hut with mattresses, shower, toilet, braai and firewood; fishing; swimming; horse-riding.

Main attractions: Cave and old mica mine with historical interest; small game.

Pertinent information: Maximum of 12 hikers at any one time. May to February are the best months. Ticks are prevalent.

The farm Welverdiend is situated 45 km south-west of Pongola and 25 km west of Magudu in the vicinity of the Mkuze River valley, and is a contrast of lowveld vegetation and the grasslands of higher ground. Duiker, reedbuck, steenbok and rhebok can be spotted on the plains or on the ridge, and at night

An eyrie-like bedroom unit of Mhlangeni Bush Camp looks out over the rugged riverine grandeur of Itala Game Reserve.

8-hour walk from the base camp at the homestead to the overnight camp in the bushveld, that will take you through middleveld, up the mountain, where you have a wonderful view of the area, down into the lowveld. An easier 9-km, 3-hour walk will take you back to the base camp on the second day. For the more energetic, an optional 3-km extension has been made to this route. Hikers can stay an extra night at the overnight camp and walk a 12-km circular route in the lowveld on the second day.

57. ITALA GAME RESERVE
LOUWSBURG

Trail details: 1. Various conducted day walks with game scout are available; 2. 3-day/4-night guided wilderness trails.

Permits/bookings: Bookings for bush camps: The Officer in Charge, Itala Game Reserve, tel. (0388) 75248/2; PO Box 42, Louwsburg 3150. Bookings for Ntshondwe Camp: The Natal Parks Board, tel. (0331) 471981, fax (0331) 471980; PO Box 662, Pietermaritzburg 3200. Bookings for the wilderness trails should also be made through the Natal Parks Board. Reservations for accompanied walks are to be made at the reserve the day before.

Facilities/amenities: 3 bush camps accommodating 4, 8 and 10 people (Thala, Mbizo and Mhlangeni); all fully equipped, game guard available by prior arrangement; camping site with cold water ablutions, flush toilets and communal kitchen; fully equipped, self-catering chalets and a luxury lodge at Ntshondwe Camp, plus a restaurant, bar, take-away kiosk, curio shop, swimming pool, conference and mini-supermarket.

Main attractions: Large variety of reintroduced game; great variety of scenery; over 400 recorded species of birds.

Pertinent information: Due to the introduction of dangerous animals, hikers are not permitted to walk on their own. No food or drink available at the bush camps or camp site. Anti-malaria precautions are advisable in the low country. Ticks can be a problem. Winter temperatures can fall way below zero at night. Summers tend to be hot.

This 29 651-ha reserve is located in the Pongola River Valley, and is reached on the R69 from Vryheid to Louwsberg. The Pongola River forms the northern border of the reserve, and several tributaries flow through the area, which is a mosaic of grassed hilltops dotted with aloes, steep valleys, open woodland savannah and bushveld.

Many large game species have been reintroduced in the area, including elephant, Cape buffalo and giraffe. The reserve is also home to impala, reedbuck, kudu, waterbuck, nyala, eland, blue wildebeest, warthog, Burchell's zebra, black and white rhino and crocodile. You can spot dassies and klipspringers on hilltops, and, if you are very lucky, you may catch a glimpse of a cheetah, leopard or hyena. For bird-watchers, the varied habitats attract over 400 species of birds.

1. A variety of guided walks through the reserve can be arranged, the length and duration of the walk and the vicinity in which it is conducted depends on where game can be spotted on a particular day and on the needs of a particular group.

2. Through the wonderland of Itala, the Natal Parks Board runs wilderness trails on demand, for 3 days and 4 nights. Eight people per trail supply their own food and sleep in beautiful bush camps along the river. Children under the age of 12 years are not permitted, and those under the age of 16 should be accompanied by a parent or guardian.

This bird's eye view over Itala is to be seen from Ntshondwe Camp.

58. NTENDEKA WILDERNESS AREA
NGOME STATE FOREST, NEAR VRYHEID

Trail details: Various circular and open-ended trails, the shortest an 8-km/3,5-hour open-ended walk (or 16-km circular route) and the longest a 28-km/1-day, open-ended trail.

Permits/bookings: For bookings and permits, apply to The Forester, Ngome State Forest, tel. (0386) 71883; Private Bag X9306, Vryheid 3100.

Facilities/amenities: Bridle paths; camp sites at fringes of wilderness with hot and cold water, toilets, thatched lapa with a large table; camping permitted for wilderness users only.

Main attractions: Indigenous forest, grassland and savannah; epiphytic orchids and rare and endangered plants and fauna; birdlife; Ntendeka cliffs; historic site.

Pertinent information: This wilderness area forms part of Ngome State Forest. The area experiences mild winters, and hot, wet, misty summers. Mists can occur suddenly in the summer. Maximum of 12 people per overnight group. At the time of going to press all state forests were being privatized and therefore the future of this trail and who the controlling authority would be was unknown.

Ntendeka Wilderness Area is a 5 230-ha reserve that is located on the R618 to Nongoma. Its principal conservation value is its indigenous high forest, exceptionally rich in plant life that exhibits strong tropical elements, unusual for an area far from the sea. This tropical environment is created by the interaction of numerous physical factors, such as the substantial annual summer rainfall, the cool, moist winds of winter, and the steep south-east-facing forested slopes which receive little frost or sun and are dissected by perennial streams.

Some of the interesting plants to look out for are *Didymochlaena truncatula*, a large fern, with 2,5-m, glossy dark green fronds, found in wet, shady kloofs, and the forest tree fern, *Alsophila capensis*. Although the forest tree fern also

197

grows in the southern Cape, it reaches the unusual height of 8 m only along the streams of Ngome.

Epiphytic ferns, more often associated with tropical jungle, also abound in the forests of the Ntendeka wilderness. Look for them above the ground, on moss-covered tree bark or in humus-filled tree cracks, as these micro-habitats are their sole source of water and nutrients. The area contains other rare species such as terblans (a tree member of the Proteaceae), bastard stinkwood, *Ocotea kenyensis*, and endemics such as the Ngome lily; both species have limited distributions.

The forest, as well as the lower, tropical grassland and savannah region of the reserve, provide good and varied habitats for many birds, including the bronze-naped pigeon, narina trogon, purple-crested lourie, longcrested and crowned eagle and the endangered bald ibis and blue swallow.

Mammals such as bushbuck, blue and grey duiker, samango monkey and vervet monkey are also prevalent. The area is rich in Zulu history and, prior to 1905, its timber, especially yellowwood, was heavily exploited.

The erosion of Peruvian Ecca sandstones of the Karoo System reveals a dolerite intrusion that forms the impressive Ntendeka cliffs (approximately 1 350 m). The rock shelter known as Cetshwayo's Refuge, situated under one of these majestic cliffs, is said to have been the place where Cetshwayo, last independent king of the Zulus, took shelter when fleeing from the British who were eventually to defeat him.

Although the wilderness area is not as well known as some others, nature lovers will be well rewarded by a visit. Several paths lead into the forest from the Ngome Forest Station. Attractive camping spots can be found in the valleys near the streams, outside the wilderness area.

The trails are marked by metal signposts at strategic junctions, and vary both in length and exertion level.

59. LANCASTER HIKING TRAIL
VRYHEID NATURE RESERVE

Trail details: 13 km/1 day; self-guided, open-ended, with variations.

Permits/bookings: Bookings to be made through Municipality of Vryheid, tel. (0381) 812133, fax (0381) 809637; PO Box 57, Vryheid 3100.

Maps/information: A map is available on request at the reserve.

Facilities/amenities: Picnic sites; toilet; bird-watching hide.

Main attractions: A variety of game; mountain scenery; plantations.

Pertinent information: An overnight hut is being planned. Summer rainfall area.

The reserve is situated on the R33 between Vryheid and Paulpietersburg and is 730 ha of grasslands and forested slopes. Eland, Burchell's zebra, oribi, impala, mountain reedbuck, bushbuck, blesbok and springbok wander through the grasslands on the plateau, and the area is also of historical interest.

The trail is marked by footprints and begins at the entrance gate, from where it follows an old wagon trail, that was built by the British soldiers during the Anglo-Boer War, up onto the plateau to

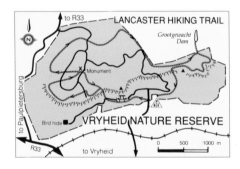

Lt Col Gawne's monument and then on to the North Gun Point, which was also built by the British. At the monument, there is an alternative route that will take you along the escarpment, offering a panoramic view of the surrounding area, and then return you to where the original trail reached the escarpment. From there it is a short walk back to the entrance gate. At North Gun Point the trail leaves the reserve and continues for another 4 km to the end point at Grootgewacht Dam. Alternatively, you can return to the entrance gate via another route that traverses the escarpment in the western part of the reserve.

An overnight hut is being planned, and the trail will be extended to 2 days.

60. BALELE HIKING TRAIL
UTRECHT

Trail details: 25 km/1,5 days; self-guided, circular.

Permits/bookings: Arrangements to walk the trail to be made through the Town Council of Utrecht, tel. (03433) 3041, fax (03433) 4312; PO Box 11, Utrecht 1980. Permit must be obtained from Balele Recreation Resort when you arrive. Brochure with map available.

Facilities/amenities: 12-bed base camp in Old Weltevreden House, with coal stove, tables, chairs, running hot and cold water, toilets, braai facilities and firewood, pots and pans, gas lamps and lanterns; overnight camp of 2 traditional beehive huts containing 12 mattresses, open cooking facilities and firewood, toilets, lanterns, drinking water, and pots and pans.

Main attractions: Remains of water furrows; large variety of indigenous trees, birds, flowers and game; 3 waterfalls; perennial mountain streams; unique rock formations.

Pertinent information: Maximum of 12 people per group. Ticks can be a problem. The trail is fairly demanding and should not be undertaken by the unfit. This is a summer rainfall area, and summers are generally hot with thunderstorms. Winters are cold with frost.

The trail is situated in the Enhlanzeni Valley in the Balele mountain range, and the starting point is about 3 km from Utrecht on the Utrecht/Wakkerstroom road. The vegetation in the valley is savannah grassveld, and the Balele Mountains are covered with aloes and a variety of indigenous trees. Keep a watchful eye out for bushbuck, baboons, dassies, duiker and steenbok.

Hikers should report to the officer in charge at the Balele Recreation Resort, and then spend the night at the Weltevreden base camp. The first day is about an 8-km walk to the overnight camp. The remains of an old furrow dating back to 1860 can be seen at the beginning of the trail, and the route then leads you up the valley to a suspension bridge across Dorpspruit, which was enlarged by the cyclone Demoina in 1984. You then follow an old Voortrekker road which will take you up to the overnight camp. There you can leave your haversacks, and take a short walk to the waterfall behind the camp, where you can rest in the beautiful surroundings and revitalize yourself in the fresh mountain water. The water here, and in the numerous mountain streams *en route*, is both safe and refreshing to drink. A 3,7-km walk further up the

Erosion-striated sandstone cliffs rise above the wealth of vegetation types in Ntendeka Wilderness Area.

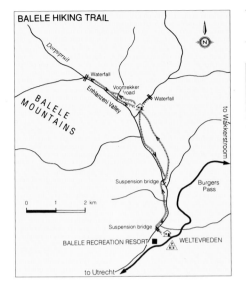

BALELE HIKING TRAIL

kloof the next day will take you to another two waterfalls where you can take an exhilarating shower in the cold mountain water. You then return to the overnight camp and follow a footpath to the suspension bridge (an easier and more straightforward route than the Voortrekker road), from where the trail follows the same course as the first day and returns you to Weltevreden.

61. BUSHMAN KRANS HIKING TRAILS
NEWCASTLE

Trail details: 3 circular routes.

Permits/bookings: For bookings contact G Conradie, tel. (03431) 53318; PO Box 1849, Newcastle 2940. Brochure and map available.

Facilities/amenities: Base camp at old farm homestead that can accommodate 30 people: bathrooms with hot and cold water and showers, beds, firewood, braai facilities, kitchen with stove, fridge, pots and kettles.

Main attractions: Indigenous forests; Bushman paintings; birds of prey; some game.

Pertinent information: Summers are warm with rainfall. The best months for walking are March to May. Ticks are prevalent in summer.

The trails are situated in the Normandien area in the foothills of the Drakensberg, 30 km from Newcastle and are designed to suit the more experienced hiker as well as the beginner. The interlinking routes, marked by arrows, wind through indigenous forest where you will find yellowwood trees and cliffs, and the two more difficult walks will take you past Bushmanskrans. Wooden rungs like footholds are believed to have been used by Bushmen to reach a beehive at the top of the krans. Troops of baboons and monkeys roam the area, and bushbuck, rhebok and duiker also make their home here. Look out for crowned and black eagles, and jackal buzzards soaring overhead. Many Bushman paintings, which, sadly, have been vandalized over the years, can be found at Bushmanskrans, and there is also a point on the escarpment from where you can see all three provinces – Inkwelo Mountain in Natal, Majuba Mountain in the Transvaal and the Orange Free State.

62. GEELHOUT TRAIL
NEWCASTLE

Trail details: 23 km/2 days; self-guided, circular.

Permits/bookings: Reservations are to be made through Glendale Farm, tel. (03435) 640; PO Box 1901, Newcastle 2940. Brochure available on request.

Facilities/amenities: 10-bed base camp with electricity, showers and toilets, stove and refrigerator/freezer; 10-bed overnight hut with drinking water and bush toilets; braai facilities at both camps.

Main attractions: Indigenous vegetation; abundant game and birdlife.

Pertinent information: Temperatures are moderate and rain falls in the summer. The best months for hiking are September to May. There is a fire hazard in the winter months of July and August. Maximum number per group is 10.

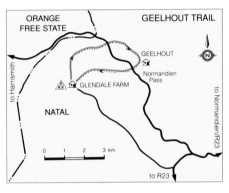

GEELHOUT TRAIL

Glendale Farm is situated in the foothills of the Drakensberg, about 50 km from Newcastle, in the Normandien area, and is 2 500 ha in extent. At Normandien there is a landing strip for private aircraft.

The farm has been conserved as a private wilderness area for many years and has a rich variety of indigenous trees and shrubs, including Natal bottlebrush, the cabbage tree, sugarbush, and Outeniqua yellowwood. A large number of game, including bushbuck, mountain reedbuck, blesbok, black wildebeest, oribi and duiker, as well as baboons, monkeys, caracal, serval and bushpig, make their home here, and the keen bird-watcher can spot more than one species of eagle, secretarybirds, honeybirds and storks.

Footprints and arrows mark the mountainous trail, which winds through an indigenous forest and leads you over streams with a few waterfalls to the overnight camp on the first day – a 12-km walk that will take about 5 hours.

The overnight hut is located next to the Normandien Pass, which leads on to Memel.

Although the 11-km route followed on the second day is shorter, it is more strenuous as it climbs to a plateau where it leads you into another indigenous forest and then back to the base camp.

63. MPATI HILL HIKING TRAIL
DUNDEE

Trail details: 3 self-guided, circular routes: 11 km, 16 km and 19 km – 1- or 2-day trail.

Permits/bookings: Reservations are to be made through Jacana Country Homes and Trails, tel. (012) 3463550, fax (012) 3462499; PO Box 5212, Waterkloof 0145. Brochure available on request. Bookings for rondavels are to be made through Dundee Municipality, tel. (0341) 22121 ext. 247; PO Box 76, Dundee 3000.

Facilities/amenities: 2 rondavels at Dundee Municipal Caravan Park are available for hikers: full ablution facilities; beds and mattresses; parking available at caravan park; overnight camp in 2-bedroom mountain cottage: beds and mattresses, full ablution facilities with cold showers, braais and firewood, pots and cooking utensils – there is no lighting at the overnight camp.

Main attractions: Battle sites; wattle plantations; game; superb views.

Pertinent information: Summers can be very hot with rainfall and thunderstorms; winters can be very cold with frost. October is the best month for walking. Maximum of 12 people per group.

Mpati Hill is where the 'Long Tom' was set up during the Anglo-Boer War, and it is situated in the foothills of the Biggarsberg. The trail, which is suitable for the unfit or inexperienced, begins in the Dundee Municipal Caravan Park and meanders about 4 km through typical Natal grassland, across streams, through indigenous forest and then reaches the overnight hut, Chase Cottage, which is set next to a mountain stream in a big wattle plantation. From there, three circular routes, that all lead you back to the overnight hut, give you the option of a 3-km, 8-km or 11-km hike. In spring, bottlebrush and aloes in flower are a lovely sight, and along

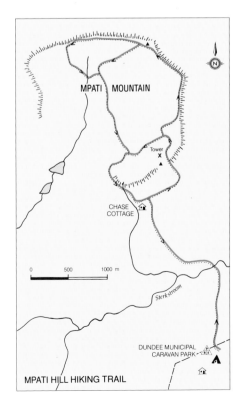

MPATI HILL HIKING TRAIL

with stopping to admire the magnificent views, hikers can look out for buck, dassies and a pair of black eagles that nest in the area. From the overnight hut, the same 4-km route takes you back to the caravan park. Hikers may walk any of the three options in one day and return to the caravan park, or stay overnight at Chase Cottage and walk a second trail the next day.

64. TALANA TRAIL
DUNDEE

Trail details: About 3,5 km/2-hours; return.

Permits/bookings: Contact the Dundee Publicity Association, tel. (0341) 22654, fax (0341) 23856; Private Bag X2024, Dundee 3000 for more information. Entrance fee for museum gives you access to the trail.

Facilities/amenities: Talana House Museum with military displays of the early inhabitants of the area, the Voortrekkers, the Anglo-Zulu and Anglo-Boer Wars; Walk 'n Tape tours available.

Main attractions: Museum and historical remains on Talana Hill.

Pertinent information: This is a fairly steep walk. The museum and trail are open 7 days a week.

The first battle of the Anglo-Boer War was at Talana, and saw British troops wearing khaki for the first time. The informative and interesting Talana Museum is housed in 10 buildings, eight of which are the original farm buildings from the late 19th century. From the museum, the steep Talana Trail follows the advance of the British troops up Talana Hill, and leads to the remains of two British forts on the top of the hill. The route is a clearly defined path that is marked by white stones. You should allow about 2 hours to climb the hill and return to the museum.

65. ORIBI HIKING TRAIL
BIGGARSBERG CONSERVANCY

Trail details: 29-km/2-day circular trail in the company of a game guard.

Permits/bookings: Reservations and permit obtainable from Jacana Country Homes and Trails, tel. (012) 3463550, fax (012) 3462499; PO Box 95212, Waterkloof 0145. Brochure with map available, or telephone (0345) 352 or 670 or 708.

Facilities/amenities: Gartmore Trail Hut as base camp accommodates 24: bathroom with hot and cold water, outside toilet, electricity, firewood and braai facilities, parking in an old wagon shed; overnight camp at Inkruip House accommodates 12 people: beds and mattresses, bathroom with toilet and hot and cold water, braai facilities.

Main attractions: Bushman paintings; archaeological finds; rich variety of flora, including over 70 identified tree species; more than 270 bird species; buck and smaller mammals.

Pertinent information: Hikers must provide their own sleeping bags. Thunderstorms in the summer and hot days, while winters are cold. Ticks can be a nuisance, and watch out for snakes. Carry water; however, water in the streams is free of bilharzia. A maximum of 12 people in a group; arrangements can be made to accommodate a bigger group.

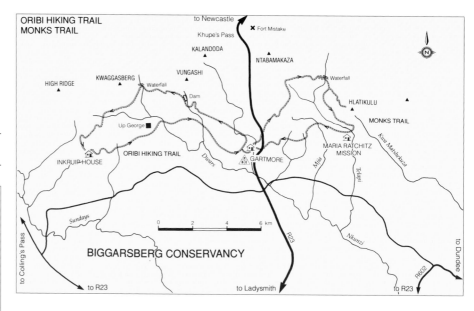

The Oribi Hiking Trail traverses the 13 400-ha Biggarsberg Conservancy which is located between Ladysmith and Newcastle, and starts at Gartmore Farm, which is on the Collingspass road off the R23. The area is steeped in history and stone implements from the Middle Stone Age and tools from the Iron Age have been found here. There is also evidence of the Nguni clans who used to inhabit the area, and Bushman paintings can be found under stone krantzes. The mountain flora is rich and fascinating and over 70 tree species have been identified. A wide variety of snakes inhabit the area, and adders and rinkhals are poisonous, so walk carefully. Oribi, rhebok, impala, mountain reedbuck, steenbok and duiker can be seen on the grass-covered slopes of the hills in the early morning or late afternoon, and at night you can hear or see blackbacked jackal, porcupine, Cape fox, serval, African wildcat, caracal and antbear. Monkeys and baboons live mainly in the forest, while near the water you may find the whitetailed mongoose, spotted necked otter and Cape clawless otter. Dassies are often seen sunning themselves on rocks, but the spotted genet, striped weasel, striped polecat, aardwolf and ground squirrel are inhabitants that are rarely seen. Over 270 species of birds have been spotted in the area as well.

The first day, the 17-km trail ascends the Vungashi Mountain and leads you to a dam where you can stop under the pine trees for breakfast. From there the route will take you through flat open grassland, paddocks, indigenous forest, and past marshes and will climb the Inkruip Mountain across the Dwars River. A final descent will lead you to the overnight camp at Inkruip House. There are some fairly steep climbs and descents along the route, and spectacular views of the area. The 12-km route on the second day is a shorter but also strenuous trail that climbs towards the Kwaggasberg, transcends the Indanyana Mountain and then continues along the back of the Vungashi Mountain. The final stretch is a walk through paddocks back to Gartmore Farm. Hikers should be fit to tackle this trail.

Route markers are yellow-painted hamerkop birds interspersed by white-washed rocks.

The black eagle, graceful in flight, favours mountainous or hilly terrain.

The Drakensberg foothills provide superb walking country.

66. MONKS TRAIL
BIGGARSBERG CONSERVANCY AREA, NEAR DUNDEE

Trail details: 21-km/2-day circular trail in company of game guard, with extra 5-km variation.

Permits/bookings: Reservations are to be made through Jacana Country Homes and Trails, tel. (012) 3463550, fax (012) 3462499; PO Box 95212, Waterkloof 1045. Or telephone (0345) 22968.

Facilities/amenities: Base camp with beds and mattresses, bathroom and toilet, hot water, and braai facilities with firewood; overnight camp with beds, mattresses, toilet, water, wood and braai facilities; both camps accommodate 24 people.

Main attractions: Maria Ratchitz Mission; waterfall; birdlife.

Pertinent information: Summers are hot, with thunderstorms. Watch out for snakes. Ticks can also be a problem. Maximum of 16 people permitted per group.

The Monks Trail traverses privately owned land in the Biggarsberg Conservancy in northern Natal. The base camp, like the Oribi Hiking Trail, is situated on Gartmore Farm, which is off the R23 from Ladysmith to Newcastle. Up to 250 species of birds have been recorded in the area, and oribi, grey rhebok, impala, mountain reedbuck, steenbok and duiker, as well as other smaller mammals, are also present. The rich mountain flora is especially lovely in spring when proteas, red-hot pokers, harebells and crocuses are in bloom.

The trail is marked by either a large stone, a pile of stones, or painted green stones. The 12-km,

6,5-hour route on the first day will take you to the overnight camp, which is a dormitory in the old Maria Ratchitz Mission (built by Trappist monks at the end of the 18th century).

Initially the trail leads you through some cultivated fields and pastures; it then ascends the slopes of a large plateau, passing through grassland interspersed by acacia thorn trees and a wide variety of indigenous bush in the kloofs. From the short grassland on the plateau, the trail descends through indigenous forest to a waterfall on the Telapi River, an ideal place to rest. An extra 5 km hike can be undertaken by the energetic to the Monk's Cross at the top of Hlatikulu Mountain – the highest peak in

Natal outside the Drakensberg – and down again to rejoin the trail. From the waterfall, the trail meanders down to the mission, following the original trail that the monks who built the mission in 1886 used.

The second day's hike is a shorter 9 km that should take you about 4,5 hours. From the mission, the trail descends into the Telapi River Valley, follows the river for a while through grassland interspersed with acacia trees, and then joins a farm track which leads to the Mjia Stream. The trail then undulates over a saddle and down to the Nkunzi River, where a short walk through some gum trees leads you back to the base camp.

Notoriously sluggish, puff adders enjoy basking in sunny spots.

NATAL DRAKENSBERG
AND LESOTHO

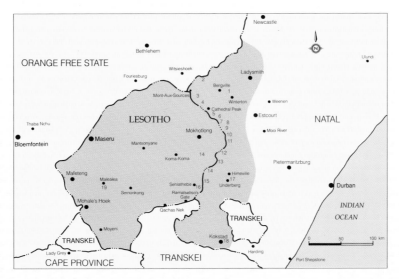

Quathlamba, a barrier of upward-pointing spears, is the Zulu name for the craggy pinnacles that form the most spectacular section of the Great Escarpment, southern Africa's major watershed. No less apt is the Dutch-derived 'Drakensberg' meaning 'mountain of the dragon', for the forbidding, jagged peaks seem a natural domain for these fabled creatures.

The Drakensberg, the highest mountain range in southern Africa, is noted for its magnificent buttresses and peaks. The numerous trails which traverse the Little 'Berg, with its enchanting waterfalls and pools and lush, forested gorges, have a magnetic attraction for mountaineers and hikers, while the magnificent views from the escarpment lure those with an adventurous spirit. Here, the summer heat is tempered by altitude and the occasional spectacular after-noon thunderstorm; the very cold winters cap the peaks in snow.

Lesotho, often referred to as the 'kingdom in the sky', is a relatively undeveloped country unexplored by hikers since it is sparsely but evenly populated by rural pastoralists and offers virtually no facilities for trailists. However, the adventurous hiker is sure to be excited by the mountaineering and trailing freedom offered in this rugged terrain. The trailist can discover, on horseback, the rich cultural heritage of the Basotho people and observe the flora and fauna unique to this mountainous region, including the only breeding population of bearded vulture in southern Africa.

All visitors to Lesotho must be in possession of a valid passport; some nationals, other than South African citizens, may also need visas. Non-South African passport holders must remember to obtain a re-entry visa for returning to South Africa. Liquor and military-like clothing or camouflage clothing should never be carried across the border. Other than in areas well away from human habitation, never drink unpurified or unboiled water.

Lesotho is a land of winter sunshine. Cloudless warm days and crisp, cold nights (often with frost) prevail from May to September. Winter also brings snow, so be prepared for intense cold; however, unseasonal snow can fall at any time of year. Summer is the rainy season with more than 85 per cent of the annual rainfall occurring between October and April.

LEFT: *Mnweni Pass winds its picturesque way beneath towering rocky walls.*

203

1. SPIOENKOP NATURE RESERVE
WINTERTON

Trail details: 1. Spioenkop Discovery Trail:
10 km/5 hours, circular; 2. Spioenkop Battlefield
Trail: 1 km/30 minutes, circular. Both are
self-guided.

Permits/bookings: Reservations for accommodation
and for the ferry to Ntenjwa rustic camp are to be
made through the Natal Parks Board, tel. (0331)
471891, fax. (0331) 471980; PO Box 662,
Pietermaritzburg 3200. Bookings for the camp and
caravan site are to be made through The Camp
Manager, tel. (03648) 81578; PO Box 140,
Winterton 3340.

Maps/information: Information and maps for the
trails are available at the reserve.

Facilities/amenities: There are 24 fully equipped
chalets at the reserve; Ntenjwa rustic camp has
accommodation for 8 people in A-frame structures
and provides hot and cold water, showers, toilet,
refrigerator, gas stove, cooking utensils, cutlery and
crockery; canoes and lock-up garages are available.
The reserve also has 30 camp and caravan sites;
picnic sites; watersports on the dam, and land
sports also available.

Main attractions: Game park; historical areas;
aloes in bloom.

Pertinent information: Bring your own food and
drink. The rustic camp can only be reached by
ferry, or a long 14-km walk. This is a summer
rainfall area. Access to the reserve is via the R74
from Bergville or Winterton.

*The vast spaces of the Drakensberg Amphitheatre lie between a hiker and the distant
blue of the Eastern Buttress in the Royal Natal National Park.*

The 4 562-ha Spioenkop Nature Reserve is 35 km
from Ladysmith and 14 km from Winterton, in the
foothills of the Drakensberg. The area was the
scene of numerous battles during the Boer War, including the Battle of Spioenkop, and is also the site
of a Late Iron Age settlement, so a walk in this
reserve is definitely recommended for those interested in history. Mountain reedbuck, steenbok, grey
duiker, kudu and hares can be spotted by the quiet

and observant hiker, as well as birds like the pied
barbet, forktailed drongo and neddicky.

Guided walks with a game guard can be arranged
at the reserve. Instead of using the ferry, the energetic can also arrange to walk to or from Ntenjwa
rustic camp – about a 14-km walk through open,

mixed woodland, sometimes along the shoreline of
the dam, and through thickets of riverine thorn
scrub. There isn't a clearly defined trail, and you
should carry plenty of water and allow a whole day
for this lengthy walk.

1. The Spioenkop Discovery Trail is an overall introduction to the ecology of the region. It is really
two trails in one: the first loop is 4 km/2 hours, and
is marked with yellow arrows. The second loop is
6 km and will take 3 to 4 hours to walk. It is
marked with red arrows and extends the first loop
to include the shoreline of the Spioenkop Dam.
From the car park, the trail passes through typical
thornveld country which is dominated by acacia
trees and aloes, which are magnificent when they
are in bloom. The trail then leads into the two
loops, neither of which is a strenuous walk, but
there are a few short, steep inclines and declines. A
booklet is available for the trail that will explain
points of interest like the water life line, areas of
erosion, and the Late Iron Age settlement – all of
which are situated on the first loop.
2. A booklet is also available to guide you around
the site of the **Battle of Spioenkop**, which took
place on 24 January 1900 when the British tried, un-
successfully, to relieve the siege of Ladysmith. You
can see the remains of the trench that the British
built and the graves of both British and Boer. Drive
to the summit of Spioenkop, where there is a car
park. Although this interesting trail is very short, it
is a climb around and up to the summit and then
down the other side and back to the car park, so it
is quite strenuous.

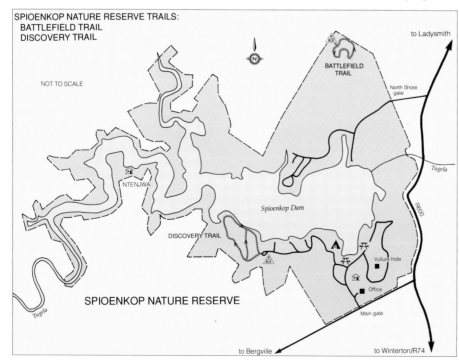

SPIOENKOP NATURE RESERVE TRAILS:
  BATTLEFIELD TRAIL
  DISCOVERY TRAIL

NOT TO SCALE

NTENJWA

BATTLEFIELD
TRAIL

to Ladysmith

North Shore
gate

Tugela

Spioenkop Dam

DISCOVERY TRAIL

Vulture hide

Office

SPIOENKOP NATURE RESERVE

Tugela

Main gate

to Bergville

to Winterton/R74

2. THE ROYAL NATAL NATIONAL PARK
BERGVILLE

Trail details: 1. A variety of short walks from Mahai, ranging in duration from 3 km/1 hour to 14 km/6 hours, return; 2. Tugela Gorge Walk: 14 km/5 hours, return; 3. Two more walks beginning from the Tugela River car park: 6 km/ 2 hours; 9 km/3,5 hours, return; 4. Otto's Walk: 3 km/1 hour, return; 5. The Lion Buttress Trail: 7 km/3 hours, return; 6. Rugged Glen to Mahai Hike: 14 km/5–6 hours, one way. All are self-guided.

Permits/bookings: Bookings for Tendele hutted camp are to be made through the Natal Parks Board, tel. (0331) 471981, fax. (0331) 471980; PO Box 662, Pietermaritzburg 3200. Bookings for Mahai and Rugged Glen camp sites: Officer in Charge, tel. (0364) 381803, PO Mont-aux-Sources 3353. Reservations for the Royal Natal National Park Hotel: tel. (0364) 381051 or write to PO Mont-aux-Sources 3353. Contact the Drakensberg Publicity Association, tel. (0364) 481557, fax. (0364) 481562; PO Box 12, Bergville 3350 for information on hotels just outside the park.

Maps/information: Permit, brochure and contour map available at the park, plus the Natal Parks Board's booklet describing all the walks and all their variations.

Facilities/amenities: Tendele hutted camp can accommodate up to 114 people in 3-, 5- and 6-bed bungalows/chalets; the luxurious Tendele Lodge accommodates 6 people; Mahai camp site caters for 400 campers and caravanners, while Rugged Glen camp site caters for 45 visitors – both camps provide ablution facilities; the 2-star Royal Natal National Park Hotel has 65 rooms; there is a curio shop/kiosk at the Visitor Centre and one at Tendele camp; there are picnic sites in the park, and horseriding and trout fishing can be arranged.

Main attractions: Free-standing peaks create spectacular mountain scenery; the Amphitheatre, a crescent-shaped rock wall; the Tugela Falls (850 m); yellowwood forests; Bushman rock art.

Pertinent information: Be especially careful of slippery conditions, rockfalls and dehydration – carry plenty of water. Notify someone at the camp before going on longer walks, or sign the hiking register at the Visitor Centre or hotel. Sign the mountain rescue register before climbing to above the 2 300-m contour. For those who want the challenge of traversing the escarpment on a hike from Mont-aux-Sources (leaving from QwaQwa) to Cathedral Peak, David Bristow, in *Drakensberg Walks*, describes one of the routes, a 62-km/4–5-day, strenuous trail; see also page 208 for a guided trail from Mont-aux-Sources, through Lesotho Drakensberg, to Cathedral Peak Hotel (58 km/5 days). See page 210 for general guidelines on hiking in the Drakensberg. Provincial licences and park permits for fishing are available from the Visitor Centre. Access to the park is via the R74 from Bergville or Harrismith.

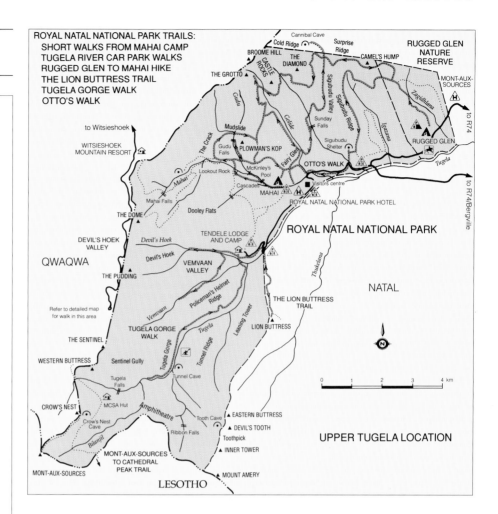

The 8 094-ha Royal Natal National Park includes the smaller, 762-ha Rugged Glen Nature Reserve. Adding to the dramatic beauty which makes the Drakensberg one of southern Africa's natural wonders is the Amphitheatre, an 8-km stretch of the escarpment wall which gives an unobstructed view of the great range of altitude in this area (1 340 to 3 048 m). Here, too, the Tugela Falls drop 850 m in three clear leaps (with a main vertical section of

Set amid varied and splendid scenery, Tendele Camp offers a range of accommodation styles.

The Amphitheatre and its gathering clouds are caught in a still mountain pool.

183 m), the river eroding the escarpment edge. The falls are the fourth highest recorded in the world. Many people use the park as a base from which to tackle The Sentinel and Mont-aux-Sources, as both are approached from QwaQwa (although the peak of Mont-aux-Sources in fact lies in Lesotho); these challenging routes are described in the relevant chapter; see page 163.

Plant life in the park is particularly rich, and in the Natal Parks Board's booklet nine communities are detailed. Contributing to the floral wealth are a number of factors such as the large range in altitude with varied topography, high rainfall, and uninterrupted periods of stability which encourage the process of evolution.

Mammals most commonly observed by hikers in this national park are baboon, mountain reedbuck, blesbok and dassies, while resident birds include black eagles, bearded and Cape vultures and jackal buzzards.

Bushmen are believed to have survived in this region until 1878; their fascinating rock paintings can be seen in the Sigubudu Shelter. It is well worth the detour to see these.

Within this exciting area, over 100 km of footpaths and more than 20 hiking routes are an open invitation to hikers of all fitness levels. The walks begin from various points in the reserve and some include short chain ladders to help the less agile over difficult places. The following is an overview of the walks that can be done in the park; for more detailed descriptions, see David Bristow's *Drakensberg Walks*.

1. Short walks that start at **Mahai camp** are:

❑ a 3-km/1-hour, return, easy route along the Mahai River past the lovely Cascades to **McKinley's Pool** – the most popular and perhaps the prettiest walk;

❑ a 5-km/2-hour hike through bracken and thick grass and past ferns, cycads, wild flowers and yellowwood trees to **Gudu Falls** where the brave can take a dip in a shockingly cold pool; the return is along the same route;

❑ a more strenuous 7-km hike to **Plowman's Kop** – and back – that will take you 2 to 3 hours and involves some climbing (with the help of a chain ladder for the steepest section). This is an extension of the route past Gudu Falls. Some highlights are the series of natural jacuzzi pools in the Gudu River on top of Plowman's Kop and the exciting return via a slippery (in wet weather) section called the Mudslide;

❑ a delightful 11-km/4-hour, return trip through **Fairy Glen** to **The Grotto**, an uphill hike, on the outward leg, that follows the Golide Stream through enchanting forest;

❑ a longer 12-km/4–5-hour, circular hike, which involves some climbing, to **Sigubudu Ridge and Valley**, a walk that affords you the opportunity to spot mountain reedbuck and grey rhebok if you start out early in the morning and move quietly. Plan a detour *en route* to visit the Sigubudu Shelter where you can see rare Bushman paintings – the signposted path leading to the shelter is near the park entrance at the beginning of the walk;

❑ a worthwhile 14-km/6-hour, return hike with some climbing (up Surprise Ridge), to the large **Cannibal Cave** where, in the mid-19th century, one of the cannibal bands that roamed the area used

to string up their victims – the cave is on private land owned by the Cavern Hotel.

2. Although the very popular **Tugela Gorge Walk** is an easy 7-km walk to the gorge and the same back again (14 km in total), the spectacular scenery can be fully appreciated only if you devote a full day to this walk. Starting from the car park near the entrance to Tendele camp, the footpath is clearly signposted. The first section winds along the contours of the slope above the Tugela ('Thukela') River, through yellowwood forested valleys and protea savannah (spring is the best time to see the splendour of the wild flowers coming into bloom). The path then merges with the river, and boulder-hopping becomes necessary. I strongly recommend a change from boots to jogging shoes to increase your agility. Further up the gorge you have the choice of climbing a sturdy chain ladder up a rock face or continuing on and subsequently wading through a wet tunnel. The tunnel is spectacular and well worth negotiating, but in times of high water it is sensible to waterproof your gear. Natural features such as the Amphitheatre, the Policeman's Helmet ridge, Devil's Tooth, the Toothpick and the Tugela Falls (fourth highest in the world) make this walk especially rewarding. Keep a look out for rain, and particularly thunderstorms, as the stream can become a raging torrent in a very short time and it would be dangerous to be trapped in the gorge in a flash flood.

3. There are two more walks from the **Tugela River car park**:

❑ a 6-km/2-hour, fairly strenuous, return hike to the dramatic **Devil's Hoek Valley**, which is often wreathed in mist, that follows the Devil's Hoek River and then one of its tributaries;

❑ and a 9-km walk to and from **Vemvaan Valley**. This second walk is also fairly strenuous and will take you about 3,5 hours; follow the Devil's Hoek path for about 1 km, then head left to the Vemvaan River and walk up the valley.

4. Beginning at the Visitor Centre, **Otto's Walk** is a 3-km/1-hour trail for which a very informative trail guide is available at the Visitor Centre. This provides a valuable introduction to the park by describing its ecology, geology, the history of the forest and its inhabitants, man's centuries-old association with the area, and by identifying trees. The route leads through forest scrub towards the Tugela River, and then continues along the northern slopes of the river, meandering through indigenous forest and more dense scrub, and then joins the road for the homeward stretch, passing a reclaimed quarry *en route*. The **Sigubudu Valley**, where rare Bushman paintings can be seen in the Sigubudu Shelter, is on your left a few hundred metres after you join the road. A signposted path will lead you to the artwork, and it is well worth making the detour.

5. From Tendele camp, there is a 7-km/3-hour hike to **Lion Buttress** and back. The route follows a steep gradient, but the magnificent views of the Amphitheatre and the river valleys make it well worthwhile. From the car park below the camp the path crosses the Tugela River and zigzags up to the guard hut where it then follows the spur to the sandstone cliffs. To the left is a large unnamed cave, and from there you climb a steep grassy gully, that can get very slippery, up to the crest of the ridge. Follow the ridge to the base of the Outer Tower.

6. Hikers can plan a walk from **Rugged Glen camp to Mahai camp**, using the paths in the park, and then return to Rugged Glen by car along the road. The walk alone is about 14 km, for which you should allow 5 to 6 hours, depending on which paths you decide to follow. Generally, the route follows a winding, undulating path, and it is well worth including a 1-km detour to visit Cannibal Cave and another further on to Fairy Glen and The Grotto (see walk 1).

Deep in the Tugela Gorge, the hurrying waters are stilled.

3. UPPER TUGELA LOCATION
NORTHERN DRAKENSBERG
(SINGATI VALLEY, NTONJELANA, MNWENI, IFIDI AND ICIDI VALLEYS)

Trail details: A variety of difficult to strenuous hikes can be undertaken in the area, the motivation of most of these being to ascend to the escarpment.

Permits/bookings: Sign the mountain rescue register at the Isandhlwana Police Post before hiking in the area.

Maps/information: David Bristow describes 6 hikes in his book *Drakensberg Walks* and provides maps. A good map to have is that compiled by Peter Slingsby. This area is so remote, that it would be a good idea to contact the head office of the Mountain Club of South Africa, tel. (021) 453412, 97 Hatfield Street, Cape Town 8001 (or check the *Yellow Pages* for a branch in your area) for advice before you set out.

Facilities/amenities: Caves provide the only shelter, but hikers may find those at lower altitudes inhabited by local tribespeople; there are no set routes or contour paths but the hiker can follow cattle paths; there is a trading store about 6 km from the police outpost.

Main attractions: The Saddle, Rockeries, Mnweni Cutback and other prominent escarpment buttresses and peaks; Mnweni Needles (free-standing peaks); Orange River source; the rivers, caves, gorges, falls and forests of the Little 'Berg are magical here.

Pertinent information: The Little 'Berg region has a fairly large rural population and both the land and the roads are in a poor state. This area has become well known for theft and attacks so be on your guard at all times, and it is advisable to hike in groups of 3 or more. Novice hikers should avoid the area as it is both remote and dangerous. Carry a compass with you and a copy of Peter Slingsby's map of the area. Access is via Bergville and all hikes start at the Isandhlwana Police Post (or you can use the Cathedral Peak area as a base). See walk number 4, page 208 for a 5-day escarpment traverse in the area. See also page 210 for notes on hiking in the Drakensberg, and map overleaf.

The upper Tugela Location is the 97 3789-ha area between the Royal Natal National Park and Cathedral Peak. This remote corner is noted for its myriad impressive buttresses and spires, but while these present fine challenges to the mountaineer and climber, the area is infrequently traversed because of its inaccessibility and lack of facilities. There are some cave shelters, but these cannot be relied on as the chances are that most of them will be occupied by shepherds or local families. Tents, therefore, are a prerequisite for those intent on tackling this mountaineering zone.

Rambling in the lower reaches, the Little 'Berg,in this area is not very rewarding as these parts are relatively heavily populated, making it difficult to achieve the sense of privacy so essential to a hiking experience. Furthermore, and more seriously, the number of people attempting to eke out an existence, coupled with poor farming techniques – especially overgrazing – and the denuding of the countryside for firewood, have led to considerable erosion. This deteriorated ecology is a very serious problem, especially because of the region's importance as a major catchment area. Not surprisingly, wildlife is scarce. Beyond these rather barren foot-

The sheer and awesome start of the Tugela's descent to the faraway sea.

hills, however, any initial disappointment is more than compensated for by the towering rock faces of the main escarpment. Several rough paths lead steeply to the top.

1. From the Isandhlwana Police Post, I suggest that you either follow the **Mnweni Cutback**, emerging at the source of the Orange River, or take the **Rockeries Pass**, starting in the Ntonjelana Valley and following the Ntonjelana's eShonalanga tributary. Although these are the easier (but still very challenging) of the numerous escarpment ascents in the area, both take a full day from the police post. Use Scaly Cave or Shepherd's Cave, or even the well-known Mponjwane Cave for the overnight stop, and then return to the police post the next day. You could combine the two routes for a 3-day round trip. The more popular and accessible Cathedral Peak area can also be used as a base to explore the Mnweni area, either via the contour path mentioned in route 4 below, or by ascending the escarpment via Mlambonja Pass (see page 210).

2. Ascents of the escarpment via the **Ifidi** and **Icidi passes** require mountaineering experience and skills, while the Gothic-like **Mbundini** and **Fangs passes** are also extremely challenging and awe-inspiring routes.

3. The escarpment traverse along this section of the escarpment is truly magnificent; see page 208 for a trail that starts at Mont-aux-Sources and ends at the road below Cathedral Peak Hotel.

4. A hike following the **contour path** along the Little 'Berg from the police post to Cathedral Peak Hotel via Sgonqweni Cave is also a worthwhile challenge. The contour path gives you access to this Little 'Berg area using the more popular Cathe-

Only lightly dusted here, the high-lying Mont-aux-Sources area has frequent heavy snow falls during the winter months.

dral Peak area as a base rather than the very remote police post at Isandhlwana.

5. The freestanding peaks are a different proposition, however, and should remain the domain of experienced mountaineers. These sharply pointed spires, pinnacles, pillars, columns and other rocky projections are fine examples of the sculpturing forces of nature and are aptly described by the Zulu word *Mnweni*, meaning 'the place of fingers'.

---

4. MONT-AUX-SOURCES TO CATHEDRAL PEAK HIKE
LESOTHO/NATAL DRAKENSBERG

Trail details: About 58 km/5 days, guided or self-guided, one-way.

Permits/bookings: For a guided trail, contact Eagle Adventures, tel. (011) 8648473; PO Box 11040, Randhart 1457.

Maps/information: David Bristow, in *Drakensberg Walks*, describes a route for the escarpment traverse for hikers who wish to do a self-guided trail.

Facilities/amenities: For those doing a guided trail, food is provided and equipment can be hired; transport from the end point back to your car can be arranged in advance; cars can be left in the car park at the Sentinel; there are caves, such as Ifidi Cave or Fangs Cave, in the area where hikers can stay if they are not already occupied.

Main attractions: The trail leads you through the most dramatic and spectacular part of the Drakensberg.

Pertinent information: Hikers should be fit for this trail. For the guided trail, hikers should be between the ages of 18 and 60, and groups are limited to a maximum of 12 people. Carry a passport and any necessary health documents. This area has become well known for theft and attacks so be on your guard at all times, and hike in groups of 3 or more. Sign the mountain rescue register before you leave. See page 210 for general notes on hiking in the Drakensberg.

Following a route that is the easiest to walk but also offers the best views, the trail traverses the escarpment along terrain that is hilly with deep valleys and high peaks, and is generally 3 000 to 3 250 m above sea level, criss-crossing the watershed-border between Lesotho and Natal/KwaZulu for most of the way. Along the way you are likely to encounter Sotho herdsmen with their cattle, sheep or goats, and there is a good chance of spotting several species of buck as well as eagles, vultures and smaller birds. Most of all, the trail will take you past the most dramatic and magnificent parts of the Drakensberg. The 11-km route on the

first day takes you from the car park in QwaQwa, past the mighty Sentinel and up the Chain Ladder to meet up with the Tugela River which it follows to its source, just below Mont-aux-Sources. The trail then heads south to meet up with the Khubedu River, which freezes up in winter and is deep enough to have to wade through in the rainy season. A steep climb up a ridge takes you to a point from where the view of the valleys below you is breathtaking. A contour path then leads to the first camp site (all camp sites are situated next to a river). Note that the route on the first day passes through QwaQwa, Lesotho and the Natal Parks

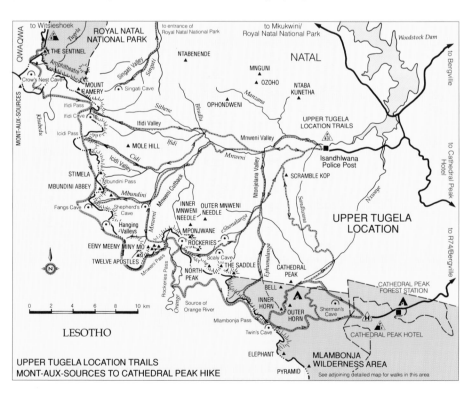

UPPER TUGELA LOCATION TRAILS
MONT-AUX-SOURCES TO CATHEDRAL PEAK HIKE

Board controlled Royal Natal National Park. The second day's hike is the shortest at 10 km, to the Mbundini Pass and Abbey where you will see peaks on the escarpment called Madonna and Her Worshippers. The Mbundini River is then crossed and a short but steep climb takes you to the remote and mysterious Mnweni Cutback area and the Hanging Valleys where the second camp site is situated. The setting of the camp is spectacular and mist plumes rise like smoke from the depths of the valley. On the third day (also an 11-km hike) the route will take you past the Eeny, Meeny, Miny and Mo peaks and on to the source of the mighty Orange River, the Senqu River, which the route then follows to the Rockeries, the massive rock tower of Mponjwane, and on to a waterfall. The camp site is low down in the valley.

Another 11-km route on the fourth day will lead you up the valley to the Saddle and then on to the Ntonjelana Pass and the magnificent Cathedral Range. Hikers can sleep overnight in Twin's Cave. The last day's hike is a strenuous 15-km route down the Mlambonja Pass to the road below Cathedral Peak Hotel (or the Natal Parks Board camp site further on), which will take you past the Mitre, Chessmen, Inner and Outer Horns, the Bell and Cathedral Peak itself. If weather and conditions allow, an alternative route along the escarpment past the Cockade, the Elephant and Cleft Peak will lead you to the descent of the awe-inspiring Organ Pipes Pass and then via the contour path and jeep track to Mike's Pass and the Natal Parks Board camp site.

5. CATHEDRAL PEAK AND MLAMBONJA WILDERNESS AREA
NORTHERN DRAKENSBERG, NEAR WINTERTON

Trail details: 1. Cathedral Peak Hike: 10 km/4–5 hours, return; 2. Various one-way hikes to the escarpment via Mlambonja Pass, Camel Ridge or Organ Pipes Pass: 10–13 km/1 day; 3. Various escarpment traverses: 37,5–40 km/2–4 days, one-way; 4. Various 1- or 2-hour, short walks; 5. Ndedema Gorge Hike: 26,5 km/3 days, circular route. All are self-guided.
Permits/bookings: Bookings for the camp site at Cathedral Peak: Officer in Charge, tel. (0364) 881880, Private Bag X1, Winterton 3340. The Cathedral Peak Hotel can be contacted at tel. (03682) ask for Cathedral Peak Hotel; PO Winterton 3340. Permits necessary to drive up Mike's Pass, to camp, for day hiking and to camp out overnight in the wilderness – obtainable from the Natal Parks Board (at the camp site) or from any of the hotels in the area.
Maps/information: Maps by Reg Pearse and Peter Slingsby are available from the hotel and from the Natal Parks Board.
Facilities/amenities: Cathedral Peak Hotel (commercial hotel); camp site in the nature reserve with ablution facilities; all-weather surface access road; picnic sites on Mike's Pass; caves for hikers on the trails.

Main attractions: Cathedral Peak, the Bell, Outer and Inner Horn and other prominent peaks; Organ Pipes Pass and Camel Ridge; the Little 'Berg (contour path); Mike's Pass (the only drive to the top of the Little 'Berg); Ndedema Gorge (natural forest and rock art); accessible region; extensive rock-climbing opportunities.
Pertinent information: This is a relatively heavily used mountaineering/hiking region. During the winter fire season, the research area is closed to those members of public who do not have special permission. Trailists are not permitted to stay overnight in caves which contain Bushman paintings. The trail up Masongwane Valley is used for education; there are no restrictions on party size. There is a limit of 12 people per party for the wilderness area, and the Natal Parks Board is investigating limiting the number of parties as well. Mountain rescue registers are kept at Natal Parks Board camp offices, the entry gate and reception office. It is advisable to carry a passport and any necessary health documents with you on hikes via major mountain passes that will take you into Lesotho. Access to the area is via Winterton. See also page 210 for general notes on hiking in the Drakensberg.

The Cathedral Peak region includes the Mdedelelo Wilderness area, and is now administered by the Natal Parks Board as part of the Natal Drakensberg Park, which stretches from Cathedral Peak in the north to Bushman's Nek in the south. Because of

its well-worn and accessible trails and the popular Cathedral Peak 'base hotel', this region is one of the prime mountaineering sections of the 'Berg. The hotel grounds are private property, so unless you are a guest, use the boom at the end of the

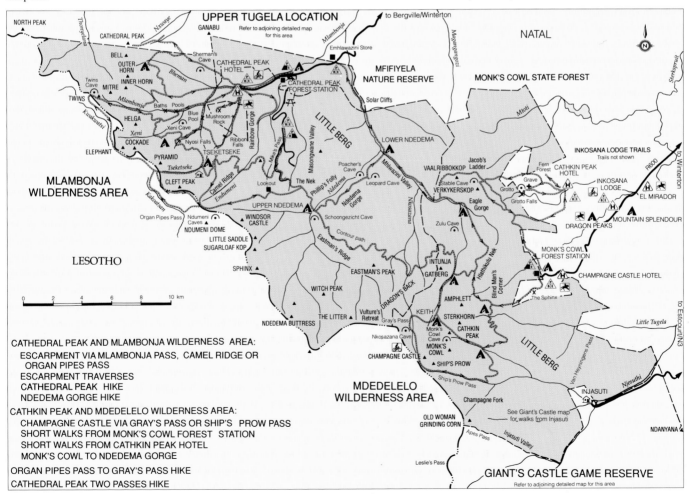

CATHEDRAL PEAK AND MLAMBONJA WILDERNESS AREA:
  ESCARPMENT VIA MLAMBONJA PASS, CAMEL RIDGE OR
    ORGAN PIPES PASS
  ESCARPMENT TRAVERSES
  CATHEDRAL PEAK HIKE
  NDEDEMA GORGE HIKE
CATHKIN PEAK AND MDEDELELO WILDERNESS AREA:
  CHAMPAGNE CASTLE VIA GRAY'S PASS OR SHIP'S PROW PASS
  SHORT WALKS FROM MONK'S COWL FOREST STATION
  SHORT WALKS FROM CATHKIN PEAK HOTEL
  MONK'S COWL TO NDEDEMA GORGE
ORGAN PIPES PASS TO GRAY'S PASS HIKE
CATHEDRAL PEAK TWO PASSES HIKE

HIKING IN THE DRAKENSBERG

1. In the interest of **conservation**, do not: leave litter behind; light fires (except at official camp sites); deface any rocks or trees in any way; disturb any plant, bird or animal (e.g. by picking flowers or removing eggs from nests); or remove anything from the environment. Only camp at officially designated sites.

2. Obtain a **permit** and sign the **walks or mountain rescue register** before you set off. In the interests of conservation and safety, do not go wandering off without official permission and always let someone know where you are going and when you expect to be back. Plan your walk carefully so that you will be back before dark. Never go off hiking into the High 'Berg without signing the mountain rescue register – it could save your life.

3. Always carry a **good map** with you, and a **compass** is also a useful navigating tool. The well-known maps of the Drakensberg are those compiled by Reg Pearse or Peter Slingsby. For up-to-date descriptions of walks and trails in the Drakensberg contact Desmond Humphrey on tel. (031) 282984. He has been hiking in the Drakensberg for over 45 years and has compiled 6 booklets that indicate where paths shown on earlier maps are no longer in use. See individual entries for information on other maps available in each area.

4. Stick to the paths and do not take short cuts – every step you take contributes to the **erosion** problem, so by staying on the paths you at least confine the problem to a specific area.

5. There are **poisonous snakes** in the Drakensberg – the puff adder, berg adder and spitting cobra (rinkhals) are the three most dangerous. Snakes avoid contact with humans as much as possible, but keep a watchful eye out for them, carry a stick and wear ankle-high boots. Generally learn as much as you can about the environment and its inhabitants before you wander off into the Drakensberg and you will not

only ensure your own safety but also minimize your impact on the environment.

6. The **unpredictable weather** in the Drakensberg is well known, and you are likely to encounter swirling mists, sudden snowfalls on a warm spring day, frighteningly spectacular thunderstorms, dehydrating heat and bitter cold. Dress sensibly so that you are prepared for sudden changes in the weather. Generally, winter days can be warm and cloudless, and nights are cold with frequent frost. Snow can be expected in winter, while 85% of the annual rain falls in summer, mainly in thunderstorms.

7. **Never hike alone** in the Drakensberg. Accidents do happen; for safety's sake, hike in groups of at least three.

8. Be alert to the problem of **theft from hikers**, particularly on the Mont-Aux-Sources plateau. The KwaZulu Bureau of Natural Resources (see address list at the back of this book) is attempting to solve the problem, but in the interim has issued the following cautions to hikers: enter the area in groups of 3 or more; never leave your equipment unguarded; if possible, use a night-watch system to guard equipment of sleeping companions; keep weapons – a prime target – strapped to the body or close at hand, and not in view or in backpacks.

9. The Natal Parks Board suggests that **the essentials** you should carry with you are a brightly coloured anorak and hat; a basic first-aid kit with sun-filter cream; a whistle and torch with reserve batteries; light nourishment such as chocolates, nuts or raisins; a water bottle with a glucose base fluid mix; a contour map, paper and pen.

10. Bushman rock art, a precious heritage that is both fragile and irreplaceable, can be found in many caves in the Drakensberg. In order to preserve this heritage, you may not light a fire or sleep in any cave that contains rock art; and you must never touch or wet the art. Look, admire and leave the site untouched and undisturbed.

Mlambonja River Valley road as a start or end point (or use the Natal Parks Board camp site further on down the road).

1. Cathedral Peak, accessible via a path from the boom at the end of the road up the Mlambonja River Valley, is 3 004 m high. This full day's strenuous trek, including rock scrambling, is well worth the effort for experienced hikers, as from the summit the panoramic view of the entire northern Drakensberg, from Mont-aux-Sources to Champagne Castle, is magnificent. It will take you a good 4 to 5 hours to make the 10-km trek to the summit so you should leave early in the morning to allow yourself plenty of time to appreciate the splendid outlook from the peak and then make the return journey home. The contour path is badly eroded in some parts of this hike so take care not to cause any further damage.

Other prominent **free-standing peaks** of the Cathedral range include the Bell (2 930 m), the Inner Horn (3 005 m) and the Outer Horn (3 006 m), Chessmen (2 987 m), Mitre (3 023 m) and the Twins (22 899 m). Each requires at least 'C' scrambling skills or advanced rope climbing.

2. If you intend hiking to the escarpment (a very strenuous full day's hike), one option is to follow the **Mlambonja River**, starting at the boom at the end of the road up the Mlambonja River valley. It is about 2 km to the Little 'Berg escarpment (about a 45-minute, moderate hike). Another 1-km walk will take you to the Xeni River and on to the 1,5-km, treacherous (especially in the wet) path that leads to the magnificent Xeni Cave. Follow the river for a while, then join up with the contour path for 2 km, which will lead you back to the river. The going then gets a lot more strenuous as you head up into Mlambonja Pass, where the ground can be boggy and slippery, for 1 km. A final 3-km climb will take you up to Twin's Cave – in total, an 11-km/6-hour hike – where you can spend the night. Another option is to ascend **Camel Ridge**, which leads you around or past Cleft Peak (3 281 m) to the top of Organ Pipes Pass. A third option is via **Organ Pipes Pass**, an ascent I well recall. After a long, hot trek through the Little 'Berg we pitched camp on the contour path at the foot of the pass – a less-than-ideal site but nowhere around was better. The night was restful – I was rudely woken in the early hours by a rather aggressive herd of Basotho cattle and, still tired and sunburnt from the previous day, we began our steep hike up the escarpment. My discomfort was soon dispelled, however, by the sheer beauty of our surroundings and I felt guilty testing the echoing reputation of the numerous rock spires giving the pass its name – not wanting to disturb the silent world of some of the Drakensberg's most prominent and most photographed peaks. Beautiful as they undoubtedly are, they are equally uncompromising, a fact borne out by the number of climbing parties that have come to grief on the brooding rock faces.

3. 'Classic' **mountaineering traverses** can be completed either on the **escarpment**, a scenically superb but strenuous trip lasting several days, or along the footpath of the Little 'Berg. The traverse on the Little 'Berg follows the 2 000-metre **contour path**, starting at and ending 2 days (40 km) later at the Injasuti Valley. This hike is easier than the escarpment traverse (but still a demanding walk that winds in and out of valleys and over spurs) and

A quiet stream near the free-standing Cathedral Peak, which reaches a height of some 3 000 metres.

View towards Mnweni; Cathedral and Cathkin ranges in distance.

enables you to appreciate the wildlife, Bushman art and the forested river valleys you pass *en route*. David Bristow, in *Drakensberg Walks*, describes a hike along the contour path from the Mlambonja River Valley road to Ndedema Gorge – a 35-km route for which he allows 3 days. See number 8, page 213 for a guided hike across the escarpment, from Organ Pipes Pass to Gray's Pass, and number 6, this page, for a very popular self-guided 37,5-km/4-day trail from Mike's Pass to the Mlambonja River Valley road via Organ Pipes and Mlambonja Pass (or vice versa).

4. Ramblers will find numerous short walks that they can do in the area. Some popular routes from the hotel or the boom at the end of the road up the Mlambonja River Valley are:

❑ a 4,2-km/2-hour, one-way walk up the Mlambonja River Valley to **Neptune's Pool** – another 1 km upstream are the **Marble Baths** where the underlying sandstone rocks have been polished by the action of the water to form smooth, marbled pools;

❑ a one-way 5,5-km/2-hour, picturesque walk to **Rainbow Gorge** – a fairytale place where rainbows and gently filtered light add to the magic of cascading waterfalls, enchanted pools and moss-covered (and slippery) boulders;

❑ a steep but rewarding 2-km/1-hour, one-way hike to **Mushroom Rock**;

❑ an undemanding 5,5-km/2-hour, one-way ramble to **Nyosi Grotto**, with a stop at the **Blue Pool**, where a refreshing swim is definitely called for.

5. Armed with a map – either one by Peter Slingsby or Reg Pearse, or both – the keen hiker can plan a day or two of hiking along the many paths in the area and allowing about an hour for every 2,5 km plus time to get back to the hotel or camp site. In *Drakensberg Walks*, David Bristow describes numerous day hikes in the area, and especially

recommends an exploration of the **Ndedema Gorge**. Mike's Pass or the Emhlawazini Store can be used as a starting point, and hikers can spend the night at a camp site at the mouth of the gorge, or at Leopard Cave a little further on if hiking from Emhlawazini Store (about an 11-km day's hike), and at the camp site or Schoongezicht Cave at the top of the gorge if starting at Mike's Pass (about a 15,5-km day's hike if you include the route through the gorge). If you use Emhlawazini Store as the starting point, follow the jeep track along the Mhlwazini River for about 4 km to the guard hut at Solar Cliffs. Cross the river, then follow the left-hand bank for another 3 km – the Mhlwazini River meets the Ndedema River at the mouth of the gorge. A zigzagging path leads through the gorge, following the river, and about halfway through the gorge meets up with the contour path which makes for easier walking. Near the mouth of the gorge, take a detour to visit Poacher's Cave where the Bushman paintings are superb. From the camp site at the head of the gorge, the contour path leads you up Phillip's Folly to the Nek, and from there a jeep track takes you through pine plantations and natural bush to Mike's Pass.

6. CATHEDRAL PEAK TWO PASSES HIKE
CATHEDRAL PEAK AND MLAMBONJA WILDERNESS AREA

This challenging but spectacular 3- or 4-day hike starts at the top of Mike's Pass and ends at the Cathedral Peak camp site (or on the road just below the hotel): it can also be walked in reverse. A jeep track leads you from Mike's Pass to the contour path, which winds up to the Nek for 3 km. From there a path will take you 2 km up to the forestry

lookout and then onto a ridge, which it becomes tricky (but necessary) to follow. From the lookout it is a 3-km hike to the magnificent Organ Pipes Pass – as its name suggests, the pass gives you the feeling of being in an awe-inspiring cathedral. The

Trail details: 37 km/3 to 4 days, self-guided, one-way. See map p. 209.

Permits/bookings: Bookings for the camp site at Cathedral Peak: Officer in Charge, tel. (0364) 881880, Private Bag X1, Winterton 3340. The Cathedral Peak Hotel can be contacted at tel. (03682) ask for Cathedral Peak Hotel; PO Winterton 3340. Permits for the wilderness area available from the Natal Parks Board.

Maps/information: Maps by Reg Pearse and Peter Slingsby available from the hotel and from the Natal Parks Board. Don't embark on this trail without a map.

Main attractions: A spectacular hike along dramatic terrain that is very popular and will take you across the escarpment where the views are breathtaking.

Facilities/amenities: Cathedral Peak Hotel (commercial hotel with horses for hire); Natal Parks Board camp site in the nature reserve with ablution facilities; all-weather surface access road; caves for hikers on the trail.

Pertinent information: This is a demanding hike. It is one-way so 2 vehicles, one at each end, are advisable – however, do not leave your vehicle in the car park at the hotel unless you have booked in there. Carry a passport and any necessary health documents, as the trail will take you into Lesotho, and a tent as the caves might already be full when you reach them – it's first come first served as far as accommodation in caves is concerned. Spring and autumn are the best times to do this hike. See page 210 for general notes on hiking in the Drakensberg.

Some of the Drakensberg's best-known names are, from the left, Champagne Castle, Monk's Cowl and Cathkin Peak.

path does become boggy as you pass beneath the Organ Pipes, and the last 500 m up to Windy Gap is quite steep. Ndumeni Dome, which means 'the mountain of storms', will be on your left and is a good place to stop for the night after a demanding 13-km hike. There are various paths that you can take that will lead you across the escarpment from Windy Gap to the popular Twin's Cave – about a 12,5-km hike. You can follow the watershed over Castle Buttress and Cleft Peak, or hike up the Kakoatsan Valley and around the peaks to Cleft Peak. From there the path follows the watershed past Tseketseke and Xeni Passes, and then follows the Kwakwatsi River. A path to the right leads to Twin's Cave. Whichever route you choose, for those who enjoy climbing, Cleft Peak, the highest point between Champagne Castle and Mont-aux-Sources is definitely worth tackling as there are spectacular views of the Drakensberg from its summit. The hike across the escarpment is strenuous with lots of ups and downs, but the breathtaking scenery makes it worth the effort. Twin's Cave is a large overhang rather than a cave and can shelter up to 30 people. To view a Drakensberg sunrise from this spot is a truly breathtaking experience – often the valleys beneath you are filled with cloud that the dawn colours in pink and gold hues. The route to the Mlambonja River Valley road from there is only 11,5 km, but the descent from the cave into Mlambonja Pass is a steep and slippery one – a very demanding 3,5 km that must be tackled with strength and care. Xeni Cave is one of the largest in the Drakensberg and it is towards this cave that the path zigzags down the Mlambonja River Valley. The last 2,5 km is a gentle walk beside the river.

7. CATHKIN PEAK AND MDEDELELO WILDERNESS AREA
NORTHERN DRAKENSBERG, NEAR WINTERTON

Reflecting on my mountaineering adventures, I recall not only scenery and wildlife, but also the experiences I have in an area. Gray's Pass was my first confrontation in Africa with snow, and the Nkosazana Cave near its summit was my introduction to the enthusiastic, dependable and very knowledgeable leaders of the MCSA, and their colleagues.

Starting off from the forestry office in brilliant Easter sunshine, clad in only a cotton shirt and shorts, I was totally unprepared for what lay ahead. Twenty km farther on and 2 000 m higher, after being near-blinded by wind-driven snowflakes, I was shivering uncontrollably and struggling to follow my companion's footprints which were moulded step-like into the rapidly forming deep drifts on the steep upper reaches of the pass.

The Nkosazana Cave, 'conveniently' situated just at the top of the pass – wet from drips and puddles as it was – and great quantities of hot soup and tea, saved me from the onslaught of hypothermia. Obviously none of the MCSA members thought there was anything unusual about the freak storm, neither did they struggle to reach the escarpment for, if they had, I doubt whether they would have been quite so high-spirited later that night!

The escarpment traverse was magnificent. Drakensberg mountaineers who never see the peaks and slopes blanketed with snow, glistening in the moonlight, miss one of the 'Berg's most elegant features. On an escarpment traverse, Ship's Prow to

Trail details: 1. Champagne Castle via Gray's Pass: 19 km/9 hours, one-way; or Ship's Prow Pass: 21 km/11 hours, one-way; 2. Two short walks from Cathkin Peak Hotel: 1 km/30 minutes, one-way hike to Fern Forest; 7 km/2,5 hours, circular to Barry's Grave and the Grotto; 3. From Monk's Cowl forest station: 3 km/1,5 hours, one-way to The Sphinx. 4. Various day walks, including 9,5 km/4 hours, one-way to Stable Cave. 5. Monk's Cowl to Ndedema Gorge: 24 km/9 hours, one-way to the top of the gorge; or 27,5 km/11 hours, one-way to the bottom of the gorge along the contour path. All are self-guided. See map p. 209.

Permits/bookings: For accommodation at Monk's Cowl: The Officer in Charge, tel. (036) 4681103, Private Bag X2, Winterton 3320. To book at Cathkin Peak Hotel, phone (036) 4681091, or write to Private Bag 12, Winterton 3340. To book at Champagne Castle Hotel, phone (036) 4681063, or write to Private Bag 8, Winterton 3340. Contact the Drakensberg Publicity Association, tel. (036) 4481557, fax. (036) 4481562; PO Box 12, Bergville for more information about hotels in the area. Permits must be obtained from the Natal Parks Board at Monk's Cowl or the Cathkin Peak Hotel to enter the wilderness area.

Maps/information: Maps available from the Natal Parks Board or any of the hotels in the area are Peter Slingsby's and Reg Pearse's, while the Cathkin Peak Hotel also has a map and brochure describing various walks available.

Facilities/amenities: Natal Parks Board camp site at Monk's Cowl can accommodate 90 people; footpaths and bridle paths; hotels and private accommodation in the vicinity; Champagne Castle Hotel, closest hotel to the mountain (horses for hire and bridle paths); Dragon Peak Park caravan complex (horses for hire, day rambles to the Sunken Forest and Sphinx); Cathkin Peak Hotel (paths to Fern Forest, Grotto waterfalls and other sights); El Mirador (arranges hikes and horses for hire); Mountain Splendour caravan and camp site complex; Inkosana Lodge (see page 214).

Main attractions: Cathkin Peak (3 149 m), Monk's Cowl (3 324 m), Champagne Castle (3 378 m); Leslie's Pass and Nkosazana Cave; Bushman caves and paintings; wildlife; Little 'Berg contour path.

Pertinent information: There is a limit of 12 people per party for the wilderness area, and the Natal Parks Board is investigating limiting the number of parties as well. Mountain rescue registers are kept at Natal Parks Board camp offices, the entry gate and reception office. No fires permitted. Hikers may not stay overnight in caves which have Bushman rock art in them. Access to the area is via Winterton on the R600. See entry number 8 on page 213 for guided walks in the area, and entry number 9 on page 214 for an escarpment traverse trail. See also page 210 for general notes on hiking in the Drakensberg.

the south provides the most difficult descent. I have also used Leslie's Pass in the Giant's Castle area, which makes a 5-day trip possible.

The free-standing peaks of this wilderness area, especially Cathkin and Monk's Cowl, are impressive landmarks and very difficult rock climbs – graded E (difficult to very difficult) through to G (very severe), with some routes requiring mechanical aids. Cathkin, named *Mdedelelo* by the Zulus, which means 'make room for him', implying a bully, is the peak after which the wilderness area is named. The most unusual peak is Intunja (2 408 m), meaning 'eye', a reference to the huge hole in its summit basalt. From Gray's Pass, non-rock climbers can ascend Champagne Castle (3 377 m), which is part of the main escarpment.

The contour path mentioned under the Cathedral Peak Nature Reserve (see page 211) traverses this wilderness area, ending at Injasuti Valley in the Giant's Castle Game Reserve. The southern boundary peak, 'Old Woman Grinding Corn' (2 987 m), separates the two reserves on the escarpment.

Here is a brief overview of some of the routes in the area.

1. To reach Champagne Castle from Monk's Cowl forest station use the Gray's Pass route (19 km and 9 hours), a winding and up and down route that involves steep climbing as you approach Champagne Castle and follows a path that is eroded in many places. It's a hard slog rather than a technically difficult climb to the summit. A very strenuous and treacherous route is via **Ship's Prow Pass** – a 21-km/11-hour hike.

From the 'station, follow the bridle path past the Sphinx and Verkykerskop, across Breakfast Stream to reach the Little 'Berg plateau. Head towards Cathkin Peak until Blind Man's Corner. To reach Champagne Castle via Gray's Pass, turn right along the contour path, which will take you around Cathkin Peak, Sterkhorn, The Tower and to Amphlett and Hlathikulu Nek. About 1,5 km further on the path descends into the Mhlwazini Valley. Keeping the Amphlett on the left, the path then follows the left-hand bank of the river for 4 km before crossing the river below the Keith Bush camp. A steep climb up Gray's Pass takes you to the upper Nkosazana River where you can see a waterfall that freezes into a solid sheet of ice in winter, and get a good view of Vulture's Retreat. Look across to The Litter to see the large colony of Cape vultures that makes it its home. A climb to the top of Champagne Castle is an appropriate end to the hike, although the view from Vulture's Retreat is better. Stay overnight in Nkosazana Cave which is near the top of the pass, about 3 km from Champagne Castle. To get to Champagne Castle via Ship's Prow Pass, turn left along the contour path at Blind Man's Corner and go on to the Vlei, a camp site, and then to Ship's Prow Stream. The path follows the stream for about 3 km, then heads left (do not go right) to ascend the pass by scrambling up unstable scree and vertical rock. About 2,5 km later you will reach the top of the pass at the head of the Nkosazana Valley. Champagne Castle will be on your right, and the 1 km ascent of the summit will be a breeze after surviving Ship's Prow Pass!

2. Two walks from Cathkin Peak Hotel are:
❏ a 1-km/30-minute, easy and enchanting one-way walk to **Fern Forest** where a picnic spot next to a waterfall invites you to rest in the shade;
❏ and a fairly easy 7-km/2,5-hour, round trip to **Barry's Grave** and the **Grotto** traverses through grass, wattle plantation and forest, and includes crossing a river under a waterfall – this route is crisscrossed by cattle paths so take care no to get lost.

3. From the Monk's Cowl forest station there is a very popular route into the Little 'Berg via **The Sphinx** and **Verkykerskop**. It is a 3-km/1,5-hour, one-way hike from the forest station to The Sphinx via the delightful Crystal Falls, and from the summit there are good views of Hlathikulu Forest and Sterkspruit Valley. The hike is fairly steep but picturesque and not too difficult.

4. Hikers can plan various day walks in the area, following established paths. A very picturesque 9,5-km/4-hour hike is that from the **Cathkin Peak Hotel to Stable Cave** via the Steilberg to the top of the Little 'Berg that leads you up steep paths, along ridges and down slopes. Alternatively, you can hike to the cave via **Jacob's Ladder** and **Van Damm's Cascade**. Refer to David Bristow's *Drakensberg Walks* for a description of more routes.

5. A hike from **Monk's Cowl** to the beautiful **Ndedema Gorge** is a 24-km/9-hour route that winds around the Hlathikulu Forest along the bridle path to Blind Man's Corner and then along the contour path around Cathkin Peak, Sterkhorn, The Tower and Amphlett to Hlathikulu Nek. Head right for about 3 km, then head left into the Mhlwazini Valley and on to Eagle Gorge (a good place to pitch a tent for the night if you want to do the hike to the gorge in 2 days). From there, the path follows the Mhlwazini River in a crisscross fashion to the Lower Ndedema camp site. Alternatively, one can follow the contour path from Monk's Cowl to the lower end of Ndedema Gorge. This is a 27,5-km route that will take about 11 hours, but it is advisable to allow 2 days and stop overnight at the camp site just before the main head of Nkosazana Gorge. Head left at Hlathikulu Nek and follow the contour path around Intunja and then up and over spurs and ridges and river valleys to round Eastman's Peak. The path then winds along Eastman's Ridge to the Upper Ndedema camp site.

---

8. ORGAN PIPES PASS TO GRAY'S PASS HIKE
MLAMBONJA AND MDEDELELO WILDERNESS AREAS, NEAR WINTERTON

Trail details: About 50 km/5 days, guided or self-guided, one-way.

Permits/bookings: Contact Eagle Adventures, tel. (011) 8648473; PO Box 11040, Randhart 1457, if you wish to do a guided trail. A permit from the Natal Parks Board or the hotel at Cathedral Peak is required to enter the wilderness area.

Maps/information: Maps by Reg Pearse and Peter Slingsby can be purchased from hotels and Natal Parks Board camps or offices in the area.

Facilities/amenities: For the guided trail, food is provided and equipment can be hired. Cars can be left in the car park at the boom at the end of the road up the Mlambonja Valley, and arrangements can be made for transport back to your car at the end of the hike. Hikers can stay in caves in the area, if they do not have Bushman rock art in them and are not already occupied.

Main attractions: The trail leads you through the most dramatic and spectacular part of the Drakensberg.

Pertinent information: Hikers should be fit. For the guided trail there is an age restriction of 18 and 60, and groups are limited to a maximum of 12 people. Carry a passport and any necessary health documents as the hike will take you into Lesotho. Permits for the wilderness area are restricted to 12 people per group, and the Natal Parks Board is investigating restricting the number of parties. Do not venture out without a good map of the area, and it is advisable to hike in groups of at least 3, with one of the party being a seasoned Drakensberg hiker. See page 210 for general notes on hiking in the Drakensberg.

The trail starts at Mike's Pass and leads you south to end at Monk's Cowl forest station, using the route that offers you the best views from the dramatic escarpment but also opts for the easiest paths to follow. A strenuous 10-km hike on the first day will take you from Mike's Pass, past the Camel and up the spectacular Organ Pipes Pass (this ascent is described in more detail on page 210). The first night is spent at a camp site below Ndumeni Dome – 'the mountain of storms' – where the weather may be unfriendly, but the view is breathtaking. All camp sites along the way are situated next to a river or stream. An 11-km route along the magnificent escarpment the next day, following established paths that are marked on Slingsby's map, will take you past Windsor Castle, the Little Saddle, the Sugarloaf, Sphinx and Ndedema Dome and Buttress to the camp site below Ndedema Cave – romantic sounding places whose names evoke the awesome mystery of the Drakensberg. A shorter, 8-km hike on the third day will take you past Eastman's Ridge down to The Litter and Vulture's Retreat and then on to the beautiful Dragon's Back to the camp site at the Nkosazane River. Look forward to spending a day exploring the waterfall at Dragon's Back, which freezes into a solid wall of ice in winter, as well as Vulture's Retreat, from where you can observe the large colony of Cape vultures, and Champagne Castle. Hikers can camp in the same spot as on the third night or move on to Gray's Pass and set up camp at Keith Bush camp. A long 16-km hike down Gray's Pass, a climb up to Hlatikulu Nek and then an easier walk down The Sphinx, Crystal Falls and to Monk's Cowl forest station awaits you on day five (a more detailed route description of this route is given above).

Well-wooded old erosion-features in the Cathedral Peak area.

9. INKOSANA LODGE TRAILS
CHAMPAGNE CASTLE

Trail details: A variety of guided trails: 1. Cathkin Peak to Injasuti Trail: 2 days; 2. Mhlwazini Valley Trail: 2–3 days; 3. Nkosazana Cave Trail: 3 days; 4. Bell Traverse Trail: 3 days; 5. Ndedema Cave Trail: 5 days, and Northern Berg Trail: 11 days.

Permits/bookings: For bookings and more information, contact Edmund Salomons, tel. (03682) ask for 3520; PO Box 60, Winterton 3340.

Facilities/amenities: Inkosana Lodge – a comfortable hostel, all food provided; transport to beginning and end of trails provided.

Main attractions: Trails in the most spectacular part of the Drakensberg under the supervision of experienced guides.

Pertinent information: Only 6–11 people per group. Bring your own sleeping bag and mat, water bottle, eating utensils, towel, torch, rucksack and clothing. See page 210 for general notes on hiking in the Drakensberg, and p. 209 for orientation.

Inkosana Lodge – an inexpensive and informal mountaineer's lodge – is on the road to Champagne Castle Hotel. Six guided trails, under the supervision of an experienced mountaineer, in the Cathkin Peak and Mdedelelo Wilderness Area are offered, ranging from 2 to 11 days.

1. The 2-day hike from **Cathkin Peak to Injasuti** is fairly easy and takes you through Wonder Valley, where you spend the night in Wonder Valley Cave. The second day is a walk through indigenous forest in the Van Heyning's Pass to Injasuti.

2. Another fairly easy hike is the 2- or 3-day **Mhlwazini Valley Trail.** The first day is an easy climb up Jacob's Ladder to Stable Cave, where you spend the night. Hospital Spruit leads you into the Mhlwazini Valley the next day, where you spend the night in Zulu Cave. The third day is spent exploring the Makurumani Forest – a haven for bird-watchers.

3. The 3-day **Nkosazana Cave Trail** is more suited to the experienced hiker as it is quite strenuous. The route on the first day takes you around Cathkin Peak to the overnight stop in the cave at Ship's Prow Pass. An ascent of the pass – the most difficult in the Drakensberg – the next day leads to Nkosazana Cave, where you spend the night. The return on the third day is via Gray's Pass and Keith Bush camp.

4. Another hike for the more experienced is the 3-day **Bell Traverse Trail.** From the Cathedral Peak Hotel, the trail leads up the Mlambonja Valley to Twin's Cave. The second day is a hike across the escarpment to Bell Cave, heading back across the Cathedral Range. An ascent of the range the next day leads you back to the hotel.

5. The 5-day **Ndedema Cave** and 11-day **Northern Berg trails** are only for the very fit and experienced.

10. GIANT'S CASTLE AREA
GIANT'S CASTLE, INJASUTI AND HILLSIDE, NEAR ESTCOURT

The 34 638-ha Giant's Castle Reserve stretches between the Injasuti and Lotheni rivers and (almost) incorporates the 3 314-m high Giant's Castle peak

Trail details: 1. Bushman's River Trail: 3,2 km/2 hours, circular; 2. Short walks from Giant's Castle: from 3 km/1 hour to 14 km/4,5 hours; 3. 1-day hikes in Giant's Castle area; 4. Short to 1-day walks in the Injasuti area; 5. Short to 1-day hikes in the Hillside area. All are self-guided.

Permits/bookings: Reservations for hutted accommodation and caves: Natal Parks Board, tel. (0331) 471981, fax. (0331) 471980; PO Box 1750, Pietermaritzburg 3200. Reservations for camp site at Injasuti: Officer in Charge, tel. (0020) ask for Loskop 1311, Private Bag X7010, Estcourt 3310. Reservations for Giant's Lodge: Natal Parks Board, tel. (0331) 471961; PO Box 662, Pietermaritzburg 3200. Enquiries about Giant's Castle hutted camp; Camp Manager, tel. (0363) 24718, Private Bag X7055, Estcourt 3310. Bookings for Lammergeyer Hide: tel. (0363) 24616, or write to Giant's Castle (see above). Reservations for Hillside camp site: Officer in Charge, tel. (0363) 24435; PO Box 288, Estcourt 3310. Permits for the wilderness area from the Natal Parks Board camps and entrance gates.

Maps/information: A comprehensive booklet on the Giant's Castle Game Reserve with a map and detailed description of all walks and hikes is available from the Natal Parks Board. There is also a comprehensive map available at Injasuti, and trail guides available at Hillside. Peter Slingsby's map can also be purchased from the Natal Parks Board.

Facilities/amenities: Hutted camp at Injasuti: 17 fully equipped 6-bed cabins; two 8-bed dormitory cabins with braai facilities. Camp site at Injasuti for 80 people with ablution facilities. Lower Injasuti Cave and Fergy's Cave with basic toilet facilities. Basic foodstuffs can be purchased at Injasuti. Giant's Castle hutted camp: self-contained accommodation for 68 people. Giant's Lodge: luxurious accommodation for 7 people. Rustic hut at Giant's Castle for 10 people with gas refrigerator and stove; no bedding. Mountain huts for hikers: Giant's Hut and Bannerman Hut for 8 people and Meander Hut for 4 people; bunk beds and mattresses provided. Picnic site near Giant's Castle hutted camp with all amenities, and Environmental Awareness Officer stationed at camp. Main Caves and Site Museum, and Lammergeyer Hide in Giant's Castle Game Reserve for 6 people. Petrol and oil available at main entrance to Giant's Castle. Trout fishing at Injasuti and Giant's Castle. Hillside camp site accommodates 150 people and has ablution facilities. Hillside rustic hut is self-contained and fully equipped for 8 people. Limited grocery supplies available for purchase. Horse trails from Hillside (see page 216).

Main attractions: Mountaineering, hiking, rambling, rock-climbing, ice-climbing and horse-riding; excellent wildlife and bird-watching area; 140 recorded bird species, including the lammergeyer (bearded vulture); stone bird hide from which cliff-dwelling species can be viewed; Bushman rock art; brown and rainbow trout fishing, with licence and permit; Giant's Castle peak; game; mountain tarns; 4 mountain passes.

Pertinent information: Visitors must provide their own food and drink. Hikers are not permitted to stay in caves containing Bushman paintings. Permits for the wilderness area are limited to 12 people per group, and the Natal Parks Board is considering limiting the number of permits per day. Provincial trout fishing licence and daily rod permit must be obtained at Injasuti or Giant's Castle for trout fishing. Hikers are advised to carry passports and the necessary health documents if trails cross the Lesotho border. Access is via Estcourt or Mooi River. See walk number 11 on page 216 for a 40-km/3-day, self-guided hike in the area. See also page 210 for general notes on walking in the Drakensberg.

with its 4-km ridge as well as the 3 409-m Mafadi Peak, the highest in South Africa. Injasuti, formerly a private resort, and Hillside are satellite camps in the northern part of the reserve. The reserve is perfect for hiking, with its rolling, grassy hills and ridges, high basaltic cliffs, wooded gorges, perennial streams and waterfalls, and dramatic scenery.

It is well worth getting your hands on the Natal Parks Board literature before you set off exploring the area along the numerous established paths; your hike will be enriched as you learn many fascinating facets of ecology, like why the ants you will encounter on some of the trails are named 'cocktail ants', why soils differ in colour, where the birth control pill originates, how ghost frogs climb waterfalls, which Giant's Castle plant is used during theatrical shows, the origin of ox-bow lakes, who lives in 'Old Man's Beard', and the astonishing fact that the human race has polluted 99 per cent of the earth's fresh water.

Other attractions of the area are the game and bird species found there: eland, black wildebeest, blesbok, reedbuck, grey rhebok, bushbuck, oribi, common duiker, red hartebeest, klipspringer, the rare black-backed jackal, more common rock dassie, and the ice rat (a small, hairy and short-tailed rodent). Over 140 species of birds have been recorded and include the endangered lammergeyer, as well as the black eagle, jackal buzzard, rock kestrel, lanner falcon, Cape vulture, crows and ravens. Then, of course, there are the Bushman paintings.

1. First impressions are very often the most lasting … and certainly this generalization is accurate regarding my introduction to the Giant's Castle Reserve. When I visited the Main Caves in the reserve, the clear visual evidence of the everyday lives and the culture of the Bushmen who, until the mid 1800s, had lived there continuously for many centuries, left an indelible impression on me. It was this experience that has greatly enhanced my appreciation of all the Bushman art and caves I have subsequently visited while hiking throughout southern Africa. Today, the Main Caves, together with taped information and a life-sized display, are part of the **Bushman's River Trail,** a self-guided stroll which, in conjunction with its booklet, provides an excellent introduction to the geology, vegetation and history of the Giant's Castle Reserve.

2. There are a variety of other short walks from the **Giant's Castle** hutted camp and in the surrounding area:

❑ Starting at the hutted camp, a 5-km/2-hour, return route will take you to the **Main Caves Forest.** On a hot summer's day, a refreshing dip in the several deep clear pools that are found in the Two Dassies Stream along the way is possible.

❑ The **Grysbok Bush Trail** is an 8-km return route that will take you about 3,5 hours. The beautiful and shy bushbuck roams the forest where it eats the wild fruits and roots that it finds there. The path is cemented where it passes through a fairly swampy grassland area that becomes boggy after summer rains. At the 4-km mark there are a series of beautiful pools that become whirlpools after heavy rains. Retrace the same route to return to the hutted camp.

❑ The **River Walk** follows the east bank of the Bushman's River, through low-lying grassland and then through light bush, across the wall of a small dam, through a gate, and up a steep paved path to the camp. It is a round trip of 3 km that will take

Oblivious to the delicate lighting patterns on the higher ground, contented cattle graze near the camp at Injasuti.

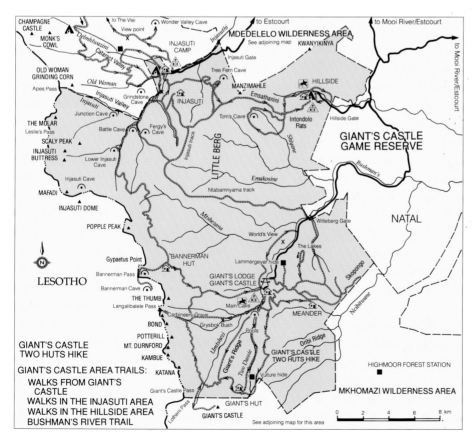

you about 1 hour. A variation of this walk leads you across Bannerman Bridge to a picnic site – a fairly steep climb – and then joins the main road to take you back to the camp at Giant's Castle. This is a 4,5-km/2-hour route.

❏ **Bergview Walk** is a 14-km hike along the Little 'Berg plateau that offers superb views of the escarpment. It is also a circular route that involves some steep climbing, and returns to the camp via the jeep track.

3. There are also a variety of 1-day hikes that you can undertake in the **Giant's Castle area**:

❏ A 19-km/7,5-hour, circular route, starting at the hutted camp, takes you past the Main Caves to Giant's Ridge and then along a contour path to **Giant's Hut**. From there the trail leads you down to the Two Dassies Stream and back to the camp. It is a 15-km/6-hour hike there and back.

❏ From the contour path, you can head right, cross four streams and take the path that leads to a break in the cliffs – a steep route that has the risk of land-slides – then head for the **summit of Giant's Castle**. It is a 6,7-km/4-hour hike from Giant's hut to Giant's Pass and another 2,8 km to the summit of Giant's Castle – in total a 19-km/8-hour, round trip from Giant's Hut and back again.

❏ **Bannerman Hut** is a strenuous 10-km/4-hour hike from the Giant's Castle camp. The ascent of Bannerman Pass follows a clearly defined path which boulder screes makes difficult in the steepest section. It is a 3,6-km/2-hour hike from the hut to

215

The Bushman's River flows past green and gentle slopes in Giant's Castle Game Reserve.

the top of the pass – so you will need to allow at least 6 hours to hike from Giant's Castle hutted camp to the top of Bannerman Pass.

❏ From Bannerman Hut you can follow the contour path northwards to the Injasuti River and the **Lower Injasuti Cave**. This is a 23,2-km/8-hour, round trip that will give you a magnificent view of the whole Injasuti Valley.

❏ The contour path can also be used as a route between **Giant's Hut and Bannerman Hut** – a fairly easy 18-km walk along a wide path that will take about 6 hours.

❏ **Langalibalele Pass** is an easy ascent of the escarpment from the contour path, and at the top of the pass you will find the Carbineer's Grave. Return along the same route to Giant's Castle hutted camp – an 8-hour/26,8-km round trip.

❏ **World's View Trail** takes you to the highest point on the Wildebeest Plateau above the Bushman's River and is worth the 14-km/4,5-hour hike there from Giant's Castle camp for the magnificent views of the Drakensberg from World's View.

❏ **Meander Hut** can be reached from Giant's Castle camp via Beacon Ridge (a 14-km/4,5-hour, round trip) or via the jeep track (a 12-km/4,5-hour route). The hut itself is wonderfully situated above the cliffs overlooking Meander Valley.

❏ The jeep track leads east from Meander Hut to **Skopongo Ridge** where there is an airstrip – a 2,5-km/1-hour, round trip from Meander Hut.

❏ A variation of the route to Meander Hut via the jeep track will lead you to a huge basalt shelf that has a series of large water-filled potholes. This circular trail is aptly named **The Lakes Trail**, and is a 14-km/5-hour hike.

❏ **Meander Hut to Giant's Hut** via the Loteni jeep track is a one-way 11,4-km/4-hour hike that involves some steep climbing.

❏ Finally, there is the 15,6-km/5,5-hour route from Giant's Castle camp to the contour path, where you turn left and continue to **Langalibalele Path**, just before Langalibalele Pass, which will lead you back to the camp.

4. In the Injasuti area, there are also a variety of short and 1-day walks:

❏ An interesting 2,5-km/1-hour stroll in the vicinity of the Injasuti camp will take you past the **Old Kraal and Dipping Tank**, through the Yellowwood Forest and back to the camp. A variation of this route visits the Forest Guard's hut and will add about 30 minutes to your walk.

❏ There are various routes that will take you to **Boundary Pool and Poacher's Stream** where the brave can take a dip in the chilly water. It takes about 1 hour to walk from the Injasuti camp to Boundary Pool, and a round trip that includes Poacher's Stream will take you about 2,5 hours, with a steep climb through a sandstone band included in the route.

❏ **Tanglewood Forest** can be visited on a 1,5-hour round trip, but involves a crossing of the Injasuti River that is dangerous at the height of the rainy season. Follow the route to Poacher's Stream but continue on to the forest instead of climbing up the sandstone band.

❏ A hike into the Mdedelelo Wilderness Area is possible from Injasuti camp, following shorter or longer routes to visit **Grindstone Caves and Cataract Valley**. A 13-km/4-hour route follows the Old Woman Stream and then crosses another stream further on and leads past a small waterfall to Cataract Valley, from where the route home follows the Delmhlwazini River.

❏ The walk to **The View Point at Van Heyning's Pass** is an 8-km/3-hour trip that is a good introduction to the surrounding landscape and major peaks as from View Point you can see all the paths in the Injasuti area.

❏ A 7-hour, round trip to **Wonder Valley via Van Heyning's Pass** will take you past patches of forest, a cave, waterfall and streams.

❏ A full day's hike is possible along the **contour path** beneath Monk's Cowl. This 21,5-km/10,5-hour route leads you from the Injasuti camp through Van Heyning's Pass and up the ridge to the contour path, and then across streams and on to

Cataract Valley, where the path will lead you back to the camp.

5. From **Hillside camp** there are also a variety of walks that you can do (although this camp is primarily for horse trails):

❏ The Natal Parks Board has an interesting brochure describing the most interesting aspects of the environment to take with you on the **Forest Walk** – a 4,5-km/1,5-hour, round trip. Guided tours are also offered on this route.

❏ **iNtondolo Forest and Flats Hike** explores the forest and wide plain – an 8-km/3-hour route.

❏ **Tom's Cave and Tree Fern Cave** are used as overnight stops for horse trails, but hikers can walk to Tom's Cave along a 17-km/6-hour, circular trail and to Tree Fern Cave via a 12-km/4-hour route (allow time to return to the camp).

---

11. GIANT'S CASTLE TWO HUTS HIKE
GIANT'S CASTLE GAME RESERVE, NEAR ESTCOURT

Trail details: 39,5 km/3 days, circular. See map p. 215.

Permits/bookings: Bookings are to be made through the Natal Parks Board, tel. (0331) 471981, fax. (0331) 471980; PO Box 662, Pietermaritzburg 3200.

Maps/information: Map of the Central Drakensberg by Peter Slingsby and a trail booklet are available from the Natal Parks Board at the camp.

Facilities/amenities: Giant's Castle hutted camp: self-contained cottages and bungalows for up to 68 people; Giant's Lodge: luxurious lodge accommodating up to 7 people; Rustic hut: accommodation for up to 10 people; gas refrigerator and stove provided; 2 huts on trail – Giant's Hut and Bannerman Hut – each accommodating 8 people, with bunk beds and mattresses; Environmental Awareness Officer at the Giant's Castle hutted camp.

Main attractions: Giant's Castle Peak; game; birdlife; relatively easy hike.

Pertinent information: A maximum of 8 people can be accommodated on this trail. Spring to autumn is the best time of the year although you can encounter mist and lingering rain, and snow has been known to fall all year round. Carry water with you. Access to Giant's Castle is via Estcourt or Mooi River. See page 210 for general notes on hiking in the Drakensberg.

This is a relatively undemanding trail that passes the foot of some of the highest peaks of the Drakensberg but follows the contour path along the minor shelf of the Little 'Berg. Three different routes will take you from the car park at Giant's Castle to Giant's Hut. Via Oribi Ridge is perhaps the easiest as the path climbs steadily to the contour path. Look out for oribi and mountain reedbuck en route, and various tarns on the ridge are sometimes visited by blue cranes when full. Just before the trail reaches the contour path, it passes the vulture hide where bones and meat are left out for the bearded vultures every Saturday and Sunday between May and September. The contour path itself winds up and down gullies, a favourite grazing area for eland. Giant's Hut is 10,5 km and about a 4-hour walk from the car park along this route. A shorter route is via Two Dassies Stream, but this

Curiously headless men seem to be on a hunt in this painting on a rock wall near Giant's Castle.

12. MKHOMAZI WILDERNESS AREA; KAMBERG, LOTENI AND VERGELEGEN NATURE RESERVES
SOUTHERN AND CENTRAL DRAKENSBERG

route becomes very steep. Another optional route is to walk via Giant's Ridge and then 2 km along the contour path. Giant's Hut is beautifully situated beneath the imposing Giant's Castle and the tarn in front of the hut adds to the peaceful picture. In the early morning you may observe game drinking at the water's edge.

On the second day the trail leads you along the contour path from Giant's Hut to Bannerman Hut, an 18-km hike. Keeping the escarpment on your left, the well-defined path winds around spurs, crosses streams and skirts the Katana, Kambue,

Mount Durnford, Potterill, Bond, Erskine and The Thumb peaks. Raptors soar above the crags, and a variety of waterbirds like egrets and storks can be found at the tarns along the way, while the grassland attracts harriers, francolins and quail. Gypaetus Point looms above Bannerman Hut and is home to the bearded vulture.

The route back to the car park at Giant's Castle hutted camp on the third day is an 11-km hike that steeply descends the Little 'Berg plateau to the grassland, continues along a spur and then descends a gully to cross the Bushman's River.

Trail details: 1. In Kamberg Nature Reserve, Mooi River Trail: 4 km/1,5 hours, circular; 2. In Loteni, Eagle Trail: 12 km/6 hours, circular, and Gelib Tree Trail: 2,5 hours, circular; 3. Hikes into the wilderness area from Loteni: from 7,5 km/3 hours to 16 km/6 or 7 hours; 4. Hikes into the wilderness area from Vergelegen: from 14 km/5,5 to 6 hours to 21 km/8 to 9 hours; 5. Pyramid Trail in Vergelegen: 3 km/1,5 hours, one-way; 6. Various hikes in the wilderness area from Mkhomazi Forest Station: from 4,5 km/1,5 hours to 11 km/3,5 to 4 hours.

Permits/bookings: Reservations for Highmoor camp site: Officer in Charge, tel. (0333) 37240; PO Box 51, Rosetta 3301. For enquiries regarding camp in the wilderness area, contact the Officer in Charge, Mkhomazi, tel. (0333) 36664; PO Box 105, Nottingham Road 3280 or the Officer in Charge, Vergelegen, Private Bag 116, Himeville 4585. Permits to enter the wilderness area are available from the Natal Parks Board. Reservations for Kamberg and hutted accommodation at Loteni: Natal Parks Board, tel. (0331) 471981, fax. (0331) 471980; PO Box 662, Pietermaritzburg 3200. Bookings for the camp site at Loteni: Camp Manager, tel. (033722) 1540; PO Box 14, Himeville 4585.

Maps/information: Peter Slingsby's map of the area can be purchased from the Natal Parks Board. Information and brochures are available at Kamberg, Loteni and Vergelegen regarding self-guided trails in those areas. David Bristow, in *Drakensberg Walks*, gives detailed descriptions of trails in the wilderness area.

Facilities/amenities: There is a small rustic camp site with cold water facilities at Highmoor; also vehicle access to the top of the cave sandstone; overnight camping is permitted in the wilderness area. At Kamberg there are five 3-bed rest huts, a community lounge, central kitchen and ablution facilities; one 6-bed, self-contained cottage; Stillerust cottage which sleeps 10 and is fully contained with gas lights, refrigerator and stove; a picnic site; a trail suitable for the handicapped (see page 218); trout hatchery and trout fishing. Loteni hutted camp has 12 chalets, each with own refrigerator, bathroom and toilet and served by 2 kitchen blocks, and 2 self-contained cottages; Simes rustic cottage accommodating 10 people; a camp site with 10 stands and ablution facilities; and a Settler's Homestead Museum. Vergelegen has no accommodation facilities, but there is access to wilderness area where camping is permitted.

Main attractions: Rainbow and brown trout fishing; swimming and horse-riding; large game animals; many caves.

Pertinent information: 1 September to 30 April is trout season. Anglers need both a provincial licence and a daily permit, both of which are available at the camps. Take your own food and drink. Permits for the wilderness area are available for a maximum of 12 people per group. Although there are many caves in the wilderness area that can accommodate hikers, it is always advisable to carry a tent with you. The road to Vergelegen is subject to flooding from December to February. Carry water with you on hikes. Access to the reserves is via Bulwer in the south or Estcourt in the north. See page 210 for general notes on hiking in the Drakensberg.

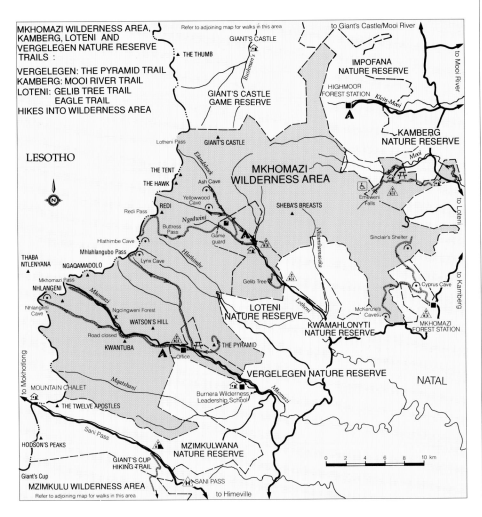

In the foothills of the Drakensberg, the Little 'Berg, the Loteni, Kamberg and Vergelegen nature reserves attract trout anglers, nature ramblers, solitude-seekers and naturalists. I spent days enjoying the rivers and streams, studying the birds, searching for antelope and admiring the backdrop of the sensational high peaks of the great Drakensberg. From Vergelegen Nature Reserve, Thaba Ntlenyana (3 482 m), the highest mountain in southern Africa, is visible.

The 54 000-ha rugged Mkhomazi Wilderness Area is bordered in the north by Giant's Castle Game Reserve (see page 215) and in the south by the Sani Pass, and includes the three reserves mentioned above.

1. The Mooi River Trail in the **Kamberg Nature Reserve** consists of a 4-km main trail as well as three 1-km loops, each taking approximately 2 hours to complete. It is one of the few trails in southern Africa planned for the physically disabled.

2. There are 2 trails in **Loteni Nature Reserve**:

❑ The newer 12-km circular **Eagle Trail** in Loteni helps to focus the walker's attention on human history, as well as the geological, botanical and ecological processes working in the reserve. It offers magnificent views of the Drakensberg and should be allocated a leisurely 6 hours to be fully appreciated. The clearly signposted trail starts about 0,5 km from the rest camp and is quite steeply graded in parts.

❑ The **Gelib Tree Trail** is a 2,5-hour, circular ramble that begins near the museum and also presents a couple of steep gradients.

3. Various hikes into the wilderness area can be undertaken from **Loteni** camp site. Don't forget to carry a good map with you.

❑ There is a one-way, 7,5-km/3-hour hike to **Ash Cave** from the camp site that follows the Lotheni River and is easy walking.

❑ To get to **Yellowwood Cave** from the camp site, follow the Lotheni River until the fork, then follow its tributary, the Ka-Masihlenga. It is a 6,5-km one-way route that will take you about 3 hours and is also fairly easy walking.

❑ **Redi Peak** can be reached from Loteni via Buttress Pass, a 13-km/7-hour, one-way route that involves some steep climbing and follows the contour path for a while. The views of Lesotho and Natal from the summit are really quite magnificent. Carry a tent with you for overnight camping.

❑ **Hlathimbe Cave** is situated at the top of Hlathimbe Pass and looks out towards The Fingers and Hlathimbe Buttress. It is a strenuous, 16-km/7-hour, one-way hike from the camp site to the cave via Redi Peak, so it is advisable to plan spending the night in the cave (or pitching a tent if the cave is already occupied).

4. Armed with Peter Slingsby's map, you can undertake various challenging hikes into the wilderness area from **Vergelegen** picnic spot or the Natal Parks Board office.

❑ **Nhlangeni Cave** on the escarpment can be reached via Nhlangeni Pass. The 21-km, one-way route follows the Mkhomazi and Nhlangeni rivers into a deep cutback. Numerous streams and caves and the rugged terrain invite you to extend the 9-hour hike to 2 days so that you can explore the area at leisure. Spend the night in Nhlangeni Cave, or pitch a tent if the cave is already occupied.

❑ From the picnic spot, you can follow the **Mkhomazi River** to its source at the top of the escarpment, a strenuous 17-km/8-hour, one-way hike that passes through the Ngcingweni Forest on the way. Carry a tent with you for the overnight stop, and remember that the summer rains tend to turn valleys into quagmires.

❑ **Lynx Cave**, another cave on the escarpment, can be reached via a number of routes, but the easiest perhaps is to follow the Mhlahlangubo omkhulu River to the Mhlahlangubo Pass – a 14-km/6-hour, one-way route that passes a number of delightful pools along the way.

5. A short and fairly easy 3-km walk from near the picnic spot in Vergelegen to the summit of **The Pyramid** will take you about 1,5 hours. The path traverses hilly ground as it leads you to the base of The Pyramid. It then spirals up to the 1 782-m summit where you can take a rest to admire the view of the surrounding countryside. Return along the same route.

6. The Mkhomazi Forest Station can also be used as a starting point for a variety of hikes into the wilderness area. Once again, don't venture out without a good map, and if you plan to stay overnight, carry a tent with you.

❑ There are some interesting old ruins near **Cyprus Cave**, which is only a 4,5-km/1,5-hour, one-way hike from the forest station. The cave can be used as an overnight stop for 6 to 8 people.

❑ **Sinclair's Shelter** on the lip of the escarpment is an 11-km/4-hour, one-way hike from the forest station, if you follow the path that passes Cyprus Cave. The shelter can also be used as an overnight stop for 6 people.

❑ **McKenzie's Caves** are also on the escarpment and the two caves can sleep about 24 people. The caves are situated on top of the Ka-Malungana Ridge which raptors use for roosting. The route from the forest station is about 11 km one way and will take 3,5 to 4 hours. A detour along the way to visit Cyprus Cave is worthwhile.

13. BURNERA TRAIL
HIMEVILLE

Trail details: Guided trails from 10 days to 3 weeks.

Permits/bookings: For reservations and further information, contact the Wilderness Leadership School, tel. (031) 428642, fax. (031) 428675; PO Box 53058, Yellowwood Park 4011. Brochure available on request.

Facilities/amenities: Accommodation in old farmhouse; transport to Burnera, food and all equipment provided, except sleeping bags and daypacks.

Main attractions: Little 'Berg ecology.

Pertinent information: Maximum of 8 people per group. Summer rainfall area with thunderstorms. Winters cold with snowfall.

The Burnera Wilderness Leadership School borders the Vergelegen Nature Reserve, which is run by the Natal Parks Board. The school runs backpacking courses of 10 days to 3 weeks duration which take place in the wilderness areas of the southern Drakensberg and focus on outdoor skills and minimum impact techniques. (See map p. 217.)

14. MZIMKULU WILDERNESS AREA AND MZIMKULWANA NATURE RESERVE
SOUTHERN DRAKENSBERG

Trail details: 1. Sani Pass, from Sani Pass Hotel: 20 km/1 day, one-way; from NHW car park: 14 km/6 to 7 hours, one-way; from Koma-Koma Bridge or Mokhotlong: 2 or 4 days, one-way; 2. From Cobham to Hodgson's Peaks: 19 km/1 day, one-way; 3. Cobham to Siphongweni Shelter: 11 km/4,5 hours, one-way; 4. Garden Castle to Rhino Peak: 11 km/5 hours, one-way; 5. Garden Castle Forest Station to Sleeping Beauty Cave: 4 km/1,5 hours, one-way; 6. From Bushman's Nek, to Sehlaba-Thebe Lodge: 14 km/5,5 to 6 hours, one-way; to Thomathu Cave: 10 km/4,5 hours, one-way.

Permits/bookings: Bookings for Cobham camp site: Officer in Charge, tel. (033722) ask for 1831; PO Box 116, Himeville 4585. For information about accommodation in private hotels in the area, contact the Drakensberg Publicity Association, tel. (0364) 481557, fax. (0364) 481562; PO Box 12, Bergville 3350, or tel. (0364) 881180. Permits for the wilderness area can be obtained from the Natal Parks Board or the hotels in the area, or from entrance gates.

Maps/information: David Bristow, in *Drakensberg Walks*, describes in detail various hikes that you can undertake in the area.

Facilities/amenities: At Cobham there is a small camp site with cold water ablution facilities, plus horse-riding and trout fishing, and access to wilderness area where camping is permitted; Garden Castle Forest Station and Bushman's Nek Police Post also provide access to the wilderness area; mountain chalet at the top of Sani Pass; hotels in the foothills (Sani Pass Hotel, Drakensberg Gardens Hotel, Bushman's Nek Hotel).

Main attractions: Rugged mountain scenery; Sani Pass; Rhino's Horn; Hodgson's Peaks; Siphongweni Shelter; skiing.

Pertinent information: Permits for the wilderness area are limited to 12 people per group and the Natal Parks Board is considering restricting the number of parties. No fires allowed. Hikers may not stay overnight in those caves that contain Bushman paintings. Remember to carry your passport and any necessary health documents with you if a trail is going to take you across the Lesotho border. Access to Cobham is via the D7 from Himeville, and to Garden Castle and Bushman's Nek via the R394 from Underberg. Sign the mountain rescue register before setting off. See number 15 on page 220 for a 5-day trail through the area (Giant's Cup Trail). See also page 210 for general notes about hiking in the Drakensberg.

My feelings for this region are probably best expressed in the following excerpt from a *Report on the Drakensberg Hike*, written for the then-Director of Forestry soon after my arrival in South Africa in 1975: 'It is extremely difficult to relate the experience of such a hike in writing, as it incorporates a total involvement of the mind, the body and the soul. Geomorphological forces create a landscape of stark columnar basalt extrusions over sandstone in a most forbidding manner; the wind blows fiercely through narrow passes; water tumbles down cliffs as waterfalls converge into rivers; and whitenecked ravens scold at the unusual invasion of their formidable domain. The weather

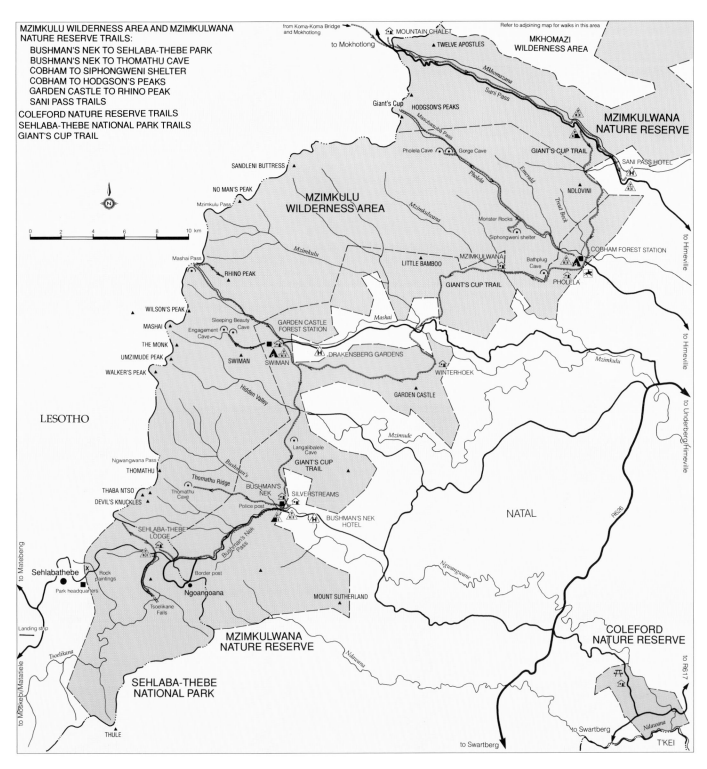

MZIMKULU WILDERNESS AREA AND MZIMKULWANA
NATURE RESERVE TRAILS:
   BUSHMAN'S NEK TO SEHLABA-THEBE PARK
   BUSHMAN'S NEK TO THOMATHU CAVE
   COBHAM TO SIPHONGWENI SHELTER
   COBHAM TO HODGSON'S PEAKS
   GARDEN CASTLE TO RHINO PEAK
   SANI PASS TRAILS
COLEFORD NATURE RESERVE TRAILS
SEHLABA-THEBE NATIONAL PARK TRAILS
GIANT'S CUP TRAIL

changes quickly and unexpectedly, and one's body shifts from perspiring and burning under the intense rays of the sun, to shivering under the shade of the clouds, to feeling the pain of hail and the discomfort of heavy rains – all of which can be experienced within the same afternoon. To an American such as myself, who has spent the majority of her hiking experiences in glaciated landscapes of the northern temperate, boreal and arctic country, the steep, V-shaped valleys, the lack of cirque lakes, and the sight of Basotho cloaked in robes, armed with primitive hunting weapons and accompanied by dogs is, in itself, an adventure comparable to none.'

The wilderness areas of the southern Drakensberg are not as well known as the northern region; paths are few and far between, the country appears wilder, the scenery more rugged and even the Little 'Berg seems more spectacular. It is a vast and remote region – a true wilderness with countless challenges for the really ambitious backpacker. This rugged region also boasts southern Africa's highest motor road, the Sani Pass (2 877 m). The 28 340-ha Mzimkulu Wilderness Area and the 22 751-ha Mzimkulwana Nature Reserve stretch southwards from Sani Pass to Bushman's Nek. Don't forget to obtain a permit before you head off into the wilderness area.

1. Tracing the upper valley of the Mkomazana River, the incredible **Sani Pass** follows a 20-km tortuous route from the luxurious Sani Pass Hotel at its foot to the Drakensberg escarpment, and then continues for 50 km into the Black Mountains to the remote village of Mokhotlong, 'the place of the baldheaded ibis', in Lesotho. The pass is regularly travelled by Basotho horsemen leading pack mules and donkeys laden with trade goods. And the only alternative to walking or riding is a fourwheel drive vehicle or trail bike, for the route up into the mountains, which is flanked by precipitous cliffs, river cascades, gorges and caves, is far beyond the capabilities of the ordinary motor car. At the top of the

*Blanketed Basotho and their worldly-wise dog
cross a stream.*

escarpment (2 900 m) is a shack, licensed to sell liquor, where mountaineers can find accommodation. During winter, snows frequently lie deep and make the added effort of taking skis well worthwhile. But whatever the season, don't forget your money, passport and vaccination certificate, as the head of the Sani Pass marks the border between South Africa and Lesotho.

The 20-km/1-day hike from the **Sani Pass Hotel to the border post** at the head of the Sani Pass follows the gravel road. Alternatively, you can leave your car at the NHW car park and hike the last 14 km, which will take you 6 to 7 hours.

From **Lesotho**, hikers can use the **Koma-Koma Bridge** on the Orange (or Senqu) River as a starting point and walk north along the fourwheel-drive track until it meets up with the track that runs from **Mokhotlong to Sani Pass**. It is a 2-day hike from the bridge to Mokhotlong, and another 2-day hike to Sani Pass. There are no facilities along the way, but the local villagers are usually helpful in pointing you in the right direction.

2. Rising from the escarpment to the south of the top of Sani Pass are **Hodgson's Peaks** (3 244 m and 3 256 m). Both can also be ascended by walking via the attractive Pholela River Valley and Masubasuba Pass, a 19-km/1-day, one-way route from **Cobham Forest Station**. Spectacle, Gorge or Pholela caves can be used as an overnight stop – each cave sleeps about 12 people.

Hikers in the region are likely to come across the cairn, dating from the mid-1800s, which marks the grave of Thomas Hodgson. At that time the southern Drakensberg was the scene of a bitter, drawn-out struggle between white pastoralists and Bushmen who reacted to the diminution of their hunting grounds by rustling the farmers' livestock. It was during one of the many skirmishes of these times that Hodgson, a farmer, was accidentally shot by one of his comrades.

3. With Peter Slingsby's map in hand and a spirit of adventure, let names like Emerald Stream, Trout Beck, The Lake District, Bushman's Rock and Hidden Valley entice you into exploring the area on paths that are not always clearly marked. David Bristow, in *Drakensberg Walks*, describes some of his personal favourite routes. **Siphongweni Shelter**, where you will find what remains of some unusual Bushman paintings of remarkable quality (vandals, however, persist in desecrating this na-

tional monument), is well worth a visit. From **Cobham Forest Station** it is an 11-km/4,5-hour, one-way hike via the Pholela River. About 7 km upstream, just before Monster Rocks, turn left and head towards the shelter.

4. The most conspicuous peak of the region is **Rhino Peak** (3 051 m) which protrudes from the escarpment. It can be reached via Mashai Pass from **Garden Castle Forest Station**, but even more skilled mountaineers will find Rhino's E to F grade climbs very challenging. The route is 11 km one way and will take you at least 5 hours, so allow time for the return journey. The well-defined path actually follows the Mlambonja River, and the ascent of the pass is a very steep one.

5. A very popular short walk in the area, that is also suitable for the novice hiker, is a 4-km/1,5-hour, one-way ramble from **Garden Castle Forest Station to Sleeping Beauty Cave**. From Swiman Hut you follow the Mashai River upstream past The Monk. About 1 km further on the cave is located on the steep slope above the river. Another 700 m upstream is a side gully that shelters **Engagement Cave**. Both caves can be safely used for overnight camping.

6. Bushman's Nek Police Post gives you access to the most southern part of the region.

❑ You can hike to **Sehlaba-Thebe National Park** in Lesotho (see entry number 16 on page 221) from the police post. Remember to get your passport stamped before you leave. The 14-km, one-way hike is a strenuous one that follows the Ngwangwane River to Bushman's Nek Pass. Keep right and head towards the border fence, and then on to Sehlaba-Thebe Lodge – it should take you 5,5 to 6 hours to reach the lodge.

❑ A well-defined path will lead you from the police post via Thomathu Ridge to **Thomathu Cave** – a 10-km/4,5-hour, one-way hike that is steep climbing most of the way. Take heart though because the last 3 km is the least steep section for the hike, as it only ascends 200 m.

❑ The area is rich in caves containing **Bushman rock art**, but the routes to these caves are not always well defined and most of the caves are not marked on any maps, so you will need to be fit and have a spirit of adventure as well as a good mountain sense and map-reading abilities to explore the area. It is not advisable to attempt to find these caves on your own or without the company of a seasoned Drakensberg hiker.

---

15. GIANT'S CUP TRAIL
SOUTHERN DRAKENSBERG, NEAR HIMEVILLE

When you think of hiking in the Drakensberg, you immediately conjure up images of a very difficult trail full of ascents on steep passes. However, the Giant's Cup section of the Drakensberg Hiking Trail is nowhere near as formidable. Starting on the Sani Pass road, near the Sani Pass Hotel (Sani Pass is the highest pass in southern Africa), the Giant's Cup Trail heads south to Bushman's Nek, a Lesotho/South African border post. Because the gradient remains flat to gentle the entire way, with only a few short, steep sections, and because all 5 days are less than 14 km each, this trail is one of the physically easier hikes in the NHWS. This was done purposely in order to allow those less fit and less adventurous than the 'Drakensberg mountain-

Trail details: 59 km/5 days, self-guided, open-ended (variations possible). See map p. 219.
Permits/bookings: Bookings are to be made through the Natal Parks Board, tel. (0331) 471981, fax. (0331) 471980; PO Box 662, Pietermaritzburg 3200. Detailed map provided. The Natal Parks Board also has a trails booklet.

Facilities/amenities: 5 huts, each accommodating 30 people, with bunks, mattresses, tables and benches, cold water and waterborne and/or pit toilets; braai facilities and parking availabel at Pholela, Swiman and Bushman's Nek; Himeville Toyota Service Station at Himeville, tel. (033722) 11, or Giant's Cup Motors, tel. (033722) 1302, will contract to transport you to the starting point or from the end of the trail.

Main attractions: Historical areas and interesting caves; rock pools for swimming; 135 species of birds; flowering plants; fishing for rainbow and brown trout.

Pertinent information: Camp-stoves are essential. Maximum of 30 people per group. At least 1 adult must accompany each group of up to 10 persons under the age of 18. Note: the environmentally based land-use plan operating in the Natal Drakensberg concentrates hiking in the trail zone, a belt ranging in altitude from approximately 1 770 m to 1 970 m, which includes the region of open grassland, wooded protea savannah and forest growing on soils derived from the Upper Beaufort Series of the Karoo System; above the trail zone, in the 'Wilderness Heart Zone', mountaineering and more strenuous hiking is available. A permit must be obtained from the Himeville Hotel if you wish to do any fishing. See page 210 for general notes on hiking in the Drakensberg.

eer' an opportunity to experience this lovely natural area. Besides the rugged mountain backdrop with views of famous peaks such as Hodgson's (3 244 m and 3 256 m), Rhino's Horn (3 051 m), Wilson's (3 276 m) and Devil's Knuckles (3 028 m), a wide variety of plants and animals make this a fascinating section of the Natal Drakensberg. Proteas

*Sani Pass and noisy motor vehicles lie far
below these hikers.*

Giant's Cup Hiking Trail passes through Cobham Nature Reserve near Himeville.

bloom in February and March, while other plants flower at various times throughout the year. Trees are labelled with their national tree list numbers. Among the variety of wildlife found in this area, eland, bushbuck, grey duiker, oribi, common and mountain reedbuck, grey rhebok, water mongoose, the bearded vulture, black and martial eagles and the secretarybird are the most commonly seen.

The first day of the trail is about a 13-km/6-hour hike to Pholela Hut (actually an old farmhouse). The starting point is at the foot of the famous Sani Pass, at the Hiking Way car park, and the first 2,5 km is through flat grassland strewn with boulders. A 120-m climb then takes you across the ridge between the Mlcomazana and Gxalingwena rivers. The trail then leads round a headland and down to Ngwenwa Pool. On a sunny day, this is a pleasant spot to stop for lunch, while when it rains, hikers can seek shelter in a cave nearby – a short climb out of the valley, at the top of the opposite slope. Refreshed, you can tackle the 4-km hike around Ndlovini Hill to Trout Beck Valley where the path crisscrosses the river at intervals and then leads you across a suspension bridge and on to the overnight stop. Day 2 is a short 9-km/3,5-hour walk to the Mzimkulwana Hut. The first 2,5 km is a climb out of the Pholela River Valley, but the next 3 km is easy walking past the Tortoise Rocks and Bathplug Cave where a small stream flows down through a hole in the cave floor. This is a good place to stop for lunch. From there the path rounds iSiphongweni Hill and gently descends to the Mzimkulwana River. Some impressive rock art can be seen at the Siphongweni Shelter which is located where the steep slope of the upper conical peak meets the northern edge of the plateau. A 12-km/5,5-hour hike on the third day will lead you to Winterhoek Hut where the oak trees are

estimated to be nearly 100 years old. A steep 4-km climb up to the plateau level of the Little Bamboo Mountain is followed by a descent to Killiecrankie Stream and the petrified forest. On a hot day in summer, the Killiecrankie pools on the route offer hot and weary hikers a refreshingly cold swim in the mountain water. The trail then follows the Garden Castle road to the overnight hut. Day 4 is nearly 13 km and will take you about 6 hours. Carry water as in the dry season you will not find any along the route. The 2-km climb up the Black Eagle Pass is hard on the legs, and the rest of the day's trail is through grassland, across a bridge above Mzimkhulu and Mlambonja rivers, and then along a meandering and undulating route to the overnight hut – Swiman. From there you tackle the final day's hike – a 12-km/4-hour walk to Bushman's Nek. An easy 3,5-km climb to Bucquay Nek is followed by a 2-km gentle descent to the Mzimude River Valley. The trail crosses the river via a suspension bridge, and then makes its way up to a saddle on Langalibalele Hill. The last section of the trail is a winding descent to Bushman's Nek, where you can spend the night at Bushman's Nek Hut, or you can continue on to the end point at the car park. It is worth spending the night here as there are numerous caves and much rock art to explore in the area. The trail may be shortened by starting at Pholela or Swiman's huts.

16. SEHLABA-THEBE NATIONAL PARK
RAMATSELISO'S GATE

Lying at an average altitude of 2 400 m, but rising to nearly 3 000 m at the Natal/Lesotho border, and located on the south-west side of the Drakensberg escarpment, is Sehlaba-Thebe ('plateau of the shield'), Lesotho's first national park. The scenery

Trail details: Hikers can use the network of footpaths and disused cattle tracks or the gravel road in the park for walking. See map p. 219.

Permits/bookings: Bookings for accommodation are to be made through Sehlabathebe Lodge Reservations, Lesotho National Parks, Ministry of Agriculture, tel. (266) 323600 or 322876; PO Box 92, Maseru 100. Only cash payments are accepted at the park.

Maps/information: The park is shown on Peter Slingsby's map of the area.

Facilities/amenities: Sehlaba-Thebe Mountain Lodge is equipped with the basic essentials and accommodates 12. A hostel with basic facilities sleeps 6. Camping is allowed in the park, but there are no facilities. There is a research station for visiting scientists.

Main attractions: Superb scenery, including fascinating rock shapes, streams, tarns and vleis, and some high peaks like Thaba Ntso (also called the Devil's Knuckles or the Three Bushmen); rare plants, endemic fish, mountain birds and some reintroduced game; trout fishing; Bushman paintings in the numerous caves and stone shelters.

Pertinent information: Bring your own bedding and food. Access by road is via Matatiele and then Qacha's Nek or Ramatseliso's Gate. Summer rains often make these roads unnavigable, and winter snow can also cut off the roads. A fourwheel-drive vehicle is essential to negotiate the track in the park. From Maseru, flights are available to Ha Paulus airstrip, and arrangements can be made for transport to the lodge: contact Air Lesotho, tel. (266) 312453; PO Box 861, Maseru 100. Hikers can walk from Bushman's Nek to the lodge (see page 220 for a description of this hike), or arrangements can be made for a guide and ponies to meet hikers at Bushman's Nek and lead/transport them to the lodge. Be prepared for unpredictable and adverse weather conditions, especially thick mists that can descend upon you very quickly.

The park is particularly rich in **Bushman rock art** – over 60 painting sites in caves and rock shelters reflect tribal ceremonies, hunting scenes and daily life of the Bushmen. On the western border of the park, near the park headquarters (which is linked to the lodge by the gravel road), is a shelter with over 130 individual Bushman paintings. It is a 9-km walk along the road from the lodge to the park headquarters, and the overhang is easily accessible from there.

A hike to **Tsoelikane Waterfall** and back to the lodge is a 1-day trip. Follow the Tsoelikane River downstream, taking a detour about halfway to climb to the summit of the Kepiseng, which will take about 20 minutes. The waterfall drops 20 m into a pool that is most inviting on a hot day.

From the lodge it is a 4- to 5-km steep hike to the first of the **Three Bushmen Peaks** (also called the Devil's Knuckles or Thaba Ntso). For the fit, the climb is worth the view of Lesotho to the west, the lowlands of Natal to the east, the summits of Walker's Peak and Rhino Peak to the north, and sheer cliffs dropping 400 m below.

17. COLEFORD NATURE RESERVE
UNDERBERG

Trail details: Short walking trails along a network of paths in the reserve.

Permits/bookings: Reservations for accommodation: Natal Parks Board, tel. (0331) 471981, fax. (0331) 471980; PO Box 1750. Pietermaritzburg 3200.

Facilities/amenities: Hutted camp with two 6-bed cottages, three 5-bed chalets, two 3-bed chalets and six 3-bed huts, all with own refrigerators, while the chalets have bathrooms and toilets; the camp also has a kitchen and ablution block; and all bedding, cutlery and crockery are provided; 'Sunnyside Cottage' accommodates 7 people and is equipped with gas stove, refrigerator, lights and basic necessities; rainbow trout fishing; horses for hire; a tennis court; facilities for croquet and deck-quoits; picnic site at river opposite Sunnyside; game- and bird-viewing hide; curio shop.

Main attractions: Game; antelope enclosures; trout fishing in rivers.

Pertinent information: Bring your own food and drink. Provincial licence and daily angling permit required; both are available at the reserve. This is a summer rainfall area.

Reflections – an ephemeral painting – in Sehlaba-Thebe National Park.

is spectacular – only the difficult access to the park keeps the number of visitors low. This fact is a definite attraction for solitude-loving backpackers. Serving as the upper catchment for the Tsoelike River, Sehlaba-Thebe National Park consists largely of sub-alpine grassland, dominated by three peaks, Baroa-baBararo ('the Three Bushmen'). Sandstone wind- and water-eroded caves, arches and pools are a photographer's playground. There are numerous pools for refreshing swims on a hot day, and both the Leqooa and the Tsoelike rivers are well known for their rainbow trout. The tiny minnow, *Oreodimaon quathlambae*, which was once thought to be extinct, is endemic to the Tsoelike catchment area. Overhead, the rare lammergeyer commands the skies.

Snakes are generally not found in highland regions and are therefore uncommon in the park. A dangerous exception, however, is the mountain adder, and climbers must be especially alert for this reptile. Its neurotoxic venom, unusual for adders as their venom is chiefly cytotoxic and haemotoxic, paralyses the eye muscles, temporarily blinding the victim. Recovery usually occurs without treatment.

In the park, as in the rest of Lesotho, rivers in flood present potential hazards, especially impeding east-west progress in the summer rainy season, so be prepared.

There are no trails in the park, but hikers can walk along the gravel road that runs through the park from the entrance in the north-west to the Ngoangoana border post in the north-east, or explore the footpaths and cattle tracks that crisscross the park. Keep in mind that there are no facilities, and no mountain rescue team to come to your aid if you should get lost or injure yourself.

This 1 272-ha reserve is pleasantly situated in the foothills of the southern Drakensberg, and the Ngwangwana and Ndawana rivers that traverse the reserve are a paradise for keen anglers in search of rainbow trout. The reserve can be reached either via the R394 from Kokstad or Underberg, or the R617 from Bulwer.

Short walking trails are laid out in the reserve. These begin at the hutted camp or Sunnyside Cottage and that explore the rivers and the surrounding grass-covered hills where game such as black wildebeest, blesbok, oribi and reedbuck graze.

18. MOUNT CURRIE NATURE RESERVE
KOKSTAD

Trail details: Crystal Springs Dam Trail: 2,2 km/ 1 hour, self-guided, circular.

Permits/bookings: Bookings for the caravan and camp site: Officer in Charge, tel. (0372) 3844; PO Box 378, Kokstad 4700.

Facilities/amenities: Camp site with ablution block and hot and cold water; picnic site with braai facilities; Crystal Dam, stocked with rainbow trout, bass and bluegill.

Main attractions: Game; Crystal Dam; Adam Kok national monument.

Pertinent inforamation: A provincial licence and daily angling permit are required to fish in the dam; both are available at the reserve. Bring your own food and drink. This is a summer rainfall area.

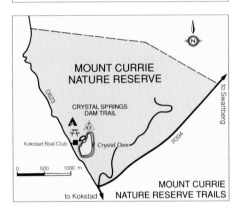

This 1 777-ha reserve is in the southern foothills of the Drakensberg and consists mainly of grass-covered hillsides. It is about 5,5 km from Kokstad via the R394 and D623 – a graded gravel road.

Game-viewing opportunities are good with antelope like grey rhebok and mountain reedbuck being most common, and springbok, blesbok, bush-buck, reedbuck, oribi and common duiker also making their home here.

Of historical interest is the memorial that marks the place where the Griquas, led by Adam Kok, erected a laager when they arrived in the area on 12 May 1803.

Visitors can walk on the short network of gravel paths in the reserve, or on cattle paths, and the hilly topography of the area gives the more energetic an opportunity to do some climbing.

The Crystal Springs Dam Trail is a pleasant 2,2-km ramble around the dam that gives you the opportunity to observe a variety of waterbirds.

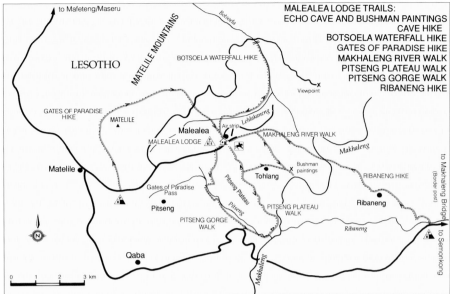

19. MALEALEA LODGE TRAILS
MAKHAKHE

Trail details: 1. Botsoela Waterfall Hike: 4 hours, return; 2. Pitseng Gorge Walk: 6 hours, return; 3. Pitseng Plateau Walk: 1 hour, one-way; 4. Makhaleng River Walk: 2-hour, return; 5. Echo Cave and Bushman Paintings Cave Hike: 3-hour, circular; 6. Ribaneng Hike: 3 hours, one-way; 7. Gates of Paradise Hike: 1-day, one-way.

Permits/bookings: For accommodation bookings, contact Maleala Lodge, tel. (266) 785336 or 785264 after hours, fax. (266) 785326; PO Makhakhe, 922 Lesotho, or PO Box 119, Wepener 9944; or tel./fax. (051) 473200.

Maps/information: Information brochures and maps available on request.

Facilities/amenities: Maleala Lodge is a self-catering rustic lodge that is used as the base for a variety of hiking and pony-trekking trails, and fourwheel-drive tours of Lesotho (see page 000 for more details about the ponytrekking trails). Pack horses and a Basotho guide can be hired. A small shop sells basic food supplies.

Main attractions: Rugged and remote country; mountain peaks, river gorges, and waterfalls; typical Basotho villages.

Pertinent information: Bring your own food and towels. To reach the lodge by road, take the A2 from Mafeteng to Morija and turn off on the B40 then the B401. There is also a small airstrip at Maleala. During the summer rains rivers can become impassable. In winter the bitter cold and frost are a hazard.

Maleala Lodge overlooks the Thaba Putsoa range of mountains, and is within hiking distance of the three highest waterfalls in Lesotho – Ribaneng, Ke-tane and Maletsunyane.

1. A 4-hour hike to **Botsoela Waterfall** and back to the lodge will take you through steep gorges and valleys via the Lehlakaneng River and then the Bot-soela River, passing remote Basotho villages along the way, to the unique twin waterfall. Try and stay close to the river bed and walk carefully as the rocks are very slippery.

2. The 6-hour **Pitseng Gorge Walk** follows the Pitseng River and will take you to magnificent overhanging rocks, pools and cascades which invite you to take a refreshing and often much-needed swim on a hot summer's day. At one point on the walk there is a very large boulder from which you have to jump into a pool of water below, which varies in depth from ankle deep to waist high. The return route is along a vehicle track and then a bridle path.

3. The Pitseng Plateau Walk is a short and easy walk for the less energetic. It will take you to the top of the plateau that overlooks the Pitseng Gorge, along the same path that is used for the return route for walk no. 2.

4. The Makhaleng River Walk is a hike from the jeep track to the Makhaleng River where you can enjoy the tranquillity of the river and its beautiful sandstone cliffs. A gorge on the right has a unique and interesting underground river tunnel that is well worth exploring.

5. Echo Cave and Bushman Paintings Cave Hike is a 3-hour, circular trip from the lodge. Follow the jeep track to Tohlang, then ask the locals to direct you to the Bushman paintings. From this point more energetic hikers can follow the Makhaleng River upstream to explore the underground river tunnel and then make their way back to the lodge via the route of the Makhaleng River Walk (see walk no. 4).

6. The Ribaneng Hike is a walk from the Riba-neng River back to the lodge along a bridle path that crosses the Ribaneng and Makhaleng rivers and then joins up with the route of the Makhaleng River Walk (see walk no. 4). Use a vehicle to get to the beginning of the hike (a 1-hour drive) as the road takes you past picturesque villages and beautiful scenery.

7. Drive to the **Gates of Paradise** for the start of an all-day hike back to the lodge. This hike will take you along the spectacular Matelile mountain range which gives you a wonderful 360-degree view of the area. The pony-trekking trails (see Special Interest section) can also be tackled on foot by more adventurous hikers who wish to explore the remote ruggedness of Lesotho.

SWAZILAND

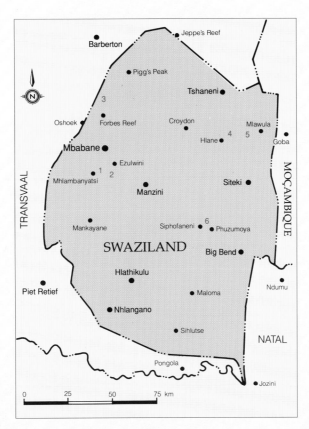

Swaziland, one of Africa's few remaining kingdoms, is a constitutional monarchy. Landlocked by Natal, the Transvaal and Mozambique, its 17 363 km^2 (similar in size to Wales) contain examples of many African ecosystems: the western mountains of the highveld with their impressive river gorges, valleys and peaks such as Emlembe, the highest at 1 863 m; rolling grasslands; and bush typical of the lowveld.

At one time, hiking trails for tourists were scarce; however, Swaziland's National Trust Commission has developed game parks and nature reserves such as Malolotja, Mlawula and Mlilwane, where the hiker is 'king'.

All visitors must be in possession of a valid passport, and nationals other than South Africans may require visas. Non-South African passport holders must have re-entry permits to return to the Republic.

Swaziland's temperate climate varies considerably with geographical region; summer rainfall is the one common feature. The north-west highlands are cooler than the south-east lowveld. Average temperatures range from 13 °C in winter to 20 °C during the summer months. Rain and humidity occur throughout the country between November and March; some areas receive as much as 2 250 mm rainfall.

The crisp, clear winter days (April to September) are perfect for hiking.

Note that bilharzia is a major health hazard and that bathing in rivers, streams and dams at the lower altitudes is not advised.

LEFT: *The verdant hills of Mlilwane Wildlife Sanctuary, scene of the popular Macobane Furrow Trail.*

Immense granite boulders, like ancient ruins, lie scattered on Meikles Mount, near Mhlane.

1. MEIKLES MOUNT
MHLAMBANYATI

Trail details: A variety of self-guided walks on roads and paths on the farm (from a short 15-minute stroll to day walks).

Permits/bookings: Bookings for accommodation: Mrs V Evans, Meikles Mount, tel. (09268) 74110; PO Box 13, Mhlambanyati, Swaziland.

Maps/information: Brochure and colour sketch map, with all roads and paths marked, and bird list are available.

Facilities/amenities: Horses for hire for guided horse-trails; natural and man-made swimming pools; fishing for yellowfish, bream and catfish; 7 fully equipped and serviced luxury cottages; small shop selling groceries, meat, dairy products and vegetables; croquet, tennis and badminton courts.

Main attractions: Indigenous forest and plantations; rare plants; mountain streams and waterfalls; small game and birdlife (120 bird species).

Pertinent information: Most rain falls in summer, when thunderstorms and mist are common. December and January are the hottest months, while July and August are the coldest and driest. The area is refreshingly cool when the surrounding countryside is hot in the summer. Anti-malaria precautions are advisable, especially in the summer months. Beware of bilharzia, crocodiles and, possibly, hippos in the rivers and dams. Carry water with you on walks. Day visitors are not permitted on the farm.

Stretching 1 341 m from the edge of the Usutu-shane River (884 m) to the top of the mountain at World's View, Meikles Mount is a small, 300-ha, secluded country estate offering guests a network of walks and rides varying in length and difficulty. The estate is 18 km from Mbabane, on the road to Mhlambanyati, and is located on granite in sour grassveld vegetation, with numerous springs and streams, some clogged by delicate rows of tree ferns. The climate is ideal for tree-growing and the owners have developed many eucalyptus stands on their grounds.

The view from the summit of World's View or Giant Rock is worth the steep climb. The hiker gazes over no less than 75 million pine trees, all belonging to the Usutu Forest, one of the largest plantations of conifers in the southern hemisphere. (As you stand in awe overlooking this gigantic man-made forest, you should bear in mind that all these trees will be ground to 100 million tons of pulp per year just to produce paper products!) Do not on any account wander into this forest. Not only are the owners reluctant to allow hikers access, but you also stand the chance of getting hopelessly lost among the trees.

The walks on Meikles Mount are varied. Many are shady paths which wind their way through plantations and firebreaks. My favourite routes include the walk to Mhlane Mountain, the ramble that takes you through the pocket of indigenous forest south-west of Mhlane, the walk through Secret Valley on the south-eastern border of the estate, and, of course, the meandering path along the river bank of the Usutushane (Little Usutu) River. Mhlane Mountain is particularly attractive due to the large granite boulders, wild flowers and its magnificent summit view of the entire estate, the Usutushane River and far beyond.

Hikers can also explore the surrounding country-side with a 5-hour walk to the Lipholo Dam wall and back, or a 2,5-hour hike around Mhlane. The Mhlane route can also be done on horseback accompanied by a guide.

A portion of the Mlilwane Wildlife Sanctuary borders the other side of the breathtaking Usutu-shane River. Although this section is not fenced, it is private property and hikers are on no account permitted to cross into Mlilwane.

Wildlife such as kudu, reedbuck, duiker, impala, warthog and monkeys may be seen by hikers on Meikles Mount, and the interesting and varied birdlife includes species like the black and Ayres hawk eagle, black sparrowhawk, helmeted guinea-fowl, pygmy kingfisher, buffstreaked chat and paradise flycatcher.

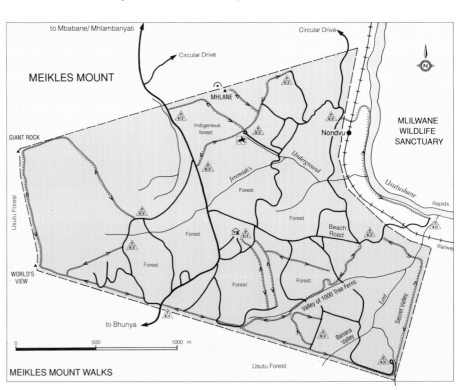

MEIKLES MOUNT WALKS

2. MLILWANE WILDLIFE SANCTUARY
MBABANE

Trail details: 1. Macobane Furrow Trail: 8 km/3–4 hours, open-ended; self-guided. 2. Guided walks.

Permits/bookings: Mlilwane Wildlife Sanctuary, tel. (09268) 61037 or 61591/2/3, fax (09268) 61594; PO Box 33, Mbabane, Swaziland. For guided walks of longer than an hour, notification the day before is preferred.

Maps/information: A variety of literature is available at the reserve.

Facilities/amenities: Horse-riding with game scouts; backpacking trail planned; interpretive centre, conservation hall, film and slide shows; game-viewing drives; Land Rover tours; rest camp with four 2-bed huts, 2 family huts and 9 traditional grass beehive huts, ablution block with showers, hot and cold water (wooden huts have refrigerators; all have bedding and towels); camp site, cabin and open-air dormitories; restaurant, with self-service cooking, overlooking the Hippo Haunt (waterhole with prolific birdlife and hippos); open camp-fire all hours; provision and curio shop; established base for the National Environmental Education programme; Reynolds Memorial Garden (aloes are spectacular); nursery.

Main attractions: Unusual variety of fauna (mixture of both highveld and lowveld species), including endangered animals; impressive variety of birds (roosting birds at the Hippo Haunt are a special attraction); magnificent scenery, especially in the northern wilderness; forest, savannah and grassveld; sacred places; old tin mine; 26-km historic furrow; the popular Mantenga Falls.

Pertinent information: Mosquitoes are a pest; malaria is possible but not prevalent, so anti-malaria precautions are advisable. It is inadvisable to swim in rivers and dams because of bilharzia, crocodiles and, possibly, hippos. Summers are generally hot, with rainfall, thunderstorms and mist. Winter days are mild, and the nights can be cold. Always carry water with you. Although there is no limit to the number of people in a group, smaller groups are preferred.

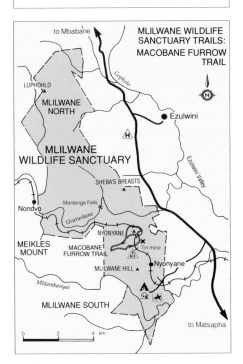

Two young white rhinos take their ease at Mlilwane Rest Camp.

Before I met Ted and Liz Reilly, I enjoyed Mlilwane; after several days with this energetic and ambitious couple, I began to appreciate fully Mlilwane Wildlife Sanctuary and its tremendous conservation achievements and contributions to the Swaziland kingdom.

Located about 24 km from Mbabane and 27 km from Manzini, the 4 545-ha reserve is divided into two parts; the well-known southern section which abounds with wildlife, and offers game drives, the Macobane Furrow Trail, the unique rest camp with its tame animals and unforgettable waterhole, and an interpretive centre and facilities for the National Environmental Education Programme; and the relative wilderness of the northern section, a rugged area of scenic landscapes and wildlife, best explored on foot.

Mlilwane lies in the Ezulwini (place of heaven) Valley, potentially the most fertile area in Swaziland. The escarpment, which forms part of the reserve, was long ago a turning point of easterly and westerly migrations of game. Spanning an altitude from 660 m to 1 437 m, the reserve represents middleveld and highveld, including montane and riverine forests, valley bushveld, broadleaf savannah and sour grassveld. This adds up to an area capable of supporting a wide variety of game; the animals include white rhino, giraffe, zebra, blue wildebeest, eland, kudu, waterbuck, sable antelope, buffalo, hippo, crocodile, wild cat, civet cat, leguaan and many more.

You can only appreciate the biological diversity of Mlilwane when you learn the incredible story of how each animal was re-introduced into a mixed farming operation: Mlilwane was developed on a family farm, previously so heavily exploited that entire habitats had to be created before wildlife could be introduced. Trees were planted, and effort was devoted to re-establishing a wetlands ecosystem. Indigenous animals, from water scorpions and frogs to impala and kudu, were introduced.

While it has always offered guided walks and horse-riding trails with Swazi game guards, the reserve also has a self-guided educational trail on offer: the *Macobane Furrow Trail*. The trail is named after Ted Reilly's father, James Weighton 'Mickey' Reilly, who was known as 'Macobane' to the Swazis. He mined tin and was the largest employer of industrial labour in Swaziland at the time, providing 800 jobs. Among his 'impossible' achievements was the building of a 26-km aqueduct on the Nyonyane mountains. The Macobane Furrow Trail follows this historic furrow, even to the extent that a boardwalk has been built along the face of a precipice where the old furrow flue carried water, and embraces the Nyonyane mountain range. The 8-km trail starts at Nature's Corner and ends at Phumalanga view; both points can be reached by vehicle, unless it has been raining. The gradient is 1 in 100, so this walk is along a contour and relatively easy. Interpretive stations, tree numbers, telescopes, Bushman caves, abundant large game and views of the old tin workings all add interest to this unusual trail.

For the physically fit, a climb up Nyonyane (1 136 m) with a game scout is highly recommended. The summit offers superb 360° views, including the Sheba's Breasts of Rider Haggard fame. The circular rock piles you encounter are actually remains of Basotho buildings from the time before the Swazis invaded. For the real wilderness seeker, arrange a guided walk to explore Mlilwane north. This highveld habitat with forests and waterfalls is home to endangered species such as klipspringer, oribi, grey rhebok, sable antelope and Addo buffalo. The sanctuary is also particularly noted for its abundance of birdlife. Luphohlo Peak, the highest point in Mlilwane, offers a view across Swaziland, from the western border near Redhill to the Lebombo mountains on the Mozambique border. A variety of other guided walks can be arranged; although there are set routes to the dam or across the plains and into the forest, these walks are flexible.

3. MALOLOTJA NATURE RESERVE
MBABANE

Trail details: A variety of self-guided, backpacking trails, from 1 to 7 days; a number of day walks, from 1 to 7 km.

Permits/bookings: For bookings: Malolotja Bookings, tel. (09268) 61178/9; PO Box 100, Lobamba, Swaziland. For more information about the trails: The Senior Warden, tel. (09268) 43060; PO Box 1797, Mbabane, Swaziland; contact The Senior Education Officer for more information about and bookings for the environmental education centre. No permit is required for day walks.

Maps/information: A brochure and map, hiking and backpacking guide, and bird and mammal checklists are available at the reserve.

Facilities/amenities: 17 camp sites on trails, with no facilities. Near main entrance gate: camping site with 15 sites and braais, thatched ablution block, and hot and cold water; 5 A-frame thatched and stone structures with 3 beds each, outside cooking facilities and ablution block; 5 fully furnished log cabins, accommodating up to 6 people each, services (bring your own food and drink). Environmental education centre; trout fishing, with permit, on Mortimer's Dam and Forbes Reef Dam; 20 km of game-viewing roads, picnic area with braai sites and toilets; skins and game meat for sale at the office when available.

Main attractions: Magnificent western highveld landscape; complex geology and dramatic mountain scenery; Swaziland's second- and third-highest peaks; breeding colonies of blue swallow, Stanley's bustard, bald ibis and blue crane; 270 species of birds; 30 species of mammals; over 1 000 plant species; Malolotja Falls (95 m, the highest in Swaziland); Barberton cycad forest; Komati River Valley; oldest mine in human history (41 000 BC).

Pertinent information: Only one party is booked per trail camp site per night; sites are small, and hold only 1 or 2 tents each. Trails are physically demanding and some require hikers to cross rivers. Backpackers are required to carry a spade, which can be rented from the office, to bury human waste. Maximum of 10 people per group. Carry water as camp sites can prove to be dry, and a compass is most useful. Summer rainfall area, and days are mild to hot with mists being common. Winter days are mild to warm and nights are very cold. Frost does occur in winter. Be prepared for sudden weather changes.

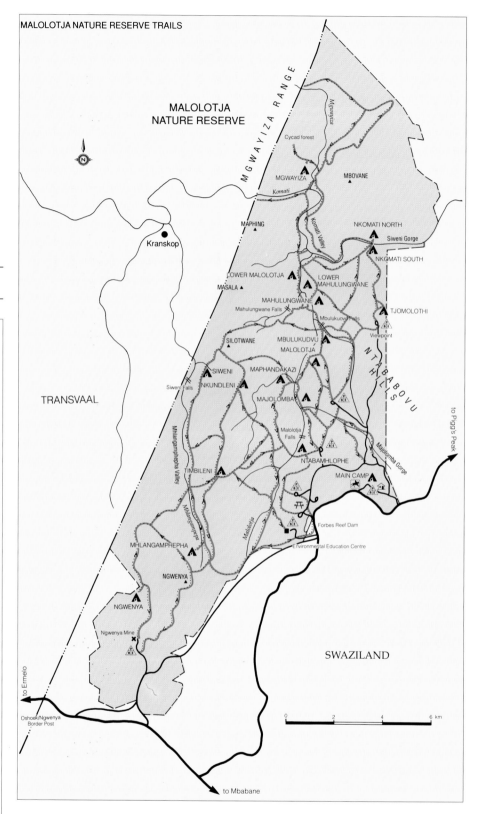

Located about 15 km from the Oshoek border, Malolotja Nature Reserve, spanning an altitude from 615 to 1 800 m above sea level and 18 000 ha in size, is Swaziland's prime hiking reserve, a paradise of highveld and middleveld topography comprising beautiful valleys, broken mountainous terrain, high peaks, plains, plateaux and deep river gorges clothed with forests and grassveld. Some of the more outstanding physical features of this area include the Malolotja Falls, the highest in Swazi-land, the Mahulungwane Falls and Mhlangamphe-pha Valley (a high valley in which the stream is lined with some impressive tree ferns), and two of Swaziland's three highest peaks, Ngwenya (1 829 m) and Silotwane (1 680 m).

Ecologically Malolotja is an essential habitat for nesting colonies of blue swallow, Stanley's bustard, blue crane and bald ibis, and the locally endangered grey rhebok, oribi and mountain reedbuck are found here. Malolotja protects many endangered plants

SWAZILAND

such as *Encephalartos laevifolius* (Kaapsehoop
cycad), *E. heeanii* (woolly cycad) and *Kniphofia
umbrina* (red-hot poker), and hosts some spectacular highveld flora including *Aloe thorncroftii,
A. chortoliriodes* var. *'boastii'* and *Disa inter-
media*, a rare orchid.

In addition to being ecologically valuable, Malolotja's geology contributes to its uniqueness. It
incorporates a representative sample of the Swaziland System, the oldest sedimentary rocks in the
world, which contains the oldest known origin of
life on earth – fossils of blue-green algae, estimated
at 3,5 billion years old. The southern end of the
reserve is rich in haematite-chert ironstones, mined
extensively in recent times for their metallic content and by Stone Age peoples for their red
pigment. Lion Cavern Mine, on the west side of
Ngwenya, is the oldest mine in the world, dating
to *c.* 41 000 BC.

Malolotja is Swaziland's last true wilderness
area and its management policies are geared for
walkers. Wilderness trails are marked with stone
cairns only and paths are not constructed, but are
cleared of bush where necessary. It is vital that you
keep consulting the map that you will be given at
the start of the trail as it is easy to get lost. Hikers
must sleep in designated tent sites and these, located next to water, are also only cleared of bush.

There are approximately 80 km of trails to
choose from. All routes must be discussed at the
tourist office before setting off. I arranged a 7-day
backpacking trip to see the whole of the reserve. I
found the backpacking trails extremely demanding
physically, although short in length. Take the times
given in the literature seriously! All trailists must
be able to read a map and navigate in poor weather
conditions. Remember, the backpacking area is
managed as a wilderness, and minimal tampering
with the environment is the policy. I discovered
two 'dry' tent sites so I recommend checking with
the warden about the water situation when arrang-
ing your route.

Each section of the reserve is different. One trail
which I found particularly lovely was the walk
from Ngwenya Camp, a tent site situated deep in
the densely forested foothills of Ngwenya Peak, to
Siweni Camp at the foot of Silotwane Mountain.
We began in the morning with a very steep
2,5-hour climb out of Ngwenya Forest. Struggling
up through broken, rugged terrain with distant
views of rural Swazi homesteads and dense forests
in deeply incised kloofs reverberating with the calls
of baboons and Knysna louries, I felt the strains
reminiscent of climbing a high Himalayan pass.
But once over the ridge, the gentle, almost magical
Mhlangamphepha Valley unfolded. Highveld rolling grassland was alive with white butterflies
feeding on a carpet of yellow daisies. Swarms of
alpine swifts feasted on these butterflies while wildebeest, blesbok and mountain reedbuck grazed on
young green grass shoots. A pair of mating blue
cranes danced in the grass and Stanley's bustards
called from afar.

The stream bed is delineated by a thin green line
of tree ferns which dance in and out of the shadows
dropped by cumulus clouds high overhead; the
wind creates a changing mosaic of patterns on these
gentle slopes; and on the horizon, the distant
Barberton mountains with their formidable peaks
and gorges disappear into the haze.

The river runs a roller-coaster course through Mahulungwane Gorge in Malolotja Nature Reserve.

The next morning I climbed Silotwane, Swaziland's third-highest peak, an exhilarating
experience that I highly recommend. Once on top,
a 360° view of the entire reserve, reaching into the
Barberton mountains of the Transvaal, unfolds.
From the summit you can really appreciate the
park's rugged topography, and the views of the
Siweni and Malolotja falls and the Komati River
Valley are spectacular. In fact, your entire backpacking route can be traced from here. A pair of
blue cranes flew below me while I was standing
there; top-lit by the sun, they appeared as a sleek
set of silver-winged jets.

In direct contrast to the southern section of the
park is the more rugged and relatively unexplored
northern section. To reach these mountains the Komati River Valley (615 m), a hot, lowveld area of
winding river and gorge, must be crossed. Remember to waterproof your pack if you have to cross the

river in the rainy season. The cycad forest on the
Mgwayiza range, with specimens reaching 7 m
high, is a highlight of this region where only fit
trailists should attempt the steep spurs between the
deeply incised, forested kloofs.

Six day walks have been set out in the reserve,
ranging from 1 to 7 km: the **Malolotja Falls Walk**
will lead you to Swaziland's highest waterfall
where you can also see a bald ibis breeding colony
(in the nesting season, hikers may not visit the site);
the **Malolotja Vlei Walk** passes the Forbes Reef
Dam and visits an upland swamp where you admire
the variety of grasses, sedges, orchids, lilies, labi-
ates and amaryllis; two **Upper Majolomba Walks**:,
the first, starting from the Silotwane viewpoint,
leads you down into the deeply forested Majolomba Gorge, then climbs the mountains at the upper
end of the river and returns you to the viewsite; the
second, starting about 3 km from the log cabins at

229

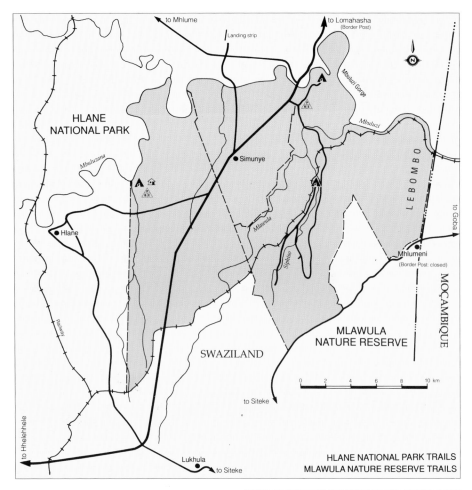

HLANE NATIONAL PARK TRAILS
MLAWULA NATURE RESERVE TRAILS

tion of scavenger species like vultures and jackals. The vegetation is typical of the lowveld – mixed bushveld and savannah – and supports game such as Burchell's zebra, rhino, warthog, kudu, waterbuck, bushbuck, nyala, duiker, and giraffe.

Guided walks can be arranged at the reserve. In the dry winter, game-viewing is particularly good in the northern part of the reserve where animals come to the river to drink.

5. MLAWULA NATURE RESERVE
MHLUME

Trail details: Network of paths for self-guided trails; also guided walks.

Permits/bookings: For information and bookings: The Officer in Charge, Mlawula Nature Reserve, tel. (0194) 38239 or 38885; PO Box 312, Simunye, Swaziland, or contact The Swaziland National Trust Commission, tel. (09268) 61178 or 61151; PO Box 100, Lobamba, Swaziland.

Maps/information: A guide book is available at the reserve.

Facilities/amenities: Land Rover tours on request; canoeing and fishing with permit (bring your own equipment); interpretive centre at the gate; two camp sites with thatched shelters, ablution blocks and hot and cold water; tented camp in mountains with ablution block.

Main attractions: Unique Lebombo mountains; views over Mozambique; endangered plant species (Lebombo ironwood, *Androstachys johnsonii*, found in dry forest) and locally endangered animal species; 'vulture restaurant' (where mammal carcasses are dumped) and hide; 300 species of birds; large game species; rhyolitic rockface communities and dramatic topography (gorges, pools and rapids); archaeology (artefacts of Stone Age peoples).

Pertinent information: Swimming in rivers or dams is not recommended because of bilharzia and crocodiles and, possibly, hippos. Ticks are prevalent. Anti-malaria precautions are advised from October to May. Birdlife is best from September/October to December. Summers are hot and humid in the area, and winters mild to warm, though winter nights can get cold.

Mlawula presents to the trailist an excitingly rich lowveld and Lebombo Mountain wilderness in eastern Swaziland, on the Mozambique border. This area has the distinction of possessing the earliest known record of our species, *Homo sapiens*, dating back 110 000 years.

Mlawula is an interesting area, archaeologically and ecologically. Along the riverbeds of the Lebombo mountains, Early Stone Age tools, one million years old, have been discovered. In the lowveld, evidence of Middle Stone Age people exists. Many of these sites are protected and an archaeological interpretive trail is planned in the Timphisini area.

Ecologically the reserve offers a diverse topography ranging from 76 m at the eastern end of the Mbuluzi Gorge to 573 m above sea level in Ndzindza in the Lebombo mountains. Dry thorn savannah in the west blends into coastal moist thickets in the east. The diversity of vegetation types produces a habitat where a great variety of animals thrive, including unusual coastal birds such as the yellow weaver, African broadbill, crested guineafowl, goldenrumped tinker barbet, and gorgeous bush shrike,

the picnic site, is a shorter and easier walk and leads you up into the higher gorges of the river; an 8-km drive from the log cabins to the Nkomati Viewpoint will take you to the start of the *Nkomati Viewpoint Trail*, which passes the Tjomolothi Camp and offers splendid views of the Nkomati River and the Pigg's Peak pine plantations; the shorter *Gold Mine Walk*. The walks will take you 2 to 3,5 hours, and for each you are required to drive to a carpark and then walk from there. Visits to the mine at Ngwenya are also possible, accompanied by a ranger and arranged a day in advance.

White rhino luxuriate in a mud wallow at Mkaya Nature Reserve.

4. HLANE NATIONAL PARK
SIMUNYE

Trail details: Guided walks.

Permits/bookings: Bookings for accommodation are to be made through The Officer in Charge, Hlane National Park, tel. (09268) 61037 or 61591/2/3, fax (09268) 61594; PO Box 216, Simunye, Swaziland. For guided walks of longer than an hour, notification the day before is preferred.

Facilities/amenities: Camp site with full ablution facilities; thatched huts with bedding and towels provided; Bhubesi Camp, fully equipped, self-catering.

Main attractions: Game; natural mortality allowed to take its course, resulting in a high incidence of scavenger species.

Pertinent information: All fences in the reserve are electrified. Anti-malaria precautions are necessary. It is inadvisable to swim in rivers and dams because of bilharzia, and you should also beware of crocodiles and, possibly, hippos. Summers are hot and wet with thunderstorms; winters are generally mild but can get cold. There is no limit to the number of people in a group for walks, but smaller groups are preferred.

Situated in the Swaziland lowveld, on the road between Manzini and Mhlume/Tshaneni, the Hlane National Park is approximately 30 000 ha in extent. Because it is one of the few conservation areas in southern Africa where natural mortality is allowed to take its course, the reserve has a high concentra-

All appears quiet at a crocodile pool in the Timphisini area of Mlawula.

and dry savannah species such as the grey lourie, marico sunbird and Bennett's woodpecker.

The bush clump grassland plateau, an area to be developed with walking trails near an escarpment overlooking Mozambique, supports oribi, zebra, duiker, wildebeest and mountain reedbuck. Water-buck are found mainly on Mbuluzi, and Ndzindza is important for supporting locally endangered species such as samango monkey, spotted hyaena, Sharpe's grysbok and the fishing owl. Ndzindza also protects endemic floral species such as *Ence-phalartos umbuluziensis*, *Aloe keithii* and *Euphorbia keithii* (Swazi euphorbia). Hippos and crocodiles occur in the Mbuluzi River on the north-ern boundary and the Mlawula River in the west. Guided walks can be arranged.

6. MKHAYA NATURE RESERVE
PHUZUMOYA

Trail details: Guided walks can be arranged.

Permits/bookings: Arrangements to visit the reserve must be made through Mkhaya Nature Reserve, tel. (09268) 61037 or 34371, fax (09268) 61594; PO Box 33, Mbabane, Swaziland.

Facilities/amenities: Spacious luxury canvas tents with pit toilet and running water; central summer house and kitchen; meals and game-viewing drives are inclusive of price; guided tours and rafting.

Main attractions: Refuge for endangered species; abundant birdlife.

Pertinent information: Summers are very hot and humid with rainfall and thunderstorms. Winter days are warm and nights are cool. Anti-malaria precautions are necessary. Beware of bilharzia, crocodiles and, possibly, hippos in the river. Most barbed wire fences in the area are electrified.

Mkhaya, a 6 200-ha lowveld reserve comprising granite sandveld (a sourveld of mixed broadleaf tree species) and dolerite or sweet acacia veld is also owned by the Reillys (see Mlilwane Wildlife

The luxury of a bath al fresco is enjoyed by a visitor to Mkhaya Nature Reserve.

Sanctuary, page 227). It is situated about 3 km from the railway bridge at Phuzumoya, which is near Siphofaneni.

Many large game species such as white rhino, wildebeest, nyala, waterbuck and tsessebe have been introduced, as well as elephant, zebra, reed-buck, roan antelope, eland, giraffe, and crocodile. Smaller carnivores in the reserve are the side-striped and black-backed jackal and spotted hyaena.

As many as 100 species of birds have been re-corded in a weekend visit, and species include the bateleur, martial, tawny, Wahlberg's, booted and crowned eagles as well as several vulture species.

Visitors staying at the reserve can arrange to walk in the area in the company of a game guard.

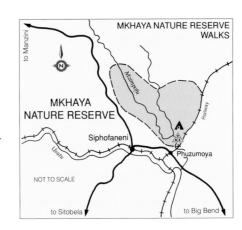

THE HIGHVELD

Most of the central and south-western Transvaal lies on the flat, grassy plateau known as the highveld. This region is South Africa's population hub and its area of greatest urban sprawl. Environmental education and relaxation from the strains of city life are provided by a system of streams (spruits), urban parks, green pockets and wild flower and bird sanctuaries which are linked by semi-urban, self-guided trails. In addition, most mountainous areas around Pretoria and Johannesburg, such as the Witwatersrand and Magaliesberg, are developed with hiking and nature trails. Educational centres and guided trails continue to grow in popularity.

The highveld climate is more predictable than in many areas of South Africa. Summers are warm, with thunderstorms common in the late afternoons. Winters are dry and sunny with cool days (perfect for hiking) but cold nights, and sometimes heavy frosts.

You can walk throughout the year; the highveld in winter is generally drab brown, spring is rejuvenating, summer is the best time for birding and autumn heralds spectacular displays of cosmos at the sides of the roads.

Bophuthatswana is presently divided into seven separate geographical units. Six units are situated between the populated gold-mining and industrial heart of South Africa and the Kalahari Desert, while the seventh area is to the south-east in wheat-growing country. Ranging in altitude between 1 000 m and 2 000 m above sea level, Bophuthatswana is flat to gently undulating, supporting highveld mountain grassveld to tropical bush, and savannah and Kalahari thornveld. Internationally acclaimed game reserves developed on these lands have reintroduced indigenous large game species and offer guided and self-guided trails.

In general, the climate is similar to a dry steppe. Bophuthatswana's rain falls mostly during the summer months, November to early April, when the days are warm to hot. Although winters are cool and frost is common, the days are sunny and pleasant for walking.

LEFT: *The cool, silvery white cascade of Retief's Kloof waterfall is a welcome sight on a hot Magaliesberg day.*

The Magaliesberg forms a natural divide between the lower-lying bushveld and the cooler highveld.

booklet, ramblers are directed to the best view-points and also learn about important geological features in the area. Both these trails are clearly marked, and offer especially pleasant walking conditions in spring and autumn.

2. MAGALIESBERG
SOUTH-CENTRAL TRANSVAAL

Trail details: Various.

Permits/bookings: Hikers are responsible for obtaining permission or permits from local governments and private landowners. Contact the Johannesburg office of the Mountain Club of South Africa for details, tel. (011) 8033716.

Facilities/amenities: Holiday resorts and camp sites; Hartebeesport Dam recreational complex.

Main attractions: Deep kloofs; rock climbing; caves; diverse plant and animal life; clean, clear water.

Pertinent information: The area is very popular during weekends and holidays. There are strict control regulations and a limited number of permits per day are issued to members of the public.

1. RUSTENBURG NATURE RESERVE TRAILS
MAGALIESBERG

Trail details: 1. Rustenburg Overnight Trail: 21 km/2 days; 2. Peglerae Interpretive Trail: 5 km/ 2 hours. Both are circular; 2 km vlei ramble.

Permits/bookings: Must be obtained from The Officer-in-charge, tel. (0142) 31050; Rustenburg Nature Reserve, PO Box 511, Rustenburg 0300. Map and brochure available on request.

Facilities/amenities: Youth camp; information centre; Kudu base hut has tap water, while visitors to Red Hartebeest overnight hut can make use of the nearby stream. Both huts are equipped with beds and mattresses for 10 people; toilet, braai area and wood.

Main attractions: Mountain scenery; wildlife; prolific birdlife; protected plants; massive quartzitic rocks.

Pertinent information: Extremes in weather; winter nights are very cold. Hikers must carry sufficient water; in summer it can be hot and dry. There is a limit of 10 hikers for this trail.

On the summit and northern slopes of the western Magaliesberg lies one of the most interesting reserves on the highveld.

1. The Rustenburg Overnight Trail through the reserve traverses a variety of habitats: the bush-clad mountain ridge which reaches an altitude of 1 690 m; a large valley basin with an extensive reed-swamp; and the western open grassland plateau. Although the ascents and descents are steep, the distances covered are relatively short (9 km and 12 km respectively) and allow leisurely walking. Reedbuck, impala, springbok, eland, sable antelope, red hartebeest, kudu and zebra are commonly seen by trailists. These species have been reintroduced to the region, but others such as the klipspringer, mountain reedbuck and grey duiker have always been present. Predators – the leopard,

endangered brown hyaena, caracal and blackbacked jackal – are largely nocturnal and therefore unlikely to be observed. Bird-watchers will identify species typical of the sour bushveld and acacia and protea woodlands, including the black eagle, Scops owl, spotted eagle owl, and redchested cuckoo, which are fairly common.

2. The Peglerae Interpretive Trail explores the northern crest of the Magaliesberg, where the rare and endemic *Aloe peglerae* occurs. Using the trail

For the highveld hiking enthusiast, the Magaliesberg provides the only suitable wilderness environment close to home. Declared a Natural Heritage Site in 1977, this range, comprising hard, resistant quartzites, and rising an average of 330 m above the surrounding plains, remains the last relatively untouched area in the south-central Transvaal.

Stretching 125 km from east to west and spanning an elevation between 1 372 m and 1 829 m, the Magaliesberg forms a conspicuous divide between the lower-lying, hot bushveld to the north

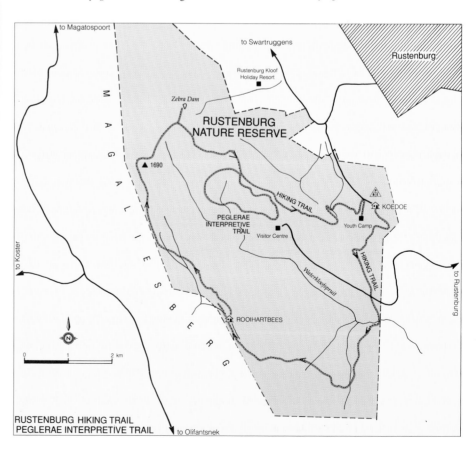

RUSTENBURG HIKING TRAIL
PEGLERAE INTERPRETIVE TRAIL

Hikers in the Magaliesberg pause where water-smoothed rocks slope down to an inviting pool.

and the cooler highveld to the south. Because flora and fauna distinct to both regions merge along the range, the Magaliesberg harbours a diversity of indigenous species. Examples of the many interesting plants are the endemic *Aloe peglerae* and the kloof-dwelling tree fern, *Cyathea dregei*.

More than 150 species of birds have been recorded, including the colourful crimsonbreasted shrike, plumcoloured starling, paradise whydah, crested barbet and a large number of raptors. The endangered Cape vulture breeds on the steep mountain cliffs. Mammals frequently seen are chacma baboons and vervet monkeys, dassies, grey duiker,

reedbuck and klipspringer. Although most of the indigenous big game has been exterminated, predators such as leopard, brown hyaena and aardwolf have managed to survive.

Numerous kloofs such as Castle Gorge, Tonquani and Cedarberg are owned or jointly owned by the Mountain Club of South Africa; they have become so popular that access to them is now strictly controlled. In addition, these areas are carefully patrolled by Mountain Club members. Summer in the Magaliesberg is characterized by hot, rainy days and cool nights; the winter days are clear and cool, the nights cold.

3. MORELETA SPRUIT HIKING TRAIL
PRETORIA

Trail details: 10 km/2,5 hours; open-ended.

Permits/bookings: Not required; the trail is always open.

Maps/information: Can be obtained from the Pretoria City Council Public Relations Department, tel. (012) 3137197; PO Box 440, Pretoria 0001.

Facilities/amenities: A number of signs and beacons mark the trail.

Main attractions: Abundant birdlife; indigenous trees; small dams; easy walking over gentle terrain.

Pertinent information: There are other urban trails in and around Pretoria, including the Walkerspruit Trail; contact the Pretoria City Council Public Relations Department for details. A water bottle is essential, especially in summer.

Much credit must go to the city fathers of Pretoria for linking the capital's attractive natural assets in a series of pleasant walking trails. The Moreleta Spruit Hiking Trail starts in Menlyn Drive and runs northwards through a variety of natural landscapes. All along the spruit are tranquil spots around natural pools, with grassy banks. The trail links many urban amenities such as the Faerie Glen Nature Reserve, Meyerspark Bird Sanctuary and the

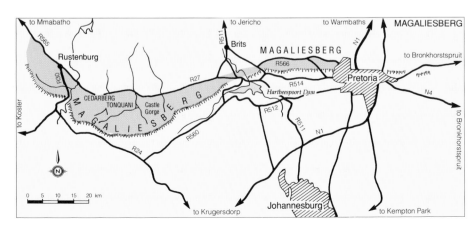

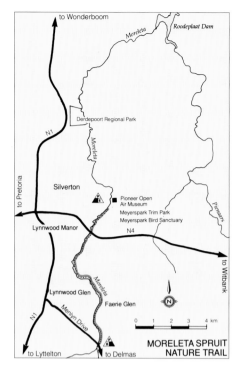

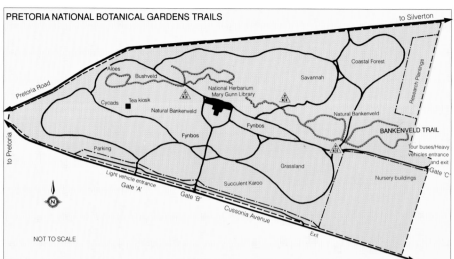

Pioneer Open-Air Museum (the oldest existing dwelling in Pretoria).

The natural environment of the trail is retained as much as possible, and, in order to achieve this, the grass is kept relatively short and the terrain levelled only where necessary. Indigenous trees have been planted along the way; these include several acacia varieties, bushwillow, white stinkwood and karee. The trail is home to varied birdlife; highveld birds are common and this is the southern limit of the habitat of several bushveld birds. The start of the trail is indicated by a sign in Menlyn Drive, and the end is on Pretoria Road opposite Pioneer House in Silverton.

4. PRETORIA NATIONAL BOTANICAL GARDEN
PRETORIA

Trail details: Bankenveld Trail: 2 km/1 hour; circular.

Permits/bookings: Not required; there is an entrance fee to the garden.

Maps/information: An annotated map offers detailed notes on the 15 viewpoints. Guided tours require prior arrangement with the curator, tel. (012) 8043200.

Facilities/amenities: Tea garden; toilets; benches; paved paths; labelled plants; nursery; kiosk; annual plant sales.

Main attractions: Full spectrum of South African flora; 50 per cent of South Africa's 1 000 tree species are represented; indigenous cycads and aloes.

Pertinent information: The garden is open to the public from 8.00 am to 6.00 pm daily. There is a suggested limit of 25 people for this walk. Members of the Botanical Society of South Africa are admitted free.

Situated 10 km east of Pretoria city centre in Cussonia Road, Brummeria, the 76-ha Pretoria National

Botanical Garden is probably the only botanical garden in the world which owes its site to the presence of a poisonous plant. Gifblaar, *Dichapetalum cymosum*, reduced the value of the land for farming, resulting in its transfer in 1946 from the university farm to the (then) Botanical Research Institute. The gardens were declared a national monument in 1979. Despite being surrounded by built-up areas, this corner of Pretoria has retained its tranquillity. Dassies sun themselves on the rocks and flocks of guinea fowl wander over the lawns. The rocky ridge is a haven to small buck, mongoose and hares, and over 185 species of birds.

The self-guided nature walk leads along the ridge skirting the gardens, where the hillside vegetation is revealed on closer inspection to be a rock garden of amazing complexity and interest. The trees are seldom more than 4 m tall; natural pruning and root growth restriction have achieved growth forms comparable with the Oriental bonsai culture. Walking in the garden is especially pleasant in winter when the many different species of aloe are in flower, and in spring when Namaqualand daisies, mesembryanthemums and vygies provide a dazzling show of colour.

5. FAAN AND NEELS VAN WYK TRAIL
ZEMVELO GAME PARK

Trail details: 32 km/2 days; circular.

Permits/bookings: Must be obtained from The Manager, Zemvelo Game Park, tel. (01212) 25728; PO Box 599, Bronkhorstspruit 1020. Map and brochure available on request.

Facilities/amenities: Overnight huts sleep 12 hikers; lapas; caravan park; swimming pool; information kiosk.

Main attractions: Game; rock formations; indigenous vegetation.

Pertinent information: Ticks are prevalent; rapidly changeable weather. There is a limit of 12 people for the trail.

Situated in the 2 096-ha Zemvelo Game Park, 25 km north-east of Bronkhorstspruit, the Faan and Neels van Wyk Trail offers hikers a 2-day route which passes through a wide variety of archaeological sites, old ruins, rock formations and graves.

The game present in the park includes kudu, impala, gemsbok, eland, blesbok, waterbuck, zebra, black wildebeest, springbok, brown hyaena and even leopard. Birdlife in the area is also varied and plentiful, with fish eagle, black eagle and kingfishers all present.

The route on the first day leads for 11 km through wild elder, cheesewood, large sour plum and spineleaved monkey orange to the overnight huts. The second day's route is 21 km long and passes through bushwillow, sugarbush protea, lavender trees, wild peach and kiepersols before arriving back at the start.

The trail is clearly marked and requires a medium level of fitness. The best months for hiking here are between September and April.

6. KRUGERSDORP GAME RESERVE
KRUGERSDORP

Trail details: Various guided trails; on average approximately 4 km/2 hours.

Permits/bookings: Must be obtained from the Krugersdorp Centre of the Wildlife Society of Southern Africa, tel. (011) 4821670; 21 Rockridge Road, Parktown, 2193.

Facilities/amenities: Accommodation in the reserve consists of 12 rondavels with 3 beds each; 6 family units with 6 beds each; caravan sites; swimming pool; picnic sites; kiosk.

Main attractions: Highveld animals; diversity of habitats.

Pertinent information: Trails are conducted on Saturday and Sunday mornings all year; they start between 6.30 am and 7.30 am, depending on the season. There is a limit of 8 people per group. These trails are free, but donations to nature conservation are welcomed.

The 1 400-ha Krugersdorp Game Reserve, conveniently situated west of Krugersdorp serves as a valuable educational trail venue on the fringes of the Witwatersrand urban and industrial sprawl. Experienced volunteer officers of the Krugersdorp Centre of the Wildlife Society lead half-day educational trails within a demarcated zone, away from public game-viewing roads.

The park's diversity of habitats (grassland, forest, bushveld and riverine vegetation) supports

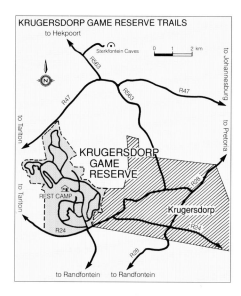

KRUGERSDORP GAME RESERVE TRAILS

reintroduced blesbok, kudu, eland, giraffe, hartebeest, roan and sable antelope, wildebeest, nyala
and waterbuck. Smaller antelope such as duiker,
steenbok, impala and springbok, as well as vervet
monkey and 143 species of birds are also present.
Lion, white rhino and buffalo are confined in separate enclosures.

*Hikers on a guided trail through the Krugersdorp
Game Reserve are likely to see giraffe.*

*Over a steep fall a river makes its way through the
Witwatersrand National Botanical Garden.*

7. ABE BAILEY NATURE RESERVE
CARLETONVILLE

Trail details: Two self-guided trails: Guinea fowl
and Avocet trails; also guided group trails.

Permits/bookings: Must be obtained from The
Education Officer, Abe Bailey Education Project,
tel. (01491) 3015; PO Box 6444, Oberholzer 2502.

Facilities/amenities: Guided trails; interpretive
centre; educational programmes; Tlatlagwe camp;
self-contained chalets.

Main attractions: A large marsh wetland habitat
with bird hide and tower; large mammals.

Pertinent information: All visits are by prior
arrangement only; snakes are prevalent;
thunderstorms are common.

Startlingly bright Haemanthus *in the
Abe Bailey Nature Reserve.*

First impressions of this reserve, which is situated
north-west of Carltonville, may be deceptive; it appears flat and monotonous. However, Abe Bailey,
one of South Africa's mining magnates, realized
the ecological value of this land, and established a
hunting lodge here. The Transvaal Branch of the
Wildlife Society has since renovated the 5 000-ha
farm for environmental education, complete with
an interpretive centre, dormitories and staff housing.

The valuable wetlands form the focal point of the
Abe Bailey Nature Reserve, which is administered
by the Transvaal Provincial Administration, and a
hide has been constructed at their edge. For bird-
watchers, the reserve boasts over 210 species;
waterbirds such as goliath and purple heron, yellowbilled stork, greater and lesser flamingo, black
crake and purple gallinule are commonly viewed
from the hide. The more conspicuous grassland
birds include whitewinged korhaan, anteating chat
and the occasional secretarybird. Cape vultures are
also sometimes seen on the reserve at the 'vulture
restaurant' when carcasses are donated by local farmers. Mammals in the reserve include Burchell's
zebra, black wildebeest, red hartebeest, springbok,
duiker, steenbok and blesbok.

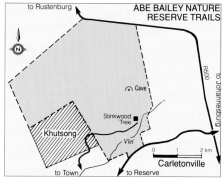

ABE BAILEY NATURE
RESERVE TRAILS

8. WITWATERSRAND NATIONAL
BOTANICAL GARDEN
ROODEPOORT

Trail details: Various guided and self-guided walks.

Permits/bookings: Not required; there is an
entrance fee to the garden.

Facilities/amenities: Interpretive centre; labelled
plants; nursery; toilets; restaurant; bird hide;
bookshop; kiosk; plants for sale (bi-annual plant
sales).

Main attractions: Witwatersrand flora; wooded
kloofs; Witpoortjie Falls.

Pertinent information: The garden is open to the
public from 8.00 am to 6.00 pm daily; guided
walks leave from the interpretive centre at 2.30 pm
and 3.30 pm every day. There are guided tours
every Sunday starting at 3.00 from the main
entrance.

The 225-ha Witwatersrand National Botanical
Garden is situated in Malcolm Road, in a beautiful
hillside site in the heart of the most densely populated part of the country. Most of this botanic
garden, which conserves one of the few remnants
of the Witwatersrand's original vegetation, has
been left in its natural state. The somewhat harsh
climate means that the appearance of the vegetation
present changes markedly with the seasons: most of
the approximately 750 mm of annual rainfall occurs in summer in the form of afternoon
thundershowers. In winter six to seven months of
drought are commonly experienced.

The characteristic cliffs of the Witwatersrand
form a dramatic backdrop to the gardens, and provide a variety of habitats and shelter from harsh
weather. The centrepiece of the gardens is the Witpoortjie Waterfall, which forms part of the

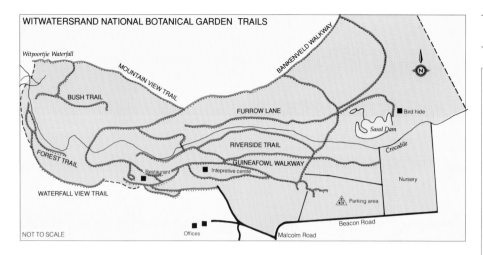

WITWATERSRAND NATIONAL BOTANICAL GARDEN TRAILS

Witpoortjie Waterfall

MOUNTAIN VIEW TRAIL

BANKENVELD WALKWAY

BUSH TRAIL

FURROW LANE

Bird hide

Sasol Dam

RIVERSIDE TRAIL

Crocodile

FOREST TRAIL

GUINEAFOWL WALKWAY

Restaurant

Interpretive centre

Nursery

WATERFALL VIEW TRAIL

Parking area

Beacon Road

Offices

NOT TO SCALE

Malcolm Road

N

Crocodile River. The river provides the gardens
with an abundant supply of water. The natural vegetation of the area is known as 'Bankenveld', which
is composed of a mosaic of grassland and savannah
with dense bush on rocky ridges, in ravines and
along streams. Major plantings in the gardens include cycads, succulents, aloes and frost-hardy
shrubs and trees.

9. KLOOFENDAL NATURE RESERVE
ROODEPOORT

Trail details: Two walks: 6 km/2,5 hours; 2 km/
2 hours; both are circular.

Permits/bookings: Not required; there is an
entrance fee to the reserve. Map available on
request.

Facilities/amenities: Amphitheatre; picnic area.

Main attractions: Birdlife; indigenous trees and
other plants; dam; national monument (Confidence
Reef mine shaft).

Pertinent information: The reserve is open daily
from 8.00 am to 6.00 pm

The tranquil 109-ha Kloofendal Nature Reserve
with its attractive kloofs, krantzes and dam is situated among the koppies of the Witwatersrand
Ridge System in the middle of the city of Roodepoort, a short drive from central Johannesburg.

The rocks of this region are more than 3 000
million years old and form part of the Lower Witwatersrand System. These ancient quartzites and
shales form the basis of the rich soils which support
the abundant indigenous plant life.

The rich vegetation in turn provides an ideal
habitat for many birds (over 120 species occur in
the reserve) and small mammals.

From the reserve's picnic site, the two demarcated walks lead into the koppies that are the main
feature of the landscape. Facets of the region's geology and gold-mining history, as well as its flora
and wildlife, are highlighted *en route*. Plants of interest include *Haemanthus hirsutus, Buddleia
salviifolia* (wild sage) and *Protea caffra*.

A visit to the Confidence Reef mine shaft, where
the first payable gold on the Witwatersrand was
discovered by Fred and Harry Struben, can be
arranged by appointment with the curator of the
Roodepoort City Museum; tel. (011) 6726641.

10. BRAAMFONTEIN SPRUIT TRAIL
JOHANNESBURG

Trail details: A complex network of self-guided
urban trails of varying lengths; each can be
completed in one day.

Permits/bookings: Not required.

Maps/information: Comprehensive brochure
available from the Johannesburg City Council
Public Relations Office, tel. (011) 4076111; Civic
Centre, Braamfontein.

Facilities/amenities: Picnic and braai sites;
benches; trail sections are marked and mapped
along the way; bird sanctuaries; botanical gardens;
boating areas.

Main attractions: Birdlife; small mammals and
reptiles; historic buildings; archaeological and
geological sites; granite outcrops; waterfalls and
natural areas.

Pertinent information: Hikers should walk in
groups, as even pairs are not regarded as safe; the
Sandton section is patrolled by mounted security
guards. Avoid wading or drinking from open water
sources as bilharzia and other diseases are present.
Summer rainfall area; thunderstorms are common
in summer; winter days are sunny.

As this book does not include city walks, I have
concentrated on the trails that pass through 'green'
areas. It is thanks to the planning and management
team of professionals and officials from the local
authorities of Johannesburg, Randburg and Sandton
that these green belts have so far survived the onslaught of urban development.

The Braamfontein Spruit, defined by its floodplain and all contiguous open spaces, is a 25-km
river course with four main tributaries: the Montgomery, Westdene, Richmond and Zoo Lake
spruits (streams). From its source on the Hillbrow
Ridge, it drains northwards through the suburbs of
Johannesburg, Randburg and Sandton, eventually
joining the Jukskei River which terminates in the
Limpopo River System.

Despite the pressures imposed by ever-encroach-
ing urban development, the environment retains
much of natural value, and plants and wildlife are
remarkably diverse. About 225 bird species frequent the river system, in addition to mammals
such as the blackbacked jackal, caracal, dassie,
spotted genet, meerkat and water mongoose.

The Witwatersrand with its typical rocky outcrops adds to the interest of the route, as do the
many noteworthy archaeological sites. Discoveries
include Stone Age overhangs, earlier Stone Age
tools 250 000 years old, rock paintings, and Late
Stone Age grindstones. The various sections of the
Braamfontein Spruit Trail are:

The Parktown/Westcliff Urban Walk takes in
magnificent mansions built in the 19th century by
the 'randlords' or mining magnates.

Dale Lace Park to Delta Park, including two
optional sections: the Parkview Link, which follows the main course of the Braamfontein Spruit;
and the Melville Koppies/Westdene Spruit Trail,
following a ridge and tributary of the Braamfontein
Spruit. The latter section includes the 66-ha Melville Koppies Nature Reserve, which is both a
national monument and a sanctuary for birds and
other wildlife. Here, among the rocky outcrops, in-

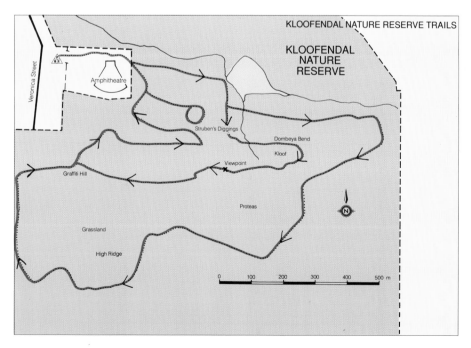

KLOOFENDAL NATURE RESERVE TRAILS

KLOOFENDAL
NATURE
RESERVE

Veronica Street

Amphitheatre

Struben's Diggings

Dombeya Bend

Kloof

Viewpoint

Graffiti Hill

Proteas

Grassland

High Ridge

N

0 100 200 300 400 500 m

digenous highveld plants flourish undisturbed; also preserved is an ancient iron-smelting furnace.

This section also includes the Johannesburg Botanical Gardens on the western shore of Emmarentia Dam. The oldest part of the gardens is the Rose Garden, which displays a fascinating collection of 4 500 roses and their hybrids from all over the world. A feature of the gardens is the plantings of culinary as well as medicinal herbs.

Delta Park to the Sandton Field and Study Centre is a suburban route along the principal course of the spruit. Delta Park, at 108 ha, is the largest open space along the trail, a relaxing place to ramble and observe birds. The 10-ha Florence Bloom Bird Sanctuary, situated in Delta Park, has viewing hides around the dam. Here you can see approximately 180 species of birds such as the paradise flycatcher, Egyptian goose, spotted eagle owl, hamerkop, bishop bird, kingfisher and woodpecker. The exotic vegetation in Delta Park includes maple, palm, eucalyptus, plane and poplar trees and fields of flowering cosmos. The Delta Environmental Centre offers environmental awareness courses and lectures on conservation-related topics.

Sandton Field and Study Centre to the Sandton boundary is a short countryside ramble.

The Montgomery Spruit Trail follows the Montgomery Spruit until it joins Westdene Spruit.

---

11. SANDSPRUIT TRAIL
JOHANNESBURG

Trail details: 16,5 km/6 hours; open-ended.

Permits/bookings: Not required.

Maps/information: An interesting and comprehensive booklet is available from the Johannesburg City Council Public Relations Office, tel. (011) 4076111; Civic Centre, Braamfontein.

Facilities/amenities: Picnic and braai sites; benches; trail sections are marked and mapped along the way; bird sanctuaries; botanical gardens.

Main attractions: Birdlife; small mammals and reptiles; historic buildings and natural areas.

Pertinent information: As with all trails situated in a metropolitan area, it is advised that hikers walk in groups. Avoid wading or drinking from open water sources as bilharzia and other diseases are present.

The Sandspruit Trail stretches over 4,5 km from Parktown to the Melrose Bird Sanctuary, and a further 12 km to Paulshof, off the Witkoppen Road. Following the course of the Sandspruit, the route takes in some of the city's loveliest parks, and provides a unique view of nature amid the urban trappings of civilization. The main source of the Sandspruit rises in The Wilds, a 20-ha park of lawns with attractive indigenous flora. The spruit then flows north through Houghton Estate, adjacent to the Killarney Golf Course and into James and Ethel Gray Park in Melrose, where the Melrose Bird Sanctuary is located. This 10-ha reserve supports over 120 highveld species, including waterbirds on its lake and reed-lined banks. Here the trail splits and you can either return to The Wilds via Paterson Park and Houghton Estate or you can continue through the various suburbs of Sandton to the confluence of the Braamfontein and Sandspruit rivers. This part of the trail is not always

clearly marked and in places some Sandton home owners have extended their gardens down to the spruit over public property, which may lead to confrontation with irate owners and/or their dogs. A small detour from the main route is known as the **Outspan Trail**, a 2,8-km walk along the Outspan Spruit to where it joins the Braamfontein Spruit at St James Street.

Space for solitude above the crowded city, on the Mervyn King Ridge Trail.

12. MERVYN KING RIDGE TRAIL
JOHANNESBURG

Trail details: 8 km/3 to 4 hours; one way.

Permits/bookings: Not required.

Maps/information: An informative brochure can be obtained from the Johannesburg City Council Public Relations Office, tel. (011) 4076111; Civic Centre, Braamfontein.

Facilities/amenities: Trail sections are marked and mapped along the way; information boards.

Main attractions: Birdlife; small mammals and reptiles; historic buildings; archaeological and geological sites of interest; well-preserved protea veld; Jukskei River.

Pertinent information: Hikers should walk in groups of not less than three.

The Mervyn King Ridge Trail is an 8-km link between historic 'old Johannesburg' and rural Johannesburg. The trail starts at the little Ockerse Street Park in Hillbrow and the route extends eastward along the Highlands and Observatory ridges before dropping down into the broad Jukskei River Valley at Bezuidenhout Park. From here it continues past Bruma Lake to its end point at Gillooly's Farm. The Mervyn King Ridge Trail extends entirely through the original 400-ha Doorn-fontein Farm. Today it features grand old houses, parks and open spaces, the Nugget Hill pedestrian bridge, historical memorials and the old observatory.

13. JUKSKEI TRAIL AND RANDLORDS HERITAGE WALK
JOHANNESBURG

Trail details: Self-guided routes of variable length; open-ended.

Permits/bookings: Not required.

Maps/information: An informative brochure can be obtained from the Johannesburg City Council Public Relations Office, tel. (011) 4076111; Civic Centre, Braamfontein.

Facilities/amenities: Picnic and braai sites; benches; recreational parks and nature reserves; trail sections are not marked.

Main attractions: Birdlife; small mammals and reptiles; historic buildings; archaeological and geological sites; open spaces.

Pertinent information: Hikers should not walk alone on any of the metropolitan trails, even pairs are not regarded as safe. Since this trail bisects the black township of Alexandra, it is advisable to first gauge the current political mood of the area, and to always walk in a group. Alternatively bypass Alexandra by skirting it on higher ground to the east (towards the N3 motorway).

The Witwatersrand ridge system forms part of the main watershed in southern Africa. A number of the so-called 'witwater' streams rise here and feed into two major river systems. The northward flowing streams, including the Jukskei, Braamfontein Spruit and Sandspruit, run into the Crocodile and then the Limpopo, which flows north-east to the Indian Ocean, and the southward flowing streams run into the Vaal and then the Orange River, which flows south-west to the Atlantic Ocean.

The Jukskei Trail begins as two separate walks: the **Mervyn King Ridge Trail**, which links Hillbrow to Bruma Lake, and the **Randlords Heritage Walk** which links Hillbrow in the west to the Jukskei Trail in the east. Although the Jukskei River rises to the north of Ellis Park in eastern Johannesburg, it is canalized for most of the way until it emerges in Bezuidenhout Park and is joined by a tributary from the Observatory Golf Course. The Jukskei Trail follows the course of the river eastwards to Bruma Lake, where it has been dammed and incorporated into a vibrant shopping and entertainment area. The trail then continues to follow the river as it flows eastwards through Bedfordview to Gillooly's Farm. From here it turns northwards around the base of Linksfield Ridge and proceeds through Edenvale, Lombardy East and Alexandra Township to Frankenwald. The route then swings westwards away from the Jukskei River to meet the Sandspruit, past its confluence with the Braamfontein Spruit, and continues on to Lone Hill, a granitic koppie which harbours an abundance of indigenous vegetation and animal life.

The Jukskei catchment area boasts archaeological sites, buildings from the gold-rush days, pre-1886 farmhouses, national monuments and historical places. The first gold found in South Africa was in the Jukskei in 1853.

14. BLOUBOSSPRUIT TRAIL
JOHANNESBURG

Trail details: 19 km/7 hours; circular.

Permits/bookings: Not required.

Maps/information: Brochure available from the Johannesburg City Council Public Relations Office, tel. (011) 4076111; Civic Centre, Braamfontein.

Facilities/amenities: Trail sections are marked and mapped along the way.

Main attractions: Birdlife; small mammals and reptiles; historic buildings; archaeological and geological sites; nature reserve; wetlands.

Pertinent information: It is advisable that hikers do not walk alone. Avoid wading in stagnant pools or drinking from open water sources as bilharzia and other diseases are present.

The Bloubosspruit Trail is a self-guided circular trail, part of which leads through the 550-ha Klipriviersberg Nature Reserve, which is accessible from Fairway Avenue in Mondeor. The trail can be walked at any time of the year, though the section through the nature reserve is guided, and is open only at 9.00 am on the second Sunday of each month.

The Klipriviersberg ridges which extend across the south of the metropolitan area of Johannesburg are composed of andesitic rocks known as the Ventersdorp lavas. These ridges contrast dramatically with the Witwatersrand ridges in terms of ecology.

The combined ridge and stream setting has provided a favourable setting for the development of early man and his ancestors. The remains of late Iron Age villages are scattered across the Klipriviersberg. Open areas along the Bloubosspruit create an exciting recreational and educational area for the urbanite, and allow for conservation of wildlife within the built-up environment.

The Bloubosspruit Trail, named after the commonly seen Transvaal bluebush, *Diospyros lyciodes*, will eventually link up with other river trails planned for the area. The well-marked trail can be joined at any point and a number of shorter routes can be selected.

15. SUIKERBOSRAND HIKING AND NATURE TRAIL COMPLEX
SUIKERBOSRAND NATURE RESERVE, HEIDELBERG

Trail details: 1. Suikerbosrand Hiking Trail: a network of trails totalling 66 km/1 to 6 days; 2. Cheetah Interpretive Trail: 4,5 km/2 hours; 3. Bokmakierie Nature Trail: 10 km or 17 km/ 4 hours or 7 hours; all are circular.

Permits/bookings: Must be obtained well in advance for the overnight trail from Suikerbosrand Nature Reserve, tel. (0151) 2181; Private Bag H616, Heidelberg 2400. Permits for any day walks available from visitor's centre at the reserve.

Maps/information: The informative map and brochure obtained at the reserve office is extremely useful.

Facilities/amenities: 6 overnight huts, each with outdoor cooking area, utensils, gas lamps, water, firewood, bunks and mattresses for 10 hikers; fully equipped cottage at the main camp; visitor centre with displays, lectures and films; picnic site; meditation hut; Diepkloof farm museum.

Main attractions: Natural area amidst the developed Vaal Triangle; reintroduced wildlife; 200 species of birds; archaeological relics and ruins; diverse topography.

Pertinent information: There is a limit of ten people for the overnight hike. Remember to take a hat as there is not much shade, and a full water bottle as there is no permanent water along the route. The terrain is hilly and hikers need to be reasonably fit.

Situated in a range of low hills approximately 50 km south of Johannesburg, this 13 337-ha reserve has been developed for resource conservation, environmental education, outdoor recreation and research. It takes its name from the sugar bush or 'suikerbossie' *Protea caffra* which grows in the hilly terrain to the east. **The Suikerbosrand Hiking Trail**, covering high hills, plateaux, kloofs, valleys and ridges, is managed as a complex of walks rather than as one continuous trail. Each of the six overnight huts must be booked individually: therefore, with the aid of the hiking series map,

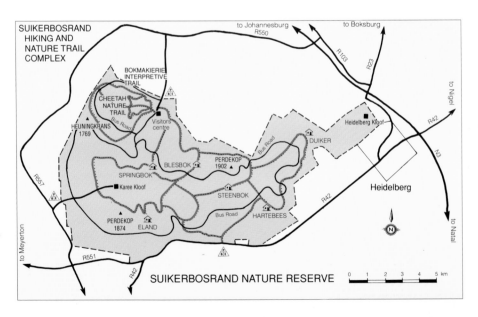

A typical highveld sky blows up above Suikerbosrand Nature Reserve.

trailists must decide beforehand on their route. Many permutations are possible; some routes are short and gentle, while others are longer and require a greater degree of endurance. In several places the trail intersects the road built for guided bus tours. To provide hikers with privacy, each of the six hiking huts is restricted to one party, irrespective of its size.

Plant communities such as aloe and acacia forest, acacia bushveld, protea savannah, vlei reedbeds and grasslands are all present in the Bankenveld vegetation covering the reserve, and these provide ideal habitats for a very diverse wildlife. Animals that have always populated the region include the grey duiker, steenbok, grey rhebok, mountain reedbuck and baboon. However, it is exciting to hike through an environment rich in large game such as blesbok, springbok, red hartebeest, black wildebeest, zebra, oribi, eland, steenbok, kudu, cheetah and brown hyaena, all of which have been reintroduced. Birds abound in the reserve: some 200 species have been recorded and here many of the bushveld birds reach the southernmost limit of their distribution. The most common birds, however, are the grassveld species such as larks, pipits, cisticolas, chats and, in summer, longtailed widows in breeding plumage. Also inhabiting the reserve are 13 species of frog.

Forefathers of the Tswana once hunted in this region; ruins and relics, some dating back to the Iron Age, remain as proof.

For day visitors the Cheetah and Bokmakierie trails are ideal. The 4,5 km **Cheetah Interpretive Trail**, an undemanding walk beginning and ending at the visitor centre, is very informative and has been designed to give visitors a better understanding of the natural history of the area, as well as some insight into earlier human habitation. **The Bokmakierie Nature Trail** also starts at the visitor centre; hikers can choose between the 10 km or the 17 km options.

The walks are clearly marked, and summer is the best time for hiking in the reserve.

16. KLIPKRAAL HIKING TRAIL
NEAR HEIDELBERG

Trail details: 27 km/2 days; circular.

Permits/bookings: Must be obtained from Jacana Country Homes and Trails, tel. (012) 346 3550; PO Box 95212, Waterkloof 0145. Brochure available on request.

Facilities/amenities: Base camp is a restored farmhouse with beds and mattresses for 16 people; shower, toilets, kitchen with cooking utensils; two lapas; wood is not supplied.

Main attractions: Stunning views over Vaal Dam; monolithic sacred rock; Iron Age settlements.

Pertinent information: Lightning and thunderstorms in summer; cold winters. There is a limit of 16 hikers for this trail (larger groups can be accommodated by prior arrangement).

The Klipkraal Hiking Trail is situated on the cattle and dairy farms of Rietfontein and Stryfontein, 35 km from Heidelberg, where the landscape is typical of the southern highveld and the hills of the Transvaal. The first day's route (15,5 km) takes hikers to the northern side of the farms where there are lovely views over the Vaal Dam. Hikers return along the loop to the base camp for the night. The second day's route (11,5 km) passes several dams where the waterbirds are plentiful.

The trail also leads past a monolithic rock, regarded by local people as sacred; its immediate environment is revered. Where the route loops, a collection of late Iron Age settlements (1600 to 1700 AD) is to be found; the inhabitants were ancestors of the early Sotho.

There are many waterbirds on the farm, and the small game which can be seen includes steenbok, grey rhebok, blackbacked jackal and blesbok. This clearly marked trail is not particularly strenuous, and is suitable for children and beginners as well as experienced hikers. The best months are from October to May.

17. THREE RIVERS NATURE TRAIL
VEREENIGING

Trail details: 12,5 km/4 to 5 hours; open-ended.

Permits/bookings: Not required.

Maps/information: Must be obtained from Eric Tofarides of the Wildlife Society, tel. (016) 46203; 170 Ring Road, Three Rivers, Vereeniging 1939.

Facilities/amenities: Toilet, water and braai facilities along the way.

Main attractions: Birdlife; bird hide in Peacehaven bird sanctuary.

Pertinent information: Hikers wishing to visit the bird hide need to obtain the key from the Wildlife Society (address above); remember to organize transport at the end of the trail or be prepared to walk 4,5 km along a tarred road back to the start. It is advisable to walk in groups of at least 4 to 6 for this trail.

This easy trail in the Vereeniging suburb of Three Rivers, leads along the Klip, Suikerbosrand and Vaal rivers. Walkers should start at either the junction of Ring Road and the Klip River, or at Riverside High School in Hawthorne Street. The terrain is level, and follows the banks of the rivers, diverging occasionally to avoid private property. The end of the trail is in Three Rivers East, behind the Fourways Garage. The route is clearly marked and offers pleasant walking conditions all year. Along the Klip River section of the trail, look out for soft, yellowish sandstone outcrops (Pelindaba Stone) in which the fossil remains of an interesting tree have been found. This tree (*Glossopteris browniara*) forms the 'missing link' between ferns and flowering plants. Further along is the Klip River Quarry which was a camp during the Stone Age, and in 1970 was declared a national monument.

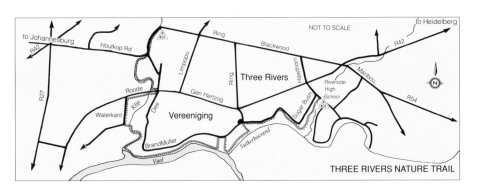

THREE RIVERS NATURE TRAIL

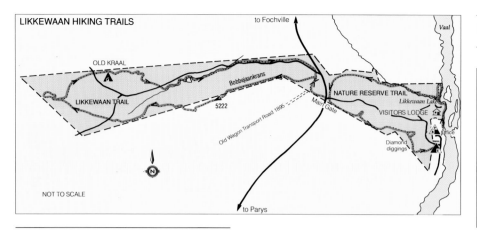

LIKKEWAAN HIKING TRAILS

18. LIKKEWAAN HIKING TRAILS
PARYS-ON-VAAL

Trail details: 1. Likkewaan Trail: 20 km/1 or 2 days, circular; 2. Nature Reserve Trail: 7 km/ 3 hours, circular; 3. River Trail: 3 km/1 hour, return.

Permits/bookings: Must be obtained from Smilin' Thru' Nature Reserve and Resort, tel. (01601) 2123; PO Box 388, Parys 9585. Map and brochure available on request.

Facilities/amenities: Overnight in Matabele kraal; holiday resort with chalets and caravan sites; swimming pool.

Main attractions: Game; prolific birdlife; lovely krantzes; geological features; alluvial diamond diggings; historic area; old wagon road.

Pertinent information: There is a limit of 30 hikers for these trails.

The Likkewaan Hiking Trails are situated on a large farm on the banks of the Vaal River, 10 km from Parys and only an hour's drive from Johannesburg. There is an abundance of indigenous fauna and flora in the area, and interesting historical and geological features. The trail brochure is extremely informative, listing the 200 species of birds present, the many wild animals to be seen, and details of the trees and vegetation to be found, as well as the background to the history and geology of the area. The farm lies close to an area which is known to geologists as the Vredefort Dome, a fascinating exposure of ancient granite surrounded by weathered ridges of quartzite belonging to the Witwatersrand System. These ridges are clearly visible from the higher vantage points on the trails and in particular on Bobbejaanskrans. Although the exact nature and origin of this exposure are not known for certain, geologists think that it occurred when a huge meteor struck the earth.

1. The Likkewaan Trail starts and ends at the Smilin' Thru' Resort, and leads through four ecosystems: riverine, vlei and marshland, grassland savannah, and wooded kloofs. For those hikers who wish to relax and do the trail over 2 days, the night is spent in a Matabele kraal (bring your own tents). The second day's route leads past Olienhoutbos (wild olive forest) and back to the start approximately 10 km further on. The first 3 km and the final 3 km are shared with the Nature Reserve Trail.

2. The Nature Reserve Trail follows the boundary of the nature reserve in which the Smilin' Thru' resort is situated.

3. The River Trail is a short walk starting from the resort and following the banks of the Vaal River. Look out for fish eagles, kingfishers, herons and other waterbirds. All the trails are easy, clearly marked and offer pleasant walking conditions all year round.

19. THE ROOIHAAS HIKING TRAIL
NEAR VENTERSKROON

Trail details: 21 km/2 days. Open-ended.

Permits/bookings: Must be obtained from Mrs R van der Walt, tel. (0148) 8572; 66 Tom Street, Potchefstroom 2520. Map and brochure available on request.

Facilities/amenities: Historic cottages (built in 1889), with electricity, braai facilities, electric stoves and a refrigerator; the mountain camp has braai facilities, hot and cold water and a swimming hole.

Main attractions: The area is of considerable historical and geological interest.

Pertinent information: 15 hikers can be accommodated at a time. Hikers should carry sufficient water for the duration of the hike.

This easily negotiated trail is situated in the region of the Vredefort Dome just outside Venterskroon and approximately 25 km west of Parys. The dome, an interesting geological phenomenon thought by scientists to have been formed by the impact of a giant meteorite, forms a semi-circular mountainous landscape, with deep ravines containing mountain streams which join the Vaal River lower down. The hilltops offer panoramic views of the Vaal River Valley and the surrounding plains.

Gold was mined here at the turn of the century, and some of the primitive mine shafts can be seen along the trail route. Several ruins of tribal settlements from the Iron Age can also be seen. The overnight camp is built on the site of one of these ancient settlements.

The trail starts at Venterskroon base camp and gradually climbs to the highest point in the region, from where the path descends through Buffelskloof to the Vaal River and a lovely swimming spot. Hikers overnight at Bergkamp mountain camp before setting out on the second day which takes in ancient ruins. The trail ends at the farmhouse, once owned by Totius (D J du Toit), a well-known Afrikaans poet. Transport back to Venterskroon can be arranged when booking.

20. BARBERSPAN NATURE RESERVE
BARBERSPAN

Trail details: Guided walks of varying length.

Permits/bookings: Must be obtained from The Manager, Barberspan Holiday Resort, tel. (0144322) ask for 28; PO Box 63, Barberspan 2765.

Facilities/amenities: Guided walk around 1 800-ha pan; caravan and camp site with braai area and toilets at the Barberspan Holiday Resort; fishing.

Main attractions: Bird hide; 351 species of birds; large mammals.

Pertinent information: The reserve is open daily from 6.00 am to 6.00 pm.

The 3 068-ha Barberspan Nature Reserve, northeast of Delareyville, is well-known for its research on the migratory habits of waterbirds; it also researches general ecology and bird behaviour. From time to time large flocks of flamingoes visit the dam, presenting a memorable sight. Bird-watching from a canoe (bring your own) is rewarding. The reserve is flat and its grasslands support black wildebeest, springbok, blesbok, zebra and ostrich as well as smaller mammals including jackal, porcupine, yellow mongoose and ground squirrel. Summer is the best time to visit the reserve.

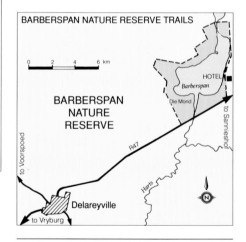

21. MARICO HIKING TRAIL
BRONKHORSTFONTEIN, WESTERN TRANSVAAL

Trail details: 27 km/2 days, circular. Shorter walks available.

Permits/bookings: Must be obtained from Barrie Erasmus, tel. (014252) 1222; PO Box 193, Groot Marico 2850. Map and brochure on request.

Facilities/amenities: Base camp is a restored farmhouse with electricity, kitchen and lapa; overnight hut with accommodation for 20 hikers; toilet and showers but no electricity.

Main attractions: Mountain scenery; game; Groot Marico River.

Pertinent information: Ticks are prevalent. There is a limit of 20 hikers for this trail. The Marico River is bilharzia free.

The Marico Hiking Trail, situated on the Omega Game Farm, 12 km south of Groot Marico in the

Reed and water of Barberspan form a habitat ideal for many waterbirds.

western Transvaal, leads through typical highveld and bushveld vegetation along the Groot Marico River and through the mountains before reaching the overnight hut, a distance of approximately 15 km. The second day is 12 km in length. Along the way hikers may spot some of the many antelope species, including gemsbok, living on the farm, and the 103 bird species present ensure some interesting sightings.

The route requires moderate exertion and should appeal to the reasonably fit as well as beginner hikers. Spring and autumn offer the most pleasant hiking conditions for this clearly marked trail; summers are hot and an early start is advised. Hikers can cool off in one of the many enticing pools in the river.

Shorter trails, varying from 30 minutes to two hours, run along the river bank.

22. BOTSALANO GAME RESERVE
NORTH OF MMABATHO

Trail details: Guided day walks by arrangement.

Permits/bookings: To visit the reserve, contact Bophuthatswana National Parks Board, Central Reservations, tel. (011) 4655423/4; P O Box 937, Lonehill 2062, South Africa. For guided trail details contact Kgama Safaris on tel. (01446) 55587; fax. (01446) 55588. Mogobe Camp offers exclusive walking trails to its guests; contact Gametrackers (Bophuthatswana), tel. (01466) 54591.

Facilities/amenities: Picnic sites and braai places; Botlhaba chalet with 6 beds; Mogobe camp with 4 safari tents on concrete aprons, each tent accommodating 2 or 3 people; paved lapa; camping area with hot and cold water, shower and toilet.

Main attractions: Large game; abundant bushveld birdlife.

Pertinent information: Botsalano is a very arid area with summer rainfall. It is a developing reserve; contact the manager for the latest details at Botsalano Game Reserve, Private Bag X2078, Mafikeng 8670. During the hunting season (April to August) the reserve may be closed to the public.

Situated close to the Botswana border approximately 30 km from Mmabatho and Mafikeng, this 5 800-ha reserve is popular with the residents of these towns, as well as with wildlife fans from afar. Botsalano's low hills with their gentle slopes and depressions are ideal habitats for game such as

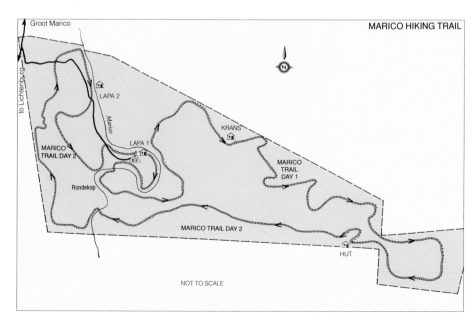

MARICO HIKING TRAIL

Groot Marico

to Lichtenburg

Marico

LAPA 2

KRANS

LAPA 1

MARICO
TRAIL DAY 2

MARICO
TRAIL
DAY 1

Rondekop

MARICO TRAIL DAY 2

HUT

NOT TO SCALE

N

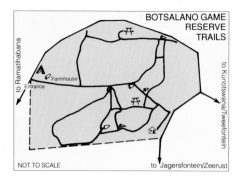

BOTSALANO GAME
RESERVE
TRAILS

NOT TO SCALE

white rhino, tsessebe, hartebeest, giraffe, impala,
eland, gemsbok, zebra, blesbok, sable antelope,
waterbuck, wildebeest, reedbuck and ostrich. Kudu,
steenbok, duiker, warthog, jackal, aardwolf, porcupine and antbear, as well as bushveld birds and
vultures, are also fairly common in the area. The
vegetation which supports this varied fauna comprises grassland, wooded grassland and woodland.
Interesting outcrops of quartzite, ironstone and
lavas of the Dominion Reef, Black Reef and Ventersdorp systems dot the landscape.

23. PILANESBERG NATIONAL PARK
BOPHUTHATSWANA

Trail details: Daily guided walks; Wilderness
Leadership Trails: 3 to 5 days.

Permits/bookings: For guided trails, contact The
Officer-in-charge, Pilanesberg National Park,
tel. (01465) 55356, at least a day in advance so that
he can arrange for a game scout to accompany you.
Sun City visitors should make reservations at the
Pilanesberg Safaris desk. Contact them directly
from any hotel in the complex or tel. (014651)
21561. Metswedi Camp offers exclusive hiking
trails to its guests; contact Gametrackers
(Bophuthatswana), tel. (01466) 54591. For the
Wilderness Experience, contact Wilderness
Leadership School, tel. (011) 4553384; PO Box
87230, Houghton 2041. Brochure available on
request.

Facilities/amenities: Within the park the Manyane,
Mankwe, Kololo, Bosele and Metswedi rest camps
provide accommodation of various levels from
tented camps to luxury bungalows; Kwa Maritane
and Bakubung time-share lodges are also located in
the park; nearby is the Sun City complex. For the
wilderness experience, hikers camp under the stars;
food and equipment supplied.

Main attractions: Abundant game and birdlife;
unusual volcanic alkaline ring complex; diverse
landscape; historically interesting sites; Iron Age
settlements; walk-in indigenous bird aviary at
Manyane gate; Pilanesberg Centre (old magistrate's
court).

Pertinent information: Ticks can be a problem in
summer. The guided walks set out at 6 am from the
camp of your choice. There is a minimum of 6 and
a maximum of 10 hikers per group. The best
months are August to May. This is a summer
rainfall area.

Approximately 42 km north-west of Rustenburg
and adjacent to the Sun City complex lies a roughly
circular mass of lava and syenite, 27 km in
diameter. Rising 600 m above Mankwe lake, the
central feature of the park, and the surrounding
bushveld plains, this mass, named Pilanesberg, is

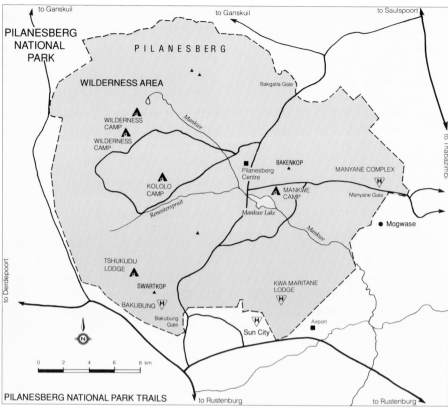

PILANESBERG NATIONAL PARK TRAILS

evidence of ancient volcanic intrusion into the
Bushveld Igneous Complex. The guided trails
stress the understanding of the entire ecological
spectrum and present an opportunity to observe the
development of this wildlife sanctuary.

Founded in 1979, this 55 000-ha reserve is the result of an imaginative and ambitious game-stocking
programme. Today over 10 000 head of game are

present, including black and white rhino, elephant,
cheetah, leopard, buffalo, giraffe and hippo.

There are about 3 500 species of birds which
thrive in the diverse habitats within the park, which
is located in a faunal transitional zone (arid western
Kalahari/ moist eastern lowveld). It is small wonder
then that this reserve has become a haven for
bird-watchers.

Established in 1979, Pilanesberg boasts a great many faunal species in its diverse habitats.

24. BORAKALALO NATIONAL PARK
JERICHO, NORTH-WEST OF PRETORIA

Trail details: Various guided wilderness trails; self-guided walks from 1 km to 4 km.

Permits/bookings: Must be obtained from the Borakalalo National Park, tel. (01461) 21102; PO Box 240, Jericho 0264, Bophuthatswana. Camps must be booked well in advance.

Facilities/amenities: Game-viewing drives; camping permitted for organized groups; 3 camps: Pitjane camp for campers and caravanners; Moretele camp with 10 fully furnished safari tents, each equipped with 2 beds, table and chairs; Phudufudu camp with 4 safari tents accommodating up to 3 people each; picnic and braai areas with ablution blocks; shop for basic supplies and curios; swimming pool.

Main attractions: Varied sand bushveld and riverine vegetation; prolific birdlife; large mammals; Klipvoor Dam with its excellent fishing (kurper, tilapia and catfish).

Pertinent information: No boating or swimming permitted on the dam; fishermen must possess a valid licence and permit, obtainable at the gate. The park is open between 6.00 am and 8.00 pm from October to March; 6.00 am to 7.00 pm from April to September.

Trailists stop to study hippo on the banks of Pilanesberg's Mankwe lake.

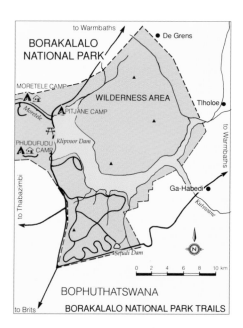

BORAKALALO NATIONAL PARK TRAILS

Thanks to the Bophuthatswana National Parks Board, the 14 000-ha Borakalalo National Park has been converted from an overused and abused recreational area into a tranquil, beautiful reserve deserving of its Setswana name, which means 'the place where the people relax'. The second-largest park in Bophuthatswana, Borakalalo encompasses a diversity of landscapes and vegetation types such as riverine bush along the Moretele (Pienaars) River, kloofs, vleis, koppies and rolling sandveld. These diverse habitats support many large mammals such as sable, roan, tsessebe, waterbuck, giraffe and zebra, as well as an astonishing 3 500 or more bird species, including abundant waterfowl on the 8 km-long Klipvoor Dam. In addition to excellent fishing, controlled canoe trails are permitted on the dam.

Borakalalo National Park, 60 km north of Brits, owes its popularity to its close proximity (only a 2-hour drive) to the Pretoria-Witwatersrand-Vereeniging area. The Bophuthatswana National Parks Board is keen to provide quality environmental education experiences for its citizens and visitors. Clearly marked, easy walks from 1 to 4 hours in duration radiate in wooded terrain from the central picnic area south of the Klipvoor Dam. They cover a riverside ramble to a gentle climb up Pitjane Koppie with its excellent views. Maps are provided at the entrance gate.

Part of the park has been set aside for wilderness trails. The Wilderness Leadership School runs weekend guided trails for groups of 6 hikers. The organization provides transport, food and camping equipment; contact them at tel. (011) 4553384; PO Box 87230, Houghton 2041. The Johannesburg Hiking Club also runs trails here; contact them on (011) 6434437.

A hornbill captures the attention of visitors to the indigenous bird aviary at the Manyane camp, Pilanesberg National Park.

NORTHERN AND EASTERN TRANSVAAL AND VENDA

The northern and eastern Transvaal comprise vast areas of South Africa's northernmost province. This region includes the land of baobab, acacia and mopane trees known as the lowveld, bordered on the north by the Limpopo River and on the east by Mozambique; and the large stretch of high land north and east of Pretoria which includes the Waterberg, Wolkberg, Magoebaskloof area, Soutpansberg and Transvaal escarpment. The highveld forms this region's southern border and the Kalahari its western border.

Facilities and amenities for trailists abound in the northern and eastern Transvaal. A plethora of constructed hiking ways along scenic mountains and through forest and woodlands have been developed under the auspices of the National Hiking Way Board, the Transvaal provincial authorities and private enterprise. The rambler will delight in the numerous short walks through indigenous forest, bushveld and wetlands, while the mountaineer is well catered for within the magnificent Wolkberg Wilderness and Transvaal escarpment areas.

Climate is predictable in the northern and eastern Transvaal, except in the mountains, which dictate their own weather. Generally, summer months (October to March) are hot and rainy, while winter (May to September) is cool, dry and sunny during the day and cold and clear at night.

Venda, Bophuthatswana and Lebowa once formed part of the Transvaal. Venda and Bophuthatswana are now independent states, while Lebowa operates as an independent homeland. Venda is relatively small and mountainous. Straddling the subtropical eastern reaches of the Soutpansberg range, it boasts an atmosphere of unadulterated Africa. Traditional settlements dot mountain slopes; Lake Fundudzi and Lwamondo Kop are not only set in beautiful surroundings but are riddled with spiritual mystery as well; here are rock art sites and sacred indigenous forest; the Sagole tribal warmwater baths, an impressive gorge on the Mutale River; and giant cycads. Big game trails are planned for the Levubu River Valley area. Visitors to Venda must be in possession of a passport or a book of life.

LEFT: *High in the remote Wolkberg, a young stream sprays out over lichen-patched boulders.*

Islands in the stream, hippo laze their day in a cooling river.

1. DIEPDRIFT HIKING TRAILS
NEAR WARMBATHS

Trail details: 1. Hippo Trail: 22 km/2 days, return;
2. Klipspringer Trail: 8 km/4 hours, circular;
3. Bontebok Trail: 6 km/3 hours; circular.

Permits/bookings: Must be obtained from Diepdrift Game Ranch, tel. (014462) 1521; PO Box 543, Warmbaths 0480. Map and brochure are available on request.

Facilities/amenities: Overnight huts with 36 beds and mattresses, hot water, toilets, lapa, and braai facilities.

Main attractions: Game; rock formations; 102 tree species; 156 bird species.

Pertinent information: Hikers must carry their own water. There is a limit of 36 hikers per trail at any one time.

Situated on the 4 000-ha Diepdrift Game Ranch approximately 50 km north-west of Warmbaths, these three trails are all clearly marked and require a medium level of fitness.

1. The Hippo Trail leads hikers through an area populated by hippo, eland, gemsbok, kudu, blue wildebeest and red hartebeest, to the overnight hut 11 km further on. The second day's route returns along the same path to the start. Keep out of the way of hippos!

2. The Klipspringer Trail takes hikers through a particularly lovely part of the farm, with interesting quartzite rock formations along the way.

3. The Bontebok Trail takes in Platklipkoppie, with its spectacular view over the surrounding countryside.

2. KRANSBERG HIKING TRAILS
NEAR THABAZIMBI

Trail details: Three routes: 16 km/9 to 10 hours; 12 km/6 to 7 hours; 10 km/4 hours. All are circular.

Permits/bookings: Must be obtained from the Trail Manager, tel. (016) 511407; PO Box 2355, Vereeniging 1930. Map and brochure available on request.

Facilities/amenities: The base camp has 3 huts, each sleeping 10 people; braai and washing-up facilities, hot and cold running water, toilets and showers are also provided.

Main attractions: Wide variety of small wildlife; many cliffs and gorges; indigenous forest; swimming holes in kloofs; beautiful vistas.

Pertinent information: Ticks are prevalent; rapidly changeable weather; hikers must carry their own water. There is a limit of 10 people per trail at any one time.

The Kransberg Hiking Trails are situated on the 2 245-ha farm Hartbeesfontein, 32 km north-east of Thabazimbi on the road to Alma. Kransberg is part of the Waterberg range. The farm is home to bushpig, dassie, klipspringer, grey rhebok and baboon. It is rare to see the nocturnal leopard, but it does make its home in the Waterberg, the wildest natural part of the Transvaal. The birdlife is prolific and includes large raptors.

Hikers have a choice of routes: an 'advanced' hike of 16 km; a 'general' hike of 12 km; and a 'relatively easy' trail of 10 km. The rugged terrain means that all three of the trails involve moderately strenuous walking; a high level of endurance is needed for the advanced route.

The 'advanced' hike is unmarked; hikers must use their map and look out for the few landmarks. The scenic route leads you through rugged terrain and takes 9 to 10 hours to complete. The 'general' route, approximately 12 km in length, takes between 6 and 7 hours to complete. There are some sharp ascents and descents along the way, and at one stage hikers pass an interesting aloe forest. This route is clearly marked. The 'easier' route shares the same start as the 'general' route, but avoids the steep ascents and descents. It takes about 4 hours to walk.

The hikes are open all year, with March to November providing the best walking conditions.

3. TAAIBOS HIKING TRAIL
NEAR VAALWATER

Trail details: 19 km/2 days, circular; there is a 1-day option.

Permits/bookings: Must be obtained from the Trail Manager, tel. (0020) 222; PO Box 185, Vaalwater 0530. Map and brochure available on request.

Facilities/amenities: 2 overnight huts with accommodation for 15 hikers each; braai facilities, firewood, cooking pots, kettle and toilets.

Main attractions: Rock art; mountain scenery; mountain pools.

Pertinent information: There is a limit of 30 people for the trail at any one time.

The Taaibos Hiking Trail is situated on the 3 300-ha Haakdoorndraai Farm, 30 km west of Vaalwater on the Ellisras road. The farm is home to a wide variety of wildlife: bushbuck, grey rhebok, kudu, leopard, brown hyaena, dassie, baboon, steenbok and duiker. The birdlife includes kingfishers, eagles, storks and hadedas.

The route starts at the Marula hut approximately 100 m from the Taaibos River, where there is a waterberry forest which is home to many birds and a surprising number of animals. The route then leads up to the top of the krantz, which affords a good view of the surrounding mountainside. Hikers then walk down to the river again and follow the trail along its banks until Tierkloof, which is situated approximately 1 km from the overnight hut: those not wishing to go any further can take a detour at this point and follow the baboon-print motif back to the start.

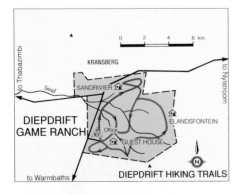

HAAKDOORNDRAAI FARM

TAAIBOS HIKING TRAIL

The second day's route leads up the krantz before descending into a kloof filled with white stinkwood trees. At John's Dam the route turns sharply back and leads through green kloofs to a braai area. The starting point is 600 m further on.

The route is clearly marked, and requires a medium level of fitness.

4. THE RHINO TRAIL
LAPALALA WILDERNESS

Trail details: 3-day guided trail.

Permits/bookings: Must be obtained from the Wilderness Trust of Southern Africa, tel. (011) 4537645; PO Box 645, Bedfordview 2008. Map, brochure and rates available on request.

Facilities/amenities: Comfortable Mogonono tented camp; all food, transport to and from Johannesburg and equipment is supplied by the trail organizers.

Main attractions: Waterberg mountains; Bushman paintings; antelope and prolific birdlife.

Pertinent information: There is a limit of 8 people per group. Hikers must wear only khaki or neutral-coloured clothing; sturdy footwear is recommended for this rugged terrain.

The Rhino Trail is situated in the 21 403-ha Lapalala Wilderness reserve, a nature sanctuary in the rugged Waterberg mountains. This is a real wilderness area that was the province's last extensive hunting grounds and was never really subdued, so it is ideal for a real bushveld adventure. The wilderness is home to white rhino, sable and roan antelope, as well as the first founder population of black rhino introduced to a private reserve in South Africa. It is a rare and unforgettable experience to see these solitary creatures. Giraffe, kudu, zebra, wildebeest, waterbuck, impala, civets, klipspringer and monkeys all live here. The prolific birdlife includes the blackheaded oriole, white helmetshrike, black eagle and green pigeon.

The trail, which is guided by an experienced field officer and operates all year round, can be adapted to the interests of each individual group.

5. SABLE VALLEY HIKING TRAIL
NEAR NABOOMSPRUIT

Trail details: 24 km/2 days; circular.

Permits/bookings: Must be obtained from Naauwpoort Farm, tel. (012) 3270442; PO Box 19279, Pretoria-West 0177; bookings must be made at least 1 month in advance. Map and brochure available on request.

Facilities/amenities: 2 overnight camps (restored farmhouses), each with 30 beds and 10 tent sites for small tents; toilets, showers, braai facilities and wood provided.

Main attractions: Indigenous forest; rock pools and waterfalls; panoramic views of the Waterberg.

Pertinent information: There is a limit of 50 hikers for this trail at any one time.

This trail is situated on the 2 000-ha farm Naauwpoort, 20 km south of Naboomspruit.

It stretches over an unusual combination of valleys, gorges, savannah and mountain streams, with crystal-clear rock pools, waterfalls and panoramic views of the northern Transvaal awaiting the hiker. The trail is not very strenuous, and children from 10 years old and upwards should have no trouble completing it.

The prolific birdlife on the farm includes, among other species, the migratory black stork, the fish eagle, black eagle, martial eagle, green pigeon, Burchell's coucal and various kingfishers and bee-eaters.

The Naauwpoort farm is also home to a number of animal species, including kudu, reedbuck, klipspringer, mountain reedbuck, brown hyaena and the civet cat. The forest is made up of a wide variety of indigenous trees.

The route is clearly marked with painted footprints, and is open all year round.

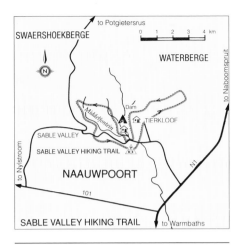

SWAERSHOEKBERGE

WATERBERGE

NAAUWPOORT

SABLE VALLEY HIKING TRAIL

6. STERKSTROOM TENT TRAIL
DOORNDRAAI DAM NATURE RESERVE

Trail details: 30 km/2 days; circular.

Permits/bookings: Must be obtained from Doorndraai Dam Nature Reserve, tel. (015423) 629; PO Box 983, Potgietersrus 0600. Map and brochure available on request.

Facilities/amenities: Nuku overnight camp with braai area, bush toilet, cold showers and tent site.

Main attractions: The reserve specializes in the protection of rare species, especially sable, roan and tsessebe; birdlife; kloofs and waterfalls.

Pertinent information: When the dam is full hikers must swim across the inlet on the second day – as bilharzia is sometimes present, it is advisable to avoid this route when the dam is full (phone ahead to check). There is a limit of 10 people for the trail per day.

Located in the foothills of the Waterberg, 43 km south-east of Potgietersrus, the 7 229-ha Doorndraai Dam Nature Reserve has sour bushveld

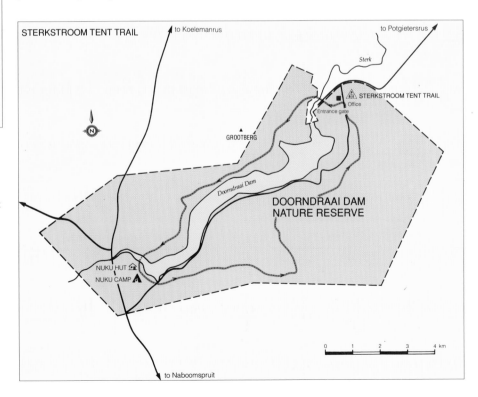

STERKSTROOM TENT TRAIL

DOORNDRAAI DAM NATURE RESERVE

A comfortable cabin on stilts, deep in the montane forest of Mapulaneng.

vegetation, comprising trees such as boekenhout, wild olive and wild syringa, while yellowwoods and wild fig are found in the kloofs. The reserve is home to reintroduced tsessebe, roan and sable antelope, as well as duiker, steenbok, kudu, klipspringer, mountain reedbuck, leopard and baboon. The dam attracts waterbirds, while raptors such as the fish eagle, Wahlberg's eagle and martial eagle can often be seen soaring overhead.

The trail begins on relatively even thornveld terrain, before hikers cross a kloof, and then the real exertion begins. The ascent to Grootberg is a relatively strenuous but scenic hike. Once hikers reach the top of Grootberg, they start westwards and downwards until they reach the overnight hut.

The second day begins with a walk eastwards through boekenhout trees and vaalbosveld, and there are good views from the top of the dam. Hikers then begin to descend towards the dam, through rooibosveld and sandveld, and head in a north-easterly direction until the reserve gate and end point is reached. This trail requires an average level of fitness, and is especially pleasant in spring and autumn.

7. MAPULANENG HIKING TRAILS
BUSHBUCK RIDGE

Trail details: 1. Trogon Trail: 16 km/6 hours; 2. Red Duiker Trail: 15 km/5 hours; 3. Swimming Pool Trail: 11 km/4 hours. All circular.

Permits/bookings: Must be obtained from the Chief Minister, Lebowa Department of Tourism, tel. (01526) 35529; Private Bag X27, Chuniespoort 0745. Map and brochure available on request.

Facilities/amenities: 3 fully equipped luxury log cabins accommodating a total of 16 hikers.

Main attractions: Indigenous forest; waterfalls.

Pertinent information: Anti-malaria precautions are necessary; ticks are prevalent; rapidly changeable weather. There is a limit of 16 hikers per trail.

Many hikers are familiar with the Blyderivierspoort Hiking Trail (see page 263). However, few are aware that just east of the canyon at the base of the escarpment is an afforested ramp called Mapulaneng. The Mapulaneng forestry region includes several plantations and large areas of unspoilt montane forest, the origin of many lowveld streams. Deep in the heart of this jungle-like environment are three secluded log cabins, situated 1 051 m above sea level. The cabins are surrounded by tall, tropical montane forest species such as yellowwood, Cape wild fig, wild peach, Cape beech, white stinkwood and Cape chestnut.

Radiating from the cabins are three circular nature trails. These are cut deep inside the forest, occasionally offering views of the distant lowveld or the towering quartzitic cliffs that shade the canopy in the late afternoon. The **Trogon Trail** runs west from the hut to Visierskop (1 796 m), the **Red Duiker Trail** takes hikers to Makapane (1 554 m). The new **Swimming Pool Trail** is in the process of being laid out; hikers should contact the Lebowa Department of Tourism for an update.

The trails display both the dry forests of the northern slopes and the wetter forests of the southern slopes. A feature of these forests is the variety of lianes and epiphytes, including members of the orchid and streptocarpus families; the forests have strong affinities with those in tropical east Africa and the Chimanimani mountains of Zimbabwe.

In summer, bird-watchers have a good chance of spotting the elusive narina trogon, as well as breeding gymnogenes and the crowned eagle, orange thrush, Knysna lourie and many more avian species. Samango monkeys, baboon, bushbuck, duiker and bushpig are all common, but not often seen. Lepidopterists will be delighted by the variety of butterflies to be found in Mapulaneng, including numerous rare, endemic species.

All these trails are easy strolling, are clearly marked, and offer pleasant hiking conditions all year round.

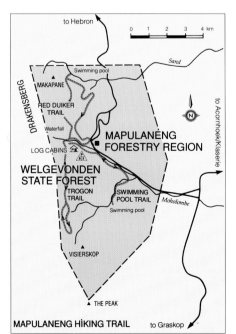

MAPULANENG HIKING TRAIL

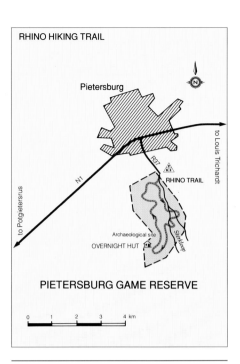

8. RHINO HIKING TRAIL
PIETERSBURG GAME RESERVE

Trail details: 18 km/1 or 2 days; circular.

Permits/bookings: Must be obtained at the entrance to the reserve. Map and brochure available on request. The overnight hut is rented out; details of tariffs available from the Pietersburg Town Council; tel. (01521) 952011.

Facilities/amenities: Overnight accommodation for 20 people; braai facilities; waterpoints; toilets.

Main attractions: Prolific birdlife; indigenous tree species marked with their national tree list numbers; wildlife.

Pertinent information: Ticks are prevalent. There is a limit of 20 people for this trail.

The Rhino Hiking Trail is situated in the 3 200-ha Pietersburg Game Reserve in Union Park, 5 km south-east of Pietersburg, where the terrain is grass-covered plains dotted with clumps of acacia bush. The trail can be walked in 1 day, or split over 2 days of 9 km per day. It starts at the entrance to the reserve, and leads through indigenous plantations, silica outcrops and archaeological features before reaching the overnight farmhouse, just before the halfway mark.

Sable antelope, waterbuck, gemsbok, nyala, tsessebe, blue wildebeest, giraffe and white rhino are all present in the reserve. The birds to be seen include the Cape vulture, saddlebilled stork and shortclawed lark (a total of 195 species of birds has been recorded in the reserve). The best months for walking are March to November. The trail is clearly marked and does not require a high level of fitness or exertion.

9. BAKONI TRAIL
BAKONI MALAPA OPEN-AIR MUSEUM, PIETERSBURG

Trail details: 8 km/3 hours; circular.

Permits/bookings: Not required; there is an entrance fee to the museum. Contact the museum at tel. (01521) 952867 for more information.

Facilities/amenities: Toilets; lapas at specified points; water at the entrance.

Main attractions: Archaeological sites; plants identified and descriptions given of their traditional uses by local peoples.

Pertinent information: Ticks are prevalent; loose rocks and pebbles on the koppies. There is a limit of 20 people per group.

This easy walk over more or less flat terrain is situated in the 126-ha Bakoni Malapa Open-air Museum, 5 km from Pietersburg. Opened in December 1992, the trail, which starts and ends at the museum entrance, is clearly marked and has information signs dotted along the route. Along the way you will see 3 archaelogical sites of old kraals and huts, the flora used in traditional medicine, the beadwork and carved utensils of the North Sotho, a demonstration of how to make a fire, and other examples of traditional life. The most pleasant months for walking here are March to November.

10. MASEBE TRAILS
MASEBE NATURE RESERVE

Trail details: 9 km/3 hours; 11 km/4 hours. Both are circular.

Permits/bookings: Must be obtained from Lebowa Tourist Department, tel. (0156) 35529; Private Bag X27, Chuniespoort 0745.

Facilities/amenities: Rest camp with two 6-bed and three 4-bed fully equipped thatched chalets; swimming pools; conference facilities; game-viewing drive; picnic site.

Main attractions: Bushman paintings; mixed bushveld; shallow caves; prolific birdlife; the Waterberg mountains.

Pertinent information: Anti-malaria precautions are necessary in the summer months. There is a limit of 12 people per group.

Situated approximately 21 km south of Marken, in the 4 542-ha Masebe Nature Reserve, the Masebe Trails, which require a low to medium exertion rate, lead through mixed bushveld and pass shallow caves and Bushman paintings. The lovely indigenous trees to be seen include paperback albizia *(Albizia tanganyicensis),* the paperbark commiphora *(Commiphora marlothii),* marula, wild fig, combretum and tamboti.

The diverse birdlife includes the black eagle, African hawk eagle, blackbreasted and brown snake eagles, hornbills and lilacbreasted rollers. Mammals to be seen are eland, kudu, impala, red hartebeest, zebra and waterbuck. The routes are clearly marked, but because these are new trails, maps and brochures are not yet available; hikers should contact the Lebowa Tourist Department at the above address for further information.

11. LIMPOPO WILDERNESS HIKING TRAIL
ALLDAYS

Trail details: 35 km/3 days (variations possible).

Permits/bookings: Must be obtained from Mr Theo Swart, tel. (01554) 464; PO Box 5, Alldays 0909.

Facilities/amenities: Two camps with long-drop toilets, cold water and firewood.

Main attractions: The Limpopo River, with its great variety of indigenous trees and rich birdlife; ancient ruins; mines.

Pertinent information: Anti-malaria precautions are necessary. The trails are organized to suit the particular interests and abilities of each individual group (there is no restriction on the number of people per group). Hikers may not cross the border into Botswana.

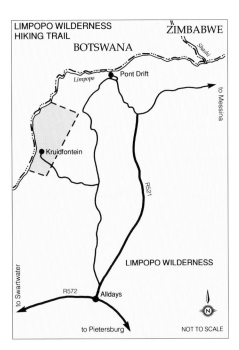

For a true wilderness experience, where there is little sign of human intrusion and the environment is absolutely unspoilt, the guided Limpopo Wilderness Hiking Trail is ideal. It is physically undemanding; the short distances covered each day encourage hikers to observe the bush and spend time at the permanent pools in the river where numerous bird species can be seen. Crocodile, hippo, bushbuck, waterbuck, impala, klipspringer and kudu are plentiful.

12. SOUTPANSBERG HIKING TRAIL:
ENTABENI SECTION, NEAR LOUIS TRICHARDT

Trail details: Option I: 48 km/3 days; Option II: 47 km/2 days; Option III: 30 km/2 days. All of these trails are circular. See map overleaf.

Permits/bookings: Must be obtained from the Department of Forestry, tel. (01551) 51152; Private Bag 2413, Louis Trichardt 0920. Map and brochure available on request.

Facilities/amenities: Kabelbaan, Entabeni and Klein Australie overnight huts, each equipped with beds and mattresses for 30 hikers, hot and cold showers, and braai facilities.

Main attractions: Indigenous forest; diverse scenery and vegetation; views of Venda; mountain environment.

Pertinent information: Ticks are prevalent; anti-malaria precautions are necessary in summer; bilharzia is present in some streams. There is a limit of 30 hikers for this trail at any one time.

The Entabeni Section of the Soutpansberg Hiking Trail passes through indigenous forest and exotic plantations. The hikes begin and end at Klein Australie Hut in Entabeni State Forest, situated approximately 40 km east of Louis Trichardt.

Bushbuck, duiker and samango monkeys are all plentiful here. The birds of the area are rather elusive, although louries and woodpeckers abound. Hikers will probably catch a glimpse of the crowned eagle, which breeds here, as this area has possibly the highest concentration of this powerful raptor in South Africa. The best months for hiking are March to October.

1. Option I takes hikers from Klein Australie Hut through various exotic gum plantations, before climbing gradually through a semi-deciduous in-

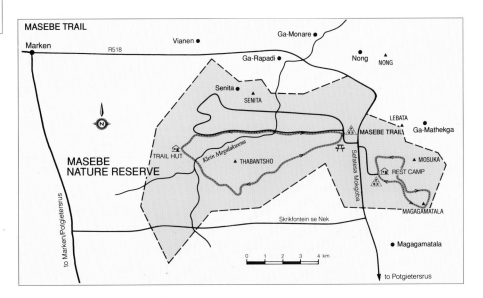

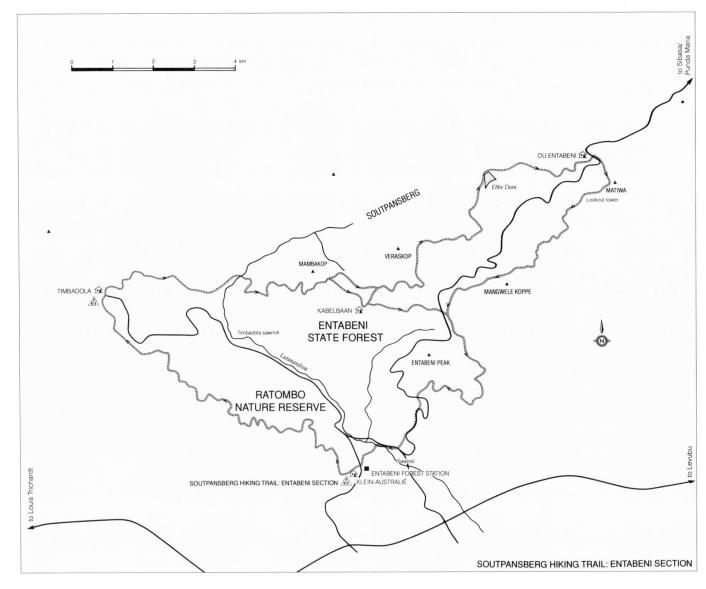

SOUTPANSBERG HIKING TRAIL: ENTABENI SECTION

digenous scrub forest, part of the 172-ha Ratombo Nature Reserve. The route then follows a steep ridge up to a lookout point over the lowveld, and then drops down to Lutanandwa Valley. There is much 'upping-and-downing' on this trail that is quite strenuous, and hikers finally climb to the top of the Escarpment and Kabelbaan overnight hut.

The second day starts with a walk through pine plantations and indigenous forest, until Ebbe Dam is reached, which is an ideal resting spot for a swim. From here the route leads through more plantations to the very picturesque Entabeni hut for the night.

On the final day of this route, hikers traverse the 880-ha Entabeni Nature Reserve until they reach

the Matiwa lookout tower, where fabulous views over Venda and the holy mountain of the Lamondo tribe can be enjoyed.

Hikers then continue through the reserve, past impressive American Coastal Redwoods and down to the start. This option is relatively easy and is suitable for families.

A sample of the dense and varied vegetation on the Hanglip section of the Soutpansberg Trail.

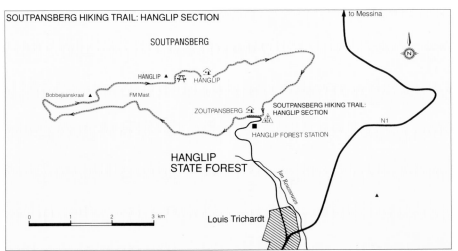

2. The first day of **Option II** combines the routes for days 1 and 2 of Option I, while the second day is the same as the third day of Option I. This is a difficult route and is recommended for very fit hikers only.

3. The first day of **Option III** is the same as the first day of Option I, while the second day of this route leads through pine plantations and eventually joins up with the same route described for the third day of Option 1. Hikers then continue through a section of the Entabeni Nature Reserve and back downhill to Klein Australie hut. This route is not particularly taxing, and is ideal for a family that enjoys hiking together.

Special permission is needed to get close to sacred Lake Fundudzi, seen here from the Mabuda-Shango Trail.

13. SOUTPANSBERG HIKING TRAIL:
HANGLIP SECTION, LOUIS TRICHARDT

> **Trail details:** Option I: 18 km/2 days; Option II: 14 km/1 day. Both are circular.
>
> **Permits/bookings:** Must be obtained from the Department of Forestry, tel. (01551) 51152; Private Bag 2413, Louis Trichardt 0920. Map and brochure available on request.
>
> **Facilities/amenities:** Information display centre and ablution block at Hanglip State Forest; Zoutpansberg and Hanglip overnight huts each with bunks and mattresses for 30 hikers, fresh water and braai facilities.
>
> **Main attractions:** Indigenous forest; aloes; open protea grassland; birdlife; diverse scenery and vegetation; Venda villages.
>
> **Pertinent information:** Ticks are prevalent; anti-malaria precautions are necessary in summer; bilharzia is present in some streams. There is a limit of 30 hikers for this trail at one time.

The Hanglip Section of the Soutpansberg Hiking Trail consists of a 1- or a 2-day route. Both options are situated in the Hanglip State Forest which nestles on the southern slopes of the Soutpansberg range. Both routes are circular and start and end at the forestry office, which is situated about 4 km north of Louis Trichardt.

1. The route of **Option I** is marked with white footprints, and takes hikers from Zoutpansberg hut through indigenous forest up the mountain to the plateau, where there are breathtaking views of the surrounding bushveld and valleys. From here the route passes through evergreen indigenous forest, with trees such as ironwood, Cape chestnut and Transvaal stinkwood. The final kilometre to Hanglip overnight hut is through open grassveld and plantation. The second day of this option leads through a natural rocky outcrop and then downhill all the way to the starting point.

2. The route of **Option II** is marked with yellow footprints. This pleasant trail follows almost the same route as the first day of the 2-day route. Once within the indigenous forest, the route branches off and after passing through the Hanglip picnic site which is most delightfully situated in a forest clearing, rejoins the 2-day trail once again.

Both the routes are relatively easy. Bushbuck, duiker, samango monkeys, louries and woodpeckers are all plentiful here. The best months for hiking are March to October.

14. MABUDA-SHANGO HIKING TRAIL
THATHE VONDO PLANTATION, SOUTPANSBERG

> **Trail details:** 53,5 km/4 days; circular.
>
> **Permits/bookings:** Must be obtained from the Department of Agriculture and Forestry, tel. (0159) 31001; Private Bag X2247, Sibasa, Venda. Map and brochure available on request.
>
> **Facilities/amenities:** The overnight camps consist of thatched structures which offer no real protection against the elements; firewood, water, refuse bins and toilets are provided; trees are marked with their national tree list numbers.
>
> **Main attractions:** Fundudzi sacred lake; Lwamondo sacred mountain; Tshamanyatsha indigenous garden.
>
> **Pertinent information:** Anti-malaria precautions must be taken. There is a limit of 30 hikers for this trail at any one time. On weekends the area is apt to get noisy.

The Mabuda-Shango Hiking Trail starts and ends at Thathe Vondo Plantation, 25 km from Thohoyandou off the Sibasa road. The trail does cross, and sometimes follows, roads such as that to the waterfall. Distances each day are relatively short, allowing hikers to walk at their leisure, enjoying the many views and absorbing the sacred significance of the trail's highlights.

The first day's route is 15,3 km long and leads through indigenous forest and past spectacular viewpoints, the first of which looks out over the Tshivhase tea estate, the Vondo Dam and the Lwamondo sacred mountain. The route continues along the Nzhelele River catchment area, through pine plantations to the Mutale River where the Fundudzi overnight rest camp is situated. The second day leads to a viewpoint overlooking the Fundudzi sacred lake, along the external fire break, past the Mwanani stream and up to the Thathe sacred forest, which served as the burial ground for Venda chiefs and headmen in the past. The trail leads through the

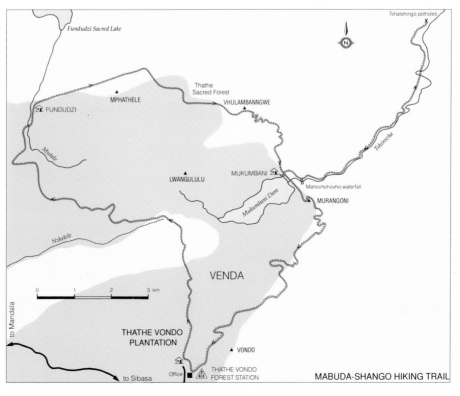

MABUDA-SHANGO HIKING TRAIL

sacred forest, renowned for its huge indigenous trees and mysterious atmosphere. The dead are believed to live in the lake, hence there are all sorts of rituals attached to it, like you should not face the lake but approach it backwards, and you should have permission from a chief or sangoma before going anywhere near the lake.

From here the route passes through the Tshamanyatsha indigenous garden, a spectacular array of indigenous flowers and ferns, before continuing to Mukumbani Dam and the overnight shelter.

The third day leads from Mukumbani Dam past the Mahovhohovho Waterfall to the Tshatshingo potholes and back along the same route to Mukumbani Dam. The fourth day's route leads past the Ndou-mhulu viewpoint and back to the start 10 km further on. This trail is clearly marked, and requires a medium level of fitness. Although it is open all year round, spring and autumn offer the best walking conditions.

15. BEN LAVIN NATURE RESERVE TRAILS
NEAR LOUIS TRICHARDT

Trail details: 1. Tabajwane Trail: 8 km/4 hours; 2. Fountain Trail: 4 km/2 hours; 3. Waterbuck Trail: 3 km/1,5 hours; 4. Tshumanini Springs Trail: 5 km/2,5 hours; all are circular.

Permits/bookings: Must be obtained at the entrance to the reserve. Map available on request.

Facilities/amenities: Camp and caravan sites; huts with firewood, linen, crockery, cutlery and refrigerators; trees labelled with their national tree list numbers; game-viewing hides.

Main attractions: Sweet and mixed bushveld vegetation; 54 mammal species, including large game; 232 recorded bird species; interesting archaeological sites.

Pertinent information: Ticks can be a problem; hikers should carry their own water. There is a limit of 6 hikers at any one time for each trail.

BEN LAVIN NATURE RESERVE TRAILS

The Ben Lavin Nature Reserve is a project of the South African Wildlife Society and is situated 12 km south-east of Louis Trichardt in beautiful bushveld country. The freedom to walk where you please exists.

The trails are all clearly marked, and only require a nominal level of fitness. Summer is an especially pleasant time for hiking in this reserve.

1. The Tabajwane Trail offers superb views of the surrounding bushveld and the Soutpansberg range, as well as possible sightings of game at waterholes, wallows and dams.

2. The Fountain Trail meanders along the banks of the Doring River, through lush riverine vegetation where bushbuck, nyala, reedbuck and leguaan are often encountered. To see kudu, impala and waterbuck, follow the **Waterbuck Trail** to the Waterbuck, Steenbok and Marsh dams.

3. The Tshumanini Springs Trail lies in the northern part of the reserve, and whereas the other three trails begin at the camp, this one starts from the Zebra Dam. Chances of seeing warthog, kudu, impala and zebra are good.

16. KRUGER NATIONAL PARK WILDERNESS TRAILS
EASTERN TRANSVAAL

Trail details: 1. Wolhuter Trail; 2. Olifants Trail; 3. Nyalaland Trail; 4. Bushman Trail; 5. Metsi-Metsi Trail; 6. Sweni Trail; 7. Napi Trail. All 8 to 15 km/ 1 to 2 days.

Permits/bookings: Must be obtained from National Parks Board offices around the country. Brochure available on request. Bookings are accepted up to a year in advance.

Facilities/amenities: Shelter, food, rucksacks, eating utensils, water bottles, beds and bedding provided.

Main attractions: One of the greatest game sanctuaries in the world.

Pertinent information: Anti-malaria precautions are necessary. Trailists meet at the relevant rest camp at 15h00 on Mondays or Fridays and return to the camp after breakfast on the final morning. There is a maximum of 8 people per trail. Hikers older than 45 must be 'walking fit'. Book well in advance for these over-subscribed trails.

A wilderness trail, which unlike a hiking trail is not confined to a set path, provides a unique encounter with nature. Large areas of unspoiled wilderness are explored on foot, under the guidance of a professional game ranger. Seven wilderness trails are available in the Kruger National Park. These vary in length and duration from 8 km to 15 km and from 1 to 2 days. A reasonable level of fitness is required for all of them, however.

1. The Wolhuter Trail is named in honour of the legendary Harry Wolhuter (famous for killing a lion with his pocket knife in 1903) and his son Henry, who were both in charge of the southern Kruger Park when they worked for the National Parks Board. The trail, started in 1978, was the park's first wilderness trail. It operates in the far southern section of the park, an area characterized by granite outcrops and *Combretum* lowveld savannah. Although this region is not known for its large herds of game because of the denser and more hilly habitat, the south has a wide variety of rarer mammal species such as roan and sable antelope, reedbuck and oribi. This area is also the chosen habitat of the white and black rhino, and these are encountered regularly by trail parties. Larger predators, such as lion, cheetah, leopard and wild dog, also occur here. A good cross-section of the birds of the park may be spotted on this trail.

The base camp for this trail accommodates hikers in wood and thatched A-frame huts which have replaced the original tents. Parties meet at the Berg-en-Dal rest camp for a short briefing by the ranger who will accompany them, and then travel to the permanent bush camp, a 1,5-hour drive away.

2. The Olifants Trail operates in the central district of the park. The camp is situated on the southern banks of the Olifants River, near its confluence with the Letaba. Except for the areas in the immediate vicinity of the river, this region is flatter than the south. Consequently, one can expect to encounter more of the large-herd species such as zebra, wildebeest and buffalo, and also their predators. Elephant, crocodile and hippo are commonly encountered, and birdlife is prolific along the river. Baobab and yellow fever trees dominate the floodplains, trees of the savannah areas of the central district are typical of Africa, i.e. acacias. Partici-

A pause along the Bushman Trail in the Kruger National Park.

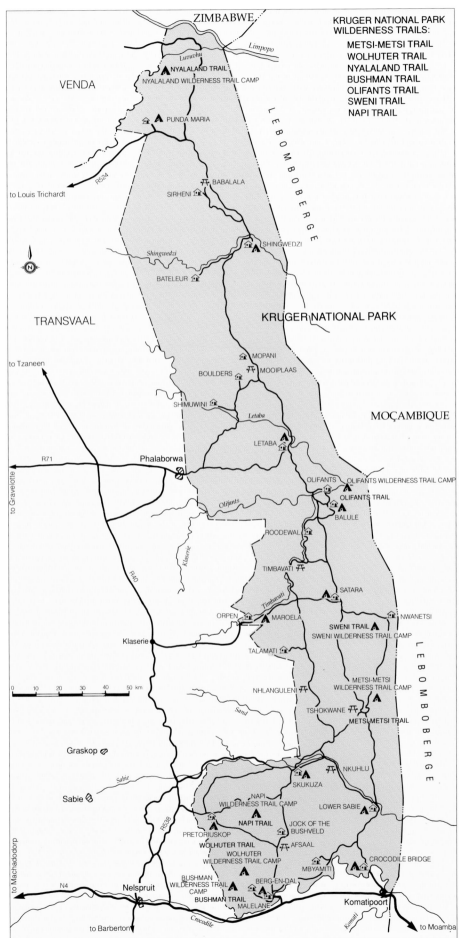

KRUGER NATIONAL PARK
WILDERNESS TRAILS:

METSI-METSI TRAIL
WOLHUTER TRAIL
NYALALAND TRAIL
BUSHMAN TRAIL
OLIFANTS TRAIL
SWENI TRAIL
NAPI TRAIL

Hikers discover that the Olifants Trail lives up to its name.

pants for this trail report at Letaba rest camp, where they are met by a ranger, and then depart for the base camp, a 1,5-hour drive away.

3. The Nyalaland Trail is a must for bird-watchers. Hikers meet at the Punda Maria reception office, from where they are transported north (1,5-hour drive) to the permanent hutted base camp. The huts, constructed under majestic ku-duberry trees so that they blend unobtrusively with their surroundings, are situated along the Madzar-ingwe Spruit, 8 km south of the Mutale/Luvuvhu River confluence in the wildest of all the wilder-ness areas of the park. This wilderness trail is named after the nyala, which is found in significant numbers in the north of the park.

The terrain is essentially sandstone, with mopane scrub dominating the area. Elephant, hippo and cro-codile are common in the vicinity of the Luvuvhu, but the outstanding feature of this region is the rich diversity of its birdlife. Rare plants and wildlife abound among the sandstone koppies. The plants include aloes such as the Zimbabwe aloe (*Aloe ex-celsa*) and Wylliespoort aloe (*Aloe angelica*), and *Euphorbia rowlandii*. The Natal red hare, yellow-spotted dassie, racquet-tailed and broadbilled rollers and the rough-scaled dark-girdled lizard are representative of the rare wildlife.

4. The Bushman Trail is located in the south-western section of the park, an area rich in Bushman rock art. The base camp is situated in a secluded valley, surrounded by granite-domed koppies, an hour's drive from the luxurious Berg-en-Dal camp. Hikers meet at the Berg-en-Dal reception office and travel by Land Rover to the

The Nyala Trail passes giant baobabs, gaunt and leafless during the clear months of winter.

permanent hutted bush camp, attractively constructed in wood and thatch. Much time is spent exploring the slopes looking for paintings. The surroundings are very similar to those on the Wolhuter Trail, so the same mammal and bird species may be seen.

5. The Metsi-Metsi Trail is located in the area east of the Nwarmuriwa Mountain near Tshokwane. The base camp is at the foot of the mountain, and a great variety of wildlife can be encountered in the area, including black rhino. The landscape varies from undulating savannah to rocky gorges and ravines. Hikers assemble at Skukuza for transportation to the base camp.

6. The Sweni Trail is situated in the wilderness area near Nwanetzi. Hikers are transported from Orpen to the base camp, which overlooks the Sweni Spruit, and which provides a view of the surrounding marula and knobthorn savannah. This area is known for its large herds of zebra, wildebeest and buffalo, and accordingly, predators such as lion and spotted hyaena are never far away. On the floodplain of the Sweni unique communities of Ilala palm (*Hyphaene natalensis*) can be seen.

7. Pretoriuskop forms the meeting place for hikers for the new **Napi Trail**, which is located approximately midway between Skukuza and Pretoriuskop. The base camp is situated on the banks of the Napi Spruit. It is cool and shady, and the sounds of riverine birdlife can be heard. The area offers varied landscapes from undulating plains and granite hills to riverine habitat. A wide variety of game can be seen and there is a large population of white rhino in the area. Black rhino are also resident and are quite frequently seen here.

17. LEOPARD TRAIL
DUIWELSKLOOF

Trail details: 22 km/2 days, circular; there are also 5 short rambles, ranging from 300 m to 8 km.

Permits/bookings: Must be obtained from the Duiwelskloof Town Council, tel. (01523) 9651; PO Box 36, Duiwelskloof 0835.

Facilities/amenities: Accommodation at the start of the trail in the caravan park; overnight hut which sleeps 12 and has bush shower and toilet, braai facilities and wood.

Main attractions: Panoramic views over the Wolkberg and Soutpansberg ranges; indigenous bush; prolific birdlife; wild flowers in summer.

Pertinent information: Heavy rains in summer; ticks, malaria and bilharzia are present – hikers must take the necessary precautions. There is a limit of 12 hikers per day for this trail.

This trail, which takes the hiker through varied vegetation, starts and ends at Duiwelskloof Holiday and Caravan Resort in the town. The first day's route ascends for 12 km to the escarpment and hut; this route is strenuous and a moderate level of fitness is required. The second day is easier and hikers travel down the escarpment via a spectacular waterfall. Along the way bushbuck, duiker, bushpig and samango monkeys may be seen. The birdlife in the area is rich; the martial eagle, tawny eagle, jackal buzzard and Knysna and purplecrested louries are all present. March to July are generally considered the best months for hiking this clearly marked trail.

White-fronted bee-eater with a dragonfly caught on the wing.

18. MODJADJI NATURE RESERVE TRAIL
BOLOBEDU

Trail details: 12 km/4 to 5 hours; circular.

Permits/bookings: Must be obtained at the entrance to the reserve.

Facilities/amenities: Information centre; kiosk; picnic and braai sites.

Main attractions: Modjadji cycad forest; Lobedu tribal history.

Pertinent information: Anti-malaria precautions are necessary; changeable weather; summers are hot and often misty.

The 530-ha Modjadji Nature Reserve, situated in the Bolobedu district of Lebowa north-east of Dui-welskloof, contains one of the most fascinating population of plants seen on any nature trail in southern Africa. Once the main diet of the prehistoric mammal-like reptiles that lived here, the Modjadji cycad (*Encephalartos transvenosus*) forms a unique natural forest which can be viewed in its prehistoric state thanks to its strict protection by succeeding generations of modjadji ('rain queens'), the hereditary rulers in the area. In fact, here the hiker has the privilege of experiencing the 'Alice in Wonderland' atmosphere of the largest concentration of a single cycad species in the world. These protected plant species not only grow in profusion in the area, but are giants in the genus of 29 species, with specimens up to 13 m high, and bearing cones that may weigh up to 34 kg. December to February sees many of these strange plants in seed.

The trail setting is superb. When mist does not obscure the view, the hiker gazes over the cycad forest to the lowveld and the Kruger National Park. Approximately 12 km of well-constructed walks drop from the cycad forest to the acacia and grass-veld below where large game such as blue wildebeest, waterbuck, nyala, impala and bushbuck, and over 170 species of birds live.

The lands of the Modjadji tribe, a matriarchal society that has produced five rain queens (only women are allowed to enter the village), surround the reserve, and the traditional vernacular architecture and culture seen on the reserve's periphery add interest to this clearly marked trail. A medium to high level of fitness is required for this trail, and autumn is the best time for hiking.

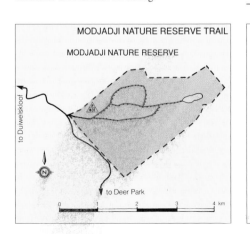

MODJADJI NATURE RESERVE TRAIL

MODJADJI NATURE RESERVE

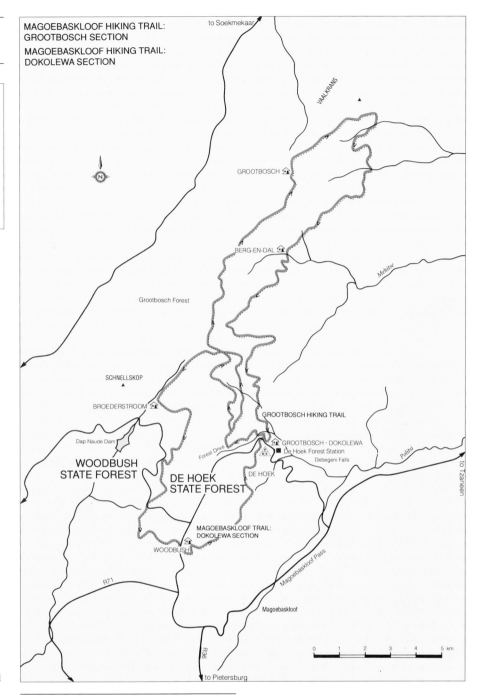

MAGOEBASKLOOF HIKING TRAIL: GROOTBOSCH SECTION

MAGOEBASKLOOF HIKING TRAIL: DOKOLEWA SECTION

19. MAGOEBASKLOOF HIKING TRAIL:
DOKOLEWA SECTION, NEAR TZANEEN

Trail details: 36 km/3 days; circular.

Permits/bookings: Must be obtained from the Department of Forestry, tel. (01551) 51152; Private Bag 2413, Louis Trichardt 0920. Map and brochure available on request.

Facilities/amenities: Grootbosch-Dokolewa hut at the start is equipped with hot and cold water, gas stove, pots, pans, flush toilet and showers; Broederstroom and Woodbush overnight huts are each equipped with a fireplace, firewood, pots, bunks and mattresses for 30 hikers, water and toilets.

Main attractions: Indigenous forests; exotic pine plantations.

Pertinent information: Ticks are prevalent. There is a limit of 30 hikers for this trail at a time.

The Dokolewa Section of the Magoebaskloof Hiking Trail passes through picturesque evergreen indigenous forests as well as plantations of exotic pine which are situated against the northern slopes of Magoebaskloof, and has some steep sections.

The trail starts at De Hoek Forest Station which is situated approximately 22 km from Tzaneen. The forest can be reached via the national road from Pietersburg. Approximately 70 km from Pietersburg, turn left to the Debegeni waterfall, and follow the gravel road for about 7 km to the Grootbosch-Dokolewa hut and the De Hoek Forest Station.

This is a well-marked trail, with distances of 14 km, 12 km and 10 km covered each day, respectively and is ideal for the whole family.

The first day of the trail is a 14-km walk from Grootbosch-Dokolewa hut to Broederstroom overnight hut. The path winds downhill through pine plantations to the bottom of the valley, from where

The route through Magoebaskloof, by road or trail, is memorable for its wealth of plantlife.

it begins climbing into the largest indigenous forest in the Transvaal, the 4 625-ha Grootbosch Nature Reserve. Samango monkeys, bushbuck, bushpig and seventy species of birds reside in the Grootbosch forest.

At first, the climb is gradual, but it gets progressively steeper. There are lovely lookout points over the lowveld along this part of the trail. Once hikers reach the plateau, the trail follows a comfortable route along the Broederstroom Valley, and on to the overnight stop.

The second day of the trail starts by crossing two mountain streams and several patches of pine plantations to the top of the plateau. The route follows the ridge, providing hikers with breathtaking scenery over the Dokolewa Valley. The route then passes the largest *Eucalyptus grandis* tree found in South Africa, before leading to the Woodbush hut for the night.

The final day's route passes a rustic monument to Mr O'Connor, the first forestry scientist in the northern Transvaal, who planted many of the first plantations in the area. The route follows the northern slopes of the Magoebaskloof along a comfortable path through picturesque indigenous forest, and finally takes the hiker back to Grootbosch-Dokolewa hut.

20. MAGOEBASKLOOF HIKING TRAIL:
GROOTBOSCH SECTION, NEAR TZANEEN

Trail details: 50 km/3 days; circular. See map p. 257.

Permits/bookings: Must be obtained from the Department of Forestry, tel. (01551) 51152; Private Bag 2413, Louis Trichardt 0920. Map and brochure available on request.

Facilities/amenities: Grootbosch-Dokolewa base hut, equipped with hot and cold water, gas stove, pots, pans, flush toilet and showers; Grootbosch lapa, a rustic shelter which can accommodate 8 people (sufficient space is available for tents); Berg-en-Dal lapa accommodates 12 hikers; both lapas have a toilet, braai area and firewood. There is no water at either lapa; you will have to carry water from marked streams to the lapa.

Main attractions: Extensive indigenous forests; limited pine plantations.

Pertinent information: Ticks are prevalent; only extremely fit hikers should attempt this strenuous trail. There is a minimum of 3 and a maximum of 12 hikers for this trail at one time. The hike is not recommended for winter as the thick forest canopy blocks out the sunlight.

The Grootbosch section of the Magoebaskloof Hiking Trail is a tent route, i.e. anything more luxurious than an open patch in the forest should be regarded as a bonus. This trail has been especially designed for hikers who enjoy a challenge. The route is extremely taxing, and is considered by many to be the hardest in the country. Distances covered are 18 km, 18 km and 14 km respectively, over rugged, mountainous terrain.

The trail starts at De Hoek Forest Station which is situated approximately 22 km from Tzaneen. The forest can be reached via the national road from Pietersburg. Approximately 70 km from Pietersburg, turn left to the Debegeni waterfall, and follow the gravel road for 7 km to the Grootbosch-Dokolewa hut and De Hoek Forest Station.

The first day of the trail follows the same route as the Dokolewa Section for 10 km. After the 10-km mark the route splits and the Grootbosch Section essentially begins here. The route follows the existing forest track for 5 km through the indigenous forest past the 'huilklip', an extraordinary natural rock which 'gongs' when hit with a stone. Shortly before the overnight site the route crosses three mountain streams in the indigenous forest. From the last river at the 18-km mark, there is a climb of 300 m to the overnight site at Grootbosch lapa (water must be carried from here to the site).

The second day takes hikers from Grootbosch lapa to the Berg-en-Dal lapa. Within the first hour hikers encounter the remains of an ancient Outeniqua yellowwood tree which blew over in a storm in 1982. It was 31 m high and nearly 7 m in circumference. After walking through the dense evergreen indigenous forest for a few kilometres, hikers are presented with a magnificent view over the lowveld, the Fanie Botha Dam in the distance to the east, and the lovely Mooketsi Valley.

At the 3,5-km mark the route takes a turn in a southerly direction and remains largely within the forest, meandering along numerous streams and traversing the Grootbosch Nature Reserve. The last stream is passed approximately 500 m from the overnight stop, and once again hikers must carry water to the lapa.

The final day of the hike takes hikers past one of the most beautiful waterfalls in the Grootbosch — really a spectacularly long series of falls and rapids with pools and cascades, followed by a very steep 3-km climb. The route then passes streams, waterfalls, forest and plantation. The trail leaves the forest rather abruptly after 11 km, and a panoramic view over De Hoek State Forest unfolds. The final 3 km comprise an easy stroll through plantations back to the end point and Grootbosch-Dokolewa hut.

Note that water is available only at the 7-km and 10-km marks.

A number of mammals such as samango monkeys, bushbuck and bushpig as well as seventy species of birds reside in the Grootbosch forest.

Sunlight is rare on this trail as you seldom get the chance to see out of the tree canopy of the largest forest in the Transvaal; hiking here in winter is not recommended. The best times to hike are from September to November and March to April.

Woodbush forestry area was once the scene of a frantic gold rush.

21. ROOIKAT NATURE TRAIL
NEW AGATHA STATE FOREST

Trail details: 11 km/5 hours; circular.

Permits/bookings: Must be obtained at the entrance to the New Agatha State Forest. Map and brochure available on request.

Facilities/amenities: Picnic area, fireplaces and toilets located at the 6-km mark.

Main attractions: Indigenous forest and plantation; impressive backdrop of the Wolkberg; swimming in the Bobs River.

Pertinent information: Changeable weather; snakes are prevalent, as in most of the Transvaal.

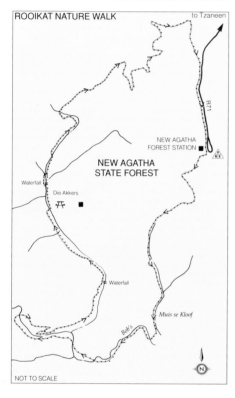

In South Africa, dense, jungle-like forest is associated mainly with the southern coastal region; however, it also grows profusely in some parts of the northern Transvaal. The New Agatha State Forest, 18 km east of Tzaneen, preserves such patches of natural forest, and here the Rooikat Nature Trail winds through 11 km of lush, evergreen woodlands along the Bobs River.

The trail is named after the rooikat, the Afrikaans name for the caracal, a large, long-eared, reddish-fawn cat. Being nocturnal, the caracal is seldom seen by hikers, although its spoor may be found. Bushbuck, duiker, baboon, vervet and samango monkeys are easier to spot, as are the water leguaans. Hikers should be on the alert for mambas, berg adders and grass snakes.

Much of this relatively easy walk passes through indigenous forest, where many of the trees are marked with their national tree list numbers. Trees such as the forest cabbage tree occur in moist wooded ravines, and hikers will see the Natal mahogany and matumi. The final part of the trail leads through a plantation before returning to the starting point at the forest station.

Near the Agatha road, plantations of fruit and forest cover the hills that stretch away towards the Wolkberg.

22. HANS MERENSKY NATURE RESERVE TRAILS
HANS MERENSKY NATURE RESERVE

Trail details: 1. Mopane Interpretive Trail: 1 km/ 30 minutes; 2. Letaba Nature Trail: 2 loops total 7 km/3 hours; 3. Waterbuck Nature Trail: 11 km/ 4,5 hours; all are circular. See map overleaf.

Permits/bookings: Must be obtained from the Letsitele Nature Conservation Office, tel. (015238) 632635; Private Bag X502, Letsitele 0885. Map and brochure available on request.

Facilities/amenities: Information centre; picnic and braai facilities.

Main attractions: Arid lowveld with associated plant and animal life; variety of trees, including marula and acacia.

Pertinent information: Do not drink stream or river water; bilharzia is present. There is a limit of 17 hikers per trail. It is necessary to take anti-malaria precautions in summer.

Transvaal Nature Conservation deserves congratulations for providing walking trails through the lovely 5 188-ha, fairly flat Hans Merensky Nature Reserve, which is situated near the Kruger National Park on the southern banks of the Great Letaba River. Before these trails were initiated, visitors could only experience the reserve by means of an organized bus tour.

The reserve was originally established in 1954 to protect sable, roan and other rare lowveld antelope. The lush mopane veld supports a very diverse wild-

A calm and colourful Letaba sunset.

life, however, and other animals such as giraffe, bushbuck, waterbuck, impala, grey duiker, zebra, blue wildebeest, tsessebe and leopard are also frequently seen.

Game-viewing is especially rewarding during the dry winter months when the vegetation dies back and many animals may be seen drinking at the waterholes along the **Waterbuck Nature Trail**. On the **Letaba Nature Trail**, particularly when using the picnic sites on the river banks, hikers must keep a wary eye out for hippos and crocodiles – never get between a hippo and the water. Needless to say, swimming is strictly prohibited. The attractive bush-veld trees in the park include species such as marula, knobthorn, mopane, rock fig, wild syringa and the candelabra tree. These provide an ideal habitat for a wealth of bush-dwelling birds. The Great Letaba River also attracts the whitebrowed coucal, fish eagle and Pel's fishing owl. Frogs such as the grey tree frog are plentiful, despite the reserve's low rainfall.

The shortest walk in the reserve is the **Mopane Interpretive Trail**, a circular route starting and ending at the visitor centre. The **Letaba Nature Trail** is a leisurely stroll in the northern part of the reserve, from the Eiland Resort through the dense riverine bush of the Letaba River. The **Waterbuck Nature Trail**, also beginning and ending at the visitor centre, takes approximately four leisurely hours and includes a visit to a hide to view animals drinking from the dam.

23. GIRAFFE HIKING TRAIL
HANS MERENSKY NATURE RESERVE

> **Trail details:** 32 km/2 or 3 days; circular.
>
> **Permits/bookings:** Must be obtained from the Letsitele Nature Conservation Office, tel. (015238) 632635; Private Bag X502, Letsitele 0885. Map and brochure available on request.
>
> **Facilities/amenities:** Information centre; 3 thatched huts, each equipped with 4 mattresses, flush toilet, cold shower, cooking pots, firewood and braai area.
>
> **Main attractions:** Arid lowveld with associated plant and animal life; variety of trees, including marula and acacia.
>
> **Pertinent information:** Do not drink stream or river water as bilharzia is present; the summers are very hot. There is a limit of 12 people for the trail.

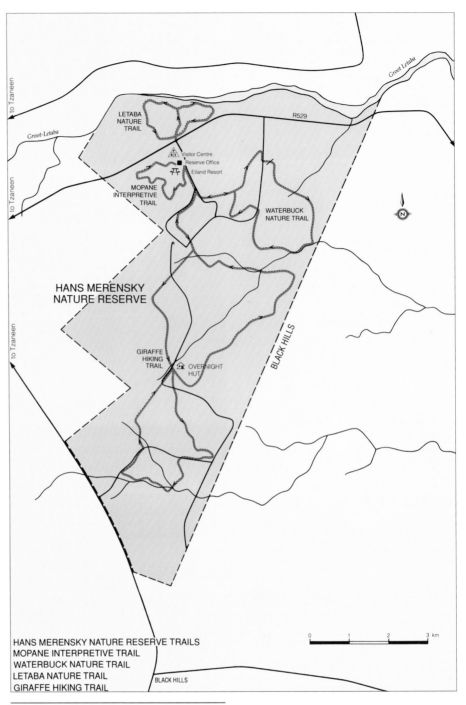

HANS MERENSKY NATURE RESERVE TRAILS
MOPANE INTERPRETIVE TRAIL
WATERBUCK NATURE TRAIL
LETABA NATURE TRAIL
GIRAFFE HIKING TRAIL

The Giraffe Hiking Trail gives hikers an option of a 2- or 3-day route in the large southern part of the 5 188-ha Hans Merensky Nature Reserve. The trail includes excellent views of the Black Hills (the series of dolerite hills on the eastern boundary), over the lowveld towards the Wartberg and Transvaal Escarpment. Much of this relatively easy walk passes through indigenous forest, where many of the trees are numbered; you will see trees such as the forest cabbage tree in moist wooded ravines, and the Natal mahogany and matumi or minger-hout, both of which are shaped into dug-out canoes by local tribesmen.

The first day's route leads from the reserve of-fice to the overnight hut, covering a distance of 9 km. The second day, which is optional, takes hikers along a circular route for 11 km and back to the hut. The last day of the walk leads for 12 km from the hut back to the starting point.

24. WOLKBERG WILDERNESS AREA
HAENERTSBURG

> **Trail details:** No set trails.
>
> **Permits/bookings:** Must be obtained from the Officer-in-charge, Serala Forest Station, tel. (0152222) 1303; Private Bag, Haenertsburg 0730.
>
> **Facilities/amenities:** Footpaths; camp site with showers, toilets and parking at the entry point at Serala; hikers staying overnight sleep out in the open (tents are essential).
>
> **Main attractions:** Pure grassland vegetation; rugged terrain; deep, densely forested ravines; endangered wildlife; rugged, variable landscape; pools, waterfalls and spectacular vistas; this is a real mountain outing.
>
> **Pertinent information:** There is a limit of 10 overnight visitors, and 60 day visitors.

The scenically delightful 22 000-ha Wolkberg Wilderness Area is situated approximately 80 km south-west of Tzaneen. The 2 127-m Wolkberg, part of the northern Drakensberg and Strydpoort ranges, with its great, vertical quartzite krantzes, countless kloofs, cool, deep and densely forested ravines, massive buttresses and folded and inter-locking spurs, was appropriately proclaimed a wilderness area in October 1977.

The 'cloudy mountain', a valuable catchment area, produces clear, silt-free water. Many streams in steep ravines flow to the Mohlapitse River, a tributary of the Olifants. The entrance to this river is through a magnificent gorge flanked by perpen-dicular, aloe-covered cliffs. Smaller branches of the Letaba River, the Thabina and the Letsitele, also originate in the Wolkberg. These rivers, with their sensational waterfalls and potholes in dolomitic

The vast and lovely landscape of the Wolkberg Wilderness Area near Tzaneen.

rock below the black quartzite layer, are refreshing after a long, tough hike.

The steep, quartzitic cliffs of the Black Reef Series provide impressive landmarks. Serala (Krugerkop), at 2 050 m the highest peak in the Wolkberg, is neighboured by Steilkoop (1 900 m), Marake (1 790 m) and Tandberg (also called the Knuckles or the Apostles), a well-known feature. Although hikers, who will be called upon to exert a medium to high fitness level, are free to travel anywhere within the wilderness, the Officer-in-charge warns that only physically competent and agile rock climbers should venture on the route from the Serala plateau over Kruger se Neus through Wonderwoud Forest and over the Tandberg as some steep scrambling is required.

The indigenous high forest pockets found in deep, wet valleys host species such as the Outeniqua and real yellowwoods, wild fig, lemonwood, wild peach and Cape beech.

Hikers have a chance of seeing klipspringer, grey rhebok, mountain reedbuck, duiker, bushbuck, genet, otter, the nocturnal caracal and vervet and samango monkeys, and if extremely lucky, leopard and brown hyaena.

The Wolkberg is rich in birdlife; the hamerkop, bat hawk, black eagle, lilacbreasted roller, blackcollared and pied barbets, pearlbreasted swallow and crested francolin are all present.

Be on the lookout for berg adders, puff adders, mambas and pythons.

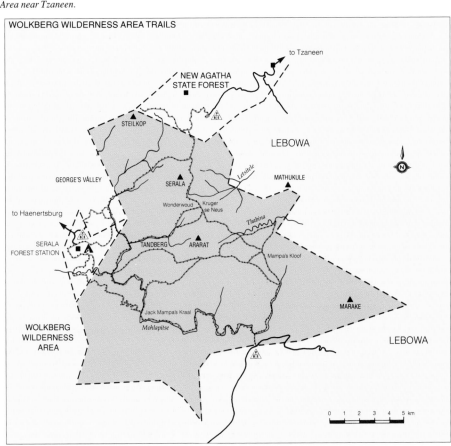

Some welcome shade along the Lekgalameetse Hiking Trail.

25. LEKGALAMEETSE HIKING TRAIL
TRICHARDTSDAL

Trail details: 29 km/2 days (open-ended) with a
40-km/3-day circular option.

Permits/bookings: Must be obtained from The
Manager, Lekgalameetse Nature Reserve, tel.
(0152302) 1514; PO Box 186, Trichardtsdal 0890.

Facilities/amenities: There is accommodation in
fully equipped log cabins for 24 hikers; braai wood
can be purchased at the office.

Main attractions: Mountain and woodland scenery;
diverse flora and prolific birdlife.

Pertinent information: Malaria precautions are
essential. There is a limit of 24 hikers for the trail.

The 18 000-ha Lekgalameetse Nature Reserve,
which incorporates the Lekgalameetse Hiking
Trail, is situated 3 km west of the tiny hamlet of
Trichardtsdal, which lies approximately 50 km
south of Tzaneen. The 2-day trail is divided into
two sections of 17 km and 12 km respectively.

The first day is very strenuous, and at times te-
dious, since most of it is spent walking on a gravel
track. The views, however, are lovely and there are
some interesting trees along the way. The second
day of the trail is very different from the first; the
route leads the hiker through an indigenous kloof
and passes through ravines and waterfalls along the
Selati River.

Hikers staying for a third day will pass into a valley before following the Makhutsi River which
leads them back to the start.

Lekgalameetse Nature Reserve is home to over
1 200 plant species, including 14 rare species, such
as *Aloe monotropa*. Fantastic yellowwoods, acacias, very large forest mahogany trees and sneeze-
woods can be seen. Game in the reserve includes
eland, bushbuck, samango monkeys, zebra, jackal,
klipspringer, mountain reedbuck, leopard and bush
babies. There are plenty of butterflies in the area as
well as 180 bird species, and hikers can look out for
wood owl, olive woodpecker, crowned and martial
eagles, Knysna lourie and narina trogon. This hike
requires a reasonable level of fitness, and is especially pleasant in spring and autumn.

26. POTLAKE NATURE RESERVE WALKS
POTLAKE NATURE RESERVE

Trail details: 7 km/2 to 3 hours; 12 km/5 to 6
hours; both are circular.

Permits/bookings: Must be obtained from the
Lebowa Tourism Department, tel. (0156) 35529;
Private Bag X27, Chuniespoort 0745. Map and
brochure available on request.

Facilities/amenities: Interpretive centre; picnic and
braai sites; toilets at the start.

Main attractions: Large game species; arid sweet
bushveld with attractive tree species; Legobwe
Mountain.

Pertinent information: Hikers must carry their own
water; the summers are very hot. There is a limit of
12 hikers per trail at any one time.

Situated 85 km south-east of Pietersburg, the 2 800-
ha Potlake Nature Reserve offers two nature trails
in the wildlife-rich, flat acacia woodland, as well as
along Legobwe Mountain (1 183 m) where the dry,
sweet bushveld looks particularly attractive in its
autumn colours. Hikers have a chance of spotting
blue wildebeest, eland, gemsbok, waterbuck, giraffe, Burchell's zebra, red hartebeest and ostrich.

These walks do not require a high level of fitness, and are clearly marked, both starting and
ending in the reserve. Walking conditions are especially pleasant in the cool, dry winter.

27. JOCK OF THE BUSHVELD TRAILS
TIMBAVATI GAME RESERVE

Trail details: Various guided trails, ranging from 3
to 5 days in duration.

Permits/bookings: Must be obtained from
Wilderness Leadership School, tel. (011) 4556805,
PO Box 87230, Houghton 2041. Map and brochure
available on request.

Facilities/amenities: Rustic trail camp; sleeping
under the stars; all transport, equipment (except
sleeping bags) and food supplied.

Main attractions: Abundant wildlife.

Pertinent information: Anti-malaria precautions are
necessary. Groups are limited to 12 people.

There are various organized trails in the 20 000-ha
Timbavati Game Reserve led by the Wilderness
Leadership School, and tailored in duration and difficulty to suit the particular interests of each group.
Some of them are geared especially towards game-
spotting while others are dedicated mainly towards
hiking, although game is prolific and will be
spotted whichever option is taken.

One of the most rewarding aspects of Timbavati
is that all the 'Big Five' are present – elephant,
lion, leopard, rhino and buffalo. Timbavati is especially well known for its white lions – these
individual animals lack melanin pigment in their
hair. Some 240 species of birds have been recorded
in the reserve, including raptors, louries, bee-eaters
and hornbills.

Timbavati is situated next to the Kruger National
Park, its climate is subtropical and its vegetation
bushveld savannah.

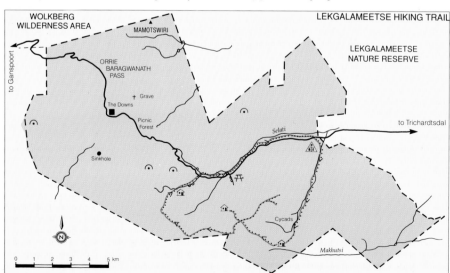

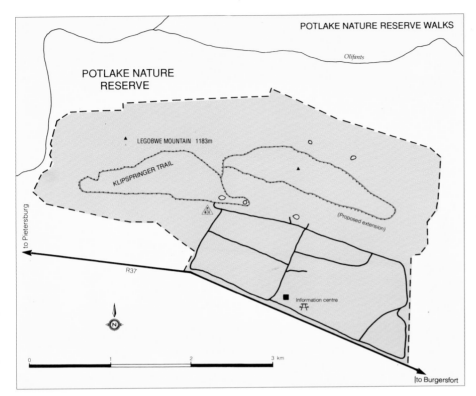

POTLAKE NATURE RESERVE WALKS

Olifants

POTLAKE NATURE RESERVE

▲ LEGOBWE MOUNTAIN 1183m

KLIPSPRINGER TRAIL

(Proposed extension)

to Pietersburg

R37

Information centre

|to Burgersfort

0   1   2   3 km

N

28. PROTEA AND YELLOWWOOD TRAILS
BLYDERIVIERSPOORT NATURE RESERVE

Trail details: 1. Protea Trail: 38,5 km/4 days;
2. Yellowwood Trail: 25 km/2 days. Both are circular. See map overleaf.

Permits/bookings: Must be obtained from The Officer-in-charge, Blyderivierspoort Nature Reserve, tel. (01315) 81216; Private Bag X431, Graskop 1270. Map and brochure available.

Facilities/amenities: Hikers on the Protea Trail stay overnight at Muilhuis, Op-de-berg and Eerste Liefde huts; hikers on the Yellowwood Trail overnight at Eerste Liefde; all huts have 10 beds and mattresses, toilets, firewood and braai facilities. There are also overnight huts at Bourke's Luck, with 20 beds and mattresses, open-air showers, toilets, fireplaces and firewood.

Main attractions: Bourke's Luck Potholes; mountain sourveld; indigenous rain forest; spectacular lowveld views, including that from the escarpment at God's Window.

Pertinent information: Bookings must be made at least three weeks in advance; there is a danger of lightning in the area approaching the Op-de-berg hut; fires are strictly prohibited. There is a limit of 10 people per trail at any one time.

Situated in the beautiful 27 000-ha Blyderiviers-poort Nature Reserve, 36 km north-east of Graskop, both these trails start and end at Bourke's Luck Pot-holes. They are routed east of the potholes, along the Inselleberg Plateau, through grassveld, bush-veld, montane and gallery forest. The diversity of vegetation is mainly the result of micro-climates within the plateau system. Wildlife is also plentiful and among the ferns, cycads, wild figs, mobola plums and orchids, hikers may spot baboon, grey rhebok, duiker and klipspringer on the krantzes. The bald ibis, a threatened species, as well as rap-

tors and the Knysna, purplecrested and grey louries, are found here.

1. From the potholes the trails run eastwards together before forking. The longer trail, the **Protea Trail** (previously known as the Muilhuis Hiking Trail), winds for approximately 12,5 km along the upper slopes of the Belvedere Valley to the first overnight hut, Muilhuis. The next day the trail continues for 6,5 km among indigenous forest to Op-de-berg, the second overnight stop. The third day is an 8,5-km walk to Eerste Liefde hut, and on the last day the trail takes hikers back to the pot-holes once more.

2. The southern track, the **Yellowwood Trail** (pre-viously known as the Eerste Liefde Hiking Trail),

leads for approximately 14 km along the Belvedere Valley to the Belvedere power station. Hikers then make a gradual descent to the Eerste Liefde over-night stop on the banks of the Belvedere River. The next day leads for approximately 11 km back to the start. Hiking conditions are especially pleasant in autumn and late spring.

29. BLYDERIVIERSPOORT HIKING TRAIL
BLYDERIVIERSPOORT NATURE RESERVE

Trail details: 65 km/5 days; open-ended.
See map overleaf.

Permits/bookings: Must be obtained from The Officer-in-charge, Blyderivierspoort Nature Reserve, tel. (01315) 29; PO Bourke's Luck 1272. Bookings for accommodation must be made well in advance and not later than 14 days before the hike. Bookings for school holidays and long weekends should be made 12 months ahead of time. If bookings are made in writing you are requested to give alternative dates and also indicate the number of hikers per group. Map and brochure available.

Facilities/amenities: Fully equipped huts sleeping 30 people; flush toilets, cold showers and wood.

Main attractions: Quartzite outcrops; breathtaking views; montane grasslands; forestry plantations; lowveld vegetation and fauna; rain forest; rivers, pools and waterfalls; dramatic landscape with a variety of natural features; wildlife.

Pertinent information: Unpredictable weather; hot days and cold nights. There is a minimum of two and a maximum of 30 people per day for this hike.

The Blyderivierspoort Hiking Trail, situated in the 27 000-ha Blyderivierspoort Nature Reserve, starts at the spectacular God's Window (5 km from Gras-kop) and ends 5 days later at Swadini (38 km from Hoedspruit). If you have never hiked before and are deciding which trail to do first, I suggest you try this one. The distances between the huts are rela-tively short (5,8 km, 13,66 km, 13,5 km, 18,3 km

A section of the immense and deeply incised Blyde River Canyon, seen from the Yellowwood Trail.

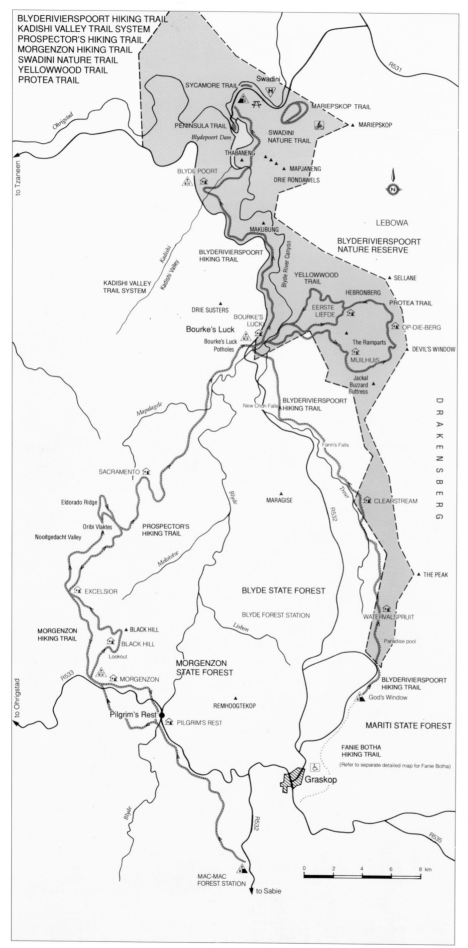

BLYDERIVIERSPOORT HIKING TRAIL
KADISHI VALLEY TRAIL SYSTEM
PROSPECTOR'S HIKING TRAIL
MORGENZON HIKING TRAIL
SWADINI NATURE TRAIL
YELLOWWOOD TRAIL
PROTEA TRAIL

Bourke's Luck Potholes at the confluence of the Blyde and Treur rivers.

and 13,8 km respectively) and the gradient of the route is very easy.

The trail offers excellent opportunities for nature study, and the comprehensive trail brochure elaborates on aspects of the ecology likely to be encountered on each of the consecutive hiking stages. Plant life is extremely interesting and diverse and, depending on aspect and altitude, varies from elements typical of Cape mountain flora to tropical vegetation. The trail also enables you to see, if you are alert and lucky, hippo, crocodile, kudu, Burchell's zebra and baboon, vervet monkeys, samango monkeys and bushbabies – the full range of South Africa's primate wildlife – when you reach the lowveld. All three species of South African lourie thrive here: the Knysna, purplecrested and grey louries.

From God's Window, at the southern end of the Blyderivierspoort Nature Reserve, the route stretches northwards, partly across privately owned land through the Blyde State Forest and then again across the reserve to Swadini in the lowveld.

The first day from God's Window to Watervalspruit hut is a short stroll with spectacular views along the escarpment and over the lowveld. The second day's hike takes hikers to Clearstream hut through the tranquil and beautiful Treur River Valley. The third day takes hikers on a pleasant walk which meanders through shady plantations to the remarkable potholes of Bourke's Luck, where the Treur and Blyde rivers meet.

On the fourth day, hikers walk to Blydepoort hut, ascending the canyon, to the Three Rondavels viewsite and overnight stop. This section of the trail is strenuous and requires a high level of endurance, as does the fifth and final day to Swadini; the route leads past Tufa Falls and the lower Kadishi River, with a variety of grassveld, forest and bushveld vegetation. The trail ends opposite the Blydepoort Dam wall at the reserve gate. It is about a 150-km drive back to the starting point.

The Three Rondavels are among many sculpted erosion-features of the Blyde River Canyon.

30. SWADINI NATURE TRAILS
BLYDERIVIERSPOORT NATURE RESERVE, NEAR KLASERIE

Trail details: 1. Sycamore Trail: 1,2 km/30 minutes, return; 2. Island Trail: 1,5 km/45 minutes, return; 3. Peninsula Trail: 2,5 km/1,5 hours, return; 4. Mariepskop Trail: 5 km/3 hours, circular. See map page 264.

Permits/bookings: Required for the Marieskop Trail only, obtained from The Officer-in-charge, Blyderivierspoort Nature Reserve, tel. (01528) 35641; PO Box 75, Swadini, Hoedspruit 1380 or from the control gate on the road to the dam.

Facilities/amenities: Information and interpretive centre; picnic and overnight facilities and a shop at nearby Sybrand van Niekerk Holiday Resort.

Main attractions: Views of Blydepoort Dam; rock formations of the eastern Transvaal escarpment; mixed sour bushveld and lowveld riverine forest flora; birdlife; geology; waterfalls.

Pertinent information: Hiking during April and May is pleasant, as the heavy rains and 'smoky' season can be avoided (the 'smoky' season is winter, when the views are often clouded by smoke from veld fires).

The Swadini interpretive centre, together with the four short walks, offer visitors a fine overall introduction to the Blyde River area.

1. The Sycamore Trail is a short, easy walk which follows the Blyde River, starting at Sybrand van Niekerk's Chalet 53 and ending at its shop.

2. The Island Trail is also a very easy walk, starting near the bridge opposite the Nature Conservator's office. It follows the stream to the waterfall and returns on the same route.

3. The Peninsula Trail follows the Ohrigstad branch of the Blydepoort Dam from the Swadini interpretive centre.

4. The Mariepskop Trail runs along the foothills of the Mariepskop. This and the Peninsula trail require good walking shoes.

31. PROSPECTOR'S HIKING TRAIL
MORGENZON STATE FOREST, PILGRIM'S REST

Trail details: 69 km/5 days; open-ended. See map page 264.

Permits/bookings: Must be obtained from the Eastern Transvaal Forest Region, tel. (01315) 41058; Private Bag X503, Sabie 1260. Map available on request.

Facilities/amenities: 4 overnight huts, all equipped with bunks and mattresses for 30 hikers, flush toilets, firewood and some cooking pots.

Main attractions: Pilgrim's Rest; old mines.

Pertinent information: Ticks can be a nuisance; hikers must carry their own water; extreme weather. The winters in this area can be bitterly cold; spring, summer and autumn are recommended for hiking. There is a limit of 30 hikers per day for this trail at any one time.

In order to link the Morgenzon Hiking Trail to the Fanie Botha and Blyderivierspoort hiking trails (see pages 268, 263 and 264 respectively), the Prospector's Hiking Trail was opened in 1983. The trail displays typical eastern Transvaal ecology: pine and eucalyptus plantations, grassveld, protea veld, wooded valleys, oribi and other antelope. The trail starts at Mac-Mac Forest Station, and ends 69 km and 5 days later at the Bourke's Luck Potholes. The route, which demands a moderate level of fitness as there are some strenuous sections, leads through the eastern Transvaal highlands over broken terrain, forested peaks, montane grasslands, rocky crests and protea veld slopes.

The first day's hike is 15,4 km long and leads from Mac-Mac to Pilgrim's Rest hut. Day 2 sees hikers travelling 8,3 km over the Blyde River and up steep Columbia Hill to Morgenzon hut. On the 15-km third day, hikers should fill their water bottles at the water spot near the 6,5-km mark. The panoramic views of this day's hike are spectacular; the distant Mariepskop, Wolkberg, Strydpoort and Waterberg ranges are all seen. Hikers overnight at Excelsior hut before starting out on the 15-km fourth day to Sacramento hut. This route is very dry; please ensure that you have sufficient water to last the day. On the fifth and final day of the hike, the route travels over grassy spurs and streams, with a sharp descent through wild pear trees and tall wild olive trees. The section around Granite Hill, where hikers must skirt irrigated fields along the bottom of the Bramble Cliffs and fight through dense riverine thicket, bramble and loose scree, is uncomfortable. Finally, hikers pass through the bustling settlement of Lebowa before arriving at the potholes and the end of the trail.

A hotel nestles amid the forested hills of Mount Sheba, near Pilgrim's Rest.

32. MORGENZON HIKING TRAIL
PILGRIM'S REST

Trail details: 36,5 km/2,5 days; circular.
See map page 264.

Permits/bookings: Must be obtained from the
Eastern Transvaal Department of Environment
Affairs, tel. (01315) 41058; P/Bag X503, Sabie 1260.

Facilities/amenities: Single hut with bunks,
mattresses, pots, toilet, water and a braai area;
rondavel with bunks and mattresses; together, the
hut and rondavel can accommodate 20 people.

Main attractions: Lovely mountain scenery; inland
tropical forest and typical grassveld vegetation.

Pertinent information: Hikers must carry their own
water; fires are allowed at the hut only. There is a
limit of 37 hikers for the trail at any one time.

The Morgenzon Hiking Trail lies 8 km from the
quaint historical town of Pilgrim's Rest, a national
monument. It provides an excellent opportunity to
see oribi: search the long grass plains carefully and
listen for the antelope's distinctive soft whistle and
sneezing. The Oribi Vlaktes is an obvious region in
which to look for these antelope, as well as grey
rhebok and birds such as Swainson's francolin and
bronze mannikins.

The trail is constructed as a figure-of-eight, and
consists of three relatively short walking days. The
first day of the trail, from the forest station to Excelsior hut, is a 13-km (approximately 6-hour) walk;
the second is a 15-km (also 6-hour) loop back to

the hut, and includes an optional 5-km circular
route to Eldorado Ridge. The last day's hike is
8,5 km (approximately 2,5 hours) and returns to
the forest station.

Black Hill (2 079 m), the highest peak in the region, is passed on the first day (I suggest you have
lunch below its lookout tower, at the stream). The

view is impressive: you can see all the way to the
Wolkberg, Strydompoort and the Waterberg. Note
also the Cape fynbos in the gully – a small remnant
of past wider distribution. The forest station is situated on the main road between Pilgrim's Rest and
Lydenburg, about 8 km from Pilgrim's Rest.

33. MOUNT SHEBA NATURE TRAILS
MOUNT SHEBA HOTEL AND NATURE RESERVE, PILGRIM'S REST

Trail details: There are 12 nature trails in the area
around Mount Sheba Hotel, varying in length from
1 km to 6 km.

Permits/bookings: Must be obtained from Mount
Sheba Hotel, tel. (01315) 81241; PO Box 100,
Pilgrims Rest 1290. Map and brochure available
on request.

Facilities/amenities: Trees labelled with their
national tree list numbers; hotel accommodation;
helicopter pad.

Main attractions: Indigenous forest; waterfalls;
110 tree species.

The climax forest, one of the last remaining stands
of indigenous Drakensberg growth, typifies the
vegetation which grew in this area many hundreds
of years ago. Some of the trees, such as yellowwoods and ironwoods, have been estimated to be
1 500 years old. Fifty-two plant families, comprising 110 tree specimens, have been identified, not
counting the numerous species of ferns, mosses,
forest creepers and parasitic figs which flourish in
the damp and shady forest.

The Mount Sheba Hotel is situated 24 km from
Pilgrim's Rest on the Lydenburg road. The hotel
brochure gives details of the 12 nature trails, all
located on a 1 600- to 2 200-m plateau in a spectacular bowl of mountains in the Transvaal
escarpment above Pilgrim's Rest, overlooking the
lowveld. The trails vary in difficulty from very
easy walking to steep. The 5-km walk to and from
Marco's Mantle waterfall is highly recommended.

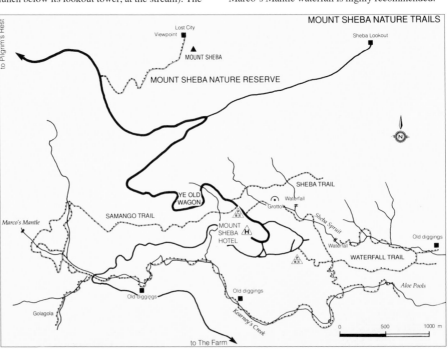

MOUNT SHEBA NATURE TRAILS

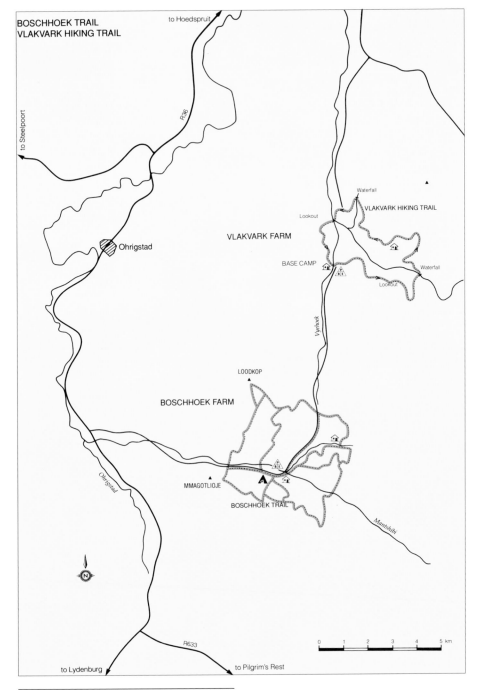

BOSCHHOEK TRAIL
VLAKVARK HIKING TRAIL

to Hoedspruit

to Steelpoort

R36

Ohrigstad

VLAKVARK FARM

Waterfall

VLAKVARK HIKING TRAIL

Lookout

BASE CAMP

Waterfall

Lookout

Vyehoek

LOODKOP

BOSCHHOEK FARM

Ohrigstad

MMAGOTLIOJE

BOSCHHOEK TRAIL

Mantshibi

N

R633

to Lydenburg

to Pilgrim's Rest

0 1 2 3 4 5 km

35. VLAKVARK HIKING TRAIL
NEAR LYDENBURG

Trail details: 2 trails, each 20 km/2 days; circular.

Permits/bookings: Must be obtained from Gerrie Stemmet, tel. (01323) 80413; PO Box 226, Ohrigstad 1122. Map and brochure available on request.

Facilities/amenities: Base camp with 24 beds, electricity, hot shower, toilet, lapa and braai wood.

Main attractions: Beautiful waterfalls; bushveld scenery; prolific birdlife; wildlife.

Pertinent information: Thunderstorms occur in summer. There is a limit of 24 hikers for this trail. Winter nights are very cold and mornings chilly.

The original Vlakvark Hiking Trail, situated on the 2 000-ha Vlakvark Farm 50 km north-east of Lydenburg on the Ohrigstad road, offers beginners a lovely introduction to the joys of hiking. The trail is not very strenuous, covering 10 km on both days, and is clearly marked.

It starts with an easy stroll through lovely trees, wild flowers and magnificent scenery down towards the first waterfall. The climb up to the hut is marked by very tall, majestic aloes. The next day begins with a descent to the river through an area of abundant flowers. The path then follows the river upstream, and climbs out of the valley. From here an easy walk leads down towards the base camp.

Kudu, bushbuck, warthog, reedbuck, duiker and klipspringer all abound, and hikers can spot a variety of birdlife including grey louries, black eagles and the jackal buzzard. Interested hikers should also enquire about the recently opened second trail.

36. DINKWANYANE HIKING TRAIL
OHRIGSTAD

Trail details: 20 km/2 or 3 days; circular. See map page 268.

Permits/bookings: Must be obtained from the Lebowa Department of Tourism, tel. (01526) 35529; Private Bag X27, Chuniespoort 0745. Map and brochure available on request.

Facilities/amenities: Camp sites; huts are planned.

Main attractions: Deep kloofs with indigenous forest and swimming holes; cliffs and geological formations; birdlife.

Pertinent information: This trail was previously known as the Strydom Tunnel Hiking Trail. There is a limit of 12 people per day.

Situated in the Transvaal escarpment in the southern slopes of the lowveld, this trail runs along the Ohrigstad River gorge where the vegetation is montane grassland and forest. Take R36 between Ohrigstad and the Strydom Tunnel onto the Bourke's Luck road (R532) for 7,5 km. The dirt road to Dinkwanyane turns off to the left and crosses the Ohrigstad River, from where the route to the starting point of the trail 5 km further on is clearly marked. The trail starts at the bottom of a spectacular wooded kloof with a lovely perennial mountain stream. The route then leads hikers along north-eastern mountain sourveld to magnificent

34. BOSCHHOEK TRAIL
OHRIGSTAD

Trail details: 21 km/3 to 4 days; circular. Each of 4 loops (10-13 km) can be walked in a day.

Permits/bookings: Must be obtained from Mr and Mrs Erlank, tel. (01323) 80061; Boschhoek Farm, PO Box 191, Lydenburg 1120. Map and brochure.

Facilities/amenities: Base camp sleeping 24 with electricity, hot and cold running water, toilets, showers and a bath; veld huts, sleeping 12, with toilets and lanterns. There is also a caravan park and camp site for casual visitors.

Main attractions: Waterfall with swimming pools; spectacular scenery.

Pertinent information: Ticks are prevalent; the weather is unpredictable. There is a limit of 24 hikers for this trail.

The Boschhoek Trail is situated on the 2 500-ha Boschhoek Farm, 18 km south-east of Ohrigstad. This trail is particularly scenic, and leads the hiker through tranquil, spectacular mountain landscapes, with abundant streams, waterfalls and natural swimming pools.

The habitat is mainly sour montane grassland with isolated trees and wooded ravines. Hikers stand a good chance of seeing game: bushbuck, grey rhebok, kudu, steenbok, grey and ordinary duiker, klipspringer, bushpig, baboon and leopard are all present on the farm.

The trail requires a low level of fitness, and offers pleasant hiking from April to July. Mr and Mrs Erlank provide a detailed route description to hikers on arrival, and the trail is clearly defined with footprint markers. Each of the 4 days' routes can be tackled as day hikes by those whose time is limited.

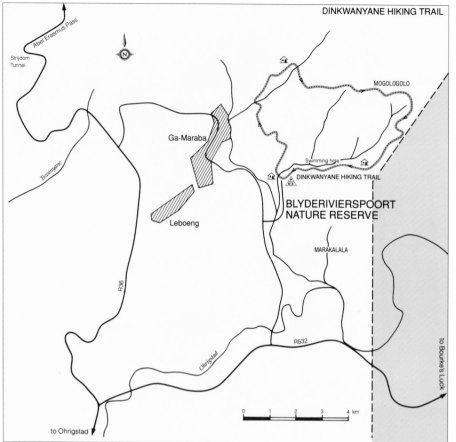

DINKWANYANE HIKING TRAIL

Abel Erasmus Pass

Strijdom Tunnel

N

MOGOLOGOLO

Ga-Maraba

Swimming hole

DINKWANYANE HIKING TRAIL

Leboeng

BLYDERIVIERSPOORT
NATURE RESERVE

MARAKALALA

R36

Ohrigstad

R532

to Bourke's Luck

0 1 2 3 4 km

to Ohrigstad

FANIE BOTHA HIKING TRAILS:
LOERIE NATURE WALK
FOREST FALLS WALK

BLYDE
FOREST STATION

to Tzaneen

Refer to separate detailed map

BLYDERIVIERSPOORT HIKING TRAIL

Jock of the Bushveld

Lisbon

Blyde

R533

REMHOOGTEKOP

R532

QUARTZ HILL

GOD'S WINDOW

Pilgrim's Rest

GRASKOP
FOREST STATION

R534

FANIE BOTHA HIKING TRAIL

N

Graskop

to Rusplaas

GROOTFONTEIN
FOREST STATION

STANLEY BUSH

to Bosbokrand

FANIE BOTHA HIKING TRAIL

GRASKOP

Kowyn's Pass

0 2 4 6 8 km

Forest Falls

to Hazyview

MAC-MAC

FOREST FALLS WALK

Blyde

MAUCHSBERG

MAC-MAC
FOREST STATION

Mac-Mac

PROSPECTOR'S HIKING TRAIL

Klein-Sabie

Mac-Mac Pools

Refer to separate detailed map

R532

MT MOODIE

HARTEBEESVLAKTE

TWEEFONTEIN
FOREST STATION

Sabie

MT ANDERSON

Elna Falls

LOERIE
NATURE WALK

Sabie

to Nelspruit

Bridal Veil Falls

Sabie Falls

R536

CEYLON FOREST STATION

Sabie

MARITZBOS

Lone Creek Falls

R537

FANIE BOTHA HIKING TRAIL

to Lydenburg

to White River

views overlooking the lowveld. Although approximately 20 km in length (divided into distances of 7 km, 10 km and 3 km – or the trail can be done in 2 or 3 days), steep gradients and rough terrain are encountered which make this trail fairly difficult. Two overnight stops are provided for tent camping only (huts are planned). The clearly marked trail is open all year round, with autumn and spring offering the most pleasant walking conditions, and does not require a high level of fitness as the distance walked each day is short.

37. FANIE BOTHA HIKING TRAILS
SABIE

Trail details: 1. Fanie Botha Hiking Trail: 76,9 km/5 days, open-ended; 2. Loerie Nature Walk: 14 km/1 day, circular; 3. Forest Falls Walk: 4 km/2 hours; circular.

Permits/bookings: Must be obtained from The Regional Director, Department of Forestry, Eastern Transvaal Forest Region, tel. (01315) 41058; Private Bag X503, Sabie 1260.

Facilities/amenities: 5 huts with bunks, mattresses and cooking pots; 30 people per night can be accommodated.

Main attractions: Old pine plantations interspersed among indigenous forest; prolific birdlife; magnificent views over the escarpment; waterfalls; high mountain aspects.

Pertinent information: Hikers should carry their own water. Groups are limited to 30 people.

Antelope such as oribi, mountain reedbuck, grey rhebok, klipspringer and duiker are all present, as are bushbuck, baboon and dassie. The prolific birdlife includes the Knysna lourie, redchested cuckoo, sombre bulbul, malachite sunbird, masked weaver and red bishop.

1. The Fanie Botha Hiking Trail starts at the Ceylon Forest Station, approximately 6 km west of Sabie. On the first day hikers travel through pine plantations, cross Lone Creek, and meander through poplar groves before reaching the Maritzbos overnight hut approximately 3 to 4 hours and 8,1 km later. The second day is a steep, strenuous walk of 12,6 km. The route winds through forests of white stinkwood, yellowwood and lemonwood, and takes in the Tarka Falls and Piper Pools. Hikers are rewarded with a pleasant view after the final uphill section, before arriving at Hartebeesvlakte hut for the night. The third day of 19,4 km takes about 7 hours, and leads through grassland and pine plantations. The trail continues along the edge of the pine plantation, and swings towards Mauchsberg Peak and the overnight hut. (The trail may be shortened before reaching the Mauchsberg by returning to the Ceylon Forest Station via a plantation path leading on to the Loerie Nature Walk.) The fourth day offers hikers a choice of walking to Graskop hut via Mac-Mac Pools or The Bonnet. Alluvial gold was discovered in this area in 1873 and the odd name of Mac-Mac was derived from the many Scotsmen who settled there. The Mac-Mac Pools are lovely, but unfortunately swarm with a plague of tourists; The Bonnet route is much shorter and easier. On the last day of the trail, the 14,5 km route is very easy walking. Hikers pass through wooded gorges and plantations, and there are

God's Window, at the end of the Fanie Botha Hiking Trail.

lovely views over the lowveld. The trail finishes at God's Window.

2. The Loerie Nature Walk starts at the Ceylon Forest Station, and leads past the Bridal Veil Falls and an old gold-mining area.

3. The Forest Falls Walk starts at the Mac-Mac picnic spot near Mac-Mac Forest Station, and takes hikers through pine plantations and past the lovely Forest Falls.

38. GUSTAV KLINGBIEL NATURE RESERVE
LYDENBURG

Trail details: 1. Ribbok Trail: 20 km/2 days; 2. Protea Walk: 12 km/5 hours; 3. Crane Walk: 9 km/3,5 hours; 4. Pedi Walk: 5 km/2 hours. All are circular routes.

Permits/bookings: Must be obtained from Lydenburg Municipality, tel. (01323) 2121; PO Box 61, Lydenburg, 1120. Map and brochure available on request.

Facilities/amenities: Overnight hut with 12 bunks, firewood, kettles, cold showers, toilets and braai facilites.

Main attractions: Archaeological sites of the Iron Age and Boer War; large game; over 100 bird species; rich variety of flora; vulture restaurant.

Pertinent information: Ticks can be a pest in summer; binoculars are recommended. There is a limit of 12 people per trail at any one time.

Situated on the outskirts of Lydenburg on the Sabie road, the 2 200-ha Gustav Klingbiel Nature Reserve plays host to an overnight hike and three

nature walks. These are not strenuous walks, but hikers should carry their own water. September to November and February to June are the best months for walking here.

More than 200 bird species can be seen in the reserve, including dabchick, blue crane, hamerkop, pied kingfisher, and whiteheaded and whitebacked vultures. Eland, zebra, kudu, impala and blue wildebeest are among the game to be spotted.

1. The Ribbok Trail is a relaxed 2-day route, with hikers having to complete only 10 km each day. The route starts behind the Lydenburg Museum, and leads deep into the reserve to the overnight hut. The following day hikers return to the start. The yellow trail-markers are easy to follow.

2. The Protea Walk takes hikers through a large protea grove, as well as to old Boer forts.

3. The Crane Walk is popular with bird-lovers. Marked in orange, the route takes hikers to the dam

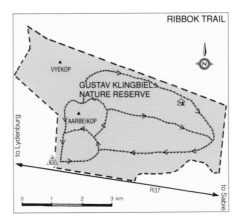

wall where many different species of birds can be seen. The vulture restaurant for the endangered Cape vulture is also visited; hikers are advised to stay well away from the feeding site when observing the birds.

4. The Pedi Walk is marked in blue, and takes hikers to the former home of the ancestor of the Pedi. Hikers should keep a look out for remnants of terraces, stone-walled tracks and old homesteads along the way. The settlement was deserted during the Difaqane war, when its inhabitants were driven away by Mzilikazi.

39. STERKSPRUIT HIKING TRAIL
LYDENBURG

Trail details: 30,6 km/2 or 3 days; circular. See map overleaf.

Permits/bookings: Must be obtained from the Lydenburg Municipality, tel. (01323) 2121; PO Box 61, Lydenburg 1120. Map and brochure available on request.

Facilities/amenities: Rooikat hut with 10 beds and mattresses, shower and flush toilet; Oribi and Klipspringer huts, each with 10 beds and veld toilet.

Main attractions: Mountain views; natural and pine plantations; waterfalls.

Pertinent information: Rapidly changeable weather; hikers must carry their own water; the trail is open from the beginning of October through to the end of May. Groups are limited to 10 hikers.

Situated in the 10 080-ha Sterkspruit Mountain catchment area 10 km south of Lydenburg, this clearly marked trail is scenic and not strenuous;

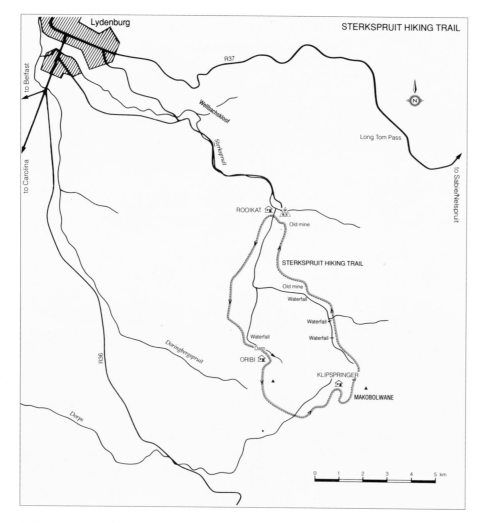

The Steenkampsberg Hiking Trail begins at the Dullstroom Dam and leads through the town of Dullstroom for 1 km before it winds its way through the veld. The 16-km route taken on the first day leads the hiker through narrow gulleys and valleys, before reaching the overnight stop. The 12-km route on the second day leads past beautiful rock formations, a vlei where wattle cranes breed, deep gulleys and numerous streams. A variety of game is also to be seen. The trail is clearly marked and is not unduly taxing.

41. CRANE CREEK TRAIL
NEAR WATERVAL BOVEN

Trail details: 10 km/3,5 hours; circular.

Permits/bookings: Must be obtained from Rod and Marylin Paterson, Crane Creek Farm, tel. (013252) 3303; PO Box 111, Waterval Boven 1195. Map and brochure on request.

Facilities/amenities: An extremely comfortable bunkhouse with accommodation for 20 hikers, equipped with basic kitchen utensils, stove, fridge, toilets, showers and indoor/outdoor braai areas (firewood supplied).

Main attractions: Beautiful gorge with waterfalls and pools; rare cycads.

Pertinent information: The trail can be tailored in length and duration according to the needs of the particular party. The trail accommodates a maximum of 20 hikers at any one time.

Situated on the 300-ha Crane Creek Farm, 15 km south of Waterval Boven on the Slaaihoek road, this guided trail, which requires a moderate degree of fitness, runs through a natural heritage site, declared for its preservation of rare cycads, including *Encephalartos humilis*. The route leads across undulating plateaux with breathtaking views and then drops for 500 m into a gorge with fantastic waterfalls and pools. Klipspringer, zebra, blesbok, bushbuck and bushpig all abound, as do the black eagle and the Knysna lourie. Walking conditions are pleasant all year round.

the 3-day option in particular is very easy. The trail is divided into the following stages: from Rooikat hut to Oribi hut (9,6 km); from Oribi hut to Klipspringer hut (7 km) and from Klipspringer hut back to Rooikat (14 km). Hikers wanting to complete the route in two days are advised not to stop at Oribi hut but to walk on to Klipspringer.

Grey rhebok, mountain reedbuck, oribi, steenbok, klipspringer, zebra, baboon, bushbuck, bushpig and grey and red duiker are just some of the many animals present in the area.

40. STEENKAMPSBERG HIKING TRAIL
DULLSTROOM

Trail details: 28 km/2 days; circular.

Permits/bookings: Must be obtained from the Dullstroom Town Council, tel. (01325) 40151/2; PO Box 1, Dullstroom 1110. Map and brochure available on request.

Facilities/amenities: Base camp site at dam, and overnight camp site, both accommodating 12 hikers; water and toilet facilities.

Main attractions: Wild flowers; waterfalls; scenic views.

Pertinent information: Winters are very cold and there is the possibility of snow and ice. There is a limit of 12 people for the trail at any one time.

The Steenkampsberg is approximately 2 000 m above sea level and has a sub-alpine climate, which is regarded as unique in South Africa by meteorologists. More than 200 species of wild flowers have been identified in this area, and October to February are the best months to see the flowers in bloom. An interesting feature of the area is that magnificent white quartzite rock formations are scattered throughout the countryside.

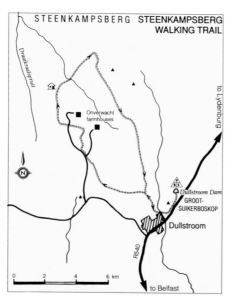

A distant gleam of river on Crane Creek Trail.

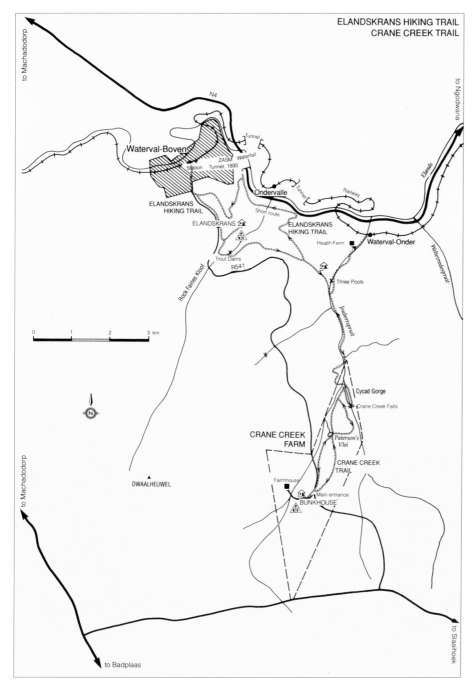

ELANDSKRANS HIKING TRAIL
CRANE CREEK TRAIL

This 90-metre drop on the Elands River gave its name to Waterval Boven.

42. ELANDSKRANS HIKING TRAIL
NEAR WATERVAL BOVEN

Trail details: 22,5 km/2 days, open-ended; one-day trail.

Permits/bookings: Must be obtained from the Elandskrans Holiday Resort, tel. (013262) 176; Private Bag X05, Waterval Boven 1195.

Facilities/amenities: Base camp; Elandskrans Holiday Resort (tariffs on request); 6 overnight huts each accommodating 8 people and with ablution facilities and firewood.

Main attractions: Horst Windish waterfall; indigenous trees; natural swimming pools; Elandskrans gorge.

Pertinent information: The trail tariff includes the train fare and the overnight hut accommodation. There is a limit of 48 people per group.

Situated 2 km from Waterval Boven in a lush setting of waterfalls and bushveld, the Elandskrans Hiking Trail is South Africa's first and only trail to include a train ride *en route*.

On the overnight trail, the hikers walk the 5 km from the resort to the overnight hut and drop off their packs, then set out to visit two waterfalls for the afternoon. The next morning the marked trail leads hikers to Waterval Onder where a 12-km train ride winds through two tunnels in the Elands Pass and skirts the historic Five Arch Bridge, the 90 m-high Elands River Falls and the abandoned 400 m-long NZASM tunnel and takes hikers to Waterval Boven. From this point it is a 1,5-km hike uphill to the resort.

The 1-day trail starts at the Elandskrans Holiday Resort and gently climbs to the plateau where it then winds through beautiful scenery to the Five Arch Bridge. From there the route follows the road

A day walk from the Elandskrans Holiday Resort brings you to the disused NZASM Tunnel, which was completed in 1893.

to the NZASM Tunnel and the Elands River Waterfall, and then the historic mountain pass back to the Elandskrans Holiday Resort.

While the longer trail is a drawcard for steam train enthusiasts who are reasonably fit, the day trail offers more to those who enjoy game- and birdspotting. Black eagle and Knysna lourie inhabit the area, as do duiker, grey rhebok and bushbuck.

43. UITSOEK HIKING TRAILS
BETWEEN WATERVAL BOVEN AND LYDENBURG

Trail details: 1. Houtbosloop route: 29,5 km/ 2 days; 2. Beestekraalspruit route: 11 km/4,5 hours; 3. Bakkrans route: 11 km/4,5 hours; all are circular.

Permits/bookings: Must be obtained from The Regional Director, Department of Forestry, tel. (01311) 52169; Private Bag X11201; Nelspruit 1200; reservations must be made at least 14 days in advance. Map and brochure available on request.

Facilities/amenities: The Uitsoek base hut accommodates 36 people, and has electricity and hot and cold running water; the Lisabon hut has 12 beds with mattresses and cold water but no electricity or firewood.

Main attractions: Outstanding mountain scenery; Nguni ruins.

Pertinent information: Very hot summers; hikers should carry their own water. There is a limit of 36 people for these trails at any one time.

Situated near the Sudwala Caves off the Houtbosloop road from Waterval Boven to Lydenburg, the access road to the Uitsoek Forest Station provides a fair indication of the beautiful landscape these trails traverse, with its folds of mountains covered in grassland and pine plantations, and beyond, layers and layers of mountains. All the trails, which were developed by the Roodepoort Hiking Club for the NHWB, begin and end at Uitsoek hut.

A comprehensive list of the many birds, animals, flora and fauna to be seen on the trails appears in the trail brochure, available on request from the Department of Forestry.

1. The Houtbosloop route begins with a strenuous 15-km hike from the foothills to the plateau. Hikers should make an early start, especially in summer. There are waterpoints at the 2,5 km, 8,4 km and 11 km marks. The ascent from the gorge to the plateau is followed by a fairly flat area and a final climb to the overnight hut. In contrast to the open mountainsides, there are lots of forests, streams and waterfalls up the kloof. Except for approximately 500 m at the start and the last 2 km, the second day's route is downhill or on the level.

2. The Beestekraalspruit route climbs gently through pine plantation, indigenous scrub forest and grassland to the cliff edge of the Beestekraalspruit, before descending gradually into the gorge with its lovely riverine forest. A feature of this route is that it crosses the stream 20 times over wooden bridges.

3. The first half of the **Bakkrans route** leads through plantation above the Houtbosloop route and through indigenous scrub forest in the gorges, before joining the Houtbosloop route at the Bakkrans Waterfall.

44. WATHABA WILDERNESS TRAILS
WATHABA FARM, NEAR MACHADODORP

Trail details: Various mountain trails.

Permits/bookings: Must be obtained from Wimpie Rauch, Wathaba Farm, tel. (013252) 2211; PO Box 389, Machadodorp, 1170. Brochure available on request.

Facilities/amenities: Large hut sleeping 24 people, with a large kitchen, long-drop toilets, bath, shower, hot water; wood, cooking and eating utensils provided.

Main attractions: Waterfalls; beautiful mountain scenery; swimming.

Pertinent information: Changeable weather. There is a limit of 24 people per group.

Situated 21 km south of Machadodorp on the Badplaas road, Wathaba Farm offers hikers the opportunity to walk anywhere on the farm. The Schoonspruit is the main natural feature of the walks. One ramble, approximately 5 km long, leads up a steep mountain slope and loops through a high plateau back down towards the Schoonspruit. Another walk leads up along a waterway and into a deep, sheer gorge, where there are two high waterfalls with deep swimming pools just a few metres away. Hikers may sleep here in the open under the stars if desired and if the weather permits, although the base camp is very comfortable and provides an excellent view of the Schoonspruit.

The hikes in the area are not particularly strenuous. Many guests, though, prefer to relax at the base camp, and spend their time swimming. The trails are open all year, and the farm is home to baboon, monkey, rooikat, jackal, bushpig, bushbuck, klipspringer, otter and many more. The birdlife is also prolific, with many raptors present.

45. KAAPSCHEHOOP HIKING TRAILS
NEAR NELSPRUIT

Trail details: 1. Coetzeestroom Trail: 38 km/ 2 days; 2. Wattles Trail: 28 km/2 days; 3. Tent Trail: 41 km/3 days; all are circular.

Permits/bookings: Must be obtained from The Regional Director, Southern Transvaal Forest Region, tel. (01311) 52169; Private Bag 11201, Nelspruit 1200; reservations must be made not less than 14 days in advance. Map available on request.

Facilities/amenities: Base camp and 3 huts each with 30 bunks and mattresses, hot water, cooking utensils and braai facilities; 2 tent camps with braai facilities and long-drop toilet.

Main attractions: Indigenous forest; excellent birdlife, this is the breeding area of the endangered blue swallow.

Pertinent information: There is a limit of 30 people per trail.

The Kaapschehoop Hiking Trails, south-west of Nelspruit, consist of two 2-day routes and one

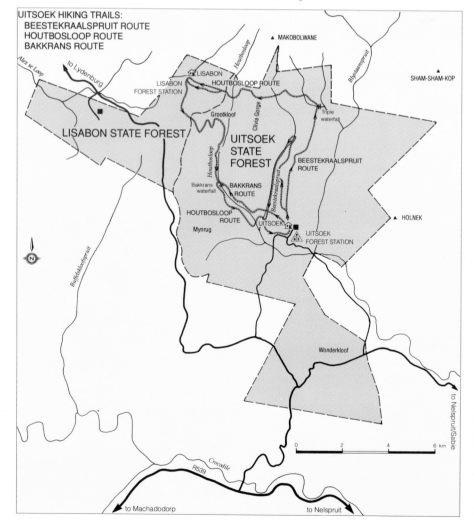

UITSOEK HIKING TRAILS:
BEESTEKRAALSPRUIT ROUTE
HOUTBOSLOOP ROUTE
BAKKRANS ROUTE

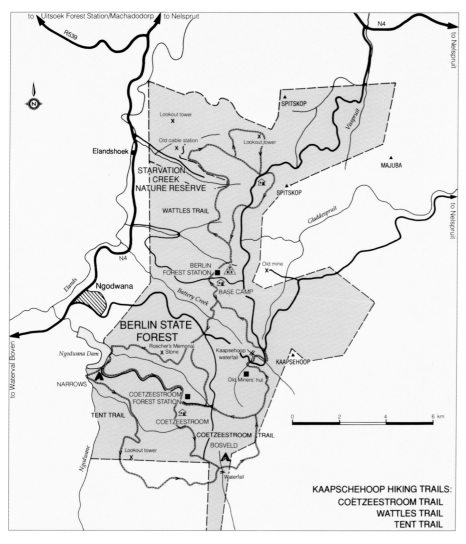

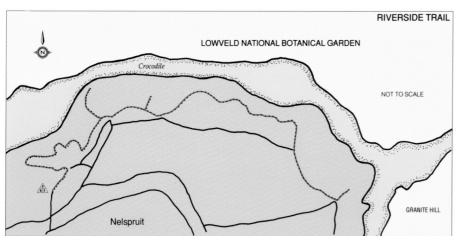

Kaapschehoop; and the longest route of 21 km via the Narrows camp. This hike is fairly strenuous.

2. The Wattles Trail leads from the base camp to Wattles hut, a distance of 19 km. The next day hikers walk the 9 km back to the base camp. This is not a strenuous hike.

3. The Tent Trail follows the same route as the Coetzeestroom Trail up until the 11-km mark, where it splits. There are 2 camp sites; Bosveld camp, 13 km from the start, and Narrows camp at the 26-km mark. This trail is fairly strenuous.

46. RIVERSIDE TRAIL
LOWVELD NATIONAL BOTANICAL GARDEN, NELSPRUIT

Trail details: 4 km/1,5 hours; circular.

Permits/bookings: Not required; there is an entrance fee to the gardens.

Facilities/amenities: Information office; toilets.

Main attractions: The indigenous flora of the Crocodile River Valley (500 plant species); pothole waterfalls; prolific birdlife.

Pertinent information: Bilharzia is present in the river; rocks can be slippery. There is a limit of 30 people per group.

Situated in the Lowveld National Botanical Garden just outside Nelspruit opposite the Sabie intersection, this short self-guided trail along the banks of the Crocodile River highlights the plant life of the region and is physically undemanding, and especially pleasant in spring and autumn. The route, starting and ending near the information office, is clearly marked, and walkers have an excellent chance of seeing some of the 245 bird species recorded in the gardens.

3-day route, which include a wide variety of natural, historic and scenic attractions; the first stock exchange in South Africa was established in the old mining town of Nelspruit.

The major part of each route winds through natural forest and along rivers. Vervet monkeys, baboon and dassies occur, as do oribi, bushbuck, grey rhebok, mountain reedbuck, bushpig and porcupine. More than 200 species of birds have been recorded. The endangered blue swallow breeds in dongas and old mine shafts in the sour grassland.

All these trails are clearly marked, and walking conditions are pleasant all year round, although the route sometimes follows logging roads where you are likely to choke from the dust; such routes should therefore be avoided in the dry season.

1. The Coetzeestroom Trail, from the base camp to Coetzeestroom hut, is approximately 17 km long. After spending the night hikers have a choice of 4 routes back to the start: a short 9-km route; a 13-km route past the miner's hut and pear orchard; a 15-km route over the northern escarpment of

Lowveld Botanical Garden near Nelspruit.

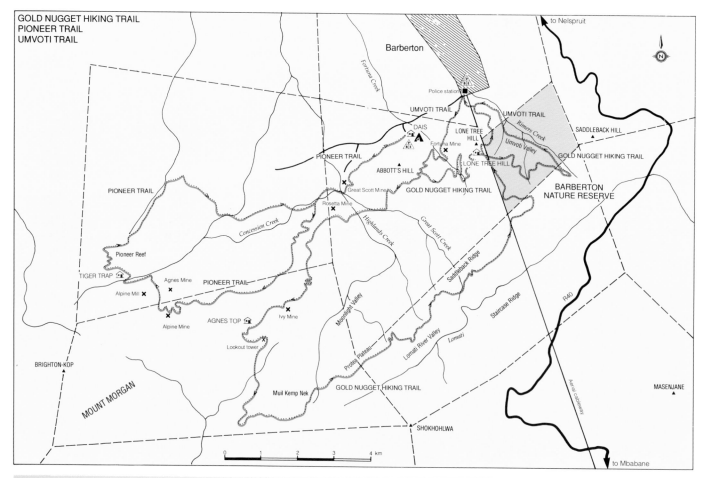

GOLD NUGGET HIKING TRAIL
PIONEER TRAIL
UMVOTI TRAIL

A wealth of historical and natural treasures awaits discovery in the lowveld countryside around Barberton.

47. PIONEER TRAIL
BARBERTON

Trail details: 28,5 km/2 days; circular.

Permits/bookings: Must be obtained from Makhonjwa Conservation Foundation, tel. (01314) 24067; PO Box 81, Barberton 1300. Map and brochure on request.

Facilities/amenities: Dais base camp (hikers must bring their own tents); overnight hut with accommodation for 20 people; toilets and showers; braai lapa.

Main attractions: Beautiful mountain scenery; signs of gold-mining activities of early pioneers; 43 species of fern.

Pertinent information: Bees are prevalent; rapidly changeable weather; bilharzia is present in the streams; hikers must carry their own water. There is a limit of 20 people for this trail at any one time.

Situated in the vast Barberton mountainland just 1 km west of Barberton, the Pioneer Trail starts and ends at the Dais base camp.

The first day's walk leads up into the Makhonjwa mountains and down rivers, streams and waterfalls for 15 km; it is strenuous and very steep in parts, but otherwise a moderate hike. The second day's route begins with an ascent up the Pioneer reef, before crossing the valley and leading downwards and eastwards towards the start of the trail. Vegetation types encountered during the course of this trail are bushveld, mountainous grassland and indigenous and riverine forest.

The atmospheric little town of Barberton is one of South Africa's earliest gold-mining centres, so along the trail you will come across evidence of those early treasure seekers.

Baboon, monkeys, klipspringer, duiker and other small animals can all be seen in the area, while the large variety of birds present includes the jackal buzzard. The trail is clearly marked, and the winter months are especially pleasant for walking.

48. UMVOTI TRAIL
BARBERTON

Trail details: 20 km/2 days; circular.

Permits/bookings: Must be obtained from Makhonjwa Conservation Foundation, tel. (01314) 24067; PO Box 81, Barberton 1300. Map and brochure available on request.

Facilities/amenities: A Boer War signalling fort serves as an overnight hut, with accommodation for 20 hikers; toilets, cold showers; firewood and braai lapa.

Main attractions: Mountain scenery; indigenous forest; spectacular views.

Pertinent information: Bees are prevalent; rapidly changeable weather; bilharzia is present in the streams; hikers must carry their own water. There is a limit of 20 people for this trail at any one time.

Starting and ending opposite the police station in Barberton, this moderate trail begins with a 10-km climb to Lone Tree Hill hut, where hikers spend the night. Next morning, the route traverses the Barberton Nature Reserve and descends at Rimers Creek, from where a short walk leads through the centre of

the historic and very attractive town of Barberton back to the start.

The route, which passes through temperate mountain grasslands and indigenous forest, is clearly marked, and is ideal for the beginner hiker or the not-so-fit. Animals to be seen include baboon, monkeys, the nocturnal porcupine, klipspringer, duiker and mongoose. This trail is open all year, although winter is generally considered to be the best time for hiking.

49. GOLD NUGGET HIKING TRAIL
BARBERTON

Trail details: 47 km/2 to 3 days; circular.

Permits/bookings: Must be obtained from the Makhonjwa Conservation Foundation, tel. (01314) 24067; PO Box 81, Barberton 1300. Map and brochure on request.

Facilities/amenities: 2 overnight huts: the Agnes Top hut (an old miner's house), where water, shower, toilets, bunks for 20 people, firewood and a braai place are provided; Lone Tree Hill hut (an old fort) contains toilets, shower, tank water, bunks for 20 people, firewood and a braai place.

Main attractions: The trail gives insight into the rugged, adventurous life of early Barberton gold miners; old mines and their associated buildings; breathtaking scenery.

Pertinent information: Hikers must carry their own water.

Starting and ending in Barberton, the Gold Nugget Trail winds along old bridle paths and past historical gold mines. The historical emphasis of the trail is unusual, and there is much to hold the attention of the naturalist; a variety of aloe and protea species, flowering plants such as the Barberton daisy and Pride-of-De-Kaap, and indigenous trees such as the tamboti, sausage tree, mobola plum, lowveld chestnut, Transvaal red milkwood and lowveld cabbage tree are encountered.

The birdlife is equally fascinating; the Barberton area is a complex ecotone environment where a varied blend of highveld, lowveld and escarpment species coexist.

This clearly marked trail is not recommended for beginners as it is strenuous. The first day covers 17 km and takes approximately 7 hours. Starting opposite the police station in the town, the route leads up and over Abbott's Hill Neck, down through a gum plantation and across the Great Scott Creek. Hikers then start ascending the mountain, and arrive at Agnes Top hut a short while later. The second day leads for 20 km along the Saddleback Ridge of the Makhonjwa mountains. There is no guarantee of water on this section; hikers must ensure that their water bottles are full when leaving the Agnes hut. The route leads through plantations and indigenous forest, and has some magnificent views overlooking the Shonameni and Moonlight valleys. From the south side of the Saddleback Ridge there is an uninterrupted view over the mountains of Mendon all the way into Swaziland. Hikers proceed up Muil Kamp Nek and Protea Plateau, before heading eastwards and down to Lone Tree Hill Fort. Hikers now have a choice of overnighting here, or proceeding downhill at the 3 km sign and following the yellow arrows back to Barberton.

Hikers spending the night at Lone Tree proceed the next morning from the 3 km sign south of the hut, traversing a nature reserve and arriving at Rimers Creek, from where a short walk leads through the centre of town back to the start. This trail is open all year, although winter is generally considered to be the best time for hiking.

50. SONGIMVELO WILDERNESS EXPERIENCE
SONGIMVELO GAME RESERVE, KANGWANE (NEAR BADPLAAS)

Trail details: Various guided trails available, ranging from 3 to 5 days.

Permits/bookings: Must be obtained from Wilderness Leadership School, tel. (011) 4556805; PO Box 87230, Houghton 2041. Brochure available on request.

Facilities/amenities: Hikers sleep in the open under the stars; all food and equipment is supplied by the organizers; transport to and from Johannesburg is included in the cost.

Main attractions: Diverse birdlife; the perennial Komati River.

Pertinent information: Ticks in summer; anti-malaria precautions must be taken. There is a limit of 8 hikers per group.

A 4-hour drive from Johannesburg, nestled in the Barberton mountainland north-west of the Swaziland border, is the Songimvelo Game Reserve

Smooth and slow, the Little Olifants River winds below the Baboon Hiking Trail.

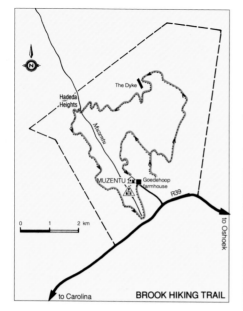

BROOK HIKING TRAIL

Wilderness Experience which consists of guided walks tailored to suit the requirements and interests of each individual group. A medium level of fitness is required for these walks.

The 65 000-ha reserve, containing afro-montane and riverine forest and savannah bushveld, sweeps dramatically up from bushveld plains and the Komati River Valley to high peaks on Swaziland's rugged northern border.

Game to be seen includes elephant, rhino, black wildebeest, hippo, antelope, giraffe and zebra in the lowlands and reedbuck and grey rhebok higher up, while 300 species of birds have been recorded, including the narina trogon. There are some archaeological sites in the area, which is rich in Iron Age settlements estimated to date back to 200 or 400 BC. There is also evidence of the Barberton Gold Rush.

51. THE BROOK HIKING TRAIL
NEAR CAROLINA

Trail details: 21,5 km /2 days; circular.

Permits/bookings: Must be obtained from HL&H Lothair District Office, tel. (013462) ask for 15; PO Box 75, Lothair 2370.

Facilities/amenities: Muzentu overnight hut sleeps 20 hikers, and is equipped with showers, toilets, stove, sink, fireplace, tables and benches.

Main attractions: Lovely brooks; abundance of flowers; breathtaking views.

Pertinent information: Hot summers; unpredictable mist; bees and ticks are prevalent. There is a limit of 20 people for this trail at any one time.

The Brook Hiking Trail is situated just off the Carolina/Oshoek road (Swaziland border). The trail traverses a beautiful part of the country where the grassland of the high plateau gives way to the tumbling valleys forming the start of river systems flowing eastwards. In the northern valley of the Komati River basin flow a number of brooks which combine to form the Muzentu stream. The twin valleys formed by these brooks are the setting of the Brook Hiking Trail.

The trail passes through open grassland and the area is home to hundreds of plant species, 50 species of bird, and many animals. The trail consists of one full day's walking of 16 km plus a half-day 5,5-km walk. The route is clearly marked by a white line down the centre of the path, and is not particularly exacting.

52. CYCAD HIKING TRAILS
NEAR MIDDELBURG

Trail details: 1. Baboon Trail: 20 km/2 days; 2. Cycad Trail: 11 km/4 hours; 3. Suikerbos Trail: 8 km/3,5 hours; 4. Tarentaal Trail: 9 km/3,5 hours; all are circular.

Permits/bookings: Must be obtained from The Manager, Cycad Hiking Trails, tel. (0132) 43 1040; PO Box 1326, Middelburg 1050. Map and brochure available on request.

Facilities/amenities: Mountain and ravine huts, each accommodating 40 hikers; toilets, showers, mattresses for hire; braai facilities.

Main attractions: Rare cycad species; prolific birdlife; mountain scenery.

Pertinent information: Bilharzia is present in the streams and rivers; hikers should carry water purification tablets; ticks and snakes are prevalent; summers are hot. There is a limit of 40 hikers per trail at any one time.

These trails are situated on the 2 000-ha Bankfontein Farm, 23 km north of Middelburg.

All the trails are clearly marked, and vary in difficulty; the Baboon Trail is the only trail where more than a rudimentary fitness is required. Leopard, hyaena, kudu, ribbok, duiker and caracal are all present in the area.

1. The Baboon Trail starts at Scheepersdal house, and leads for 9 km to the ravine huts, passing cliffs, ravines and mountain scenery. The second day's route leads from the ravine huts to the mountain huts, and back to the start.

2. The Cycad Trail starts at the mountain huts, and passes fascinating prehistoric cycads (*Encephalartos*

Eugene-maraisii and *Encephalartos lanatus*), before ending near the start of the Baboon Trail.

3. The Suikerbos Trail starts at Scheepersdal house, and winds towards Loskop on the upper plateau, before returning to the starting point along the bank of the Olifants River.

4. The Tarentaal Trail starts where the Cycad Trail ends, and gives hikers a taste of both river and plateau before joining up with the Baboon Trail.

53. BOTSHABELO TRAILS
BOTSHABELO NATURE RESERVE, MIDDELBURG

Trail details: 1. Klein Aasvoëlkrans Trail: 12 km/ 6 to 7 hours return (shorter Oorbietjie optional route); 2. Botshabelo Trail: approximately 8 km/4 hours; 3. Eland Trail: 24 km/2 days; all are circular.

Permits/bookings: Must be obtained from the Municipality of Middelburg, tel. (0132) 21337; PO Box 14, Middelburg 1050.

Facilities/amenities: Overnight huts accommodating 6 hikers each; drinking water, pots, firewood, mattresses and rubbish bags are provided; refreshments for sale.

Main attractions: Klein Olifants River Valley; rare plants; cycads; wide variety of wildlife; Fort Merensky; south Ndebele village.

Pertinent information: Bilharzia is present; swimming in the river is not recommended. Hikers must carry their own water (2 litres per person per day is recommended in summer). There is a limit of 12 people for each trail.

The 2 306-ha Botshabelo Nature Reserve is situated 12 km outside Middelburg.

1. The Klein Aasvoëlkrans Trail is a pleasant, easy walk. Clearly marked with white footprints, it leads firstly towards the Klein Olifants river gorge, and there is a very good chance of spotting game such as oribi, duiker, klipspringer and baboon in the early morning. Birdlife is also prolific and includes the African fish eagle and steppe buzzard; it is suggested that hikers take along a pair of binoculars. Presently, the path cuts through the gorge to

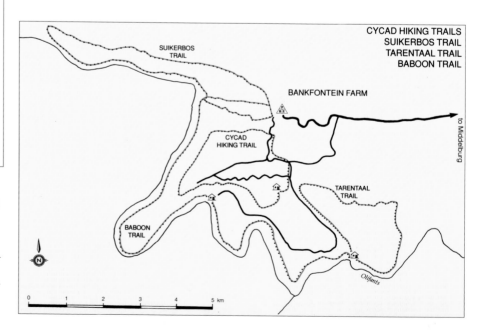

CYCAD HIKING TRAILS
SUIKERBOS TRAIL
TARENTAAL TRAIL
BABOON TRAIL

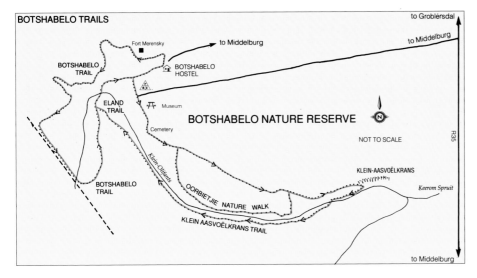

BOTSHABELO TRAILS

to Groblersdal

to Middelburg

Fort Merensky

to Middelburg

BOTSHABELO
TRAIL

BOTSHABELO
HOSTEL

ELAND
TRAIL

Museum

Cemetery

BOTSHABELO NATURE RESERVE

N

NOT TO SCALE

R35

KLEIN-AASVOËLKRANS

Keerom Spruit

BOTSHABELO
TRAIL

OORBIETJIE NATURE WALK

KLEIN AASVOËLKRANS TRAIL

to Middelburg

the river, where there are some lovely spots for a rest. The route then leads back to the start.

2. Ramblers can walk the entire trail or opt for a shorter loop, the **Oorbietjie Nature Walk**, which will return them to the parking area in approximately 4 hours. The endemic Olifants River cycad grows within a plant community which hosts an interesting diversity of indigenous trees and shrubs.

3. **The Botshabelo Nature Trail**, situated just north of the Klein Aasvoëlkrans Trail, offers, in addition to the natural features seen on the Klein Aasvoëlkrans Trail, views of Fort Merensky, Botshabelo (a Sotho word meaning 'place of refuge') village and the South Ndebele open-air museum. The mission station for the Berlin Mission Society was established here in 1865 and given the name Botshabelo. In the early 1900s some 3 000 people lived there, and the mission prospered until World War I, when funds from Germany dried up. The fort was built in expectation of an attack by Sekhukhune, a local chief who persecuted Christians; however, it was only ever used briefly by the British in the Anglo-Boer war.

4. **The Eland Trail** takes hikers from the mission station over a distance of 16 km through a cycad forest and along the Klein Olifants River, before reaching the overnight huts. The second day follows the trail markers for 8 km back to the start. The Eland Trail requires a higher level of fitness than the Klein Aasvoëlkrans and Botshabelo trails.

54. NGODWANA TRAIL
NGODWANA DAM

Trail details: 12 km/5 hours, circular; there is a short route of 1,5 hours. See map p. 247.

Permits/bookings: Sappi Forests office, tel. (01318) 54551; situated behind the shopping centre in Ngodwana. A simple map is available on request and a brochure will be available at the end of 1993.

Facilities/amenities: Picnic site.

Main attractions: Birdlife at the dam; picnic site; swimming hole.

Pertinent information: As pepper ticks abound in the area, it is suggested that hikers wear long pants and/or apply insect repellent to their legs; there is a limit of 12 people on the trail per day, and no-one is allowed on the trail before sunrise or after sunset.

The longish Ngodwana Trail begins near the parking area at the Ngodwana Dam. It crosses the Ngodwana River and climbs through aloes and dolomite rock formations, past an old limestone mine, to a high viewpoint. It then descends through grassland to riverine bush and the Ngodwana River, where there is a delightful swimming hole and a picnic site. Oribi, mountain reedbuck, bushbuck and grey rhebok can be seen, especially after the grass had been burnt in spring. The trail returns above the Ngodwana Dam, where it joins up with the short route leading down to the water's edge.

The Ngodwana Dam has attracted a variety of waterbirds, including a pair of fish eagles, and is deservedly popular with bird-watchers as a result.

55. MASHONAMIEN FOREST TRAILS
GROOTGELUK PLANTATION, NEAR NGODWANA

Trail details: Mashonadien Trail: 6 km/2,5 hours, circular; a short route, which takes about 30 minutes, is available. See map p. 247.

Permits/bookings: Must be obtained from Sappi Forests Office, tel. (01318) 54551; situated behind the shopping centre in Ngodwana. A simple map and a list of the area's flora and fauna are available on request.

Facilities/amenities: Small camp site; braai facilities; picnic tables and toilets at halfway mark.

Main attractions: Indigenous forest, waterfalls, endless vistas along the Escarpment.

Pertinent information: As pepper ticks abound in the area, it is suggested that hikers wear long pants and/or apply insect repellent to their legs; there is a limit of 12 people on the trail per day, and no-one is allowed on the trail before sunrise or after sunset. It may be necessary to paddle or wade across the rivers in the rainy season (November to March).

Nature's powers of restoration are nowhere better depicted than in the Mashonamien Forest and Heritage Area, 30 minutes' drive from Ngodwana. An increased demand for mining timber at the end of the Boer War led to large-scale exploitation of the indigenous forest in this area until about 1907. However, the only evidence of this are relic sections of narrow-gauge railway line and machinery used to process the logs and transport them out of the gorges. The slopes are once again covered by a

mosaic of deciduous scrub and semi-deciduous woodland, while the moist areas of the upper valley harbour high evergreen montane forest.

The name Mashonamien is a corruption of the Swazi, 'Shona emini', meaning 'where the sun sets early' – an appropriate description of this mountainous area where a trail has recently been laid. You will need to request instructions on how to reach Mashonamien when you book at Ngodwana.

The trail itself is easy and gentle, apart from one brief steep section. It begins near the car park, where the vegetation is scrub interspersed with deciduous trees. For the most part, the route follows a stream in the forested Mashonamien Valley, crossing and recrossing it. Points of interest have been marked and several remnants of logging activity can be spotted along the way. Hikers eventually reach the old steam engine which once powered the belt-drive bush mill. This is an ideal spot for a rest, as picnic tables and toilets are provided.

The return leg of the trail runs parallel to and above the outward leg, traversing steep cliffs of lava; if you examine these you will find that the lava contains inclusions (called amygdales) which were once gas bubbles. Lower down, the route crosses an extensive scree slope comprising lava boulders; the fragments in these indicate that a violent eruption must have splintered the existing rock, which fell back down and was embedded in new lavas. One of the common trees on the edge of the scree slope is the Transvaal bottlebrush.

Near the end of the route there are the remains of stone dwellings, possibly those of turn-of-the-century woodcutters.

56. KALKOENKRANS TRAILS
NEAR BADPLAAS

Trail details: Guided trails of flexible length/duration, according to demand. See map p. 247.

Permits/bookings: Book with trail leader Mr G Combrink, tel. (01344) 31954, or through Sappi Rooihoogte forestry office, tel. (01344) 32802. A brochure is available on request.

Facilities/amenities: Trail includes farm breakfast before starting out and a braai on return. Accommodation is offered in an old farmhouse.

Main attractions: Varied flora and fauna.

Pertinent information: Trails are likely to be restricted in periods of severe fire hazard, for the protection of the forests.

The Kalkoenkrans conservation area is a 13 000-ha expanse of plantation, indigenous forest and grassland, reached via Sappi's Rooihoogte plantation, on the Badplaas/Carolina road. It is in this varied environment that guided hiking and horse trails have recently been established.

Kalkoenkrans features a great diversity of flora – ranging from highveld grassland to forests where tree ferns flourish – and fauna, including blesbok. It also boasts a wealth of birdlife and two magnificent waterfalls where a pair of crowned eagles and a colony of bald ibises (hence the *kalkoen*) nest.

The trails begin and end at the farmhouse, but are otherwise designed to accommodate the interests of the hiking party. Hikers can cool off in the farm dam at the end of the day's hike.

NAMIBIA

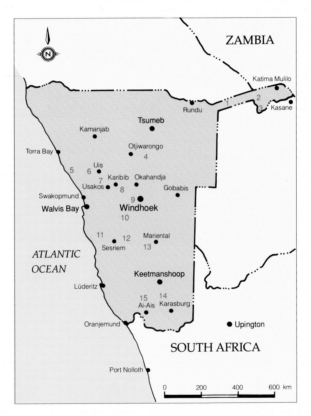

Namibia is a vast, sparsely populated land situated north of the Orange River, and is bordered by Angola in the north, Botswana in the east, South Africa in the south and the Atlantic Ocean in the west. The Khoikhoi named this huge territory (823 144 km² – almost four times the size of Great Britain) 'Namibia', which means 'plain'. Despite its vast and harsh desert to semi-desert waterless environment and the long distances between population centres, Namibia continues to draw outdoor enthusiasts. Endless rocky plains, desert dunes, desolate coastlines, dry riverbeds, animals adapted to desert conditions, rewarding birdlife and unusual plants offer the trailist a sense of beauty and tranquillity.

In the desert areas a unique blend of natural colours and angles combines with wide horizons and pollution-free skies to produce magnificently aesthetic lighting: crimson glowing dunes, silver shining pans, pastel mountains at dawn and dusk, and brilliant wild flowers after the rains. Photography here is a dream.

To the north, the region is well-watered and is becoming more accessible to tourists. The Caprivi is a place of rare adventure that resembles the Okavango Delta and although no formal trails exist at present, this wilderness area is earmarked for development.

Hikers must be prepared for extremes in temperature. The midsummer hiker experiences hot days (temperatures may rise to above 40°C) and cool nights; winter is a more agreeable time to visit Namibia, when the days are comfortably warm, although at night the temperature can fall to several degrees below freezing point.

The interior of Namibia has two rainy seasons: the short one, between October and December, when rain falls sporadically, and the main rainfall period, accompanied by thunderstorms, between mid-January and April. During this time, be wary of potential flash-flooding.

It is wise to walk during the cooler parts of the day, in the early morning and late afternoon.

LEFT: *A true desert, the Namib is noted for its immense dunes, some of which are seen here near Sossusvlei.*

Sunset over the east Caprivi, and fishermen chug slowly home on the still Zambezi River.

2. MADUMU NATIONAL PARK
CAPRIVI

Trail details: Guided walking safaris only.

Permits/bookings: Must be obtained from Kalizo Fishing & Photographic Safaris (Pty) Ltd, Central Reservations, tel. (011) 7644606; PO Box 195, Wilgeheuwel 1736. See also Fish Eagle Trail, p. 295.

Facilities/amenities: Mvubu Lodge accommodates 10 people in luxury permanent tents. Meals are provided *en route* and equipment and luggage portaged ahead by vehicle/boat.

Main attractions: Big game; prolific birdlife.

Pertinent information: There is a limit of 10 people per group. Anti-malaria precautions are essential. For more information on Madumu National Park contact the Ministry of Wildlife, Conservation and Tourism, tel. (061) 63131; Private Bag 13346, Windhoek.

Originally a forest reserve, the 85 000-ha Madumu National Park, proclaimed in 1990, encompasses the Madumu Malapo grasslands, and extends some 25 km into the forest area and for about 45 km along the Kwando River, adjoining the Caprivi Game Reserve. Visitors may spot hippo and crocodile in the oxbow lake in front of the lodge, and elephant coming to drink. Big game migrates through this area between Botswana, Zambia and Angola, and concentrates within the park, mainly in the winter months, drawing a myriad predators.

Apart from riverine woodland and reedbeds, there are extensive areas dominated by mopane and other tree species. The birdlife is particularly abundant in the riverine belt.

3. MAMILI NATIONAL PARK
LINYANTI SWAMPS, CAPRIVI

Trail details: Guided walking safaris only.

Permits/bookings: Must be obtained from Kalizo Fishing & Photographic Safaris (Pty) Ltd, Central Reservations, tel. (011) 7644606; PO Box 195, Wilgeheuwel 1736. See also Fish Eagle Trail, p. 295.

Facilities/amenities: There are no facilities in the park itself, but the tour organizers provide tented camps.

Main attractions: Prolific birdlife; the opportunity to explore remote and unspoilt locations.

Pertinent information: There is a limit of 10 people per group. Anti-malaria precautions are essential. For more information on Mamili National Park contact the Ministry of Wildlife, Conservation and Tourism, Private Bag 13346, Windhoek; tel. (061) 63131.

1. WEST CAPRIVI GAME RESERVE
CAPRIVI

Trail details: Guided walking safaris only.

Permits/bookings: Must be obtained from Kalizo Fishing & Photographic Safaris (Pty) Ltd, Central Reservations, tel. (011) 7644606; PO Box 195, Wilgeheuwel 1736. Kalizo also operate photographic, bird-watching and boating safaris, or a combination of these. Brochure available on request.

Facilities/amenities: Sitwe camp, on the banks of the Kwando River, has five 2-person chalets and a camp site for 10 people.

Main attractions: Prolific wildlife and birdlife; unspoilt vegetation; tranquillity.

Pertinent information: There is a limit of 10 people per group. Anti-malaria precautions are essential. For more information on the West Caprivi Game Reserve contact the Ministry of Wildlife, Conservation and Tourism, tel. (061) 63131; Private Bag 13346, Windhoek.

This large 600 000-ha game reserve is bounded in the west by the Kavango River (the source of the Okavango River and swamps), and in the east by the Kwando River, source of the Chobe River. To the north it is bounded by Angola, with its large forests, and to the south by Botswana.

Walks in this area cover two distinct ecosystems: the wide flood plains of the Kwando with its accompanying papyrus swamps and palm islands, and the teak forests growing on fossil dune lines of the ancient Kalahari. In the past the inter-dune valleys were watercourses and today these are dotted with small shallow pans along their length. These fill up in the wet seasons and slowly dry out during the summer months.

The flood plains are home to lechwe, sitatunga antelope, hippo, crocodile, wild dog, huge herds of buffalo and other game. Elephant move down to the flood plains from the forests to drink, and stay on the plains for months on end. In the teak forests elephant, roan and sable antelope, buffalo and kudu are found. Predators such as lion, leopard and cheetah wander between the forests and the swamplands.

The birdlife in the area is prolific: wattled crane, slaty egret and Pel's fishing owl are just some of the many species present.

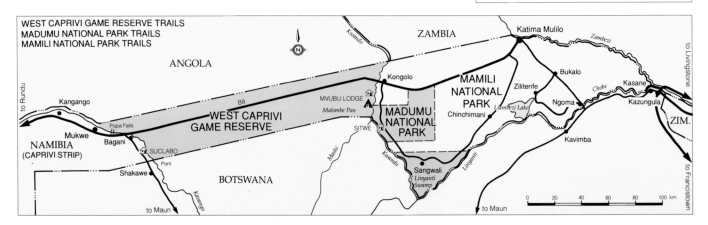

The recently proclaimed 35 500-ha Mamili National Park protects 40 000 ha of flood plain and swampland formed by the Kwando River changing course to a north-easterly direction due to the Magwegana fault line, part of the Great Rift Valley system. Two islands – Nkasa and Lupala – are situated in this vast swampland of papyrus and grassy flood plains, which is extremely hot and humid in summer. The Linyanti River and a network of hippo channels hold water throughout the year. Elephant, hippo, red lechwe, sitatunga, lion, buffalo, spotted hyaena and leopard occur. Game migrates into this area from the Savuti area of Botswana in times of drought and adds to the resident multitudes. The birdlife is a major attraction, with such species as wattled crane, fish eagle, swamp boubou, collared palm thrush, Bradfield's hornbill, Pel's fishing eagle, whitecrowned plover and slaty egret all present.

4. WATERBERG PLATEAU PARK
NEAR OTJIWARONGO

Trail details: 4-day guided wilderness trail; circular. A self-guided 4-day/42-km wilderness trail opened in June 1993.

Permits/bookings: Must be obtained well in advance from The Director of Tourism, Reservations, tel. (061) 36975; Private Bag 13267, Windhoek 9000.

Facilities/amenities: Base camp with 4 rustic huts sleeping 2 people each; rest camp with bungalows; a camp site with shop and swimming pool. Overnight shelters at Otjozongomba (where hikers spend 1 night) and Otjomapenda (where they spend 2 nights).

Main attractions: Interesting sandstone formations; rock engravings; rich and varied vegetation, animal and birdlife in a wilderness atmosphere; the park is refuge to the only breeding colony of Cape vultures in Namibia.

Pertinent information: The guided trails run from Thursday to Sunday afternoon every second, third and fourth weekend from 1 April to 30 November. The form the route takes is flexible, and depends on the requirements of each group, but distances covered do not exceed 15 km per day. There is a minimum of 3 and a maximum of 10 hikers per group. The hot, wet months are October through to April.

Like some strange archaeological relic, a termite mound explains the name of Anthill Way.

The unique 40 000-ha Waterberg Plateau Park is situated approximately 30 km east of Otjiwarongo. In this land of scenic surprises, the table mountain formation of the Waterberg Plateau, abruptly rising about 200 m above the surrounding plains, forms yet another striking contrast. The plateau, a remnant of the original crust which existed before the surrounding land eroded away, hosts an interesting gradation of vegetation from the summit down through the sandstone cliffs and slopes of the mountain to its base. Large trees grow around the free-flowing springs which are a special feature of this park. In fact, a whole series of frog species has evolved within the numerous springs.

Animals relocated to the huge, undisturbed mountain plateau include the endangered sable, roan, buffalo and black and white rhino. The trails are led by armed game rangers who are well-acquainted with the park and the area.

5. UGAB HIKING TRAIL
SKELETON COAST PARK

Trail details: Guided trail of between 50 and 60 km/ 3 days; circular. See map p. 282.

Permits/bookings: Must be obtained from The Director of Tourism, Reservations tel. (061) 36975; Private Bag 13267, Windhoek. Brochure available on request.

Facilities/amenities: Mile 108 camp site (approximately 30 km south of the entrance gate to the park) can accommodate hikers before they start the trail. No facilities *en route*; hikers must supply all their own food and equipment.

Main attractions: Rugged wilderness-like environment; fascinating geology; canyonlands; sand dunes; unique desert flora; large game, and smaller animals uniquely adapted to desert life; interesting birdlife; desert and riverine vegetation.

Pertinent information: Mosquitoes can be a problem but there is no malaria at present. A medical certificate issued 40 days prior to commencement of hike is required, and is checked at the Ugab River mouth at the start of the trail. The route is flexible, and can be adjusted to the requirements and interests of the particular group. Groups are limited in size to a minimum of 6 and a maximum of 8 hikers. The trail is open only from March to August. Mid-May to June (after the rainy season) are the best months to hike. Be prepared for extremes in temperature.

Although the Ugab Hiking Trail can extend approximately 40 km inland from the mouth of the Ugab river, it is tailored to suit varying group stamina, interests, enthusiasm and weather conditions. Located in the dry river course of the Ugab River Valley, the trail runs along the southern boundary of the Skeleton Coast Park, an immense area of more than a million and a half hectares, composed of sand dunes, gravel plains and wild, desolate coastline. Inland the park boasts a rare, silent beauty of jagged mountains, canyons and interesting wildlife.

WATERBERG PLATEAU PARK TRAILS

TRAIL CAMP

TRAIL CAMP

Also refer to the Brandberg and Spitzkoppe map

Park Headquarters

D2512

to Grootfontein

WATERBERG PLATEAU PARK

Wilderness Area

WILDERNESS TRAIL

REST CAMP

N

to C22/Otjiwarongo

0 2 4 6 8 10 km

As hikers follow the river course upstream from the mouth, an ever-changing landscape emerges. The open, granitic gravel plains are followed by folded rocky outcrops composed of biotite schists (a metamorphic rock of dark brown to black mica) interlayered with marble bands. These mountains are sliced by 125 million-year-old dolerite dykes and are edged on the southern river banks by sand dunes. Overnight camps in this impressive canyon landscape are chosen at random, often in a rocky side-canyon under a large and spreading ana tree (*Faidherbia albida*).

Desert flora and fauna compete with landform for the hiker's attention. Camel thorn and ebony trees provide shade and shelter while shrubs such as brack-bush, Bushman's candle and euphorbias, and smaller plants such as the vygies, are common. Along the marshy areas of the riverbed, various sedge-like plants and reeds form evergreen oases.

Hikers have a good chance of spotting gemsbok, springbok, Hartmann's mountain zebra and black-backed jackal, while black rhino, lion and cheetah pass through the trail area occasionally. Warthog, Cape hare, striped polecat and honey badger, as well as a healthy snake population (including horned adder), lizards, chameleons and insects especially adapted to desert conditions are present. Bird-watchers will be delighted by Rüppell's korhaan and Ludwig's bustard, resident raptors such as augur buzzards, chanting goshawks and rock kestrels, lappetfaced vultures and, of course, all the smaller birds of bush and river valley.

6. THE BRANDBERG
NORTH-WESTERN NAMIBIA

Trail details: No demarcated trail as such, but the 1,5-hour walk to the famous 'White Lady' rock painting is popular and fairly easy to follow. For mountaineers, an extended backpacking trip to Königstein Peak is possible.

Permits/bookings: Not required.

Facilities/amenities: Informal camp sites with no facilities provided.

Main attractions: The 'White Lady' and other rock paintings; rugged rock scenery; spectacular sunrises and sunsets; unusual plants.

Pertinent information: Water is severely limited in this area; because of the rugged terrain and extremes in temperature, the inexperienced or unfit must not attempt long hikes or climbs in the Brandberg; mosquito repellent and sunscreen lotion are essential. Hikers should always take plenty of water with them.

One of the many exquisite rock paintings that adorn Schlangen-Höhle in the Brandberg.

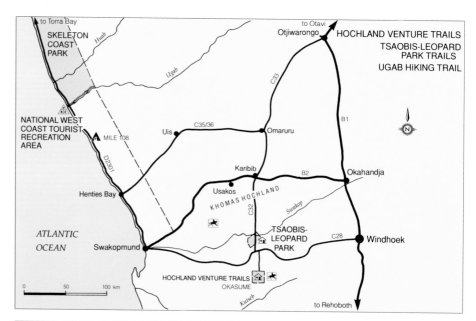

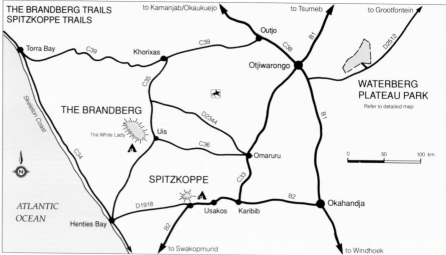

The Brandberg, situated approximately 40 km west of Uis in central Damaraland, is an impressive granite massif towering 2 000 m above the surrounding semi-desert steppe of grass and bush. Considering the Brandberg's other names – Desolate or Forsaken Mountain, and Fire Mountain – one can understand why only the toughest mountaineers climb Königstein Peak (2 579 m), the highest point in Namibia.

By far the most popular walk in the Brandberg is the ramble along the main ravine which leads to the White Lady, one of the most famous rock paintings in Namibia, and one which has over the years evoked a myriad hypotheses as to its origin and, most especially, its meaning.

Rambling at the base of the Brandberg reveals rare and unusual plants such as cobas, a thickset succulent tree which bears a red, grape-like fruit containing poisonous oxalic acid, and the African moringa, another conspicuous, thick-set tree with edible bark, stem and roots.

Only mountaineers of long standing should attempt longer hikes in the Brandberg – its excessive daytime temperatures, bitterly cold nights, the lack of water (except in hidden springs and waterholes) and its jumble of rock, ravine and natural rubble combine to create a formidable goal.

Descending Weyerbrunn in the west Brandberg.

282

7. SPITZKOPPE
NEAR USAKOS

Trail details: No demarcated trails.

Permits/bookings: Not required at present, but may be introduced once the camp sites have been developed; contact The Director of Tourism, Reservations, tel. (061) 36975; Private Bag 13267, Windhoek, for the latest information.

Facilities/amenities: Informal camp sites with no facilities; it is planned to establish camp sites in this area in the future.

Main attractions: Interesting rock formations; rock art; semi-precious stones.

Pertinent information: Hikers should always take plenty of water with them.

Rising as abruptly as it does from the surrounding plains, it is easy to understand why the Spitzkoppe – a volcanic granite 'Matterhorn', capped with 700 m-high sheer, naked stone – draws expert rock climbers, photographers, artists and nature lovers. Although the Spitzkoppe is a challenge to mountaineers, the impressive granite dome-shaped mountain does not present any opportunities for serious hikers. Many hours can, however, be spent exploring the fascinating rock formations and interesting flora.

8. TSAOBIS-LEOPARD NATURE PARK
NEAR KARIBIB

Trail details: Rambling anywhere in the reserve is permitted; 1-hour walks to 2-day hikes are possible.

Permits/bookings: Tsaobis-Leopard Nature Park, tel. (062252) 1304; PO Box 143, Karibib 9000, Namibia.

Facilities/amenities: There are 10 fully self-contained bungalows; swimming pool.

Main attractions: Chuos mountains; wildlife; wide, open spaces.

Pertinent information: Hikers who wish to camp out in the park overnight must give the manager at least two weeks' notice so that water points can be organized. Hikers should always carry plenty of water with them. Spring and autumn are the best months for walking, when the days are hot and the nights cool. In winter there is a possibility of pre-dawn temperatures falling to below freezing. Rain is possible from October to December (short rains) and mid-January to April (frequent thunderstorms).

To visit the 35 000-ha Tsaobis-Leopard Nature Park, travel south from Karibib for 52 km to the Swakop River bridge – the entrance to the park is 800 m beyond the bridge on the right-hand side. Within the main camp, there are several species of wild animals (in large enclosures) which have been hand-reared and are therefore approachable for photographs.

Mountain zebra, kudu, gemsbok, springbok, klipspringer and giraffe are all present in the park and may be seen by trailists.

The park was established in 1969 by Dr August Juchli, a Swiss conservationist, for the breeding and studying of leopards. However, due to years of drought, leopards are not readily observed on trails.

All walks start and end at the main camp.

A natural arch in the Spitzkoppe reveals a view of the Pondok Mountains.

9. DAAN VILJOEN GAME PARK
NEAR WINDHOEK

Trail details: 1. Wag-'n-Bietjie Trail: 3 km/ 1-1,5 hours, open-ended; 2. Rooibos Trail: 9 km/ 3,5 hours, circular. Rambling anywhere in the reserve is permitted.

Permits/bookings: Hikers obtain a permit at the park office on arrival.

Facilities/amenities: Bungalows; caravan and camp sites; picnic sites; restaurant and shop; swimming pool; trees labelled with their national tree list numbers.

Main attractions: Abundant wildlife and birdlife, especially when the dam is full; game-viewing drives; fishing.

Pertinent information: Winter nights can be extremely cold. April to September are the best months for walking in the area.

Situated 24 km west of Windhoek at an altitude of 2 000 m, the Daan Viljoen Game Park is an excellent stopover *en route* to other hiking and scenic areas in Namibia.

Essentially an area for rambling, bird-watching and game-viewing, the reserve is bounded in the west by the rolling hills of the Khomas plateau and in the east by the Windhoek Valley. Hikers are likely to see a number of the mammals that typify the Namibian highlands – mountain zebra, gemsbok, kudu, blue wildebeest, red hartebeest, eland, springbok, impala and baboon. Bush-dwelling birds and waterfowl are also attractions and the best places for bird-watching are around the dam and the rest camp area.

The **Wag-'n-Bietjie Trail** is very easy, and is especially suitable for families with children, while the **Rooibos Trail** is slightly more difficult. Both are clearly marked.

The vegetation of this reserve is mostly highveld savannah with occasional low trees and shrubs.

In Daan Viljoen Game Park – water in a dry land.

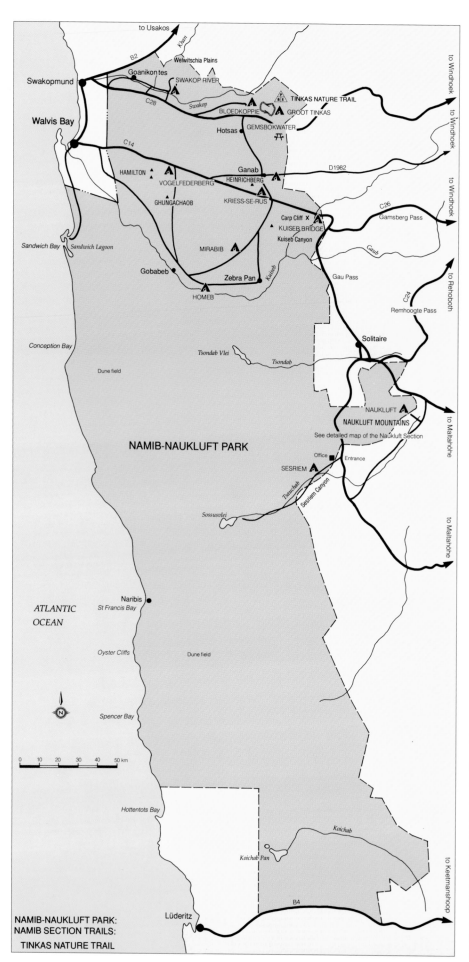

NAMIB-NAUKLUFT PARK:
NAMIB SECTION TRAILS:
TINKAS NATURE TRAIL

10. HOCHLAND VENTURE TRAILS
NEAR WINDHOEK

Trail details: Day walk: 6 km/3 hours; overnight route: 30 km/4 days, with shorter options; both are circular. See map p. 282.

Permits/bookings: Must be obtained from Hochland Venture Trails, tel. (061) 64285; PO Box 2869, Windhoek. Brochure available on request.

Facilities/amenities: The lodge at the farm is equipped with all facilities for 10 hikers; overnight shelters on the trail offer protection from rain and wind, and braai facilities, toilet and shower.

Main attractions: Gamsberg; flora and fauna, including Hartmann's mountain zebra, kudu, gemsbok, steenbok and grey duiker.

Pertinent information: There is a limit of 10 hikers at one time. Open all year round, November to March can be extremely hot; hikers should always take plenty of water and sunhats with them. Medical health certificates and indemnification are required. Horse riding trails can be arranged on request.

Hochland Venture Trails operate from the farm Okasume in the Khomas Hochland, approximately 130 km west of Windhoek. Visitors travel along the Daan Viljoen main road from Windhoek for 112 km, and then take the turn-off southwards for a further 18 km until the farm is reached.

The trails afford hikers an ideal opportunity to experience the fascinating scenery and flora typical of the Khomas Hochland, an upland plateau which lies some 1 800 m above sea level. Along the route hikers are rewarded with expansive views of the Namib Desert to the west, and the 2 347-m high Gamsberg (a familiar landmark in the Khomas Hochland) to the south. On account of the undulating terrain traversed on the overnight route, only fit hikers should select this option.

11. NAMIB-NAUKLUFT PARK, NAMIB SECTION
WEST-CENTRAL NAMIBIA

Trail details: Tinkas Nature Trail: 15 km/4-5 hours, circular; walking opportunities at Sandwich Lagoon, Sesriem Canyon, Sossusvlei and Kuiseb Canyon.

Permits/bookings: Permits are necessary to camp at designated camp sites or when travelling on signposted roads in the Namib section of the park; make enquiries with Ministry of Wildlife, Conservation and Tourism, tel. (061) 63131; Private Bag 13346, Windhoek. Permits not required by travellers using proclaimed roads passing through the park. Permits to visit Sandwich Lagoon are available from various sources in Swakopmund and Walvis Bay; no camping allowed.

Facilities/amenities: Camp sites in the Namib section of the park usually do not have firewood or water. However, shaded camp sites with tapped water, fireplaces, hot and cold water ablutions, as well as a petrol station, are available at Sesriem.

Main attractions: Coastal desert and escarpment, including Sandwich Lagoon, Sossusvlei, Kuiseb and Sesriem canyons.

Pertinent information: A fourwheel drive vehicle is required to reach the start of the Tinkas Trail, as well as Sandwich Lagoon and Sossusvlei.

A long, long trail – soon to be erased by the winds – marks the dune crest at Sossusvlei.

In 1978 the borders of the Namib Park and the high-land plateau of the Naukluft Mountain Zebra Park were 'merged' to form one huge reserve, covering an area of over 2 million ha. The park was further enlarged to almost 5 million ha in 1986 when Consolidated Diamond Mines made available formerly restricted diamond territories to the south-west. The Namib is the world's oldest and driest desert; its annual rainfall of less than 25 mm falls mostly in brief cloudbursts.

Of particular interest in the Namib section are Sandwich Lagoon, Sossusvlei, Sesriem Canyon and Kuiseb Canyon, which are richly endowed with unusual wildlife such as the barking gecko (heard at night), the desert gerbil, and the Namaqua chameleon, which preys on desert toktokkies (a species of wingless tenebrionid beetle).

Rambling is allowed at all the above-mentioned places in the Namib section of the park, provided that you have obtained the necessary permit.

The clearly marked **Tinkas Nature Trail**, starting and ending near Groot Tinkas in the north of the park, is a fairly strenuous trail which enables the fit visitor to explore this fascinating area on foot. The route traverses the Namib plains, winding past weathered granite rock formations and along usually dry river courses. Typical Namib vegetation can be seen, as can some of the smaller creatures inhabiting the area. **Sesriem Canyon** lies

4 km south of the delightful camp site, on the edge of a vast dune field. A track leading from the car park allows you to walk up the 1-km gorge, which contains a natural swimming pool after good rains. The gorge is 30 m deep in places and narrows to just 2 m wide.

The final 5 km to **Sossusvlei**, a clay pan 65 km south-west of Sesriem, can be undertaken only in a fourwheel drive vehicle; the tourist office at Sesriem must be advised of your anticipated departure and return times. The huge crested dunes in the vicinity are best seen – or explored – at sunrise.

A fourwheel drive vehicle is also essential to reach **Sandwich Lagoon,** a birder's paradise covering about 20 km^2. At the fence to the north of the lagoon you are free to explore the shore on foot, provided you do not disturb the birdlife.

Twenty kilometres west of the Kuiseb Canon camp site is the turn off to the **Carp Cliff** viewpoint, providing spectacular views of the Kuiseb Valley and the Great Escarpment. A 15-minute walk from here leads to a large overhanging cliff, Carp Cliff, where two German geologists who feared internment during World War II lived, with their dog, for over 2 years in a hostile environment; they described the experience in *The Sheltering Desert*. The Kuiseb Canyon and Valley is inhabited by mountain zebra, gemsbok, springbok, klipspringer, leopard and brown hyaena.

Only the hardiest plant-forms survive in the Namib.

Rocky terrain on the Olive Trail in the Namib-Naukluft Park.

12. NAMIB-NAUKLUFT PARK, NAUKLUFT SECTION
WEST-CENTRAL NAMIBIA

Trail details: 1. Naukluft Hiking Trail: 120 km/ 8 days, as well as shorter options, including a 58-km/4-day option; 2. Waterkloof Trail: 13 km/5 to 6 hours; 3. Olive Trail: 10 km/4-5 hours. All are circular.

Permits/bookings: Permits for the Naukluft Hiking Trail, as well as bookings (well in advance) for the Naukluft camp site, must be obtained from the Director of Tourism, Reservations, tel. (061) 36975; Private Bag 13267, Windhoek.

Facilities/amenities: Naukluft camp site has hot and cold showers, toilets, fireplaces, firewood and dishwashing facilities; during the trail hikers sleep in rustic shelters, with drinking water but no wood; take camp-stoves.

Main attractions: The Naukluft Mountain massif; spectacular scenery; endemic Hartmann's mountain zebra; interesting birdlife.

Pertinent information: Medical forms are forwarded with confirmation of reservation for the Naukluft Hiking Trail, and should be completed by a medical doctor not more than 40 days prior to the trail date; these forms must be handed in at the start of the trail. A minimum of 3 and a maximum of 12 people per day are permitted on the Naukluft Hiking Trail. Hikers should take as much water as they can carry. Camp-stoves are required as there is no wood. The trails are open from 1 March to 31 October each year.

The **Naukluft Hiking Trail**, Namibia's first official hiking trail, opened in June 1989, takes hikers over extremely rugged, mountainous terrain where, on average, distances covered are around 15 km each day. The hike begins from the Naukluft camp site and follows the dry riverbed of the Naukluft for

a few kilometres before climbing up a barren mountain, where the terrain levels out, affording the opportunity to absorb the magnificent views of the Naukluft Valley far below. Shortly afterwards, a steep ascent takes hikers up Heartbreak Pass.

The second day's route also starts with a fairly steep ascent, but then continues along undulating terrain to Bergpos. Cathedral Fountain, about 20 minutes from Bergpos, is a good place for a rest before descending Ubusis Kloof. Here, several waterfalls must be negotiated, and a fair amount of boulder-hopping is necessary.

The third leg of the trail takes hikers back up Ubusis Kloof to Bergpos, and follows an easy route across the plateau to the overnight shelter. After about half of the fourth day's hike, a steep descent takes hikers into the main valley, where boulder-hopping is again necessary. The final 2 km of Day 4 is along a gravel road leading to the overnight stop. Day 5 begins with a steep ascent up Broekskeur and passes over hills dotted with kokerboom trees, moringas and euphorbias. The final

11 km of this route follow a flat jeep track to the overnight shelter.

The sixth day's route is very exacting indeed. It climbs steeply up the river valley before descending to Tufa Tavern where hikers spend the night. The second-last day of the trail takes hikers up to the plateau, and then along to Bakenkop, the highest point on the trail, where the views are quite spectacular.

The final day's route leads along undulating, seemingly endless hills and down a tributary of the Naukluft River, where several fascinating tufa formations ('waterfall limestone' containing inviting pools) can be seen. From these formations, it is a 20-minute walk to the end of the trail.

The two circular day walks marked out for visitors to the Naukluft camp site are the **Waterkloof Trail**, which starts at the camp site, and the **Olive Trail**, which is signposted about 3 km from the park office. Both trails are quite strenuous, and hikers should carry at least 2 litres of water per person.

Map

NAMIB-NAUKLUFT PARK: NAUKLUFT SECTION TRAILS
NAUKLUFT HIKING TRAIL
WATERKLOOF TRAIL
OLIVE TRAIL

NAMIB-NAUKLUFT PARK: NAUKLUFT SECTION

to Walvis Bay
Solitaire
Abbabis
C14
NAUKLUFT MOUNTAINS
Bullsport
to Maltahöhe
Also refer to Namib Section map
C36
Quartz Valley
TUFA
Tufa Cave
DIE VALLE
BAKENKOP
Melkbosvlakte
KAPOKVLAKTE
Never Ending Hills
WATERKLOOF TRAIL
OLIVE TRAIL
Office
Broekskeur
Entrance
NAUKLUFT HIKING TRAIL
TSAMS-OST
NAUKLUFT
Zebrakloof
Heartbreak Pass
ADLERHORST
Koedoevlakte
PUTTE
Ubusis Kloof
BERGPOS
Cathedral Fountain
to Sesriem/Solitaire Road
UBUSIS
D854
to Sesriem/Maltahöhe
to C36
0 2 4 6 8 10 12 14 16 km

13. HARDAP RESORT AND GAME PARK
NEAR MARIENTAL

Trail details: A day walk with 9-km/3-hour or 15-km/5-hour options; circular.

Permits/bookings: Not required if staying at the resort, otherwise must be obtained from the Ministry of Tourism, Reservations; tel. (061) 36975; Private Bag 13267, Windhoek.

Facilities/amenities: Game-viewing drives; fishing; rest camp with bungalows, restaurant, and caravan and camp sites; watersports.

Main attractions: Rich birdlife on the dam; scenic setting of stone koppies and thorn trees.

Pertinent information: Hikers should always take plenty of water with them. April to September provide the best walking conditions here, with warm days and the possibility of pre-dawn temperatures falling to below freezing. Short rains are possible from October to December, and from mid-January to April thunderstorms occur.

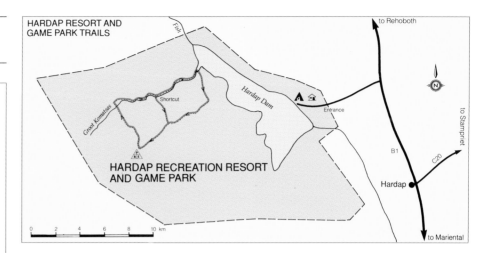

Hardap Resort and Game Park is reached by travelling north on the B1 road from Mariental. The trail, which is defined by yellow footprint markers, is situated in the north-western part of the game park, and leads through rocky, mountainous terrain and riverbeds. The ruins of Namibia's first school can be seen along the way.

The park plays host to red hartebeest, Hartmann's mountain zebra and birds of prey. Black rhino have been reintroduced into the park and hikers should be aware of their presence and steer clear of these irascible creatures.

14. OAS HIKING TRAIL
OAS HOLIDAY FARM, SOUTHERN NAMIBIA

Trail details: 36 km/3 days; circular. No map available.

Permits/bookings: Book with Mantie Oberholzer, tel. (06342) ask for 4321 Stinkdoring; PO Box 4, Karasburg 9000.

Facilities/amenities: Base hut accommodating 11 hikers, with mattresses and hot water; kitchen hut with a stove and refrigerator; overnight huts with braai facilities; veld toilet and drinking water.

Main attractions: Karas mountains; 27 natural pools; birdlife; game.

Pertinent information: There is a minimum of 3 and a maximum of 11 hikers for this trail. Hikers should always take plenty of water and a sunhat with them.

The OAS Hiking Trail is situated on the 12 016-ha OAS Holiday Farm, 84 km from Karasburg on the road between the Kalahari Gemsbok National Park and Ai-Ais. The route, which traverses the Karas Mountains, is not particularly strenuous – the distances covered each day are 12,5 km, 11 km, and 10 km respectively and water is available on each of the 3 days.

Along the way hikers may spot rosyfaced lovebirds and the magnificent black eagle, as well as herds of kudu and gemsbok. Smaller game such as springbok, steenbok and klipspringer also live here. Camel thorn trees grow along the seasonal water courses.

The trail, which is clearly defined with horse motifs, is open from 1 April to 31 October each year, although the holiday farm itself is open year-round.

Rock and water in bright sunshine along the day walk in the Hardap Game Park.

15. FISH RIVER CANYON
SOUTHERN NAMIBIA

Trail details: 90 km/5 days (80 km/4 days if the short cuts are followed); open-ended.

Permits/bookings: These must be obtained well in advance (18 months) from The Director of Tourism, Reservations, tel. (061) 36975; Private Bag 13267, Windhoek. Map and brochure available on request. A medical certificate is required.

Facilities/amenities: Hobas camp site, conveniently situated at the start of the trail, has 12 sites, a swimming pool, communal ablution facilities and a small kiosk; there are no facilities on the trail.

Main attractions: Spectacular and unique canyon scenery; hot springs; wilderness atmosphere.

Pertinent information: This is a very demanding trail and should under no circumstances be attempted by beginner or unfit hikers who do not have a high degree of heat tolerance. Medical forms forwarded with confirmation of the reservation should be completed by a medical doctor not more than 40 days prior to the trail date. These forms must be handed in at the start of the trail. Day-time temperatures in this area are high, even in winter, when the nights are cold. There is a minimum of 3 and a maximum of 40 hikers for this trail at any one time. Hikers should always take plenty of water as the supply varies with rainfall. Mosquitoes can be a problem at times. The hiking season is from May to the end of August.

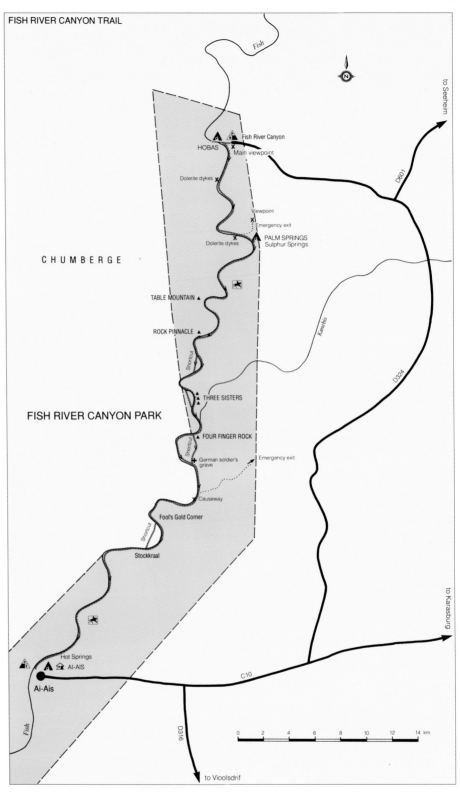

FISH RIVER CANYON TRAIL

A 'chain gang' descending into the Fish River Canyon.

Descending into geological history, experiencing magnificent sunrises and sunsets, being totally surrounded by the Fish River's sensational wind- and water-hewn sculptures: this is what hiking the Fish River Canyon is all about, an endeavour which will always remain one of the 'specials' in your trailing accomplishments.

The Fish River rises in the Naukluft mountains, south-east of Swakopmund, and travels 800 km before flowing into the Orange River. For approximately 65 km along its route, the river has sliced an impressive gash through the surrounding plateau. The canyon itself is a combination of two geological processes: the upper section, a huge trough with a flattish floor, is the result of faulting, while the lower is attributed to water erosion as the Fish River has cut back into the upper canyon's floor. Many other natural eroding forces, such as sand-blasting winds, have worked on the canyon's sides, carving out crags, buttresses and turrets in the ancient rock strata. These eroding forces reveal, in the deepest parts, the Archaean granite and

A bend in the river. All the lonely, rocky vastness of the mighty Fish River Canyon.

gneisses of the Basement Complex – of rock more than 1 800-million years old.

The hike officially begins at the main viewing point, about 80 km north of Ai-Ais, where you scramble down an eroded track for approximately 45 to 90 minutes to the canyon's floor. Once you arrive at the Fish River, simply follow its meandering course, zigzagging across the stream to be on whichever bank offers the easiest walking. The hike is slightly downhill all the way; the only factors presenting physical difficulties are the stretches of small round rock or soft sandy banks. The amount of water in the riverbed often determines the mood of the hike, the difficulty of the river crossings and the quantities of water hikers must carry. On very hot days, walking should be limited to between dawn and 11.00 am and after 3.00 pm.

Although there are no obligatory overnight stops, the best areas are obvious. The most used is an area of hot sulphur springs among some isolated palm trees. These palms are believed to have been planted during the First World War by escaping German prisoners.

There are plenty of birds in the canyon, especially water-associated species such as the fish eagle and pied kingfisher. Mammals are not frequently seen but it is possible to spot klipspringer, dassie, baboon and mountain zebra. Fishermen may try their luck for yellowfish, catfish, carp or blue kurper, while hikers more interested in plants can identify the scattered vegetation which varies from the unusual kokerboom and wild fig to the many species of thorn tree.

Most hikers terminate their hike where the river reaches Ai-Ais, a thermal spring rich in mineral waters around which a resort has been built.

The beach and eroded slopes and rockfaces show the heights from which the Fish River carved its canyon.

BOTSWANA

Botswana is synonymous with wilderness. The country's 580 000-km² area is bordered by Namibia in the west, Zimbabwe in the east and South Africa in the south. This vast area is inhabited by less than one million people; a commendable 17 per cent of the country is under the control of the Department of Wildlife and National Parks. Here roam the greatest wildlife herds in southern Africa, together with varied birdlife.

Although landlocked, Botswana boasts the world's largest inland delta. The Okavango, drowning 16 000 km² of potential desert, receives floodwaters from the Angolan highlands, 1 000 km away. These waters transform the delta into a paradise of animals and tropical plants, with ecosystems as varied as dry savannah and riparian woodland, mopane forest, reedbeds and permanent swamp. The waterless Kalahari, covering two-thirds of the country, contains grassed and bare pans, dry riverbeds and grasslands, all rich in wildlife.

Entry to Botswana requires a valid passport or travel document for some non-South African and non-Commonwealth nationals. Visas must be obtained before entering the country, as they are not available at the border. Visitors are required to pass through a border post or an airport which is gazetted as a port of entry.

The rains fall as short thunderstorms from November to March or April, and the temperature ranges from 38 °C in the day to 19 °C at night. In the dry winter (May to September), when skies are clear, temperatures may reach 28 °C, but sometimes fall to below freezing at night.

Although you can travel farthest in the delta in late June and July, other months have their advantages: birdlife excels from November to April and tigerfish bite in October; October and November are probably the best months for game-viewing. Flood waters reach Shakawe in January/February and Maun in around June.

LEFT: *Small in a vast landscape – Tuli Block elephants at home.*

One way of crossing the Limpopo is by Mashatu's cableway.

1. MASHATU GAME RESERVE
EASTERN BOTSWANA

Trail details: Guided walks. See map p. 294.

Permits/bookings: Facilities at this reserve are available only to guests, hence a booking is essential. Contact Rattray Reserves, tel. (011) 7892677; PO Box 2575, Randburg 2125.

Facilities/amenities: Majale Lodge provides luxurious, all-inclusive accommodation, swimming pools and a conference room; bush camps offer luxury tents.

Main attractions: Game-viewing drives; night game-viewing with a spotlight; wide variety of wildlife; 375 species of birds.

Pertinent information: Casual visitors are not admitted to the reserve. The maximum number of guests at any one time is 30. Take precautions against malaria. Visitors must be in possession of all necessary travel documents.

Mashatu Game Reserve, covering some 30 000 ha, is one of the largest privately owned conservation areas in southern Africa. Located in the north-eastern Tuli Enclave, this area lies between the Shashe and Limpopo rivers in southern Botswana, 600 km north of Johannesburg via Pietersburg to Pont Drift. The adjacent area in Zimbabwe is known as the Tuli Conservation Area. Road access is from either South Africa via Alldays, or from Gaborone; alternatively, customs and immigration clearance can be arranged for those guests choosing to fly in to the local airfield.

The Tuli Enclave is steeped in history. Inhabited by the Maphungubwe tribe during the Iron Age, once a hunting ground of the legendary Frederick Courteney Selous, and having close historical associations with ancient Zimbabwean cultures, the area boasts many artefacts left by hunters, prospectors and missionaries.

The reserve encompasses a great diversity of landscapes, consisting mostly of acacia woodland and mopane, grassland and some riverine forest.

Renowned for its large elephant population of some 600 animals, Mashatu is home to other large mammals, including lion, leopard, jackal, cheetah, sable, eland, impala, wildebeest, waterbuck and buffalo. The reserve is a paradise for bird-watchers with 375 species having been recorded. Guests have the opportunity to see the wildlife at close proximity by participating in either game-drives or guided walks that are conducted by the reserve's experienced staff. Part of the 5-day Rhino and Elephant Trail also operates within the reserve's boundaries (see next entry).

Summers last from October until April; it is very hot and the area receives most of its annual rainfall at this time. Winters days are generally warm, but nights can be cold.

SAFARIS IN BOTSWANA

There are no self-guided, constructed hiking trails or walks in Botswana. Most of the country is a vast wilderness, alive with game, birds and smaller forms of life. Crocodiles and hippos are plentiful in the rivers. While the aim of the trailist in Botswana should be intimate encounters with nature, walking without a guide is not advisable. It is very difficult however, for a private party to organize a canoeing trip or safari on their own.

Canoeing is restricted to the rivers; canoes are not viable and not permitted in the swamps. The only way to negotiate the Okavango Swamps and its floodplains, which are dominated by high reeds and choked with vegetation that wraps around paddles, is by mokoro. These locally-made dugouts are guided by skilled and experienced polers.

To find a safari company that best suits your needs, contact a reputable travel agent who will be able to recommend experienced safari operators. Most companies boast 'the ultimate safari programme and services of professional game rangers and camp staff'. Activities during safaris usually include walking, boating, game-viewing drives and bird-watching.

A baobab keeps watch over mounds of rock that suggest some ancient lost city of the wilds.

2. THE RHINO AND ELEPHANT TRAIL
LAPALALA WILDERNESS/MASHATU GAME RESERVE

Trail details: 5-day guided trail. See map p. 294.

Permits/bookings: Can be obtained from the Wilderness Trust of Southern Africa, tel. (011) 4537645, fax (011) 4537649; PO Box 645, Bedfordview 2008. A brochure and rates are available on request.

Facilities/amenities: Luxury safari tents with *en suite* bathroom facilities; all food, and transport from and to Johannesburg is provided by the trail organizers; evening meal in a boma.

Main attractions: Elephants and other large animals; prolific birdlife; ruins and artefacts of archaeological interest.

Pertinent information: Group size is limited to a maximum of 8 people. Participants must have valid passports and visas for entry into Botswana (and re-entry to South Africa, where applicable). Wear neutral-coloured clothing. Precautions against malaria are necessary. Ticks are prevalent. Both Lapalala Wilderness and Mashatu Game Reserve are privately owned and casual visitors will not be admitted.

This 5-day guided trail comprises 2 sections, the first being the Rhino Trail which takes place in the Lapalala Wilderness in the northern Transvaal (for details see page 249).

On the third morning of the trail, members of the group are taken on a short drive across the South African border into the vast open spaces of Botswana's Mashatu Game Reserve (see previous entry), which is located in the north-eastern Tuli Enclave.

This trail can be arranged to suit the interests of the individual group. From the camp you explore the surrounding area, in the company of a guide,

Sabre-horned gemsbok breast the tall grass in the Central Kalahari Game Reserve.

both on foot and by open fourwheel drive vehicle, returning to base each night. A minimum distance of approximately 10 km is covered each day.

The 30 000-ha reserve is famous for its large herds of elephant, which can be seen anywhere in the area; however, they are particularly easy to spot during the dry season when they come to drink at the pools along the banks of the Limpopo River. Summers (from October to April) are hot and humid with much of the annual rainfall occurring during these months; winters are warm and dry, although nights are cold.

The trail, which requires a medium level of fitness, is best from February to November.

3. KALAHARI BUSHMAN HIKING TRAIL
NORTH-WEST OF GABORONE

Trail details: 7-day guided tour, which includes 40 km of walking. See map p. 294.

Permits/bookings: A booking is essential; contact the Taaibos Hiking Trail, tel. (0200) and ask for Bulgerivier 222 (after hours); PO Box 185, Vaalwater 0530. Alternatively write to Kalahari Bushman Trails, PO Box 110, Mahalapye, Botswana. A brochure and rates are available on request from these addresses.

Facilities/amenities: Tour organizers provide all transport, tents (which must be shared), mattresses, chairs and cooking utensils.

Main attractions: Central Kalahari Game Reserve; opportunity to observe the traditional Bushman way of life; wildlife.

Pertinent information: You must supply your own food and refreshments, bedding, water bottle and medical supplies. The trail operates once a fortnight from April to September only. Ensure that you have the correct travel documentation for entry into Botswana and return to South Africa. Anti-malaria precautions are necessary.

This unusual trail combines travelling in a fourwheel drive vehicle to interesting places that you then explore on foot. The route starts on Day 1 at the base camp of the Taaibos Hiking Trail near Vaalwater (see page 248). Fourwheel drive vehicles are loaded up here in preparation for an early start the next morning.

On the second day you are driven to Dithopo Ranch in Botswana via Mahalapye; this stop is your last chance to get provisions for the remainder of the journey. Dithopo Ranch in the Kalahari is a government project, set up to farm game. It is here that you have the chance to enjoy your first walk of 4 km, with the possibility of spotting eland.

Day 3 commences with a 10-km walk through the ranch grounds before you leave Dithopo to

People of the land, this young Bushman family has decided to settle long enough to require a shelter.

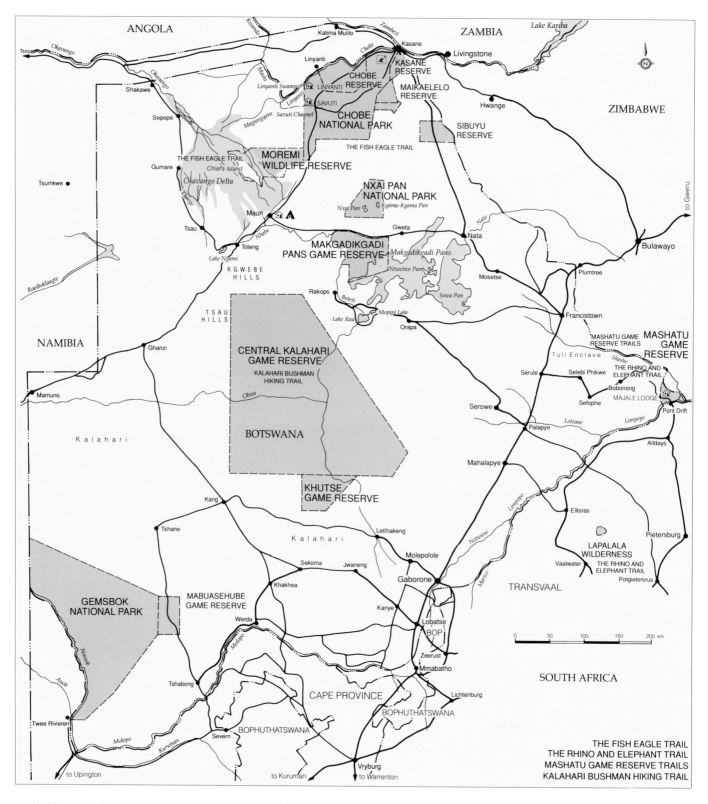

travel 150 km to the Central Kalahari Game
Reserve. This 51 800-km^2 game reserve is still
home to groups of Bushmen, so there is very
limited public access. Only a restricted number of
scientists and a small number of tour operators are
permitted entry; anyone found in the area without
permission is liable for severe penalties. Overnight
camp is at Xuba-Xuba where a Kalahari Bushman guide has erected several Bushman
shelters, which provide alternative accommodation
to tents.

The highlight of the following day is a 10-km
walk with Togela as guide. This is an opportunity
to see how the Bushmen survive in this harsh
environment without food and water, to observe
their hunting skills, and to spot some of the
animals that share this reserve with them – blue
wildebeest, gemsbok, springbok, eland, lion,
cheetah, wild dog, leopard and hyaena. A game-
viewing drive in the evening offers a further chance
to view local wildlife. Overnight camp is again
at Xuba-Xuba.

Day 5 sees another move, this time to set up
camp at Lebong Pan 100 km from Xuba-Xuba. An
8-km walk around the edge of the pan offers the
chance of spotting red hartebeest, ostrich, vulture
and ground squirrel.

Heading back towards South Africa, Day 6
involves a 200-km drive to the Limpopo Valley,
where you can enjoy an 8-km walk among the
wildlife. The last evening of the trip is spent
camping on the riverbanks, before you return to
Taaibos base camp the following day.

Lily pads and leisure in the great maze of waterways that is the immense inland delta of Okavango.

4. THE FISH EAGLE TRAIL
OKAVANGO SWAMPS/CHOBE NATIONAL PARK OR LINYANTI

Trail details: 5-day guided trail.

Permits/bookings: Book with the Wilderness Trust of Southern Africa, tel. (011) 4537645; PO Box 645, Bedfordview 2008. A brochure is available.

Facilities/amenities: Food and utensils, camping equipment, mosquito nets, sleeping bags, linen, mattresses and tents, showers and toilets. Flights from Johannesburg via Maun to the Okavango Delta are included in the cost of the trail.

Main attractions: Okavango wilderness; canoeing in dugouts through the Okavango Delta, one of the richest areas in Africa for wildlife and birdlife.

Pertinent information: Groups are restricted to a maximum of 8 people. Trails depart from Johannesburg at 6.00 am on scheduled dates from April to October. Take precautions against malaria. Binoculars, insect repellent and sunscreen lotion are recommended. Maximum baggage allowance is 7 kg; a complimentary flight bag is provided. Khaki or neutral-coloured clothing is recommended. A valid passport and entry visa to Botswana are necessary. Non-South African citizens must ensure that they are in possession of a re-entry visa to South Africa. You must sign an indemnity form before participating in this trail.

The Okavango River, which rises in Angola and flows 1 000 km south towards the Kalahari, forms a 16 000-km^2 inland delta in its lower reaches. This is the venue of the Fish Eagle Trail. These immense swamplands house a wealth of fauna reputed to be unsurpassed elsewhere in Africa.

A 'wilderness trail' such as this, led by an experienced trails officer and tracker, is the best and safest way to enjoy the Okavango Swamps, especially if your time is limited. The venue is reached by air from Johannesburg, and from the bushveld airstrip in the swamps you travel by mokoro dugout to a secluded tract of land near Chief's Island, your sleeping base for your stay. Mornings are spent walking on different islands, afternoons in the dugouts exploring the swamps. Meals are prepared by your officer over an open fire.

Three habitat types – water channels and lagoons; bands of large forest trees and bushy swathes along waterways; and dry woodlands – provide myriad niches for the diversified and specialized fauna. The lechwe, a typical representative of the Okavango, provides a good example of such adaptation. This swamp-dwelling buck has well-developed lateral hooves which, by providing wider and more stable 'platforms', facilitate the animal's passage over marshy terrain.

The Fish Eagle Trail also includes 2 days at either Savuti in the Chobe National Park, or at nearby Linyanti. The choice of which destination to visit is arranged with the trail organizers according to your preference. From either Savuti or Linyanti, you can enjoy game-drives; however, walking is not permitted within the boundaries of Chobe National Park. Lion are often seen at Savuti, as well as spotted hyaena, cheetah and wild dog.

If you choose to explore Linyanti, you will be able to participate in guided walks, enjoy barge trips on the Linyanti River and try your hand at fishing for tigerfish, bream and barbel. The twisting waterways of the river, lined with papyrus and wild date palms, also conceal hippo and crocodile. There are over 300 species of birds in the area including the African hawk eagle, scarletchested sunbird, white pelican and carmine bee-eater.

Covering an area of 12 000 km^2, Chobe National Park is mostly flat. It includes a number of natural pans which are dry for much of the year. Surface water is provided by the Chobe and Linyanti rivers during the dry season. Chobe has a large elephant population, and is also home to herds of buffalo and white rhino. Sable and roan antelope, oribi, blue wildebeest and Chobe bushbuck can also be seen, as well as the puku, an antelope which is restricted to flood plains and not known in any other location south of the Zambezi.

ZIMBABWE

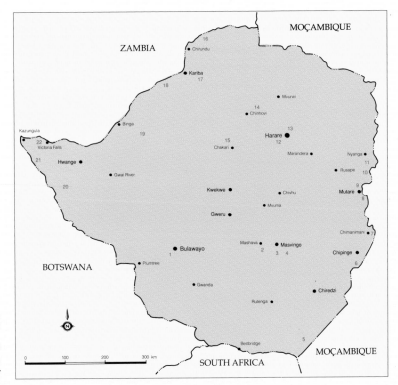

Zimbabwe, with its huge land mass of 390 245 km^2 (the equivalent area of the American state of California and three times the size of England), has gradually, since attaining independence in 1980, regained its former reputation as one of Africa's most lovely, diverse and hospitable outdoor attractions. Zimbabwe is landlocked between Zambia and Mozambique in the north and east, and Botswana and South Africa in the west and south. Twelve per cent of the land is preserved for parks and game sanctuaries, a heritage providing endless opportunities for rambling, wilderness backpacking and game-viewing on foot.

Here you will find the exquisite Victoria Falls; the Hwange National Park, an elephant haven; wildlife-rich Lake Kariba and its surrounding bushveld reserves; the Great Zimbabwe national monument (Zimbabwe Ruins);

highveld semi-urban parks; and the Eastern Highlands, the backpacker's mecca where mountain wonderlands such as the Chimanimanis beckon the energetic. Canoeing and white-water rafting trips have also been introduced on the mighty Zambezi River.

Visitors staying less than six months enter Zimbabwe with few formalities: a valid passport, return ticket or enough money to purchase one, and visas for certain nationals. If entering Zimbabwe by car, ensure that your vehicle's documentation is in order, as long delays can result if this is not correct.

Zimbabwe's climate is subtropical. The coldest months are between May and August,

when the temperature averages 13 °C, dropping in the highlands. The hot season is from September to December; October and November are the hottest months, with temperatures often reaching more than 32 °C. The rains begin in November and end in mid-March. Average annual rainfall varies between 300 and 1 500 millimetres.

Unfortunately incidences of theft from tourists have become more common in Zimbabwe, so visitors should never leave valuables or possessions in unattended vehicles. Also be aware that bilharzia is possible in all rivers and dams and therefore swimming in and drinking these waters should be avoided. Malaria is also a serious problem. It is essential to obtain current information on which medication is necessary and to take reasonable precautions to avoid being bitten.

LEFT: *Below the falls on the Inyangombe River, msasa trees grow thickly around the ripple-swept pool.*

Like bold cuboid sculpture, balancing rocks in Matobo National Park take on the shapes the viewer wants to see.

1. MATOBO NATIONAL PARK
NEAR BULAWAYO

Trail details: A network of marked trails.

Permits/bookings: Reservations for accommmodation can be made through the Department of National Parks and Wild Life Management, tel. (092634) 706077; PO Box 8151, Causeway, Harare.

Facilities/amenities: Chalets which are fully equipped, except for cutlery and crockery; camp and caravan sites, with ablution blocks; picnic sites; tennis court; shop selling groceries, tinned goods, bread and milk; fishing, with permit, is allowed in the dams.

Main attractions: High granite outcrops weathered into scenic formations; caves with Bushman paintings; 300 species of birds; abundant wildlife.

Pertinent information: All waters in the park are infested with bilharzia. Boil all drinking water. Beware of snakes, particularly the black mamba. Winter is mild, with sunny days and cool nights; thunderstorms are common in summer during the rainy season (December to mid-March). Visitors should ensure they have sufficient petrol with them, as the nearest service station is in Bulawayo.

Matobo National Park lies 54 km south of Bulawayo. A corruption of an Ndebele term, Matobo means 'the bald heads', an appropriate description of the ancient boulder-strewn granite hills of the park. The powerful feeling of primeval wilderness is reinforced by the world-famous balancing rock formations, worn into their weird shapes by more than 2 000 million years of erosion.

The geology of the region is fascinating, and the Matobo National Park is also a naturalist's delight, with a myriad of intriguing discoveries awaiting the enthusiastic rambler. Black eagles abound; the park has the densest eagle population known anywhere in the world. This is not surprising as the rocky terrain provides an ideal habitat for the dassie, the almost exclusive prey of this raptor. Martial and crowned eagles also occur, but only in small numbers. Also prolific are klipspringer and *Platysaurus capensis*, the teasingly tame, rainbow-coloured rock lizard.

Some 300 species of birds have been recorded in the park. In addition to the 32 species of raptors breeding in the Matobo Hills, another interesting resident of the area is the boulder chat. This is one of the few areas in southern Africa where this species can be seen.

Acacia-mopane woodland lies thickly in the valleys, while aloes, cycads and numerous wildflowers flourish in the rocky terrain.

Within the boundaries of the park is a 16 500-ha game park which is home to a variety of game, including leopard, giraffe, black and white rhino, zebra, impala, warthog and sable. Entry permits can be obtained from the attendant at the park; however, due to the presence of potentially dangerous animals, walking is not allowed here.

The Matobos also contain huge caves, well decorated with fine examples of Bushman art, while World's View, the summit of the great granite dome, is the site of Cecil John Rhodes' grave, and that of his friend, Dr Leander Starr Jameson. Also buried here in a Grecian-style mausoleum are the remains of Allan Wilson and his men, who went in pursuit of Lobengula after the king fled Bulawayo in November 1893. They fought to the last man against a Matabele impi, and Cecil Rhodes decided to erect a memorial here in their courage. Here you may well encounter some of the rock lizards, which are almost tame and come swarming up to visitors in the hope of being fed.

Marked day walks to the cave paintings and a trail system provide opportunities for interesting rambles in some areas of the park.

2. MUSHANDIKE SANCTUARY
MUSHANDIKE DAM, MASVINGO

Trail details: Short rambles in the sanctuary.

Permits/bookings: A booking is required for the camp site; contact the Department of National Parks and Wild Life Management, tel. (092634) 706077; PO Box 8151, Causeway, Harare.

Facilities/amenities: Camp and caravan sites with fireplaces and communal ablution facilities; good gravel roads; fishing, with licence, in dam for black bass, bream and catfish.

Main attractions: Antelope and birdlife; irrigation dam; Bushman rock shelters; ecological training centre and wild herbivore domestication project.

Pertinent information: Although the access roads and internal roads in the sanctuary can be negotiated by all types of vehicles, they are subject to seasonal flooding. The sanctuary is open daily from sunrise to sunset.

Located 26 km west of Masvingo on the Zvishavane to Bulawayo road, is the 417-ha Mushandike Sanctuary. Rambling here is rather 'tame' compared with many of Zimbabwe's more remote parks. However, for the family or inexperienced trailist, walks through the *Brachystegia* woodlands, koppies and *Hyparrhenia* grasslands are enjoyable, and encounters with browsing animals such as sable, kudu, waterbuck, klipspringer, grysbok and duiker are likely, as are sightings of the large flocks of flamingoes. The Mushandike Dam attracts large numbers of waterfowl, such as Egyptian geese, herons, cormorants and redbilled teals.

Mushandike Sanctuary houses the Natural Resources College run by the Department of National Parks and Wild Life Management. It is also the site of a project to domesticate wild herbivores such as eland; this is the reason for the large paddocks in the sanctuary. Note that this area is not open to the public.

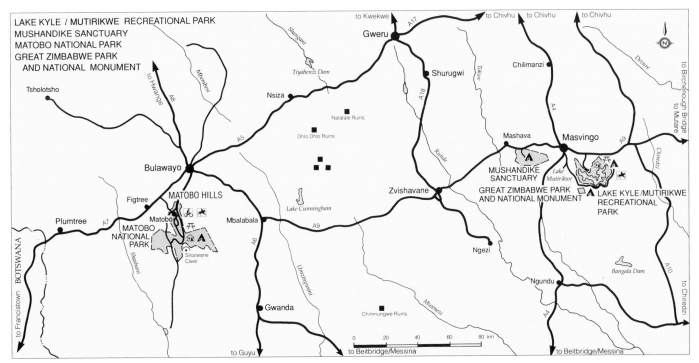

LAKE KYLE / MUTIRIKWE RECREATIONAL PARK
MUSHANDIKE SANCTUARY
MATOBO NATIONAL PARK
GREAT ZIMBABWE PARK
AND NATIONAL MONUMENT

3. GREAT ZIMBABWE PARK AND NATIONAL MONUMENT
MASVINGO

Trail details: Short walks around the ruins.

Permits/bookings: Not required.

Facilities/amenities: Camp and caravan site, with an ablution block; Site Museum.

Main attractions: Great Zimbabwe ruins; museum.

Pertinent information: The ruins are open daily from 8.00 am to 5.00 pm; the museum closes at 4.30 pm.

These immense ruins lie 27 km south-east of Masvingo. The most impressive single complex of ruins south of the Sahara Desert, these stone structures were built by the Karanga people between the 11th and 15th centuries AD. The city served as the capital of a kingdom that dominated the central plateau and both the ivory and gold trades, and is thought to have had a population of some 30 000 people. The ruins are dominated by a conical tower resembling a grain bin. This forms the centre of a complex including a large elliptical building, a wall and outer huts. The wall has a circumference of 249 m and is over 10 m high and 5 m thick in parts.

Visitors can wander at will around the ruins. One attractive route is up to the Acropolis where there are spectacular views of the main temple and nearby Lake Mutirikwe. As well as rambling around the ruins, visitors can learn more about the ancient city by viewing the interesting exhibits in the Site Museum, including displays of prehistory and history of Zimbabwe, local artefacts and Zimbabwe soapstone birds.

This is a good area to see bird species typical of *Miombo/Brachystegia* woodland. Watch out for Meyer's parrot, the blackcollared and crested barbets, greater honeyguide and miombo rock thrush. In summer, black saw-wing swallows breed around the edges of the woodland.

Science may have explained much of Great Zimbabwe, but the power and mystery still fascinate.

4. LAKE MUTIRIKWE RECREATIONAL PARK
SOUTH OF MASVINGO

Trail details: Game-viewing walks in designated areas. See map page 299.

Permits/bookings: For accommodation, contact the Department of National Parks and Wild Life Management, Tel. (092634) 706077; PO Box 8151, Causeway, Harare.

Facilities/amenities: Fully equipped lodges; camp and caravan sites; a number of privately owned resorts; picnic sites with ablution blocks; fishing with a permit is allowed.

Main attractions: Recreation area, including game enclosure; good bird-watching.

Pertinent information: Beware of crocodiles and bilharzia in the lake. The park is open daily from 6.00 am to 6.00 pm. The nearest shop and petrol station are in Masvingo.

Lake Mutirikwe (formerly known as Lake Kyle), Zimbabwe's second largest man-made lake, covers a total area of 16 900 ha. It is bordered on the north by a 8 900-ha game park. The rolling hills, covered by *Brachystegia* woodlands, koppie vegetation and grassland enhance the park's pleasant setting. Although kudu and reedbuck occur naturally, most antelope, buffalo, giraffe and other large species were introduced; the white rhinos, for instance, were brought all the way from Umfolozi Game Reserve in Natal (see page 190). Birdlife in the bays and inlets along the secluded wooded shores is abundant, and includes the whitebreasted cormorant, grey heron, Egyptian goose and fish eagle.

Rambling in this park is not strenuous, and is suitable for the family, the not-so-fit and the less experienced naturalist.

5. GONAREZHOU NATIONAL PARK
SOUTH-EAST ZIMBABWE

Trail details: 1. Mabalauta Trail: 4 days/3 nights; 2. Pombadzi Trail: 4 days/3 nights; 3. Sibonja Trail: 4 days/3 nights; 4. Rundi Trail: 5 days/ 4 nights. All are guided, circular. See map p. 302.

Permits/bookings: Required from the Department of National Parks and Wild Life Management, tel. (092634) 706077; PO Box 8151, Causeway, Harare.

Facilities/amenities: Game-viewing on foot; chalets; camp sites (cleared areas only).

Main attractions: Large concentration of big game; river landscapes; Chilojho Cliffs.

Pertinent information: This national park is strictly for Zimbabweans, except if you have a work permit for Zimbabwe or come from an African country. Accessing the park at Chipinda Pools via Tswiza should be avoided, due to security considerations and the poor condition of the road. Instead use the Masvingo-Beitbridge road. Some roads in the park are only suitable for a fourwheel drive vehicle. Anti-malaria precautions are necessary. Bilharzia is present. Groups are limited to 6 people. According to current reports, this park has been very badly affected by drought; the Department of National Parks and Wild Life Management will continue to assess the situation and may close it again if this is deemed necessary. Unescorted driving on game-viewing roads is not permitted.

Adjoining Mozambique in south-eastern Zimbabwe, this vast 5 000 km², remote park, whose name means 'the horn (tusk) of the elephant' can be a wonderful experience. Large tuskers, reintroduced black rhino, nyala, suni, hippo, hartebeest and giraffe are just a few of the game species which can be seen in this lowveld reserve.

Much of the dense riverine vegetation has been damaged by elephants; other vegetation includes large tracts of rugged mopane tree savannah and acacia woodlands. Baobabs grow on the lower slopes of the magnificent sandstone Chilojho Cliffs which rise above and range alongside the Lundi River for 32 km. The cliffs glow a vibrant red when touched by the rays of the setting sun.

Over 400 species of birds have been recorded in Gonarezhou. Raptors, such as the hooded, white-backed and whiteheaded vultures, are common throughout the park. The pans support many waterbirds, including egrets, storks and ducks.

Wilderness trails, offered by the Department of National Parks and Wild Life Management, operate in the Mabalauta and Chipinda Pools regions.

1. Mabalauta Trail The afternoon before the trail commences, participants meet the officer guiding the trail for a briefing on the route.

Day 1's walk commences at Nyamature Track turn off and heads to Nyamature Pool on the Mwenezi River. Overnight camp is set up here. In the afternoon, trailists have the chance to walk downstream to the confluence of the Mwenezi and Mawange rivers and explore this area of beautiful riverine woodland.

The following day's route leads downstream along the Mwenezi River for 6 km past Nyamasi-kana Pool, through the picturesque Samalema Gorge to Makokwani. Because of the numerous permanent pools, game is abundant here.

The third day sees trailists heading west to the Machisamba River, then proceeding downstream. This river is a permanent source of water, attracting large numbers of game in the dry season. Vegetation along the riverbanks varies from ironwood thickets to patches of riverine woodland.

On Day 4, trailists continue downstream along the Machisamba River through a deep, narrow gorge to rejoin the Mwenezi River. Walking some 4 km along this river's banks, walkers have the opportunity to see a large whitefronted and carmine bee-eater colony, which is active only from October to December. The trail continues for a further 3 km past Buffalo Bend, an area renowned for its huge trees, back to base camp.

2. The Pombadzi Trail covers the Pombadzi River area on the north bank of the Rundi River. The first day is spent walking towards the Pombadzi River through mopane woodland. Day 2 follows the river's western bank towards Masikandro Pool, while Day 3's walk returns along the eastern side of the Pombadzi river. On Day 4 trailists return to Nyahungwe Camp. Vehicles can be left at the base camp for the duration of the trail.

3. The Sibonja Trail follows both the north and south banks of the Rundi River, taking in two major dry season watering points – Massassanya Dam and Bengi Weir. Large concentrations of game can be found at both locations, while Bengi Weir is a favourite drinking place for local elephants. The average distance walked per day is between 10 and 15 km.

4. The Rundi Trail starts at Chinguli Camp; vehicles can be left there. The first day's route follows the north bank of the Rundi River, where walkers can enjoy superb views beneath the Chilojho Cliffs. Day 2's trail is through riverine forest from Nyahungwe to Lisodo, and the third day's walk continues down the Rundi River as far as Pokwe Pool. The following day trailists can enjoy a walk around Machaniwa Pan where a wide variety of birds, especially waterfowl, make their home.

The final day of the trail involves a walk around Tamboharta Pan, before participants are transported back to Chinguli Camp to collect their vehicles.

Due to its longer duration, a reasonable level of fitness is required to walk this trail.

6. CHIRINDA FOREST BOTANICAL RESERVE
CHIPINGE, EASTERN HIGHLANDS

Trail details: A network of pathways. See map page 302.

Permits/bookings: Not required.

Maps/information: For details, contact the Department of National Parks and Wild Life Management, tel. (092634) 706077; PO Box 8151, Causeway, Harare.

Facilities/amenities: Picnic sites.

Main attractions: Evergreen montane forest, noted for ironwoods, wild figs and red mahogany trees, and including a number of tropical plants; also noted for butterflies and moths which feed on rotting vegetation.

Pertinent information: The reserve is open from sunrise to sunset. This is a summer rainfall area, but mist can occur at any time of year. There are no internal roads in the reserve. Chirinda borders on Mozambique; due to the political turmoil in that country, it is strongly recommended that you do not stray across the border.

Zimbabwe's tallest indigenous tree, the 66 m-tall, 400-year-old red mahogany, along with a diverse selection of evergreen montane plants, is preserved at Chirinda. This reserve is located south-east of Masvingo and close to the Mount Selinda Mission. More than 100 tree species, as well as a mass of mosses, ferns, creepers and tree orchids, grow here in dense profusion. Also found is the rare blue orchid, *Callianthus natalensis*.

Many rare or elusive birds and mammals are present, including the trumpeter hornbill, Knysna and Livingstone's louries, the rarely-seen crested guineafowl, Swynnerton's robin, Swynnerton's red squirrel, sun squirrel, samango monkey, tree civet and blue duiker. Tropical plants occurring as far afield as Madagascar and Nigeria are present in Chirinda, the 'place of refuge', thus contributing to the theory that in bygone times much of the continent of Africa was blanketed by continuous rainforest vegetation.

At the main entrance to the reserve is a monument to Charles Francis Swynnerton, a naturalist who lived in the forest for two decades at the turn of the century. He kept extensive records and much of what is known of the reserve's flora and fauna stems from his detailed observations.

Spring is the best time to visit the reserve, for then the ironwoods are in bloom – a mass of white,

The memorial to naturalist Charles Swynnerton is in the forest where he lived for two decades.

less than a day's hike from the mountain chalet and it is a scramble to the summit. Fraser's Falls, a very high, impressive waterfall, can also be reached within a day from the chalet.

The Chimanimanis are also popular because of the lovely camp sites amidst the diverse plant communities which flank fast-flowing perennial streams, some of which hold trout.

Although the vegetation of Chimanimani is basically dry sub-montane forest and grassy flats, many hikers compare the rock formations and plant life to those of the Western Cape. The mountain ranges support proteas and pincushions, everlastings and ericas, and cedars and yellowwoods on sedimentary rock. Chimanimani has its own endemic *Podocarpus* trees, in addition to endemic amphibians and reptiles. Interspersed with its temperate flora are tropical ferns and orchids.

In the secluded kloofs and slopes of these grand mountains live sable, eland, bushbuck, klipspringer and the rare blue duiker, along with the baboon and its arch enemy, the leopard. Spectacular and diverse birdlife is also present. Watch out for a unique and isolated population of bokmakierie, discovered in the 1960s, the scarce swift, blue swallow, Augur buzzard and Gurney's sugarbird. Beware of whitenecked ravens; these birds are known to raid unattended backpacks.

8. BUNGA FOREST AND VUMBA BOTANICAL RESERVES
SOUTH-EAST OF MUTARE, EASTERN HIGHLANDS

Trail details: A network of footpaths in both reserves. See map page 302.

Permits/bookings: For accommodation bookings and further information, contact the Department of National Parks and Wild Life Management, tel. (092634) 706077; PO Box 8151, Causeway, Harare.

Facilities/amenities: No accommodation at Bunga; at Vumba, there is a camp and caravan site, with ablution facilities, a swimming pool, picnic sites and a tearoom.

Main attractions: Dense indigenous forest; monkeys and forest buck; excellent bird-watching; landscaped gardens at Vumba.

Pertinent information: The reserve is open daily from sunrise to sunset; however, it is sometimes temporarily closed due to bad weather.

pea-like blossoms. Butterflies, especially abundant during and after the rains, can be seen, together with moths, feeding on rotting vegetation. As there are no roads in the reserve, visitors can ramble along the pathways enjoying the tranquillity of this magnificent evergreen forest.

7. CHIMANIMANI NATIONAL PARK
EASTERN HIGHLANDS

Trail details: Footpaths leading through the park. See map page 302.

Permits/bookings: Not required.

Facilities/amenities: Small mountain chalet with minimal furnishings, limited cooking utensils, cold showers and toilet; Mutekeswane base camp at the foot of the mountains (no advance booking possible); camping is permitted anywhere in the wilderness area, but caravans are not allowed; information office at base camp.

Main attractions: Rugged grandeur of Zimbabwe's mountain wilderness; endemic plants and animals; beautiful streams.

Pertinent information: Access on foot only. Camping at camper's own risk; trailists are advised to check political conditions and safety precautions with the local office of Chimanimani National Park, tel. (0926326) 555; Private Bag 2063, Chimanimani, Zimbabwe. The border with Mozambique is unfenced, therefore it is possible to wander across it; however, this is strictly forbidden. Drizzle can be expected at any time of the year. The region is subject to sudden storms and/or mist. The nearest supplies of food and petrol are at Chimanimani village.

The 2 400-m rugged quartzite and sandstone Chimanimani mountains derive their name from that of the pass through which the Musapa River flows. This pass is known to the Ndawu tribe as *Tschimanimani*, meaning 'to be squeezed together'. One of southern Africa's most beautiful wilderness regions, there has been no development in the park and every effort has been made to preserve its unspoilt character. There is access to the foot of the range by car from Chimanimani village. This road is gravel and can be classed only as fair; it leads to the base camp some 19 km from the village.

Numerous paths radiate from the Mutekeswane base camp. The game scout on duty is available to advise you on the best routes to take. The main way into the range follows the ancient slave trade and traditional gold pedlars' route from Chimanimani village over the western slopes, across the inner valley, down via Skeleton Pass into Mozambique and on to the coastal ports. The first 3 hours of strenuous walking along this path bring you to Chimanimani's only mountain chalet. This simple structure comprises 2 dormitories, bunkbeds, a fireplace in a communal room, limited cooking utensils and a cold shower. Although the hut cannot be booked in advance, it is crowded only on weekends and during school holidays.

The central range, one of the three parallel north-south ranges within the national park, is the climbing area. It contains numerous caves for over-nighting, well-trodden paths, plenty of water, natural swimming holes and waterfalls. The landscape is dominated by Point 71 (2 440 m), Turret Towers (2 399 m) and Uncontoured Peak (2 213 m). The base of Turret Towers is reached in

A rustic bridge in Vumba Botanical Reserve.

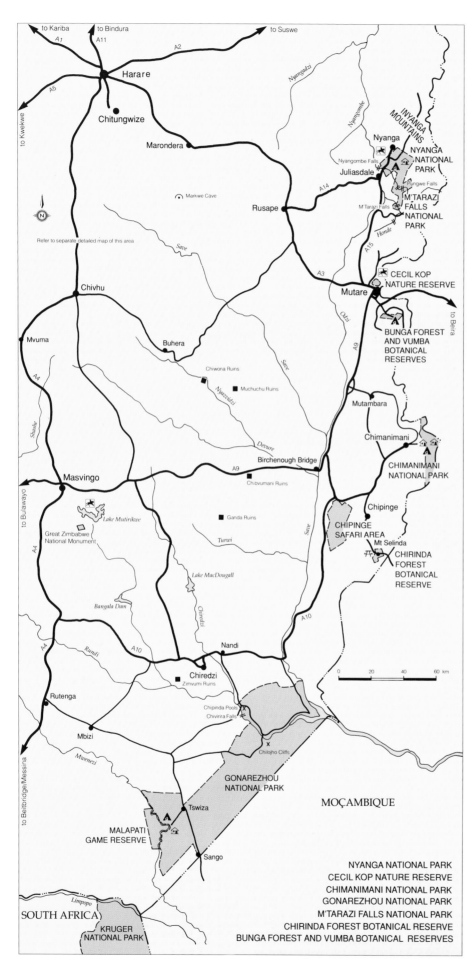

NYANGA NATIONAL PARK
CECIL KOP NATURE RESERVE
CHIMANIMANI NATIONAL PARK
GONAREZHOU NATIONAL PARK
M'TARAZI FALLS NATIONAL PARK
CHIRINDA FOREST BOTANICAL RESERVE
BUNGA FOREST AND VUMBA BOTANICAL RESERVES

Located in the beautiful Vumba Mountains, Bunga Forest Reserve lies 27 km south of Mutare and covers an area of 1 588 ha. Vegetation is the main attraction of this reserve; its steep hills are forested with evergreen trees. Birdlife in the reserve is prolific. Species found mainly in the forest canopy include the Knysna lourie, emerald cuckoo, white-eared barbet, Cape batis, silverycheeked hornbill and the rare Chirinda apalis. Some small mammals are also present, such as the samango monkey, bushpig and tree civet.

The nearby 42-ha Vumba Botanical Reserve contains a 32-ha botanical garden, while the remaining land is covered by indigenous forest. The bright flowers of aloes, cycads, fuchsias, lilies, orchids, proteas and azaleas adorn the landscaped gardens. Many of the plants and trees in Vumba's gardens cannot be found elsewhere in Zimbabwe. Bird species present include the bronze sunbird, Nyasa crimsonwing and Roberts' prinia. Proteas in the gardens attract Gurney's sugarbird and the malachite sunbird.

In both reserves, there are well-maintained footpaths allowing visitors to ramble at will.

9. CECIL KOP NATURE RESERVE
MUTARE

Trail details: Cleared pathways.

Permits/bookings: Not required.

Facilities/amenities: Viewing platform, hides and a road system; rambling and pony riding; trees labelled with their national tree list numbers; educational programmes, Rupert Fothergill open-air classroom.

Main attractions: Mountain grassland, forest, open woodland and vlei; large game; birdlife.

Pertinent information: Open sunrise to sunset. Winter (May to August): mild, sunny days and cool nights; frost possible. Summer (September to December): thunderstorms possible. October and November are the hottest months. December to mid-March is the rainy season.

Under the auspices of the Manicaland Branch of the Wildlife Society of Zimbabwe, 1 700 ha of public commonage on the northern perimeter of the city of Mutare have been preserved as the Cecil Kop Nature Reserve. Rising from 1 036 m to 1 707 m, the Cecil Kop range comprises a variety of plant communities, including montane grassland, evergreen forest, open msasa woodland and grassy vleis. These habitats are rich in species peculiar to Zimbabwe's eastern districts, for example, the blue duiker, sun squirrel, samango monkey, Gurney's sugarbird, Nyasa crimsonwing and grey waxbill. Fortunate walkers may spot the elusive bat hawk in this area. Whitefaced whistling ducks and redbilled teals are common around the dams.

The reserve is divided into two areas: the primary game and wild areas (stocked with elephant, white rhino, eland, buck, giraffe and tsessebe), which offer viewing platforms, hides and a road system; and the wilderness area (481 ha), where rambling and pony riding on cleared trails among 'non-dangerous' game are permitted. Interesting trees are numbered.

The reserve's major asset has been its overwhelming popularity as the venue for educational programmes serving schoolchildren throughout Zimbabwe. A museum education officer leads trails and uses the Rupert Fothergill open-air classroom for informal lectures.

10. M'TARAZI FALLS NATIONAL PARK
SOUTHERN BOUNDARY OF NYANGA NATIONAL PARK

Trail details: Short walking trails.

Permits/bookings: Not required.

Maps/information: For further details, contact The Warden, Nyanga National Park, tel. (09263298) 274; Private Bag T 7901, Mutare.

Facilities/amenities: Nature rambles; carpark and picnic/braai site near the falls.

Main attractions: Wilderness comprising montane moorland and mist forest; M'Tarazi Falls.

Pertinent information: Administered as a unit with Nyanga National Park. Opening hours are from 7.00 am to 6.00 pm. This is a high rainfall area; mist can occur at any time of year.

The main feature of this 2 495-ha national park, adjacent to Nyanga National Park south-east of Harare, is the M'Tarazi Falls, which, at a height of 762 m, are the highest in Zimbabwe. There is a pleasant walk down to the viewpoint over the falls, where there are superb views not only over this highlight but also over the Honde Valley. Tea and coffee are the two main crops grown in this fertile area.

The park comprises upland heath and montane mist forest. Forest dwellers here include the blue duiker, samango monkey and crowned eagle.

11. NYANGA NATIONAL PARK
EASTERN HIGHLANDS

Trail details: A network of paths.

Permits/bookings: For accommodation, contact the Department of National Parks and Wild Life Management, tel. (092634) 706077; PO Box 8151, Causeway, Harare.

Facilities/amenities: Fully equipped lodges; camp sites and caravan parks; trout fishing, with a licence; recreation facilities, including tennis, boating and pony trails (see Special Interest section); hotels.

Main attractions: Mountain landscapes; stone ruin terraces; Zimbabwe's highest mountain and waterfall; scenic drives.

Pertinent information: Camping is permitted only in the tourist camping grounds, not in the park itself. This is a high rainfall area, reaching approximately 2 200 mm in December. Most of the park lies at an altitude of between 2 000 and 2 300 m; hence the climate is invigorating and warm clothing is necessary, especially at night.

Nyanga National Park, located south-east of Harare, covers a total land area of 47 100 ha; this includes the adjacent M'Tarazi Falls National Park. Although not as popular for mountaineering as the Chimanimani range, Nyanga, lying at the northern

end of a long mountain chain, has its own particular character and boasts superb views stretching all the way to Mulanje in Malawi. The park, with its pine plantations, fruit orchards and holiday resorts, is much more developed than the highlands to the south, but nevertheless has many refreshing walks through moist and sub-montane forest, grassland and heathlike scrub similar to the fynbos of the Western Cape.

Within Nyanga National Park, the famous Pungwe Falls (243 m) and M'Tarazi Falls (at 762 m, Zimbabwe's highest), as well as many others, can be reached via a short, signposted walk from the hotels, or by car. Zimbabwe's highest peak, Inyangani (2 593 m), is reached via a clear, beaconed path from the carpark, which is located about a quarter of the way up the mountain. The walk, which takes approximately 1-1,5 hours, is closed during periods of heavy rains, usually in the summer, between December and February. Thick mist during this time creates dangerous hiking conditions and inexperienced trailists could easily lose their way and fall over Inyangani's steep cliffs.

Wildlife is fairly prolific and treats in store for nature ramblers include possible sightings of the samango monkey and blue duiker.

The park is home to 276 species of birds. In the grassland, visitors should watch out for the stonechat, wailing cisticola and broadtailed warbler. The fortunate walker may spot the secretarybird, blue swallow and scarce swift in the hills. Several species of raptor are present here, including the lanner falcon, rock kestrel and crowned eagle.

A view of Zimbabwe's eastern highlands in Nyanga National Park.

12. ROBERT McILWAINE
RECREATIONAL PARK
SOUTH-WEST OF HARARE

Trail details: Walking trails at Bushman Point.

Permits/bookings: Reservations for accommodation can be made through the Department of National Parks and Wild Life Management, tel. (092634) 706077; PO Box 8151, Causeway, Harare.

Facilities/amenities: Lodges and chalets; camp and caravan sites; recreational facilities include swimming pools, tennis and volleyball courts; picnic sites.

Main attractions: Recreation park with a variety of resort facilities; plentiful birdlife; game area with large mammals.

Pertinent information: Open sunrise to sunset. It is strongly recommended that anyone staying in the camp or caravan sites should lock their property in their car at night, or whenever they are away from the site; cases of theft have been reported. Visitors staying in the chalets and lodges should note that these are located in the game park, the gates of which are locked between 6.00 am and 6.00 pm. Nearest food supplies are at Norton 24 km away; the nearest petrol is at Turnpike Garage 16 km away. Visitors contemplating fishing or boating on the lake should be aware that both bilharzia and crocodiles are present.

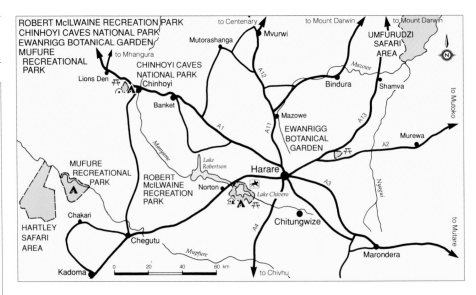

Situated only 32 km west of the capital, the 5 500-ha Robert McIlwaine Recreational Park is a favourite playground of Harare's residents. The park incorporates Lake Chivero (formerly Lake McIlwaine) and a 1 600-ha game park. Most of the animals have been introduced from other areas and include giraffe, white rhino, tsessebe, eland, sable and Burchell's zebra.

The park is one of the best areas close to Harare for birdwatching. Species that make their home in *Miombo/Brachystegia* woodland are well represented; look out for the spotted creeper, mashona hyliota, violetbacked sunbird and miombo rock thrush. Waterbirds are prolific and you may see Goliath and blackcrowned night herons, little

bittern, Hottentot teal and southern pochard. Fish eagles breed around the lake shore, while Wahlberg's eagle and the blackbreasted snake eagle are some of the more common raptors found in the park.

An area at Bushman Point has been set aside for walking; enquire at the Tourist Reception Office in the park for further information.

Pony trails are offered daily (see Special Interest section for details).

13. EWANRIGG BOTANICAL
GARDENS
NEAR HARARE

Trail details: A network of paths through the Gardens.

Permits/bookings: Not required.

Facilities/amenities: Picnic sites and fireplaces.

Main attractions: Indigenous woodland; exotic aloes and cycads; water garden.

Pertinent information: The Gardens are open from 8.00 am to sunset.

Ewanrigg Botanical Gardens, located 41 km northeast of Harare on the Shamva road, were established in 1920 by Basil Christian, who bequeathed them to the nation in 1950. He named them after his brother Ewan who was killed in the Second World War – 'rigg' is Welsh for ridge. The Gardens are best known for their brilliant aloes and prehistoric cycads, many of which do not occur naturally in the area. Other species to be found there include cacti, fuchsias, Barberton daisies and bougainvillaeas. Some 40 ha of the Gardens' total area is cultivated, while the remaining 200 ha are left to natural vegetation.

Some 275 species of birds have been recorded in the Gardens and surrounding area. Possibly the most noticeable are the sunbirds that are attracted to the aloes, especially during the winter months when these plants are in flower. Watch out for black, whitebellied, scarletchested and miombo doublecollared sunbirds.

Visitors can enjoy walks along the many paths laid out through the Gardens, which are probably at their best from June to August, when seasonal blooms provide a riot of colour.

Restful Robert McIlwaine Recreational Park is conveniently close to the city of Harare.

Its seasonal splendour is among the attractions of Ewanrigg Botanical Gardens.

Going about their quiet and stately business, elephants cross Mana Pools at dawn.

14. CHINHOYI CAVES NATIONAL PARK
CHINHOYI

Trail details: Paths to the caves.

Permits/bookings: Not required. A small entrance fee is charged to see the caves. For more details, contact the Department of National Parks and Wild Life Management, tel. (092634) 706077; PO Box 8151, Causeway, Harare.

Facilities/amenities: Caravan and camp site; picnic site; restaurant.

Main attractions: Deep, flooded calcite caves formed by erosive action of water on soft limestone.

This small park, located at the foot of the Hunyani Hills, north-west of Harare, is a popular stopping-off spot on the way to Mana Pools or Lake Kariba. The main feature of the park is the unusual and very beautiful Chinhoyi Caves. Sleeping Pool in the main cave maintains a temperature of 22° C and is thought to be between 88 and 91 m deep. Pottery and human remains dating from roughly 650 AD have been found in and close to the park.

A silent pool in Chinhoyi Caves.

15. MUFURE RECREATIONAL PARK
ZIMBABWE MIDLANDS

Trail details: 3 days/2 nights; guided.

Permits/bookings: Bookings for the trail, and for accommodation before and after the trail, can be made with the Department of National Parks and Wild Life Management, tel. (092634) 706077; PO Box 8151, Causeway, Harare. Book up to 6 months in advance.

Facilities/amenities: Camp site; on the trail hikers sleep under the stars.

Main attractions: Small game; fishing in the river; this area is undeveloped and away from the normal tourist routes.

Pertinent information: Participants must be over 16 years of age. Groups are restricted to a maximum of 6 people. This is a malarial area; take the necessary preventative medication. Water purifying tablets are a necessity.

This wilderness trail, run by the Department of National Parks and Wild Life Management, operates once a month during the dry season (May to October). Exact dates are available from the department and generally coincide with the full moon. Expect to carry your own equipment; request a list of necessary supplies when you make your booking. You will need a fourwheel drive or another strong type of vehicle to reach Hartley A safari area, where the trail begins. Make sure you are at the office by 10 am on the first day.

Located in the Zimbabwe midlands roughly 160 km from Harare and 50 km north-west of Chegutu, Mufure Recreational Park is completely undeveloped and few people are able to visit the area. This is a major part of its charm and if you enjoy getting away from normal tourist haunts, then this park will appeal to you. In a scenic, hilly area with an open valley, big game animals are not common; instead the focus is on sable, kudu and smaller mammals.

Because this is a wilderness area, it is imperative for everyone's safety that you always follow the Trail Officer's instructions. Remember that he is experienced in this environment, and is responsible for the wellbeing of both you and the game.

16. MANA POOLS NATIONAL PARK
ZAMBEZI RIVER

Trail details: 4 days/3 nights; guided, circular. See map page 306.

Permits/bookings: A permit and booking are required from the Department of National Parks and Wild Life Management, tel. (092634) 706077; PO Box 8151, Causeway, Harare.

Facilities/amenities: Nyamepi Camp (camp and caravan sites with full ablution facilities); lodges, including Mana Tree Lodge; primitive fishermen's camps; private safari camps, offering walking tours, situated along the riverbanks.

Main attractions: Prolific bush and river birdlife; varied and abundant mammal life; attractive floodplains; good fishing for tigerfish, bream and giant vundu.

Pertinent information: Fishermen and trailists must be wary of crocodiles. Anti-malaria precautions are necessary. Park is open 1 May to 31 October. Maximum of 6 people per group permitted for walking trails. Driving off the roads in the park is prohibited.

Mana Pools National Park, in the extreme north of Zimbabwe, stretches southwards from the Zambezi River to its escarpment. The park's isolated location contributes greatly to its wilderness atmosphere, thus enhancing its appeal to true lovers of nature. Wandering on foot through the riverine and mopane acacia woodland is very rewarding, for

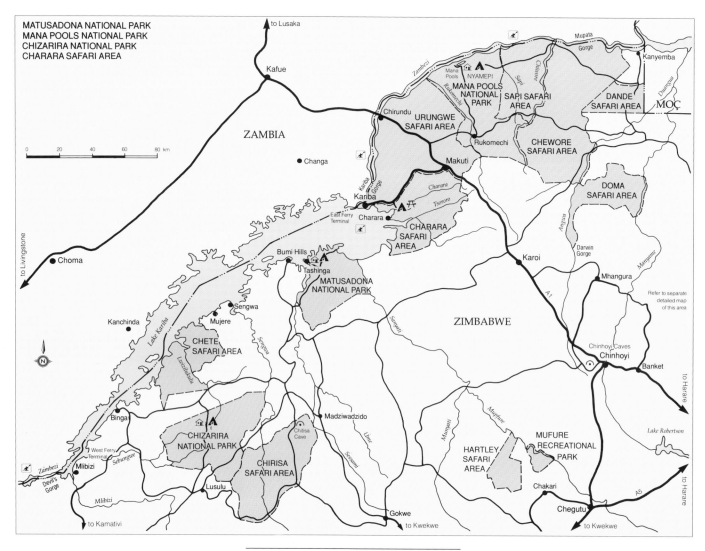

MATUSADONA NATIONAL PARK
MANA POOLS NATIONAL PARK
CHIZARIRA NATIONAL PARK
CHARARA SAFARI AREA

you are likely to encounter, among a wide range of animals, elephant, hippo, buffalo, black rhino, eland, impala, lion, leopard, wild dog and crocodiles, as well as a great many birds.

Wilderness trails are available in both southern and northern areas of the park. The southern trail leaves from the Nyakasikana Gate, where you will be met by your trail leader. Walkers must be at this point by 12 pm on the first day of the trail; note that it is safe to leave your car here.

The northern area trail begins at Nyamepi Camp. Leading along the Zambezi floodplain, it offers excellent walking through completely undeveloped areas and ample opportunities for game-viewing.

Mana means 'four', a reference to the park's most outstanding feature – the group of four small lakes and pools within the fertile river terraces. Any exploration of these crocodile-infested pools is at the trailist's own risk and can be further hampered by mosquitoes, tsetse flies and the year-round heat. However, if you are willing to bear these inconveniences, the bird-watching and game-viewing are superb – especially when the large herds and lion prides come down from the hills of the escarpment to drink.

Mana Pools is one of the best places in Zimbabwe to see the western banded snake eagle, while a further 387 species of birds have been recorded in the park, including carmine and whitefronted bee-eaters, the horus swift and bluecheeked bee-eater.

17. CHARARA SAFARI AREA
LAKE KARIBA

Trail details: Game-viewing on foot.

Permits/bookings: Bookings for accommodation can be made through the Department of National Parks and Wild Life Management, tel. (092634) 706077; PO Box 8151, Causeway, Harare.

Facilities/amenities: Camp ground with ablution block and braai places; slipway for launching boats; game-viewing platform; picnic sites; angling for tigerfish and tilapia.

Main attractions: Diverse wildlife, especially large game; Lake Kariba scenery.

Pertinent information: A fourwheel drive vehicle is necessary to negotiate the reserve's roads. Movement around the reserve can be difficult during the rainy season (December to March). Take precautions against malaria. Crocodiles are present in the lake.

Bordering the north-east shore of Lake Kariba, the 1 700 km² Charara Safari Area provides the opportunity of watching many animals as they come down to the water to drink. A variety of game species can be seen close to the camp, which is located only 100 m from the water's edge. Visitors can expect to see elephant, buffalo, leopard, lion, black rhino, kudu and waterbuck. The safari area overlies

rich deposits of coal, copper, mica, chrome and tin and although the inevitable mining scars are present, the *Brachystegia* woodland is relatively untouched by man.

18. MATUSADONA NATIONAL PARK
SOUTHERN SHORES OF LAKE KARIBA

Trail details: Guided walks and wilderness trails.

Permits/bookings: Can be obtained from the Department of National Parks and Wild Life Management, tel. (092634) 706077; PO Box 8151, Causeway, Harare.

Facilities/amenities: Backpacking trails conducted by private companies; game scouts provided for private walking trips; 3 exclusive camps, each accommodating 12 people; camp sites on the shore at Sanyati West and Tashinga (on the Ume River); fishing for tigerfish, bream and vundu.

Main attractions: Large mammals; scenic lake shore with winding, tree-lined creeks and waterfalls; Zambezi escarpment; Sanyati Gorge.

Pertinent information: Roads are suitable for fourwheel drive vehicles only. Beware of crocodiles (there are approximately 400 adult crocodiles living in the waters around the park). Tsetse fly is present. Entry by boat is allowed throughout the year; entry by road only between 1 May and 31 October; float planes are common vehicles of access.

Matusadona is a wilderness area of 1 407 km² on the southern shores of Lake Kariba, with the Matuzviadohna Hills running through the park.

A beautiful way to incorporate this national park into a trailing experience is to canoe along the shoreline; advise the Department of National Parks and Wild Life Management of your intentions in advance and they will recommend a qualified guide (canoeing unaccompanied is not permitted). Watch for elephant, buffalo, impala, kudu and waterbuck and, of course, the thriving aquatic birds. Fish eagles, cormorants and darters use the dead trees in the water as roosting and nesting sites. Then ramble through the *Commiphora-Combretum* thickets along the lower plains and the *Brachystegia* woodland on the escarpment, where rhino, eland, sable, roan and lion are frequently seen. Many of these animals are 'refugees' saved from drowning during 'Operation Noah', one of the most successful wildlife rescue projects of all time, when the Zambezi Valley, which swarmed with wildlife, began to flood with the filling of Lake Kariba.

Fothergill Island (Private Bag 2081, Kariba, Zimbabwe) and Tiger Bay (PO Box 102, Kariba, Zimbabwe) are two of a number of private lodges which organize walking safaris and sailing or canoe trips to Matusadona. For example, Fothergill offers a guided, 3- to 5-day wilderness backpacking trip into the rugged Matusadona mountains. Tiger Bay, on the Ume River, offers short walks, a 4-day hike and also environmental education courses for youngsters. Each lodge concentrates on different areas of the park, and trails can be adapted to suit the needs and interests of the group.

19. CHIZARIRA NATIONAL PARK
NORTH-WEST ZIMBABWE, SOUTH OF LAKE KARIBA

Trail details: 3 days/2 nights. Both trails are guided and circular.

Permits/bookings: A permit and booking are required from the Department of National Parks and Wild Life Management, tel. (092634) 706077; PO Box 8151, Causeway, Harare.

Facilities/amenities: Two wilderness camp sites.

Main attractions: Large variety of big game; spectacular and varied mountain scenery; streams, gorges and views over the Zambezi Valley.

Pertinent information: *Chizarira* is a Batlonka word meaning 'barrier'. Access is difficult, and possible by fourwheel drive vehicle only. Petrol and other supplies are only available at Binga, 90 km from the park's headquarters. Wilderness trails are limited to 6 people per group.

For outdoor enthusiasts seeking a 'real' wilderness experience, Chizarira's relatively undeveloped, magnificently diverse and rugged terrain is an unforgettable experience. Chizarira lies in the remote north-west of Zimbabwe where *Brachystegia-Colophospermum* woodlands, scrub savannah and *Hyparrhenia* grassland clothe the slopes bordering the steep Zambezi escarpment. Wildlife, too, is diverse and includes many 'refugees' displaced from the Zambezi Valley when the river was dammed to create Lake Kariba. The most notable inhabitants are tsessebe, waterbuck, roan antelope, buffalo, black rhino, elephant, lion and leopard.

A wooded wilderness buttress in Chizarira National Park.

This national park is a paradise for anyone with an interest in raptors. Crowned, black and martial

The southern shores of Lake Kariba at Matusadona are really high-lying slopes of the old Zambezi River Valley.

eagles, Augur buzzards and peregrine and lanner falcons are resident here, but the species many enthusiasts want to see is the rare Taita falcon.

The Department of National Parks and Wild Life Management offers several different wilderness trails here during the dry season.

The Nyagangara Trail starts at Kasikili Spring and leads through Ngalani to Nyagangara spring. The following day is spent exploring this beautiful area which includes the Nyagangara Gorge, with panoramic views of the Zambezi Valley. A well-worn game trail provides the path which leads back to Kasikili Spring.

The Machininga Trail is a new area open to visitors, and is well worth exploring. The starting point of the trail is a 1,5-hour drive from the Chizarira headquarters and accessible only in a fourwheel drive vehicle. Trailists spend the night before and the night after the walk at Machininga Spring. Note that there are no facilities here and camping equipment is essential. From the spring, the walk takes a circular route through Kabombo and Sinompas springs and back past the Mberere River.

20. HWANGE NATIONAL PARK
NORTH-WESTERN ZIMBABWE

Trail details: Guided trails varying in length.

Permits/bookings: A permit and booking is required from the Department of National Parks and Wild Life Management, tel. (092634) 706077; PO Box 8151, Causeway, Harare.

Facilities/amenities: Foot safaris; waterhole platforms; 4 camps offering hut accommodation and caravan and camp sites; three 'exclusive' camps (Deka, Bumbusi and Lukosi); Hwange Safari Lodge offering vehicle, foot and night safaris, and tree hides; network of game-viewing drives.

Main attractions: Large concentrations of big game, which are attracted to the natural pans; prolific birdlife (401 species, which is half the Zimbabwe list).

Pertinent information: Anti-malaria precautions are necessary. Groups are limited to a maximum of 6 people. May to November, the dry season, is the best time for game-viewing. Book well in advance, as accommodation in the park is very popular.

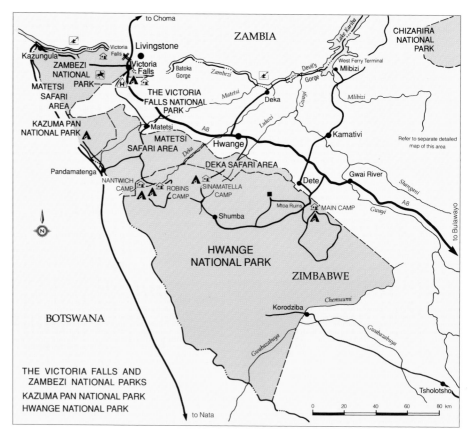

The moving shadows of sunset in Hwange National Park.

For the trailist, Hwange's principal attractions are the 'exclusive' camps and guided trails. Exclusive camps are fully equipped, permanent accommodation units for groups of not more than 12 people who, for the period of their stay, have sole use of the area within a 5-km radius of their accommodation, for game-viewing. Guided trails or foot safaris are operated within the park. A maximum of 6 trailists is taken on a walking safari accompanied by an experienced ranger.

Walks starting from the Sinamatella Camp last for 5 days and 4 nights. Accommodation or a camp site should be booked for the night before and the night after the trail. On the walk, nights are spent in the open where it can be extremely cold in winter.

Trails commencing from Robins Camp vary in length. A fourwheel drive vehicle is recommended to get to the camp, where walkers spend the night preceding and the night following the hike. Remember to book accommodation here well in advance.

Walking in Hwange, the largest of Zimbabwe's national parks and one of the great elephant sanctuaries of Africa, is a very rewarding experience, as it is reputed to have the greatest variety as well as one of the densest populations of wild animals in the world.

The largest area of the park is covered by Kalahari sand, supporting bushveld savannah and grassy plains, the natural habitat of many herding animals. But it is probably the region's large natural pans, rich in salts, sodium, lime and other minerals, that play the greater part in attracting many of the animals. The pans are continuously enlarged by animals wallowing in the mud and drinking at their edges. North of the main watershed, a hilly area of granite outcrops with mopane woodland, is the popular haunt of the elephants; consequently, this area suffers extensive damage from large herds.

In addition to elephants, trailists may see many of the 70 species of large animals such as buffalo, giraffe, lion, reintroduced black and white rhino, wildebeest, ostrich, warthog, spotted and brown hyaena, jackal, hippo and crocodile. The diversified antelope population includes hartebeest, eland, sable, roan, impala, kudu, waterbuck, tsessebe and gemsbok. Present but not readily seen are Hwange's 7 cm-long pygmy mouse and the South African hedgehog.

The birdlife, especially migrants, is prolific and diverse, due to the range of habitats in the park. Species occuring throughout the park include white-headed vulture, yellowbilled kite, tawny eagle and swallowtailed bee-eater. Often seen close to the camps are knobbilled duck, redbilled francolin and crowned crane.

21. KAZUMA PAN NATIONAL PARK
NORTH-WEST ZIMBABWE

Trail details: 3 days/2 nights; guided.

Permits/bookings: A booking is required from the Department of National Parks and Wild Life Management, tel. (092634) 706077; PO Box 8151, Causeway, Harare. Bookings are also necessary for accommodation in the park before and after the wilderness trail.

Facilities/amenities: Two designated areas are available for camping; these sites have water but no other facilities.

Main attractions: Open grassland savannah with seasonally flooded natural pans; excellent birdlife; a variety of game.

Pertinent information: The park is open from March to the end of December. Groups are limited to a maximum of 6 people. Take precautions against malaria. Roads in the park are in poor condition and can only be negotiated by a fourwheel drive vehicle.

A relatively small national park of 31 300 ha, Kazuma Pan is situated 80 km south-west of Victoria Falls. It consists of an open grassland depression surrounded by teak forests, and is quite unlike other Zimbabwean bush. Because it includes a series of pan depressions, large numbers of game which migrate from Botswana can be seen here, especially from September through to the first rains in December. Less common species often seen in the area include white rhino, cheetah, oribi, roan antelope and tsessebe. When water is scarce, buffalo and elephant are also present in large numbers and lion are a fairly common sight. The pan also provides an excellent home for a large variety of waterbirds, including marabou and openbilled storks, the African spoonbill and rufousbellied heron.

Wilderness trails, led by an experienced member of the park's staff, are available during the dry season. Contact the Department of National Parks and Wild Life Management for this year's dates. Trailists drive to Matetsi headquarters; although the road is rough, it is negotiable for normal saloon

cars. From here, transport is provided to Kazuma Pan (an additional fee is charged). Check-in time on the first day of the trail is 8.00 am, so it is advisable to stay the night before and the night after the trail at Robins Camp.

22. THE VICTORIA FALLS AND ZAMBEZI NATIONAL PARKS
ZAMBEZI RIVER, WESTERN ZIMBABWE

Trail details: Paths to Victoria Falls; guided walks.

Permits/bookings: Bookings for accommodation in the national parks are required; contact the Department of National Parks and Wild Life Management, tel. (092634) 706077; PO Box 8151, Causeway, Harare.

Facilities/amenities: Kandahar, Mpala Jena and Sansimba fishing camps in Zambezi National Park; hotels, chalets, lodges, camp and caravan sites in Victoria Falls Village.

Main attractions: One of the world's largest and most sensational waterfalls.

Pertinent information: Raincoat, umbrella and waterproof camera are useful. Summer (November to March) is rainy and very hot, while winter (June and July) is cool and dry, and frosts are possible at night; pack accordingly. During the peak-flow winter months spray can obscure the falls, so between August and November are recommended as the best months for photography.

The Zambezi River rises in the north-west Zambian highlands and flows eastwards through the flat Barotse plains, gaining momentum in rocky gorges, until it takes its magnificent leap over a chasm eroded in basalt rock. It is difficult to describe the sheer size and grandeur of the Victoria Falls. The Kololo name *Mosi oa Tunya* ('the smoke that thunders') captures their evocative spirit and power; when David Livingstone first saw them in 1855 he exclaimed that 'scenes so lovely must have been gazed upon by angels in their flight', and named the spectacle in honour of his queen.

Today, while following what is one of Africa's most awe-inspiring nature walks, the Victoria Falls

The streaming splendour of the main falls.

are seen from the very safe network of paths leading through the Rain Forest, along the opposite bank of the gorge into which the river plunges.

The dense and luxuriant riparian forest which flourishes in the moisture from the falls' spray is also worthy of attention. The attractive herbaceous plants towered over by fig, ebony, waterberry and olive trees are of great botanical interest.

A cruise on the river provides a good vantage point from which to see some of the area's birdlife, which includes the African skimmer, rock pratincole and whitecrowned plover. Several pairs of the rare Taita falcon breed in the gorge below the falls. Other species in the area include the trumpeter hornbill, collared palm thrush, black swift, blue waxbill and brown firefinch.

For people planning their first visit to Victoria Falls, I recommend the first half of summer (November or December) as the best time; although these are very hot months, the waters are at their lowest level, comparatively little spray is produced and consequently the geological formation of the region can be better appreciated. At peak flood times (March and April) water volumes increase thirty-fold, making the spray so dense that the bottom of the 103 m-deep chasm and the full 1 708 m-width of the falls are difficult to see. If possible, try to experience the majestic atmosphere of the falls under full moon or in the late afternoon when rainbows arc through the sprays.

The Zambezi National Park starts at the Victoria Falls and includes 46 km of the Zambezi River upstream of the falls, as well as a large area south of the river. The park is noted for fishing, large mammals and crocodiles. Visitors wishing to explore this park on foot should contact the Department of National Parks and Wild Life Management in Harare for permission and details.

Below the tempestuous falls, the Zambezi runs smooth and quiet through its sculpted gorge.

ZAMBIA

Zambia is a large, land-locked, 1 300-m high plateau whose 750 000-km^2 area is about the same size as France, Switzerland, Austria and Hungary combined. An independent republic since 1964, Zambia has demarcated an impressive one-third of the country for national parks and game management areas. The country's natural assets offer the intrepid hiker an ideal setting for guided walking trails: such as the wildlife-rich Luangwa Valley (the tail end of the Great Rift Valley) in eastern Zambia which is renowned world-wide for its walking safaris; the Kafue National Park with its diverse landscape in the west; endless expanses of flat *Brachystegia* forested plateau dotted with occasional hills throughout the country; the majestic

Victoria Falls; and inland beaches along Lake Tanganyika and Lake Kariba. Of these, it is still the Luangwa Valley and the Kafue National Park that are the prime areas for game-viewing walking safaris.

Visas are not required for visitors from Commonwealth countries, but all other visitors must have a visa; South Africans can be issued with a visa at the point of entry. Yellow fever and cholera vaccination certificates are required for visitors arriving from infected areas, and all visitors must take anti-malaria precautions. Tsetse flies are found in some areas, so carry an

insecticide spray with you. It is advisable to boil all water before you drink it. Visa and health requirements fluctuate so you should check the information with the authorities before your visit.

Although tropical, Zambia's high plateau ameliorates temperatures. The exception is in the Zambezi and Luangwa River valleys where heat and humidity can be uncomfortable in the summer. Trailists should avoid the hot, wet months between December and March; rather walk in the cool, dry season from May to August or the warmer, more humid months from September to November. Indeed, some camps and lodges have to close during the rainy season (June to October/November) as the roads become inaccessible.

LEFT: *Victoria Falls, on the Zambia-Zimbabwe border, by far the largest in Africa, and one of the great waterfalls of the world.*

A tiny settlement lies at the hub of radiating streams and footpaths on the flood plains of Kafue.

Trail details: Guided half-day walks (10 to 15 km). See map p. 314.

Permits/bookings: Reservations for accommodation: **New Kalala Lodge and camp:** tel. and fax (1) 223390; PO Box 33018, Lusaka; **Chunga Safari Lodge and camp:** tel. (1) 225352 or 2218827; **Kafwala camp:** Wildlife Conservation Society of Zambia, tel. (5) 223467 or 222743; PO Box 80632, Kabwe; **David Shepherd camp:** tel. (1) 254226; PO Box 30255, Lusaka; **Lufupa Lodge, Lufupa and Kafwala Rapids camps** and **Shumba bush camp:** tel. (1) 221197/8 or 222075 or 223628, fax (1) 222198 or 221157; PO Box 31322 or 30984, Lusaka; **Musungwa Safari Lodge, Nanzhila and Ngoma camps:** tel. (1) 273493 or 274233, fax (1) 274233; PO Box 31808, Lusaka; **Nanzhila tented camp:** tel. (3) 323235, fax (1) 323224; Livingstone; or contact the Zambia National Tourist Board, tel. (1) 229087/8/9, fax (1) 225174; PO Box 30017, Lusaka. Brochures and rates available on request. Permits for the park can be obtained at entrance gates.

Facilities/amenities: Full catering accommodation at Shumba bush camp on the Busanga Plain, Lufupa camp at the Kafue-Lufupa confluence, Kafwala camp overlooking the Kafwala Rapids, Chunga Safari camp on the Kafue River, at Musungwa Safari Lodge and New Kalala camp at Lake Itezhi-tezhi, at Nanzhila in the southern section of the park, and at Nanzhila tented camp in the south. Self-catering accommodation also available at Lufupa, Chunga Safari camp, Kafwala, Kafwala Rapids, Ngoma, Nanzhila and the David Shepherd camp. Musungwa Safari Lodge accommodates 72 and has facilities such as restaurant, bar, swimming pool, conference room, curio shop, river and lake cruises, visits to local villages, game-viewing drives, camping at Musungwa or on Chongo Island, tennis, squash, windsurfing, parasailing and waterskiing; Nanzhila accommodates 8, offers game-viewing drives, and has camping facilities. Shumba, Lufupa and Kafwala offer day and night game-viewing drives, and hunting or photographic safaris can be arranged. Kalala camp accommodates 8 people, and offers cruises on the river and lake.

Main attractions: Prolific birdlife; big game; few visitors in relation to park size; hot springs overlooking the Nanzhila Plain; Lake Itezhi-tezhi.

Pertinent information: Access to the park by road is via Mumbwa (from Lusaka) or Kalomo (from Livingstone), and there is an airstrip at Ngoma. Some camps close during the rainy season (November to May); check when booking.

1. LUNGA-LUSWISHI GAME MANAGEMENT AREA
WESTERN ZAMBIA

Trail details: Walking safaris. See map p. 314.

Permits/bookings: Reservations for accommodation can be made through Summit Safaris, Leopard Lodge, tel. (1) 216689 or 216318; PO Box 33419, Lusaka.

Facilities/amenities: Full catering 14-bed lodge and four 2-bed lodges, each with bathroom, at Leopard Lodge; game-viewing drives; fishing; access to hot springs.

Main attractions: Plenty of game in the area, including a variety of antelope.

Pertinent information: Beware of bilharzia. Access from Lusaka by road is via Mumbwa. Leopard Lodge is open all year round.

North of the Kafue River and north-west of the Kafue National Park (see below) lies the Lunga-Luswishi Game Management Area. Sable, impala, waterbuck, puku, yellow-backed duiker, eland, kudu and bushbuck graze the open grassland, while hippo inhabit the river.

The privately run Leopard Lodge is in the south of the area, almost on the border of the Kafue National Park, and offers guided walking safaris to suit the abilities of the particular group.

2. KAFUE NATIONAL PARK
WESTERN ZAMBIA

At 22 500 km² Kafue National Park is one of the largest game sanctuaries in Africa. The birdlife really is prolific here with over 600 species inhabiting the flood plains and river banks. In the rainy season (November through to May), when some areas become inaccessible, countless species of waterfowl converge on the deluged Busanga flood plains to breed.

The meandering Kafue River travels for more than 240 km through the park, and offers good game fishing in the form of pike, bream, silver barbel and catfish, while the Lufupa and Lunga rivers, both tributaries of the Kafue, also water the region. Countless hippos and crocodiles inhabit these rivers.

The Big Five (lion, leopard, elephant, rhino and buffalo) are all found here, as are large herds of antelope such as waterbuck, impala, kudu, roan and sable. The red lechwe, a beautiful and graceful antelope, is endemic to the area and is found in herds mostly around the Busanga flood plains. Another unusual antelope is the shy sitatunga, which lives in the swamps. Visitors can also see baboon, warthog, wild pig and hartebeest, as well as predators like hyaena and wild dog, in the park.

Trees of a drowned forest protrude above the blue waters of Lake Itezhi-Tezhi, a focus for abundant wildlife.

Guided walks under the supervision of a game scout and guard are offered from most of the lodges in the park. These walking safaris are not overly strenuous and are usually conducted in the early morning or late afternoon.

In the wet months of November to March when abundance of water disperses the herds of game, **Chundukwa** offers walking safaris geared for bird enthusiasts from their two tented camps at Nanzhila in the southern part of the park. The walks are 10 to 15 km per day. Walking safaris with traditional porters can also be arranged. Backpacking safaris, where you carry equipment and personal effects on your back but staff is provided to set up camp and prepare meals, cover about 10 km a day. Nanzhila camp is situated in a very unspoilt piece of Africa. Visitors can venture out on guided walks to look for herds of larger game or smaller buck such as oribi and reedbuck. Cheetah, lion and wild dog all prowl the plains in search of prey and water.

For the bird enthusiast or keen photographer, specialist walking safaris can be arranged from **Musungwa Safari Lodge**, which is beautifully situated on the shores of Lake Itezhi-tezhi, 1 km from Musa gate.

3. TONGABEZI CAMP
ZAMBEZI RIVER, UPSTREAM OF VICTORIA FALLS

Trail details: Walks in the area of Victoria Falls. See map p. 314.

Permits/bookings: Reservations for accommodation: tel. (3) 323235 or 323235, fax (3) 323224; Private Bag 31, Livingstone. Brochure and rates on request.

Facilities/amenities: Full-catering accommodation in luxury tented camp for 14 at Tongabezi with luxury honeymoon suite available; for 8 at Sindabezi Island camp; and for 6 at fly-camp on Livingstone Island. Livingstone has 3 good museums worth visiting; Maramba Cultural Village and Makuni Village, both in the area of the falls, can also be visited; see Special Interest section for canoeing and white water rafting trips in the area.

Main attractions: Victoria Falls and gorges.

Pertinent information: Children under 12 are not welcome. Visitors can fly into Livingstone in Zambia or Victoria Falls in Zimbabwe; transport will be arranged to Tongabezi.

The privately owned and very popular Tongabezi Camp is 25 km upstream from the magnificent Victoria Falls – one of the seven natural wonders of the world. The best time for viewing the falls is between August and December, when the water level is lowest and the mist created by the falling water does not obscure the view.

Visitors can set out on a delightful day's outing at the falls where they visit Livingstone Island, walk along Knife Edge Bridge and to Boiling Pot, and then enjoy an informal picnic, with waiter in attendance, in view of the falls – right on the edge of Eastern Cataract.

Keen walkers can arrange to be guided, in groups of 4, in an exploration on foot of the gorges below the falls, or in the area of the falls and adjacent game park – the Mosi-oa-Tunya ('the smoke that thunders') National Park. The walks are easy and relaxed, focusing on local flora and fauna, and the luxury of a porter is provided to carry along a picnic and drinks.

The rare Taita falcon may be spotted in the densely vegetated gorges by the observant hiker, while buffalo, duiker, warthog, bushbuck and vervet monkey inhabit the park.

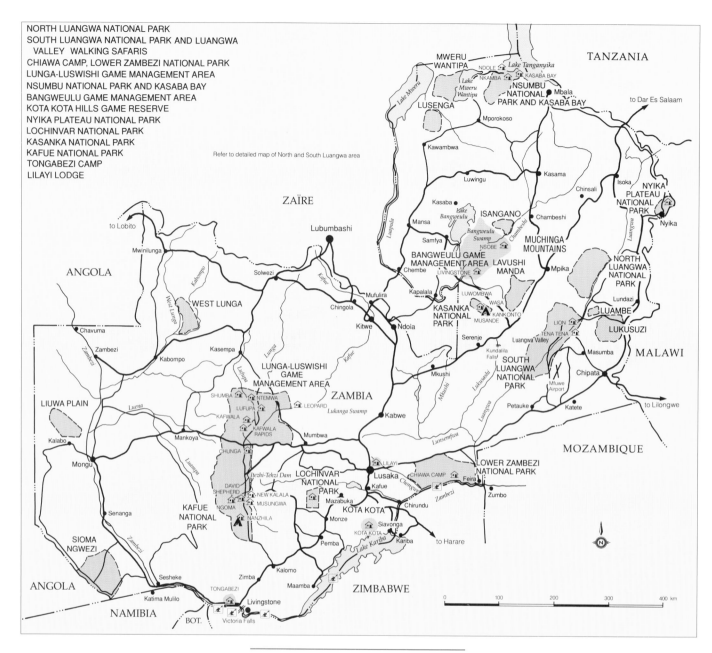

NORTH LUANGWA NATIONAL PARK
SOUTH LUANGWA NATIONAL PARK AND LUANGWA
 VALLEY WALKING SAFARIS
CHIAWA CAMP, LOWER ZAMBEZI NATIONAL PARK
LUNGA-LUSWISHI GAME MANAGEMENT AREA
NSUMBU NATIONAL PARK AND KASABA BAY
BANGWEULU GAME MANAGEMENT AREA
KOTA KOTA HILLS GAME RESERVE
NYIKA PLATEAU NATIONAL PARK
LOCHINVAR NATIONAL PARK
KASANKA NATIONAL PARK
KAFUE NATIONAL PARK
TONGABEZI CAMP
LILAYI LODGE

Refer to detailed map of North and South Luangwa area

Puku are found only in a very small area of the flood plain.

4. KOTA KOTA HILLS GAME RESERVE
VICTORIA FALLS REGION/ZAMBEZI VALLEY/LAKE KARIBA

Trail details: Guided walking safaris of 7 km/ 6 hours; 23 km/3 days; 49 km/6 days.

Bookings/permit: Write to Kota Kota Fund Committee, Private Bag W88, Lusaka for more information and bookings.

Facilities/amenities: Lodge accommodating 16 people; restaurant; private airstrip; swimming pool; day and night game-viewing drives; visits to Victoria Falls can be arranged.

Main attractions: 'Big Five' game; 300 bird species; stunning scenery; fishing.

Pertinent information: There is a limit of 8 to 16 people per group. This area is extremely hot towards the end of the dry season (September and October) and hikers must carry water with them. Canoeing and helicopter trips are possible – enquire at the reserve.

This 8 500-ha reserve, 300 km from Lusaka, is open all year, but is best in the months of May to December; mid-summer months tend to be extremely hot and uncomfortable.

Guided walking safaris from 1 to 6 days in duration can be arranged to meet the needs of the particular group. The basic route takes the visitor from the lodge to the radio station and on to Crocodile Bay, returning to the lodge via elephant thickets. A shorter route is from Tonga village to the radio station and then back to the lodge. These walks are not too strenuous (on average, 7 or 8 km are tackled in a day).

Keen bird-watchers will welcome the opportunity to observe some of the 300 different species found here, including the Taita falcon and the fish eagle, while the 'safari' enthusiast can experience the thrill of tracking big game like elephant, lion or buffalo on foot. The elusive leopard (more likely to be spotted at night during a game-viewing drive), as well as hippo, crocodile and the magnificent sable antelope, are some of the other animals that are found in the reserve.

5. LOCHINVAR NATIONAL PARK
KAFUE FLATS

Trail details: Guided game walks.

Permits/bookings: Contact Africa Bound, tel. (1) 216509 or 229154 ext. 22, 38 or 42, fax (1) 224267; PO Box 31567, Farmers House, Cairo Road, Lusaka. Permit for the park obtainable at the entrance gate.

Facilities/amenities: Old lodge accommodates 20 people; new lodge accommodates 60. Both are full-catering.

Main attractions: Prolific birdlife; game; Gwisho hot springs; archaeological sites.

Pertinent information: Access to the park is via Monze. Beware of bilharzia.

This 410-km^2 park is located on the flood plains south of the Kafue River. Over 400 species of birds, including many waterbirds, and game such as lechwe, blue wildebeest, Burchell's zebra and hippos can all be seen in the area. Close by are the Gwisho Hot Springs and Sebanzi Hill, both archaeological sites – the first of a Stone Age settlement, the latter of an Iron Age village.

Under the supervision of a game guard, visitors are encouraged to leave the comfort of the vehicle on game-viewing or bird-watching drives and explore the park on foot for a true taste of Africa.

6. LILAYI LODGE
NEAR LUSAKA

Trail details: 10-km/1,5- to 3-hour guided walks.

Permits/bookings: Reservations to be made through Lilayi Lodge, tel. (1) 228682/3, fax (1) 222406; PO Box 30093, Lusaka. Brochure and rates are available on request.

Facilities/amenities: 12 full-catering luxury chalets; conference facilities; game-viewing drives; horse-back safaris on request; trips to local villages.

Main attractions: Numerous game species; a variety of trees and birds.

Pertinent information: Transfer from airport in Lusaka can be arranged. Children under 12 can be accommodated on request. The best months are May to October.

Just 20 minutes' drive from Lusaka is Lilayi Lodge, situated on a private game ranch which supports 16 varieties of antelope, including impala, waterbuck, puku, eland, kudu, roan and sable antelope, and the unique lechwe. Burchell's zebra can also be seen, and night drives give the guest the opportunity to look out for small mammals such as civet, serval, porcupine, aardvark and pangolin.

The vegetation is miombo or munga woodland, with open areas of acacia or bauhinia. Over 230 species of birds, including many raptors and migrants, have been identified, and the calls of Heuglin's robin, turaco, cuckoo, guinea fowl and francolin can be heard in the early morning and evening. Guided walking safaris that cover about 10 km in 1,5 to 3 hours, depending on the group, are the best way to view the game on the ranch. Guests who wish to do so can also arrange to walk around the ranch unescorted.

Wasa Lodge is reflected in the waters of Lake Wasa, in Kasanka National Park.

7. CHIAWA CAMP
LOWER ZAMBEZI NATIONAL PARK

Trail details: Walking safaris.

Permits/bookings: Reservations to be made through G & G Safaris, tel. (1) 288290 or 261588, fax (1) 262683; PO Box 30972, Lusaka. Brochure and rates on request.

Facilities/amenities: Full-catering tented camp; game-viewing trips by boat or vehicle; night drives; angling in Zambezi.

Main attractions: Unspoilt wilderness area; wealth of big game and prolific birdlife.

Pertinent information: Groups are limited to 8–12 people. Transfer from Lusaka can be arranged. Access by road from Lusaka is via Chakwenga. The camp is open from the beginning of May to the end of October.

Chiawa is the only camp in the 1 092-km^2 Lower Zambezi National Park, which is situated in the wilderness area of the Lower Zambezi Valley. The area between the miombo woodland-covered hills and the Zambezi River is dominated by mopane and acacia, and hosts a wide variety of game species. One of the largest elephant populations in Africa can be found here, including some 'Big Tuskers'; the area is also home to hippo, buffalo, zebra, lion, leopard, cheetah, hyaena and a great variety of birds, such as huge colonies of carmine bee-eaters and the lone fish eagle.

Walking safaris under the supervision of an armed and experienced game guard are designed to suit the abilities of a particular group.

8. KASANKA NATIONAL PARK
EASTERN ZAMBIA

Trail details: Guided walks.

Permits/bookings: Reservations can be made through Inter-continental Travel, tel. (1) 263951 or 260705 or 260706, fax (1) 252178; PO Box 320187, Lusaka. Brochure and rates on request.

Facilities/amenities: Full-catering Wasa camp with 4 twin-bed rondavels; full-catering Luwombwa camp with accommodation for 10 in rondavels; full-catering Musande camp with accommodation for 12 in luxury safari tents; Kankonto camp site with full-catering service available; boating and fishing; excursions to the David Livingstone Memorial, Kundalila Falls, Nsalu Cave and Bangweulu Game Management Area (see overleaf) can be arranged.

Main attractions: Wilderness area; antelope; abundant birdlife; fishing.

Pertinent information: Air charters from Lusaka can be arranged. Access by road from Lusaka is via Serenje. The park is open all year round.

This 420-km^2 park is one of Zambia's smallest, but it encompasses eight lakes and four rivers, including the beautiful Luwombwa. A mixture of forest and swamp is home to some highly specialized mammals and birds, such as the rare shoebill stork and the blue monkey. Elephant, hippo, hartebeest, sable, bushbuck, reedbuck, waterbuck, warthog, baboon, jackal, hyaena and leopard all inhabit the area, and the lakes and rivers are ideal for fishing trips. Guided walks have been designed for the visitor

South Luangwa National Park is where walking safaris really began.

10. SOUTH LUANGWA NATIONAL PARK AND LUANGWA VALLEY
EASTERN ZAMBIA

Established in 1938, the South Luangwa National Park is 9 050 ha in extent and most of it lies west of the Luangwa River. One of the largest and most varied concentrations of wildlife in the world can be found in the park, and the variety of walking safaris offered by the operators of the lodges and camps gives you a unique opportunity to experience wild Africa on foot. Indeed, the walking safari has its birthplace in the South Luangwa National Park, where the hiker can walk at a leisurely pace, accompanied by an armed game scout, among wild animals in their natural habitat. Elephants are plentiful, as are lions and leopards, hippos and crocodiles. Few black rhino occur but amongst the variety of wildlife are Cape buffalo, zebra, kudu, puku, impala, waterbuck and roan antelope; the visitor can also see Cookson's wildebeest and

to explore some of the park's most interesting habitats to not only observe the mammals and birds but also to examine the fascinating wealth of plant life. Adventurous hikers can creep through the 'mushitu' forest, where trees up to 30 m in height form a closed canopy; easier walks are those that skirt the grassy plains where herds of antelope graze or explore the lakes and rivers which are inhabited by hippo, crocodile and waterbirds. It is worth spending some time quietly observing the unique and shy swamp-dwelling sitatunga from a hide built for that purpose before heading back to the camp.

9. BANGWEULU GAME MANAGEMENT AREA
EASTERN ZAMBIA

Trail details: Guided walks. See map p. 314.

Permits/bookings: For more information, contact **Shiwa Safaris**, tel. (1) 611171; Private Bag E3295, Lusaka; or **Getaway Safaris**, tel. (1) 217230 or 213678; PO Box 32212, Lusaka; or **Kasanka Wildlife Conservation**, PO Box 36657, Lusaka.

Facilities/amenities: Full catering Nsobe camp accommodates 10 in chalets, each with own bathroom; Livingstone camp has self-catering accommodation for special-interest groups; game-viewing drives are offered, and there are game-viewing and bird-watching hides.

Main attractions: True wilderness area with magnificent flood plains and marshes.

Pertinent information: From Lusaka, access by road is via the Mpiksa road. The camps are open from 5 May to 1 December as roads in the area are impassable in the rainy season.

Seventeen rivers flow into the Lake Bangweulu basin. These vast wetlands support a large and interesting variety of bird species (more than 400), including the rare shoebill stork, which breeds in the papyrus swamps here. The unique lechwe and shy sitatunga, as well as the clawless otter, tsessebe, reedbuck, buffalo, elephant, lion and leopard, add to the rich variety of wildlife in the area. Visitors can explore the area on foot, accompanied by a game guard.

Trail details: Half-day guided walks.

Permits/bookings: For **Kapani Lodge, Luwi and Nsolu bush camps:** tel. (62) 45015, fax (62) 252178; PO Box 100, Mfuwe; for **Tena Tena and Nkwali bush camps:** tel. (62) 45017, fax (62) 45076; PO Box 320154, Lusaka; early booking is essential for the very popular Tena Tena camp; for **Chinzombo Safari Lodge:** Save the Rhino Trust; tel. (1) 211644, fax (01) 45076; PO Box 320169, Lusaka; for **Chamilandu and Kuyenda bush camps:** tel. (62) 45074, fax (62) 45076; PO Box 59, Mfuwe; for **Manze bush camp:** tel (62) 45053, fax (62) 45076; PO Box 85, Mfuwe; for **Kakuli and Muchenja bush camps:** tel. (1) 224427/57, PO Box 37783, Lusaka; for **Chichele and Mfuwe lodges:** tel. (62) 45018 or 45062; PO Box 69, Mfuwe; for **Chibembe Safari Lodge and Nsefu bush camp:** tel. (1) 220122, fax (1) 220166; PO Box 35058, Lusaka.

Facilities/amenities: Kapani Lodge accommodates 16 in 4 *en suite* twin-bed stone chalets, and has a swimming pool and curio shop; Luwi rustic bush camp accommodates 6 in 4 thatched, bamboo rooms, and has a shady dining area and separate hot shower and flush toilet; Nsolu bush camp accommodates 6 in 4 *en suite* grass huts with verandahs; all 3 camps are fully catering and serviced; day and night game-viewing drives are offered; a visit to a crocodile farm or a local village, as well as leisurely picnic drives or a nature walk can be arranged from Kapani. Tena Tena camp accommodates 12 in 6 *en suite* 2-bed tents under a thatched roof; a low, unobtrusive electric fence around perimeter of camp is switched on at night; Nkwali camp accommodates 12 in 6 *en suite* twin-bed chalets; both camps have a wildlife library, offer day and night game-viewing drives, and are full catering and serviced. Chinzombo Safari Lodge accommodates 18 in *en suite* thatched chalets, and has a dining room and bar, swimming pool and curio shop; day and night game-viewing drives, all-day safaris with picnic lunches and visits to a local village are offered; Chamilandu bush camp has 4 *en suite* mopane wood, reed and grass chalets and is fully catering; Kuyenda bush camp has reed and grass huts with modern toilet facilities, and offers game-viewing drives; both bush camps have bar facilities and each accommodates 6. Manze bush camp has *en suite* rondavels and is fully catering. Kakuli and Muchenja bush camps each have 5 to 7 twin-bed bamboo and thatch huts with mosquito nets, separate toilets and showers, dining room and lounge, and paraffin lamps for lighting; day and night game-viewing drives are offered. The luxurious

Chichele Lodge has an air-conditioned dining room, fully stocked bar, video, swimming pool and curio shop; guests can visit a crocodile farm or a cultural village; Mfuwe Lodge offers accommodation in 12 twin-bed chalets and also has a restaurant, bar, swimming pool, curio shop, video and conference facilities; game-viewing drives are offered at both places. Chibembe Safari Lodge accommodates 40 in *en suite* wooden chalets with verandahs; the camp has a swimming pool; day and night game drives are offered, with a special Sundowner Drive; day trips to Bangweulu Swamps via a 5-seater aircraft can be arranged; Nsefu bush camp is the oldest tourist camp in Zambia, and consists of 6 *en suite* 2-bed thatched rondavels; game can be viewed at the waterhole from the bar at the camp or a hide next to the waterhole; game-viewing drives are also offered.

Main attractions: Abundant birdlife; wilderness atmosphere; close contact with big game; crystal clear water stream at Tena Tena.

Pertinent information: Luwi and Nsolu are only open from 1 June to 31 October as they are inaccessible when it rains; guided walks at Kapani, Luwi and Nsolu are for a maximum of 6 people, and are only conducted in the dry season, from June to November. Walking safaris from Tena Tena and Nkwali are conducted from June to October; children under 12 are not permitted, but exceptions may be made for a group booking. Chinzombo is open from April through to early January, while Chamilandu and Kuyenda are open from June to October; walks are only conducted in the dry season, for up to 7 people; children under 12 are not permitted on walks. Tsetse flies are present in the area of Manze bush camp; there is a limit of 6 hikers per group. Tsetse flies are also present in the region of Kakuli and Muchenja bush camps; there is a limit of 6 to 8 people per group; no children under 12 are allowed on walks; the camps are only open in the dry season, from June to the end of October. There is a limit of 7 people per walking group at Chichele and Mfuwe; walks are only conducted between the beginning of June and the end of October. Chibembe and Nsefu are only open from the beginning of June to the end of October. Visitors can fly in to Mfuwe airport where transport to the lodge or safari camp can usually be arranged. Be prepared for an extra fee of 15% sales tax plus a 10% service charge to be added to your accommodation bill. Some daily rates do not include national park daily fees; sometimes an extra fee is charged for guided walks; drinks are usually not included in your daily fee.

Thornicroft's giraffe, both of which are endemic to the area. About 400 species of birds, with migrants visiting the area in the 'green' season, make the Luangwa Valley a paradise for bird-watchers.

Kapani Lodge is owned by Norman Carr, well-known conservationist and author with over 50 years' bush experience, and is located just outside the park. It overlooks a quiet lagoon beside the Luangwa River, and is a mere 5 km from the park entrance gate, and a 35-minute drive from Mfuwe airport. The guided walks of about 4 km/3 hours from Kapani usually take place in the morning, with the trained guides pointing out features of interest, including local bushlore. The walks are flexible, and can be tailored to suit the interests of each particular group.

For those wanting to experience a wilderness atmosphere on foot rather than from a vehicle, the **Luwi** and **Nsolu bush camps** are ideal. Close contact with big game, and especially the opportunity to observe lions on foot, makes the guided walks of about 4 km/3 hours from these camps very exciting. The camps are situated in an isolated section of the park in open savannah woodland, within an hour's drive of Kapani. Approximately 10 km apart, they nestle under shady evergreen trees on the banks of the Luwi Sand River, a tributary of the Luangwa River. **Luwi camp** is situated near a large oxbow lagoon teeming with hippo and crocodile, while **Nsolu camp** is near a hide overlooking a waterhole where game-viewing is very rewarding.

Situated inside the park in the remote Nsefu sector on the east bank of the Luangwa River, under an evergreen mahogany grove, is **Tena Tena** – the only fully tented camp in the park. Relaxed bush walks with expert guides and armed game scouts are conducted from 6.30 am to 10.30 am and cover about 6 km, and guests can venture out on a late afternoon walk at 4.00 pm The emphasis is on flexibility, and hikers are likely to see Cookson's wildebeest and eland in the area. **Nkwali** is 30 km south of Tena Tena, just outside the park in the all-weather Mfuwe area, and is an informal camp with shared facilities. It is just 30 minutes' drive from the park entrance and the setting of the camp is secluded and in a beautiful wooded area facing the Luangwa River. Walks of about 6 km/4 hours through the grassy plains and woodlands – excellent game country – have hikers looking out for Thornicroft's giraffe, elephants and puku, or the purplecrested lourie. Special safaris can be organized in advance for artists or photographers from Tena Tena or Nkwali.

Chinzombo Safari Lodge and the bush camps are owned by the Save the Rhino Trust, which was established in 1980 to help combat commercial poaching of not only the nearly extinct black rhino, but also elephant. Located in a shady grove of magnificent ebony and mahogany trees on the banks of the Luangwa River, **Chinzombo Safari Lodge** is both attractive and comfortable. Walks of 3 to 4 hours are conducted in the morning and afternoon in the park and the adjacent game management areas under the supervision of a professional safari guide and an armed wildlife scout. The route is dictated by the wishes of the group, and hikers can track down the unique Thornicroft's giraffe or Cookson's wildebeest. **Chamilandu** and **Kuyenda**, the two bush camps, are located further south in a remote wilderness area, and are ideal bases from

NORTH LUANGWA NATIONAL PARK
SOUTH LUANGWA NATIONAL PARK
AND LUANGWA VALLEY WALKING SAFARIS

which to explore the area on foot on 3- to 4-hour walks. Chamilandu is reserved exclusively for walking safaris. Special interest groups such as ornithologists or photographers can be catered for at Chinzombo, Chamilandu and Kuyenda.

Manze bush camp offers safaris that take hikers through mopane and riverine woodland, open grassland, palm groves and deciduous thickets, in order to see as wide a variety of game as possible. Walks range from 6 to 16 km; there are no set routes as the safari operators adapt each outing to suit the interests of each particular group.

Kakuli faces a beautiful open plain by the Luangwa River, while **Muchenja** is situated further north amongst a cluster of age-old ebony trees by the river.

Walks of 6 to 8 km/3 hours are conducted under the supervision of a guide and armed game scouts, and the route varies according to the presence of game and the special interests of the group.

Mfuwe Lodge is located on the tree-shaded banks of a lazy lagoon, adjacent to the Luangwa River, while **Chichele Lodge** is perched on top of a hill that overlooks the Luangwa flood plain. Walking safaris of about 8 km/3 hours, in the company of an armed game scout and a qualified guide, are conducted from both lodges in the dry season. From Mfuwe, the walks explore savannah woodland and riverine-vegetated areas, and the best months are June to August. The walks from Chichele are a little more strenuous and explore the riverine vegetated locations.

Chibembe Safari Lodge is situated under enormous Natal mahogany and thorn trees, just across the Luangwa River and outside the South Luangwa National Park, while **Nsefu** is located well within the park on a sweeping bend of the river with a breathtaking view and remarkable wildlife. Game-viewing walks are conducted in the morning and afternoon and last about 3 to 4 hours.

11. WALKING SAFARIS
SOUTH LUANGWA NATIONAL PARK

Trail details: 1- to 3-day walking safaris; 7- to 10-day portered walking safaris. See map p. 317.

Permits/bookings: Contact **Shenton Safaris**, tel. or fax (62) 290146; PO Box 57, Mfuwe; or **Wilderness Trails**, tel. (1) 220122, fax. (01) 220166; PO Box 35058, Lusaka; or **Robin Pope Safaris**, tel. (1) 45017, fax (1) 45076; PO Box 320154, Lusaka; or **Chinzombo Safaris**, tel. (1) 211644, fax (1) 226736; PO Box 30106, Lusaka. Brochure and rates on request.

Facilities/amenities: Shenton Safaris: full-catering Lion camp with 4 luxury, thatched, 2-bed *en suite* chalets; day and night game-viewing drives offered, and picnics as well as visits to a local village can be arranged; game-viewing hides are also available. Wilderness Trails: fully staffed bush camps are set up each year with hot showers and bar facilities; luggage is carried by porters. Robin Pope Safaris: mobile camp moved by truck with support vehicle; accommodation in mosquito-proof tents, each sleeping 2, with folding camp beds and comfortable bedding, and bucket shower and bush toilet; all catering provided and camp fully staffed. Chinzombo Safaris: all camping equipment and catering provided and carried by porters; accommodation in spacious stand-up tents with air mattresses and comfortable bedding.

Main attractions: Wide variety of game; abundant birdlife (400 species); true safari experience in wilderness.

Pertinent information: Shenton Safaris: limit of 6 people per group; June to September are the best months; the daily fee is all inclusive. Wilderness Trails: groups are limited to 7 people and no children under 12 are permitted; advanced booking is necessary, and at least 1 night prior to the walking safari must be spent at Chibembe; the safaris are run between June and October. Robin Pope Safaris: Groups are limited to 4 to 6 people; daily rates are all inclusive, but do not include daily national park fees. Chinzombo Safaris: operated for a maximum of 6 people from July to September.

Walking safaris of 1 to 10 days are offered by various tour operators in the South Luangwa National Park (see entry 10 on page 316) and give the hiker the opportunity to really experience Africa and encounter a rich variety of wildlife, including lion, leopard, buffalo, elephant, spotted hyaena, Thornicroft's giraffe, Cookson's wildebeest, puku, honey badger, hartebeest, hippo, crocodile, Burchell's zebra, kudu and other game, on foot. Keen birdwatchers can keep binoculars at hand and look out for Pel's fishing owl, carmine bee-eaters and pelicans amongst the over 400 species of birds that inhabit the park.

Shenton Safaris' Lion camp is situated in a part of the park where the vegetation varies from riverine to mopane woodland. Guests are taken on a 25-km/1-day guided hike to Old Lion camp; a shortcut to reduce the length of the walk to 12,5 km can be taken across a vast plain. After spending the night at the old camp, intrepid hikers can undertake to hike back to New Lion camp, or the less energetic can be transported back to Chinzombo by vehicle. Both camps are situated on the banks of the Luangwa River under cool riverine shade, deep inside the park. Trees in the area include mahogany, African ebony and sausage trees.

Wilderness Safaris will take hikers on a 3-day **'walk on the wild side'** into a wilderness area where riverine/riparian woodland is dotted with small streams and lagoons for a true safari experience.

Robin Pope Safaris offer 5-day **walking mobile safaris** in a remote area of the park, close to the boundary on the Mupamudzi River (a tributary of the Luangwa). A camp is set up in advance of the walking party. Participants walk 10 to 15 km per day; and although these safaris are exclusively for hikers, the less energetic can hitch a ride with the support vehicle to get to the next camp. In the morning, the group hikes 6 to 10 km to the next camp; afternoon tea is followed by another walk around the camp of 2 to 3 km. Unusual antelope like oribi, roan, hartebeest and reedbuck reside in the area.

The **portered walking safaris** offered by **Chinzombo** explore the wilderness areas of the park for 7 to 10 days. The trip is led by two naturalists, while armed scouts and a retinue of porters accompany the group for an old-fashioned safari experience that emulates the travels of hunters and explorers into the unmapped hinterlands a century ago.

12. NORTH LUANGWA NATIONAL PARK
EASTERN ZAMBIA

Trail details: 15-to 20-km walks. See map p. 317.

Permits/bookings: Contact Shiwa Safaris, tel. or fax (1) 611171; Private Bag E395, Lusaka for more information.

Facilities/amenities: Kapishya Hot Springs camp has *en suite* pole and grass chalets, each with a verandah; Buffalo camp provides accommodation for 8 people in spacious safari tents with private facilities. Guests can visit the hot springs, or Shiwa House (a 40-room mansion built in the 1920s), or can enjoy bird-watching walks, go river-rafting or embark on an expedition up Nachipala Hill where David Livingstone took bearings in 1867.

Main attractions: True wilderness area with abundant birdlife and wildlife; hot springs.

Pertinent information: Beware of bilharzia, and note that nights can be cool. Safaris into the North Luangwa National Park are only run from June to October. Six people per group is the ideal size for these walking safaris.

Waterbuck linger on the bed of a receding river in South Luangwa National Park.

A typical rural settlement, close to the Lusaka-Luangwa road.

North Luangwa National Park is a 4 636-km^2 wilderness area that has recently been opened to visitors and is often referred to as the last remaining 'real' African park. It is bordered by the rugged Muchinga Escarpment in the west and the mighty Luangwa River in the east. The Kapishya Hot Springs camp is situated outside the park, on the estate of Shiwa Ngandu, which boasts an incongruous English mansion in the middle of Africa. The camp is situated on the banks of the Manshya River, 26 km west of the magnificent Shiwa House, which overlooks the 'Lake of the Royal Crocodiles'. Buffalo camp is situated in the park, on a bend of the Mwaleshi River where buffalo and other plains game come to drink. Both camps are used as a base for walking safaris into the wilderness area of the North Luangwa National Park, which, with its mopane woodlands and open plains, riverine forest, thickets and lagoons, is superb walking country. Lion, elephant, buffalo, leopard, hippo, antelope, waterfowl, birds of prey, storks, kingfishers, ibises and bee-eaters are just some of the creatures that make their home here.

13. NYIKA PLATEAU NATIONAL PARK
EASTERN ZAMBIA

Trail details: Walking safaris. See map p. 314.

Permits/bookings: Contact Robin Pope Safaris, tel. (62) 45017, fax (62) 45076; PO Box 320154, Lusaka. Brochure and rates on request.

Facilities/amenities: Fully catering accommodation at Tena Tena (see entry 10 on page 316), and in a colonial resthouse in Nyika. Day and night game-viewing drives are offered.

Main attractions: Beautiful scenery; remote wilderness area.

Pertinent information: The safaris are offered from June to October for 4 guests; no children under 12 are permitted.

The unique Nyika Plateau National Park is the smallest in Zambia at 80 km^2, and extends into Malawi. The hilly area with its numerous streams makes a stark contrast to the flat bush areas of the Luangwa Valley, and is superb walking country. Excellent plains game includes roan antelope, eland, reedbuck and duiker, while leopard and serval can also be spotted. The walking safaris offered by Robin Pope include 5 days at Tena Tena in the South Luangwa National Park (see entry 10 on page 316) and 5 days on the Nyika Plateau where the keen hiker can venture out each day on foot, accompanied by an experienced trail guide, and explore this magnificent area.

14. NSUMBU NATIONAL PARK AND KASABA BAY
LAKE TANGANYIKA

Trail details: Guided walks. See map p. 314.

Permits/bookings: For reservations, contact Circuit Safaris, tel. (2) 212277 or 214447; PO Box 21491, Kitwe. Brochure and rates on request.

Facilities/amenities: Kasaba Bay Lodge with 14 *en suite* chalets and Nkamba Bay Lodge with 9 *en suite* chalets; Ndole Bay Lodge with 14 *en suite* chalets; all lodges have swimming pools; 12-hole golf course at Kasaba; crocodile farm; fishing; Kalambo Falls.

Main attractions: Lake Tanganyika; fishing.

Pertinent information: Beware of crocodiles and tsetse flies. Visitors can fly to Mpulungu and be transferred by boat to their destination.

The 2 020-km^2 Nsumbu National Park encompasses about 80 km of lakeshore, from deserted stretches of beach to vertical cliffs and rocky coves. Away from the lake, like much of Zambia, the rugged hills of the plateau are covered mainly by miombo woodland and small areas of open woodland. Game in the park includes a variety of antelope – roan, sable, eland, the rare blue duiker and shy swamp-dwelling sitatunga – as well as hartebeest, buffalo and zebra; lions, including some magnificent black-maned males, and leopards are often spotted at night on drives; and the lake itself teems with crocodile, hippo, waterbirds and a variety of fish. The elephants of Nsumbu are a major attraction – during the dry season herds pass the lodges as they follow ancestral routes to the lake, and at Kasaba Bay they wander through the lodge on their way to the water almost every night. The lack of a good road network makes game-viewing by vehicle difficult, but the area offers hikers superb opportunities for guided walks.

Hikers on a mobile walking safari near Tena Tena camp.

MALAWI

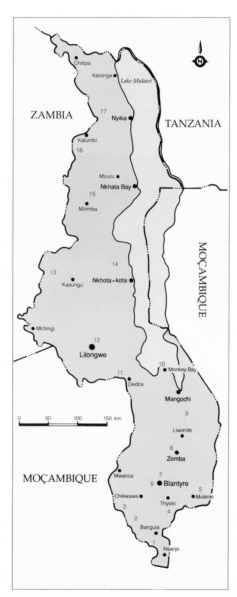

Malawi is a small country: 901 km in length and varying from 81 to 161 km in width, little more than twice the size of the Kruger National Park. Bordered by Tanzania in the north, Moçambique in the east and Zambia in the west, Malawi embraces a diversity of natural environments. Lake Malawi with its shores of long sweeping beaches, rocky headlands and sheltered coves, the highland plateau of Nyika, and the often mist-shrouded mountain massifs of Zomba and Mulanje are just a few of the natural features in this country of limitless walking and hiking potential.

Although Malawi is one of the most densely populated countries in Africa, this does not in the least detract from its value as an outdoors haven. Malawians are among the most helpful and courteous people I have met and their natural charm is likely to remain an outstanding impression of your visit. There is no doubt in my mind why Malawi is affectionately known as 'the warm heart of Africa'.

Malawi lies not far south of the equator and there are times of the year, especially along the shores of the lake and in the Shire River Valley in the summer months, when the sticky heat is unpleasant. However, because of the country's diverse topography, you can always escape into

the high mountains with their cool glades and streams which provide a beautiful retreat from the oppressive humidity of the lowlands. Most rain falls from December to March, and the frequent thunderstorms take the edge off the heat; from time to time the 'Chiperone', a cool misty cloud, blows up from the Moçambique plains to cool the southern parts of the country.

From June to July the weather is generally cool and dry and, in many ways, this is the finest time of the year for hiking. April and May, after the rains, offer excellent walking conditions. August and September are pleasantly warm, while October to March is extremely hot. It should be remembered that during the summer rainy season many roads become impassable.

Malawi has two social codes which are surprisingly well enforced and which apply equally to visitors and residents. In public places, women must wear skirts which cover their knees, although this is unnecessary in the more remote places such as Zomba, Mulanje, Dedza, Viphya and Nyika, as well as the lakeshore resorts. It is always wise to carry a skirt with you, especially if you are likely to walk through villages. A simple cotton skirt that can double as a pillow case when camping overnight on hiking trips is fine. The other restriction applies to men's hairstyles: long hair (covering the neck and ears) is illegal.

When buying provisions, it is also worth bearing in mind that hikers who hire porters are generally expected to provide basic food for them for the duration of the hike.

All visitors require valid passports; some nationals (including South Africans) do not need visas. In general, immigration formalities are minimal for visitors intending to stay less than three months.

The Shire River races towards the cataracts in Majete Wildlife Reserve.

kudu, impala, duiker, samango monkey and banded mongoose are some of the common species present.

The Wildlife Society of Malawi has a guide booklet for their 2,5-km nature trail, which is in the vicinity of the chalets. Visitors can also walk from the car park to the viewing hides on their own. However, if hikers want to wander further afield, they must be accompanied by a game scout at all times.

3. MAJETE WILDLIFE RESERVE AND SHIRE RIVER CATARACTS
CHIKWAWA

> **Trail details:** Guided walks to prime game-viewing areas; walks on footpaths.
>
> **Permits/bookings:** Permits must be obtained from the Department of National Parks and Wildlife, tel. 723505, fax 723089; PO Box 30131, Lilongwe 3 for the reserve. A permit is not required to visit the cataracts.
>
> **Facilities/amenities:** Minimal camping facilities (wood-burning stove) in reserve; shallow bathing pools in the river; 4-bed chalet at the confluence of the Mkulumodzi and Shire rivers; picnic site at Kapichira Falls.
>
> **Main attractions:** Kapichira Falls; waterbirds; miombo and riverine woodland; cataracts; fishing for tigerfish and vundu; grave (national monument) of Richard Thornton, Richard Livingstone's geologist; birdlife; baobabs.
>
> **Pertinent information:** Anti-malaria precautions are essential. Some roads are not recommended for use after heavy rains. The most accessible of the falls are Kapichira Falls (southern end) and Mfumba Falls (northernmost major falls).

1. MWABVI WILDLIFE RESERVE
SOUTHERN REGION

> **Trail details:** Guided walks.
>
> **Permits/bookings:** These are necessary and must be obtained from the Department of National Parks and Wildlife, tel. 723505, fax 723089; PO Box 30131, Lilongwe 3.
>
> **Facilities/amenities:** 2 twin-bedded rondavels; small camp site; basic ablution facilities; open wood fires for cooking.
>
> **Main attractions:** Mwabvi Gorge; Mulaki hills; sandstone outcrops; Mwabvi and Thanguzi rivers; water holes; Nyantoko Hill; birdlife; view of Zambezi River.
>
> **Pertinent information:** Malaria is present – precautions must be taken.

This small reserve in the southernmost part of Malawi, approximately 130 km from Blantyre, is situated in the hot lower Shire Valley and comprises, for the most part, mopane woodland. The reserve is drained by the upper Thangadzi River. It is extremely isolated and very difficult to reach as the roads leading to it are in bad condition (and in some cases they are non-existent since the 1989 floods).

The scenery is spectacular and rugged, with several permanent water holes, the most dramatic being the steep-sided Mwabvi Gorge, home to many shade-loving plants. Kudu, sable, suni and warthog, as well as nyala, buffalo and a few remaining black rhino can be found in the reserve; while the evergreen thicket along the rivers is a good place to spot a variety of bird species.

The guided walks, in the company of a game scout, must be arranged in advance with the Department of National Parks and Wildlife.

Human settlements in the southern part of Mwabvi pose a threat to its long-term viability.

2. LENGWE NATIONAL PARK
SOUTHERN MALAWI

> **Trail details:** 2,5-km self-guided nature trail. Guided walks are also available.
>
> **Permits/bookings:** Day visitors must obtain a permit from the Park Warden on arrival; overnight visitors must book in advance with the Department of National Parks and Wildlife, tel. 723505, fax 723089; PO Box 30131, Lilongwe 3.
>
> **Maps/information:** Booklet for nature trail available from the Wildlife Society of Malawi, tel./fax 643765; PO Box 1429, Blantyre.
>
> **Facilities/amenities:** Game-viewing and bird-watching hides; picnic shelter; limited chalet accommodation; network of game-viewing drives; newly constructed bar.
>
> **Main attractions:** Diverse wildlife; prolific birdlife, especially good in December and January.
>
> **Pertinent information:** After heavy rain the roads in the park are extremely hazardous. Visitors must bring their own food, which the camp staff will cook on request. Anti-malaria precautions are essential. Bilharzia is present. The nearest food and fuel supplies are 18 km away at Nchalo.

Lengwe National Park is a wonderful small (887 km^2) reserve situated 74 km south-west of Blantyre. Its flat, lowland alluvial plain is covered by thicket and riparian forest, and its wildlife is abundant and diverse; of special interest is the nyala. Lengwe was originally proclaimed to protect a population of this large, beautifully marked antelope, which is found in great numbers in the park, where it reaches the northernmost limit of its distribution.

Livingstone's suni and the crested guineafowl are other species with limited distributions which can readily be seen here. Sharp eyes will spot them drinking at forested waterholes. Buffalo, bushbuck,

From Blantyre, the drive down to the Shire area is spectacular. The road descends via a 1 000-m escarpment of hairpin bends to a hot land of baobabs, prolific birdlife, and the lazy Shire River. The 691-km^2 Majete Wildlife Reserve is situated between the Shire, Mwanza and Mkulumadzi rivers. Visitors can reach the reserve via the M8 from Blantyre until Chikwawa, and then by turning right and continuing for approximately 23 km.

A large part of the vegetation in the area consists of miombo woodland, with some riverine forest, and extensive bamboo thickets in the western section. Elephant, leopard, kudu, waterbuck, sable, Sharpe's grysbok, Burchell's zebra, warthog and hippo are present in the reserve, although not often seen, as game is sparse in Majete.

Crossing the river at Chikwawa, a 23-km road leads to the impressive Kapichira Falls, situated at the southern end of the cataracts on the Shire's descent to the lowlands. The magnificent falls are a bird-watcher's paradise (over 600 species of birds have been recorded, of which the carmine bee-eater, colonizing the river banks, is the most vividly outstanding), and there is good fishing below the falls for the angler. Kapichira Falls were the first of the Shire River's 64-km stretch of cataracts encountered by David Livingstone when he attempted to reach Lake Malawi by riverboat.

Arrangements can be made through the Department of National Parks and Wildlife to go on guided walks in the reserve, and hikers can explore the river and cataracts, including Kapichira Falls, freely along the footpaths in the area.

Estate workers amid the emerald green of tea plantations near Thyolo Mountain.

4. THYOLO MOUNTAIN
SOUTH OF BLANTYRE

Trail details: Footpaths through the forest.

Permits/bookings: Permission to enter the area is necessary, and must be obtained in advance from Satemwa Tea Estate, tel. 472233 or 472276; PO Box 6, Thyolo.

Facilities/amenities: None.

Main attractions: Prolific birdlife; significant area of sub-montane evergreen forest.

Pertinent information: The paths are indistinct. Anti-malaria precautions are essential.

Thyolo (or Cholo) Mountain is situated 50 km south of Blantyre, and rises to 1 462 m. The area is very special for bird-watching; it is one of the few places where the Thyolo alethe and whitewinged apalis can be seen, and the greenheaded oriole is also present. The sub-montane forest is under threat from illegal woodcutters and one can only hope that this unique patch does not disappear.

It is 14 km from the main road to the forest, and due to the maze of tea roads it is easy to get lost – ask for directions at the estate gate.

5. MULANJE MOUNTAIN
SOUTHERN REGION

Mount Mulanje, south-east of Blantyre, is the highest massif in south-central Africa. About 20 km beyond the village of Mulanje, a minor road to the left leads to the mountain. One of the best aspects of Mulanje is that any reasonably fit person can hike and climb the mountain, as the steep footpaths to the plateau, requiring a 1 000- to 1 500-m ascent,

Trail details: Hiking trips lasting between 7 and 9 days; a network of paths.

Permits/bookings: Must be obtained well in advance from the Ministry of Forestry and Natural Resources, tel. 465218; PO Box 50, Mulanje. It is vitally important to check and confirm your bookings regularly before departure; double and even triple bookings are common! To book the Likhabula forestry cottage, tel. 465218; for the church hostel, tel. 465262.

Information/maps: Contact the Mountain Club of Malawi for details of mountain climbing opportunities and availability of huts: tel. 634436; PO Box 240, Blantyre.

Facilities/amenities: Huts at Lichenya and Thuchila plateaux, and at Ruo, Sombani and Madzeka basins, accommodating 4–20 hikers and equipped with tables, chairs, cooking places, firewood, water, emergency first-aid kit and toilets; a small complex in the Likhabula Forestry Depot, at the base of the mountain, which has a forestry cottage with 4 rooms and 9 beds, plus a lounge and kitchen – this is a good base for hiking (in the same complex a church hostel runs 3 self-catering chalets); the Red Route shelter (at base of Sapitwa Peak), made of corrugated steel with an earthern floor, accommodates 8 people at a very tight squeeze, and no amenities are provided; porters can be hired.

Main attractions: Beautiful mountain area; montane evergreen forest, including the Mulanje cedar; wild flowers and birdlife; trout fishing.

Pertinent information: Huts have watchmen who will perform minor chores and who should be tipped. If you have hired porters, you are also expected to provide them with a small tip each, plus basic food for the duration of the hike. The Malawi Mountain Club maintains its own equipment (beds, mattresses, lamps, utensils and porters' blankets) under lock and key at each hut; club members or reciprocal members can obtain keys. Mid-April to the end of July is the best climbing season, although wet, misty conditions and night frosts can occur. High temperatures are experienced between August and November with thunderstorms between November and April. Anti-malaria precautions are essential.

Their fields tilled, villagers can enjoy the unrivalled view of Mount Mulanje.

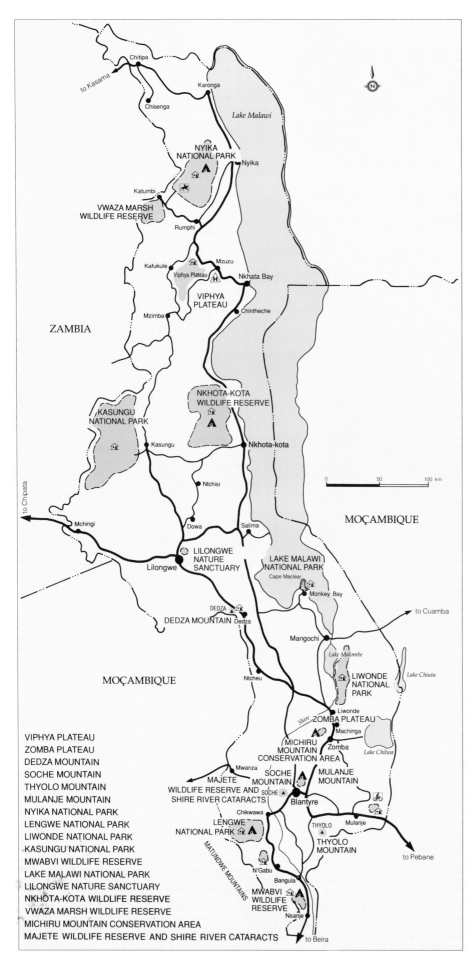

can be negotiated with the aid of porters. Once on the 1 830- to 2 133-m plateau, the numerous footpaths and firebreaks make for relatively easy going. Huts are approximately half a day's walk apart, allowing time to climb Mulanje's high peaks, 20 of which reach 2 500 m or more. The highest point, Sapitwa (3 002 m), is a reasonable day's round-trip from the Red Route shelter, and involves considerable rock scrambling. The route is marked with painted arrows.

Mulanje is blessed with such topographic and ecological diversity that everybody, from the nature explorer to the rock climber, is well catered for. Divided by the Ruo River's deep valley, the 26- by 22-km massif consists of rolling, grassy uplands; deep, forested kloofs and gullies; rocky, boulder-strewn peaks, and montane evergreen forests which host the 46-m tall endemic Mulanje cedar. These almost impenetrable, jungle-like montane forests, with their bubbling sounds of water and clear bird calls and songs, are strikingly primeval in atmosphere. The Mulanje cedars are still exploited today, but, because they are so large, they must be sawn into planks first, before they can be taken down the mountain.

Wild flowers are a constant source of beauty. As a result of the varying altitudes, aspects and moisture regimes, the species are highly diversified; some flowers are endemic, while many resemble those found in Cape fynbos.

Mammals and snakes are not numerous on the Mulanje plateau, the former because of indiscriminate hunting, the latter because of the altitude. Bird-watching is both exciting and frustrating when you try to spy on forest species. The hiker who sits quietly near a path in the rain forest may be fortunate enough to spot the rameron pigeon, Livingstone's lourie, whitetailed flycatcher, scarce swift and longtailed wagtail (along the rivers) and other elusive species. The augur buzzard, lanner falcon and rock kestrel are frequently seen on the wing. At night, the soothing hoot of owls can be heard at Likhabula Lodge.

6. SOCHE MOUNTAIN
BLANTYRE

Trail details: Two nature walks: 3-hour circular walk; 45-minute one-way climb to the summit.

Permits/bookings: Not required.

Facilities/amenities: None.

Main attractions: Views; *Brachystegia* woodland; sub-montane evergreen forest; riparian woodland.

Pertinent information: Anti-malaria precautions are essential. The footpaths are very indistinct.

Soche Mountain overlooks the towns of Blantyre and Limbe, its conspicuous boulder standing regally at the summit, at an altitude of 1 530 m. Visits to the mountain, which is only 6 km from Blantyre centre, make an excellent half-day outing.

Drive along Kapeni Road in Blantyre until just before the top of the hill, where you turn right onto an untarred road. This road passes the Soche Secondary School and leads eventually to a stone quarry, where you may park your car. Approximately 250 m from the quarry, there is a path which runs past eucalyptus trees and cultivated plots, eventually joining a major path which runs either around the circumference of the reserve, or up to the summit of the mountain.

If you are looking for gentle exercise, the 3-hour circular route leading around the circumference of the forest reserve is ideal.

For more energetic walkers who wish to take in the views from the summit, the upward path winds across a gently undulating riverine valley, before heading upwards towards the summit. The occasional red arrow painted on rocks should confirm that you are on the right track, and approximately 45 minutes after setting out you should reach the summit. The final ascent to the beacon should not be undertaken by those afraid of heights, and if the weather is rainy or stormy it is best not to approach the exposed beacon at all.

The views from the beacon are magnificent, with the vista taking in the whole of Blantyre and Limbe, and Zomba and Mulanje in the distance. Aerial displays by the whitenecked raven, augur buzzard, lanner falcon and redwinged starling provide the animated entertainment.

The lower slopes of Soche Mountain are covered with *Brachystegia* woodland, where hikers may see a variety of birds, including the cardinal woodpecker, spotted creeper and rock cisticola. The higher slopes, which are covered in riparian evergreen forest, are home to the starred robin and yellowstreaked bulbul. There is much animal life in the reserve, and hikers walk to the bark of suspicious monkeys crashing their way through the trees. Return to the starting point by retracing your steps down the mountain.

Dense plantations are among the forests on the well-watered Zomba plateau.

7. MICHIRU MOUNTAIN CONSERVATION AREA
BLANTYRE

Trail details: 5 circular trails varying in duration from 30 minutes to 5 hours.

Permits/bookings: Not required, but large groups must give written notice in advance of their arrival to The Co-ordinator, Michiru Mountain Conservation Area, PO Box 619, Blantyre.

Facilities/amenities: Environmental education project; picnic and braai site; overnight camp sites in cleared areas; curio shop at office.

Main attractions: Largest natural woodlands near Blantyre (*Brachystegia* forest, riparian forest and sub-montane forest); splendid views from ridge walks; 200 bird species; animal life.

Pertinent information: Anti-malaria precautions are essential. May to October is the dry season with rain from November/December to March/April.

The 5 000-ha Michiru Mountain Conservation Area, adjacent to Blantyre and situated on the edge of the Rift Valley, is an exciting environmental education and recreation centre. This scientifically managed, diverse area comprises the largest natural woodlands near Blantyre: steep slopes of *Brachystegia* forest, riparian forest in stream valleys, and patches of sub-montane forest near the 1 473-m summit. Eucalyptus and pine plantations are also grown in the area.

Ridge walking yields superb views over the plains to the Kirk Range, the mountains around Ncheu and Dedza, and to Mulanje and Zomba.

As an environmental education project, three areas receive emphasis: forestry, farming and wildlife. The forestry reserve portrays a good example of successful wood plantations. The farming area covers about 400 ha devoted to raising dairy cattle for milk, butter and cream. In addition to maize and bananas grown for silage, several freshwater ponds provide good waterfowl habitats.

The wildlife section of the park has 5 main trails: Trail 1, along the lower part of the Mikwawa River, highlights the park's indigenous trees. Trails 2 and 3 wind about the base of Michiru Mountain and into the Mikwawa River Valley, passing hyaena caves, and crossing the river and its streams many times. The fourth trail ascends the peak, while the fifth trail runs along the mountain's summit to Tumbulumbu Hill. Night hiking to see nocturnal animals such as hyaena, leopard, serval, wildcat, civet, genet, jackal, porcupine, bushpig and galago, can be arranged.

8. ZOMBA PLATEAU
SOUTHERN REGION

Trail details: Various nature trails.

Permits/bookings: Must be obtained from the Malawi Department of Forestry, tel. 652555; PO Box 5493, Limbe.

Maps/information: Contact the Wildlife Society of Malawi, tel./fax 643765; PO Box 1429, Blantyre.

Facilities/amenities: 24 km of circular drives with a lookout at KuChawe Inn; camp site with water and toilets within walking distance of the hotel.

Main attractions: Panoramic views; waterfalls and kloofs; indigenous forest patches; abundant birdlife; fishing for rainbow trout.

Pertinent information: The area is subject to climatic extremes; very hot weather from August to November; thunderstorms from November to April; very heavy mist in winter. Anti-malaria precautions are essential.

From the town of Zomba, a narrow tarred road winds steeply upwards through thick forest to the top of Zomba Plateau, a syenitic rock massif rising 1 000 m above the surrounding plains. Zomba Plateau is the oldest forest reserve in Malawi, covered with conifers of Mulanje cedar, cypress and Mexican pine. All along the nature trails, roads and climbing routes that crisscross the plateau, hikers are rewarded with magnificent views.

The plateau is a forest reserve with streams, pools, pine and cedar stands, indigenous montane evergreen forest and grassland. Various peaks rise from the 1 830-m table, notably the striking Chiradzulu or Zomba Peak (2 088 m), Norimbe and Chagwa. Rock climbing is possible on Zomba's steep cliffs. To the east and south, the plateau is bounded by a sheer 762-m scarp, while to the west it is bounded by one of the main Rift Valley faults – a truly spectacular 1 220-m drop to the Shire River Valley floor.

The entire plateau is a mountain reserve, crisscrossed by mountain streams. There are cool pine forests, wide umbrella trees, mosses, ferns and creepers, and a variety of wild flowers.

In Mulunguzi Dam and the many streams there is excellent trout fishing. The circular road around the plateau offers breathtaking views of Mulanje across the broad Phalombe Plain, the Shire River with the Kirk Range on the horizon, as well as of Lake Chilwa to the east.

The Chingwe's Hole Nature Trail, with its informative guidebook to the natural history of the plateau (especially emphasizing orchids, succulents, fungi and birds), is one of my favourite short walks. It begins at Chingwe's Hole, which was once used as a burial place for thieves and outcasts, on the western side of Zomba Plateau. This trail, together with the Mulunguzi Nature Trail and other nature trails are projects of the Wildlife Society of Malawi, which has done a fine job promoting ecological awareness of natural areas remaining on the plateau.

Lake Malawi's Cape Maclear is a favourite venue for snorkellers.

10. LAKE MALAWI NATIONAL PARK
CAPE MACLEAR

Trail details: There are no formal trails, but this is a wonderful area for rambling.

Permits/bookings: Must be obtained from the Department of National Parks and Wildlife, tel. 723505, fax 723089; PO Box 30131, Lilongwe 3. Ask for available literature.

Facilities/amenities: The Golden Sands camp consists of 6 basic rondavels with 3 beds in each, and 5 chalets; no food or cutlery is provided, but beds and linen are; hotels nearby.

Main attractions: Nankumba Peninsula and offshore islands; over 450 species of tropical freshwater fish (largest number of species in any freshwater lake in the world); dramatic lake scenery, beaches, dunes and reed marshes; missionary graves at Cape Maclear (historical monument); prolific birdlife.

Pertinent information: Anti-malaria precautions are essential. The best way to visit the park is by boat.

9. LIWONDE NATIONAL PARK
LIWONDE

Trail details: Guided walks.

Permits/bookings: Must be obtained from the Department of National Parks and Wildlife, tel. 723505, fax 723089; PO Box 30131, Lilongwe 3. For details of the Mvuu camps contact Central African Wilderness Safaris, tel. 723527, fax 723548 in Lilongwe; or tel. (011) 8841458, fax 8836255 in Johannesburg.

Facilities/amenities: Boats permitted on the river; river cruises offered; comfortable Chinguni guesthouse near park entrance with 5 double rooms, dining room, kitchen and bar – bedding, cooking and eating utensils provided; rondavel camp on Shire River with basic facilities only – guests must bring their own food, bedding and cooking and eating utensils; Mvuu self-catering camp and Mvuu luxury camp are planned for mid-1993, to be run by Central African Wilderness Safaris – 8 fully equipped double units (linen provided) and ablution block.

Main attractions: Shire River scenery; swamp, flood plain, palm savannah, woodland and thicket; varied birdlife.

Pertinent information: Anti-malaria precautions are essential. Central African Wilderness Safaris control all boating and walking activities from the Mvuu camps, while Chinguni remains under the jurisdiction of Malawi National Parks. Bring your own provisions.

The 548-km^2 Liwonde National Park, 64 km from Zomba, is situated on the southern end of Lake Malawi, a land of flood plain grasslands, reed swamps and floating meadows. The Shire River wends its way along the western boundary of the park, and palm trees, sausage trees and huge baobabs grow in profusion before giving way to mopane woodland.

The park, which is a prime bird-watching area, is home to the only population of Lilian's lovebird in Malawi, as well as a wide variety of woodland species and aquatic birds such as Pel's fishing owl, the palmnut vulture, Livingstone's flycatcher and Böhm's bee-eater. The lush grazing on the plains attracts waterbuck and reedbuck, while the mopane bush plays host to sable, impala, kudu, duiker and oribi. Elephant, hippo, crocodile, lion and leopard all live in the park in large numbers, and for this reason unaccompanied walking is strictly prohibited. (Liwonde's elephants have a reputation for being the most vicious on the subcontinent, due to inefficient poaching methods which enrage the wounded animals.)

Two places of interest to hikers, which the armed scouts will be happy to point out, are the Chisuse and Kalunga waterholes. Another interesting and lovely spot to visit is Chiunguni Hill, a volcanic cone open on one side, from which magnificent views can be enjoyed.

There is a network of untarred roads, which unfortunately are inaccessible during the rainy season (November to May). While these roads are closed during the rains, the park remains open throughout the year and access to Mvuu camp is possible by boat. August to October are the best months for visiting the park.

The 88-km^2 Lake Malawi National Park is reached along the M15, from which the mostly untarred S39 branches off approximately 6 km south of Monkey Bay. Travellers continue on the S39 for approximately 18 km to Cape Maclear.

Lake Malawi National Park is the first park in the world to give protection to a tropical deep-water rift valley lake. The park incorporates the Nankumba Peninsula and its offshore islands, the Mwenya and Nkhudzi hills and Nkhudzi Spit, the latter a low-lying marshland and sandy bar. Although no formal trails have yet been established, this area is wonderful rambling country, and the lake's crystal-clear waters and dazzling tropical fish make snorkelling a unique experience. The brightly coloured 'mbuna' fish of the Cichlid family is the one most obvious to snorkellers, as it feeds off algae found on rocks close to the shore.

One rambling option is to traverse the headland from Monkey Bay to Cape Maclear. Although this is a hot, dry walk, following inland valleys and wooded rocky hills instead of the shoreline, once

Late afternoon in Lake Malawi National Park, where a traditional dugout and a more modern boat share a common purpose.

A distant, misty view from the top of Dedza Mountain, which rises to more than 2 000 metres.

you reach Cape Maclear you can refresh yourself in Lake Malawi.

The lake contains the largest number of fish species of any lake in the world – over 450, of which about 350 are endemic (latest research suggests that there could be as many as 1 000 species). The prolific fish eagles readily fly down to fish thrown out for them. Vervet monkeys and bushbuck inhabit the woodland; klipspringer may be spotted on the rocky outcrops of the mainland; and crocodiles and hippos live in the reed marshes. In addition to rambling around the hills of Cape Maclear and snorkelling in the lake, you can ask the local fishermen to take you out in their dug-out canoes to fish: the succulent, delicate flesh of the lake bream, chambo, makes an excellent evening braai. I was fascinated by the fishermen's skill in filleting and roasting my dinner on the hot coals.

The little cemetery at Cape Maclear contains the graves of Dr Black (a medical missionary), the South African missionary Shadrack Ngunana, and other victims of fever, and remembers those individuals of the 'Old Livingstonia' mission, situated here from 1875–81.

11. DEDZA MOUNTAIN
DEDZA

Trail details: No formal trails, but visitors can walk on the forestry roads and footpaths.

Permits/bookings: Must be obtained from the Ministry of Forestry and Natural Resources, tel. 465218; PO Box 50, Mulanje.

Facilities/amenities: Dedza resthouse accommodates 6 people, and can be used as a base for exploring the 2 189-m high mountain.

Main attractions: Rocky cliffs; indigenous flora; pine plantations.

Pertinent information: Anti-malaria precautions are essential. May to October is the dry season.

The town of Dedza is situated 275 km from Blantyre on the main road, and gives you access to Dedza Mountain, a forest reserve, which rises to 2 189 m. Like that at Mulanje and Zomba, the birdlife is outstanding and the flora varied and interesting. Look out for an excellent array of ground orchids. Hikers can walk along paths in the forest, which are not very distinct.

12. LILONGWE NATURE SANCTUARY
LILONGWE

Trail details: Two short trails of 2 km and 3 km/ 1 hour each.

Permits/bookings: Not required. Brochure available at the entrance on request.

Facilities/amenities: Education centre; bird hides.

Main attractions: Abundant and varied birdlife; Lingadzi River; acacia and *Combretum* woodland; prolific ground orchids.

Pertinent information: From time to time there are wildlife displays at the education centre. The sanctuary is open all year round for day use only.

The Malawian authorities are to be commended for setting aside this 119-ha site, between the old town and the new capital of Lilongwe, as a nature centre and wildlife sanctuary. It functions as a venue for environmental education as well as relaxation. Wildlife in this small woodland reserve is amazingly diverse, with more than 200 bird species, small mammals such as the lesser galago (*nagapie* or Senegal bushbaby), greater bushbaby and duiker, and large mammals like bushbuck, leopard and hyaena. In addition, the Lingadzi River, home of crocodile, otter and 14 species of fish, flows through the sanctuary. The area is excellent for ground orchids.

There is a network of footpaths, two of which have been developed as self-guided nature trails which wind through acacia and *Combretum* woodland and along the bamboo-sheltered Lingadzi River. Both of the trails are laid out on flat terrain, but the paths are indistinct. Each can be completed with ease in approximately one hour.

13. KASUNGU NATIONAL PARK
CENTRAL REGION

Trail details: 10 km; guided.

Permits/bookings: Must be obtained from the Department of National Parks and Wildlife, tel. 723505, fax 723089; PO Box 30131, Lilongwe 3.

Facilities/amenities: Game-viewing drives on untarred roads; Lifupa Lodge with rondavels, restaurant and bar overlooking Lifupa water hole; fully equipped tents; swimming pool; petrol; passenger vehicle for hire.

Main attractions: Iron-smelting kiln on Dwangwa River; prolific birdlife; geometric rock paintings near Solonje Hill.

Pertinent information: The park is closed from January to March. Anti-malaria precautions are essential. The roads in the park are very muddy in the wet season.

Kasungu National Park is located approximately 55 km west of the town of Kasungu, in Malawi's central region. The entrance to the 2 070-km^2 park is reached via 38 km of the mainly untarred D187 road, from the turnoff to Kasungu.

The park contains a 280-km network of game-viewing roads as well as a 10-km guided walking trail. Although walking is not an emphasized activity, ask the game warden to point out game and places of interest. The route takes in an old iron-smelting kiln, and geometric rock paintings.

Elephant, hippo, buffalo, cheetah, kudu, lion, spotted hyaena, wild dog, buffalo, warthog, eland, oribi, common duiker, zebra, Lichtenstein's hartebeest, puku, roan and sable antelope and reedbuck all inhabit the park, and bird-watchers are well catered for, with 200 species present.

14. NKHOTA-KOTA WILDLIFE RESERVE
NKHOTA-KOTA

Trail details: Guided walks through the reserve.

Permits/bookings: Must be obtained from the Department of National Parks and Wildlife, tel. 723505, fax 723089; PO Box 30131, Lilongwe 3. Ask for available literature.

Facilities/amenities: Camp sites – bring your own tents – at Bua (on the river) and Chipata (at the foot of the mountain); 2-bed rondavel also available at each camp.

Main attractions: Scenery and vegetation, *Brachystegia* to dense rain forest on Chipata Mountain; excellent fishing in Bua River (licence required); rich birdlife.

Pertinent information: Animals are difficult to spot but the scenery is excellent. Malaria and bilharzia are both present – precautions must be taken. During the rainy season, access is only possible in a fourwheel drive vehicle.

The Nkhota-kota Wildlife Reserve lies to the east of the town of Nkhota-kota, and can be reached via a short cut on the M10 (untarred) to Lilongwe. The oldest wildlife reserve in Malawi, it covers 1 802 km^2, and lies in the hills of the Rift Valley escarpment, dominated by Chipata Mountain. The scenery is spectacular, and there is a wide variety of game such as elephant, buffalo, zebra, crocodile, leopard, lion and sable antelope (game is generally difficult to spot here due to the woodland and rain

forest vegetation). The birdlife is rewarding, especially around Bua River and the waterfalls.

15. VIPHYA PLATEAU
MZUZU

Trail details: Nature walks on indistinct footpaths in the forests.

Permits/bookings: These are not currently required, but this may possibly change in the future (various landowners control the area). Contact the Malawi Department of Tourism, tel. 620300; PO Box 402, Blantyre for further details. To book for the Kasito resthouses, tel. 343222, fax 343208 (booking in advance is essential).

Facilities/amenities: 2 delightful Kasito self-catering resthouses near Chikangawa and Luwawa dams, each accommodating 10 people in 5 double rooms; Mzuzu hotel nearby.

Main attractions: Beautiful and enormous vistas; Kamuzu viewpoint; Elephant Rock; heavily forested slopes; outstanding birdlife – this is a good area for spotting the whiteheaded saw-wing swallow, one of Malawi's specials.

Pertinent information: Anti-malaria precautions are essential. May to October is the dry season with rain occurring from November/December to April.

Like Mulanje, Zomba and Dedza, Viphya Plateau, south of Mzuzu via the main road, has outstanding birdlife and a variety of interesting flora. Hikers can walk along forest paths. Kamuzu viewpoint, 30 km south of Mzuzu and signposted from Mzuzu main road, overlooks a 17 000-km^2 area of pine forests and indigenous woodland. On a clear day Lake Malawi is visible.

16. VWAZA MARSH WILDLIFE RESERVE
KATUMBI

Trail details: 2-km trail; self-guided. Guided walks can be arranged with a game scout.

Permits/bookings: Must be obtained from the Department of National Parks and Wildlife, tel. 723505, fax 723089; PO Box 30131, Lilongwe 3.

Facilities/amenities: Game-viewing and bird-watching on foot, accompanied by a game guard; 5 tents on raised concrete slabs with thatched canopies, each with 2 beds; rustic toilets and showers; camping with minimal facilities.

Main attractions: One of the highest densities of animals in Malawi marshland; mixed mopane/ *Brachystegia* woodland and rocky hills; Lake Kazuni; rich birdlife.

Pertinent information: Fourwheel drive vehicle is necessary during the rainy season (November/December, March/April), although recent reports suggest that in very wet weather even a fourwheel drive vehicle will be of no use. Malaria and tsetse fly are present (take precautions).

To reach the 1 000-km^2 Vwaza Marsh Wildlife Reserve, travel along the S85 from Rumphi in the direction of Nyika. Approximately 10 km past Rumphi, turn left onto the untarred S49 and continue for a further 19 km to the reserve entrance.

Vwaza Marsh Nature Reserve contains a wide variety of habitats, including miombo and mopane woodland, rocky hills, and marshland. The animals present include roan antelope, impala, warthog, lion, leopard, buffalo and elephant, all of which are concentrated chiefly in the woodland of the flood

The creased sides of Nganda Hill rise up beyond the flat grasslands of Nyika National Park.

Lowlands and their encircling mountains, seen from Jalawe Viewpoint, Nyika.

plains of the South Rukuru River. There are a variety of birds living around Lake Kazuni and in the marsh, where hippos may also be seen. Waterbirds that can be observed include the redwinged pratincoles and the rare European marsh harrier in the summer. The 2-km self-guided trail leads along Lake Kazuni from the tent camp to a hide near Uyuzi Hill and back. Guided trails can be arranged to suit the interests of the particular group.

17. NYIKA NATIONAL PARK
NEAR RUMPHI

Trail details: Guided wilderness trails combining hiking and game-viewing; self-guided day walks.

Permits/bookings: Must be obtained from the Department of National Parks and Wildlife, tel. 723505, fax 723089; PO Box 30131, Lilongwe 3. Ask for available literature. To book for the Zambian resthouse, contact Central African Wilderness Safaris, tel. 723527, fax 723548.

Facilities/amenities: 224 km of game-viewing tracks for vehicles; dams with fishing for rainbow trout; Chelinda Game Camp with chalets, a camp site, a shop, and (sometimes) petrol; cabin in Juniper Forest; Zambian self-catering resthouse, beautifully situated just off the main road to Chelinda, has 4 double rooms, lounge and kitchen.

Main attractions: Large herds of game; birdlife; undulating montane grassland; evergreen forest.

Pertinent information: Visitors may hike unaccompanied, but if they plan to camp out a guide must be arranged; the paths are indistinct and it is easy to get lost; the high altitude may affect people with heart conditions. Although the resthouse is in Zambia, there are no border formalities for guests wishing to visit the park.

Visitors to Nyika National Park enter through the Thazima gate, which is situated approximately

55 km north-west of Rumphi. (The road from Rumphi is untarred and in bad condition; during the rains a fourwheel drive is best.) The largest of Malawi's national parks at 3 134 km^2, Nyika includes most of the high-lying Nyika Plateau in Malawi's northern region. I was fortunate to arrive at Nyika to find that there was no petrol available. Fortunate? Yes, for I was left with no alternative but to walk the dirt roads, taking short cuts on the myriad game paths which cross the highest (2 135 m on average, rising to 2 400 m in places) and most extensive plateau in central Africa.

Nyika is bounded on all sides by steep scarps, and to the north-east forms the main wall of the Rift Valley. The plateau is also a major watershed and here Malawi's northern rivers have their source in the wide, flat dambos, reminiscent of the peat bogs of the temperate northern hemisphere. Owing to its high altitude, the park is much cooler than the rest of Malawi.

Various guided trails have been designed, ranging from 1 to 5 days, and visitors are free to walk anywhere in the park as long as they are accompanied by a trained game scout. A lovely short 1-hour ramble takes hikers to Chisanga Falls, and a close-up of the North Rukuru River as it plunges through chasms and forests down the western escarpment.

Rivers, shallow valleys with evergreen forest and undulating montane grassland provide an excellent environment for viewing wildlife. Hikers will easily identify southern reedbuck and herds of eland, zebra and especially roan antelope, and the very observant may spot bushbuck, warthog, bushpig, klipspringer, and baboons. Nyika is home to the largest concentration of leopard in Malawi, and they are often seen, especially in the vicinity of Chelinda camp at night.

For the bird-watcher, Nyika is a must. The large birds such as the wattled crane and Stanley's bustard (known as Denham's buzzard in Malawi) are

particularly impressive, while redwing francolin occur in the grasslands, and cinnamon dove, bar-tailed trogon and starred robin can be spotted high in the forest canopy.

Malawi high-road – the footpath to Jalawe Hill.

SPECIAL INTEREST TRAILS

MOUNTAIN-BIKING TRAILS

Mountain bike riding is relatively new in Africa. It has been my observation that mountain bikers come from two entirely different disciplines. The first group view bikes as a healthy extension of exercise, by which they can cover more distance per day than by walking but which still allow an intimate experience with nature. The second group stems from a world of motorbikes and fourwheel drive vehicles. These people love the out-of-doors but also enjoy testing their machinery on challenging terrain. Irrespective of which group you fit into, all riders should adopt the following suggestions on safe and considerate riding – crucial for the sport's future.

PREPARING FOR THE TRAIL

Once you have bought a mountain bike there are a few other pieces of equipment you should consider. A pair of gloves will save the skin on your hands from the inevitable scrapes of a fall. They also absorb sweat and enhance your handlebar grip. If you think your head is worth protecting, wear a bike helmet – in fact, it is foolhardy not to. In order to enjoy comfortable rides, purchase padded shorts.

You will need to carry a first-aid kit for yourself, and one for your bike. Pushing an injured bike for 20 km and then trying to hitchhike with it was my first and last experience of riding without a repair kit. Before your ride, make sure that your bike is working properly, and that the tyres have the correct air pressure for the terrain (on tar: 5 bar; on gravel: 3 to 3.5 bar). The chain should be well lubricated and the brake pads flush with the rim when applied and not rubbing the tyre. I use inner-tube liners to protect my tubes from thorns and sharp rocks. The following tools should be carried on a remote or multi-day ride.

- a spare tube and a patch kit
- tyre levers
- bicycle pump
- allen keys
- adjustable end wrench
- small screwdriver
- chain rivet tool
- spoke wrench
- spare chain links
- spare cable for brakes and derailleur
- lubricant, tiny tube
- a small rag (or be willing to destroy your shirt)

LEFT: *Magnificent views towards Robertson.*

If you share tools with your riding partners, check before you set off that they fit your bike. A good bike maintenance book, bike repair shop or simple trial and error will show you how to use these tools. Knowing how to repair your bike on the trail is essential as there are no AA services in the bicycle backcountry.

TOURING

A mountain bike is the ideal touring bike as it is inherently strong and reliable; the riding position is comfortable and handling easy. The best pannier configuration for extended touring is two medium-sized panniers mounted on the front forks and two mounted on the rear carrier. This gives a well-balanced load with a low centre of gravity. The secret to enjoyable touring is to pack only what is really needed and to keep weight to a minimum. The total weight should not exceed 7 kg. Plan your route carefully and allow time for lunch stops, sightseeing and finding suitable accommodation.

ON THE TRAIL

Basic Riding Techniques:
❏ When descending steep hills keep your weight low by lowering your saddle or by leaning behind it. Your front brake has more stopping power than your back brake but a sudden application can send you flying over the handlebars.
❏ On rugged trails and roads, relax your grip and let the bike absorb the bumps. Soft tyres go a long way to making your ride more comfortable.
❏ To reduce saddle soreness, keep your crotch off the saddle when riding bumps.
❏ When ascending a steep hill, your rear wheel may slip. To avoid this you need the correct mixture of balance and proper gear selection. When approaching a hill, shift gears before heading up it.

Low-impact Riding:
This information was compiled in collaboration with the Responsible Organised Mountain Pedallers (ROMP) of Cape Town. They can be contacted at tel. (021) 4614019; PO Box 23190, Claremont 7735, Cape Town.

This style of riding must serve as a prerequisite to all offroad excursions. If the following guidelines are not heeded, you may experience your favourite areas blooming with restrictive signs, permit systems and gun-toting law enforcement rangers – all because the public refused to abide by a code of ethics and behaviour which is committed to conserving the integrity of the African land.

1. Ride only on open trails
If a trail sign indicates 'no biking' don't ride there. If you do, you will be helping to promote an image of mountain bikers as irresponsible and unworthy of access to natural areas. If permits or authorization are required, get this before you set out. Respect private and public property; landowners who permit mountain bikes would like you to leave things (such as gates) as you find them.

2. Respect other users
Anticipate that hikers, joggers or horses may be around corners and moderate your speed. I have witnessed a horse rearing up and bucking off its rider when confronting a mountain biker. A well-tuned bike is very quiet – people and horses appreciate a warning that you are approaching. Simply screaming 'bicycle' is not enough. Approach slowly and, if necessary, dismount and walk your bike. If bikers want to win the favour of other trailists, they must be considerate of others' experience.

3. Consider the environment
Be aware of the ground you are riding on. In many regions the soil is particularly fragile and can be easily damaged. Many trails have earthen, log or stone waterbars directing water off the trail, thus retarding erosion. Bikers who ride over these structures tend to dislodge them. Preferably, stop and lift your bike over waterbars and steps. Bikers should also avoid riding on wet trails and roads. Not only will the mud clog your derailleur and brakes, but riding through it creates ruts, accelerating erosion. If your wheels lock up and skid when riding down a very steep trail, it is best to dismount and walk your bike – locking brakes contributes to needless trail damage. Try to avoid times when trailheads are overcrowded, as riding two or more abreast on a single-file trail leads to erosion.

If you are riding on a multi-day trail, take rest stops and make camp only at previously impacted sites. Never camp closer than 100 m from water as it sustains wildlife too. If you wash, do it away from the water source and rinse off so that the soapy water flows into sand. Cook on a campstove. If campfires are permitted, keep them small and consider making your fire in a container to keep it from scarring the soil. Use wood which is provided or even better carry it in. Never strip trees of bark, or cut or pull down branches – you will be interfering with natural processes.

Carry out 'more' than you carry in. Remove your own litter and then carry out litter your fellow human beings left behind. If there are no toilets at a camp site, bury your waste in a 15-cm 'cathole' and then burn your toilet paper (be careful not to start a fire). In a heavily used, confined area such as a narrow kloof, a beach or along a river, you should carry out all human bodily waste and toilet paper in a plastic bag.

The wide, sandy tracks of De Hoop Nature Reserve can be tackled by riders of all ages.

MOUNTAIN-BIKE TRAILS

The trails have been graded in terms of the effort and skill required to ride them. A trail can be easy, moderate or difficult in terms of effort and technical or non-technical in terms of the skills required. On a technical trail you are likely to encounter steep slopes, rocky ground, streams and logs which require skill to negotiate.

The Cape has a variety of nature areas which permit mountain bikers to ride on organized demarcated routes, as does the Rietfontein Conservancy in the Orange Free State; there are also a few marked trails in other areas in southern Africa, from the Ciskei through to Malawi. The adventurous should consider buying a map which details all the old gravel roads which lead one through the countryside and plotting their own ride. There are literally hundreds of kilometres of public gravel road to explore in southern Africa. In addition, you can choose your own style of accommodation, opting for camp sites or hotels. Remember to set reasonable distances and to avoid the midday heat.

1. JONKERSHOEK STATE FOREST
NEAR STELLENBOSCH, WESTERN CAPE

Trail details: about 4 hours.
Permits/bookings: Booking not required, but permits must be purchased at the gate. To find out if the reserve is open, tel. (02231) 78063.
Pertinent information: Party size is unlimited. The forest is only open during winter months (April to September). There are no facilities.

This beautiful valley offers a variety of jeep tracks for moderate and non-technical riding. Consider hopping off your bike and walking into the forested kloofs. See map on page 61.

2. TABLE MOUNTAIN
CAPE TOWN, CAPE PENINSULA

Trail details: 6 km of marked jeep track.
Pertinent information: Maximum party size is 5. No permit or bookings are required, but phone ROMP at (021) 4614019 for more information. There are no facilities available.

This trail offers moderate riding with steep sections on the jeep track below Tafelberg Road. See map on page 55.

3. SILVERMINE NATURE RESERVE
NEAR MUIZENBERG, CAPE PENINSULA

Trail details: A demarcated 6-km loop.
Permits/bookings: No booking required. Permits purchased at the gate.
Facilities/amenities: Picnic sites with braai facilities.
Pertinent information: Maximum party size is 5.

This 6-km circular route in the southern section of the reserve is difficult and technical in places. See map on page 56.

4. CAPE OF GOOD HOPE NATURE RESERVE
TIP OF CAPE PENINSULA

Trail details: 20 km of tar and gravel roads.
Permits/bookings: No booking required, but there is an entrance fee. For more information, tel. (021) 7801100.
Facilities/amenities: Picnic sites, restaurant and kiosk.
Pertinent information: There is no limit to party size. For a leisurely guided ride through the reserve, contact Eco Adventures, tel. (021) 7801353 (Terry), fax (021) 7826026 (Lynn).

This 7 750-ha reserve is a popular tourist attraction and offers spectacular views over its 40 km of coastline. Primarily a scenic and botanical reserve, it also supports small numbers of game including eland, bontebok, rhebok and Cape mountain zebra. See map on page 59.

5. GRABOUW STATE FOREST
NEAR GRABOUW, SOUTH-WESTERN CAPE

Trail details: 8 hours of riding on various routes which are well marked.
Permits/bookings: Permits obtainable from ROMP, tel. (021) 4614019 or 6892838, at least 24 hours beforehand.
Pertinent information: There are no facilities, and no limit to party size.

This pine forest is situated on the slopes of the Hottentots Holland mountains, 55 km from Cape Town, and provides moderate, non-technical riding along forestry roads. It is important to note that it is open to ROMP members only and heavy fines are imposed on non-permit holders – bikers and bikes alike. See map on page 67.

6. CALEDON NATURE RESERVE
CALEDON, SOUTH-WESTERN CAPE

Trail details: 5 km.
Permits/bookings: No booking required, but there is an entrance fee.
Facilities/amenities: A tea room and public toilets.

There is a 5-km mountain bike trail in the gardens, which are the venue of an annual mountain bike race which provides some difficult and technical riding. Be particularly aware of people walking through the gardens. See map on page 70.

7. SALMONSDAM NATURE RESERVE
NEAR STANFORD, SOUTH-WESTERN CAPE

Trail details: 5 km.
Permits/bookings: No booking required for the trail, but for accommodation bookings, tel. (0283) 770062.
Facilities/amenities: Accommodation in cottages and a camp site; picnic sites with braai facilities.
Pertinent information: There is no limit to party size.

This small reserve is great for a winter weekend getaway and offers a difficult ride up to the mountain top along a jeep track. The best time to tackle this ride is winter as the summer tends to be hot and dry. See map on page 71.

8. DE HOOP NATURE RESERVE
NEAR BREDASDORP, SOUTH-WESTERN CAPE

Trail details: 4 km to 30 km.
Permits/bookings: No booking required, but to book accommodation, tel. (02922) 782. A permit is obtainable at the gate.
Facilities/amenities: Accommodation in chalets and a camp site; picnic sites with braai facilities.
Pertinent information: No limit to party size.

De Hoop has fantastic birdlife on the large vlei and a rugged coastline. The jeep tracks make for easy riding which can be sandy in places, and bikers can choose from a variety of routes. See map on page 77.

9. ANYSBERG TRAIL
ANYSBERG NATURE RESERVE, NEAR LADISMITH, SOUTH-WESTERN CAPE

Trail details: 2 days.
Permits/bookings: For bookings, contact Cape Nature Conservation, tel. (0443) 291739; Private Bag X658, Oudtshoorn 6620.
Facilities/amenities: Overnight accommodation in an old farm house; water available.
Pertinent information: Maximum party size is 12. Payment must be made in advance.

This easy, non-technical trail exposes one to interesting veld communities and archaeological sites.

10. HOOPOE TRAILS
BREEDE RIVER VALLEY, NEAR BONNIEVALE, SOUTH-WESTERN CAPE

Trail details: 5 routes of 25 to 66 km; 2 fun routes.
Permits/bookings: For bookings, contact Christa van der Merwe, tel. (02346) 2995; PO Box 353, Bonnievale 6730.
Facilities/amenities: Accommodation in cottage.
Pertinent information: The cottage sleeps a maximum of 10. A map is provided.

Five signposted routes that vary in length and difficulty traverse farm land and take the biker into the Langeberg and Riviersonderend mountains, or the less energetic can tackle one of two fun rides.

11. KAROO NATIONAL PARK
NEAR BEAUFORT WEST, KAROO

A mountain bike trail in the Nuweberg Mountain range is being planned. For more information, tel. (0201) 52828/9. Also see the entry for Karoo National Park on page 136, which gives details about accommodation and facilities available, as well as describing some of the flora and fauna found in this national park.

12. ROOIHEUWEL FARM
NEAR BEAUFORT WEST, KAROO

Trail details: About 50 km.
Permits/bookings: For bookings, contact Flip Vivier, tel. (02022) 661; PO Box 237, Beaufort West 6970.
Facilities/amenities: Accommodation in 2 homesteads.
Pertinent information: Maximum party size is 24. Pets are allowed.

This Karoo farm, which includes part of the Nuweveld mountains, offers a range of routes; some are easy, others give fourwheel drive vehicles trouble.

13. SWARTBERG TRAIL
SWARTBERG NATURE RESERVE, NEAR PRINCE ALBERT, SOUTHERN CAPE

Trail details: 3 days one-way or 6 days return.
Permits/bookings: For bookings, contact Cape Nature Conservation, tel. (0443) 291739; Private Bag X658, Oudtshoorn 6620.
Facilities/amenities: Accommodation in 2 overnight huts and a camp site; water available at all three.
Pertinent information: Maximum party size is 20. Payment must be made in advance.

The rugged Swartberg range and the desolate Gamkaskloof Valley offer views on this moderate, non-technical trail. There is a possibility of snow in winter and extreme heat in summer. See map on page 87.

14. ROCK JUMPER AND KAMMANASSIE TRAILS
LANGKLOOF NATURE RESERVE, NEAR UNIONDALE, SOUTHERN CAPE

Trail details: 1. Rock Jumper Trail: 2 days; 2. Kammanassie Trail: 3 days.
Permits/bookings: Bookings can be made through Cape Nature Conservation, tel. (0441) 742160, fax (0441) 742619; Private Bag X6546, George 6530.
Facilities/amenities: Overnight camping permitted.
Pertinent information: Maximum party size for both trails is 12. Payment must be made in advance.

1. Rock Jumper Trail This 2-day trail is moderately difficult and technical but rewards one with breathtaking views on the home ground of the Cape mountain zebra.
2. Kammanassie Trail You will need fairly good handling skills on this moderately difficult 3-day trail. Keep an eye open for archaeological sites and the Cape mountain zebra.

15. KNYSNA FOREST TRAIL
KNYSNA, SOUTHERN CAPE

Trail details: 2 days.
Permits/bookings: Bookings can be made through the Regional Director of Forestry, tel. (0445) 23037, fax (0445) 825461; Private Bag X12, Knysna 6570.
Facilities/amenities: Overnight accommodation at the Diepwalle Forest Station in hikers' hut or camp in tents; ablution facilities but no hot water.
Pertinent information: Maximum party size is 12. Payment must be made in advance.

Be on the lookout for the forest's three remaining elephants which roam this beautiful area. Riding is on forestry roads which are open to motorized vehicles, including the odd logging truck. See map on page 94.

16. KNYSNA WILDERNESS TRAIL
SEDGEFIELD/KNYSNA AREA, SOUTHERN CAPE

See entry under horseback trails on page 338.

17. HARKERVILLE STATE FOREST
BETWEEN KNYSNA AND PLETTENBERG BAY, SOUTHERN CAPE

Trail details: 28 km of marked routes.
Permits/bookings: Permits must be obtained in advance from the Regional Director of Forestry, tel. (0445) 23037; fax (0445) 825461, Private Bag X12, Knysna 6570.
Pertinent information: Maximum party size is 12. There are no facilities.

If riding through indigenous Cape forests and gazing at splendid coastal scenery sounds right for you, consider this easy, non-technical route. See map on page 92.

18. COMMANDO DRIFT NATURE RESERVE
NEAR CRADOCK, EASTERN CAPE

The walking trails in the reserve (see entry for Commando Drift Nature Reserve on page 112) can be used for mountain-biking by previous arrangement. Contact the Officer in Charge, tel. (0482) 3925 for more information. See map on page 113.

19. SETHUNZINI MOUNTAIN BIKE CHALLENGE
NEAR LADY GREY, SOUTHERN DRAKENSBERG

Trail details: 70 km/3 days and 4 nights.
Permits/bookings: For bookings, contact Rocky and Lindy Cloete, Sethunzini Trails, tel. (05552) ask for 272; PO Box 64, Lady Grey 5540.
Facilities/amenities: Accommodation in homesteads and/or bush camps; meals, backup and guide provided.
Pertinent information: Maximum party size is 12.

I am not sure that you can call this trail a challenge with the 5-star pampering you are likely to receive, however the riding is moderately difficult. See map on page 123.

20. KATBERG MOUNTAIN BIKING TRAILS
BALFOUR, CISKEI

Mountain-biking trails of several hours to 1 day are offered in the Katberg Forest area, starting from the Katberg Protea Hotel. Mountain bikes are provided for ease of handling on these rugged mountain tracks. Although routes are mapped out, riders are free to plan their own route along plantation roads. See entry on page 114 for more information about the area.

21. FLORA RIDE
KORANNA CONSERVANCY, NEAR MARQUARD, EASTERN ORANGE FREE STATE

Trail details: 1. Pink Trail: 28 km; 2. Blue Trail: 35 km.
Permits/bookings: Contact Jacana Country Homes and Trails, tel. (012) 3463550, fax (012) 3462499.

Facilities/amenities: Basic accommodation in barn or cottage, ablution facilities, hot water; bikes can be hired.
Pertinent information: A maximum of 28 can be accommodated. Summer temperatures can be extreme.

These 2 circular mountain-biking trails follow farm roads and traverse grasslands in the Koranna Conservancy with the majestic Korannaberg as a backdrop. Both trails are designed to cater for families wanting to enjoy mountain-biking together. See map on page 146.

22. KORANNA TWO MOUNTAIN BIKE TRAILS
KORANNA CONSERVANCY, NEAR MARQUARD, EASTERN ORANGE FREE STATE

Trail details: 36 km, or a shorter route.
Permits/bookings: Contact Jacana Country Homes and Trails, tel. (012) 3463550, fax (012) 3462499.
Facilities/amenities: Basic accommodation in barn or cottage, ablution facilities, hot water; bikes can be hired.
Pertinent information: A maximum of 28 people can be accommodated.

In October, during the Cherry Trail Sports Festival, this challenging ride is a great favourite with mountain bikers. For those who do not feel confident enough to tackle the devastating downhill called 'Suicide Hill', a short cut can be taken back to base camp at the S-junction. A variety of hiking trails are also available in the Koranna Conservancy. For information see entries on pages 148 to 150.

23. CHERRY TRAIL CHALLENGE
NEAR MARQUARD, EASTERN ORANGE FREE STATE

Trail details: 66 km/2 days.
Permits/bookings: Contact Jacana Country Homes and Trails, tel. (012) 3463550, fax (012) 3462499.
Facilities/amenities: Accommodation in cottages with ablution facilities and hot water provided; guides are available for groups larger than 10; bikes can be hired.
Pertinent information: Maximum party size is 23. Be aware that summer temperatures can be extreme.

This challenging trail is used annually during the Cherry Trail Challenge Mountain Bike Rodeo, and it takes you through the Rietfontein Conservancy and across farms in the area. The trail is graded as moderate to difficult and must be ridden with experienced mountain bikers.

Nature's vibrant carpet of spring blossoms attracts many cyclists to Namaqualand.

24. RIETFONTEIN RIDE
RIETFONTEIN CONSERVANCY, NEAR MARQUARD, EASTERN ORANGE FREE STATE

Trail details: 1. Black Trail: 10 km; 2. Green Trail: 20 km; 3. Yellow Trail: 37 km; 4. Blue Trail: 50 km.
Permits/bookings: Contact Jacana Country Homes and Trails, tel. (012) 3463550, fax (012) 3462499.
Facilities/amenities: Overnight accommodation is available in cottages with ablution facilities and hot water; bikes can be hired.
Pertinent information: Ask about some interesting hikes to historical Boer sites in the area.

For those who want a leisurely pleasure ride, or for the inexperienced, these trails are ideal. They all start and end in Marquard, and traverse the Rietfontein Conservancy, which is typical eastern Free State countryside. There is interesting bird and animal life in the area. See map on page 150.

25. WOLWERAND RIDE (RED TRAIL)
RIETFONTEIN CONSERVANCY, NEAR MARQUARD, EASTERN ORANGE FREE STATE

Trail details: 1 day.
Permits/bookings: Contact Jacana Country Homes and Trails, tel. (012) 3463550, fax (012) 3462499.
Facilities/amenities: Accommodation available in cottages in Marquard with ablution facilities and hot water; bikes can be hired.
Pertinent information: The 4 cottages sleep 9, 5, 6 and 4 respectively.

A climb up Wolwerand and a great downhill *en route* make this trail fit for the experienced rider. Marquard is the starting and end point of the route. See map on page 160.

26. SPARROWFARM TRAILS
GOLDEN GATE VALLEY, NORTH-EASTERN ORANGE FREE STATE

Trail details: From 1-hour rides to 50-km/2-day trail.
Permits/bookings: Can be obtained from Gary Thorpe, tel (011) 4621587.
Facilities/amenities: Accommodation in a dormitory with communal ablution facilities and hot water available; camping is also permitted.
Pertinent information: Ideal group size is 6 to 24. April to November are the best months.

For the most part, rugged paths are used for these trails. Only the fit should attempt the 2-day trail, which involves a 7-km climb up a mountain pass, followed by a 3-km descent. A variety of other activities are also available at Sparrowfarm, including horse-riding, paragliding and excursions in fourwheel drive vehicles.

27. THE DRIFTERS INN TRAILS
WINDMILL FARM, BETWEEN BERGVILLE AND HARRISMITH, NORTH-EASTERN ORANGE FREE STATE

Trail details: 20 km/1 day and 30 km/2 days.
Permits/bookings: Contact Drifters, tel. (011) 8881160, fax (011) 8881020; PO Box 48434, Roosevelt Park 2129.
Facilities/amenities: The Drifters Inn and a stone hut for overnighting on the 2-day trail.
Pertinent information: Maximum party size is 10.

The riding on this trail is moderately easy.

28. BLANERNE GAME-VIEWING TRAILS
NEWCASTLE, NORTHERN NATAL

Trail details: 4 trails varying in length and difficulty.
Permits/bookings: From Pam Mitchell Innes, tel. and fax (03621) 747; Blanerne, PO Box 52, Elandslaagte 2900.
Facilities/amenities: Tented camp, toilets and hot-water pulley showers in thatched enclosure; luxury accommodation also available. Self-catering, but a guide, camp attendant and landrover are available for an extra charge.
Pertinent information: Groups are limited to 8 people.

Bikers have the run of this 55 000-ha cattle farm which has 14 species of game and 240 species of birds. Streams, mountains, pools and a waterfall add to the enjoyment of the country experience.

29. CATHEDRAL PEAK
NATAL DRAKENSBERG PARK, DRAKENSBERG

Cathedral Peak is the only part of the Natal Drakensberg Park zoned for mountain bikers (limited to 12 per group), who should familiarize themselves with the park's code of ethics for responsible riding. Cycling along the 70 km of jeep tracks is moderate and non-technical. See page 208 for more information about Cathedral Peak.

30. CHAMPAGNE VALLEY
CHAMPAGNE CASTLE, DRAKENSBERG

A range of 1-day trails that average 25 km each can be undertaken from Inkosana Lodge for a maximum of 12 people, either self-guided, or Mr Salomons can guide those unfamiliar with the bike trails. See page 214 for more information about Inkosana Lodge. See map on page 209.

31. MOUNTAIN BIKE ADVENTURES
LESOTHO

This mountainous land was the venue of a recent Mongoose Challenge in which 3 mountain bikers rode from Tele Bridge to the Sani Pass, over 500 km away, in 6 days. They conquered 5 rugged mountain passes which sometimes became little more than a donkey track winding up the tortuous peaks. Lesotho offers a lot of great riding but you will have to take the initiative of buying a map and plotting a route which suits you. Remember temperature extremes are common and good fitness and backup are essential.

32. MARIEPSKOP FORESTRY AREA
NEAR GRASKOP, EASTERN TRANSVAAL

Trail details: 20 km of forestry roads.
Permits/bookings: Permission for access from the Forester in Charge, tel. (01528) 32581. To book accommodation, tel. (0156) 35529.
Facilities/amenities: Camping at the Blyde River site or one of two forestry chalets (5 persons) at Mariepskop.
Pertinent information: The chalets and camp site accommodate a maximum of 40.

The Mariepskop Forestry Area, 490 km from Johannesburg, provides for fairly difficult, non-technical riding on local mountain slopes largely covered in pine plantations.

33. MATOBO NATIONAL PARK
NEAR BULAWAYO, ZIMBABWE

Trail details: Several trails are laid out in the park.
Permits/bookings: Contact The Warden, Private Bag K 5142, Bulawayo for bookings.
Facilities/amenities: Lodges, chalets, a caravan and camp site with full ablution facilities; picnic sites.
Pertinent information: This is a malaria and bilharzia area; take anti-malaria precautions and it is essential to boil all drinking water.

Cycling in the park is on exciting, varied terrain suitable for all riders. The biker can see game, Bushman caves and Rhodes's grave in this beautiful remote area. See map on page 299.

34. CHAMBE PATH
MULANJE MOUNTAIN, NEAR BLANTYRE, MALAWI

Trail details: 10 km/6 hours.
Permits/bookings: Contact the Department of Forestry, tel. (0903) 465218; PO Box 50, Mulanje for bookings.
Facilities/amenities: No facilities.
Pertinent information: Cash payment to the tourist attendant is required on arrival. The trail is closed May–July and November–March. This is a malaria area so take anti-malaria precautions.

To travel 10 km in 6 hours means that this technical and difficult trail is for the super-fit and courageous. Travelling through the indigenous forest and experiencing some breathtaking views should be just reward. See map on page 324.

CANOEING AND RIVER-RAFTING TRAILS

Generally, sunburn is a greater danger than drowning when you go canoeing and river-rafting! This is because the operators who offer trips on the various rivers – from the Doring in the Cape to the Zambezi – provide adequate safety equipment, lessons and guidance. Life jackets are a must on all river trips and are generally supplied by the operator. No experience is needed, and some operators cater for the very young or old, and the disabled on quieter stretches of river. However, you will have to be reasonably fit and a competent swimmer to tackle white-water rafting as the chances are very good that you are going to end up in the water – although experience is not required as you are well drilled in techniques and safety procedures before you are allowed near the river. Rapids are graded 1 to 6 – with grade 1 being a very gentle rapid that even the timid can tackle without fear, and grade 6 being un-runnable – you get off the river and carry the raft past the rapid!

Take adequate protection against the sun, and carry plenty of soft drinks with you – not all operators provide soft drinks. Remember that you will need to waterproof all your gear.

Where trails are unguided (see the Bushmans River Trail and the Kowie River Trail, page 336), it is advisable that you be a proficient swimmer and have at least one person in your party who has canoeing experience.

Zambezi River
Anti-malaria precautions are necessary if visiting the area, while yellow fever and cholera inoculations are recommended if visiting Zambia. Bilharzia is a hazard, especially in stagnant or slow-moving water, and there are crocodiles and hippos in the river. Take adequate protection against the sun, especially between September and March.

As the river forms the border between Zambia and Zimbabwe, you should carry with you your passport and entry/exit visas for both Zimbabwe and Zambia. Operators who offer trips from either the Zimbabwian or Zambian side both use the same stretch of river, and sometimes cross over into the other country.

1. ORANGE RIVER
FROM NOORDOEWER THROUGH RICHTERSVELD RESERVE, CAPE/NAMIBIAN BORDER

Trail details: 4 to 6 days.
Permits/bookings: Contact any of the following: **Aquatrails**, tel. (021) 7945808, fax (021) 7941765, 8 Oak Farm Crescent, Constantia 7800; **River Rafters**, Cape, tel. (021) 725094/5, fax (021) 725241, PO Box 14, Diep River 7856, or Transvaal, tel. (011) 7922353, fax (011) 7922833, PO Box 68132, Bryanston 2021; **Felix Unite**, Cape, tel. (021) 7626935/6, fax (021) 7619259, PO Box 96, Kenilworth 7745, or Transvaal, tel. (011) 8039778, fax (011) 8039603; **River Runners**, Cape, tel. (021) 7622350, or fax (021) 7611373, PO Box 583, Constantia 7848, or Transvaal, tel. (011) 4032512, PO Box 31117, Braamfontein 2017.
Facilities/amenities: Unless it rains, you sleep under the stars on the riverbank each night; generally all canoeing or rafting equipment, camping equipment and meals are supplied; some offer kayaking lessons – check with tour operators to confirm.
Pertinent information: March to October are the best months as summers are very hot with rain falling in short showers – the greatest hazard on the trip is sunburn, so take adequate protection. Group sizes vary from 15 to 30 people. Remember that you will need a passport and visa.

Between Noordoewer and the Fish River junction the mighty Orange River wends its way through a vast desert wilderness – the Richtersveld Reserve area. Lush greenery fringes the river in stark contrast to the mountainous moonscape of the surrounding desert. The trails are not strenuous as the rapids in the river are graded 1 to 2 and distances travelled vary from 15 to 20 km a day, so they require no experience or great level of fitness.

The developing Richtersveld National Park, on the South African side of the Namibian border, plans to offer canoeing trails down the Orange River. For further information, contact the National Parks Board in Cape Town, tel. (021) 222810, PO Box 7400, Roggebaai 8012; or Pretoria, tel. (012) 3431991, PO Box 787, Pretoria 0001.

2. ORANGE GORGE
ORANGE RIVER, CAPE/NAMIBIAN BORDER

Trail details: 3 to 5 days.
Permits/bookings: For bookings and more information, contact **River Rafters**, tel. (021) 725094/5, fax (021) 725241, PO Box 14, Diep River 7800; **Felix Unite**, tel. (021) 7626935/6, fax (021) 7619259, PO Box 96, Kenilworth 7745.
Facilities/amenities: Guides, all canoeing equipment and food are provided.
Pertinent information: You must be a confident swimmer for this trail, which is run from mid-March to mid-January. Remember that you will need to take your passport and visa.

For the more adventurous, there are canoeing trips on this stretch of the Orange River (north of Pofadder), from Pella to Goodhouse, where the rapids are graded 1 to 3, as the river flows swiftly through a maze of channels between reed islands.

3. ORANGE RIVER
NEAR AUGRABIES FALLS, NORTH-WESTERN CAPE

Trail details: 3 to 6 days.
Permits/bookings: Contact **River Rafters**, tel. (021) 725094/5, fax (021) 725241, PO Box 14, Diep River, Cape Town 7800; or **Sunwa Ventures**, tel. (011) 7885129, PO Box 41952, Craighall 2024.
Facilities/amenities: Guide, all equipment and food provided; overnight accommodation at base camp or camping on banks of river; kayaking lessons offered.
Pertinent information: No experience needed and average fitness required.

These 3- to 6-day canoeing trips on the Orange River start about 20 km downstream of the Augrabies Falls and take you as far as the Namibian border. See map on page 135.

4. TWO SHIPS TRAIL
ORANGE RIVER AND BUSHMANLAND, NEAR AUGRABIES FALLS, NORTH-WESTERN CAPE

Trail details: 2,5-day canoeing trip followed by 2,5-day camel or horse trail.
Permits/bookings: Contact **Camel Runners**, tel. (011) 4032512 or 3397183, fax (011) 3391380; PO Box 31117, Braamfontein 2017.
Facilities/amenities: Guides and all equipment and food provided; overnight accommodation at base camp and camping out on trail.
Pertinent information: The trail is offered from October through to May. A pony cart is provided for children. Party size is limited to 8 to 20, with no children under 8 permitted; no children under 14 on camels, and under 12 on horses.

Participants paddle down the Orange River from the base camp, 20 km down-river from the Augrabies Falls, for 40 km, and then transfer to camels or horses for a 40-km trail through Bushmanland. See map on page 135.

5. DORING RIVER
NORTHERN CEDARBERG, WESTERN CAPE

Trail details: 2 or 4 days.
Permits/bookings: Contact one of the following: **River Rafters**, Cape, tel. (021) 725094/5, fax (021) 725241,

Canoeists enjoy a tranquil stretch of the Orange River.

PO Box 14, Diep River 7856, or Transvaal, tel. (011) 7922353, fax (011) 7922833, PO Box 68132, Bryanston 2021; **River Runners**, Cape, tel. (021) 7622350, fax (021) 7611373, PO Box 583, Constantia 7848, or Transvaal, tel. (011) 4032512; PO Box 31117, Braamfontein 2017; **Felix Unite**, tel. (021) 7626935/6, fax (021) 7619259, PO Box 96, Kenilworth 7745.
Facilities/amenities: Accommodation in rustic bush camps or camp sites; guides, all equipment and food provided; kayaking lessons offered by River Runners.
Pertinent information: Maximum of 40 people for River Rafters, and 30 people for Felix Unite. Check whether children under 12 are permitted. Trails are run from June to September, depending on rainfall. A wetsuit is required.

These trails give you the opportunity to do some exhilarating white-water canoeing and rafting on grade 2 to 3 rapids. On quieter stretches of the river you can explore the area in search of Bushman paintings. See map on page 85.

6. LANGEBAAN LAGOON
CAPE WEST COAST

Trail details: 1 to 2 hours.
Permits/bookings: Bookings can be made at least 24 hours in advance through the information officer at the West Coast National Park, tel. (02287) 22144.
Facilities/amenities: Guide and 5 double canoes provided.
Pertinent information: Mornings are the best time for this trail, before the south-easter starts blowing.

This canoe trail is a must for bird-watchers. Participants paddle from the lodge at Langebaan to Skaape Island where, from the canoes, they can observe the variety of marine and breeding birds on the island before paddling back to the lodge.

7. BREEDE RIVER
NEAR SWELLENDAM, SOUTH-WESTERN CAPE

Trail details: 1 to 2 days.
Permits/bookings: Contact **Breede River Adventures**, tel. (021) 4610033, fax (021) 4614344, 104 Upper Maynard Street, Vredehoek 8001; or **Aquatrails**, tel. (021) 7945808, fax (021) 7941765, 8 Oak Farm Crescent, Constantia 7800.
Facilities/amenities: Accommodation in cottages or rustic bush camps; food, guides and all equipment supplied; Breede River Adventures offer conference facilities.
Pertinent information: Summers are pleasant in this area, and winters cold and wet, so take a wetsuit. Maximum of 20 for Aquatrails. Canoeing on the Breede is suitable for the disabled.

The Breede is the largest river in the Western Cape and offers picturesque countryside and safe and leisurely rafting and canoeing experiences that are suitable for the whole family. Rapids are graded 1 and 2.

8. THE WINE ROUTE CANOEING AND RAFTING ADVENTURE
BREEDE RIVER, SOUTH-WESTERN CAPE

Trail details: 1 day.
Permits/bookings: Contact **Felix Unite**, tel. (021) 7626935/6, fax (021) 7619259, PO Box 96, Kenilworth 7745; or **River Rafters**, tel. (021) 725094/5, fax (021) 725241, PO Box 14, Diep River 7856.
Facilities/amenities: Guides, all equipment, food and wine are provided.
Pertinent information: The trails are offered from mid-October to mid-March. Group size is 20 to 40 for Felix Unite.

A leisurely canoeing trip through the Worcester Valley, where the rapids are graded 1 and 2, combined with wine tasting and a buffet lunch on the banks of the river.

A fast-flowing rapid on the Orange River.

The Zambezi is considered one of the world's most exciting and challenging rivers for white-water rafting.

9. BUSHMANS RIVER CANOE TRAIL
BUSHMANS RIVER, EASTERN CAPE

Trail details: 30 km/2 days.
Permits/bookings: Contact J and A-M Snyman,
tel. (0464) 81223; PO Box 88, Kenton-on-Sea 6191.
Facilities/amenities: Equipment and overnight
accommodation in hut provided.
Pertinent information: Maximum party size is 12.
Children under 15 must be accompanied by an adult in
the canoe.

Participants paddle upstream on the winding and
unspoilt Bushmans River for 15 km to the overnight
hut and then back again the next day. A short walking
trail from the hut is also available.

10. KOWIE CANOE TRAIL
WATERS MEETING NATURE RESERVE,
PORT ALFRED, EASTERN CAPE

This trail offers people the exciting and unusual
opportunity of combining a 3-hour canoeing trip with
a 12-km/4-hour walk. For further information, see the
entry and map for the Kowie Hiking/Canoe Trail on
page 110.

11. TUGELA RIVER
NORTHERN NATAL

Trail details: 1 to 4 days.
Permits/bookings: Contact **Sunwa Ventures**, tel. (011)
7885120, PO Box 41952, Craighall 2024; **Felix Unite** in
Cape, tel. (021) 7626935, fax (021) 7619259, PO Box 96,
Kenilworth 7745, or in Transvaal, tel. (011) 8039778,
fax (011) 8039603, or in Natal, tel. (0331) 65018,
fax (0331) 69616.
Facilities/amenities: All equipment and meals supplied;
accommodation in bush camps provided.
Pertinent information: You need to be a confident
swimmer for these trails, but no previous canoeing
experience is necessary. Felix Unite does not permit
children under 16, and only runs trails from September to
March. Sunwa Ventures restrict party size to 30.

Forming the traditional boundary between Natal and
Zululand, the Tugela River offers exciting possi-
bilities for white-water rafting. Sunwa Ventures offer
trails on the stretch of the river near Colenso, whereas
Felix Unite operates in the Tugela Gorge where the
rapids are graded 2 to 4 for what is reputed to be the
best white-water rafting in South Africa. See map on
page 205.

12. VAAL RIVER
NEAR PARYS, TRANSVAAL

Trail details: Guided river-rafting. Number of days spent
on the river is flexible.
Permits/bookings: Contact Sunwa Ventures, tel. 7885120;
PO Box 41952, Craighall 2024.
Facilities/amenities: Accommodation in bush camp with
all facilities; all equipment and meals provided.
Pertinent information: The camp can accommodate up to
40 people.

Experienced guides take guests down the Vaal River
in 2-person canoes. Most of the river is calm and
serene, but a few rapids, with interesting names like
the Knucklecrusher and Groepswoeps, do lend excitement to the trip.

13. HADEDA CREEK TRAIL
VAAL RIVER, PARYS, TRANSVAAL

Trail details: Guided 2-day canoeing trips.
Permits/bookings: Contact River Rafters, in the Cape
tel. (021) 725094/5, fax (021) 725241, 35 Kendal Road,
PO Box 14, Diep River 7856; or in the Transvaal,
tel. (011) 7922353, fax (011) 7922833; PO Box 68132,
Bryanston 2021.
Facilities/amenities: Tented accommodation at Hadeda
Creek; all equipment supplied.
Pertinent information: The camp can accommodate up to
30 people.

Canoeing on the Vaal River in 2-person inflatable
canoes – shooting down exciting rapids, and exploring hidden channels that are overhung with willows
– is on offer.

14. CHOBE RIVER
CAPRIVI, NAMIBIA

Trail details: 5-day canoeing safari.
Permits/bookings: Contact Kalizo, tel. (011) 7644606;
PO Box 195, Wilgeheuwel, Roodepoort 1736.
Facilities/amenities: Guides and all equipment and food
provided; accommodation in tented camps.
Pertinent information: Maximum of 6 people per group.
Remember that you will need a passport. See page 280 for
general notes on the area.

Glide leisurely down the meandering Chobe River in
this remote wilderness area through teak and hard-
wood forests, dense riverine vegetation and swamps,
and spot big game like elephant, hippo and a variety
of antelope. See map on page 294.

15. UPPER ZAMBEZI RIVER
KAZUNGULA TO VICTORIA FALLS

Trail details: Canoeing and rafting: 1 to 3 days; about
20 km per day.
Permits/bookings: In Zambia, contact **Makora Quest**,
tel. (3) 321679 or 320401, fax (3) 320732, PO Box
60420, Livingstone; or **Tongabezi Canoeing Safaris**,
tel. (3) 323235, fax (3) 323224, Private Bag 31,
Livingstone. In Zimbabwe, contact **Shearwater
Adventures**, tel. (4) 737512, fax (4) 735716,
PO Box 3961, Harare; or **Bushlife**, tel. (4) 48548 or 45752
or 45868, fax (4) 48265, PO Box CH84, Harare.
Facilities/amenities: Most operators supply all canoeing
or rafting, and camping equipment, as well as all meals
and drinks, and transport to and from the nearest centre;
some include the opportunity to try kayaking.
Pertinent information: Groups of 6 to 9 are usually
catered for, and some trips do not allow children under
16. Participants need not be experienced, but should be
reasonably fit.

The mighty Zambezi River is the very essence of
Africa. Between Kazungula and Victoria Falls lies the
65-km stretch of the Upper Zambezi River where
rapids that test your strength and courage are interspersed with calm and peaceful channels, sometimes
less than 2 m wide, and enchanted islands. See map
on page 314.

16. ZAMBEZI RIVER
BELOW THE VICTORIA FALLS TO LAKE KARIBA

Trail details: White-water rafting: 13 km to 22 km.
Extended trips of up to 7 days also possible.
Permits/bookings: In Zambia, contact **Sobek Whitewater
Adventures**, tel. (1) 224248, fax (1) 224265, PO Box
30263, Lusaka; or **Safari Par Excellence**, tel. (3) 321679,
fax (3) 320732, PO Box 60420, Livingstone. In
Zimbabwe, contact **Shearwater Adventures**, tel. (4)
737512, fax (4) 735716, PO Box 3961, Harare; or **Safari
Par Excellence**, tel. (4) 700911/2 or 736674 or 720527,
fax (4) 722872, PO Box 5921, Harare. In South Africa,
contact **Safari Par Excellence**, tel. (011) 7879756 or
7879500, fax (011) 7879757, PO Box 1395, Randburg
2194; or **Sunwa Ventures**, tel. (011) 7885120,
PO Box 41952, Craighall 2024.
Facilities/amenities: Guides, instruction and all equipment
supplied, and some tours also include a light lunch and
refreshment; extended trips are run in expedition style
with all canoeing and camping equipment, meals and
drinks supplied.
Pertinent information: Most tour operators can
accommodate up to 20 people, but children under 16 are
not permitted. Depending on the rains, high-water runs
are usually operated from June to mid-July and
mid-December to March; low-water runs are usually
offered from July to mid-December. Between February
and June the level of the water is usually dangerously
high. Participants need not have experience, but should be
reasonably fit.

Below the Victoria Falls, the Zambezi River becomes
a fury as it drops about 19 m through 24 km of sinuous,
tortuous gorges, sometimes only 12 m wide, creating
some of the biggest white-water rapids to be found
anywhere in the world – 23 rapids that are graded 3
to 6 (it is necessary to portage around the unrunnable
grade 6 rapid 9). From the gorges, as the river wends
its way to Lake Kariba, rapids are interspersed with
long calm stretches of water. See map on page 314.

17. LAKE KARIBA
NORTHERN ZIMBABWE

Trail details: Short trips or longer safaris in either canoes
or yachts.
Permits/bookings: In Zimbabwe, contact **Fothergill Island
Safaris**, tel. Kariba (61) 2253, PO Box 2081, Kariba; or
Bushlife, tel. (4) 48548 or 45752 or 45868, fax (4) 48265,
PO Box CH84, Harare; or **Sailing Safaris**, tel. (61) 2645,
Lake Kariba. Contact the relevant tour operator for more
detailed information.
Pertinent information: Take anti-malaria precautions and
be wary of bilharzia in the water. Although Kariba is a
lake, remember that during a storm it can be as dangerous
as the open sea.

Forming the bridge between the Upper and Lower
Zambezi River, Lake Kariba is 5 000 km^2 of island-

studded water. Bays, inlets, river estuaries and forests make its shores a fascinating wonderland to explore, and the adjoining wilderness area is teeming with game. See map on page 314.

18. LOWER ZAMBEZI RIVER
FROM LAKE KARIBA TO KANYEMBA

Trail details: 1- to 9-day canoeing trips; travelling about 20 km per day.
Permits/bookings: In Zambia, contact **Zambezi River Safaris**, tel. (1) 287748 or 287817 or 230576, fax (1) 230576, PO Box 30050, Lusaka; or **Sobek Canoe Adventures**, tel. (1) 224248, fax (1) 224265, PO Box 30263, Lusaka; or **Tongabezi Canoeing Safaris**, tel. (3) 323235, fax (3) 323224, Private Bag 31, Livingstone; or **Safari Par Excellence**, tel. (3) 321679, fax (3) 320732, PO Box 60420, Livingstone. In Zimbabwe, contact **Shearwater Adventures**, tel. (4) 737512, fax (4) 735716, PO Box 3961, Harare; or **Bushlife**, tel. (4) 48548 or 45752 or 45868, fax (4) 48265, PO Box CH84, Harare; or **Safari Par Excellence**, tel. (4) 700911/2 or 736674 or 720527, fax (4) 722872, PO Box 5921, Harare. In South Africa, contact **Wild Frontiers**, tel. (011) 7022132 or 7022246, fax (011) 7021131, PO Box 844, Halfway House 1655; or **Drifters**, tel. (011) 8881160, fax (011) 8881020, PO Box 48434, Roosevelt Park 2129; or **Goliath Safaris**, tel. (011) 7885549, fax (011) 7886675, PO Box 52900, Saxonwold 2132; or **Safari Par Excellence**, tel. (011) 7879756 or 7879500, fax (011) 7879757, PO Box 1395, Randburg 2194, South Africa.
Facilities/amenities: Accommodation provided in fully equipped camps; canoes and all equipment, meals and drinks are supplied.
Pertinent information: The limit to the number of people in a group varies from 4 to 20, and children under 15, or sometimes 16, are generally not permitted. This stretch of the river is so calm and peaceful that it is easy paddling all the way. The best months for canoeing are from March to December.

The Lower Zambezi River, 280 km from Lake Kariba to Kanyemba on the Moçambique border, is perfect canoeing country. The river flows gently through remote wilderness, creating vast, panoramic floodplains, channels and steep gorges, and spreads to 4 km at its widest point. The beautiful Mana Pools are *en route*, as is the austere and remote Mupata Gorge. You can observe herds of impala, waterbuck, elephant and buffalo and the endangered black rhino, as well as a wide variety of bird species. See map on page 314.

HORSEBACK, PONY-TREKKING, AND CAMEL TRAILS

Many of these trails cater for inexperienced riders – the horses or ponies are well trained, the guides are accustomed to novices and the route is chosen according to the ability of the group, so it is very important that you should be completely honest with your guide about your riding experience. However, bear in mind that a 4-day horse-trail is not the time to discover that you don't like horse-riding, so some experience is sensible if you are planning a longer trail. It is not advisable to tackle trails of more than 1,5 hours without some prior preparation, or the discomfort of unused muscles protesting will detract from your enjoyment of the trip – in fact, by the end of the first day you will probably be barely able to walk. A hot mustard bath is always good for easing aching muscles at the end of a ride, so stock up before you set out on a horseback trail! Wear suitable clothing – comfortable long pants and boots, which must have a heel, and a hard hat – and always prepare for unpredictable weather.

1. KALAHARI GEMSBOK NATIONAL PARK
NEAR UPINGTON, NORTHERN CAPE

The park is considering the viability of camel trails. For information, contact the National Parks Board in Cape Town (021) 222810; or Pretoria (012) 3431991.

2. KAMEELDORING TRAIL
BUSHMANLAND, NEAR AUGRABIES FALLS, NORTH-WESTERN CAPE

Trail details: 5-day, 85-km camel trail.
Permits/bookings: Contact Camel Runners, tel. (011) 4032512, fax (011) 3391380; PO Box 31117, Braamfontein 2017.

Facilities/amenities: Guides and all equipment and meals provided; accommodation at base camp and camping out on trail; horses and pony carts optional.
Pertinent information: Party size is 10 to 20 per group with no children under 8 allowed. No children under 14 on camels and under 12 on horses.

This unique trail traverses the remote Bushmanland area where the Orange River is fringed with lush green vegetation and the Nama plateau offers a stark and rugged contrast. See map on page 135.

3. TWO SHIPS TRAIL
ORANGE RIVER AND BUSHMANLAND, NEAR AUGRABIES FALLS, NORTH-WESTERN CAPE

See the entry for Two Ships Trail on page 335.

4. CEDARBERG WILDERNESS TRAIL
CEDARBERG MOUNTAINS, WESTERN CAPE

Trail details: 1- or 2-day (weekend) trails.
Permits/bookings: Contact Horse Trail Safaris, tel. (021) 734396; PO Box 126, Ottery 7808.
Facilities/amenities: Accommodation in rustic bush camp; guide, food and all equipment provided.
Pertinent information: Maximum party size is 10. Although novice riders can be accommodated, because of its length the trail is best suited to experienced riders.

The rugged and beautiful Cedarberg range offers imposing rock formations, caves, cool streams, Bushman paintings, dense mountain fynbos and magnificent views from little-known peaks. When the weather is clear, you can visit the observatory and do some stargazing. See map of the area on page 43.

5. K'TAAIBOS HORSE TRAILS
WESTERN CAPE

Trail details: 3 days.
Permits/bookings: Contact K'Taaibos Adventures, tel. (02281) 51541, fax (02281) 51525.
Facilities/amenities: Guide, equipment and food provided.
Pertinent information: Maximum party size is 7.

Participants can spend 3 days exploring the West Coast, starting from Elands Bay, or head off into the mountains near Citrusdal for a 3-day safari experience. See map on page 42.

6. WEST COAST WILDERNESS TRAIL
VERLORENVLEI BIRD SANCTUARY, CAPE WEST COAST

Trail details: 2 days; return.
Permits/bookings: Contact Horse Trail Safaris, tel. (021) 734396; PO Box 126, Ottery 7808.
Facilities/amenities: Guide, all necessary equipment and meals are provided.
Pertinent information: Maximum party size is 10. Although novice riders can be accommodated, because of its length the trail is best suited to experienced and practised riders. Stables are at Lambert's Bay.

Explore the quiet shores of the Verlorenvlei Bird Sanctuary and examine Bushman paintings on this trail. Participants ride along the desolate 18-km stretch of beach on the West Coast (from Lambert's Bay to Eland's Bay), which has imposing sand dunes, and then take canoes up the Verlorenvlei River to Muishoek where you camp overnight, before making the journey back to Lambert's Bay by canoe and horseback. See map on page 42.

7. NOVICE TRAILS
OTTERY, NEAR CAPE TOWN, CAPE PENINSULA

Trail details: 1 or 2 hours.
Permits/bookings: Contact Horse Trail Safaris, tel. (021) 734396, PO Box 126, Ottery 7808.
Facilities/amenities: Guide and all equipment provided.
Pertinent information: These short trails are particularly suitable for the novice rider, and riding lessons are given at the stables in Ottery.

A 1-hour outride from the stables at Ottery, or a 2-hour Muizenberg beach ride where you can see buck, tortoises and mongooses.

The rolling foothills of the Drakensberg make ideal horse-riding country.

A guided trail through the rugged grasslands of the eastern Cape.

8. NOORDHOEK BEACH
NOORDHOEK, CAPE PENINSULA

Trail details: 1,5-hour beach ride.
Permits/bookings: Contact Horse Trail Safaris, tel. (021) 734396, PO Box 126, Ottery 7808.
Facilities/amenities: Guide and all equipment provided.
Pertinent information: Trails leave at 8.00 am, 10.00 am, 2.00 pm and 4.00 pm, and are suitable for the novice rider.

An exhilarating ride along the endless expanse of Noordhoek Beach. See map on page 56.

9. MONTAGU TO DE DOORNS
MONTAGU, WESTERN CAPE

Trail details: 2 or 4 days.
Permits/bookings: Contact Horse Trail Safaris, tel. (021) 734396; PO Box 126, Ottery 7808 for bookings.
Facilities/amenities: Overnight accommodation in a barn in Montagu, and camping on trail.
Pertinent information: This trail was in the planning stage at the time of writing, so contact Horse Trail Safaris for more information. See map on page 76.

10. WORCESTER GAME TRAIL
WORCESTER, WESTERN CAPE

Trail details: 1- or 2-day (weekend) trails.
Permits/bookings: Contact Horse Trail Safaris, tel. (021) 734396; PO Box 126, Ottery 7808.
Facilities/amenities: Guide, all necessary equipment and food are provided.
Pertinent information: Maximum party size is 10. Although novice riders can be accommodated, because of its length the trail is best suited to experienced and practised riders. Stables are on the Nuy road.

This trail offers the opportunity to observe varieties of wildlife, including buzzards, hawks and black eagles, jackals and caracal, or perhaps the shy Cape mountain leopard in the Robertson area of the Karoo.

11. KNYSNA WILDERNESS TRAIL
SEDGEFIELD/KNYSNA AREA, SOUTHERN CAPE

Trail details: 4-day horse and canoe trails.
Permits/bookings: Contact Horse Trail Safaris, tel. (021) 734396; PO Box 126, Ottery 7808.
Facilities/amenities: Base camp at Lake Pleasant with conference facilities; guide, all equipment and food are provided.
Pertinent information: Maximum party size is 10. Although novice riders can be accommodated, because of its length the trail is best suited to experienced and practised riders.

Explore the coastal zone of the Goukamma Nature Reserve with its beautiful beaches, indigenous forests and mystical rivers on horseback. Birds, monkeys, bushbuck, otters and fish eagles abound in this diverse stretch of the southern coast. See map on page 93.

12. BENGHOIL HORSE AND HIKING TRAILS
NEAR CATHCART, EASTERN CAPE

Trail details: Optional, according to group, but usually weekend trails.
Permits/bookings: Contact Benghoil Horse and Hiking Trails, tel. (04562) ask for 2203; PO Box 142, Cathcart 5310 for bookings.
Facilities/amenities: Accommodation for 8 in rustic thatched lodge with all modern conveniences; catering provided for large groups.
Pertinent information: Autumn is the best time for these trails, but they are offered all year round. The trails are suitable for children.

Mountain-bred horses are used for these guided trails. Discover Bushman paintings at 6 sites, and enjoy the wealth of cycads, birds and game.

13. SETHUNZINI HORSE TRAIL
NEAR LADY GREY, SOUTHERN DRAKENSBERG

Trail details: 4-day/5-night trail. Shorter options, e.g. weekend packages, are available.
Permits/bookings: Contact Jacana Country Homes and Trails, tel. (012) 3463550, fax (012) 3462499.
Facilities/amenities: Guide and all equipment and food provided; fishing, kloofing and skiing (in winter) possible.
Pertinent information: Maximum party size is 10.

Sturdy mountain ponies are used for this trail that winds through the scenically magnificent Witteberg range, where the rugged mountains of the southern Drakensberg rise to about 95 m. Explore the riverside caves for Bushman paintings, and look out for the Cape vulture. See map on page 123.

14. KATBERG MOUNTAIN HORSE TRAILS
BALFOUR, CISKEI

Horse trails in the Katberg Forest area start from the Katberg Protea Hotel. They are 0,5 hours to 1 day in duration, depending on the experience of the riders. A 0,5- to 1-hour route leads through the lower Katberg Forest, while a popular trail is that to the top of the Katberg Pass. See page 114 for more information.

15. MPOFU GAME PARK
BALFOUR, CISKEI

Trail details: 1- to 2-day pony trails.
Permits/bookings: Contact the Manager, tel. (040452) ask for 11; PO Box 647, Fort Beaufort 5720.
Facilities/amenities: Accommodation available in lodge; trails are guided.
Pertinent information: Maximum party size is 8. Trails run from mid-August to end of March (which is non-hunting season).

This area with its numerous veld types and forested kloofs is still being developed as a conservation area.

16. MARIA MOROKA NATIONAL PARK
THABA NCHU, BOPHUTHATSWANA

Trail details: 1,5 hours; longer trails by arrangement.
Permits/bookings: Contact Debbie Jackson, tel. (05265) 2161; Thaba Nchu Sun, PO Box 114, Thaba Nchu 9780 for bookings.
Facilities/amenities: Guide and all equipment provided.
Pertinent information: No previous experience is required. No children under 12 permitted, unless they are accomplished riders.

These short horse rides take you into the Maria Moroka National Park where you have the opportunity of getting really close to game such as zebra, eland, rhino, red hartebeest and blesbok.

17. GOLDEN GATE HIGHLANDS NATIONAL PARK
NEAR CLARENS, NORTH-EASTERN ORANGE FREE STATE

Riders can hire horses from the stables at Gladstone's Buttress for a variety of short trails. See entry on page 158 for further information about the park and map on page 159.

18. SPARROWFARM TRAILS
GOLDEN GATE VALLEY, NORTH-EASTERN ORANGE FREE STATE

Half-day to 3-day horseback trails are also offered by Sparrowfarm Trails (see entry on page 334 for further information) and are suitable for novice and experienced rider alike. At least one experienced rider must accompany a group for the half-day trail, and the longer trails are guided.

19. BOKPOORT HORSE SAFARIS
NEAR CLARENS, NORTH-EASTERN ORANGE FREE STATE

Trail details: 1. Bokpoort Trail: 10 km; 2. Oumas Kraal Trail: 30 km/2 days or 45 km/3 days; 3. Snow Hills Trail: 50 km.
Permits/bookings: Contact Jacana Country Homes and Trails, tel. (012) 3463550, fax (012) 3462499.
Facilities/amenities: All equipment and meals provided (self-catering optional); accommodation at base camp on Bokpoort farm or at Oumas Kraal mountain hut, De Rots hut or Snow Hills old homestead; horse cart offered on Oumas Kraal Trail.
Pertinent information: Party size is 2 to 8. Snow Hills Trail is for the skilled and adventurous rider, but the other 2 trails are suitable for the inexperienced.

1. The Bokpoort Trail, for novice and experienced riders, is an easy 10 km that takes you to a waterfall where there is a beautiful panoramic view of the Clarens mountains and the surrounding area. After enjoying a braai at the waterfall, you return to the Bokpoort farm. The route follows that used for the hiking trail (see page 161).
2. Oumas Kraal Trail is especially suited to novice riders and covers 15 km per day. The trail explores the 20 000-ha Clarens Conservancy.
3. The Snow Hills Trail is for the more skilled and adventurous rider and traverses typical grassland areas, indigenous forest and ravines. About 25 km is covered each day, and the trail explores the wilderness area behind Golden Gate stretching to Lesotho. See map on page 160.

20. RIETFONTEIN HORSE RIDE
MARQUARD DISTRICT, EASTERN ORANGE FREE STATE

Trail details: 12 km/1 day or 52 km/2 days, with several variations.
Permits/bookings: Contact Jacana Country Homes and Trails, tel. (012) 3463550, fax (012) 3462499.
Facilities/amenities: Overnight accommodation in cottages in Marquard and on the trail; stabling for horses is provided.
Pertinent information: Take your own provisions. You must provide your own horse.

A variety of trails traverse the Rietfontein farm, and the 52-km route can be done in one day as an endurance ride. See map on page 150.

21. FRANSHOEK MOUNTAIN HORSE TRAIL
WITTEBERG CONSERVANCY, EASTERN ORANGE FREE STATE

Trail details: 29 km/1 day; short 2-hour rides are also possible.
Permits/bookings: Contact Christian Findlay, tel. (05192) 3938; PO Box 603, Ficksburg 9730.
Facilities/amenities: Accommodation at Franshoek Mountain Lodge, or overnight in cave.
Pertinent information: Maximum party size is 10.

In the company of a guide, riders enjoy this beautiful mountain trail. See map on page 153. A 2-day hike starting at Franshoek Lodge is also possible; see page 154 for details.

22. QWIBI HORSE TRAIL
NEAR MELMOTH, NORTHERN NATAL

Trail details: 2-day/2-night trails (weekend).
Permits/bookings: Contact Jacana Country Homes and Trails, tel. (012) 3463550, fax (012) 3462499.
Facilities/amenities: Guide and all equipment (including camping) supplied.
Pertinent information: Groups of 4 to 6 can be accommodated. Take your own provisions.

This trail takes you through the Nooitgedacht farm and the newly proclaimed Opate Game Reserve – Zululand bushveld country where the birdlife is prolific, with an abundance of raptors. The area is also rich in history as it is here in these hills that battles were fought between Dingaan and Shaka, and that the Voortrekkers collected and fought for cattle.

23. NDANYAAN MOUNTAIN TRAILS
NEAR NEWCASTLE, NORTHERN NATAL

Trail details: 1,5 or 3 or 4 days.
Permits/bookings: Contact John Whipp, tel. (03431) 23028; PO Box 447, Newcastle 2940.
Facilities/amenities: Accommodation in tented camps with bush showers and toilets; all food provided.
Pertinent information: Children under 16 only permitted if they are experienced riders.

Trails cover about 20 km per day and are flexible, but generally riders will be taken through *Protea caffra* groves, across the Ncandu River, and then through open grassland and natural mountain forest.

24. ROYAL NATAL NATIONAL PARK
NORTHERN DRAKENSBERG

Riders can undertake 2- or 3-hour horse trails from Rugged Glen Camp. The guided trails leave 3 times a day; all-day trails can be arranged. See entry on page 205 for more information about the reserve and a map.

25. CATHEDRAL PEAK HOTEL HORSE RIDES
CATHEDRAL PEAK AREA, DRAKENSBERG

Guided horse rides for groups of 10 to 12 are offered daily – a beginners' ride is for 1 hour and a 2-hour ride for the experienced – in the vicinity of the hotel. See page 209 for more information about the area and a map.

26. DRAGON PEAK HORSE RIDES
CHAMPAGNE CASTLE AREA, DRAKENSBERG

The Dragon Peak caravan and camping resort offers guided horse rides for groups of 8 to 12 on the weekends and during holiday seaons. There is a half-hour ride for beginners and 1-hour rides for intermediate and experienced riders.

27. CHAMPAGNE CASTLE HOTEL HORSE RIDES
CHAMPAGNE CASTLE AREA, DRAKENSBERG

Guided horse rides for beginners and experienced riders in the vicinity of the hotel are offered daily – the beginners' ride is for 1 hour and 9 riders, the ride for the experienced is for 1,5 hours and 5 riders. See page 214 for more information and map on page 209.

28. HILLSIDE
GIANT'S CASTLE RESERVE, NATAL DRAKENSBERG PARK

Trail details: 2, 3 or 4 days.
Permits/bookings: Contact the Natal Parks Board, tel. (0331) 471981, fax (0331) 471980; PO Box 1750, Pietermaritzburg 3200.
Facilities/amenities: Accommodation either at base camp or in caves.
Pertinent information: Maximum party size is 8; children under 14 are not permitted. Bring your own food. Trails are run from September to June.

These guided horseback trails explore the foothills of the Drakensberg. See map on page 215.

29. GATESHEAD LODGE
SOUTHERN DRAKENSBERG

Trail details: 16 to 18 km/1 to 4 days.
Permits/bookings: Contact Gateshead Lodge, tel. (04542) 7211 or 7502; PO Box 15, Barkly East 5580.
Facilities/amenities: Self-catering accommodation in fully equipped farmhouses.
Pertinent information: Best months are from September through to April.

A variety of circular trails lead from Gateshead Lodge and explore the Gateshead Conservancy and neighbouring farms. The 4-day trail involves some steep climbing and then a steep downhill, so should only be attempted by the fit and experienced. Shorter trails are available for the novice rider.

30. FRASERS LODGE
SEMONKONG, LESOTHO

Trail details: 1. Maletsunyane Falls Pony Trek: 4 to 5 hours; 2. Semonkong Village Pony Trek: 3 to 4 hours; 3. Methodist Church Hospital Pony Trek: 2 to 3 hours; 4. Ketane Falls Trek: 2 days.
Permits/bookings: Can be obtained from Frasers Lodge, tel. (05192) 2730 or 3106, fax (05192) 3313; PO Box 243, Ficksburg 9730.
Facilities/amenities: Self-catering cottages and a restaurant at Semonkong Lodge; camp at Ketane Falls with food provided.
Pertinent information: Winters can be very cold. A 4-day, 3-night trek from Qaba Lodge can be done by arrangement. There is an additional charge for guides.

Explore the Maluti mountains and visit the Maletsunyane Falls, the highest in Lesotho, on these pony-trekking trails.

31. MATELILE PONY-TREKKING TOURS
MAFETENG DISTRICT, LESOTHO

Trail details: 1. Botsoela Falls Trek: 4 hours; 2. Ribaneng Falls Trek: 2 days; 3. Trek to Lesotho's Great Falls: 4 days.
Permits/bookings: Contact the Lesotho Tourist Board, tel. (09266) 322896; PO Box 1378, Maseru 100.
Facilities/amenities: Ponies for hire from Matelile Pony Owners' Association Pony Trekking Centre; accommodation in Basotho villages.
Pertinent information: Winters can be very cold. Minimum of 5 per group.

1. The 4-hour trek to **Botsoela Falls** includes a stop to view Bushman paintings and rock pools.
2. The adventurous **Ribaneng Falls Trek** takes you past streams and through traditional Basotho villages.
3. Trek to **Lesotho's Great Falls**: Ribaneng, Ketane and Maletsunyane, and visit Bushman paintings and traditional Basotho villages along the way.
See map on page 223.

32. MALEALEA LODGE
NEAR MAKHAKE, LESOTHO

Trail details: Pony treks, ranging from 1 hour to 6 days.
Permits/bookings: Contact Malealea Lodge, tel. (09266) 785336, fax (09266) 785326; PO Makhake, 922 Lesotho.
Facilities/amenities: Basic accommodation in huts for longer trails; Malealea Lodge is used as a base for shorter trails; self-catering and self-guided trips are optional.
Pertinent information: Winters can be very cold. Minimum of 3 people per group.

All the hiking trails mentioned in the entry on page 223 can be used for pony trekking. In addition, the adventurous can embark on longer trails, such as the 2-day Ribaneng Pony Trek to visit the Ribaneng Falls, extended to a 4-day trail to take in the Ketane Falls, which can be further extended to 6 days to visit the Maletsunyane Falls. See map on page 223.

33. BASOTHO PONY-TREKKING
MOLIMO NTHUSE PASS, LESOTHO

Trail details: 1. Leboela Falls Trek: 2 hours; 2. Qiloane Falls Trek: 4 hours; 3. Maletsunyane Falls Trek: 7 days.
Permits/bookings: Contact Basotho Pony Trekking, tel. (09266) 314165; PO Box 1027, Maseru.
Facilities/amenities: Accommodation available in Basotho villages (there is a small fee for pitching a tent); guides can be hired; self-catering.
Pertinent information: Winters can be very cold. Minimum of 4 per group. Bring a small bag of charcoal with you as wood can be very scarce in Lesotho.

Although no riding experience is required, these trails are not for the faint-hearted as the mountainous terrain is rugged and facilities are few.

34. MEIKLES MOUNT
NEAR MBABANE, SWAZILAND

Guests can go on a guided horseback trail around Mhlane Mountain. See entry on page 226 for more information on Meikles Mount.

35. MALOLOTJA NATURE RESERVE
NEAR MBABANE, SWAZILAND

Half-day guided horse trails are also offered at Malolotja Nature Reserve. See entry on page 228 for more information about the reserve.

36. EQUUS TRAILS
WATERBERG MOUNTAINS, NORTHERN TRANSVAAL

Trail details: 2 to 5 hours; 5- to 10-night wilderness trails.
Permits/bookings: Contact Equus Trails, tel. (01536) 50230, fax (01536) 50108; PO Box 57, Marken 0605.
Facilities/amenities: Experienced trail leaders as guides; accommodation in tented bush camp with hot showers and meals provided; wilderness trails backed up by fourwheel drive vehicle; camps are run for school children.
Pertinent information: Maximum party size is 10.

A variety of shorter trails is offered: a beginners' trail (outside the big game area), trails that include breakfast, a picnic or sundowners, and a moonlight trail. For the hardy, the wilderness trail is a real adventure.

37. KALKOENKRANS HORSE TRAILS
NEAR CAROLINA, EASTERN TRANSVAAL

Guided horse trails that follow the same routes and offer the same facilties as the walking trails (see page 277) are offered. For more information and bookings, tel. Mr G Combrink, (01344) 31954 or Sappi Rooihoogte forestry office, tel. (01344) 32802.

38. NAMIB DESERT HORSE RIDING
NAMIB DESERT, FROM KHOMAS HOCHLAND TO SWAKOPMUND, NAMIBIA

Trail details: 400 km/9 days.
Permits/bookings: For bookings and further information, contact A and W Fritzsche, tel. (0628) ask for Friedental 1111, fax (061) 38890; PO Box 20706, Windhoek 9100.
Facilities/amenities: Guide and all equipment provided.
Pertinent information: Trails are conducted from February to April and July to September.

The trail starts on a farm in the Khomas Hochland, 65 km from Windhoek, and leads you past slopes where leopards and zebras hide, and through the Namib Desert where you can see the strange Welwitschia Plain and Moon Valley, and on to Swakopmund on the coast. See map on page 282.

39. DUSTERNBROOK HORSE TRAILS
KHOMAS HOCHLAND, NAMIBIA

Trail details: 3 to 5 days.
Permits/bookings: Contact Johann Vatz, tel. (061) 32572, fax (061) 34758; PO Box 870, Windhoek 9100.
Facilities/amenities: Accommodation on Dusternbrook farm or in tents.
Pertinent information: Minimum of 4 persons per group.

Participants can either stay on Dusternbrook farm and embark on daily horse trails to explore the area, or they can spend 3 to 5 days camping out in the Khomas hochland and ride from ranch to ranch. See map on page 282.

40. OAS GUEST FARM
NEAR KEETMANSHOOP, NAMIBIA

Trail details: 27 km/2 days.
Permits/bookings: For bookings and further information, contact Mantie Oberholzer, tel. (06342) ask for Stinkdoring 4321; PO Box 4, Karasburg 9000.
Facilities/amenities: Equipment and camping facilities (in a large room) with toilet; drinking water supplied.
Pertinent information: The trail is closed from the beginning of April to the end of October. Maximum party size is 11.

The trail is in a scenic mountainous area, and the historical site of German graves is *en route*. See map on page 288.

41. FISH RIVER CANYON HORSE TRAILS
SOUTHERN NAMIBIA

Trail details: 70 km/5 nights.
Permits/bookings: For bookings and more information, contact Saddle Runners, tel. (021) 7622350, fax (021) 7611373; PO Box 583, Constantia 7848.
Facilities/amenities: Guide, equipment and food provided.
Pertinent information: Passport and visa required. Trail is run from mid-June to end of October.

Although no experience is needed for this exploration of the Fish River Canyon the trail is designed for the adventurous who don't mind 'roughing it' and sleeping under the stars. See map on page 288.

42. ZAMBEZI HORSE TRAILS
ZAMBEZI NATIONAL PARK, NORTH-WESTERN ZIMBABWE

Trail details: Morning or afternoon rides for novice or experienced riders; full-day rides; overnight horse trails; Zambezi 2-night trail; 3-night trail; 4-night Masuwe trail. All trails are guided.
Permits/bookings: Contact Shearwater Adventures, tel. 735712, fax 735716; PO Box 3961, Harare.
Facilities/amenities: Transfers from Victoria Falls Hotel or Shearwater office; novice riders collected from Illala Lodge; soft drinks supplied on all trails; meals and luxury tented accommodation supplied on overnight trails.
Pertinent information: 2 to 5 people per group, unless special arrangements have been made. No children under 16, except ride for novices which can accommodate children over 8 (those under 12 must have had at least 1 year's riding lessons and be accompanied by a parent or elder).

Many freshwater springs around its base give the Waterberg Plateau its name and help vegetation flourish.

Overnight stops are in the Zambezi National Park, Woodlands Safari Camp and Masuwe Lodge. These trails are an excellent way to explore the Zambezi area. March to May are the best months as temperatures are moderate, and the land is still fresh and green from the summer rains. See map on page 308.

43. MATOBO NATIONAL PARK
NEAR BULAWAYO, ZIMBABWE

Trail details: A variety of pony trails can be arranged.
Permits/bookings: Permits can be purchased at gate. For further information contact The Warden, Matobo National Park, tel. Matopos 0-1913, Private Bag K 5142, Bulawayo; or tel. Matobo 9 or contact the tourist office which is located at Hazelside.
Facilities/amenities: A variety of accommodation offered; all equipment provided for pony trails.

The Matobo Hills (the Matopos) is a 2 000-km^2 area of gigantic wind-sculpted rock formations, cool green wooded valleys and lakes. Here Cecil Rhodes is buried atop a colossal granite dome, and thousands of ancient rock paintings remain as witness to the people who once lived here. The park is well worth exploring on a pony trail. See map on page 299.

44. LAKE MUTIRIKWE RECREATIONAL PARK
NEAR MASVINGO, ZIMBABWE

Trail details: Guided pony trails in the game park.
Permits/bookings: Permits available at the gate. For further information, contact The Warden, Private Bag 9136, Masvingo.
Facilities/amenities: Accommodation is available at the park; all equipment provided.

On the northern shores of Lake Mutirikwe (formerly Lake Kyle) visitors can explore the game park on horseback to view a variety of antelope species as well as white rhino and giraffe. The landscape consists of undulating and broken hill country, covered with grass and woodland. See map on page 302.

45. CECIL KOP NATURE RESERVE
NEAR MUTARE, EASTERN ZIMBABWE

Trail details: Pony trails in the wilderness area.
Permits/bookings: For further information, contact the Manicaland branch of the Wildlife Society of Zimbabwe, tel. Mutare 61537 or 61570; PO Box 920, Mutare.
Facilities/amenities: The Wildlife Society runs educational programmes for school children in the reserve.

Visitors can arrange to explore the wilderness area on horseback. The reserve consists mainly of montane grassland, evergreen forest, woodland, grassy vleis and man-made dams. Various antelope species as well as elephant, white rhino and giraffe inhabit the area. See map on page 302.

46. NYANGA NATIONAL PARK
NEAR MUTARE, EASTERN ZIMBABWE

Trail details: Guided half-day or full-day pony trails.
Permits/bookings: Permits can be purchased at the gate. For further information, contact The Warden, Nyanga National Park, tel. Nyanga 274 or 384; Private Bag T 7901, Mutare. All pony trails must be booked at the park the day before.
Facilities/amenities: A variety of accommodation is available in the park; all riding equipment supplied for pony trails; participants must take along their own food and drink.
Pertinent information: Children under 16 must be accompanied by an adult, and children under 7 are not permitted on the trails.

The half-day trails are conducted in the morning or afternoon and last about 1,5 hours. These guided trails will take you through the park to visit places like Nyangwe Fort, the Pit Structures, the Experimental Fruit Station and the exotic plantations. All-day trails are conducted in the Warrendale area and are only for experienced riders. See map on page 302.

47. ROBERT McILWAINE RECREATIONAL PARK
NEAR HARARE, ZIMBABWE

Trail details: Half-day guided pony trails.
Permits/bookings: Permits available at the gate. For further information, contact The Warden, tel. Norton 2329; Private Bag 962, Norton.
Facilities/amenities: A variety of accommodation is available in the park; all riding equipment is provided.

These guided pony trails, available for day visitors and residents, are conducted in the morning or afternoon and take you through the game park. See map on page 304.

48. HORSEBACK SAFARIS
NYIKA NATIONAL PARK, MALAWI

Trail details: 1. Base Camp Safari; 2. Mobile Camping Safari; 3. Mobile Luxury Safari.
Permits/bookings: Contact Heart of Africa Safaris, tel. (265) 740848, fax (265) 740848 or 740207; PO Box 8, Lilongwe.
Facilities/amenities: Fully catering accommodation in chalets for Base Camp Safari and tented camps for Mobile Luxury Safaris; semi-catering tented camps for Mobile Camping Safari; a guide and scout accompany each group.
Pertinent information: These safaris are flexible, and guests can choose a combination of the three.

These 3 types of safaris, where you embark on half- or full-day rides from the comfort of the base camp or you camp out, with or without the luxury full service and all amenities, are designed to suit the needs of most tourists who wish to explore the wilderness on horseback. Whichever option you choose, this is the ideal way to explore Malawi's largest park, much of which is inaccessible by vehicle. See map on page 324.

TRAILS FOR THE DISABLED

The National Botanical Institute in South Africa has been at the forefront of designing trails for the visually disabled and people in wheelchairs, while in Natal, the Wildlife Society has been instrumental in opening trails for the disabled in places like Glenholme Nature Reserve. Of special interest is the trail being established at the Palmiet Nature Reserve: the longest such trail to date, it gives the visually disabled the opportunity to tackle a 6-km route. In the future there should be more trails for the disabled in South Africa as the National Parks Board in the Cape, tel. (021) 222810, the Ecodisabled Committee for the Eastern Transvaal (contact Rob Filmer of Blyde River Nature Conservation, tel. (01315) 81215) and Disabled Adventures (contact Carol Schafer, tel. (021) 5314592) are all turning their attention to establishing such trails.

1. KIRSTENBOSCH NATIONAL BOTANICAL GARDEN
CAPE TOWN

Trail details: 1. Braille Trail: 45 minutes; 2. Fragrance Trail: 10 minutes; 3. Wheelchair route: 45 minutes.
Permits/bookings: None are required, but contact the information officer at Kirstenbosch, tel. (021) 7621166, for information.
Facilities/amenities: Car park, restaurant, toilets, curio shop, information office.
Pertinent information: The garden is open all year round, and there is an entrance fee. See map on page 53.

The world-renowned Kirstenbosch has special trails for the blind and those confined to wheelchairs.
1. The Braille Trail is roped and traverses a forest area. Labels *en route* are printed in braille.
2. The Fragrance Trail is a 10-minute walk through a fragrant garden where the visually disabled can touch a variety of plants. Labels in the garden are printed in braille.
3. The Wheelchair route starts at the restaurant and leads through the fragrance and herb gardens to the lawn section, where it then visits the aloes and oak trees and leads back to the restaurant through the Peninsula section.

2. KAROO NATIONAL PARK
NEAR BEAUFORT WEST, SOUTHERN KAROO

The park has established a braille trail of 800 m. For further information, tel. (0201) 52828/9. See also entry for Karoo National Park page 136 and map on page 137.

3. KENNETH STAINBANK TRAIL
KENNETH STAINBANK NATURE RESERVE, DURBAN, NATAL

Trail details: 500 m.
Permits/bookings: Guided trails for school groups can be arranged; contact the Senior Ranger, tel. (031) 421125; PO Box 53048, Yellowwood Park 4011. There is an entrance fee.
Facilities/amenities: A car park, public toilets and picnic site with braai facilities.
Pertinent information: There is no limit to party size.

A concrete path specially designed for people in wheelchairs leads along the stream bank, across a bridge to the picnic site. A variety of interesting visual and tactile displays that interpret the surroundings are placed along the route for the disabled. See map on page 175.

4. DURBAN BOTANIC GARDENS
DURBAN, NATAL

Trail details: A walk for the visually disabled through the herb garden.
Permits/bookings: Entrance to the Gardens is free and no bookings are required.
Facilities/amenities: Public toilets, an information kiosk and tearoom.
Pertinent information: There is no limit to party size.

For the visually disabled, the aromatic herb garden with its varied scented and textured plants, many of them used in traditional Zulu medicine, is a delight to stroll through. Labels are printed in braille and ordinary type.

5. PALMIET NATURE RESERVE
DURBAN, NATAL

The Palmiet Nature Reserve is establishing a 6-km trail for the visually disabled that forms part of the D'M.O.S.S. network of trails (see page 174) and should be open by the end of 1993. A tapping rail, hand railing at dangerous sections and guide ropes leading to signs in braille that give pertinent information at points of interest along the route will all form part of the trail.

6. GLENHOLME TRAIL FOR DISABLED AND BLIND PERSONS
GLENHOLME NATURE RESERVE, KLOOF, NATAL

Trail details: 250 m.
Permits/bookings: Contact the Wildlife Society of Southern Africa, tel. (031) 213126; 100 Brand Road, Durban 4001 for more information.
Facilities/amenities: Public toilets, car park and picnic sites with braai facilities.
Pertinent information: There is no limit to party size.

The peaceful and tranquil Glenholme Nature Reserve has a specially designed trail, part of which is on an elevated walkway through swampy forest, with guide rails and braille plaques for people in wheelchairs and the visually disabled. See map on page 174.

7. KAMBERG NATURE RESERVE
NATAL DRAKENSBERG PARK, DRAKENSBERG

The beautiful Kamberg Nature Reserve has a 1,5-km trail along the river for people in wheelchairs. See entry on page 217 for more information about the reserve and a map.

Trail options in Kirstenbosch Botanic Garden.

8. BONNET HERBS FARM
GRASKOP, EASTERN TRANSVAAL

The Bonnet Herbs farm has a 50- to 100-m roped braille route that is wide enough to accommodate wheelchairs and that leads through the herb display garden. A brochure in braille is also available. Sadly, the trail has been unused for years, so contact Professor Brown, tel. (01315) 71079 to find out if the trail is still open and what other facilities are offered.

UNDERWATER TRAIL

We hope that this pioneering scuba-diving trail willl be the first of many in southern African waters.

1. STORMS RIVER MOUTH
TSITSIKAMMA NATIONAL PARK

Trail details: Unmarked snorkelling and scuba-diving trails along 2 reefs.
Permits/bookings: No bookings are required but an entrance fee is charged. Phone the park at (042) 5411652 for more information. Scuba divers are required to sign in and out at reception.
Facilities/amenities: Emergency equipment is available; during the school holidays, a boat is available to take snorkellers out to the reefs; Beacon Isle is closest for the hiring of equipment; while divers can fill up their tanks at the Tsitsikamma Diving Club, tel. (042) 5411753.
Pertinent information: A minimum of 2 per party. November to January are the best months. Minimum qualification required is Open-water 2 or the equivalent.

Unfortunately, due to the erosion of the reefs, the trail markers for the 2 trails along the reefs have been removed. However, a map which marks the trails is still available at the reception office, and the information officer is always glad to give divers and snorkellers advice. See map on page 98.

STOP PRESS

The new trails that follow are arranged as they are in the main section of the book, namely geographically from the west to the east of the subcontinent. Walks and hiking trails are followed by a variety of special interest trails.

WALKS AND HIKING TRAILS

CAPE

LIESBEEK RIVER WALK
CAPE TOWN

Trail details: 8 km; one-way.
Permits/bookings: Not required.
Facilities/amenities: None.
Pertinent information: At the time of going to press, some parts of this walk were still under construction.

The Liesbeek River runs from Kirstenbosch Botanical Gardens to a confluence with the Black River, before flowing into the sea at Paarden Eiland. This walk covers an 8-km stretch along the river banks, starting at the Sans Souci Bridge in Newlands and continuing through Rondebosch to the Liesbeek Parkway. Because the route is intersected by many streets, ramblers can join up with or leave the trail wherever they wish. Despite its urban setting, the area supports some wildlife; the water mongoose, the grey mongoose and clawless otter, as well as roughly 90 bird species have been spotted there. Of historical interest are Valkenberg Manor, Josephine Mill and the Koornhoop Farmstead. The walk is part of the 'Greening of the City' scheme.

BRANDVLEI DAM-KWAGGASKLOOF HIKING TRAIL
WORCESTER, SOUTH-WESTERN CAPE

Trail details: 45 km/2 days; circular.
Permits/bookings: Must be obtained from Worcester Publicity Association, tel. (0231) 71408; 75 Church Street, Worcester 6850.
Facilities/amenities: A semi-detached house, sleeping 18, with braai facilities, running (cold) water and 2 toilets.

This new trail is situated between Worcester and Rawsonville. It runs around the Brandvlei and Kwaggaskloof dams. The prolific birdlife and the proteas are two of the attractions.

MOOIVALLEI HIKING TRAIL
BONNIEVALE, SOUTH-WESTERN CAPE

Trail details: 12 km/4 hours; circular.
Permits/bookings: Bookings are not required. For further information, contact the Bonnievale Publicity Association, tel. (02346) 2105.
Facilities/amenities: None.
Pertinent information: Carry water.

This trail is situated on a farm outside Bonnievale, where one can admire the fynbos and birdlife in the tranquil surroundings.

THARFIELD TRAIL
PORT ALFRED, EASTERN CAPE

Trail details: Length and duration varies according to the proficiency of the group; guided, return.
Permits/bookings: Contact T G Webb, tel. (0464) 711083; Tharfield Farm, Port Alfred 6170.
Facilities/amenities: None.
Pertinent information: Group size is restricted to a minimum of 4 and a maximum of 8 people.

This trail is on the farm Tharfield, located some 15 minutes' drive from Port Alfred. The owner guides you, personally, through virgin riverine forest along the Riet River. Look out for oribi and bushbuck. Crowned eagle, gymnogene and jackal buzzard can also be spotted. Tharfield House, dating back to 1835, is of historical interest.

AARDVARK HIKING TRAIL
BEAUFORT WEST, KAROO

Trail details: A 4-day mountain hike and various 1-day routes; circular.
Permits/bookings: Mr. P M Vivier, tel. Hugorus (02022) 661; PO Box 237, Beaufort West 6970.
Facilities/amenities: Facilities for 12 in each of 2 farmhouses; self-catering.

These trails are located on a private farm, 16 km off the Leeu-Gamka to Fraserburg road in the Karoo. The 4-day hike leads through the Nuweveld Mountains, covering distances of between 10 and 14 km per day. There are interesting birds to be seen and plants to be identified on this farm. One can also engage in general farming activities.

NATAL/LESOTHO

LA MOINA HIKING TRAIL
HATTINGSPRUIT, NEAR DUNDEE, NATAL

Trail details: 2 day-walks/2-5 hours; 2-day trail/21 km. All circular.
Permits/bookings: Must be obtained from La Moina Park, tel. (0341) 23792; Canarvon, PO Hattingspruit 3081.
Facilities/amenities: A-frame huts with mattresses, can accommodate 50 people; hot showers, toilets, gas stove and braai facilities. Larger chalets also available.

This private farm comprises 1 000 ha of bushveld with mountain streams, a variety of buck and 85 species of birds. Hattingspruit is north-west of Dundee, off the route R68.

SOUTH BERG ADVENTURES HIKING TRAILS
SOUTHERN DRAKENSBERG

Trail details: 2-day, 3-day and 4-day guided trails/2-5 hours. All circular.
Permits/bookings: Must be obtained from South Berg Adventures, tel. (0374) 422 – all hours.
Facilities/amenities: Thatched, fully furnished Little Stream Cottage serves as home base for all hikes: full amenities and meals provided; Thule Cave and Eagle's Nest Cave serve as mountain overnight venues, mattresses and camp food only; Sehlaba-Thebe Lodge in the Sehlaba-Thebe National Park, Lesotho, offers full amenities and meals. See page 221 for details of park.
Pertinent information: Limit of 8 people; mountainous terrain demands certain degree of fitness. Hikes are

conducted around weekends only; trails closed between June and September due to heavy snowfalls. Bookings for Lesotho hikes should be made well in advance to secure accommodation at the Lodge.

Hikes are conducted through the more remote scenic areas, with spectacular views, rare bird species, buck, wild flowers and interesting Bushman paintings.

MOLUMONG TOURS
MOKHOTLONG, LESOTHO

Trail details: From Underberg, a 4-wheel drive vehicle takes you to the Molumong Resthouse in Lesotho, the starting point for various day trails.
Permits/bookings: Must be obtained from Underberg Hideaways, tel. (0331) 443505; 27 Ashby Road, Pietermaritzburg 3201.
Facilities/amenities: Furnished resthouse with 5 bedrooms, fully equipped kitchen and braai facilities. Hikers may choose self-catering option or full board accommodation.
Pertinent information: Resthouse accommodates 10 persons. Minimum of 3 persons per tour party. Four-wheel drive tours operate over weekends only, but longer bookings can be arranged. Valid passports essential.

Underberg, beneath the southern Drakensberg, is at the intersection of the R617 and R626.

TRANSVAAL

BUFFALO SPRINGS NATURE TRAIL
BUFFALO SPRINGS FARM, NEAR NORTHAM

Trail details: 5 trails, up to 5 hours in duration; circular.
Permits/bookings: Must be obtained from Neil Posthumus-Meyjes, tel. (01537) 22516; PO Box 133, Chromite 0362. Map and brochure available on request.
Facilities/amenities: Cottage with 8 beds, hot showers, toilets and braai facilities.
Pertinent information: Limit of 15 people. Carry water, as there is no natural water along trail. Trails are closed June and July.

Terrain is mountainous; great variety of game and birdlife (identification list available) can be seen. The farm is 45 km from Northam, north of Rustenburg.

BUFFELSKLOOF TRAILS
BUFFELSKLOOF FARM, NEAR POTCHEFSTROOM

Trail details: Rooihaas and Summer trails, each 21 km/ 2 days; circular.
Permits/bookings: Must be obtained from Dome Trails Conservation Group, tel (0148) 8572; or write to PO Box 525, Kroonstad, 9500.
Facilities/amenities: Base camp; mountain camp with beds, small kitchen, hot showers and toilets. Lapa accommodating 40 people available; shower, toilet and braai facilities.

River and mountain environment offering wonderful views; interesting plant, bird and wildlife. Also 1,5-hour boat cruise on Vaal River. Buffelskloof is 30 km south of Potchefstroom, off the R53.

BOSVELD HIKING TRAIL
ORION GAME FARM, ZEERUST

Trail details: 10 km/15 km, each 2 days; also guided walking safaris and day walks. Circular.
Permits/bookings: Must be obtained from Orion Game Farm, tel. (01428) 23350; PO Box 151, Zeerust 2865. Brochure and map available on request.
Facilities/amenities: Eiland hiker's hut/20 people: Water cart, bush toilet and braai facilities; wood for sale. Maroela Camp/60 people: 8 bedrooms with beds, 2 lapas, hot showers, toilets and braai facilities; kitchen with fridge, freezer, gas stove and cooking utensils for hire; wood for sale. Taaiboshuis/10 people: Fully equipped private farmhouse and lapa.
Pertinent information: All trails and facilities must be booked in advance. Carry water.

Both a game and nature reserve, this 3 000-ha private farm is also of geological and archaeological interest. The farm is 24 km north of Zeerust, off the R505.

GROENKLOOF HIKING TRAIL
PRETORIA

Trail details: Up to 21,5 km/2 days; circular.
Permits/bookings: Must be obtained 3 weeks in advance from Pretoria City Council, Parks and Recreation Department, tel. (012) 3137198; PO Box 1454, Pretoria 0001. Brochure and map available.
Facilities/amenities: Base camp with bunkbeds, lights, cooking utensils and braai facilities; cold showers and toilets.
Pertinent information: Take light raincoat and warm clothing. Snake kit essential. Carry water.

Trail leads through Groenkloof Nature Reserve near Pretoria; extensive birdlife, zebra and blesbok can be seen by hikers.

KAREEBOSRAND CONSERVANCY
NEAR PRETORIA

Trail details: Large range of day walks; 2-day hiking trails. Circular.
Permits/bookings: Must be obtained from The Secretary, Kareebosrand Conservancy, tel. (011) 6591298/1934; PO Box 68633, Bryanston 2021.
Facilities/amenities: Basic camp site, cold showers, bush toilets; unfurnished cottage with electricity and flush toilet.

This green belt of 10 000 ha is crossed by the Jukskei, Crocodile and Hennops rivers, and stretches into the foothills of the Schurweberg. It is of great botanical and geological interest, and has contains 270 species of birds, as well as blesbok and eland. The conservancy lies south of Hartebeespoort Dam, and can be reached from the R28.

TOUCHSTONE TRAIL
TOUCHSTONE GAME RANCH, NEAR POTGIETERSRUS, NORTHERN TRANSVAAL

Trail details: 18,5 km/2 days; circular.
Permits/bookings: Must be obtained from Touchstone Game Ranch, tel. (01536) 50230; PO Box 57, Marken 0605. Map available on request.
Facilities/amenities: Base camp; first overnight stop in wooden cabins with bunkbeds; second overnight stop in tented camp; both have cold shower, toilet as well as braai facilities.
Pertinent information: Limit of 12 persons.

Trail crosses hilly bushveld terrain with magnificent views; birdlife, buck, hyaena and giraffe can be seen. The ranch is near Marken on the R518, north-west of Potgietersrus.

ELANDSVALLEI HIKING TRAIL
NEAR NELSPRUIT, EASTERN TRANSVAAL

Trail details: 21,5 km/2 days; circular.
Permits/bookings: Must be obtained from Jacana Country Homes & Trails, tel. (012) 3463550/1/2; PO Box 95212, Waterkloof 0145.
Facilities/amenities: Base camp and overnight camp, each with 20 beds; bush toilets, hot showers, gas cooker, braai facilities and wood.

Pertinent information: Maximum of 20 hikers permitted. Be cautious of hippos in Elands River; trail can be slippery in wet season.

The trail covers mountainous terrain and offers great views, swimming in a weir, visits to a waterfall and caves and sightings of various members of the cat family. Off the N4, 30 km from Nelspruit, 20 km from nGwodana.

KHOKA MOYA WILDLIFE ENCOUNTERS
MANYELETI GAME RESERVE, EASTERN TRANSVAAL

Trail details: Three options on offer: short, guided walks for maximum of 8 guests; a guided backpacking trail for 4-8 people for a minimum of 2 days; 4 to 5-day wildlife encounter. All circular.
Permits/bookings: Reservations for guided day walks and wildlife encounter: Safariplan, tel. (011) 8861810; PO Box 4245, Randburg 2125; for backpacking trails, tel. (01528) 35874.
Facilities/amenities: Khoka Moya Trails Camp accommodates 8 guests; fully equipped, all meals provided. Backpacking and wildlife encounter trails: reeded boma, showers, 'skybeds' (sleeping platforms) overlooking Mohlwareng Dam; all meals provided.

The 23 000-ha Manyeleti Game Reserve shares its borders with Kruger National Park, Timbavati and Sabie-Sand. The game to be seen in gentle rolling grasslands includes rhino and elephant. To get there, turn into the Orpen gate at Kruger; the Manyeleti entrance is signposted at the 35,8-km marker peg.

PUNGWE TRAILS CAMP
MANYELETI GAME RESERVE, EASTERN TRANSVAAL

Trail details: Variety of guided day walks; circular.
Permits/bookings: Must be obtained from Lowveld Environmental Awareness Trails, tel. (01311) 51995; PO Box 2797, White River 1240.
Facilities/amenities: 4 2-bedded safari tented units under thatched roof with showers, toilets and all meals supplied.
Pertinent information: Minimum stay of 2 nights for a limit of 10 people. Malarial precautions should be taken.

Manyeleti Game Reserve borders on Kruger National Park; excellent game-viewing. For directions on how to get there, see previous entry.

MOHOLOHOLO FOREST CAMP & WILDLIFE REHABILITATION CENTRE
KLASERIE, EASTERN TRANSVAAL

Trail details: Guided and self-guided day trails of various lengths; circular.
Permits/bookings: Must be obtained from Brian Jones, Moholoholo Forest Camp, tel. (01528) 35236; PO Box 58, Klaserie 1381.
Facilities/amenities: Fully equipped farmhouse with 12 beds, can accommodate 80 people on self-catering basis; alternatively, fully equipped log cabin in Quinine Forest, all meals provided.

Trails pass through acacia woodland and rain forest. Game is plentiful and 350 species of birds can be spotted, including the rare Taita falcon. Klaserie lies east of the Blyderivierspoort Nature Reserve, at the intersection of R40 and R531.

SALPETERKRANS HIKING TRAIL
NEAR LYDENBURG, EASTERN TRANSVAAL

Trail details: 27 km/2 days; circular.
Permits/bookings: Must be obtained from Chris/Wilna Davel, Draaikraal Farm, tel. (0132732), ask for 1230; PO Box 151, Roossenekal 1066.
Facilities/amenities: 2 mountain huts with 12 beds; paraffin lamps, hot showers, toilets and braai facilities. Shop next to office sells basic provisions.
Pertinent information: Limit of 20 people.

Trail passes through Salpeterkrans Mountains and the Klip River flows through valley with stunning views; buck, birdlife and Cape clawless otter can be seen. The farm is 100 km north of Middelburg, off the route R555.

TIMBAVATI WILDERNESS TRAILS
TIMBAVATI NATURE RESERVE, EASTERN TRANSVAAL

Trail details: Guided day trails from base camp over 4-night period, circular; night drives are included.
Permits/bookings: Must be obtained from Timbavati Wilderness Trails, tel. (031) 2071565, PO Box 70137, Overport 4067.
Facilities/amenities: Fully equipped wooden, thatched chalets with beds, hot bucket-showers and bush toilets; all meals provided.
Pertinent information: Limit of 8-10 people; malarial precautions must be taken.

Trails are conducted through game reserve, which is on the eastern border of Kruger National Park; game includes lion, cheetah, rhino and elephant, as well as small mammals and birdlife. To get there, turn off the R40 at Acornhoek and head for Kruger Park.

UMLANI BUSHCAMP
TIMBAVATI NATURE RESERVE, EASTERN TRANSVAAL

Trail details: Guided day walks, circular; night drives are included.
Permits/bookings: Must be obtained from Umlani Trails, tel. (012) 3293765; PO Box 26350, Arcadia 0007.
Facilities/amenities: Fully equipped thatch-and-reed base camp with 5 double huts, showers and toilets; all meals are supplied.
Pertinent information: Malarial precautions should be taken by trailists.

The camp is situated on the banks of the Shlaralumi River which flows during good rains, but is usually dry. Trails are conducted through the game reserve, therefore big game is plentiful; good bird-watching hide. Transport to Umlani can be arranged from Hoedspruit, on the R40; Metavia supply 3 flights a week to Hoedspruit.

SPECIAL INTEREST TRAILS

MOUNTAIN-BIKING TRAILS

CAPE

CITRUSDAL-CEDARBERG MOUNTAIN BIKE TRAILS
CITRUSDAL

Trail details: Ten different trails ranging from 15 to 60 km in distance and 50 minutes to 4 hours in duration.
Permits/bookings: Not required; however, for further information write to Mountain Bike Trails, Private Bag X11, Citrusdal 7340.
Facilities/amenities: For accommodation in Citrusdal, contact Tourist Information, tel. (02662) 610. Maps are also available on request.
Pertinent information: Cars are not permitted on these trails. Ensure that you close all gates behind you.

Ten permanent mountain-bike trails have been established around the Citrusdal area. They run through private land, and follow farm roads, jeep tracks and paths. The trails, which are linked up by public roads, offer a range of routes to suit all levels of fitness and varying ability.

The Citrusdal Cedarberg Fat Tyre Festival is held every September for 3 days; details can be obtained by contacting ROMP, tel. (021) 4614019, or writing to the above address.

AARDVARK MOUNTAIN-BIKING TRAIL
BEAUFORT WEST, KAROO

Trail details: Various 1-day routes and a longer mountain ride.
Permits/bookings: Can be obtained from Mr PM Vivier, tel. Hugorus (02022) 661; PO Box 237, Beaufort West 6970.
Facilities/amenities: Facilities for 12 in each of 2 farmhouses; self-catering.

Mountain bikers may use the same trails as the hikers and the same facilities are available to them (see entry on page 343).

NATAL

KWEZINTABA TOURS MOUNTAIN BIKING
UNDERBERG AND HIMEVILLE

Trail details: Various daily and overnight routes/between 6 and 70 km; circular.
Permits/bookings: Bikes can be hired from Kwezintaba Tours, tel (033701) 1017, who will advise on routes, or directly from the farmers themselves.
Facilities/amenities: Self-catering overnight farmers' cottages available; to be arranged at time of booking.

There are both scenic and challenging routes, varying from good gravel roads to mountainous tracks. A bus service runs from Durban and Pietermaritzburg to Underberg; arrangements can also be made for visitors to be picked up from the airport.

HORSE-RIDING TRAILS

CAPE

ROZENDAL RIDING TRAILS
STELLENBOSCH, WESTERN CAPE

Trail details: From 4 hours to 3 days.
Permits/bookings: Rozendal Riding Trails, tel. (021) 8838737; PO Box 160, Stellenbosch 7600.
Facilities/amenities: Picnic sites; wine-tasting.

Rides are organized to various wine farms and to the Jonkershoek State Forest (see page 61, in the main section, for a map of the area). Panoramic views, as well as the opportunity to picnic and taste wines make for an enjoyable ride. Two- to 3-day rides are being planned. The stables can be found opposite the Lanzerac Hotel in the Jonkershoek Valley.

VINEYARD HORSE TRAILS
STELLENBOSCH, WESTERN CAPE

Trail details: 1-hour to overnight trails; guided.
Permits/bookings: Bookings are essential and can be obtained from Vineyard Horse Trails, tel. (021) 9812480; PO Box 397, Brackenfell 7560.
Facilities/amenities: All trails, regardless of duration, include refreshments.
Pertinent information: Wear appropriate clothing. Transport from any location in the Cape Peninsula to the stables can be arranged in advance.

Stables some 20 km from Stellenbosch serve as a base for these rides. Trails are led by experienced guides and cater for all levels of riding experience. Routes of varying lengths lead through the vineyards of the Bottelary Hills, and there are magnificent views over the surrounding winelands. A range of different trail options includes full- or half-day trails, a champagne breakfast trail and an evening and moonlight trail. One of the routes follows the Vineyard Hiking Trail (see page 60, main section).

An overnight trail, with accommodation and meals provided, is also offered; the overnight chalet, located in the Koopmanskloof Nature Reserve, is accessible by road. Experienced riders can participate in competitions and winter hunts.

NATAL

UNDERBERG HIDEAWAYS PONY-TREKKING
SOUTHERN DRAKENSBERG / COBHAM & COLEFORD NATURE RESERVES

Trail details: Daily outrides for both novice and experienced riders, in co-operation with local farming community; pony-treks in the southern Berg, Lesotho; overnight bridle trail between farms is being planned in Nottingham Road/Kamberg area.
Permits/bookings: Must be obtained from Underberg Hideaways, tel. (0331) 443505. For details, see Molumong Tours on page 342.

Four-wheel drive transport to Lesotho, and transport to farms, is available from Underberg.

TRANSVAAL

MAGALIESBERG MOUNTAIN TRAILS
MAGALIESBERG, NEAR PRETORIA

Trail details: 1-hour to 4-day trails.
Permits/bookings: Bookings can be obtained from Magaliesberg Mountain Trails, tel. (011) 7923132 or (01211) 31404; PO Box 568, Brits 0250.
Facilities/amenities: Glenwoods Stable will provide all meals and bedding, if required. Riding equipment is also available.

Close to both Pretoria and Johannesburg, off the R27, Glenwoods offers a variety of trails, including weekend, moonlight and sunrise trails. There are also 'junior camps', which are 5 days long. Remember to take walking shoes, for possible hikes. Although food is provided, drinks are not. See main section, page 235, for a map of the area.

TRAILS FOR THE DISABLED

CAPE

LIESBEEK RIVER WALK
CAPE TOWN

Trail details: 8 km; one-way.
Permits/bookings: Not required.
Facilities/amenities: None.

This trail runs along the banks of the Liesbeek River and is accessible to people confined to wheelchairs. For more detailed information about the route, see entry on page 342.

FURTHER READING

GENERAL

Books

Bradt, H. *et al. Backpacker's Africa. Bradt Publications, United Kingdom, 1990 (third edition).*

Bristow, D. *Best Hikes in Southern Africa.* Struik Publishers, Cape Town, 1992.

Dearlove, T. *Wilderness Walks.* Struik Publishers, Cape Town, 1992.

Joyce, P. *Guide to Southern African Safari Lodges.* Struik Publishers, Cape Town, 1993.

Koornhof, A. *Dive Sites in Southern Africa.* Struik Publishers, Cape Town, 1993.

Olivier, W. and Olivier, S. *The Guide to Backpacking and Wilderness Trails.* Southern Book Publishers, Johannesburg, 1989.

Olivier, W. and Olivier, S. *The Guide to Hiking Trails.* Southern Book Publishers, Johannesburg, 1991.

Reader's Digest Illustrated Guide to the Game Parks and Nature Reserves of Southern Africa. Compiled and published by the Reader's Digest Association of South Africa (Pty) Limited, Cape Town, 1991 (second edition).

Ryan, B. *National Parks of South Africa.* Struik Publishers, Cape Town, 1993.

Stevens, U. *The South African Backpacker's Cookbook.* Struik Publishers, Cape Town, 1992.

Stuart, C. and Stuart, T. *Guide to Southern African Game and Nature Reserves.* Struik Publishers, Cape Town, 1992 (second edition).

Van Eeden, J., comp. and ed. *The South African Mountain Leadership Guide.* Mountain Club of South Africa, northern Transvaal section, 1991.

Magazines

Africa Environment & Wildlife. Black Eagle Publishing, Cape Town.

Getaway. Ramsay, Son and Parker (Pty) Ltd., Cape Town.

Great Outdoors. Promedia Publications, Silverton.

Hiking Africa. Promedia Publications, Silverton.

SA Hiker. Promedia Publications, Silverton.

Spoor. The Hiking Federation of South Africa, Groenkloof, Pretoria.

BIRDS

Chittenden, H., comp. *Top Birding Spots in Southern Africa.* Southern Book Publishers, Johannesburg, 1992.

Maclean, G.L. *Roberts' Birds of South Africa.* The trustees of the John Voelcker Bird Book Fund, Cape Town, 1985 (fifth edition).

Newman, K. *Newman's Birds of Southern Africa.* Southern Book Publishers, Johannesburg, 1992.

Sinclair, I. *Field Guide to Birds of Southern Africa.* Struik Publishers, Cape Town, 1993 (second edition).

Sinclair, I. *Southern African Birds: A Photographic Guide.* Struik Publishers, Cape Town, 1993.

Sinclair, I., Hockey, P. and Tarboton, W. *Sasol: Birds of Southern Africa.* Struik Publishers, Cape Town, 1993.

FAUNA

Liebenberg, L. *A Field Guide to Animal Tracks of Southern Africa.* David Phillip Publishers, Cape Town, 1991.

Van der Elst, R. *Guide to the Common Sea Fishes of Southern Africa.* Struik Publishers, Cape Town, 1993 (third edition).

FIRST AID

The British Red Cross Society. *South African Practical First Aid.* Struik Publishers, Cape Town, 1993.

The St John Ambulance Association and Brigade, authorized manual of the St John Ambulance and Red Cross Society. *The South African First Aid Manual.* Struik Publishers, Cape Town, 1993.

FLORA

Acocks, J.H.P. *Veld Types of South Africa.* Botanical Research Institute, 1988.

Berzac, P., Campbell, G.K., Huckett, B.I. and Pammenter, N.W. *In the Mangroves of Southern Africa.* Natal Branch of the Wildlife Society of South Africa, 1986 (third edition).

Wild Flowers of South Africa. Compiled under the auspices of the National Botanical Gardens of South Africa, Kirstenbosch. Struik Publishers, Cape Town, 1993.

De Winter, B., Vahrmeijer, J. and von Breitenbach, F. *The National List of Trees.* J.L. van Schaik Ltd, 1978 (second edition).

Van Wyk, P. *Photoguide to Trees of South Africa.* Struik Publishers, Cape Town, 1993.

Von Breitenbach, F., comp. *National List of Indigenous Trees.* Dendrological Foundation, Pretoria, 1990.

Von Breitenbach, F., comp. *National List of Introduced Trees.* Dendrological Foundation, Pretoria, 1989.

INVERTEBRATES

Filmer, M. *South African Spiders: An Identification Guide.* Struik Publishers, Cape Town, 1993.

Migdoll, I. *Field Guide to Butterflies of Southern Africa.* Struik Publishers, Cape Town, 1992.

Quickelberg, C. *Familiar South African Butterflies.* Natal Branch of the Wildlife Society of South Africa, 1986.

MAMMALS

Stuart C. and Stuart T. *Southern, Central and Eastern African Mammals: A Photographic Guide.* Struik Publishers, Cape Town, 1992.

Stuart, C. and Stuart T. *Field Guide to the Mammals of Southern Africa.* Struik Publishers, Cape Town, 1992.

Walker, C. *Signs of the Wild: A Field Guide to the Spoor and Signs of the Mammals of Southern Africa.* Struik Publishers, Cape Town, 1993 (third edition).

MAPS

Government Printer's Maps of South Africa, central source: Government Printer, Private Bag X85, Bosman St, Pretoria 0001.

REPTILES

Branch. B. *Field Guide to the Snakes and Other Reptiles of Southern Africa.* Struik Publishers, Cape Town, 1992.

Branch, B. *Photoguide to Snakes of Southern Africa.* Struik Publishers, Cape Town, 1993.

BOTSWANA

Newman, K. *Newman's Birds of Botswana.* Southern Book Publishers, Johannesburg, 1989.

MALAWI

Hough, J. *Malawi's National Parks and Game Reserves.* Wildlife Society of Malawi, Blantyre, 1989.

Maurel, M. *Visitors' Guide to Malawi.* Southern Book Publishers, Johannesburg, 1990.

Newman, K., Johnson-Stewart, N. and Medland, B. *Birds of Malawi.* Southern Book Publishers, Johannesburg, 1992.

Shorter, C. *An Introduction to the Common Trees of Malawi.* Wildlife Society of Malawi, Lilongwe Branch, 1993.

NAMIBIA

Olivier, W. and Olivier, S. *Visitors' Guide to Namibia.* Southern Book Publishers, Johannesburg, 1989.

Spectrum Guide to Namibia. Compiled and edited by Camerapix, Nairobi, Kenya, 1993.

Willetts, D. and Amin, M. *Journey through Namibia.* Camerapix, Nairobi, Kenya, 1993.

SOUTH AFRICA

WESTERN CAPE

Anderson, T. *Day Walks in and around Cape Town.* Struik Publishers, Cape Town, 1993 (fourth edition).

Bristow, D. *Western Cape Walks.* Struik Publishers, Cape Town, 1991.

Brossy, S. *A Walking Guide for Table Mountain.* Shirley Brossy, Cape Town, 1991 (fourth edition).

Brossy, S. *A Walking Guide for the Hout Bay to Simon's Town Mountains.* Shirley Brossy, Cape Town, 1991 (second edition).

Lundy, M. *Best Walks in the Cape Peninsula.* Struik Publishers, Cape Town, 1991.

Lundy, M. *Weekend Trails in the Western Cape.* Human and Rousseau, Cape Town, 1992.

Moll, G. *Table Mountain, A Natural Wonder.* The Wildlife Society of South Africa, 1987.

Paterson-Jones, C. *Table Mountain Walks.* Struik Publishers, Cape Town, 1991.

SOUTHERN CAPE

Paterson-Jones, C. *Garden Route Walks.* Struik Publishers, Cape Town, 1992.

Wagner, P. *Otter Trail and Tsitsikamma Coastal National Park.* Struik Publishers, Cape Town, 1993 (second edition).

TRANSKEI

Butchart, D. *A Guide to the Coast and Nature Reserves of Transkei.* The Wildlife Society of South Africa, Cape Town, 1989.

NATAL

Bristow, D. *Drakensberg Walks.* Struik Publishers, Cape Town, 1990 (2nd impression).

Hilliard, O.M. *Trees and Shrubs of the Natal Drakensberg.* University of Natal Press, Pietermaritzburg, 1992 (second edition).

Irwin, D. and Irwin, P. *A Field Guide to the Natal Drakensberg.* Rhodes University, Grahamstown, 1992 (second revised edition).

Killick, D. *A Field Guide to the Flora of the Natal Drakensberg.* Jonathan Ball Publishers, Johannesburg, 1990.

Little, R.M. and Bainbridge, W.R. *Birds of the Natal Drakensberg Park.* Natal Branch of the Wildlife Society of South Africa, 1992.

Nichols, G. and Fairall, M. *Day Walks in and around Durban and Pietermaritzburg.* Struik Publishers, Cape Town, 1992.

Shepherd, O. *Wild Places of Natal.* Natal Branch of the Wildlife Society of South Africa, 1989.

Shepherd, O. *Wild Walks of Natal.* Natal Branch of the Wildlife Society of South Africa, 1990.

Wager, V. *Dwindling Forests of the Natal Coast.* Natal Branch of the Wildlife Society of South Africa, 1989.

TRANSVAAL

Braack, L. *Field Guide to Insects of the Kruger National Park.* Struik Publishers, Cape Town, 1992.

Braack, L. *Kruger National Park – A Visitor's Guide.* Struik Publishers, Cape Town, 1993.

Braack, L. *Kruger National Park Checklist.* Struik Publishers, Cape Town, 1993.

Braack, L. *Wildlife of the Kruger National Park and other Lowveld Reserves.* Struik Publishers, Cape Town, 1993.

De V. Pienaar, U., Joubert S.C.J., Hall-Martin, A., De Graaff, G. and Rautenbach, I.L. *Field Guide to the Mammals of the Kruger National Park.* Struik Publishers, Cape Town, 1993.

Ryan, B. *Day Walks in and around Johannesburg and Pretoria.* Struik Publishers, Cape Town, 1992 (second edition).

Ryan, B. and Isom, J. *Go Birding in the Transvaal.* Struik Publishers, Cape Town, 1990.

Sinclair, I. and Whyte, I. *Field Guide to the Birds of the Kruger National Park.* Struik Publishers, Cape Town, 1991.

Van Wyk, B. and Malan, S. *Field Guide to the Wild Flowers of the Witwatersrand and Pretoria Region.* Struik Publishers, Cape Town, 1988.

Van Wyk, P. *Field Guide to the Trees of the Kruger National Park.* Struik Publishers, Cape Town, 1993.

ZIMBABWE

Irwin, M.P.S. *The Birds of Zimbabwe.* Quest Publications, Harare, 1981.

Solomon, D. and Williams, J. *Birdwatch Zimbabwe.* Harare, Zimbabwe, 1991.

Spectrum Guide to Zimbabwe. Compiled and edited by Camerapix, Nairobi, Kenya, 1991.

Steyn, P. *Hwange Birds.* Longman Zimbabwe (Pvt) Ltd, Harare, 1992 (third impression).

USEFUL ADDRESSES

SOUTH AFRICA

Cape Nature Conservation, for referrals to nature reserves under the jurisdiction of Cape Nature Conservation:
Western and Southern Cape region, Bellville: tel. (021) 9487490.
Eastern Cape region, Port Elizabeth: tel. (041) 3909111.
Northern Cape region, Kimberley: tel. (0531) 22143.

Hiking Federation of South Africa:
Head Office, PO Box 1420, Randburg 2125; tel. (011) 8866524 or 8866507, fax (011) 8866013.
Western Cape region: Mr D Rousseau, PO Box 1, Sanlamhof 7532; tel. (021) 9472851.
Eastern Cape region: Mr H Parry, PO Box 27355, Greenacres, Port Elizabeth 6057; tel. (041) 306420.
Griqualand West region: Mrs F de Kock, PO Box 318, Kimberley 8300; tel. (0531) 611189.
Orange Free State region: Mr R de Klerk, PO Box 2709, Welkom 9460; tel. (057) 3521523.
Eastern Transvaal region: Mr B de Souza, PO Box 81, Barberton 1300; tel. (01341) 24067.
Southern Transvaal region: Mr H Rees, PO Box 5318, Weltevreden Park 1715; tel. (011) 8494286.

Mountain Club of South Africa:
Cape Town section: 97 Hatfield St, Cape Town 8001; tel. (021) 453412.
Tygerberg section: PO Box 2125, Bellville 7535.
Stellenbosch section: PO Box 152, Stellenbosch 7600.
Hottentots Holland section: PO Box 1100, Somerset West 7130.
Paarl/Wellington section: PO Box 2645, Paarl 7620.
Worcester section: PO Box 373, Worcester 6850.
Eastern Province section: PO Box 1274, Port Elizabeth 6000.
Orange Free State section: PO Box 1291, Bloemfontein 9300.
Natal section: PO Box 4535, Durban 4000.
Northern Natal section: PO Box 1362, Newcastle 2940.
Transvaal section: PO Box 1641, Houghton 2041.
Northern Transvaal section: PO Box 1418, Pretoria 0001.

Natal Parks Board, PO Box 662, Pietermaritzburg 3200; tel. (0331) 471981.

National Hiking Way Board, Private Bag X93, Pretoria 0001; tel. (012) 3103839, fax (012) 3200949.

National Parks Board, PO Box 787, Pretoria 0001; tel. (012) 3431991, fax (012) 3430905; or PO Box 7400, Roggebaai 8012; tel. (021) 222810, fax (021) 246211.

ROMP (Responsible Organized Mountain Pedallers), PO Box 23190, Claremont 7735; tel. (021) 4614019.

Transvaal Nature Conservation, Private Bag X209, Pretoria 0001; tel. (012) 3233403.

Wildlife Society of South Africa:
Western Cape branch: PO Box 30145, Tokai 7966; tel. (021) 7011397.
Eastern Province branch: 2B Lawrence St, Central Port Elizabeth; tel. (041) 559606.
Border branch: PO Box 7608, East London 5200; tel. (0431) 439409.
Northern Cape branch: PO Box 316, Kimberley 8300.
Orange Free State branch: PO Box 2099, Bloemfontein 9300; tel. (051) 366909.
Natal branch: 100 Brand Road, Durban 4001; tel. (031) 213126, fax (031) 219525.
Transvaal branch: PO Box 44344, Linden 2104; tel. (011) 4822430, fax (011) 4822436.
Johannesburg Office: PO Box 44189, Linden 2104; tel. (011) 4821670, fax (011) 4822436.

NAMIBIA

Dorsland Voetslaners, PO Box 730, Windhoek, Namibia 9000; tel. (061) 51325.
The Director of Tourism, Private Bag 13267, Windhoek, Namibia 9000; tel. (061) 36975; or Namibia Tourism, Private Bag 13346, Windhoek, Namibia 9000; tel. (061) 2849111, fax (061) 221930; or PO Box 11405, Johannesburg 2000, South Africa; tel. (011) 3317055, fax (011) 3312037; or PO Box 738, Cape Town 8000, South Africa; tel. (021) 4193190, fax (021) 215840.
Mountain Club of South Africa, Namibian section: PO Box 662, Windhoek 9000.

ZIMBABWE

Zimbabwe Tourist Development Corporation, PO Box 9398, Johannesburg 2000, South Africa; tel. (011) 3313137, fax (011) 3316970.
Department of National Parks and Wild Life Management, PO Box 8151, Causeway, Harare, Zimbabwe; tel. (092634)706077.

MALAWI

Mountain Club of Malawi, Mr G Wallace, PO Box 240, Blantyre; tel. (09265) 65329.

HIKING CLUBS IN SOUTH AFRICA

CAPE

Bellville Hiking Club, PO Box 1089, Oakdale 7534.
Breede Valley Hiking Club, PO Box 271, Worcester 6850; tel. (0231) 21392.
Cumhike, Cape Union Mart, Shop 500, Tyger Valley Centre, Bellville 7530; tel. (021) 9462290.*
Disabled Adventures, 15 Kingfisher Walk, Pinelands 7405; tel. (021) 5315044.*
East Cape Adventure and Hiking Association, PO Box 43, Swartkops 6210; tel. (041) 731070.
Footloose Hiking Club, PO Box 4028, Cape Town 8000; tel. (021) 582816.*
Gantouw Hiking Club, PO Box 316, Strand 7140; tel. (024) 552258.

Helderberg Hiking Club, PO Box 857, Somerset West 7130.
Hottentots Holland Hiking Club, PO Box 5325, Helderberg 7135; tel. (024) 24784.
Kathu Rambling Club, PO Box 973, Kathu 8446; tel. (0595) 31664.
Kimberley Hiking Club, PO Box 318, Kimberley 8300.
Klein Karoo Voetslaanklub, PO Box 62, Oudtshoorn 6620; tel. (021) 241483.*
Matzikama Hiking Club, PO Box 696, Vredendal 8610; tel. (0271) 32050.*
Paarl Hiking Club, PO Box 567, Suider-Paarl 7624; tel. (02211) 589959.*
Sanlam-Staptoerklub, PO Box 1, Sanlamhof 7532; tel. (021) 947911.*
Sapstap, 32 15th Avenue, Boston, Bellville 7530; tel. (021) 4621850.*
Stellenbosch Hiking Club, 17 Het Heerenhof, Oudebaan, Stellenbosch 7600; tel. (02231) 72647.*
Swartland Hiking Club, 20 Rainier Street, Malmesbury 7300; tel. (0224) 21820.*
Trails Club of South Africa, PO Box 104, Diep River 7856; tel. (021) 4102020.*
Trotters Hiking Club, PO Box 7329, Roggebaai 8012; tel. (021) 7050282.*
Tuff Trax Hiking Club, PO Box 24511, Lansdowne 7780; tel. (021) 6916639.*
Valley Outdoor Club, 7 Boekenhout Avenue, Paarl 7646; tel. (02211) 621515.*
Viking Hiking Club, PO Box 162, Tafelsig, Mitchells Plain 7785; tel. (021) 314234.*

NATAL

Durban Rambling Club, PO Box 1063, Durban 4000; tel. (031) 729590.
Eshowe Ramblers Club, 33 Clark Avenue, Eshowe 3815; tel. (0354) 42509.
Mountain Backpacking Club, 16 Lawrence Drive, Westville 3630; tel. (031) 863970.

ORANGE FREE STATE

Bloemfontein Hiking Club, PO Box 779, Bloemfontein 9300; tel. (051) 227057.
Bothaville Hiking Club, PO Box 216, Bothaville 9660; tel. (01414) 3674.
Kroon Hiking Club, PO Box 1616, Kroonstad 9500; tel. (0562) 26992.
Momentum Hiking Club, PO Box 659, University of the Orange Free State, Bloemfontein 9300.
Orange Free State Hiking Trails Association, Mr D Odendaal, PO Box 8910, Bloemfontein 9300; tel. (051) 479511.
Panorama Hiking Club, PO Box 28982, Danhof 9310; tel. (051) 484931.
Schoeman Park Hiking Club, 4 Captain Proctor Street, Bloemfontein 9301.
Welkom Hiking Club, PO Box 400, Welkom 9460; tel. (0171) 22786.*

TRANSVAAL

Akasia Hiking Club, PO Box 59809, Karenpark 0118; tel. (012) 5492684.*
Alswel Hiking Club, 368 Christoffel Street, Pretoria West 0183; tel. (0122) 792505.*
Backpackers and Hikers of South Africa, PO Box 60, Magalieskruin 0150; tel. (012) 574684.*

BHS Hiking Club, PO Box 3173, Pretoria 0001; tel. (012) 209911.
BKS Stapklub, 160 Camelia Lane, Murrayfield 0184; tel. (012) 832937.*
Bokmakierie Hiking Club, PO Box 1818, Heidelberg 2400; tel. (0151) 5141 x205.*
Boksburg Hiking Club, PO Box 752, Boksburg 1460; tel. (011) 8994257.*
Bontpoot Voetslaanklub, PO Box 12470, Onderstepoort 0110; tel. (012) 5491101.*
Bootleggers Hiking Club, PO Box 719, Edenvale 1610; tel. (011) 4075214.*
Boots Stapklub, 83 Van Wouw Street, Groenkloof 0181; tel. (012) 464032.*
Bush Buddies, PO Blackhill 1032; tel. (011) 4075214.*
Club International, PO Box 160, Wingate Park 0153; tel. (011) 3922431.
Corpus Christi, 4 Park Gardens, Floreana, Pretoria North 0182; tel. (012) 553353.
Cresta Hiking Club, PO Box 5423, Weltevredenpark 1715; tel. (011) 6791069.
Cycad Hiking Club, PO Box 93, Middelburg 1050; tel. (0132) 23250.
Drag-a-Bag Hiking Club, PO Box 5016, Boksburg North 1459; tel. (011) 8642610.*
Drosters Hiking Club, PO Box 810, Klerksdorp 2570; tel. (018) 25704.
East Rand Hiking Club, PO Box 12226, Benoryn 1504; tel. (011) 8492574.*
F.O.R. Stapklub, P/A Fed. Onderwysraad, Private Bag X2651, Arcadia 0007; tel. (012) 3251593.*
Fochville North Hiking Club, PO Box 186, Fochville 2515; tel. (01492) 2566.*
Footloose Stapklub, Private Bag X33, Johannesburg 2000.*
Footprint, PO Box 329, Naturena 2064; tel. (011) 8352271.*
Footsloggers Hiking Club, PO Box 3276, Edenvale 1610; tel. (011) 4523871.
Glenhazel Hiking Club, 37 Long Avenue, Glenhazel 2192; tel. (011) 4403288.*
Goue Arende Hiking Club, 747 Belmont Street, Suiderberg 0082; tel. (012) 702020.
GST Stapklub, 292 Mund Street, Silverton 0127; tel. (012) 8419111.*
Hamba Gahle Ramblers Club, PO Box 11213, Randhart 1457; tel. (011) 8641333.*
Happy Hikers, 248 Nigel Road, Selcourt Springs; tel. (011) 4936225.*
Happy Hikers, 1272 Fontana Road, Queenswood 0186; tel. (012) 735018.*
Hazyview Hiking Club, PO Box 565, Hazyview 1242; tel. (0131762) ask for 5111.
Hiking Academy, 10 Berg Road, Witkop Ridge, Boksburg 1459; tel. (011) 8942445.*
Ignikuri Stappers, PO Box 5011, Horison 1730; tel. (011) 7634488.*
ISM Hiking Club, PO Box 1419, Johannesburg 2000; tel. (011) 7281881.*
Johannesburg Hiking Club, PO Box 2254, Johannesburg 2000; tel. (011) 6164315.*
Kalender Hiking Club, PO Box 28591, Sunnyside 1032; tel. (012) 571812.*

Kameeldrift Hiking Club, 658 Stasie Street, Pretoria North 0182; tel. (012) 5423261.*

Kanniwari Voetslaanklub, Tweefontein Colliery, Pk Coalville 1033; tel. (013586) 351.*

Kilometre Eaters Hiking Club, PO Box 934, Boksburg 1460; tel. (011) 526634.*

Klipspringer Hiking Club, PO Box 633, Pretoria 0001; tel. (012) 9911518.*

Kloof Voetslaanklub, PO Box 190, Westonaria 1780; tel. (011) 7531397.*

Kolot Hiking Club, Private Bag X1, Valhalla 0137; tel. (012) 6636014.

Laeveld Wandelklub, PO Box 1929, Nelspruit 1200; tel. (01314) 24067.*

LNR Voetslaanklub, Private Bag X293, Pretoria 0001; tel. (012) 571280.*

Lowveld Hiking Club, PO Box 1929, Nelspruit 1200; tel. (01314) 24067.

Madeliefie Hiking Club, 220 Dey Street, New Muckleneuk 0181; tel. (012) 466735.*

Mannekrag Hiking Club, PO Box 623, Montana 0151; tel. (012) 576390.*

Megawatt Exploration Society, PO Box 67362, Bryanston 2021; tel. (011) 7052896.*

Mountain Roamers Hiking Club, 78 Wilmington Crescent, Lyndhurst 2192; tel. (011) 8642660.*

Ndaba Hiking Club, PO Box 276, Broederstroom 0240; tel. (01211) 31781.*

Nomads Mountain Club, Collins In 1250, Waverley 0186; tel. (012) 731555.*

Nooitgedacht Hiking Club, PO Box 509, Muldersdrift 1747; tel. (011) 6590584.

NPI Hiking Club, PO Box 3971, Pretoria 00101; tel. (012) 703631.*

Ore Hiking Club, PO Box 16041, Atlasville 1465; tel. (011) 9734587.

Oventuur Adventure Club, PO Box 15666, Lynn East 0039; tel. (012) 6620424.*

Padvinders Hiking Club, PO Box 38628, Garsfontein 0042; tel. (012) 647476.*

Pakstappers, PO Box 23735, Innesdale 0031; tel. (012) 3292118.*

Panorama Rambling Club, Department of External Affairs, Private Bag X152, Pretoria 0001; tel. (012) 282711.*

Paraketlos Voetslaanklub, PO Box 26229, Arcadia 0007; tel. (012) 872320.*

Plodders Hiking Club, 134 Rabie Street, Fontainbleau 2194; tel. (011) 7871108.*

Potchefstroom Voetslaan Klub, PO Box 2680, Potchefstroom 2520; tel. (0148) 8794.

Pretoria Wanderers, PO Box 24721, Innesdale 0031; tel. (012) 5491321.*

Radio Hiking Club, PO Box 44576, Linden 2195; tel. (011) 7824875.*

Remskoen Hiking Club, PO Box 51115, Wierda Park 0149; tel. (012) 644490.*

Rugsak-en-Steuwels, PO Box 28560, Sunnyside 0132; tel. (011) 9782162.*

SAA Hiking Club, PO Box 2588, Kempton Park 1620; tel. (011) 3931150.*

SABC Hiking Club, PO Box 91114, Auckland Park 2006; tel. (011) 7142569.

Safari Hiking Guild, PO Box 7320, Birchleigh 1620; tel. (011) 9723204.

Snuffel Stappers, 35 Dieter Street, Birchleigh North 1619; tel. (011) 7732963.*

Spring-Back Voetslaanklub, PO Box 2488, Springs 1560; tel. (011) 8132220.*

Springs Hiking Club, PO Box 2121, Springs 1560; tel. (011) 562770.*

Stapkasia Hiking Club, 15 Henderson Street, Orchards X 11, 2192; tel. (012) 5492003.*

Stapsaam Hiking Club, 674 10th Avenue, Gezina 0084; tel. (012) 3356040.*

Togs Hiking Club, PO Box 552, Kelvin 2054.*

Trail Rovers Hiking Club, PO Box 12076, Elspark 1418; tel. (011) 8642014.*

Turbo Trappers, PO Box 58313, Karenpark 0118; tel. (012) 5491511.*

Vaaldriehoek Voetslaanklub, PO Box 595, Vanderbijlpark 1900; tel. (016) 8895100.*

Viva Hiking Club, 268 Vaandrager Street, Dorandia 0182; tel. (012) 555518.*

Vuurvliegie Adventure Club, PO Box 29250, Sunnyside 0132; tel. (012) 3332208.*

Waterkloof Voetslaanklub, PO Box 7504, Bonaero Park 1622; tel. (012) 6618862.*

West Gold Hiking Club, 65 First Street, Fochville 2515; tel. (01491) 702309.*

Witbank Obees Hiking Club, PO Box 12552, Leraatsfontein 1038; tel. (0135) 081411.*

X-City Hiking Club, 44 Hakea Crescent, Vanderbijlpark 1900; tel. (016) 324975.*

Yskor Hiking Club, PO Box 34048, Erasmia 0023; tel. (012) 782511.

GLOSSARY

This short glossary provides definitions and explanations of ecological, geological and mountaineering terms, used in the text, and translations of Afrikaans terms which hikers may encounter.

Basalt a hard, dark-coloured rock of volcanic origin.

Basement complex deposits of chiefly metamorphic and igneous rocks under the stratified rocks of a region. Basement or Primitive formations date back to the beginning of geological history.

Batholith a great mass of granite or other igneous rock intruded below the surface, commonly along the axis of a mountain range, sometimes exposed by erosion.

Beaufort series the geological zones which lie above the Ecca series in the Karoo system, and which contain fossil reptiles.

Cataract a large, steep waterfall.

Climbing grades: A a walk; **B** a rock scramble; **C** a rock climb with good hand-holds; **D, E,** etc., rock climbs requiring ropes and sometimes, in higher grades, artificial aids.

Cretaceous the last geological period of the Mesozoic era, characterized by the formation of chalk deposits, dinosaurs becoming extinct and the development of flowering plants.

Dolerite a coarse-grained basalt.

Dywka the oldest and lowest of the major geological zones within the Karoo system, which shows evidence of a great ice age.

Ecca the geological zone which lies above Dwyka in the Karoo system, and which is rich in fossil plant remains.

Endemic indigenous within a localized area.

Family a group of related animals or plants ranking below an order and above a genus.

Faultline a line which marks the intersection of a fault plane with the earth's surface.

Folded mountains mountains with bends and flexures formed by tremendous pressures after their stratification.

Food chain a series of organisms interrelated by the fact that each member feeds on another and in turn forms food for another organism in the series.

Food web a group of interrelated food chains.

Genus a group of related plants or animals, generally consisting of two or more species, but sometimes a single species, possessing certain common structural characteristics distinct from any other group. A genus ranks below a family and above a species.

Geophyte a plant which survives the winter by storing its food in deep subterranean buds.

Gneiss a coarse-grained, metamorphic rock composed of quartz, feldspar and mica or hornblende. It is distinguished from granite by its foliated or laminated structure.

Gondwanaland one of two ancient supercontinents produced by the first split of the larger supercontinent Pangaea about 200 million years ago, forming what are now Africa, South America, Australia, Antarctica and the Indian subcontinent.

Graben a rift valley (see 'Rift valley')

Granite a hard, igneous rock comprising grains of other rocks, chiefly quartz and feldspar, and usually with one or more minerals, such as mica or hornblende.

Igneous produced by intense heat or volcanic action.

Inselberg a residual stump or core of a mountain rising above a surrounding plain, mainly the result of wind erosion.

Karoo system gently inclined beds of rock, dating from late Carboniferous to Triassic times, which cover the greater surface of the interior of South Africa. The Karoo system is composed of stratified formations of shale and sandstones and volcanic rock intrusions.

Kloof a ravine, steeper than a valley but less steep than a gorge.

Krantz a rock precipice.

Liane common name for a climbing or twining plant.

Nek a narrow pass

Peneplain a formerly mountainous or hilly area so reduced by erosion as to be almost a plain.

Permo-Triassic era the period between 190 and 280 million years ago.

Pleistocene the geological epoch commonly called the Ice Age, followed by the Recent (Holocene) and characterized by vast glaciation of the northern hemisphere and the evolution of man.

Pre-Cambrian the earliest geological division of time in the earth's history.

Poort a narrow pass through a mountain.

Quartzite a metamorphic, granular rock formed from siliceous sandstone.

Quaternary the geological period marked by the onset of glaciation and including the Pleistocene and Recent (Holocene) epochs.

Resource conservation the preservation from impairment or wise use of all significant objects and features of nature.

Rift block a mass of displaced rock between two faults, lifted above or sunk below the general level.

Rift valley a valley formed by the subsidence of land between two nearly parallel faults.

Sandstone a sedimentary rock formed by the consolidation of sand, the grains being held together by a cement or silica or the like.

Schist a crystalline metamorphic rock composed mainly of mica. It splits easily into layers.

Shale band a layer of shale sandwiched between sandstone or other rocks, prominent in the Cape folded mountains. Because shale has better water retention, a higher nutrient content and is less porous then sandstone, the shale band supports different vegetation to its neighbouring sandstone layers.

Slate a fine-grained, bluish-grey metamorphic rock formed from shale. It flakes easily into thin, smooth layers.

Spoor footprints, tracks, scents or droppings of animals, including those of man.

Stormberg series a geological subdivision of the Karoo system following the Beaufort series; it contains four geological stages itself.

Temperature inversion an atmospheric condition in which a layer of warm air develops above a layer of cool air.

Topocadastral map a map which indicates both the surface features of a region, and the extent and ownership of land.

Upwelling the movement of nutrient-rich, cold oceanic waters upwards to replace warmer surface waters blown away by off-shore winds. Upwelling of the Benguela Current, which originates in sub-Antarctic water and which is rich in nutrients, diatoms and phytoplankton, is responsible for the productivity of the Atlantic coast of South Africa and Namibia.

Vlakte flat land, usually grassed or, if in fynbos, covered mainly with restios.

Voetslaanpad hiking trail.

Wag-'n-bietjie literally meaning 'wait a bit', referring to trees with thorns that entangle your clothes and tear at your skin; for example, *Ziziphus mucronata.*

Wandelpad nature walk.

Xerophyte a plant that loses very little water and can grow in deserts or very dry ground.

INDEX

Bold type denotes main entries.
See also page 36 for a directory
of trails by area.